ICSEA 2016

The Eleventh International Conference on Software Engineering Advances

August 21 - 25, 2016

Rome, Italy

ICSEA 2016 Editors

Luigi Lavazza, Università dell'Insubria - Varese, Italy

Mira Kajko-Mattsson, Stockholm University & Royal Institute of Technology, Sweden

Krishna M. Kavi, University of North Texas, USA

Radek Koci, Brno University of Technology, Czech Republic

Stephen Clyde, Utah State University, USA

Printed from e-media with permission by:

Curran Associates, Inc.
57 Morehouse Lane
Red Hook, NY 12571

CURRAN ASSOCIATES INC. proceedings.com

Some format issues inherent in the e-media version may also appear in this print version.

Printed by Curran Associates, Inc. (2016)

International Academy, Research, and Industry Association (IARIA)
412 Derby Way
Wilmington, DE 19810

Phone: (408) 893-6407
Fax: (408) 527-6351

petre@iaria.org

Additional copies of this publication are available from:

Curran Associates, Inc.
57 Morehouse Lane
Red Hook, NY 12571 USA
Phone: 845-758-0400
Fax: 845-758-2633
Email: curran@proceedings.com
Web: www.proceedings.com

TABLE OF CONTENTS

ICSEA 1: SOFTWARE ENGINEERING TECHNIQUES, METRICS, AND FORMALISMS I

ICSEA 2: SOFTWARE ENGINEERING TECHNIQUES, METRICS, AND FORMALISMS II

ICSEA 3: ADVANCES IN SOFTWARE TESTING

ICSEA 4: ADVANCES IN FUNDAMENTALS FOR SOFTWARE DEVELOPMENT I

ICSEA 10: BUSINESS TECHNOLOGY

ICSEA 11: SOFTWARE ENGINEERING FOR SERVICE COMPUTING

ICSEA 12: ADVANCED DESIGN TOOLS FOR DEVELOPING SOFTWARE

ICSEA 13: SOFTWARE SECURITY, PRIVACY, SAFENESS

ICSEA 14: AGILE AND LEAN APPROACHES IN SOFTWARE ENGINEERING

ICSEA 2016

Forward

The Eleventh International Conference on Software Engineering Advances (ICSEA 2016), held on August 21 - 25, 2016 in Rome, Italy, continued a series of events covering a broad spectrum of software-related topics.

The conference covered fundamentals on designing, implementing, testing, validating and maintaining various kinds of software. The tracks treated the topics from theory to practice, in terms of methodologies, design, implementation, testing, use cases, tools, and lessons learnt. The conference topics covered classical and advanced methodologies, open source, agile software, as well as software deployment and software economics and education.

The conference had the following tracks:

- Advances in fundamentals for software development
- Advanced mechanisms for software development
- Advanced design tools for developing software
- Software engineering for service computing (SOA and Cloud)
- Advanced facilities for accessing software
- Software performance
- Software security, privacy, safeness
- Advances in software testing
- Specialized software advanced applications
- Web Accessibility
- Open source software
- Agile and Lean approaches in software engineering
- Software deployment and maintenance
- Software engineering techniques, metrics, and formalisms
- Software economics, adoption, and education
- Business technology
- Improving productivity in research on software engineering

Similar to the previous edition, this event continued to be very competitive in its selection process and very well perceived by the international software engineering community. As such, it is attracting excellent contributions and active participation from all over the world. We were very pleased to receive a large amount of top quality contributions.

We take here the opportunity to warmly thank all the members of the ICSEA 2016 technical program committee as well as the numerous reviewers. The creation of such a broad and high quality conference program would not have been possible without their involvement. We also kindly thank all the authors that dedicated much of their time and efforts to contribute to the ICSEA 2016. We truly believe that thanks to all these efforts, the final conference program consists of top quality contributions.

This event could also not have been a reality without the support of many individuals, organizations and sponsors. We also gratefully thank the members of the ICSEA 2016 organizing committee for their help in handling the logistics and for their work that is making this professional meeting a success.

We hope the ICSEA 2016 was a successful international forum for the exchange of ideas and results between academia and industry and to promote further progress in software engineering research. We also hope Rome provided a pleasant environment during the conference and everyone saved some time for exploring this beautiful historic city.

ICSEA 2016 Advisory Committee

Herwig Mannaert, University of Antwerp, Belgium
Mira Kajko-Mattsson, Stockholm University & Royal Institute of Technology, Sweden
Luigi Lavazza, Università dell'Insubria - Varese, Italy
Roy Oberhauser, Aalen University, Germany
Elena Troubitsyna, Åbo Akademi University, Finland
Davide Tosi, Università dell'Insubria - Como, Italy
Luis Fernandez-Sanz, Universidad de Alcala, Spain
Michael Gebhart, iteratec GmbH, Germany
Krishna M. Kavi, University of North Texas, USA
Radek Koci, Brno University of Technology, Czech Republic
Stephen Clyde, Utah State University, USA

ICSEA 2016 Research Institute Liaison Chairs

Oleksandr Panchenko, Hasso Plattner Institute for Software Systems Engineering - Potsdam, Germany
Teemu Kanstrén, VTT Technical Research Centre of Finland - Oulu, Finland
Osamu Takaki, Gunma University, Japan
Georg Buchgeher, Software Competence Center Hagenberg GmbH, Austria

ICSEA 2016 Industry/Research Chairs

Herman Hartmann, University of Groningen, The Netherlands
Hongyu Pei Breivold, ABB Corporate Research, Sweden

ICSEA 2016 Special Area Chairs

Formal Methods
Paul J. Gibson, Telecom & Management SudParis, France

Testing and Validation
Florian Barth, University of Mannheim, Germany

Web Accessibility
Adriana Martin, National University of Austral Patagonia (UNPA), Argentina

Software engineering for service computing
Muthu Ramachandran, Leeds Beckett University, UK

ICSEA 2016 Publicity Chairs

Sébastien Salva, University of Auvergne, Clermont-Ferrand, France

ICSNC 2016

Committee

ICSNC Advisory Committee

Eugen Borcoci, University Politehnica of Bucarest, Romania
Sathiamoorthy Manoharan, University of Auckland, New Zealand
Leon Reznik, Rochester Institute of Technology, USA
Masashi Sugano, Osaka Prefecture University, Japan
Zoubir Mammeri, IRIT, France
Xavier Hesselbach, UPC, Spain
Svetlana Boudko, Norsk Regnesentral, Norway
Ben Lee, Oregon State University, USA

ICSNC 2016 Research Institute Liaison Chairs

Song Lin, Yahoo! Labs / Yahoo Inc. - Sunnyvale, USA
Habtamu Abie, Norwegian Computing Center - Oslo, Norway

ICSNC 2016 Industry/Research Chairs

Rolf Oppliger, eSECURITY Technologies - Guemligen, Switzerland
Jeffrey Abell, General Motors Corporation, USA
Christopher Nguyen, Intel Corp., USA
Javier Ibanez-Guzman, RENAULT S.A.S. / Technocentre RENAULT - Guyancourt, France

ICSNC 2016 Special Area Chairs

Mobility / vehicular
Maode Ma, Nanyang Technology University, Singapore

Pervasive education
Maiga Chang, Athabasca University, Canada

ICSNC 2016 Technical Program Committee

Habtamu Abie, Norwegian Computing Center - Oslo, Norway
M. Ilhan Akbas, University of Central Florida, USA
Fakhrul Alam, Massey University, New Zealand
Jose M. Alcaraz Calero, University of the West of Scotland, UK
Pedro Alexandre S. Gonçalves, Escola Superior de Tecnologia e Gestão de Águeda, Lisbon
Mikulas Alexik, University of Zilina, Slovak Republic
Abdul Alim, Imperial College London, UK
Shin'ichi Arakawa, Osaka University, Japan

Seon Yeob Baek, The Attached Institute of ETRI, Korea
Michael Bahr, Siemens AG - Corporate Technology, Germany
Ataul Bari, University of Western Ontario, Canada
João Paulo Barraca, University of Aveiro, Portugal
Mostafa Bassiouni, University of Central Florida, USA
Roberto Beraldi, "La Sapienza" University of Rome, Italy
Luis Bernardo, Universidade Nova de Lisboa, Portugal
Robert Bestak, Czech Technical University in Prague, Czech Republic
Carlo Blundo, Università di Salerno - Fisciano, Italy
Eugen Borcoci, Politehnica University of Bucarest, Romania
Svetlana Boudko, Norsk Regnesentral, Norway
Martin Brandl, Danube University Krems, Austria
Thierry Brouard, University of Tours, France
Dario Bruneo, Università di Messina, Italy
Francesco Buccafurri, University of Reggio Calabria, Italy
Dumitru Dan Burdescu, University of Craiova, Romania
Carlos T. Calafate, Universitat Politècnica de València, Spain
Juan-Carlos Cano, Universitat Politècnica de València, Spain
Aparicio Carranza, NYC College of Technology, USA
Jonathon Chambers, University Loughborough - Leics, UK
Maiga Chang, Athabasca University, Canada
Hao Che, University of Texas at Arlington, USA
Jen-Jee Chen, National University of Tainan, Taiwan, R.O.C.
Tzung-Shi Chen, National University of Tainan, Taiwan
Feng Cheng, Hasso-Plattner-Institute at University of Potsdam, Germany
Jong Chern, University College Dublin, Ireland
Stefano Chessa, Università di Pisa, Italy
Stelvio Cimato, Università degli studi di Milano - Crema, Italy
Nathan Clarke, University of Plymouth, UK
Jorge A. Cobb, University of Texas at Dallas, USA
Sebastian Damm, FH Aachen, Germany
Danco Davcev, University "St. Cyril and Methodius" - Skopje, Macedonia
Vanesa Daza, University Pompeu Fabra, Spain
Sergio De Agostino, Sapienza University, Italy
Jan de Meer, smartspace®lab.eu GmbH || University (A.S.) of Technology and Economy HTW, Germany
Eli De Poorter, Ghent University - iMinds, Belgium
Carl James Debono, University of Malta, Malta
Edna Dias Canedo, Universidade Federal da Paraíba (UFPB), Brazil
Jawad Drissi, Cameron University - Lawton, USA
Jaco du Toit, Stellenbosch University, South Africa
Wan Du, Nanyang Technological University (NTU), Singapore
Gerardo Fernández-Escribano, University of Castilla-La Mancha - Albacete, Spain
Carol Fung, Virginia Commonwealth University, USA
Marco Furini, University of Modena and Reggio Emilia, Italy
Pedro Gama, Truewind, Portugal
Thierry Gayraud, LAAS-CNRS / Université de Toulouse, France
Sorin Georgescu, Ericsson Research - Montreal, Canada
Katja Gilly, Universidad Miguel Hernández, Spain

Copyright Information

The Uncomfortable Discrepancies of Software Metric Thresholds and Reference Values in Literature

Eudes de Castro Lima, Antônio Maria P. de Resende
Department of Computer Science
Universidade Federal de Lavras (UFLA)
Lavras, Minas Gerais, Brasil
e-mail: comp.eudes@gmail.com, tonio@dcc.ufla.br

Timothy C. Lethbridge
School of Information Technology and Engineering
University of Ottawa
Ottawa, Canada
e-mail: tcl@eecs.uottawa.ca

***Abstract*— Software metrics perform a crucial role in the software industry because they provide measures needed to control software process and product, such as software quality, complexity, maintainability, and size. Measuring software allows one to diagnose whether the project is within expected norms or there is a deviation. However, many publications present metrics but omit thresholds or reference values that would give guidance about their ideal limits and range. Metrics might be used more frequently and effectively if they were accompanied by reliable reference values. We therefore present a Systematic Literature Review to find research that presents such reference values and thresholds. The keyword search phase of the systematic review generated 6.654 articles from IEEE Xplore, ACM Digital Library, Ei Compendex, SCOPUS, and Elsevier Science Direct. Further filtering narrowed this to only 19 articles actually disucssing thresholds and reference values. We present an analysis of these papers, including a comparison highlighting discrepancies in the reference values and thresholds. The results serve as a starting point to guide further research.**

Keywords- software metrics; software measures; thresholds; reference values; systematic literature review.

I. INTRODUCTION

In medicine, when a blood test is done, the values obtained are compared with their respective reference intervals printed beside the results. If there is any abnormality in the results then the doctor makes a diagnosis, defines the disease, and determines the type and dose of medicine the patient should take. There are reference values for most tests, allowing the diagnosis of patients. However, in software engineering, there is still a long journey to obtain these values and achieve maturity based on measures.

Software metrics perform an important role in the software industry because they provide measures for software features, such as maintainability, reusability, portability, readability, correctness, complexity and so on. These measures provide the software engineer, software architects and project managers the current state of the software. The measures allow diagnosing of projects, products and processes, and check whether the values of measures are within the expected norm or there is unexpected deviation.

Over the years, a variety of software metrics [1]-[11] and automated tools for measuring [12][13][14] have been proposed. However, despite the importance of software metrics, most have not been widely applied in industry [15][16]. It is believed that one reason is the lack of reference values and thresholds for most metrics [17].

A threshold defines a point that should (or not) be exceeded due to (un)desirable effects involved. A reference value or range gives objectives for what should be achieved or defines value sets classified qualitatively; for instance the classification could be bad, regular and good. In this paper, the term 'reference value' will be used for both in most of what follows, unless context requires otherwise.

In some cases, the reference values are known, but not widely accepted. This causes an uncertainty which, according to [16], inhibits the popularization of software metrics.

Reference values for metrics enable interpretation of the results of measurement. It is through comparing measures to reference values that software engineers can verify that the project, product and process meets a desired standard or, that the project is improving, worsening or stable.

Various authors [18]-[22] have proposed reference values for software metrics and techniques for deriving them. There are articles, such as [19][21][23], which provide benchmarks based on "experience" (tacit knowledge) without any statistical or technical analysis that supports the claim. However, since they were obtained in a specific context, published reference values tend not to be generalizable beyond the context of their inception.

In this work, the results of a systematic literature review (SLR) of software metrics are presented, focusing on reference values. The SLR selection process resulted in selection of 19 articles, out of 6.654 considered. In subsequent sections we summarize these articles and present the reference values cited or calculated in the articles . We discuss certain differences in metric interpretations. We also comment on the amount and type of software used to calculate and validate the reference values. We then present a comparison of the discrepancies among reference values proposed in those articles. Finally, we suggest future work that would promote improvements in software metrics and measurements.

The SLR methodology has proven very useful software engineering researchers. It provides a documented and repeatable process to identify the state of the art about some issues of researchers' interest.

The structure of this paper is as follows. Section II describes SLRs in general, the SLR construction process, the protocol used and the results obtained from this SLR. Section V presents the comparison analysis and discussion of the articles as a group. Section VI presents the main conclusions obtained in this work, as well as contributions and future work.

II. SYSTEMATIC REVIEW PROCESS

A systematic literature review is an evidence-based technique originating in medicine and medical sciences [24]. This technique has been employed in several areas including software engineering.

An SLR involves several distinct activities [25]. In the literature, it is possible to find different suggestions for the number and order of activities undertaken in a systematic review. In [24][25][26] the authors present an SLR process consisting of three main phases: planning, execution and analysis of results. This section presents the application of the SLR, following the three-phase approach.

1. Planning

This section presents the planning phase.

- *Objectives:* To perform a survey of scientific papers that discusses software metrics that have ranges or specific reference values associated with them.
- *Research questions:* What software metrics have values or ranges of reference assigned to them? What values or ranges have been identified in the literature?
- *Keywords:* The following keywords were adopted: Software metric, measure, measuring, threshold, reference value, value, range, limit.

  Search string: the search string was compiled from the keywords, linking them logically: (software) AND (metric OR metrics OR measure OR measures OR measuring) AND ("reference value" OR "reference values" OR ranges OR thresholds OR limits OR range OR threshold OR limit).
- *Search method sources:* Web sites of virtual scientific libraries.
- *List of research sources:* IEEE Xplore (http://ieeexplore.ieee.org), Elsevier Science Direct (www.sciencedirect.com), Scopus (www.scopus.com), ACM Digital Library (http://dl.acm.org), and EiCompendex (www.engineeringvillage2.org).
- *Types of articles:* Papers considered are those relating to software metrics, including comparisons and analyzes.
- *Language of articles:* The articles must be in English.
- *Criteria for inclusion or exclusion of articles:* Articles should: i) Be available for download as full papers; ii) Provide reference values for software metrics; and iii) Have been published between the years 1990 and 2015.

It is known that the search string used can return a lot of articles or limit the results as well. So, in this investigation, the results expected are papers that contain the words present in search string. A string search containing the name of a specific metrics was not used. For instance, Depth Inheritance Tree, Response for Classes, Coupling Between Objects, Number of Children, Weighted Methods per Class, LCOM and others could be inserted in the search string. Considering the amount of metrics, the length of the search string, the volume of articles that need to be retrieved and the data need to be processed, the work must be separated for each metric.

2. Execution

The execution was divided into four steps, as suggested in [27] called initial selection, primary selection, secondary selection, and obtaining and evaluation of scientific papers.

- *Initial selection (obtaining of articles):* Searches are conducted in databases defined in the protocol; then the results are summarized according to previously established criteria. This process is iterative, i.e. the search can be readjusted and run again, if the results are not reasonable.
- *Primary selection:* This is the first filtering of the results. Usually the Title and Keywords of articles are read to verify compliance with the criteria for inclusion and exclusion.
- *Secondary selection:* This is the second filtering of the results. This step aims to eliminate irrelevant results by reading the abstracts and conclusions of the articles, and checking compliance with the criteria for inclusion and exclusion.
- *Results organization:* The results are tabulated in a way that favors a quick visual analysis.

Step 1 – Initial selection

The initial selection was conducted by searching in the databases mentioned above. Filters were carried out during searching activity to restrict the results according to year (the period between 1990 and 2015), language (English), and discipline (computer science and/or software engineering). Scientific articles were searched for using our search strings applied to titles, abstracts and keywords.

Because of the characteristics of the search engines for some databases, the search strings defined in the protocol required slight change, but their semantics were retained. In some situations, it was necessary to include the query string parameters. For instance, in the ACM Digital Library it was necessary to divide the search string into three, to obtain a plausible result for analysis. The searches were performed on November 10 and 26, 2014.

Table I presents the exact search strings used in the SLR for each database.

As a result of that search, 6.654 scientific articles were found, as shown in the second column of Table II. The tool JabRef version 2.7.2 [28] was used to manage the list of articles.

TABLE I. SEARCH STRINGS USED IN PRIMARY SELECTION

Databases	Search strings	
IEEE Xplore	((software) AND (metric OR metrics OR measure OR measures OR measuring) AND ("reference value" OR "reference values" OR ranges OR thresholds OR limits OR range OR threshold OR limit))	
Elsevier Science Direct	pub-date > 1989 and TITLE-ABS-KEY((software) AND (metric OR metrics OR measure OR measures OR measuring) AND ("reference value" OR "reference values" OR ranges OR thresholds OR limits OR range OR threshold OR limit))[All Sources(Computer Science)]	
Ei Compendex	(((((software) AND (metric OR metrics OR measure OR measures OR measuring) AND ("reference value" OR "reference values" OR ranges OR thresholds OR limits OR range OR threshold OR limit)) WN KY) AND (({computer software} OR {software engineering}) WN CV)) AND (((english) WN LA) AND (1990-2015) WN YR))	
Scopus	TITLE-ABS-KEY((software) AND (metric OR metrics OR measure OR measures OR measuring) AND ("reference value" OR "reference values" OR ranges OR thresholds OR limits OR range OR threshold OR limit)) AND PUBYEAR > 1989 AND (LIMIT-TO(LANGUAGE, "English")) AND (LIMIT-TO(SUBJAREA, "COMP"))	
ACM Library	String 1	("software measure*") AND ("reference value*" OR range* OR threshold* OR limit*)
	String 2	("software measuring") AND ("reference value*" OR range* OR threshold* OR limit*)
	String 3	("software metric*") AND ("reference value*" OR range* OR threshold* OR limit*)

TABLE II- RESULTS AFTER APPLYING SELECTIONS

Data Bases	Initial Selection	Primary Selection	Secondary Selection			Selected
			Irlvt	Rpt	Incompl	
IEEE	3.266	91	80	0	0	11
Elsevier	180	27	24	0	0	3
Compendex	1.254	33	19	11	0	3
Scopus	1.687	54	37	16	0	1
ACM	267	37	33	3	0	1
Total	**6.654**	**242**	**193**	**30**	**0**	**19**

Step 2 – Primary selection

After the initial selection was performed (step 1), the scientific articles were submitted to primary selection, where *titles*, *keywords* and *abstracts* were filtered and analyzed manually.

During filtering, it was found that a large proportion of the articles belonged to other areas of computer science and did not meet the purposes of this SLR. Hence, the number of scientific articles decreased from 6654 (obtained in the initial selection) to 242. This is shown in column 3 of Table II.

In an SLR, it is usual for the initial search to return a large number of irrelevant articles that neither respond to the research questions nor are unrelated to the theme in question [26].

Step 3 – Secondary selection

In secondary selection, the 242 scientific articles selected in the primary selection (Step 2) passed an inspection in which both *introductions* and *conclusions* were read. At this stage, relevance, repetitiveness and completeness were checked.

Out of 242 articles selected earlier, 193 papers were considered irrelevant, because they did not correspond to the objectives of this SLR; 30 articles were considered repeated, because they were found in more than one database; no article was considered incomplete, and all items surveyed were available. Finally, 19 scientific articles passed the selection criteria. In other words, 19 papers were found that had clearly stated an intent to define or analyze thresholds or reference values in their title, abstract or introduction. Table II presents a summary of the results in its rightmost four columns.

Step 4 - Obtaining and evaluation of scientific papers

Those 19 papers were read and discussed one by one, and data were gathered in order to show the state of the art around the research theme. Table III presents the relevant scientific articles that answer the research questions set out in the protocol. Section 3 presents the analysis and discussion of papers identified.

3. Results analysis

This SLR indicates that the number of papers discussing reference values for software metrics has increased in recent years. One of the factors contributed to that increase is likely the market demand for quality products. The SLR shows that 57.8% of scientific papers were published since 2009.

TABLE IV - RELEVANT INFORMATION OF ARTICLES IDENTIFIED IN SLR.

ID	Classification	Articles or tools referenced	Values empirically validated	Technique	Context
A	Type I	[13]	no	experience	specific
B	Type II	[10]	no	distribution analysis	generic
C	Type I	[18]	no	statistical analysis	specific
D	Type I	[9][21]	negative	experience	specific
E	Type II	[31]	negative	statistical analysis	specific
F	Type I	ISM	no	logistic regression	specific
G	Type II	-	yes	distribution analysis	specific
H	Type I	[44]	no	experience	generic
I	Type II	-	yes	statistical analysis	specific
J	Type II	[21]	yes	statistical analysis	specific
K	Type II	-	no	statistical analysis	specific
L	Type II	-	yes	statistical analysis	specific
M	Type II	-	no	ROC courves	specific
N	Type II	-	no	experience	generic
O	Type II	[45]	no	ROC courves	specific
P	Type II		no	experience	specific
Q	Type II	[45]	no	statistical analysis	generic
R	Type I	[31][46] [23][9]	no	learning machine	specific
S	Type II	[13]	no	experience	specific

A total of 66 metrics having thresholds were identified from the 19 papers. Among the metrics identified, there are metrics specific to the OO paradigm as well as traditional metrics adapted to the OO paradigm, such as LOC and cyclomatic complexity. In total, 57.4% of the papers refer to OO metrics specifically and 82.5% of them come from the CK metrics suite [4].

The IEEE Xplore database presented the most relevant articles for this research, with 58% of studies. The databases with the lowest number of relevant studies were Scopus and the ACM Library, with 5% of scientific articles each. Table IV summarizes the articles analyzed. The first column gives the reference number (see Table III).

TABLE III. RELEVANT ARTICLES THAT ANSWER THE RESEARCH QUESTIONS SET OUT IN THE PROTOCOL.

ID	Year	Title	Ref.	Base
A	2009	An outlier detection algorithm based on object-oriented metrics thresholds	[29]	IEEE
B	2010	Deriving metric thresholds from benchmark data	[18]	IEEE
C	2011	Benchmark-Based Aggregation of Metrics to Ratings	[30]	IEEE
D	2000	Thresholds for object-oriented measures	[31]	IEEE
E	2002	The optimal class size for object-oriented software	[32]	IEEE
F	2009	Clustering and Metrics Thresholds Based Software Fault Prediction of Unlabeled Program Modules	[33]	IEEE
G	2003	A metrics suite for measuring reusability of software components	[34]	IEEE
H	2007	Observing Distributions in Size Metrics: Experience from Analyzing Large Software Systems	[35]	IEEE
I	1997	Software metrics model for quality control	[36]	IEEE
J	2010	A Quantitative Investigation of the Acceptable Risk Levels of Object-Oriented Metrics in Open-Source Systems	[37]	IEEE
K	2014	Extracting relative thresholds for source code metrics	[38]	IEEE
L	2011	Identifying thresholds for object-oriented software metrics	[20]	Elsevier
M	2011	Class noise detection based on software metrics and ROC curves	[39]	Elsevier
N	2011	Improving the applicability of object-oriented class cohesion metrics	[40]	Elsevier
O	2010	Finding software metrics threshold values using ROC curves	[22]	Compendex
P	1992	Software metrics for object-oriented systems	[19]	Compendex
Q	2005	An empirical exploration of the distributions of the Chidamber and Kemerer object-oriented metrics suite	[41]	Compendex
R	2011	Calculation and optimization of thresholds for sets of software metrics	[42]	Scopus
S	2010	Estimation of Software Reusability: An Engineering Approach	[43]	ACM

The second column categorizes the papers into: i) Type I - studies that use existing reference values to achieve a goal, such as outlier detection and predicting failures, and ii) Type-II studies that aim to establish or optimize reference values. Among the identified articles, 31.6% use existing thresholds and 68.4% aim to identify or optimize thresholds as shown in Table IV.

The thresholds classified as Type I and presented by selected papers were gathered from tool documentation or from other studies that they had referenced. The thresholds obtained from tools such as: McCabe IQ, or ISM are hard to reproduce because the tools are not readily available and some thresholds were determined "by authors experience".

The labels "no", "yes" and "negative" shown in Table IV mean respectively that "there was no validation", "there was validation", or "there was validation, but the result states that the reference values are bad values". Articles D and E [31][32] had negative validation, representing 10.5% of the articles. A total of 21.1% of articles validated the thresholds and reference values, and 68.4% did not validate them. These results are undesirable, because only 21.1% validated values and only article L [20] out of 21.1% were classified as general context. The other articles were considered neither validated nor general. Software engineering should have well validated thresholds in order to support software engineers during the development process.

Other articles had used the thresholds to validate only the method used to discover thresholds, but they did not validate their own thresholds as presented. This was the case for articles R and S [42][43].

Regarding the techniques used to obtain the thresholds, as Lanza and Marinescu indicated in [16], there are two main approaches: professional experience and statistical analysis. Of the articles analyzed, 31.6% obtained thresholds through experience, i.e., the authors determined arbitrarily and subjectively the thresholds, and 68.4% obtained them through statistical analysis. Methods like machine learning and error models were classified as statistical analysis approaches.

The context was classified as generic and specific. The 'generic' label indicates the reference values fulfill all of the following criteria: a) Three or more systems; b) more than 50% of systems are developed by people different from the authors, c) more than one domain, and d) more than one programming language. Otherwise the label 'specific' is used. A total of 79% of selected papers were classified as specific, and 21% were classified as general.

During the analysis process, several methods were found to calculate thresholds. These include experience, statistical analysis, error models, clustering, distribution analysis, and machine learning.

Most of the papers would not be amenable to replication due to incomplete details such as missing versions of systems, names of systems, details about applied metric interpretation to measure software and so on. Those details should be included in articles. In fact, it is necessary to establish a protocol to guide authors to supply that information, allowing replication and validation of research of this kind.

Several articles did not define precise instructions for how metrics were counted in papers. For instance, what is the difference between 'comments' and 'lines of comments'? How were lines of comment blocks counted? And how were lines counted that had both code and comment?

Another difficulty faced was determining whether a value refers to a minimum or maximum, for instance in Schneidewind's article (1997) [36].

In [37], the authors used three versions of Eclipse to determine values. However, using different versions of the same software will not result in the same level of generality as if completely different systems had been used. The same argument can be made when multiple systems in the same domain are analyzed.

In next section, some metrics are analyzed considering the values found in the articles. The reference values presented by article E [32] are results from a negative validation meaning that values are invalid to use.

III. COMPARING REFERENCE VALUES PRESENTED BY PAPERS

After reading all selected papers, the gathered reference values are presented in tables below with columns labelled metric, reference, value, and nature of measure. Respectively, each table contains the name of the metric evaluated, the reference to the paper that presented the reference value, the reference value presented or proposed to the metric mentioned, and the nature of measure that represents the meaning of the value presented like maximum, minimum, desirable, good, bad, typical, etc.

In this section, the reader will note the existence of different reference values for the same metric.

1. Weighted Methods per Class (WMC)

Two interpretations for the WMC metric were found. The first interpretation, called here WMC1, is calculated by summing the complexity of each method in a class and assuming the complexity of each method is 1. That means the WMC is a simply counting the number of methods (each method has complexity 1). The second interpretation, called here WMC2, is calculated by summing the McCabe Cyclomatic Complexity of the methods.

Table V presents just one reference value that was found for WMC1 and several different values for WMC2. For the same interpretation, the WMC2 threshold could be 20 or 100 as cited and calculated, respectively, in [22]. This situation makes the work of software engineers difficult, since they will not know what value should be used as a threshold in their projects.

TABLE V - VALUES OF WMC METRIC

Metric	Ref.	Value	Nature of Measure
WMC1 - Counting methods	A	14	Max
WMC2 - Sum complexities	D	100	Max
	K	100	Max
	K	20	Max
	N	24	Max
	N	100	Max
	R	100	Max
	S	20 and 100	Desirable and Max
WMC - not defined	K	32	80% quantiles (relative threshold)

2. Depth of Inheritance Tree (DIT)

The papers presented moderate differences among suggested DIT thresholds. This metric measures the maximum depth of the inheritance hierarchy in a system. In Table VI, it is observed that values from 6 to 10 are most commonly found to be the maximum suggested value or upper threshold. This is still a large range, so further research is needed to determine how much worse a system would be if it had a DIT of 10 vs. 6.

TABLE VI - VALUES OF DIT METRIC.

Ref.	Value	Nature of Measure
A	7	Max
D	6	Max
L	2	Typical
Q	10	Max
Q	6 (in Java or C++)	Max
S	3 and 6	Desirable and Max

3. Cyclomatic Complexity (CC)

The Cyclomatic Complexity metric is the number of linearly independent paths in program flow and has significantly different reference values in the papers studied, as shown in Table XII.

TABLE XII - VALUES OF CICLOMATIC COMPLEXITY METRICS.

Metrics	Ref.	Value	Nature of Measure
Cyclomatic Complexity Per Method	B	<=6]6;8]]8;14] >14	low risk moderate risk high risk very-high risk
	F	10	It was impossible check it, because original reference on web is not available
	M	P1 - 3 P2 - 5 P3 - 5 P4 - 3 P5 - 4	Best value for each dataset P1, P2,..., P5
	P	10	Max
	R	C - 24 C++ - 10 C# - 10	Max
Cyclomatic Complexity per Module	P	100	Max Value, considering 10 methods and each one supporting max complexity equal 10.
Design Complexity Per Module - Number of paths including calls to other modules	M	P1 - 3 P2 - 3 P3 - 3 P4 - 3 P5 - 3	Best value for each dataset P1, P2,..., P5

4. Number of Children (NOC)

NOC represents the number of children that any given class has. In Table VIII, it is observed once again that there are different values for the maximum value or upper threshold ranging from 3 to 10.

TABLE VIII - VALUES OF NOC METRICS.

Ref.	Value	Nature of Measure
A	3	Max
Q	10	Max
Q	]4, 6[Java and <6 C++	Desirable and Max

5. Lack Of Cohesion Methods (LCOM)

LCOM measures lack of cohesion and has several interpretations and different names as shown in Table IX. As different cohesion views appeared over time, new metrics were developed. Article [40] explains the subtle difference among the various LCOM metrics.

TABLE IX - VALUES OF LCOM 1, 2, 3, 4, 5 AND LOCM METRICS.

Metric	Ref.	Value	Nature of Measure
LCOM1	N	42 and 21	Mean and 75th percentile
LCOM2	L	0, [10;20] and >20	Intervals mean: Good, Regular and Bad
	N	27 and 8	Mean and 75th percentile
LCOM3	N	1.67 and 2	Mean and 75th percentile
LCOM4	N	1.62 and 2	Mean and 75th percentile
LCOM5	N	0.76 and 1	Mean and 75th percentile
LOCM (McCabe Tools)	A	75	Max
LCOM (not defined)	K	36	80% quantiles (relative threshold)

6. Operator and Operand Countings

Halstead`s metrics count Unique Operators, Unique Operands, Total Operators and Total Operands as shown in Table X. There are different reference values for each dataset from NASA in [39] called P1,..., P5 in this paper. Halstead used these direct measures to calculate indirect measures, for instance, volume of software can be used to indicate complexity. The higher the volume of software, the higher its complexity.

TABLE X - VALUES OF COMPLEXITY OPERATOR AND OPERAND METRICS.

Ref	Value to UNIQUE		Value to TOTAL	
	Operator Count	Operand Count	Operator Count	Operand Count
F	25	0	125	70
I	10	33	26	21
M	P1 – 7 P2 – 12 P3 – 15 P4 - 18 P5 - 15	P1 – 7 P2 – 17 P3 – 19 P4 - 21 P5 - 20	P1 - 13 P2 - 42 P3 - 54 P4 - 53 P5 - 50	P1 - 8 P2 - 27 P3 - 36 P4 - 57 P5 - 34

7 *Response For a Class (RFC), Coupling Between Object Classes (CBO), Fan-in, Afferent Coupling (AC) and Number of Function Calls (NFC)*

Metrics shown in Table XI to Table XIII are related to method calling. Fan-in is known as afferent coupling and Fan-out is known as efferent coupling.

There are different values for the same metric in this case too. For instance, Table XI shows in its first line the maximum value is 2 and in line 6 the maximum value is 13.

TABLE XI - VALUES OF CBO AND METRICS.

Ref.	Value	Nature of Measure
A	2	Max
D	5	Max
J	5	Max
J	9	Max
O	5	Max
O	13	Max
R	5	Max

In Table XII, there are discrepancies among values. For instance, the RFC maximum value starts with 0 and ends with 222.

TABLE XII - VALUES OF RESPONSE FOR CLASS (RFC).

Ref.	Value	Nature of Measure
A	100	Max
D	100	Max
J	100	Max
J	40	Max
K	49	80% quantiles - relative threshold
O	100	Max
O	44	Max
R	100	Max
S	[50;100] and 222	Desirable and Max

TABLE XIII - VALUES OF FAN-IN, AFFERENT COUPLING (AC) AND NUMBER OF FUNCTION CALLS (NFC) METRICS.

Metric	Ref.	Value	Nature of Measure
FAN-IN	B	10, 22 and 56	70%, 80%, 90% percentiles
AC	L	1, [2;20] and >20	Intervals mean: Good, Regular and Bad
NFC- Number of Function Calls	R	5	Max

8. *Number of Attributes, Methods and Parameters*

Metrics shown in Table XV measure characteristic related to classes and methods like number of attributes and methods per class and the number of parameters in a method signature. Some variations are considered, such as whether modifiers are public or private . The maximum value of 0 for the public attributes measure was presented in paper H, due to suggested good practices for OO modeling. Values originating from good practices could be called theoretical recommendations. However, paper H considers 0 as good, but accepts up to 10 as the regular situation, when considering the distribution analysis of dozens of open source systems. Those values could be called practical recommendations.

TABLE XV - VALUES OF NUMBER OF ATTRIBUTES, NUMBER OF METHODS AND NUMBER OF PARAMETERS.

Metric	Ref.	Value	Nature of Measure
Number of Attributes	E	39	Invalid Threshold. Do not use.
	K	0.1	75th percentile (relative threshold)
Number of Public Attributes	L	0, [1;10], >10	Intervals mean: Good, Regular and Bad
	H	0	Max
	K	0.1	75th percentile (relative threshold)
Number of Methods (NM)	B	29, 42 and 73	70%, 80% 90% quantiles
	E	1	Invalid Threshold. Do not use
	R	20	Max
	K	16	80% quantiles (relative threshold)
Number of Public Methods	H	[5;10]	Min and Max Interval
	L	[0;10], [11;40], >40	Intervals mean: Good, Regular and Bad
Number of Parameters (NP)	B	10, 22, 56	70%, 80% 90% percentiles

These reference values have not been widely accepted for the following main reasons: a) The thresholds that have been found cannot distinguish 'good' from 'bad' values, they just present statistical results; b) the thresholds originate from studies of only one (or a few) application domains, geographical regions, or groups of companies, reducing the generalizability of results; c) There are important discrepancies among thresholds proposed in different scientific papers; d) The papers do not explain why a new threshold proposed is better (or worse) than older ones. They just show numbers and assert their new numbers as new suggested thresholds.

Article [20] seems to have reference values that are more reliable, considering the number of systems and domains, but it considers only Java systems.

Some reference values that were proposed omit explanations of how they were calculated or the reason for those values. Sometimes, it was stated that the values were established based on author's experience [13][19], suggesting for us to close our eyes and just trust. Therefore, there is a long distance to be walked in this journey to improve metrics and their use.

During this analysis, no evidence was found regarding whether different kinds of software (e.g., CPU bound vs. I/O bound) should have the same thresholds or reference values. A similar question arises regarding whether software employing particular frameworks, or generated by code-generation tools should be expected to have reference values consistent with software that does not employ such technologies. For example, such software might contain attributes and methods that are empty or not used.

In [33] the authors showed different values for five projects (Table X). There were significant differences among the values for certain metrics in different articles. So, the question arises of whether it is even possible calculate a single threshold or reference value in many cases.

Furthermore, in articles [31] and [32] the authors show negative results for those validations. The first one [31] demonstrates that there was no *threshold effect* (sudden effect change at some threshold) in some metrics. The second one [32] demonstrates there is no empirical evidence for the "Goldilocks Conjecture" that there is a 'sweet spot' for a given metric. Even if these are valid conclusions, surely there must be negative effects at some extreme values. In other words, even if Goldilocks found that all the beds were comfortable, she likely still would not have wanted to sleep on a board or on quicksand.

This context, without reference values that are generic, brings to mind learning processes like machine learning, neural networks, fuzzy systems, and so on. Those methods, without generic values for training, have to be trained in each context and must have their application limited to that context only.

Considering the current scenario without generic thresholds and reference values, more effort needs to be applied to find reasonable values.

We found no articles presenting values of metrics that simultaneously take into consideration dimensions such as domain, architecture, language, size of system, size of developer teams, modeling approach, code generation technology, build system, or delivery system. We believe that reference values may be quite different depending on where systems are situated in the space defined by the above dimensions. Additionally, there were no papers comparing metrics in several independent systems or different versions of the same system. By independent systems, we are referring to systems produced by others than those that are collecting, calculating or validating thresholds or reference values. In some cases, it was not clear whether the systems studied were independent of the evaluators.

Many reference values found should be used only with caution, because, for instance, either they do not have validation, or their measurement cannot be repeated, or they might be specific to a certain type of system, and hence not generic.

As mentioned earlier, it is also important to consider how a metric is interpreted or implemented and what impact this has on reference values. For instance, when the metric LOC is applied, it is necessary to define how blank lines, comments, and statements in more than one line will be counted.

There are also likely to be inherent differences in reference values for different programming languages. For example, some object-oriented languages might intrinsically need different numbers of classes, or different depths of inheritance due to such features as inner classes and multiple inheritance. Other feature differences could lead to different numbers of attributes, methods, and so on.

Thus, we recommend that a Metrics Research Protocol should be developed. This would promote consistent research and enable the exchange of 'big data' in this field among many researchers. It would be similar to what has happened in biology (e.g., genomics), particle physics, and so on.

There are some metrics for which there likely should be no natural limit and for which a more complex system would always have higher values. For instance, this would apply to LOC, number of classes, number of methods, and number of attributes in a system. For such metrics, the reference values should suggest averages or medians per unit, where the unit might be the class.

The situation described in this paper indicates that the software engineering community must conduct considerable additional research if it wants to be considered a true branch of engineering.

IV. Conclusion and Future Work

The main objective of this study was to conduct a survey of software metrics that have reference values or thresholds associated with them. For this, a systematic literature review was performed to identify, interpret, and evaluate the relevant scientific articles available.

During the conduct of the SLR, 6654 scientific articles were identified after searching of IEEE Xplore, EiCompendex, Elsevier Science Direct, Scopus and the ACM Library. The primary selection obtained 242 papers, based on scanning titles and keywords. With further refinement, 193 papers were classified irrelevant, 30 were classified repeated, and none were classified incomplete. Finally, the SLR resulted in 19 articles read and analyzed completely.

The original questions that motivated this SRL were: a) What software metrics have reference values or ranges assigned to them? b) What values or ranges were identified in the literature? Both of these questions were answered, and details were discussed throughout this paper. However, our analysis showed that the values are not yet generic enough or sufficiently validated to be useful.

The major contributions of this work are: i) the identification of a set of measures that have reference values ii) the summary of measures, values, systems evaluated, domains and languages involved, and technical validation, of these iii) critical evaluation of 19 articles.

The main conclusions of this paper are: i) There are conflicts among the most reference values; ii) There are several non-reproducible research papers in the field; iii) There are reference values based on weak or absent validation; iv) The selected reference values are for the most part not generalizable; v) There is little comparison between reference values and discussion of how one value is better than another; vi) The thresholds found cannot be used to distinguish 'good' from 'bad' values, they mainly represent statistical results; and vii) The scientific community should establish a protocol to determine what authors should consider minimum information and procedures that a paper must have when they study and purpose thresholds and reference values for software metrics.

Thus, the values presented in papers should not be trusted. The lack of reference values for software metrics persists. Additional investigation involving other articles not covered in this SLR and new statistical analysis involving multiple software systems must be conducted. Considering the discrepancies among values presented in this paper, we assert that the issue involving metrics and their thresholds and reference values is completely open and deserves more effort.

The possible threats to validity of this study include the limitations of search engines of the digital libraries, and lack of retrieval due to insufficient detail in the title, abstract or keywords of the papers. Other valid articles without keywords in the titles or provided keywords might not have been found. The authors will conduct a new SLR involving the name of each metric and also conduct a statistical analysis of more than 100 open source software projects.

Software metrics have played a key role in organizations. Even though there has been a growth of research related to software metrics and thresholds in the last few years, this issue still needs further research and publications that provide support to software engineers.

Various actions should be taken as future work:

i) Perform a backward and foward SLR considering the set of articles discussed in this paper as the starting point. This might uncover important information that may have been abandoned over time, as well as complementary data about thresholds and methods.

ii) Perform a comparative analysis in order to identify discrepancies among thresholds selected in the literature, considering software both within various domains and across domains.

iii) Study and conduct research to establish thresholds for metrics of interest, creating quality protocols useful as for reference.

iv) Evaluate evolution of measures between different versions of the same software, of the same domain and different domains in order to get average values and uncover discrepancies.

v) Compare different metrics tools in order to look for discrepancies in the same metrics applied in the same projects, to understand why they produce different values, and to enable creation of warnings and advice about their use.

vi) Develop and propose a protocol to facilitate research into reference values for various metrics and software types, and for specific software instances to assure sharing of data and replicability.

vii) Model thresholds as an n-dimensional problem considering different domains, sizes, languages, paradigms, kinds of system and so on.

viii) Develop a comparative analysis about correlation among similar metrics in order to identify distinct behaviors even though those metrics assess the same software attribute (characteristic).

The software engineering research groups from UFLA and UOttawa continue their work in advancing all these proposals. In particular, we are extending the Umple technology [47, 48] to compute metrics for state machines and networks of associations embedded in code, and will develop systematic reference values for these metrics.

Finally, the results obtained in this SLR served to understand the state of the art and serve to guide subsequent studies related software metrics and thresholds.

ACKNOWLEDGMENT

The authors thank the CNPq / Brazil for financial support and the Research Groups on Software Engineering, Federal University of Lavras (PQES / UFLA) and the University of Ottawa is research environment.

REFERENCES

[1] F. B. E. Abreu and R. Carapuça, "Object-Oriented Software Engineering: Measuring", in *Proc. of 4th Int. Conf. on Software Quality*. Milwaukee: American Society for Quality, pp. 1-8, 1994.

[2] A. J. Albrecht, "Measuring Application Development Productivity", in *Proc. of first IBM Application Development Symposium*, New York: IBM, pp. 83-92, 1979.

[3] J. Bieman and B. Kang, "Cohesion and Reuse in an Object-Oriented System", in *Proc. of Symposium on Software Reusability (SSR'95)*, New York: ACM, pp. 259-262, 1995.

[4] S. Chidamber and C. Kemerer, "A metrics suite for object oriented design", *IEEE Transactions on Software Engineering*, v. 20, n. 6, pp. 476-493, 1994.

[5] J. A. Dallal and L. C. Briand, "A Precise Method-Method Interaction-Based Cohesion Metric for Object-Oriented Classes", *ACM Transactions on Software Engineering and Methodology*, v. 21, n. 2, pp. 1-34, 2012.

[6] G. Gui and P. D. Scott, "New Coupling and Cohesion Metrics for Evaluation of Software Component Reusability", *In Proc. of 9th Int. Conf. for Young Computer Scientists* (ICYCS' 2008), Hunan: IEEE, pp.1181-1186, 2008.

[7] M. Halstead, *Elements of software science*. New York: Elsevier, 1977.

[8] S. Henry and D. Kafura, "Software Structure Metrics Based on Information Flow", *IEEE Transactions on Software Engineering*, v. -7, n. 5, pp. 510-518, 1981.

[9] M. Lorenz and J. Kidd, *Object-oriented software metrics*. Englewood Cliffs, NJ: PTR Prentice Hall, 1994.

[10] T. McCabe, "A Complexity Measure", *IEEE Transactions on Software Engineering*, v. -2, n. 4, pp. 308-320, 1976.

[11] H. Washizaki, H. Yamamoto, and Y. Fukazawa, "A Metrics Suite for Measuring Reusability of Software Components", in *Proc. of 9th Int. Symposium on Software Metrics*, Sydney: IEEE Computer Society, pp. 211-223, 2003.

[12] CCCC - Cccc.sourceforge.net, "Software Metrics Investigation", 2015. [Online]. Available: http://cccc.sourceforge.net/. [accessed: 13-July-2016].

[13] McCabe IQ. "MaCabe software". Available: http://www.mccabe.com/pdf/McCabe%20IQ%20Metrics.pdf. [accessed: 13-July-2016].

[14] A. Terceiro et al, "Analizo: An Extensible Multi-Language Source Code Analysis and Visualization Toolkit", in *Proc. of the Brazilian Conf. on Software 2010*, Salvador: SBC, pp. 1-6, 2010.

[15] N. Fenton and M. Neil, "Software metrics: successes, failures and new directions", *Journal of Systems and Software*, v. 47, n. 2-3, pp. 149-157, 1999.

[16] M. Lanza and R. Marinescu, *Object-Oriented Metrics in Practice: Using Software Metrics to Characterize, Evaluate, and Improve the Design of Object-Oriented Systems*. New York: Springer, 2006.

[17] E. Tempero, "On Measuring Java Software", in *Proc. of 31th Australasian Computer Science Conference*, Wollongong: CRPIT, pp. 7-7, 2008.

[18] T. L. Alves, C. Ypma, and J. Visser, "Deriving Metric Thresholds from Benchmark Data", in *Proc. of the 10th IEEE Int. Conf. on Software Maintenance*, Timisoara: IEEE Computer Society, pp. 1-10, 2010.

[19] J. C. Coppick and T. J. Cheatham, "Software Metrics for Object-Oriented Systems", in *Proc. of 20th ACM Computer Science Conference*, New York: ACM, pp. 317-322, 1992.

[20] K. Ferreira, M. Bigonha, R. Bigonha, L. Mendes, and H. Almeida, "Identifying thresholds for object-oriented software metrics", *Journal of Systems and Software*, v. 85, n. 2, pp. 244-257, 2011.

[21] L. H. Rosenberg, R. Stapko, and A. Gallo, "Risk-Based Object Oriented Testing", in *Proc. of 24th Annual Software Engineering Workshop*, Greenbelt: NASA, 1 CD-ROM, 1999.

[22] R. Shatnawi, W. Li, J. Swain, and T. Newman, "Finding software metrics threshold values using ROC curves", *Journal of Software Maintenance and Evolution: Research and Practice*, v. 22, n. 1, pp. 1-16, 2010.

[23] V. A. French, "Establishing Software Metric Thresholds", in *Proc. of 9th Int. Workshop on Software Measurement*, Mont-Tremblant, pp. 1-10, 1999.

[24] J. Biolchini et al, Systematic review in software engineering. Rio de Janeiro: UFRJ, Technical Reports RT - ES, 679/05 , 31 p., 2005.

[25] B. Kitchenham, Procedures for performing systematic reviews. Keele: Keele University, Technical Report TR/SE-0401; NICTA Technical Report, 0400011T.1, 33 p., 2004.

[26] B. Kitchenham and S. Charters. Guidelines for performing systematic literature reviews in software engineering. Keele: EBSE Technical Report EBSE-2007-01, 57 p., 2007.

[27] T. Dyba, T. Dingsoyr, and G. K. Hanssen, "Applying Systematic Reviews to Diverse Study Types: An Experience Report", in *Proc. of 1st Int. Symposium on Empirical Software Engineering and Measurement*, Washington: IEEE Computer Society, pp. 225-234, 2007.

[28] Jabref, "JabRef reference manager", 2015. [Online]. Available: http://www.jabref.org. [accessed: 13-July-2016].

[29] O. Alan and C. Catal, "An Outlier Detection Algorithm Based on Object-Oriented Metrics Thresholds", in *Proc. of the 24th Int. Symposium on Computer and Information Sciences,* Guzelyurt: IEEE Computer Society, pp. 567-570, 2009.

[30] T. L. Alves, J. P. Correia, and J. Visser, "Benchmark-Based Aggregation of Metrics to Ratings", in *Proc. of the 21th Int. Workshop on Software Measurement; Int. Conf. on Software Process and Product Measurement*, Nara: IEEE Computer Society, pp. 20-29, 2011.

[31] S. Benlarbi, K. El Emam, N. Goel, and S. Rai, "Thresholds for Object-Oriented Measures", in *Proc. of 11th Int. Symposium on Software Reliability Engineering*, San Jose: IEEE Computer Society, pp. 24-38, 2000.

[32] K. El Emam et al., "The optimal class size for object-oriented software", *IEEE Transactions on Software Engineering*, v. 28, n. 5, pp. 494-509, 2002.

[33] C. Catal, U. Sevim, and B. Diri, "Clustering and Metrics Thresholds Based Software Fault Prediction of Unlabeled Program Modules", in *Proc. of 6th Int. Conf. on Information Technology New Generations*, Las Vegas: IEEE Computer Society, pp. 199-204, 2009.

[34] H. Washizaki, H. Yamamoto, and Y. Fukazawa, "A Metrics Suite for Measuring Reusability of Software Components", in *Proc. of 9th Int. Symposium on Software Metrics*, Sydney: IEEE Computer Society, pp. 211-223, 2003.

[35] R. Ramler, K. Wolfmaier, and T. Natschlager, "Observing Distributions in Size Metrics: Experience From Analyzing Large Software Systems", in *Proc. of 31th Annual Int. Computer Software and Applications Conference*, Beijing: IEEE Computer Society, pp. 299-304, 2007.

[36] Schneidewind, N. F. "Software Metrics Model for Quality Control", in *Proc. of 4th Int. Software Metrics Symposium*, Albuquerque: IEEE Computer Society, pp. 127-136, 1997.

[37] R. Shatnawi, "A Quantitative Investigation of the Acceptable Risk Levels of Object-Oriented Metrics in Open-Source Systems", *IEEE Transactions on Software Engineering*, v. 36, n. 2, pp. 216-225, 2010.

[38] P. Oliveira, M. T. Valente, and F. L. Paim, "Extracting Relative Thresholds for Source Code Metrics", *Software Maintenance, Reengineering and Reverse Engineering (CSMR-WCRE), 2014 Software Evolution Week - IEEE Conference on*, pp.254-263, 2014.

[39] C. Catal, O. Alan, and K. Balkan, "Class noise detection based on software metrics and ROC curves", *Information Sciences*, vol. 181, no. 21, pp. 4867-4877, 2011.

[40] J. Al Dallal, "Improving the applicability of object-oriented class cohesion metrics", *Information and Software Technology*, vol. 53, no. 9, pp. 914-928, 2011.

[41] G. Succi, W. Pedrycz, S. Djokic, P. Zuliani, and B. Russo, "An Empirical Exploration of the Distributions of the Chidamber and Kemerer Object-Oriented Metrics Suite", *Empirical Software Engineering*, v. 10, n. 1, pp. 81-104, 2005.

[42] S. Herbold, J. Grabowski, and S. Waack, "Calculation and optimization of thresholds for sets of software metrics", *Empirical Software Engineering*, v. 16, n. 6, pp. 812-841, 2011.

[43] T. R. G. Nair and R. Selvarani, "Estimation of Software Reusability: An Engineering Approach". ACM SIGSOFT Software Engineering Notes, New York, v. 35, n. 1, p. 1-6, 2010.

[44] K. Wolfmaier and R. Ramler, "Common Findings and Lessons Learned from Software Architecture and Design Analysis", in *Proc. of 11th IEEE Int. Software Metrics Symposium*, Como: IEEE Computer Society, pp. 1-8, 2005.

[45] L. H. Rosenberg, "Applying and Interpreting Object Oriented Metrics", in *Proc. of 10th Software Technology Conference*, Utah, pp. 1-18, 1998.

[46] T. Copeland, *PMD applied*. Alexandria, Va.: Centennial Books, 2005.

[47] T. C. Lethbridge, A. Forward, and O. Badreddin, "Umplification: Refactoring to Incrementally Add Abstraction to a Program", in *Conference on Reverse Engineering*, Boston, pp. 220-224, 2010.

[48] Cruise Group, "Umple: Merging Modeling with Programming", 2016. [Online]. Available: http://www.umple.org. [accessed: 13-July-2016].

[49] M. Young, The Technical Writer's Handbook. Mill Valley, CA: University Science, 1989.

CERTICS - A Harmonization with CMMI-DEV Practices for Implementation of Technology Management Competence Area

Fabrício Wickey da Silva Garcia
Faculty of Computing
Federal University of Pará
Castanhal, Pará, Brazil
e-mail: fabriciowgarcia@gmail.com

Sandro Ronaldo Bezerra Oliveira
Graduate Program in Computer Science
Federal University of Pará
Belém, Pará, Brazil
e-mail: srbo@ufpa.br

Clênio Figueiredo Salviano
"Renato Archer" Information Technology Center
Campinas, São Paulo, Brazil
e-mail: clenio.salviano@cti.gov.br

Abstract—**This paper proposes a harmonization between a product quality model and a software process model used in the industry, CERTICS (a national Brazilian model) and CMMI-DEV (an international model). The focus of this harmonization is on the Competence Area of Technology Management of CERTICS, which addresses the key question of whether "the software is kept autonomous and technologically competitive". The results of the harmonization are examined step by step, as well as including a review of the harmonization, and were assisted by an expert on the CERTICS and CMMI-DEV models. Thus, this paper aims to correlate the structures of the two models to reduce the implementation time and costs, and to stimulate the execution of multi-model implementations in software development.**

Keywords-software engineering; software quality; technology management; CERTICS; CMMI-DEV; harmonization.

I. INTRODUCTION

The growing use of software in companies means that most manual work is now automated, as well as most business routines [1]. This can be regarded as a benefit since the adoption of software products generates a greater demand for goods and services. The increase in demand leads to a proportional increase in customer requirements. Thus, the requirement for greater quality in software products is increasing, since these customers are becoming more selective with regard to the software products they find acceptable [2].

There are several certified models on the market to ensure the quality of the software products, such as the Capability Maturity Model Integration (CMMI) [3], the International Organization of Standardization / International Electrotechnical Commission (ISO / IEC) 15504 [4] and Six Sigma [5]. In Brazil, there are two models that are gaining prominence, which are Brazilian Software Process Improvement (MPS.BR) [6], and the Certification of National Technology Software and Related Services (CERTICS) [7].

Brazil is a country, which has one of the world's largest range of software products, and every day the requirements of customers regarding the quality and complexity of products is increasing. From this standpoint, it can be observed that companies are increasingly seeking maturity in their software processes so that they can reach international standards of quality and productivity, which are essential for survival in the IT market. However, the cost of certification for a company can be up to US$ 400,000, which is not feasible for micro, small and medium-sized firms, and is a characteristic of Brazilian IT Enterprises. Because of this, the Department of Information Technology of the Ministry of Science, Technology and Innovation launched a number of Government and marketing initiatives, which led to a more aggressive stance to export-oriented software. These involved the creation of models to comply with the features required by national companies, and the recent investment policies for the training and expertise of professionals [6][7].

Despite the wide range of certification models, many companies seek to make improvements in their processes and products by using more than one of these models. The reason for this is that the practices included in a single one cannot fully comply with their requirements for improvement. The great difficulty in the implementation of more than one model is that each has a different kind of structure, which causes conflicts and problems about how to understand the models, which will be implemented in the company. These implementation problems that are found in more than one model can only be reduced by achieving a harmonization between them. This task will help to identify the similarities and differences between the models [8]. This harmonization is fully accepted by the regulatory bodies as a means of obtaining quality in the products and services related to software.

The research question of this paper is about how CERTICS (product quality model) and CMMI-DEV (process quality model) can help to bring about an organizational improvement in an integrated way by using the assets (practices, processes and others) that these models possess. Thus, this research is driven by the need for materials that guide the implementation process of the multi-models (CERTICS and CMMI-DEV) in companies, by providing assets to identify their strengths and weaknesses. Furthermore, this research aims to show the relationship between the CERTICS and CMMI-DEV quality models, by harmonizing their features to show the level of adhesion between their structures and support organizations that want to implement them together. The description of the main objective concerns the application of the practices defined in the quality models for the software process and product.

The extent of the business / scientific problem and its

challenges is revealed by the number of existing models that focus on improving the quality of software development. The harmonization can help to identify the common features of these models, by providing the software company with an instrument to guide the joint implementation of its practices, and thus reduce time and costs. Thus, the means of tackling this problem is to determine how many assets (practices, processes and others), which are needed to support the implementation of different models, can be applied together in the software company.

In this paper, there are discussions related to the details of the harmonization of the CERTICS model of technology management competence area with the CMMI-DEV model. In describing the similarities between the structures of the models, the coverage criteria and evaluation are performed to validate the correctness of the harmonization between the models. Thus, the purpose of this paper is to design an instrument that can guide the joint implementation of the practices contained in the two models (CMMI and CERTICS).

Several questions need to be addressed in this research: these include the way the nature and scope of the investigated problem are related to the software quality and the improvement of the process and product. They also involve an attempt to ensure that, within the scope of the process improvement in practice, the improvement of the software products can be achieved.

According to CTI Renato Archer [7], the model of CERTICS provides benefits to Brazilian software development companies that seek to gain preference in government procurement and market differentiation, and thus create a positive image of the company as an innovator of software development and technological progress in the country. Until April 2016 this model had 29 products certified and registered on the site [7].

CERTICS is composed of four competence areas. The choice of the Technology Management area for this work was based on the fact that it involves establishing action-driven strategies for research and development (R&D). This includes the absorption and / or acquisition of existing software to be embedded in technologies, based on autonomous and technological innovation. This area makes use of the results of R&D in domain ownership software, together with the relevant technologies used in software. This means that the technological innovations and decision-making capacity in the key software technologies must be introduced to ensure that the software remains technologically competitive [7].

Thus, it is expected that the results of this research will: a) reduce the burden of companies with joint implementation models, b) reduce inconsistencies and conflicts between models, and c) reduce costs through this kind of implementation. The difficulty is how to harmonize two models that are defined by different organizations and decide which practices should be integrated. Finally, this research is constrained by being concentrated in one CERTICS competence area and, for this reason, an expert has been invited to evaluate the harmonization.

This paper is structured as follows. Section II examines some related works, which carry out the harmonization of two or more models, and the two models of this research are discussed in detail. Section III outlines the harmonization of the Technology Management Competence Area of CERTICS with regard to CMMI-DEV practices. Finally, Section IV concludes with some final considerations. These include the results obtained and the limitations of this research, followed by some suggestions for possible future work.

II. Related Works and Background

This section provides an overview of the concepts of the CMMI-DEV and CERTICS models and some related works.

A. Related Works

The work of Baldassarre *et al.* [9] proposes a harmonization model that aims to support and guide companies in the integration, management and alignment of software development and quality management practices, or those that are concerned with improving existing ones. This is possible by mapping the ISO 9001 and Capability Maturity Model Integration for Development (CMMI-DEV) model, using the Goal Question Metrics (GQM) for the definition of operational goals. In this work, the statements of ISO 9001 can be reused in the CMMI assessments.

In [10], Pelszius and Ragaisis put forward a scheme for mapping and matching the maturity levels of the CMMI-DEV model and ISO / IEC 15504. The authors investigated which maturity level of a model was ensured by each level of another one. Thus, the mapping was divided into the following stages: (i) the elements of the CMMI-DEV Process Areas were mapped with the ISO / IEC 15504 process indicators, (ii) a summary of each level mapped by the models, i.e. the CMMI practices were mapped in relation to the ISO / IEC 15504 outputs, (iii) calculating the percentage of the ISO / IEC 15504 process attributes, (iv) defining the indicators that express the capability of each process, such as N for Non-Performed, P for Partially Performed, L for Largely Performed and F for Fully Performed, (v) establishing the capabilities of the ISO / IEC 15504 processes, and (vi) determining the organizational maturity of the ISO / IEC 15504, by ensuring a CMMI-DEV maturity level.

In [11], Garcia-Mireles *et al.* show the results of harmonizing the processes and product quality models. A different approach is adopted in this work, where guidance is given by the improvement goals of the software product quality control. Four stages were defined for the mapping between the process models, which are: (i) analysis models, (ii) definition of mapping, (iii) implementation of mapping, and (iv) evaluation of mapping results.

Finally, in Araújo's work [8] there are two mappings: the first is between the MPS Reference Model for Software (MR-MPS-SW) [6] and the Brazilian Test Process Improvement (MPT.Br) [12] models, and the second is made with the MR-MPS-SW and CERTICS models. On the basis of the results of this research, it was found that the first mapping showed a great adherence to the models used, while the second mapping showed that the MR-MPS-SW is only slightly adherent to the CERTICS model.

The existence of many frameworks and works dealing with the harmonization of practices included in different quality models, led to the joint implementation and evaluation of these models. It also helped the regulatory bodies to accept the existence of practices that are not yet present in the versions of their models. This brings about improvements in the the organizational process without the need for individual interventions by the large number of models.

B. The CERTICS Model

CERTICS is a Brazilian evaluation methodology that seeks to determine whether or not software is the result of technological development and innovation in the national sphere. In this way, it seeks to assess whether the product developed "creates or expands technological skills that are related to the country, or contributes to the creation of business based on knowledge. This leads to an increase in technological autonomy and innovative capacity." [7].

The CERTICS methodology was designed on the basis of the ISO / IEC 15504-2 standard [4] and aims to define a minimum set of requirements related to technological development and innovation in the country [7].

The CERTICS model is composed of four Competence Areas and sixteen Outcomes. The Competence Areas include the details about the concepts of the resulting software that is used for technological innovation and the development of the country. Each Competence Area has a key feature that describes characteristics that must be reached in order to fulfil the requirements of the model. The competence areas are as follows:

- **Technological Development (DES),** key question - "Is the software the result of technological development in Brazil?",
- **Technology Management (TEC),** key question - "Does the software remain technologically autonomous and competitive?",
- **Business Management (GNE),** key question - "Does the software leverage knowledge-based business and is it driven by these business?", and
- **Continuous Improvement (MEC),** key question - "Is the software the result of continuous improvement originating in the management of personnel, processes and knowledge to support and enhance their development and technological innovation?".

The Competence Areas have a set of outcomes, which, when implemented, must satisfy the goals of the model. The model also provides guidance about how to implement each outcome, as well as a list of examples of work products that illustrate what is desirable to fulfill each outcome [7]. In the domain of this work area, the Outcomes of the Technology Management Competence Area are:

- **TEC.1. Use of Results from Technological R&D -** the software development uses results from Technological Research and Development,
- **TEC.2. Appropriation of Relevant Technologies**, the relevant technologies used in software are appropriated by the Organizational Unit,
- **TEC.3. Introduction of Technological Innovations**, - the introduction of technological innovations in software are stimulated and kept at the Organizational Unit, and
- **TEC.4. Decision-Making Capacity** - the Organizational Unit has a decision-making capacity for the key technologies in the software.

C. The CMMI-DEV Model

CMMI is a maturity model for process improvement that is created by Software Engineering Institute (SEI) to integrate knowledge areas in a single model, such as Systems Engineering (SE), Software Engineering (SW), Integrated Products and Process Development (IPPD) and Supplier Sourcing (SS) [3].

Currently the CMMI is in version 1.3 and is composed of three models, which are: CMMI for Development (CMMI-DEV), which is concerned with development processes, CMMI for Acquisition (CMMI-ACQ), whose focus is on acquisition processes, as well as product and / or services sourcing, and CMMI for Services (CMMI-SVC), which deals with service processes such as maintenance and evolution.

The CMMI structure consists of several elements that are grouped into three categories, which are: a) required components (Specific and Generic Goals), b) expected components (Specific and Generic Practices) and c) informative components (Subpractices, Examples of Work Products, and others). These components assist in the interpretation of the model requirements. Thus, the CMMI-DEV is composed of twenty-two process areas, which consist of its purpose and specific goals for each area supplemented by generic goals, since they are related to all the process areas. The specific goals define unique characteristics for each process area, while the generic goals define characteristics that are common to all the process areas. Each specific goal has a set of specific practices, which are activities that must be taken into account to ensure that the goal is satisfied. Similarly, the generic goals have generic practices.

III. The Harmonization between CERTICS and CMMI-DEV Models

The CERTICS and CMMI-DEV models have different structures, each of which has a set of specific requirements, however, despite the particular features of each model, it can be inferred that the models have elements that can influence the fulfillment of some of the requirements that can be found in both models, according to Table I.

The CERTICS model is formed of Competence Areas, which have a set of practices (outcomes) that must be implemented so that it can fulfill the requirements of the model. Similarly, the CMMI-DEV model has an element called Process Area, which is also composed of many practices that must be implemented to fulfill their goals; these practices are called Specific and Generic Practices.

TABLE I. ELEMENTS THAT CAN INFLUENCE THE FULFILLMENT OF THE CERTICS AND CMMI-DEV REQUIREMENTS.

CERTICS Elements	CMMI-DEV Elements	
Competence Area	Process Area	
Key Questions	Specific Goals (SG)	Generic Goals (GG)
Outcomes	Specific Practices (SP)	Generic Practices (GP)
Guidelines	Subpractices	Generic Practice Elaborations
Evidences from Processes related with Software	Example of Work Products (WP)	

The Key Questions of the CERTICS model are similar in some respects to the Specific Goals and Generic Goals of CMMI-DEV, because these three elements have a set of characteristics that must be identified in a company to ensure that it fulfills the requirements of the model. Thus, the Outcomes of the CERTICS model have goals that can be equated with the Specific Practices and Generic Practices of CMMI-DEV, since these features represent the details of the requirements with regard to what should be performed as a practice to ensure the goals of these models are achieved.

It should be noted that when guiding the implementation process of these models, both have some elements that help to bring about a correct implementation of the requirements of the models. In the CERTICS model there are Guidelines and in CMMI-DEVthere are Subpractices and Generic Practice Elaborations, which offer guidance about how to implement each kind of model item.

Similarly, it was found that the Evidence of the CERTICS model also had goals that can be equated with the Example Work Products of CMMI-DEV, because these elements can act during the implementation of the models as a reference-point for what can be used so that it can provide evidence that the requirements of each model have been fulfilled.

The set of supporting concepts adopted in this paper defines a set of technologies that can be integrated to assist in the software process appraisal and improvement. In this domain, there are tools, techniques, procedures, processes, roles, methodologies, frameworks, languages, standards, patterns, and so on.

A. The Conformance Analysis of the Competence Area of Technology Management

The competence area of Technology Management has four outcomes, which are designed to ensure that the software remains autonomous and technologically competitive [7].

1) TEC.1: Use of Results from Technological R&D

The TEC.1 outcome seeks to analyze the technologies used in the software development to find out whether the results of the research and technological development (R&D) were applied to the development of the software product.

For this reason, when the CMMI-DEV model was analyzed, it was noted that the CMMI-DEV does not cover this outcome because the model does not require the results of the research and development (R&D) results in its implementation. To obtain this outcome, it would be necessary for the CMMI-DEV practices to provide the use of technological resources, such as those of any project that seeks to define the technical solutions based on R&D, partnerships or investment indicators in R&D related to the software product.

2) TEC.2: Appropriation of Relevant Technologies

The TEC.2 outcome seeks to determine whether the relevant technologies in software development that have been used, are appropriate for the organizational unit. In assessing whether this outcome has been achieved, the organizational unit must demonstrate that action taken for the appropriation of technological knowledge is present in the software, (such as the training of its professionals). Thus, this outcome needs a set of CMMI-DEV Process Areas and Practices to achieve its goals.

In the ***Project Planning (PP)***, the SP.2.3 focuses on data management planning, and the SP.2.5 and SP.2.6 ensure that the planning of the professionals involved in the project is based on their professional profiles and skills as well as the involvement of the stakeholders.

In the ***Project Monitoring and Control (PMC)***, the Specific Practice SP.1.1 allows the monitoring of the practices that were planned in PP.SP.2.5 and PP.SP.2.6, while the SP.1.4 allows the monitoring of data management based on the project plan.

In the ***Organizational Training (OT)***, the SP.1.1 seeks to maintain the training on the basis of organizational strategies and needs. The SP.1.2 determines what the training needs are in the business and what the projects are, while the SP.1.3 seeks to establish and maintain the tactical training plans, as well as the quality of this training to meet the needs that are fulfilled by the SP.1.4. Moreover, with the SP.2.1 it can ensure that the training takes place in accordance with the tactical training plan. The records of these training sessions can be kept by the SP.2.2, while the SP.2.3 makes it possible to evaluate the effectiveness of the training in the company.

The ***Generic Practice GP.2.5*** seeks to ensure that the professionals are able to handle the technology used in the company, by providing training that is suited to the needs of the company.

The coverage in TEC.2 was complete, because the CMMI-DEV had met the requirements of this outcome.

3) TEC.3: Introduction of Technological Innovations

The focus of this outcome is on technological innovation, because it seeks to find out whether the organizational unit has taken steps to introduce and encourage the use of technological innovation in software development. To this extent, this outcome needs a CMMI-DEV Process Area and Practice to achieve its goals.

In the ***Organizational Performance Management (OPM)***, with the SP.2.1 it can initiate and categorize the suggested improvements.

The coverage in TEC.3 was not complete because the

CMMI-DEV does not have practices for conducting the professional activities for members of the project that set up the schemes for technological innovation. Another requirement is the incorporation of innovative ideas that arise from joint ventures with R&D teams, as well as the software made available for technological innovation.

4) TEC.4: Decision-Making Capacity

The TEC.4 outcome seeks to determine whether the organizational unit has decision-making powers with regard to the relevant technologies that are presented in the software product. Hence, to ensure that this outcome is fulfilled, it is necessary for the organizational unit to prove that it has the authority to make changesin the relevant technologies that are present in the software. Thus, this outcome needs a set of Process Areas and Practices of CMMI-DEV to achieve its goals.

In the ***Organizational Performance Management (OPM)***, the Specific Practice SP.2.2 allows the improvements to be analyzed with regard to the possible effects of achieving the quality goals of the organizational process performance. The SP.2.3 is concerned with validating the improvements selected. In the case of the SP.2.4, it can select and prepare the improvements for implementation in the company, on the basis of an evaluation about costs, benefits and other factors.

The coverage of this outcome was partial because the CMMI-DEV has practices that allow the suggested improvements to be analyzed by selecting, implementing and validating these improvements, but the CMMI-DEVprovides no evidence to support the updates of the relevant technologies that can be found in the software and that can allow a decision to be made in the organizational unit.

B. The Evaluation of the Harmonization of Technology Management

The peer review technique was employed to evaluate the harmonization between the requirements of the CERTICS and CMMI-DEV models outlined in the last section, This was overseen by an expert, who has over five years of experience with the implementation of quality models in software development companies, and has recognized certification in CERTICS and CMMI-DEV models. The expert received the document that contains the harmonization of CERTICS and CMMI-DEV models, and carried out the review in accordance with a set of criteria, which were defined on the basis of Araújos's work [8], as shown in Table II.

When reviewing the harmonization of Technology Management (TEC) Competence Area, the expert detected a problem, which was classified as General (G). It was suggested that an analysis should be conducted of all the CMMI-DEV specific and generic practices that have been mapped in the TEC area with the aim of determining whether they are listed and described at the end of the document. If any mapped practice had not been listed, the expert suggested that it should be included in the document, as a means of enabling the goal of these practices to be understood.

TABLE II. CRITERIA DEFINED FOR THE HARMONIZATION EVALUATION.

Criteria	Definition
TH (Technical High)	Indicates that a problem in a harmonization item was found and, if not changed, would impair the system.
TL (Technical Low)	Indicating that a problem in a harmonization item was found and a change would be appropriate.
E (Editorial)	Indicating that a Portuguese language error was found or the text can be improved.
Q (Questioning)	Indicating that there were doubts about the content.
G (General)	Indicates that in general a commentary is needed.

In TEC 2, the expert found a problem that was classified as TL. Since in this outcome a Generic Practice was unnamed, the expert suggested that its name should be included in the harmonization document.

The expert did not find any problem classified as TH, E or Q.

C. How should the Harmonization be used?

The purpose of the harmonization of CERTICS and CMMI-DEV models is to help businesses that wishing to obtain certifications through multi-model implementations or even by making evaluations of the two models. The use of harmonization can optimize costs, time and effort because the models now have their structures harmonized and interrelated.

It was possible to find and highlight the differences and similarities included in the requirements of CERTICS and CMMI-DEV models. In this way, it can be seen that although some requirements of the models are similar or even complementary, it is not always possible for them to fulfil their goals in the same way. According to Association for Promoting Excellence in Brazilian Software (SOFTEX) [6], this may occur because of the different level of requirements found in some of the practices, outcomes and expected results of the models.

The harmonization spreadsheets have become an important support tool in the joint evaluation or implementation of the models, because they provide inputs that allow adaptation / harmonization in the frameworks of the models and in their expected results, practices and outcomes. This can enable the multi-models to be implemented in companies.

As a result, the company saves time from the implementation of joint models, because it will not have to spend time on separately analyzing the frameworks of the models. This means that it has to determine in what way a model can suit another one. This is because all the structures and requirements, which are the same for all the models, have been identified, harmonized and documented in the harmonization spreadsheet of the models.

IV. CONCLUSION AND FUTURE WORK

This research study has examined the harmonization of Technology Management Competence Area included in CERTICS with CMMI-DEV practices. To achieve its goals, this research sought to identify the similarities and differences between the CERTICS and CMMI-DEV frameworks by investigating their harmonization. To avoid problems of understanding and inconsistencies, an expert in the models evaluated the harmonization by the peer review technique. The results of this review were analyzed and suggested changes should be implemented to eliminate inconsistencies and problems of understanding problems, which were detected by the expert. The document with the complete harmonization generated after the peer review, including all the CERTICS Competence Areas is available in [13].

The usability of the harmonization of the two models can be corroborated by numerous certifications registered in the CERTICS website [7] about products developed by Brazilian software companies that have also made appraisals of their processes that are outlined in the CMMI website [3]. This shows that there is national interest in the two models.

The lessons learned from this research stem from the fact that there is an analytical and comparison domain between the models. Thus, it is recommended that more than one person perform it, so that any conflicts or uncertainties can be discussed and solved by a peer review.

One drawback of this study is that the harmonization has not been evaluated in a software development company; it has only been evaluated by peer review. An evaluation of the harmonization in a company is being completed in Brazil, and its processes are in accordance with the practices of CMMI-DEV Maturity Level 3. As a result, it is possible to determine whether the harmonization contributed positively or negative to a multi-model implementation. Another drawback is the fact that the peer review has only been performed by a single expert, which means that it can only be a limited view of the results obtained from the research. However, this expert is a part of a team that specifies the CERTICS model, and he has extensive experience with the implementation of the CMMI-DEV model, and reduces the bias of the results obtained from the review.

In the future, we intend to continue expanding this research, and apply it to other enterprises, and thus allow the positive and negative aspects of the use of harmonization in a CERTICS multi-model implementation with the CMMI-DEV to be quantified. Another future study concerns the definition of the complete cycle of a harmonization based on the research results of Araújo's work [8] and the SOFTEX guide [14].

So far now that the case study has not been completed, it is possible to perceive that the benefits of joint implementation are as follows: a reduction in costs and time to fulfill the expected results and practices in CERTICS and CMMI-DEV models, creation of unified and standardized evidences to achieve the two models, and the standardization of technical language, which is employed in these models, to define the software development process.

ACKNOWLEDGMENT

The authors would like to thank the Dean of Research and Postgraduate Studies at the Federal University of Pará (PROPESP/UFPA) by the Qualified Publication Support Program (PAPQ) for the financial support.

REFERENCES

[1] A. G. Cordeiro and A. L. P. Freitas, "Prioritization of requirements and evaluation of software quality as perceived buyers", Ciência da Informação, v. 40, n. 2, Brazil, pp. 24-35, 2012.

[2] itSMF UK, "An Introductory Overview of ITIL® 2011", The IT Service Management Forum UK, London, 2011.

[3] SEI, "CMMI for Development (CMMI-DEV)", Version 1.3, Software Engineering Institute, Carnegie Mellon University, USA, 2010, Available in http://www.cmmiinstitute.com. Retrieved: july/2016.

[4] ISO/IEC, "ISO/IEC 15504-2: Information Technology – Process Assessment - Part 2 -Performing an Assessment", Geneve, 2003.

[5] G. Tennant, "Six Sigma - SPC and TQM in Manufacturing and Services", Gower Publishing, Burlington, 2001.

[6] SOFTEX, "Brazilian Software Process Improvement (MPS.BR) - General Guide: 2016", Brazil, 2016.

[7] CTI Renato Archer, "Reference Model for the CERTICS Evaluation – Detailing Document", Centro de Tecnologia da Informação Renato Archer, Brazil, 2013, Available in http://www.certics.cti.gov.br. Retrieved: july/2016.

[8] L. L. Araújo, "Mapping between MPS.SW and MPT.BR and CERTICS", Dissertação de Mestrado, COPPE/UFRJ, Brazil, 2014.

[9] M. T. Baldassarre, D. Caivano, F. J. Pino, M. Piattini, and G. Visaggio, "Harmonization of ISO/IEC 9001:2000 and CMMI-DEV from a theoretical comparison to a real case application", Springer Science+Business Media. v.20 pp. 309-335, 2011.

[10] S. Pelsdziusand S. Ragaisis, "Comparison of Maturity Levels in CMMI-DEV and ISO/IEC 15504", Applications of Mathematics and Computer Engineering, pp. 117-122, 2011.

[11] G. A. García-Mireles, M. Á. Moraga, F. García, and M. Piattini, "Towards the Harmonization of Process and Product Oriented Software Quality Approaches", Springer-Verlag Systems, Software and Services Process Improvement, pp.133-144, 2012.

[12] SOFTEX RECIFE, "MPT.Br Brazilian Test ProcessImprovement – Model Reference Guide", s.l. : SOFTEX RECIFE, 2011.

[13] F. W. da S. Garcia, "An Approach to Software Quality Multi-Models Implementation adopting CERTICS and CMMI-DEV", Dissertação de Mestrado, PPGCC/UFPA, Brazil, 2016.

[14] SOFTEX, "Implementation Guide - Part 11: Implementation and Evaluation of MR-MPS-SW: 2012 Together with CMMI-DEV v1.3", Brazil, 2012.

An Investigation on the Relative Cost of Function Point Analysis Phases

Luigi Lavazza
Dipartimento di Scienze Teoriche e Applicate
Università degli Studi dell'Insubria
Varese, Italy
email: luigi.lavazza@uninsubria.it

Abstract— **Function Point Analysis (FPA) is widely used, especially to quantify the size of applications in the early stages of development, when effort estimates are needed. However, the measurement process is often too long or too expensive, or it requires more knowledge than available when development effort estimates are due. To overcome these problems, early size estimation methods have been proposed, to get approximate estimates of Function Point (FP) measures. In general, early estimation methods (EEM's) adopt measurement processes that are simplified with respect to the standard process, in that one or more phases are skipped. EEM's are considered effective; however there is little evidence of the actual savings that they can guarantee. To this end, it is necessary to know the relative cost of each phase of the standard FP measurement process. This paper presents the results of a survey concerning the relative cost of the phases of the standard FP measurement process. It will be possible to use data provided in the paper to assess the expected savings that can be achieved by performing an early estimation of FP size, instead of properly measuring it.**

Keywords- functional size measurement; Function Point Analysis; IFPUG Function Points; measurement process; cost of measurement.

I. INTRODUCTION

FPA [1][2][3][4] is widely used. Among the reasons for the success of FPA is that it can provide measures of size in the early stages of software development, when they are most needed for cost estimation.

However, FPA performed by a certified FP consultant proceeds at a relatively slow pace: between 400 and 600 FP per day, according to Capers Jones [5], between 200 and 300 FP per day according to experts from Total Metrics [6]. Consequently, measuring the size of a moderately large application can take too long, if cost estimation is needed urgently. Also, the cost of measurement can be often considered excessive by software developers. In addition, cost estimates may be needed when requirements have not yet been specified in detail and completely.

To overcome the aforementioned problems, EEM's that provide approximate values of FP measures have been proposed. A quite comprehensive list of such methods is given in [7].

The goal of the work presented here is to assess the cost of the measurement activities (detailed in Section II.B). However, as mentioned in the introduction, there is little agreement on the cost of FP measurement: for instance, Capers Jones [5] and Total Metrics [6] provide quite different evaluations. Therefore, it appeared more viable to pursue an evaluation of the *relative* cost of the measurement phases. In this way, we will be able to assess how much we save -in terms of measurement effort, hence ultimately of money- by skipping a measurement phase, i.e., by not performing one of the activities of the standard measurement process. In fact, if a manger knows that applying the standard measurement process in her organization takes X PersonHours per FP, and a simplified measurement process allows for saving 70% of the effort, she can easily conclude that in her organization the application of the simplified process will take 0.7X PersonHours.

The paper is structured as follows. Section II reports a few basic concepts of FPA. Section III describes how the surveys was carried out, illustrates the results of the survey and discusses the threats to the validity of the study. Section IV accounts for related work. Finally, Section V draws conclusions and briefly sketches future work.

II. FUNCTION POINT ANALYSIS CONCEPTS

FPA aims at providing a measure of the size of the functional specifications of a given software application.

A. *The model of the software being measured according to FPA*

FPA addresses functional specifications that are represented according to a specific model. The model of functional specifications used by FPA is given in Fig. 1. Briefly, Logical files are the data processed by the application, and transactions are the operations available to users. The size measure in FP is computed as a weighted sum of the number of Logical files and Transactions. The weight of logical data files is computed based on the Record Elements Types (RET), i.e., subgroups of data belonging to a data file, and Data Element Types (DET), i.e., the elementary pieces of data; besides, the weight depends on whether the data file is within the boundaries of the application, i.e., it is an Internal Logic File (ILF) or it is outside such boundaries, i.e., it is an External Interface File (EIF). The weight of transactions is computed based on the Logical files involved –see the FTR (File Type Referenced) association in Fig. 1– and the DET used for I/O; besides, the weight depends on the "main intent" of the transaction. In fact, depending on the main intent, transactions are classified as External Inputs (EI), External Outputs (EO) or External Queries (EQ).

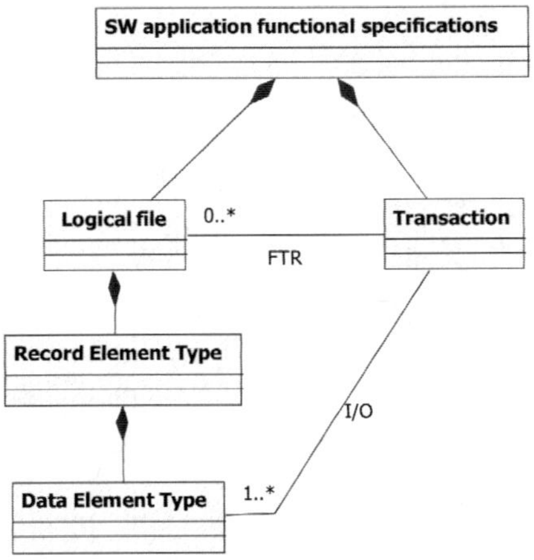

Figure 1. The model of software used in FPA.

B. The FPA measurement process

According to the International Function Point User Group (IFPUG) measurement manual [3][4], the measurement process includes the following phases:

1. Gathering the available documentation concerning functional user requirements;
2. Identifying application boundaries;
3. Determining the measurement goal and scope;
4. Identifying Elementary Processes (Transactions) and Logical Data Files;
5. Classifying transactions as EI, EO or EQ; classifying files as ILF or EIF; identifying RET, DET, FTR and determining complexity;
6. Calculating the functional size;
7. Documenting and presenting the measurement.

The EEM's tend to skip as many as possible of the steps listed above. The idea is straightforward: the less phases have to be performed, the faster and cheaper is the process. However, some activities –namely, those involved in phases 1, 2 and 4– are preparatory of the real measurement and cannot be skipped. Similarly, phase 7 can hardly be avoided. In any case, it should be noted that the simplification of the measurement process can affect phases 1 and 7 as well: on the one hand, a simplified process requires less documentation concerning Functional User Requirements (FUR); on the other hand, documenting and presenting a simplified measurement is easier and faster than documenting the full-fledged measurement.

As a final observation, the extent of phase 7 depends on the context and the goal of measurement: for instance, if an organization is measuring the size of the application to be developed for "internal" purposes, the documentation can be kept to a minimum; on the contrary, if the functional size measures have to be used in a bid or in establishing the price of a contract, the documentation to be produced has usually to be quite detailed, and the presentation of the measures and measurement has also to be accurate. In practice, the cost of phase 7 depends more on the context and goal of the measurement than on the fact that the standard process or a simplified process were used.

In conclusion, EEM's address mainly phases 4, 5 and 6. However, there is hardly any evidence of how much you save if you skip any of these phases. On the contrary, some evidence exists that by simplifying the measurement process, some measurement error is introduced [19].

III. Experiment and Results

A. The survey

The investigation described here was performed via a questionnaire, which was filled by people that are experienced in IFPUG Function Point measurement.

The questionnaire was published on the kwiksurveys site [20]. The questionnaire was publicized via several channels:

- An invitation to fill out the questionnaire was sent to the Italian Function Point User Association (www.gufpi-isma.org);
- A similar invitation was sent to the Nesma association [21];
- Finally, a question was published on ResearchGate [22], and experts were redirected to the questionnaire URL.

The questionnaire is reported in the appendix. It can be noticed that the questionnaire targets both the IFPUG [3][4] and the Nesma [9] measurement processes. In fact, according to Nesma, *"[Since 1994,] owing to [...] the intensive cooperation between the Nesma and the IFPUG, the counting guidelines of the NESMA and the IFPUG continuously came closer and closer. [...] With the publication of IFPUG CPM 4.2 (2004) the last major differences between IFPUG and NESMA disappeared."* Therefore, mixing data concerning the current IFPUG and Nesma measurement processes is perfectly safe, and the results found apply equally well to both measurement methods.

The questionnaire was published in November 2014, and answers were collected until April 2015.

B. The Results of the survey

31 answers were collected. Even if the number is not very large, it is nonetheless sufficient to get a reasonably reliable assessment of the relative cost of FP measurement activities.

Of the respondents, 21 are certified Function Point Specialist (CFPS), and 4 are certified Function Point Practitioner (CFPP). Only 6 have no certification; however, of these, 2 use NESMA Function Points, therefore it is reasonable that they do not need an IFPUG certification.

The experience of the respondents is also quite reassuring: 20 respondents have been using FP measurement for over 10 years; only two for less than 5 years.

It should be noted that the questionnaire does not ask for a specific percentage for each phase; instead, it asks to specify in what range the actual percentage of effort belongs. This choice was due to two reasons: 1) the free version of the questionnaire provided by kwiksurveys does not support the collection of numeric values, and 2) it is unlikely that a respondent knows the exact fraction of effort that is spent in each phase, while it is much more probable that he/she can indicate the correct range.

TABLE I. ANSWERS CONCERNING RELATIVE PHASE COSTS

Respondent	Phase 1	Phase 2	Phase 3	Phase 4	Phase 5	Phase 6	Phase 7
1	11-15%	0-5%	0-5%	26-30%	36-40%	0-5%	16-20%
2	16-20%	6-10%	0-5%	36-40%	6-10%	0-5%	16-20%
3	6-10%	0-5%	0-5%	6-10%	46-50%	0-5%	11-15%
4	0-5%	0-5%	0-5%	66-70%	0-5%	0-5%	0-5%
5	0-5%	6-10%	6-10%	36-40%	16-20%	0-5%	0-5%
6	0-5%	0-5%	46-50%	31-35%	0-5%	0-5%	0-5%
7	6-10%	6-10%	0-5%	21-25%	26-30%	0-5%	11-15%
8	26-30%	11-15%	6-10%	11-15%	11-15%	0-5%	11-15%
9	16-20%	0-5%	0-5%	21-25%	21-25%	0-5%	11-15%
10	0-5%	0-5%	0-5%	46-50%	31-35%	0-5%	0-5%
11	31-35%	0-5%	0-5%	21-25%	16-20%	11-15%	0-5%
12	0-5%	0-5%	0-5%	16-20%	0-5%	0-5%	11-15%
13	0-5%	0-5%	0-5%	21-25%	46-50%	0-5%	0-5%
14	0-5%	0-5%	0-5%	41-45%	26-30%	0-5%	0-5%
15	11-15%	6-10%	0-5%	36-40%	11-15%	0-5%	0-5%
16	6-10%	0-5%	0-5%	51-55%	16-20%	0-5%	0-5%
17	6-10%	6-10%	0-5%	26-30%	6-10%	36-40%	6-10%
18	0-5%	0-5%	0-5%	36-40%	36-40%	0-5%	0-5%
19	6-10%	6-10%	0-5%	11-15%	11-15%	0-5%	41-45%
20	31-35%	16-20%	6-10%	26-30%	11-15%	0-5%	0-5%
21	16-20%	6-10%	6-10%	16-20%	11-15%	6-10%	16-20%
22	16-20%	0-5%	0-5%	61-65%	0-5%	0-5%	0-5%
23	0-5%	56-60%	16-20%	66-70%	51-55%	0-5%	11-15%
24	6-10%	6-10%	11-15%	26-30%	11-15%	11-15%	0-5%
25	11-15%	6-10%	0-5%	21-25%	21-25%	11-15%	6-10%
26	6-10%	0-5%	0-5%	41-45%	21-25%	0-5%	6-10%
27	41-45%	6-10%	0-5%	6-10%	6-10%	6-10%	11-15%
28	6-10%	16-20%	6-10%	31-35%	11-15%	0-5%	16-20%
29	11-15%	0-5%	0-5%	66-70%	11-15%	0-5%	0-5%
30	21-25%	0-5%	0-5%	21-25%	21-25%	6-10%	0-5%
31	0-5%	0-5%	0-5%	6-10%	6-10%	0-5%	0-5%

The collected data concerning the relative effort required by each measurement phase are given in Table I.

When information is collected via questionnaires, it is always possible that some respondents do not provide correct data. Therefore, before proceeding to the analysis of the collected data, it is necessary to remove unreliable answers from the dataset. In our case, the following problems were considered:

1) The sum of the efforts spent in each phase must be 100%. Having asked for ranges, we expect that the sum of the lower bounds of the ranges is $\leq$ 100% (but close to 100%) and that the sum of the upper bounds is $\geq$ 100% (but close to 100%). Respondents 12, 23 and 31 do not satisfy these conditions: total effort is in [27%, 60%] range for respondent 12, in [200%, 230%] range for respondent 23 and in [12%, 45%] range for respondent 31. These are clearly meaningless indications, therefore they have been excluded from the dataset.
2) Among the remaining respondents, it is easy to spot a few outliers. Respondent 19 declared a fraction of effort for phase 7 (Documenting and presenting the measurement) that is almost half the total effort and more than double than the other respondents'. Respondent 27 declared an abnormally large amount of effort dedicated to phase 1 (Gathering the available documentation concerning FUR): such a large effort may be required in specific contexts, but is not representative of the general case (as other respondents clearly show). To preserve the representativeness of the data, the answers provided by the mentioned respondents have been excluded from the dataset.
3) Respondents 4 and 5 declared that they use (EEM's). Their answers were removed from the dataset, since we

are interested in the relative cost of the standard measurement process.

To analyze the data in Table I, the following procedure was adopted:

1) For every phase, the mean values of the lower bound and upper bound of the given ranges were computed. Let MLB_i and MUB_i be the means of the upper and lower bound, respectively, for phase i.
2) For every phase, $M_i = (MLB_i + MUB_i)/2$ was computed. Being the midpoint between MLB_i and MUB_i, M_i indicates the more likely value for the fraction of effort spent in the ith phase, according to respondents.
3) It was then found that $\Sigma_{i=1,7}\ M_i = 91.4\%$. This is not acceptable, since the sum of the efforts dedicated to the measurement phases must equal the total measurement effort. Therefore, we computed a weighted version of M_i: $WM_i = 100\ Mi/91.4$, so that $\Sigma_{i=1,7}\ WM_i = 100\%$. WM_i is assumed to indicate the most likely value for the fraction of effort spent in the ith phase.

The values of MLB_i, MUB_i M_i and WM_i are given in Table II.

TABLE II. MEAN VALUES OF PHASE RELATIVE COSTS

Phase	MLB_i	MUB_i	M_i	WM_i
1	10.8%	15.0%	12.9%	14.1%
2	3.5%	8.1%	5.8%	6.4%
3	3.4%	8.1%	5.8%	6.3%
4	30.8%	34.8%	32.8%	35.9%
5	18.8%	22.9%	20.9%	22.8%
6	3.4%	8.1%	5.8%	6.3%
7	5.3%	9.8%	7.5%	8.2%

Since in general the mean is affected by the smallest and largest values in the observed population, we repeated the procedure described above using the medians of upper and lower bounds. The results obtained are given in Table III.

TABLE III. MEDIAN VALUES OF PHASE RELATIVE COSTS

Phase	MLB_i	MUB_i	M_i	WM_i
1	8.5%	12.5%	10.5%	15.8%
2	0.0%	5.0%	2.5%	3.8%
3	0.0%	5.0%	2.5%	3.8%
4	26.0%	30.0%	28.0%	42.1%
5	16.0%	20.0%	18.0%	27.1%
6	0.0%	5.0%	2.5%	3.8%
7	0.0%	5.0%	2.5%	3.8%

The results of the analyses provide some useful indications concerning the relative cost of the phases of FP measurement, performed according to the IFPUG or Nesma process.

The results concerning the relative efforts derived using the means and the medians are fairly close: this fact supports the hypothesis that values reported in Tables II and III are actually representative of the real relative effort per phase.

The fact that more than half the effort is concentrated in phases 4 and 5 also appears to confirm the reliability of results. In fact, it is popular wisdom that most measurement effort is required by the analysis of data and processes, which is concentrated in phases 4 and 5.

C. Threats to validity

A first threat to the validity of the study is due to the number of datapoints that were collected. Although it was possible to collect only 31 datapoints, we strived to guarantee the representativeness of the collected data by eliminating outliers, as well as data that appear incorrect. In any case, the size of the dataset that was finally analyzed (containing 24 datapoints) is not smaller than many datasets used for empirical software engineering studies.

Concerning the statistical analyses that were performed in this study, they are so simple that it is unlikely that any serious threat to statistically validity actually applies. One could observe that confidence intervals for the mean values could have been computed, but having already asked for ranges rather than specific values, computing confidence intervals would have been sort of overkilling.

Most respondents (23) are from Italy, four are form the Netherlands and the remaining ones are from Brazil, Switzerland and Belgium. The lack of geographic dispersion could be a limit for the generalizability of results. However, most respondents are certified Function Point Specialists or certified Function Point Practitioners, thus we can assume that they all follow the process specified in the official manuals [3][4][8][9]. If so, our results should be applicable to all the measurements performed according to the standard counting practices.

IV. RELATED WORK

There is not much literature concerning the cost of functional size measurement. A couple of documents report about the total cost of FP measurement [5][6], but none provides information concerning how the total effort is spread among the various measurement phases.

Some indications are provided by the proposers of EEM's. For instance, it was reported that "*the E&Q size estimation technique has been proved in practice to be quite effective, providing a response within ± 10% of the real size in most real cases, while the savings in time (and costs) can be between 50% and 90% (depending on the comprised aggregation level) with respect to corresponding standard measurement procedures.*" [18]

It was also reported that "*the results found with NESMA estimated fall within a reach of -6% to +15% of the corresponding result found with a NESMA detailed approach, and NESMA estimated FSM is performed 1,5 times as fast as a NESMA detailed FSM.*" [12]

These evaluations are probably optimistic to some extent. However, they are not precise enough to be used for decision making: for instance, it is not clear if the reported savings are evaluated with respect to the whole measurement process or only with respect to the core part (phases 4-6).

V. CONCLUSIONS

The measurement process of IFPUG (and Nesma) FP is often considered too expensive and time consuming. To overcome this problem, EEM's have been proposed, to obtain faster and cheaper approximate measure estimates.

However, it is quite difficult to estimate how much measurement effort can be actually saved by using an EEM instead of the standard measurement process. This knowledge would be clearly quite important for managers who have to choose whether to perform a full-fledged measurement or an approximate estimation.

Since EEM's indicate what phases of the measurement process they allow to skip, to be able to evaluate the saving yielded by EEM's we need to know the relative cost of the measurement phases that compose the standard IFPUG measurement process. To this end, a questionnaire was proposed to professional measurers, and the collected answers were analyzed.

The results of the analysis are reported in this paper (see Section B).

Most EEM's allow for skipping phases 5 and 6. Among such methods are the NESMA estimated [8][11][12], Early&Quick Function Point [10], simplified Function Point [14] (not to be confused with the Simple Function Point method, which is a proper functional size measurement method, not an EEM method[17][15][16]), ISBSG average weights (which assigns to each basic functional component the average weight that type of component has in the ISBSG dataset [13]).

According to the values given in Tables II and III, we can see that EEM's that allow to skip phases 5 and 6 are expected to save 28–30% of the measurement effort. Actually, as previously mentioned, also phases 1 and 7 are expected to become faster and simpler when EEM's are used. However, the analysis reported here does not support the evaluation of savings in phases 1 and 7, which are largely dependent on the context.

Future work includes:

- Extending the dataset, especially with answers from non-European countries, to make the dataset representative of a larger community of IFPUG users.
- If possible, collecting real effort data from the field, instead of subjective indications provided by measurers. This would make it possible to analyze not only the relative cost of measurement phases, but also the actual cost of measurement.
- Characterizing the contexts in which measurement is performed, to support the empirical evaluation of the dependency of the relative cost of measurement phases on the context.

ACKNOWLEDGMENT

The work presented here has been partly supported by the FP7 Collaborative Project S-CASE (Grant Agreement No 610717), funded by the European Commission and by the "Fondo di Ricerca d'Ateneo" of the Università degli Studi dell'Insubria.

REFERENCES

[1] A. J. Albrecht, "Measuring Application Development Productivity", Joint SHARE/ GUIDE/IBM Application Development Symposium, pp 83–92, 1979.

[2] A. J. Albrecht and J. E. Gaffney, "Software function, lines of code and development effort prediction: a software science validation", IEEE Trans. on Software Eng., vol. 9, pp. 639–648, 1983.

[3] International Function Point Users Group, "Function Point Counting Practices Manual - Release 4.3.1", 2010.

[4] ISO/IEC 20926: 2003, "Software engineering – IFPUG 4.1 Unadjusted functional size measurement method – Counting Practices Manual", ISO, Geneva, 2003.

[5] C. Jones, "A new business model for function point metrics", http://concepts.gilb.com/dl185, 2008. Last access June 12th, 2016.

[6] "Methods for Software Sizing – How to Decide which Method to Use", Total Metrics, www.totalmetrics.com/function-point-resources/downloads/R185_Why-use-Function-Points.pdf, August 2007. Last access June 12th, 2016.

[7] L. Santillo, "Easy Function Points – 'Smart' Approximation Technique for the IFPUG and COSMIC Methods", IWSM-MENSURA, pp. 137–142, 2012.

[8] ISO/IEC, ISO/IEC 24750:2005, Software Engineering "NESMA Functional Size Measurement Method, Version 2.1, Definitions and counting guidelines for the application of Function Point Analysis. International Organization for Standardization, Geneva, 2005.

[9] NESMA, "Counting Practice Manual, Version 2.1", 2004.

[10] "Early & Quick Function Points for IFPUG methods v. 3.1 Reference Manual 1.1", April 2012.

[11] nesma, Early Function Point Analysis, July 15, 2015, http://nesma.org/freedocs/early-function-point-analysis/ Last access June 12th, 2016.

[12] H. S. van Heeringen, E. W. M. van Gorp, and T. G. Prins, Functional size measurement accuracy versus costs is it really worth it? Software Measurement European Forum, May 2009.

[13] ISBSG, Worldwide Software Development–the Benchmark. Release 5, International Software Benchmarking Standards Group, 1998.

[14] R. Meli and L. Santillo, Function Point Estimation Methods: a Comparative Overview, FESMA conference, pp. 2009.

[15] L. Lavazza and R. Meli. "An Evaluation of Simple Function Point as a Replacement of IFPUG Function Point." IWSM-MENSURA 2014. IEEE, pp. 196–206, 2014.

[16] F. Ferrucci, C. Gravino, and L. Lavazza, "Assessing Simple Function Points for Effort Estimation: an Empirical Study", 31st ACM Symposium on Applied Computing – SAC 2016, Pisa, April 4-8, pp. 1428–1433, 2016.

[17] Simple Function Point Association, Simple Function Point - Functional Size Measurement Method Reference Manual v01.01, March 2014, http://www.sifpa.org/en/sifp-method/manual.htm. Last access June 12th, 2016.

[18] L. Santillo, M. Conte, and R. Meli. "Early & Quick function point: sizing more with less." 11th IEEE International Symposium on Software Metrics, 2005. IEEE, 2005.

[19] L. Lavazza and G. Liu, An Empirical Evaluation of Simplified Function Point Measurement Processes, Int. Journal on Advances in Software, vol. 6, n. 1-2, pp. 1-13, 2013.

[20] Kwiksurveys site, https://kwiksurveys.com/s.asp?sid=azttngx1iibno6450647#/ Last accessed June 12th, 2016.

[21] nesma association, www.nesma.org. Last accessed June 12th, 2016.

[22] ResearchGate, http://www.researchgate.net/ Last accessed June 12th, 2016.

APPENDIX - THE QUESTIONNAIRE

A survey about the relative effort required by the phases of Functional Size Measurement

A. *About you...*

Question	Possible answers
Are you a certified Function Point Specialist (CFPS)?	Yes/No
Are you a certified Function Point Practitioner (CFPP)?	Yes/No
How many years of experience do have in FP counting?	Less than 5 Between 5 and 10 More than 10
How many FP per year do you count on average?	No more than 200 Between 200 and 1000 Between 1000 and 5000 More than 5000

B. *Relative effort required by the phases of functional size measurement*

According to your experience, what is the relative effort required by the phases of functional size measurement? Please, specify how big is the percentage effort for each phase, according to your experience. Please note that here we consider the measurement performed at the beginning of the project, based on functional user requirements.

Thanks a lot for your answers! If you have any additional comment or remark, or if you want to be informed on the results of the survey, please send an email to: luigi.lavazza@uninsubria.it

Question	Possible answers
Phase 1: gathering the available documentation concerning functional user requirements	0-5%, 6-10%, 11-15%, 16-20%, 21-25%, 26-30%, 31-35%, 36-40%, 41-45%, 46-50%, 51-55%, 56-60%, 61-65%, 66-70%, 71-75%, 76-80%, 81-85%, 86-90%, 91-95%, 96-100%
Phase 2: Identifying application boundaries	0-5%, 6-10%, 11-15%, 16-20%, 21-25%, 26-30%, 31-35%, 36-40%, 41-45%, 46-50%, 51-55%, 56-60%, 61-65%, 66-70%, 71-75%, 76-80%, 81-85%, 86-90%, 91-95%, 96-100%
Phase 3: Determining the measurement goal and scope	0-5%, 6-10%, 11-15%, 16-20%, 21-25%, 26-30%, 31-35%, 36-40%, 41-45%, 46-50%, 51-55%, 56-60%, 61-65%, 66-70%, 71-75%, 76-80%, 81-85%, 86-90%, 91-95%, 96-100%
Phase 4: Identifying Elementary Processes (Transactions) and Logical Data Files	0-5%, 6-10%, 11-15%, 16-20%, 21-25%, 26-30%, 31-35%, 36-40%, 41-45%, 46-50%, 51-55%, 56-60%, 61-65%, 66-70%, 71-75%, 76-80%, 81-85%, 86-90%, 91-95%, 96-100%
Phase 5: Classifying transactions as EI, EO or EQ; classifying files as ILF or EIF; identifying RET, DET, FTR and determining complexity	0-5%, 6-10%, 11-15%, 16-20%, 21-25%, 26-30%, 31-35%, 36-40%, 41-45%, 46-50%, 51-55%, 56-60%, 61-65%, 66-70%, 71-75%, 76-80%, 81-85%, 86-90%, 91-95%, 96-100%
Phase 6: Calculating the functional size	0-5%, 6-10%, 11-15%, 16-20%, 21-25%, 26-30%, 31-35%, 36-40%, 41-45%, 46-50%, 51-55%, 56-60%, 61-65%, 66-70%, 71-75%, 76-80%, 81-85%, 86-90%, 91-95%, 96-100%
Phase 7: Documenting and presenting the measurement	0-5%, 6-10%, 11-15%, 16-20%, 21-25%, 26-30%, 31-35%, 36-40%, 41-45%, 46-50%, 51-55%, 56-60%, 61-65%, 66-70%, 71-75%, 76-80%, 81-85%, 86-90%, 91-95%, 96-100%
Please, specify what measurement method the given data you gave apply to	IFPUG NESMA Other
Please, specify if the given data take into account some type of simplification	No simplification Nesma estimated Nesma indicative Early & Quick FP Other

A Pattern Language for Application-level Communication Protocols

Jorge Edison Lascano[1,2], Stephen Wright Clyde[1]
[1]Computer Science Department, Utah State University, Logan, Utah, USA
[2]Departamento de Ciencias de la Computación, Universidad de las Fuerzas Armadas ESPE, Sangolquí, Ecuador
email: edison_lascano@yahoo.com, Stephen.Clyde@usu.edu

Abstract—**Distributed applications depend on application-layer communication protocols to exchange data among processes and coordinate distributed operations, independent of underlying communication subsystems and lower level protocols. Since such protocols are application-specific, developers often must invent or re-invent solutions to reoccurring problems involving sending and receiving messages to meet specific functionality, efficiency, distribution, reliability, and security requirements. This paper introduces a pattern language, called CommDP, consisting of nine design patterns that can help developers understand existing reusable solutions and how those solutions might apply to their situations. Consistent with other pattern languages, the CommDP patterns are described in terms of the problems they address, their contexts, and solutions. The problems and consequences of the solutions are evaluated against four desirable qualities: reliability, synchronicity, longevity, and adaptability for scalable distribution.**

Keywords-design patterns; pattern languages; communication protocols.

I. INTRODUCTION

At the application level, a distributed system is two or more processes sharing resources and working together via network communications to accomplish a common goal [1][2]. Such systems are ubiquitous in today's Internet-connected world and are found in virtually every application domain, such as personal productivity tools, social media, entertainment, research, and business. Even single-user software systems that appear to be non-distributed may in fact communicate with other processes in the background to download updates, track usage statistics, or capture error logs, and are therefore actually distributed systems.

In general, the developers of a distributed system try to increase its overall throughput, reliability, and scalability by hosting data and/or operations on multiple machines, while minimizing network traffic, congestion, and turn-around times. Exactly how they do this depends heavily on the nature and requirements of the application. In some cases, developers may choose to distribute instances of one type of resource, e.g., image files in a peer-to-peer shared photo library. In other situations, developers may group resources such that all instances of a single type are on one server. Still in other cases, developers can take hybrid approaches, distributing certain types of resources among peers and hosting other types on dedicated servers. A closely related design issue deals with the granularity of the distributed resources, i.e., data and operations. From a data perspective, the possible choices range from whole databases to individual records or even individual fields within records. From an operations perspective, the choices range from entire subsystems to atomic operations. With today's programming languages, many developers follow the object-oriented paradigm, encapsulating operations with data and making choices for granularity that range from entire sets of objects to object fragments [3].

Besides deciding on the granularity and distribution of resources (data, operations, or objects), developers often have to consider requirements for security, fault tolerance, maintainability, openness, extensibility, scalability, and dynamic quality of service [2]. The degree to which an application possesses these desirable characteristics is primarily a consequence of architectural design choices, which, in turn, place new requirements on inter-process communications.

The problem is not that existing application-level communications protocols are poorly designed and implemented; rather, the problem is that application developer has to re-invent or re-design them for every new application.

In this paper, we will refer to an exchange among two or more processes for a particular purpose as a *conversation*. A single conversation may be short and simple, like querying a stock's price, or it could be long and complex, like the streaming of a video. The rules that govern a particular type of conversation are a *communication protocol* and a collection of protocols is called a *protocol suite* [4][5].

Application-layer communication protocols (ACPs) are often defined on top of other protocols. For example, the *Hypertext Transfer Protocol* (HTTP), which is an ACP, is defined on top of the *Transmission Control Protocol* (TCP) [1]. Many higher level ACPs, like webservice-based ACPs, are in turn defined on top of HTTP [1]. Section II provides additional background on protocols and protocol suites, as well as a brief discussion on layered communication subsystems.

Because requirements for ACPs can come from an application's (a) functional requirements, (b) architectural design, and (c) use of lower layer protocols, coming up with effective designs can be challenging. Fortunately, the problems that developers are likely to encounter are not uncommon and have known solutions. The key is to capture this knowledge in a way that developers can easily find it and adapt it to a new application. This is precisely what design patterns can do [6].

Unfortunately, design patterns for communication protocols at application layer have yet not been gathered, correlated, and formally organized into a cohesive and thorough collection. To this end, this paper introduces a system of design patterns, i.e., a pattern language, for ACPs, called CommDP. The patterns in CommDP come from a variety of sources and are by themselves not new ideas, as is the case for all newly documented design patterns [7]. Section III provides more background information on design patterns and pattern languages, as well as information about related work.

Since designing ACPs is different from designing executable software, it is necessary to discuss desirable qualities for protocols. Section IV introduces four, namely reliability, synchronicity, longevity, and adaptability for scalable distribution. Section V presents a design pattern template that incorporates these characteristics into the definition of communication problems and the consequences of pattern solutions.

Section VI-A introduces three communication idioms that act as conceptual building blocks for all the ACP patterns in CommDP. We then provide an overview of the ACP patterns in Section VI-B. Additional details for the CommDP patterns are available on-line[1].

Patterns are rarely used in isolation; instead, developers typically weave multiple pattern instantiations together to create complete solutions [8]. A system of patterns, i.e., a pattern language, not only includes a collection of patterns, but relationships among them that help developers know how they might be effectively combined [9]. Section VI-C provides a digest of these relationships for CommDP. Finally, in Section VII, we summarize the value of CommDP and outline our future research direction.

II. Protocols and Protocol Suites

Software and electrical engineers model, design, and implement inter-process communications in layers. Fig. 1 shows a simple 5-layer model commonly favored by those

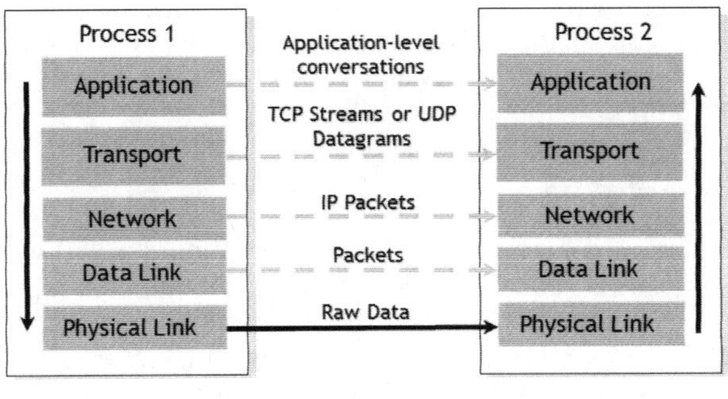

Figure 1. 5-Layer Model for IP-based Communications

who work with IP-based protocols [1][10]. There are several other common models, such as the 7-layer OSI model [11]. A conversation between Process 1 and Process 2 can be discussed at any layer and, for each layer, it must adhere to agree upon protocol(s) for that layer. For example, if Process 1 were a web browser, Process 2 were a web server, and the conversation a simple web-page request, then the application-layer protocol would be HTTP, the Transport-layer protocol would be TCP, and the Network-layer protocol would be IP.

Besides providing a convenient way for discussing protocols, layered models establish a basis for creating substitutable software communication subsystems. Since we are addressing ACPs in this paper, we do not deal directly with design and implementation of these software components. Nevertheless, we assume that appropriate communication subsystems exist at the transport layer for streaming of unstructured data and transmitting datagrams (semi-structured data). Section V relies on this reasonable assumption to define four communication idioms.

At the application layer, a protocol governs why, when, and how processes interact with each other to accomplish a common goal. Specifically, an ACP should define the following:

1. the processes involved in the interaction in terms of the roles they play during a conversation;
2. the possible sequences of messages for valid conversations;
3. the structure of the messages;
4. the meaning of the messages; and
5. relevant behaviors of the participating processes.

Because processes in a distributed system typically have to communicate with each other for many different tasks, e.g., authentication, resource sharing, and coordination, it is common for a distributed system to require multiple ACPs, i.e., an ACP suite.

III. Design Patterns and Pattern Languages

Christopher Alexander et al. defined a pattern as a reusable solution to a reoccurring problem [9]. Kent Beck and Ward Cthe detailsunningham started to apply the concept of pattern languages to software engineering in 1987 [12], and the idea was later popularized by Eric Gamma et al. with their landmark language of 23 patterns [6]. Since then, pattern languages have been documented for many areas of software engineering, including architectural design [13][14], user-interface design [15], event handling [16][17][18], and concurrency [19]-[25]. There are even patterns specifically for distributed computing [8], distributed objects [26][27][28], communication software [29][30], RESTful and SOAP web services [31], cloud computing [32], and distributed real-time and embedded systems [33]. However, to date, no pattern language has been published specifically for ACPs.

There are two hoped-for benefits of pattern languages that are important to ACP design. First, they create a vocabulary that enables developers to discuss complex ideas in a few words [28]. Second, they allow developers of all experience levels to benefit from expert reusable solutions [34].

IV. Qualities of Communication Protocols

Like software, ACP suites, as whole, should possess certain desirable qualities that contribute to the overall success of a system. Some of these desirable qualities come directly

[1] http://commdp.serv.usu.edu/

from the software arena. For example, cohesion is the degree to which the elements of a software component align with a single purpose [35]. Cohesion and its definition can apply almost directly to ACPs, but this is a subject for future research (see Section VII). Another desirable software quality directly applicable to ACPs is modularization. Modularization is the degree to which a system is divided up into independent components [36]. When a system has good modularization, developers do not have to look very far beyond a component to understand it or reason about it. We believe the same to be true for ACPs, but the details of modularization applied to ACPs are also a subject for another paper (see Section VII).

Although we believe cohesion and modularization are important qualities for ACPs, they do not directly help in describing reoccurring communication problems nor are they good discriminators for reusable solutions, because all pattern solutions should, by definition, have good cohesion and modularization. So, we turn our attention to four other qualities with discriminating definitions for ACPs, namely: reliability, synchronicity, longevity, and adaptability for scalable distribution.

A. *Reliability*

For an ACP, reliability is the degree to which a process that sends a message as part of a conversation obtains an assurance that the intended recipient(s) received it, entirety and uncorrupted, and reacted as prescribed in the ACP. At the application level, reliability is typically achieved by the recipients returning messages that provide the sender with confirmation that the message was received and/or processed. When such return messages fail to arrive in a timely fashion, reliable ACPs will require the sender to retransmit the original message.

In Section VI, where we present an overview of the ACP patterns in CommDP, we rank each of the patterns in terms of reliability using the following 3-point rubric:

Rank/Criteria

3 The problem (P) addressed by the pattern is primarily concerned with reliability and the solution (S) can make the following guarantees under normal and extreme conditions:

  a. The sender can distinguish between successful and failed conversations.
  b. The receiver can distinguish between successful and failed conversations.
  c. In successful conversations, any process X that sends a message M to process Y, gives a timely assurance to X (in some subsequent message) that Y received M.
  d. In successful conversations, for any process X that sends a message M to process Y, if M is supposed to trigger a non-trivial behavior in Y, then X receives a timely assurance that Y successfully handled M.

2 P is concerned with reliability and S can guarantee at least (a) and (c) from above in normal situations.

1 P is not concerned with reliability and S doesn't limit reliability.

Clearly, there are other conceivable problem/solution criteria for reliability not listed above, such as a reoccurring problem where reliability is a major concern and a solution that doesn't address it. However, we don't include such meaningless classifications because they wouldn't help classify patterns with expert, reusable solutions.

B. *Synchronicity*

In the most general sense, synchronization deals with the coordinated execution of actions in a distributed system and what the state information is necessary for that coordination. This broad definition encompasses, but is not limited to, the common view among programmers that synchronous communications occur when the sender of a message stops and waits for a response from the message receiver [37]. However, this is not the only way to achieve synchronization. Some other common mechanisms are logical clocks [38][39], vector clocks [40][41], vector timestamps [42], optimistic concurrency controls [43], and timing signals.

To evaluate the synchronization requirements for ACPs, we consider: (a) what are the actions that need to be coordinated, (b) where will those actions be executed, and (c) what kind of state information is needed to achieve the desired coordination. A distributed system may perform many different tasks comprised of numerous operations, but rarely all of them have to be fully coordinated. In fact, the more independent the individual operations are, the more a system can maximize concurrency and increase throughput. From a coordination perspective, where the operations take place is actually more important than what the operations do. For example, if all of the actions occur in just one process, then that process may not need to know anything about the state of the other process. Once developers know what operations have to be coordinated and where they will execute, they can consider what local or global state information the coordination logic will need.

To rank synchronicity for ACP patterns, we will use the following definitions:

- *C* is a conversation involving a closed set of processes, $C.P = \{p_1, \ldots, p_n\}$, and a set of messages, $C.M = \{m_1, \ldots, m_n\}$, such that $sender(m_i) \in C.P \wedge receivers(m_i) \subseteq C.P$ for $1 \leq i \leq n$ where $sender(m_i)$ is the process that sent message m_i and $receivers(m_i)$ is the set of processes that received m_i.
- *A* is a set of operations, $\{a_1, \ldots, a_n\}$ that run on $C.P$ and whose execution requires coordination, e.g., ordering, simultaneous execution, etc.
- *h(a)* is the host process for operation, a, where $a \in A$ and $h(a) \in C.P$
- *s(a)* is the state information that *h(a)* needs to coordinate *a's* execution with the rest of the operations in *A*.
- *H(A)* is the set of host processes for all operations in *A*

Below is an informal 3-point rubric for ranking synchronicity for CommDP patterns using these definitions. We believe that a more rigorous ranking system would have value beyond the categorization of ACP patterns, and its full definition is beyond the scope and purpose of this paper.

Rank/Criteria

3 The problem (P) addressed by the pattern deals with situations where $|H(A)| > 1$ and the solution (S) can guarantee that for all $a \in A$, h(a) receives s(a) via messages, $m_i \in C.M$, in time to do the prescribed coordination.

2 P deals with situations where $|H(A)| = 1$ and S can guarantee that for all $a \in A$, h(a) receives s(a) via messages, $m_i \in C.M$, in time to do the prescribed coordination.

1 P is not concerned with synchronicity, e.g., $|A| = 0$, and S does not limit synchronicity.

C. *Longevity*

Longevity is the degree to which an ACP can support long-running conversations caused by long-running operations. The primary problem for conversation with long-running operations is that there could be huge span of times when processes are uncertain of each other's states. Consider a simple request/reply conversation where some process A sends a request to B, but B takes a long time to execute the requested operation and sends back a reply. While waiting for the reply, process A doesn't know if B received the request, has failed, or is just taking a long time. ACPs that support long-running operations include mechanisms for exchanging state information independent of results.

We rank the longevity for ACP patterns according to the following 3-point rubric:

Rank/Criteria

3 The problem (P) addressed by the pattern is primarily concerned with long-running conversations and the solution (S) can guarantee the following in successful conversations:
   a. Participants made aware of each other's states in periodically.
   b. Each participant in the conversation can detect when other participants are no longer available or accessible.

2 P is concerned with long-running conversations and S provides for (a).

1 P is not concerned with long-running conversations and S doesn't limit longevity.

D. *Adaptability for Scalable Distribution*

ACPs can support scalability by providing location transparency and/or replication transparency [42], and by allowing resources (data, operations, or objects) to be distributed across multiple hosts. To understand location and replication transparency, consider a website with a large number of resources. It can support scalability by placing the various resources on an expandable collection of backend servers and use a front-end server to distribute requests from browsers. If the browser doesn't need to know where a resource is actually located, then the system supports location transparency. Similarly, as traffic increases, the system could replicate resources across multiple backend servers. If the client doesn't have to know that replicas exist, then the system supports replication transparency. Both location and replication transparency simplify scalability.

Another technique for supporting scalability is allowing complex resources to be broken up into smaller resources and distributed across multiple servers. One approach for doing this is to untangle cross-cutting concerns, like security or logging, from complex operations and host these pieces of functionality on proxies [44][42].

Here is a simple rubric for the adaptability for scalable distribution.

Rank/Criteria

3 The problem (P) addressed by the pattern is primarily concerned about scalability or the distribution of action or resources and the solution (S) can provide two or more of following:
   a. Location transparency for shared resources distributed across multiple hosts
   b. Load balancing with shared resources replicated across multiple hosts
   c. Untangling of cross-cutting concerns into separate actions

2 P is concerned with scalability or distribution of resources and S provides at least one (a), (b), or (c).

1 P is not concerned with scalability or distribution and S doesn't limit them.

V. Template for Communication-Protocol Patterns

To document the patterns in CommDP, we have developed a template, loosely based on the way Gamma, Helm, Johnson and Vlissides documented their patterns [34], referred to here as the GoF template. The main goal is to keep the documentation as simple as possible, while still capturing the details of the pattern. Following are the elements of CommDP pattern template.

A. *Name*

As with the GoF template, the name uniquely identifies the pattern. Since the name will become part of the vocabulary for the pattern language, it is important that it captures the essence of the pattern, distinguishes it from other patterns, and is as concise as possible.

B. *Intent*

The intent is an abstract for the pattern. It summarizes the problem, the context, and the solutions, particularly in terms of reliability, synchronicity, longevity, and adaptability for scalable distributes.

C. *Description*

The description consists of three subsections that explain the problem, context, and solution. The problem subsection relates closely to the Motivation part in the GoF template, in that it explains the nature of the reoccurring communication-protocol design problem. This subsection should highlight the problem's need for reliable communications, synchronization, long-running conversations, or scalable distribution. The context subsection is like the Applicability in the GoF template, capturing information when the pattern may or may not be applicable and assumptions about distributed systems in which the communications will take place. The solution is analogous to the Structure in the GoF template. It focuses on the describing protocol design ideas and how they can be adapted.

D. Consequences

As with the GoF template, the consequences are important part of CommDP pattern definitions because developers will use them to determine if the pattern is a good fit for a particular situation. The consequences of CommDP patterns are described in terms of the qualities discussed in Section 4. The rankings provide a general classification, and pros explain the consequences in more detail.

E. Known Uses

Like the GoF template, this part references known instances of the pattern in production systems

F. Aliases and Related Work

The section combines two elements of the GoF template by the similar names.

G. References

This section contains a bibliography for the citations made elsewhere in the pattern definition.

VI. CommDP

A design pattern is composed of a set of patterns and idioms that are used together to solve a design engineering problem.

A. ACP Idioms

Before launching into a description of CommDP's patterns, it is important to first introduce three fundamental building blocks for all ACPs: point-to-point send, multicast, and broadcast. These are idioms instead of patterns because their usage depends on the lower layer communication protocols and because, by themselves, they do not address the qualities discussed in Section 4.

A *point-to-point* send is the transmission of a single message from one process to another, such as a message sent over a TCP connection or via a UDP datagram. An underlying communication subsystem may provide some reliability relative to the transmission but, at the application-level, a single message does not allow the sender to know if the receiver processed the message or anything about the receiver's state, nor does it help with longevity or adaptability for scalable distribution.

A *multicast* send is the transmission of a single message to a set of receiving processes [45]. It can be implemented at virtually any layer in communication hierarchy, including the physical layer. Mechanisms for identifying the group of receiving processes vary from sender determined to receiver subscriptions. By themselves, multicast are idioms for ACPs. The same is true for *broadcasts*, which also transmit messages to multiple receivers [45].

B. ACP Patterns

Table I. COMMDP PATTERNS lists the nine patterns currently in CommDP, along with their rankings from their consequences relative to the characteristics discussed in Section 4 (R=Reliability, S=Synchronicity, L=Longevity, and A=Adaptability for Scalable Distribution). Their full definitions are available on [http://commdp.serv.usu.edu].

The *Request-Reply* pattern is undoubtedly the most common. It addresses the problem where a process, A, needs to access or use shared resources in another process, B, with a reasonable degree of reliability and synchronicity. The solution consists of A sending B a message (i.e., a request) and B sending back a message (i.e., a reply) after processing the request, as you can see in Fig. 2. For A, this simple mechanism provides a modest level of reliability and synchronization, because the reply proves that B received the request and can provide relevant information about B's state. Furthermore, if A does not receive a reply within a specific amount of time (i.e., a timeout), it can resend the request. It can continue to timeout and retry until it eventually receives a reply or it exceeds some maximum number of retries. This "timeout/retry" behavior is the essence of the request-reply pattern.

TABLE I. COMMDP PATTERNS

Name	Consequences			
	R	S	L	A
Request-Reply	2	2	1	1
Request-Reply-Acknowledge	3	3	1	1
Idempotent Retry	3	1	1	1
Intermediate State Messages	3	3	3	1
Second Channel	1	3	3	1
Front End	1	1	1	3
Proxy	1	1	1	3
Reliable Multicast	3	3	1	2
Publish-Subscribe	2	1	1	3

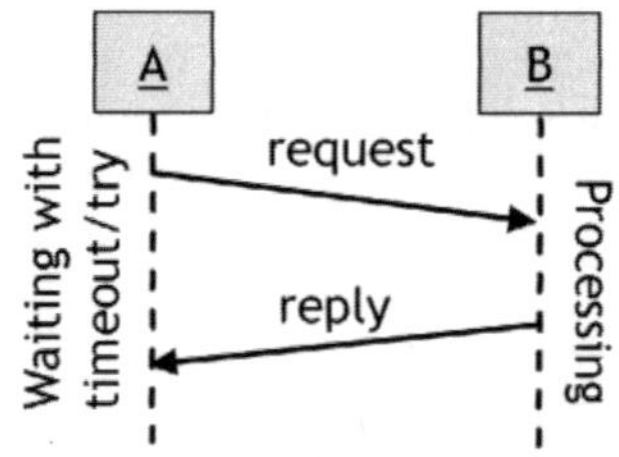

Figure 2. Request-Reply Message Sequence

The *Request-Reply-Acknowledge* pattern extends this solution with a third message (an acknowledgement) that A sends to B after receiving the reply, and gives B a timeout/retry behavior with respect to its sending of the reply and waiting for an acknowledgement, see Fig. 3. This pattern is useful in situations were significant processing may occur on A after receiving the reply or when it is problematic for B to reprocess duplicated requests caused by A's timeout/retry behavior. With this pattern, instead of reprocessing a duplicate request, B can simply cache its replies and resends them to A when necessary. The acknowledgement tells B that A has received the reply and, thus, can remove it from its cache. This pattern offers more reliability and synchronization than request-reply, but at the cost of an additional message.

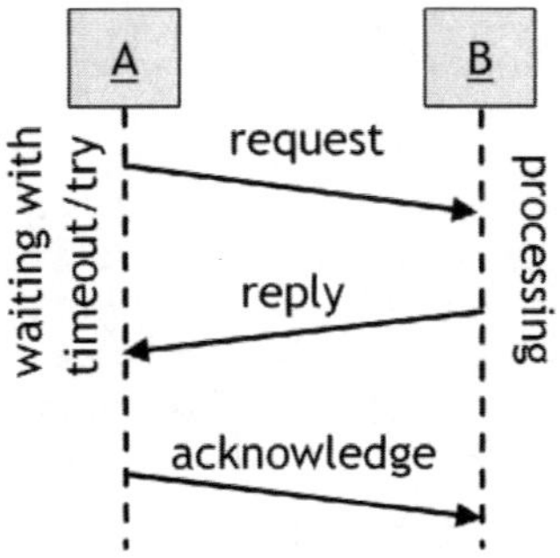

Figure 3. Request-Reply-Acknowledge Message Sequence

The *Idempotent Retry* pattern [46] captures a different solution to the problem of processing duplicate requests. Like Request-Reply, its solution consists of A sending a request to B with a timeout/retry behavior and B sending a reply back to A. But, unlike Request-Reply, the semantics of the protocol dedicate the processing of the request must be idempotent. This pattern applies to situations where the requested processing is relatively light, i.e., less expensive than caching replies.

The next pattern, *Intermediate State Message*, is also similar to Request-Reply, but addresses the problem of long-running conversations due to request actions taking substantial amounts of time to complete. To solve this problem, it has B send A one or more intermediate messages that reflect its current state. For example, B may send a message immediately after receiving the request to let A know that it got the request, another message when the processing is 10%, another at 20% complete, and so on. Each intermediate message provides state information about B, which improves synchronization in the presence of time-consuming actions, see Fig. 4.

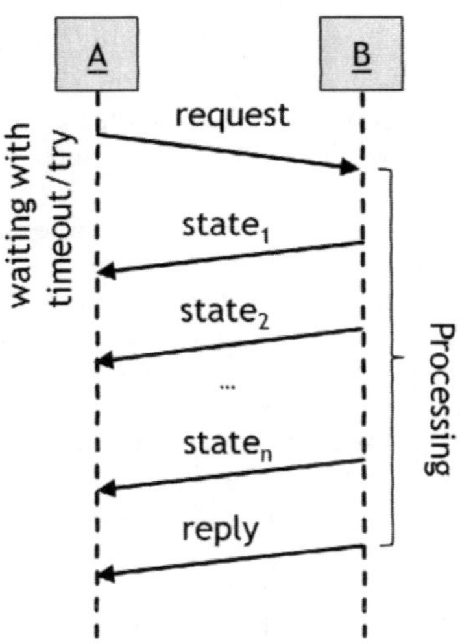

Figure 4. Intermediate State Message Sequence

The *Second Channel* pattern is also for situations involving long-running conversations, but ones dominated by significant amounts of data transfers instead of time-consuming actions. Because the large data transfers can delay intermediate state messages, this pattern's solution suggests opening a second communication channel between A and B that is dedicated to data transfer, leaving the original communication channel available for intermediate state or control messages, as it is shown in Fig. 5. The File Transfer Protocol (FTP) and its variations are classical examples of this pattern[10][45].

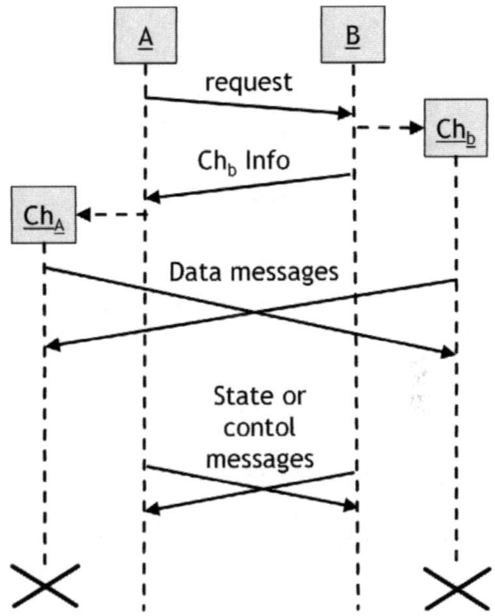

Figure 5. Second Channel Message Sequence

The *Front End* pattern addresses the problems of making the location of shared resource transparent to the client, allowing the number of resources to change dynamically. It has a resource client send requests to a front-end process that automatically redistributes them to appropriate resource managers, B processes. After processing the request, a resource manager replies back to the client directly, for a graphic description of this pattern, you can see Fig. 6. The front-end process can use a variety of criteria to decide how to redistribute requests, including request type, resource type or identity, and resource manager load. By itself, this pattern's

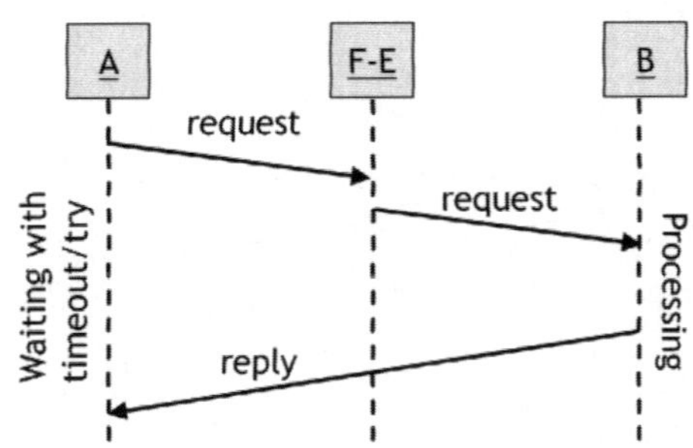

Figure 6. Front End Message Sequence

primary focus is on the distribution and scalability of resources.

Like the Front End, the *Proxy* pattern, presented in Fig. 7, introduces a process between a resource client and a resource manager. However, the intermediate process, called a proxy, serves other functional purposes besides re-distribution of the requests, for example it may provide authentication, access control, audit logging, and data transformation functionality. Also, the resource manager returns replies through the proxy to client, completely isolating the client from the resource manager.

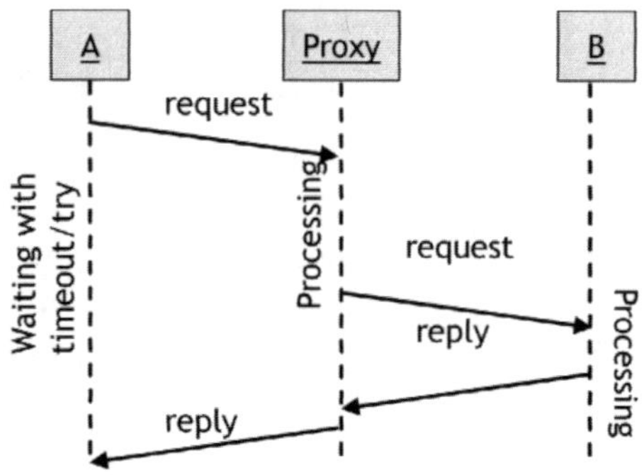

Figure 7. Proxy Message Sequence

The *Reliable Multicast* pattern builds on the multicast idiom to provide reliability and synchronization among a group of processes. Its solution is a protocol that starts with a process A sending a request message to a group of process, $B=\{b_1, .., b_n\}$. Each process b_i sends a reply back to A when it receives the request and is ready to process it. After A receives reply from all B processes, then A will multicast a go-ahead message back out to all B message indicating that they can proceed with the processing of the request, shown in Fig. 8. In this way, the execution of the request is synchronized among all of the B processes. If A fails to receive a reply from every B process, it can resend the request to some or all of them until it gets a reply from all of them or terminates the conversation

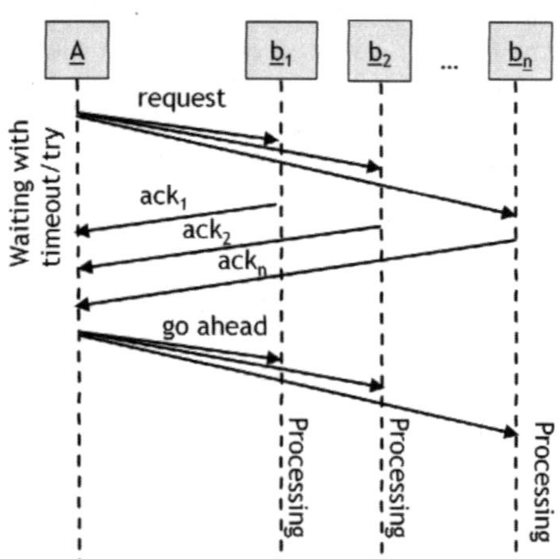

Figure 8. Reliable Multicast Message Sequence

as failed. This pattern focuses on providing strong reliability and synchronization, but can also help with scalable distribution of resources.

Finally, the *Publish-Subscribe* [8] pattern is a powerful mechanism for decoupling message senders (publisher) from message receivers (subscribers). With this pattern, an intermediate process acts as a store-and-forward buffer for message transmission with the capabilities for managing subscribers and delivering individual message to multiple subscribers.

C. CommDP: Pattern Relationships and Composition

Patterns are rarely used in isolation; instead, developers combine their solutions to solve complex problems. Virtually any of the CommDP patterns could be combined with any other pattern, but the more useful combinations are ones that have complimentary characteristics, like Request-Reply with Second Data Channel or Request-Reply Acknowledge with Front End.

To ensure that the CommDP pattern set was as minimal as possible, we did not include in any pattern in CommDP that was simply an aggregation of two or more patterns. For example, there is a common type of distributed system that deals with information flow and processing. In such systems, a process A might send a request to B through a series of intermediate proxy-like processes that transform or augment data in request on its way to B. At each intermediate step, a reply is sent back to A, informing it of the message's process. Eventually, when the transformed message arrives at B and processes it, then B sends a final reply message back to A. This particular solution offers good reliability, synchronization, longevity, and adaptability to scalable distribution, but it is actually just a composition of the Proxy pattern (applied perhaps multiple times) and the Intermediate State Message pattern.

VII. SUMMARY AND FUTURE WORK

CommDP pulls together reusable solutions to reoccurring design problems with ACPs, filling a much needed gap in the knowledge base for developers of distributed systems. We have characterized the nature of the problems that the CommDP patterns address and the consequences of their solution in terms of four desirable qualities, namely: reliability, synchronicity, longevity, and adaptability for scalable distribution. These qualities are both instructive and discriminating, in that they can help a developer understand the solutions and choose the most appropriate solution for a given situation. However, more work needs to be done to formalize these qualities and to solidify their sufficiently and completeness relative communication-protocol design. So this is one of our research group's immediate goals.

We also hope to investigate other qualities, like cohesion and modularization that might be valuable for protocol design even if they are not good discriminators for design patterns. Being able to reason about assess, and teach these qualities more formally will help developers create better distributed systems.

Finally, over time, we hope the expand the patterns in CommDP, without adding any that are just compositions of existing patterns, to encompasses a boarder range of reusable solutions for ACPs.

REFERENCES

[1] G. Coulouris, J. Dollimore, T. Kindberg, and G. Blair, *Distributed Systems: Concepts and Design*, 5 edition. Boston: Pearson, 2011.

[2] "Distributed computing," *Wikipedia, the free encyclopedia*. 27-Feb-2016.

[3] S. W. Clyde, "Object mitosis: a systematic approach to splitting objects across subsystems," in , *Proceedings of the Third International Workshop on Object Orientation in Operating Systems, 1993*, 1993, pp. 182–185.

[4] "Communications protocol," *Wikipedia, the free encyclopedia*. 10-Apr-2016.

[5] "protocol | computer science," *Encyclopedia Britannica*. [Online]. Available: http://www.britannica.com/technology/protocol-computer-science. [Accessed: 20-Apr-2016].

[6] E. Gamma, R. Helm, R. Johnson, J. Vlissides, and G. Booch, *Design Patterns: Elements of Reusable Object-Oriented Software*, 1 edition. Addison-Wesley Professional, 1994.

[7] J. O. Coplien and N. B. Harrison, *Organizational Patterns of Agile Software Development*. Upper Saddle River, NJ: Prentice Hall, 2004.

[8] F. Buschmann, K. Henney, and D. C. Schmidt, *Pattern-Oriented Software Architecture Volume 4: A Pattern Language for Distributed Computing*, Volume 4 edition. Wiley, 2007.

[9] C. Alexander, S. Ishikawa, M. Silverstein, M. Jacobson, I. Fiksdahl-King, and S. Angel, *A Pattern Language: Towns, Buildings, Construction*. New York: Oxford University Press, 1977.

[10] C. White, *Data Communications and Computer Networks: A Business User's Approach*, 7 edition. Boston, MA: Cengage Learning, 2012.

[11] "ISO/IEC 10026-1:1992 - Information technology -- Open Systems Interconnection -- Distributed Transaction Processing -- Part 1: OSI TP Model." [Online]. Available: http://www.iso.org/iso/iso_catalogue/catalogue_ics/catalogue_detail_ics.htm?csnumber=17979. [Accessed: 20-Apr-2016].

[12] K. Beck and W. Cunningham, "Using Pattern Languages for Object-Oriented Programs," in *Object-Oriented Programming, Systems, Languages, and Application*, Sep. 1987.

[13] F. Buschmann, R. Meunier, H. Rohnert, P. Sommerlad, and M. Stal, *Pattern-Oriented Software Architecture Volume 1: A System of Patterns*, Volume 1 edition. Chichester ; New York: Wiley, 1996.

[14] D. Schmidt, M. Stal, H. Rohnert, and F. Buschmann, *Pattern-Oriented Software Architecture Volume 2: Patterns for Concurrent and Networked Objects*, Volume 2 edition. Chichester England ; New York: Wiley, 2000.

[15] J. Tidwell, *Designing Interfaces*, 2 edition. Sebastopol, CA: O'Reilly Media, 2011.

[16] D. C. Schmidt, "Reactor: An Object Behavioral Pattern for Concurrent Event Demultiplexing and Dispatching," in *Pattern Languages of Program Design*, New York, NY, USA: ACM Press/Addison-Wesley Publishing Co., 1995, pp. 529-545.

[17] I. Pyarali, T. Harrison, and D. Schmidt, "Asynchronous Completion Token: an Object Behavioral Pattern for Efficient Asynchronous Event Handling," in *Proc. 3rd Annual Conference on The Pattern Languages Programs*, 1997, pp. 1-7.

[18] I. Pyarali, T. Harrison, D. C. Schmidt, and T. D. Jordan, "Proactor - An Object Behavioral Pattern for Demultiplexing and Dispatching Handlers for Asynchronous Events," in *Pattern Languages of Program Design (J. O. Coplien and D. C. Schmidt, eds.)*, Reading, MA: Addison-Wesley, 1995.

[19] M. K. Douglas C. Schmidt, "Leader/Followers - A Design Pattern for Efficient Multi-threaded Event Demultiplexing and Dispatching," in *7th Pattern Languages of Programs Conference*, Allerton Park, Illinois, 2000.

[20] D. C. Schmidt, "Strategized locking, thread-safe interface, and scoped locking," *C Rep.*, vol. 11, no. 9, 1999.

[21] R. G. Lavender and D. C. Schmidt, "Active Object an Object Behavioral Pattern for Concurrent Programming" in *Pattern Languages of Program Design 2 edited by John Vlissides, Jim Coplien, and Norm Kerth.*, Boston, MA: Addison-Wesley, 1996.

[22] D. C. Schmidt, "Monitor Object," in *Pattern-Oriented Software Architecture (F. Buschmann, K. Henney, D. C. Schmidt)*, vol. 4, West Sussex PO19 8SQ, England: John Wiley & Sons Ltd, 2007, pp. 368-369.

[23] D. C. Schmidt and C. D. Cranor, "Half-Sync/Half-Async," presented at the Second Pattern Languages of Programs, Monticello, Illinois, 1995.

[24] D. C. Schmidt, N. Pryce, and T. H. Harrison, "Thread-Specific Storage for C/C+," *More C Gems*, vol. 17, p. 337, 2000.

[25] D. C. Schmidt and T. Harrison, "Double-checked locking," in *Pattern languages of program design*, vol. 3, 1997, pp. 363–375.

[26] L. Rising, *Design Patterns in Communications Software*, 1 edition. Cambridge ; New York: Cambridge University Press, 2001.

[27] P. Jain and D. C. Schmidt, "Service Configurator: A Pattern for Dynamic Configuration of Services," in *Proceedings of the 3rd Conference on USENIX Conference on Object-Oriented Technologies (COOTS) - Volume 3*, Berkeley, CA, USA, 1997, pp. 16–16.

[28] R. C. Martin, D. Riehle, and F. Buschmann, *Pattern Languages of Program Design 3*, 1 edition. Reading, Mass: Addison-Wesley Professional, 1997.

[29] L. Rising, *Design Patterns in Communications Software*, 1 edition. Cambridge ; New York: Cambridge University Press, 2001.

[30] D. C. Schmidt, "Using design patterns to develop reusable object-oriented communication software," *Commun. ACM*, vol. 38, no. 10, pp. 65–74, 1995.

[31] R. Daigneau, *Service Design Patterns: Fundamental Design Solutions for SOAP/WSDL and RESTful Web Services*, 1 edition. Upper Saddle River, NJ: Addison-Wesley Professional, 2011.

[32] C. Fehling, F. Leymann, R. Retter, W. Schupeck, and P. Arbitter, *Cloud Computing Patterns: Fundamentals to Design, Build, and Manage Cloud Applications*. Springer Science & Business Media, 2014.

[33] "Patterns for Distributed Real-time and Embedded Systems." [Online]. Available: https://www.dre.vanderbilt.edu/~schmidt/patterns-ace.html. [Accessed: 04-Mar-2016].

[34] E. Gamma, R. Helm, R. Johnson, J. Vlissides, and G. Booch, *Design Patterns: Elements of Reusable Object-Oriented Software*, 1 edition. Addison-Wesley Professional, 1994.

[35] E. Yourdon and L. L. Constantine, *Structured Design: Fundamentals of a Discipline of Computer Program and Systems Design*, 1st ed. Upper Saddle River, NJ, USA: Prentice-Hall, Inc., 1979.

[36] "Modularity," *Wikipedia, the free encyclopedia*. 11-Apr-2016.

[37] M. Burrows, "The Chubby Lock Service for Loosely-coupled Distributed Systems," in *Proceedings of the 7th Symposium on Operating Systems Design and Implementation*, Berkeley, CA, USA, 2006, pp. 335–350.

[38] L. Lamport, "Time, Clocks, and the Ordering of Events in a Distributed System," *Commun ACM*, vol. 21, no. 7, pp. 558–565, Jul. 1978.

[39] M. Raynal, "About Logical Clocks for Distributed Systems," *SIGOPS Oper Syst Rev*, vol. 26, no. 1, pp. 41–48, Jan. 1992.

[40] F. Mattern, "Virtual time and global states of distributed systems," in *Parallel and Distributed Algorithms*, 1989, pp. 215–226.

[41] C. Fidge, "Logical Time in Distributed Computing Systems," *Computer*, vol. 24, no. 8, pp. 28–33, Aug. 1991.

[42] G. Coulouris, J. Dollimore, T. Kindberg, and G. Blair, *Distributed Systems: Concepts and Design*, 5 edition. Boston: Pearson, 2011.

[43] H. T. Kung and J. T. Robinson, "On Optimistic Methods for Concurrency Control," *ACM Trans Database Syst*, vol. 6, no. 2, pp. 213–226, Jun. 1981.

[44] M. Voelter, "Patterns for Handling Cross-cutting Concerns in Model-Driven Software Development," in *ResearchGate*, 2005.

[45] A. S. Tanenbaum and D. Wetherall, *Computer networks*, 5th ed. Boston: Pearson Prentice Hall, 2011.

[46] R. Daigneau, *Service Design Patterns: Fundamental Design Solutions for SOAP/WSDL and RESTful Web Services*, 1 edition. Upper Saddle River, NJ: Addison-Wesley Professional, 2011.

A Concise Classification of Reverse Engineering Approaches for Software Product Lines

Rehman Arshad,Kung-Kiu-Lau
School of Computer Science, University of Manchester
Kilburn House, Oxford Road, Manchester, United Kingdom
e-mail: rehman.arshad, kung-kiu.lau @manchester.ac.uk

***Abstract*—Reverse engineering in product lines means identification of feature locations in the source code or formation of the non-redundant feature model from descriptive documents. The feature identification can be represented by feature to code trace, graphical notations or tools based view. For adopting a specific approach, it is very important to know how it works, the kind of expertise needed to use it, the kind of tool support that is there, the format of the required input for using that approach, the output notation that it can provide, the related shortcomings that cannot be avoided and the kind of pre-requisite work each approach demands. Based on these parameters, this paper provides a classification of the reverse engineering approaches related to software product lines. Such classification can help the product line engineers or relevant researchers to narrow down the practical options for their implementation and to obtain the better understanding of reverse engineering in product lines.**

Keywords: Product Line Engineering; Reverse Engineering; Static Analysis; Dynamic Analysis; Textual Analysis; Hybrid Analysis; Feature Location.

I. INTRODUCTION

"The output of a reverse engineering activity is synthesized, higher-level information that enables the reverse engineer to better reason about the system and to evolve it in an effective manner" [1]. Usually, the result of reverse engineering is in higher notation of abstraction in order to understand the system. Output can be a model, graphical chart, re-structured code or some notation that can express the system in a feasible way.

The idea behind a software product line is to make different customized software products by using same platform that can support different variations in all the products. The process of constructing and managing such common platform (product line) is known as product line engineering [2].

A product line is usually composed of features ranging from few dozens to several hundreds [2]. These features are related to each other by well-defined constraints [3]. Without very extensive documentation and trace, it is almost impossible for product line engineers to understand the composition of code in terms of features. The process of reverse engineering in product lines is used for finding the feature locations in the code or for constructing a non-redundant feature model from descriptive documentation. With the evolution of the product line, the major purpose of reverse engineering is to keep code and variability modelling synchronised and understandable.

One of the concerns for product line practitioners and programmers is to know the difference in applicability of different reverse engineering approaches according to domain, available in-house expertise, tool support and required notation of extraction after reverse engineering. This short survey provides a basic classification for software product line engineers and programmers to know the difference between reverse engineering approaches for product lines, the tools that come with some approaches, kind of output provided by each approach, kind of input needed by each approach, associated shortcomings to each approach, prerequisites for implementing an approach and kind of expertise needed in order to implement an approach. Such comparison between these approaches will help in the selection of an approach over others on the basis of compatibility with all such parameters. This classification can also help novices to understand what it takes to do reverse engineering for software product lines.

The term technique and approach should not be confused in this survey. One approach can use various well-defined techniques for its implementation where as an approach is the way in which a process uses many techniques in order to get the results, e.g., *Language Independent Approach* [4] is an approach of reverse engineering that is based on techniques of Formal Concept Analysis (FCA) and Latent Semantic Indexing (LSI). Similarly, *Static Analysis* is a kind of analysis technique in reverse engineering and this technique can be used by multiple software product line reverse engineering approaches. The presented classification in this paper can help the product line engineers and relevant researchers to narrow down the practical options for their implementation instead of wasting time on comparing all such options.

The remainder of this paper is organised as follows. Section 2 explains the related work. Section 3 includes the framework of classification. Section 4 includes the classified approaches based on the framework. Section 5 provides available tool support for each approach and major shortcomings of approaches. Section 6 is the final section that includes conclusion.

II. RELATED WORK

There are hundreds of approaches in the reverse engineering but most of them are not applicable in the domain of product lines. In this paper only the approaches that meet the following criteria have been selected: they are for product lines in particular, related to product variants, relevant to feature identification/formation in the complex system families and tackle the variability of the product variants. Therefore, many well-known general reverse engineering techniques like LSI [5], Probabilistic Latent Semantic Indexing (PBLSI) [6] and NL-Queries [7] are not part of this paper. These techniques can be part of complex reverse engineering approaches related to software product lines but as standalone techniques they are not relevant. This is because a product line is constructed in terms of features and their variations, and general techniques cannot produce results in terms of features and variants. It is not the intention of this paper to include the approaches that use (*reuse*) artefacts to construct a product line. Approaches with the sole purpose of reverse engineering are considered only, therefore approaches like *clone and own* are not part of this classification because they are mainly used to *reuse* not to *reverse engineer*.

This paper covers more than thirty approaches of reverse engineering in the field of software product lines. Each approach uses many techniques of reverse engineering. Techniques like LSI, FCA, etc., do not belong to a specific domain. The way an approach uses these techniques determines whether the approach is suitable for product lines or not. Few surveys have classified reverse engineering techniques but none have done it solely for software product lines and their angle of interest is quite different, e.g., Bogdan Dit's survey [8] is the closest one because it covers the identification of feature locations. Work of Michael L. Nelson [9] covers automation of reverse engineering in legacy system. Purpose of M. Spiros and K. Moshe's survey [10] is to classify the tool support for specific operating systems. Such classifications and surveys cannot help in the domain of software product lines. They cannot help in deciding the applicability of reverse engineering because they do not discuss the classification parameters with respect to software product lines. A classified tool of reverse engineering may be great from operating system's point of view but can be useless for software product lines at the same time. Overall, no such survey exists at the moment that has discussed the reverse engineering from software product line's point of view.

III. Framework of Classification

Table I. shows the framework of classification in terms of different parameters. The parameters used for classification are;

- Analysis Technique
- Required input notation
- Generated output notation
- Phase Compatibility
- Required Expertise
- Pre-Requisite Implementation

These parameters are selected by considering their importance for applicability of practical implementation. Analysis techniques define the type of analysis used by an approach for reverse engineering. Required input notation classifies the approaches based on the input they require for execution. Generated output notation classifies the approach based on the type of output produced by each approach. Phase compatibility means whether an approach is suitable for construction or maintenance of a product line. Required expertise groups the approaches based on the kind of techniques they use and pre-requisite implementation classifies the approaches based on the kind of work they require before implementation. Further classification of these parameters is presented in Table I.

TABLE I. REVERSE ENGINEERING: FRAMEWORK OF CLASSIFICATION

Parameter of Classification	**Classification**	
Analysis Technique	Static	
	Textual	
	Dynamic	
	Hybrid	
Req. Input Notation	Source Code	
	Feature Set	
	Description	
Output Notation	Feature Model	
	Code	
	View Based	Concept Lattices and Graphs
		Feature to Code Trace
Phase Compatibility	Construction	
	Maintenance	
Required Expertise	Profiling	
	FCA	
	LSI	
	Vector Space Modelling (VSM)	
	Domain Knowledge	
	Natural Language Processing (NLP)	
Pre-Requisites	Profiling (Code Instrumentation)	
	Approach Centric	

IV. Classification of Reverse Engineering Approaches for Software Product Lines

This section will classify the reverse engineering approaches for software product lines based on analysis technique, input notation required by each approach, output notation, phase compatibility, prerequisite implementation required by each approach and expertise required by each approach. All these classification parameters are presented in the following sections.

A. Classification based on Analysis Technique

Analysis techniques in reverse engineering are classified as follows: [8]

- Static Analysis Techniques
- Textual Analysis Techniques
- Dynamic Analysis Techniques
- Hybrid Analysis Techniques

1) Static Analysis Techniques: Static feature location techniques are based on structural information of the code. They consider control flow, data flow and dependencies in the code to identify features. These techniques work by building a model of states of the program and then determine all possible routes of the program at each step. To design such approach one has to keep the balance between preciseness and granularity and some abstraction is used to consider which steps should be added in the static analysis model [11].

These techniques are based on the control structure of the source code, hence their result has very good recall but the major drawback is lack of precision. False positive results are very common in static techniques as these techniques work on user-defined model of control flow rather than the actual trace of the program. The biggest advantage is the future re-usability.

The output of such techniques can be a configuration matrix, a dependency graph or re-formation of the actual source code. Usually, these techniques are used to extract a dependency matrix between the source code and features in order to understand the relation between code and the variability model composed by features. RecoVar [12], Language Independent Approach [4], Dependency Graph [13], Concern Graph [14], Automatic Generation [15], Concern Identification [16] and Semi-Automatic Approach [17] are some of the approaches related to the product line engineering based on static analysis.

2) Textual Analysis Techniques: Few researchers [18] referred textual as a static technique but it is quite different from a standard static technique. Textual analysis does not need any abstraction model and uses the query-based input to match the words with identifiers and comments in the code.

Most textual analysis reverse engineering techniques produce feature locations as an output. These code locations are displayed either by concept lattices (if Formal Concept Analysis is used) or by dependency graphs. Examples of such approaches are Combining

FCA with IR [18] and Source Code Retrieval [19]. Few approaches produce feature models from the provided description or the feature-set as description. Examples of these approaches include Evolutionary Algorithms [20], Reverse Engineering Feature Models [40] and Feature Models from Software Configurations [21]. Few textual based approaches also extract and show the code in terms of variability, e.g., Product Variants [22] and few represent domain concepts after extracting them from the code in order to provide understanding of the code in simple domain terms, e.g., Natural Language Parsing [23].

The biggest problem is the user designed queries that are responsible for almost the whole analysis and quality or accuracy of the output. Another problem is *polysemy* and implicit implementation of the feature across many locations.

3) Dynamic Analysis Techniques: Dynamic analysis uses execution trace of the program to follow and identify the feature locations by following running code. Test scenarios or profiling is needed in order to design an execution trace with respect to some feature. Profiling is instrumentation of the code and it is a difficult task. Usually one scenario can only involve one feature, hence in case of hundreds of features, dynamic analysis becomes more complex. For every new profiling, old results are useless whereas in static we can reuse the rules of abstraction as many times as we want with continuous refinement.

Dynamic analysis output is always a trace that shows feature locations in the code. This relation is represented either as concept lattices or view-based tools. The abstraction level of code in the trace varies from approach to approach. Dynamic Feature Traces [24], Feature to code trace [25], Focused views on Execution Traces [26], Software evolution Analysis [27], Trace Dependency Analysis [28], Featureous [29], Embedded Call-Graphs [30], Scenario-Driven Dynamic Analysis [31] and Concept Analysis [32] are examples of product line approaches based on dynamic analysis.

4) Hybrid Analysis Techniques: A hybrid analysis in reverse engineering can be a combination of Dynamic-Static, Dynamic-Textual, Textual-static or Dynamic-Textual-static analysis. Hybrid analysis can join *recall* of static and *precision* of dynamic analysis. *Recall* is required in order to make dynamic analysis reusable in the future. So a static analysis can obviate the collection of certain information and dynamic can run over that collection in order to get better results. Also, many approaches like [33] use one analysis technique just to rank the elements of the code so this ranking of feature relevancy will be considered in the final results in order to increase accuracy.

Hybrid techniques provide feature locations either by using concept lattices or graphs. Static and Dynamic Analysis [34], Cerberus [33], Sniafl [35], Locating Features in Source Code [36], Using Landmarks and Barriers [37] and A Heuristic-Based Approach [38] are examples of reverse engineering approaches based on hybrid analysis.

Few approaches that cannot be fit in the classification are the ones that are dependent on pure data mining in order to correlate product variants to dependency graphs in order to predict the influence of one feature on others, e.g., [39]. The selection of analysis technique is based on many parameters like availability of the abstraction model, trade-off between false positive and accuracy, availability of profiling to run every feature and most importantly the kind of reverse engineering needed. The whole classification of this section is summarised in Table II.

B. *Classification based on Input and Output*

After selecting an appropriate analysis technique on grounds of compatibility and associated shortcomings, it is very important to know about required input notation and generated output notation of each approach. Some input notations are not compatible with some product lines implemented form and a lot of work is needed in order to transform code into specific input notation. To avoid extra work, one can select an approach that is most appropriate for the environment. The required input notation can be classified as *Source Code*, *Feature Set* and *Description Based Input*. *Feature Set* means configuration matrix or product-feature mapping in some notation where *Description* includes user Queries, Document-Corpus and Textual Input like natural language text etc.,

Similarly, output can also be classified into *Feature Model*, *Generated Code* and *View Based Output*. View Based Output can further be classified into concept Lattices or graphical notations and ranked Based Mapping or Feature to Code Trace.

Few approaches produce feature models as output [20] [21] [40]. Few transform code into core and variability parts [4] [22]. Few approaches generate feature-code trace [15] [17] [19] [23]- [25] [28] [31]- [36] [38]. Few generate output in the form of concept lattices or graphs [12]- [14] [16] [18] [27] [30] [37]. Concept lattices are different from general graphs because they are generated by defining the FCA and can be manipulated by changing the formal contexts whereas general graphs usually show variability models extracted from the code.

Hybrid approaches in this category use one analysis technique to reinforce the results and then use another technique on the generated output of the first one. Such hybrid approaches show results in the form of ranked based mapping where each mapping has a value based on its validity. Ranked based mapping is also a trace but it includes the ranking of the traces. Few approaches like [26] [29] generate both

TABLE II. REVERSE ENGINEERING:CLASSIFICATION OF REVERSE ENGINEERING APPROACHES BASED ON ANALYSIS

Reverse Engineering Approaches	**Analysis Classification**
RECoVar [12], Language Independent Approach [4], Dependence Graph [13], Concern Graphs [14], Concern Identification [16], Automatic Generation [15], Semi-Automatic Approach for Extraction [17]	Static
Product Variants [22], Natural language Parsing [23], Evolutionary Algorithms [20], Software Configurations using FCA [21], Source Code Retrieval [19], Combining FCA with IR [18], Reverse Engineering Feature Models [40]	Textual
Dynamic Feature Traces [24], STRADA [25], Call-Graphs [30], Focused views on Execution Traces [26], Concept Analysis [32], Trace Dependency Analysis [28], Scenario Driven Dynamic Analysis [31], Featureous [29], Software Evolution Analysis [27]	Dynamic
Static and Dynamic Analysis [34], Cerberus [33], Heuristic-Based Approach [38], Landmarks and Barriers [37], Locating Features in Source Code [36], SNIAFL [35]	Hybrid

TABLE III. REVERSE ENGINEERING: CLASSIFICATION BASED ON REQUIRED INPUT

Required Input	**Reverse Engineering Techniques**
Source Code	RECoVar [12], Call-Graphs [30], Concern Identification [16], Scenario Driven Dynamic Analysis [31], Featureous [29], Language Independent Approach [4], Semi-Automatic Approach for Extraction [17], SNIAFL [35], Static and Dynamic Analysis [34], Cerberus [33], Bug Localization [19], Focused views on Execution Traces [26], Heuristic-Based Approach [38], Dependence Graph [13], Software Evolution Analysis [27], Concern Graphs [14], Concept Analysis [32]
Feature Set	Product Variants [22], Natural language Parsing [23], Dynamic Feature Traces [24], Evolutionary Algorithms [20], Software Configurations using FCA [21], Static and Dynamic Analysis [34], STRADA [25]
Description (Queries, Document-Corpus, Textual input)	Cerberus [33], Landmarks and Barriers [37], Locating Features in Source Code [36], Source Code Retrieval [19], Trace Dependency Analysis [28], SNIAFL [35] Combining FCA with IR [18], Automatic Generation [15], Reverse Engineering Feature Models [40]

TABLE IV. REVERSE ENGINEERING: CLASSIFICATION BASED ON GENERATED OUTPUT

Generated Output		**Reverse Engineering Techniques**
Feature Model		Evolutionary Algorithms [20], Software Configurations using FCA [21], Reverse Engineering Feature Models [40]
Code		Product Variants [22], Language Independent Approach [4]
View-Based	Concept Lattices or Graphical notations	Combining FCA with IR [18], Landmarks and Barriers [37], Call-Graphs [30], Concern Identification [16], Dependence Graph [13], Concern Graphs [14], Software Evolution Analysis [27], RECoVar [12], Focused views on Execution Traces [26], Featureous [29]
	Ranked Based Mapping or Feature to Code Trace	Cerberus [33], SNIAFL [35], Source Code Retrieval [19], Scenario Driven Dynamic Analysis [31], STRADA [25], Natural language Parsing [23], Trace Dependency Analysis [28], Concept Analysis [32], Dynamic Feature Traces [24], Static and Dynamic Analysis [34], Locating Features in Source Code [36], Heuristic-Based Approach [38], Semi-Automatic Approach for Extraction [17], Focused views on Execution Traces [26], Featureous [29], Automatic Generation [15]

trace and graphical views. Table III. and IV. show the classification based on these parameters.

C. Classification based on Phase Compatibility, Pre-requisite Implementation and Required Expertise

Table V. shows the pre-requisites for implementing an approach. Pre-requisites have classified into approach centric process, i.e., *macro constant's selection, landmarks method selection, domain concepts, corpus extraction* and *profiling*. Profiling is the most common pre-requisite. RECoVar [12] is an approach that requires selection of the macro constants before it can be applied. It shows code based variability by extracting a model from the code. Users have to define the macro constants in the code to use them in conditional compiling while generating the model. Such macro constants can be *if-def* blocks or anything that can define a variation in pre-compilation and they are called variation points. Another approach Landmarks and Barriers [37] demands selection of *landmark* methods. Landmark methods are those that have a key role in execution of a feature. Hence, in order to select landmark features one must have to know that feature composition in terms of code. *Barrier* methods are those methods that do not have major importance from a feature point of view and they have to be selected in order to decrease the size of generated variability graph. Combining FCA with IR [18] demands generation of the document corpus by LSI. Document corpus is the generation of the part of the code that matches the user queries and it should be in vector space form which is a well known form in LSI. FCA uses this notation to start matching and producing the output in the form of concept lattices. Dependence Graph [13] needs identification and selection of the nodes that should be included in the search graph in order to search the implementation of a feature. The relevant code parts cannot be selected unless one has the knowledge and some familiarity with the domain and composition of the features in terms of code. So some code understanding and domain knowledge is must before executing this approach. In case of Reverse Engineering Feature Models [40], domain knowledge is needed because domain expert have to select the parent of each feature at each step and correct decisions require code and domain knowledge.

Table VI. shows the phase compatibility classification. *Phase Compatibility* shows whether an approach is suitable to use in the construction of a product line or in the maintenance of a product line. There are several approaches that are not designed for the maintenance or evolution but for the construction of a product line and hence they should be used for this purpose, e.g., approaches that can produce *Feature Models* are more appropriate to use in

TABLE V. REVERSE ENGINEERING: PRE-REQUISITE REQUIREMENTS

Pre-Requisite Implementation	Reverse Engineering Techniques
Profiling	Dynamic Feature Traces [24], Scenario Driven Dynamic Analysis [31] Trace Dependency Analysis [28], Featureous [29], Locating Features in Source Code [36], Static and Dynamic Analysis [34], Cerberus [33], STRADA [25], Call-Graphs [30], Focused views on Execution Traces [26], Concept Analysis [32], Heuristic-Based Approach [38], Software Evolution Analysis [27]
Macro Constants Selection	RECoVar [12]
Selection of Landmark Methods	Landmarks and Barriers [37]
Document corpus extraction for LSI	Combining FCA with IR [18]
Understanding of Domain Concepts	Dependence Graph [13], Reverse Engineering Feature Models [40]

constructing a product line rather than maintaining one because a non-redundant *Feature Model* can be achieved from requirement text or product lines initial product-feature documentation. Evolutionary Algorithm [20], Software Configuration using FCA [21] and Reverse Engineering Feature Models [40] are examples of such approaches.

Table VII. shows required expertise that are grouped as FCA, LSI, NLP, Profiling, VSM and Domain Knowledge. Product Variants [22], Concept Analysis [32], Combining FCA with IR [18] and Locating Features in Source Code [36] require the knowledge of FCA. FCA demands the designing of a formal context in which objects are defined in order to generate the model. Product Variants [22], Cerberus [33], Combining FCA with IR [18] and Heuristic-Based Approach [38] require the knowledge of LSI. LSI is a well known textual technique, mostly used in search engines. Natural language Parsing [23] requires Natural Language Processing which is a well established research domain on its own. Dynamic Feature Traces [24], Scenario Driven Dynamic Analysis [31], Trace Dependency Analysis [28], Featureous [29], Locating Features in Source Code [36], Static and Dynamic Analysis [34], Cerberus [33], STRADA [25], Call-Graphs [30], Focused views on Execution Traces [26], Concept Analysis [32], Heuristic-Based Approach [38] and Software Evolution Analysis [27] require profiling. SNIAFL [35] requires the knowledge of VSM. VSM is a special kind of LSI. Finally, Dependence Graph [13] and Reverse Engineering Feature Models [40] need the domain knowledge and the reasons are as stated in the previous section.

V. Available Tool Support, Language Constraint and Shortcomings

This section explains *Primary Tool*, *Secondary Tool*, *Evaluation Language* and *Major Shortcoming* related to each approach. Primary Tool attribute means tools that are specifically made for the approach where secondary Tool means third party tools that are not designed for the specific approach but help in implementing one. Most of the tools are academic where Reverse Engineering Feature Models [40], Focused views on Execution Traces [26] and Featureous [29] have professional tools. Table VIII. and Table X. show the primary tools and secondary tools availability for each approach.

TABLE VI. REVERSE ENGINEERING: PHASE COMPATIBILITY WITH SOFTWARE PRODUCT LINES

Approaches	Phase Compatibility
RECoVar [12], Dependence Graph [13], Concern Graphs [14], Concern Identification [16], Automatic Generation [15], Natural language Parsing [23], Bug Localization [19], Combining FCA with IR [18], Dynamic Feature Traces [24], STRADA [25], Call-Graphs [30], Focused views on Execution Traces [26], Concept Analysis [32], Trace Dependency Analysis [28], Scenario Driven Dynamic Analysis [31], Featureous [29], Software Evolution Analysis [27], Static and Dynamic Analysis [34], Cerberus [33], Heuristic-Based Approach [38], Landmarks and Barriers [37], Locating Features in Source Code [36], SNIAFL [35]	Maintenance
Product Variants [22], Semi-Automatic Approach for Extraction [17], Evolutionary Algorithms [20], Software Configurations using FCA [21], Language Independent Approach [4], Reverse Engineering Feature Models [40]	Construction

TABLE VII. REVERSE ENGINEERING: REQUIRED EXPERTISE

Approaches	Required Expertise
Product Variants [22], Concept Analysis [32], Combining FCA with IR [18], Locating Features in Source Code [36]	FCA
Product Variants [22], Cerberus [33], Combining FCA with IR [18], Heuristic-Based Approach [38]	LSI
Natural language Parsing [23]	NLP
Dynamic Feature Traces [24], Scenario Driven Dynamic Analysis [31], Trace Dependency Analysis [28], Featureous [29], Locating Features in Source Code [36], Static and Dynamic Analysis [34], Cerberus [33], STRADA [25], Call-Graphs [30], Focused views on Execution Traces [26], Concept Analysis [32], Heuristic-Based Approach [38], Software Evolution Analysis [27]	Profiling
SNIAFL [35]	Vector Space Modelling
Dependence Graph [13], Reverse Engineering Feature Models [40]	Domain Knowledge

Evaluation language shows the language in which an approach has been experimented and validated. Approaches that generate feature models and require description based documents as input are language independent, e.g., Evolutionary Algorithms [20] and Software Configurations using FCA [21]. Few approaches like RECoVar

TABLE VIII. REVERSE ENGINEERING: PRIMARY TOOL SUPPORT

Approach	Primary Tool
RECoVar [12], Evolutionary Algorithm [20], Feature Models from Software Configurations [21], CERBERUS [33], Source Code Retrieval [19], Combining FCA with IR [18], Heuristic-Based Approach [38], Dependence Graph [13], SNIAFL [35], Trace Dependency Analysis [28], Locating Features in Source Code [36], Scenario-Driven Dynamic Analysis [31]	NA
Product Variants [22]	Progmodel
Natural Language [23]	Patch Tool
Language Independent [4]	ExtractorPL
Semi Automatic Approach [17]	CIDE
Dynamic Feature Traces [24]	DFT
Static and Dynamic Analysis [34]	Customised BIT
STRADA [25]	STRADA
Focused Views on Execution Traces [26]	CGA-LDX
Concept Analysis [32]	Customised GCC
Software Evolution Analysis [27]	Trace Scrapper
Concern Graphs [14]	FEAT
Automatic Generation [15]	EclipsePlug-in
Concern Identification [16]	CoDEx
Featureous [29]	Featureous
Using Landmarks and Barriers [37]	Prototype Tool
Embedded Call Graphs [30]	Call Graph Prototype
Reverse Engineering Feature Models [40]	CDT TOOLS (LVAT)

[12] are methodologies and hence they can be applied in any language but the approaches like Focused views on Execution Traces [26], Featureous [29] and Call Graph [30] are language dependent as their tools are dependent on the programming language they have designed for. Table IX. shows the evaluation language of each approach.

One major shortcoming is the inability of an approach to consider cross cutting constraints (CTC), e.g., Semi-Automatic Approach for Extraction [17] and Language Independent Approach [4]. Few approaches like Software Configurations using FCA [21] consider CTC but they cannot produce feature model beyond two levels of hierarchy. Results of Dynamic Feature Traces [24], STRADA [25], Source Code Retrieval [19], Concept Analysis [32], Combining FCA with IR [18], Heuristic-Based Approach [38] and Trace Dependency Analysis [28] are highly dependent on the user defined input. This input is approach centric and can be code knowledge, profiling, test scenarios or setting the formal context. More detail is expressed in Table XI. Language constraint, availability of tool and relevant shortcomings are the primary factors to consider one approach over the others.

VI. Conclusion

This paper has presented a concise classification of reverse engineering approaches in software product lines. Individual reverse

TABLE IX. REVERSE ENGINEERING: EVALUATION LANGUAGE OF APPROACHES

Approach	Evaluation Language
Product Variants [22], RECoVar [12], Evolutionary Algorithm [20], Feature Models from Software Configurations [21]	Language Independent
Natural Language [23], Language Independent [4], Semi Automatic Approach [17], Dynamic Feature Traces [24], Static and Dynamic Analysis [34], CERBERUS [33], STRADA [25], Source Code Retrieval [19], Combining FCA with IR [18], Heuristic-Based Approach [38], Software Evolution Analysis [27], Concern Graph [14], Automatic Generation [15], Concern Identification [16], Featureous [29], Using Landmarks and Barriers [37]	JAVA
Concept Analysis [32], Embedded Call-Graphs [30], Locating Features in Source Code [36], SNIAFL [35], Dependence Graph [13]	C
Source Code Retrieval [19], Focused Views on Execution Traces [26], Reverse Engineering Feature Models [40], Scenario-Driven Dynamic Analysis [31], Embedded Call-Graphs [30], Trace Dependency Analysis [28]	C++

TABLE X. REVERSE ENGINEERING: SECONDARY TOOL SUPPORT

Approach	Secondary Tool
Product Variants [22], Natural Language [23], Language Independent [4], Semi Automatic Approach [17], Dynamic Feature Traces [24], STRADA [25], CERBERUS [33], Focused Views on Execution Traces [26], Dependence Graph [13], Software Evolution Analysis [27], Concern Graphs [14], Automatic Generation [15], Locating Features in Source Code [36], Featureous [29], Concern Identification [16], Embedded Call Graphs [30], Using Landmarks and Barriers [37], Reverse Engineering Feature Models [40]	NA
RECoVar [12]	Treeviz, Orange
Feature Models from Software Configurations [21]	FAMA, SPLOT
Source Code Retrieval [19]	Gibbs, LDA++
Combining FCA with IR [18]	SrcML, Columbus
Trace Dependency Analysis [28]	Rational Coverage
Scenario-Driven Dynamic Analysis [31]	JGraph
Evolutionary Algorithm [20]	BETTY
Static and Dynamic Analysis [34]	SA4J
Concept Analysis [32]	Graphlet
Heuristic-Based Approach [38]	MoDeC
SNIAFL [35]	SMART

TABLE XI. REVERSE ENGINEERING: MAJOR SHORTCOMING OF APPROACHES

Approach	Major Shortcoming
Language Independent Approach [4], Semi Automatic Approach [17]	CTC not considered
Dynamic Feature Traces [24], STRADA [25], Source code Retrieval [19], Concept Analysis [32], Trace Dependency Analysis [28], Heuristic-Based Approach [38], Combining FCA with IR [18]	Result dependency on user defined input
RECoVar [12], Reverse Engineering Feature Models using Landmarks and Barriers [37], Dependence Graph [13]	Require code understanding
Natural Language [23], Evolutionary Algorithm [20]	High computation cost
Product Variants [22]	Non-re-usability if feature set changes
Feature Models from Software Configurations [21]	Extract Feature Model for two levels of hierarchy
Static and Dynamic Analysis [34]	Work for only one feature at a time
CERBERUS [33], Locating Features in Source Code [36]	No tool support
Focused Views on Execution Traces [26]	Only work for C/C++ code
Software Evolution Analysis [27], SNIAFL [35], Scenario-Driven Dynamic Analysis [31]	Method implementation neglected
Concern Graphs [14], Concern Identification [16]	Intra-method flow of calls neglected
Automatic Generation [15]	Implicit features neglected
Featureous [29]	JAVA tool dependency
Embedded Call-Graphs [30]	C/C++ tool dependency

engineering techniques that cannot produce results in terms of features and variants of a product line were not considered. The primary aim of this short guide is to present such information that can narrow down the practical options of implementation for the product line engineers so they can discard the non-feasible options of reverse engineering. The reverse engineering in product lines is considered as extraction of artefacts from the code of a product line. However, current approaches do not propose to extract something architectural or in a component notation. Reverse engineering is focused on variability management and features locations at the moment. Future work in this domain can include the approaches that can extract executable architecture from a product line code in order to reuse it across many systems. Hence, the concept of reverse engineering in software product lines should consider the architectural extraction in future.

REFERENCES

[1] A. C. Telea, "Reverse engineering–recent advances and applications," *Ed. Intech 2012.*

[2] K. Pohl, G. Böckle, and F. Van Der Linden, *Software Product Line Engineering: Foundations, Principles, and Techniques*. Springer, 2005.

[3] F. vd Linden, K. Schmid, and E. Rommes, "Software product lines in action: The best industrial practice in product line engineering. secaucus."

[4] T. Ziadi, C. Henard, M. Papadakis, M. Ziane, and Y. Le Traon, "Towards a language-independent approach for reverse-engineering of software product lines," in *Proceedings of the 29th Annual ACM Symposium on Applied Computing*, pp. 1064–1071, ACM, 2014.

[5] S. Deerwester, S. T. Dumais, G. W. Furnas, T. K. Landauer, and R. Harshman, "Indexing by latent semantic analysis," *Journal of the American society for information science*, vol. 41, no. 6, p. 391, 1990.

[6] T. Hofmann, "Probabilistic latent semantic indexing," in *Proceedings of the 22nd annual international ACM SIGIR conference on Research and development in information retrieval*, pp. 50–57, ACM, 1999.

[7] E. Hill, L. Pollock, and K. Vijay-Shanker, "Automatically capturing source code context of nl-queries for software maintenance and reuse," in *Proceedings of the 31st International Conference on Software Engineering*, pp. 232–242, IEEE Computer Society, 2009.

[8] B. Dit, M. Revelle, M. Gethers, and D. Poshyvanyk, "Feature location in source code: a taxonomy and survey," *Journal of Software: Evolution and Process*, vol. 25, no. 1, pp. 53–95, 2013.

[9] M. L. Nelson, "A survey of reverse engineering and program comprehension," *arXiv preprint cs/0503068*, 2005.

[10] J. Raymond, J. Canzanese, O. Matthew, M. Spiros, and K. Moshe, "A survey of reverse engineering tools for the 32-bit microsoft windows environment," *Drexel University*, 2005.

[11] M. D. Ernst, "Static and dynamic analysis: Synergy and duality," in *WODA 2003: ICSE Workshop on Dynamic Analysis*, pp. 24–27, Citeseer, 2003.

[12] B. Zhang and M. Becker, "Recovar: A solution framework towards reverse engineering variability," in *Product Line Approaches in Software Engineering (PLEASE), 2013 4th International Workshop on*, pp. 45–48, IEEE, 2013.

[13] K. Chen and V. Rajlich, "Case study of feature location using dependence graph.," in *IWPC*, pp. 241–247, Citeseer, 2000.

[14] M. P. Robillard and G. C. Murphy, "Concern graphs: finding and describing concerns using structural program dependencies," in *Proceedings of the 24th international conference on Software engineering*, pp. 406–416, ACM, 2002.

[15] M. P. Robillard, "Automatic generation of suggestions for program investigation," in *ACM SIGSOFT Software Engineering Notes*, vol. 30, pp. 11–20, ACM, 2005.

[16] M. Trifu, "Improving the dataflow-based concern identification approach," in *Software Maintenance and Reengineering, 2009. CSMR'09. 13th European Conference on*, pp. 109–118, IEEE, 2009.

[17] M. T. Valente, V. Borges, and L. Passos, "A semi-automatic approach for extracting software product lines," *Software Engineering, IEEE Transactions on*, vol. 38, no. 4, pp. 737–754, 2012.

[18] D. Poshyvanyk and A. Marcus, "Combining formal concept analysis with information retrieval for concept location in source code," in *Program Comprehension, 2007. ICPC'07. 15th IEEE International Conference on*, pp. 37–48, IEEE, 2007.

[19] S. K. Lukins, N. A. Kraft, and L. H. Etzkorn, "Source code retrieval for bug localization using latent dirichlet allocation," in *Reverse Engineering, 2008. WCRE'08. 15th Working Conference on*, pp. 155–164, IEEE, 2008.

[20] R. E. Lopez-Herrejon, J. A. Galindo, D. Benavides, S. Segura, and A. Egyed, "Reverse engineering feature models with evolutionary algorithms: An exploratory study," in *Search Based Software Engineering*, pp. 168–182, Springer, 2012.

[21] R. Al-Msie'Deen, M. Huchard, A.-D. Seriai, C. Urtado, and S. Vauttier, "Reverse engineering feature models from software configurations using formal concept analysis," in *CLA 2014: Eleventh International Conference on Concept Lattices and Their Applications*, vol. 1252, pp. 95–106, 2014.

[22] Y. Xue, Z. Xing, and S. Jarzabek, "Feature location in a collection of product variants," in *Reverse Engineering (WCRE), 2012 19th Working Conference on*, pp. 145–154, IEEE, 2012.

[23] S. L. Abebe and P. Tonella, "Natural language parsing of program element names for concept extraction," in *Program Comprehension (ICPC), 2010 IEEE 18th International Conference on*, pp. 156–159, IEEE, 2010.

[24] A. D. Eisenberg and K. De Volder, "Dynamic feature traces: Finding features in unfamiliar code," in *Software Maintenance, 2005. ICSM'05. Proceedings of the 21st IEEE International Conference on*, pp. 337–346, IEEE, 2005.
[25] A. Egyed, G. Binder, and P. Grunbacher, "Strada: A tool for scenario-based feature-to-code trace detection and analysis," in *Companion to the proceedings of the 29th International Conference on Software Engineering*, pp. 41–42, IEEE Computer Society, 2007.
[26] J. Bohnet, S. Voigt, and J. Dollner, "Locating and understanding features of complex software systems by synchronizing time-, collaboration-and code-focused views on execution traces," in *Program Comprehension, 2008. ICPC 2008. The 16th IEEE International Conference on*, pp. 268–271, IEEE, 2008.
[27] O. Greevy, S. Ducasse, and T. Girba, "Analyzing feature traces to incorporate the semantics of change in software evolution analysis," in *Software Maintenance, 2005. ICSM'05. Proceedings of the 21st IEEE International Conference on*, pp. 347–356, IEEE, 2005.
[28] A. Egyed, "A scenario-driven approach to trace dependency analysis," *Software Engineering, IEEE Transactions on*, vol. 29, no. 2, pp. 116–132, 2003.
[29] A. Olszak and B. N. Jørgensen, "Featureous: a tool for feature-centric analysis of java software," in *Program Comprehension (ICPC), 2010 IEEE 18th International Conference on*, pp. 44–45, IEEE, 2010.
[30] J. Bohnet and J. Döllner, "Analyzing feature implementation by visual exploration of architecturally-embedded call-graphs," in *Proceedings of the 2006 international workshop on Dynamic systems analysis*, pp. 41–48, ACM, 2006.
[31] M. Salah, S. Mancoridis, G. Antoniol, and M. Di Penta, "Scenario-driven dynamic analysis for comprehending large software systems," pp. 71–80, IEEE, 2006.
[32] T. Eisenbarth, R. Koschke, and D. Simon, "Derivation of feature component maps by means of concept analysis," in *Software Maintenance and Reengineering, 2001. Fifth European Conference on*, pp. 176–179, IEEE, 2001.
[33] M. Eaddy, A. V. Aho, G. Antoniol, and Y.-G. Guéhéneuc, "Cerberus: Tracing requirements to source code using information retrieval, dynamic analysis, and program analysis," in *Program Comprehension, 2008. ICPC 2008. The 16th IEEE International Conference on*, pp. 53–62, IEEE, 2008.
[34] A. Rohatgi, A. Hamou-Lhadj, and J. Rilling, "An approach for mapping features to code based on static and dynamic analysis," in *Program Comprehension, 2008. ICPC 2008. The 16th IEEE International Conference on*, pp. 236–241, IEEE, 2008.
[35] W. Zhao, L. Zhang, Y. Liu, J. Sun, and F. Yang, "Sniafl: Towards a static noninteractive approach to feature location," *ACM Transactions on Software Engineering and Methodology (TOSEM)*, vol. 15, no. 2, pp. 195–226, 2006.
[36] T. Eisenbarth, R. Koschke, and D. Simon, "Locating features in source code," *Software Engineering, IEEE Transactions on*, vol. 29, no. 3, pp. 210–224, 2003.
[37] N. Walkinshaw, M. Roper, and M. Wood, "Feature location and extraction using landmarks and barriers," in *Software Maintenance, 2007. ICSM 2007. IEEE International Conference on*, pp. 54–63, IEEE, 2007.
[38] F. Asadi, M. Di Penta, G. Antoniol, and Y.-G. Guéhéneuc, "A heuristic-based approach to identify concepts in execution traces," in *Software Maintenance and Reengineering (CSMR), 2010 14th European Conference on*, pp. 31–40, IEEE, 2010.
[39] B. Zhang and M. Becker, "Reverse engineering complex feature correlations for product line configuration improvement," in *Software Engineering and Advanced Applications (SEAA), 2014 40th EUROMICRO Conference on*, pp. 320–327, IEEE, 2014.
[40] S. She, R. Lotufo, T. Berger, A. Wasowski, and K. Czarnecki, "Reverse engineering feature models," in *2011 33rd International Conference on Software Engineering (ICSE)*, pp. 461–470, IEEE, 2011.

A UML-based Simple Function Point Estimation Method and Tool

Geng Liu, Xingqi Wang, Jinglong Fang
School of Computer Science and Technology
Hangzhou Dianzi University
Hangzhou, China
email:{liugeng, xqwang, fjl}@hdu.edu.cn

Abstract—**Function Point Analysis (FPA) is used to measure the size of functional user requirements of software applications. However, the measurement process of FPA is slow, expensive and complex. The Simple Function Point (SiFP) method has been proposed as a replacement of FPA that is much faster and cheaper to apply. However, no tools supporting Simple Function Point measurement have yet been proposed. In this paper, we aim at building a tool to facilitate SiFP measurement. Specifically, we propose a measurement based on UML models of requirements, including use case diagrams and domain model (class diagrams). The proposed methodology –including a set of guidelines for domain modeling and the mapping between SiFP measure components and UML elements – makes SiFP measurement much easier to perform. In fact, the proposed methodology is usable in the early requirements definition stage, when only use case diagram and the primary class diagram illustrating the domain model (including classes' names and relationship among classes) are available. We used 17 academic sample applications to validate our proposal. The result shows that our method and tool can be used to replace manual Simple Function Point measurement in the early phases of the software development cycle to measure the functional size of software project.**

Keywords— Functional Size Measures; Simple Function Point; SiFP; UML; Object-oriented measures.

I. INTRODUCTION

Function Point Analysis (FPA) [1][2][3] aims at measuring the size of Functional User Requirements (FUR) of software applications. Being based on FUR, which are available in the early phases of development, these measures are widely used to estimate the effort required to develop software applications. FPA was originally introduced by Albrecht to measure data-processing systems by quantifying the functionality the software provides to the user, from the information view, by quantifying the volume of data flow and the storage [4].

The basic idea of FPA is that the "amount of functionality" released to the user can be evaluated by taking into account the data used by the application to provide the required functions, and the transactions (i.e., operations that involve data crossing the boundaries of the application) through which the functionality is delivered to the user. Data are user identifiable groups of logically related data, and are classified as Internal Logical Files (ILF) or External Interface Files (EIF). A transaction is a set of actions seen as one cohesive unit of work. FPA differentiates three types of transactions: External Input (EI), External Output (EO), and External Inquiry (EQ). The size of each data function depends on the type of contents; the size of each transaction depends on the number of data files used and the amount of data exchanged with the external. The sum of the sizes of data and transactions is the size of the application in Unadjusted Function Points (UFP).

Organizations that develop software are interested in Function Point measurement process that is reliable, rapid and cheap, and that fits well in their development processes. However, performing FPA requires a thorough exploration of FUR, to identify and possibly weigh basic functional components. Therefore, the measurement process can be quite long and expensive. In fact, FPA performed by a certified function point consultant proceeds at a relatively slow pace: between 400 and 600 function points (FP) per day, according to Capers Jones [5], between 200 and 300 FPs per day according to experts from Total Metrics [6]. Consequently, measuring the size of a moderately large application can take too long, if cost estimation is needed urgently. Also, the cost of measurement can be often considered excessive by software developers.

In addition, at the beginning of a project, size estimation would be necessary for bidding and planning. But, FURs have not yet been specified in detail and completely, namely the available information is often incomplete and insufficient. So the customer is only able to do approximate measurements. The accuracy of a FP measure grows with the completeness and precision of FUR specifications. When we can measure with the highest accuracy, we no longer need that measure. The situation is described by the paradox illustrated in Fig. 1.

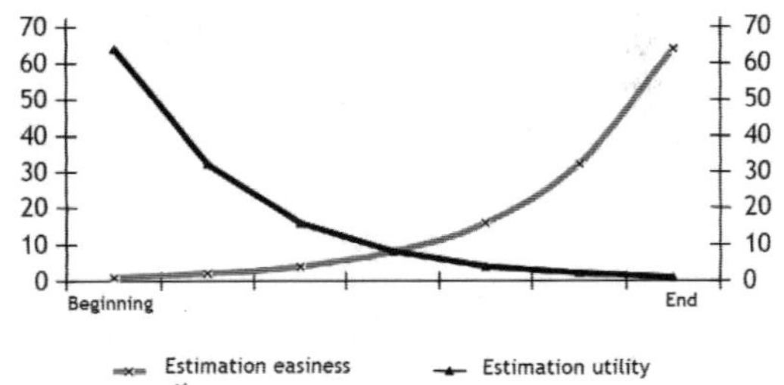

Fig. 1. Paradox of estimation and informations about estimation

Given the above situation, many simplified methods, such as Early & Quick Function Points（E&QFP) [7], Estimated NESMA [8], Simplified FP[9], ISBSG [10], ILF model [11], and Early FP [12], have been proposed. The SiFP method [13][14][27] is different from the other methods mentioned above, as it does not aim at providing approximate estimation of FP measures; rather, it defines a brand new functional size measure, to be used in place of traditional FP.

In this paper, we propose some rules for building UML models in a SiFP-oriented way. Since SiFP counting is based on the identification of Unspecified Generic Elementary Process (UGEP) and Unspecified Generic Data Group (UGDG), which basically correspond to system data and process, we exploit the ability of UML to represent such information by establishing an explicit relation between SiFP elements and UML language constructs. We also define some rules to measure the SiFP size of an application from use case diagrams and the domain model, and develop a tool to automatically measure SiFP on the base of XMI/XML files abstracted from UML model. Throughout the paper we take for granted that the reader knows at least the basics of FPA measurement and is familiar with basic UML concepts.

The rest of the paper is organized as follows: Section II explains the background knowledge about SiFP. Section III describes the empirical study. The validity of the study is discussed in Section IV. Related work is presented in Section V. Finally, Section VI draws some conclusions and outlines future work.

II. BACK GROUND KNOWLEDGE-SIFP

This section presents a brief summary of the SiFP method. For full details and explanations of the method, see the reference manual [13].

SiFP method was proposed by the Simple Function Point Association, Italy. Its basic idea is that a notion of complexity based on the number of logical data file or cross reference among transaction and file or subgroup of data in a file is not significant to the goal of representing functional size and of estimation effort or cost. In order to measure the functional size of an application, it is not necessary to identify several types of transactions and files.

The SiFP method defines the generic software model as shown in Fig.2, which highlights the components related to the functional requirements of "moving" data, "processing" data and data "storage".

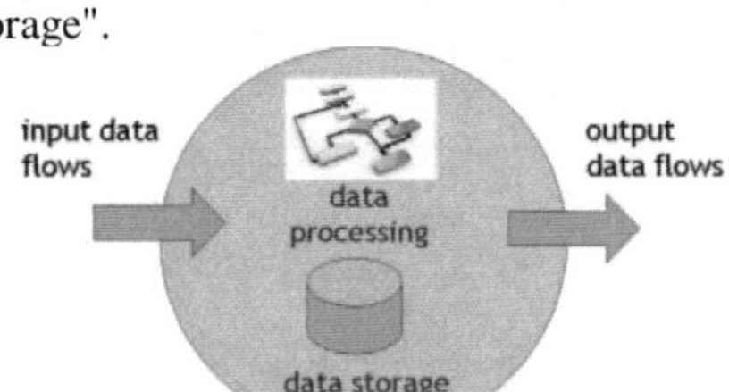

Fig. 2. Theory of SiFP [13]

The SiFP method defines and uses only two basic functional components (BFCs): UGEP and UGDG, see Fig.3. An UGEP is defined as: "*An atomic set of functional user requirements conceived for processing purposes. It refers to an informational or operational goal considered significant and unitary by the user and includes all automated, mandatory and optional activities needed to meet the goal. After an UGEP is concluded, the measurable software application (MSA) to which it belongs must be in a logically consistent state.*" [13] An UGDG is defined as: "*An atomic set of user requirements having a storage purpose. It refers to a single logical data set of interest to the user, for which information must be kept persistently.*"[13]

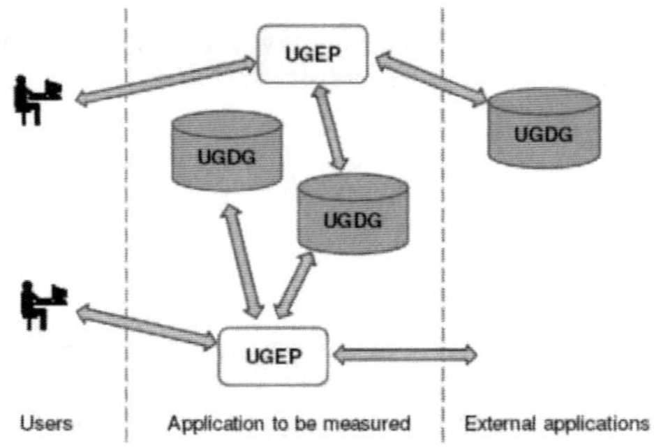

Fig. 3. BFC Types [14]

In the case of the UGEP, the term "unspecified" highlights that it is not necessary to distinguish whether a process is mainly for input, or output, or what is its primary intent of data processing. Similarly, in the case of the UGDG, it means that it is not necessary to distinguish between internal and external logical storage with respect to the boundary of the MSA.

On the other hand, the term "Generic" indicates that for any BFC there is no need to identify subcomponents in order to determine BFC's complexity: all the BFCs weight equally within the same type of BFC. Future developments of the methodology may lead to define different functional weights for each specific BFC depending on elements related to the processing component of transactional BFCs that, at present, is not quantitatively taken into account.

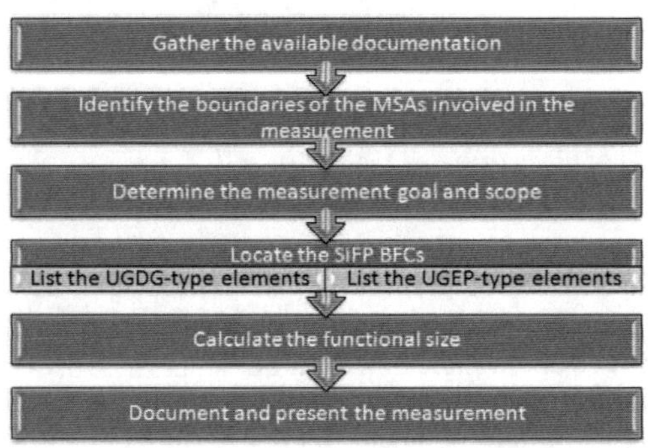

Fig. 4. SiFP measurement process [13]

The SiFP measurement process is represented in Fig.4. It is a 6-step process:

– Gather the available documentation;

– Identify application boundary;

– Determine the measurement goal and scope;

– Locate elementary processes (UGEP) and logical data files (UGDG);

– Calculate the function size using function SiFP = 4.6 UGEP + 7 UGDG;

– Document and present the measurement.

III. THE EMPIRICAL STUDY

In this section, we introduce UML-based SiFP estimation method through a case study and present briefly the Tool SiFPOOTool developed by us.

A. The case introduction

We use as the case a reduced version of a real Information System by Lavazza [15], since it is concise and its size is appropriate. Its functional size in FP is already measured, so we do not need to do it again. In our case, a system class diagram that involves composition and specification/generalization meets our needs. The only drawback of this system for our study is that the use case diagram is relatively simple; the relationships among the use cases just involve the general association. But, overall, it is suitable for our objectives.

This GymIS is an information system for Gym management. The application offers annual and monthly subscriptions. The client who subscripts the annual service only needs to pay 12 times the cost of a month but have the right of receiving 13 months service. The client and subscription data are stored in the system database. The former is characterized by name, age, profession, address, and SSN. Clients can also be updated, but, once inserted, they are never removed from the system. A subscription is characterized by the duration, the subscription date, the subscribing client, the set of optional services to which the client subscribed (their cost adds up to the cost of the basic subscription). Among the optional services there is the possibility to get a monthly medical check.

The functions that the application must provide are the following: record a new client, update the client data, record a new subscription, record the payment by a given client for a given month, compute and print how much is due by every client for the previous months, compute the number of subscriptions that include the given service in a given period, and record the results of a health check. The detailed requirements for the transactions are not presented here. The complete FURs of the GymIS can be found in [15]; they were measured according to FPA rules on the basis of a traditional description. The result was that the application is 67 FP.

B. SiFP-oriented modeling

UML-based SiFP estimation method works well only if the given models incorporate all the required information at the proper detail level and the modeling and measure rules are defined according to the SiFP theory. In this sub-section we define the SiFP-Oriented modeling methodology as a set of guidelines. For the purpose of modeling, we use UML as defined in [16]. We do not define extensions or force the semantics of the language. This choice contributes to minimizing the impact of the measurement-oriented modeling on the development process, and to make the adoption of the method as seamless as possible.

Usually, the activity of creating OO models is not sequential; rather, it is often iterative, with several refinements, deletions, extensions, and modifications of the model. In order to keep the presentation clear, we present the modeling methodology as a sequence of conceptual steps.

Step 1: Present application boundary

The first objective of the model is to represent the application boundaries and the external elements that interact with the system to be measured.

A use case diagram is a graphic depiction of the interactions among the elements of a system. A use case diagram contains four components. The boundary defines the system of interest in relation to the world around it. The actors are usually individuals involved with the system defined according to their roles. The use cases are the specific roles played by the actors within and around the system. The last component is the relationships between and among the actors and the use cases. UML provides use case diagrams, which are well suited for our purposes. The boundary of the use case diagrams can be directly taken as the boundary of the MSA.

The correspondence between the SiFP concepts and the elements of UML use case diagrams is schematically described in Table I.

TABLE I. MAPPING OF THE ELEMENTS BETWEEN SIFP AND UML

SiFP	UML
Application boundary	Boundary of the object that owns the use cases
UGEP	Use case
User	Actor
UGDG locating out of the system boundary	Actor

Step 2: Present UGEP using use case

Use Case Diagrams indicate –as actors– the elements outside the boundary with which the application interacts; most important, use case diagrams show the transactions. We represent each UGEP as a use case.

Rule 1: Each use case must represent the smallest unit of activity that is meaningful to the user(s), and must be self-contained and leave the business of the application being counted in a consistent state.

Rule 2: Relationship among the use case, extension, include, generalization, must be correctly presented.

Rule 3: A use case that cannot be instanced must be noted as "abstract" stereotype. The base use case of a cluster of use case formatted by generalization must be noted as "abstract" stereotype.

By applying the rules above to the GymIS the use case diagram reported in Fig. 5 is obtained.

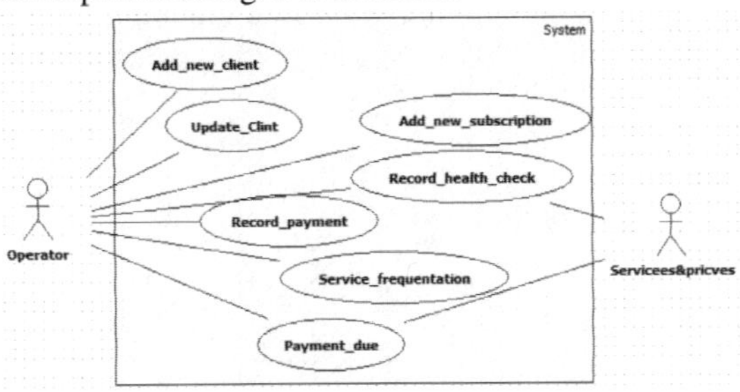

Fig. 5. Use case diagram of the GymIS

Step 3: Present UGDG using domain class

Usually, the methods proposed in the literature for measuring the functional size of UML models map the concept of data functions onto (sets of) classes. The difficulties in matching classes and logic files are exemplified very well in [18], where four different manners of identifying logical files are defined, according to the different possible ways to deal with aggregations and generalization/specializations relationships.

Although in several cases it is possible to identify a class as a logic file, it is also quite common that a single logic file corresponds to a set of classes.

In object-oriented development process, such as ICONIX processes [17], the modeling process of static model can be split into three stages: 1) requirements definition, 2) analysis, conceptual design and technical architecture, 3) design and coding. The obtained models are domain model, updated domain model and Class model -as shown in Fig. 6- which separately correspond to three types of diagram: domain class diagram, updated domain class diagram and class diagrams.

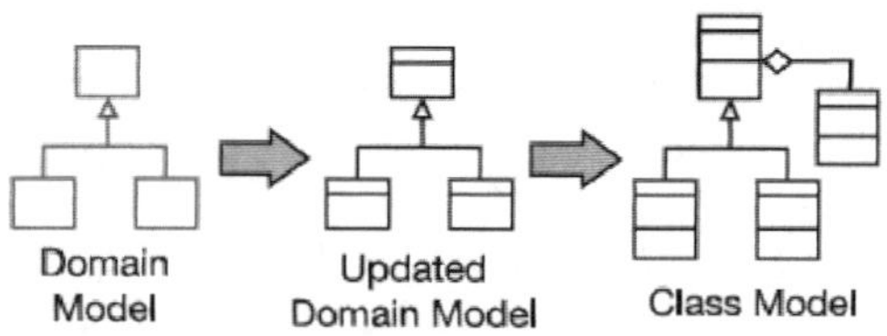

Fig. 6. Static domain model of OO development using ICONIX process

Information presented by domain diagram contains names of the entity objects, and the relationships among these entity objects; updated domain class diagram is added boundary objects and controllers. Also the attributes of each entity class abstracted from use case specification are equipped; Class diagram contains all the information mentioned above, and some controllers are changed into one or more operations and those operations are assigned to corresponding class. Analysis and comparison about different types of objects at different stages is shown in Table II. Through the above analysis we can see the domain class diagram already fully meets the demand for measuring the data "storage" part of SiFP except that it doesn't have the ability to present the UGDG located outside the system boundary.

TABLE II. ANALYSIS ADN COMPARISON ABOUT DIFFERENT TYPES OF OBJECTS

		Domain Model	Update Domain Model	Class Model
Stereotype of Class	Entity	Yes	Yes	Yes
	Controller	/	Yes	Yes
	Boundary	/	Yes	Yes
Information about entity class	Class Name	Yes	Yes	Yes
	Relationship	Yes	Yes	Yes
	Attributes	/	Yes	Yes
	Methods	/	/	Yes
Suitable for SiFP measure		Yes	Yes	Yes

Since for any BFC there is no need to identify subcomponents in order to determine BFC complexity. We define some rules as following:

Rule 4: SiFP does not distinguish between internal and external UGDG, but in order to facilitate the later statements, we divided UGDG into two types: external UGDG and internal UGDG. Internal UGDG is the UGDG that locates inside of the system boundary, external UGDG locates outside of the system boundary.

Rule 5: Entity classes that appear in the domain model diagram are the candidates for UGDG. Entity classes appear in domain model must be complete, namely, no entity class be missed. Each entity class should have its name, and the relationships among the entity classes should be complete.

Rule 6: Each entity class must be noted as stereotype <<Entity>>.

Rule 7: In general, a UGDG corresponds to an entity class (see the class User and Payments in Fig.7). A relevant exception is given by clusters of classes that are connected by composition relations (see the set classes consist of HealthRecord and Result in Fig.7), or generalization relations (see the classes Subscription, MonthScription and AnnualScription in Fig.7). A cluster of classes that are connected by composition or generalization relations is defined as one UGDG.

TABLE III. MAPPING OF THE ELEMENTS

SiFP	UML	Class(es)	#UGDG
UGDG	association	1	1
UGDG	aggregation	1	1
UGDG	composition	a cluster of	1
UGDG	generalization	a cluster of	1
UGDG locating out of the system boundary	logic data component	1	1

Rule 8: When necessary, add to the domain model one or more special class(es) to present the external system logical data: these class(es) are named as external UGDG(s) and are stereotyped <<XUGDG>> (see class otherSystem in Fig.7). A class diagram with added special classes is called an extended class diagram.

By applying the rules above to the Gym IS, the extended class diagram reported in Fig. 7 was obtained.

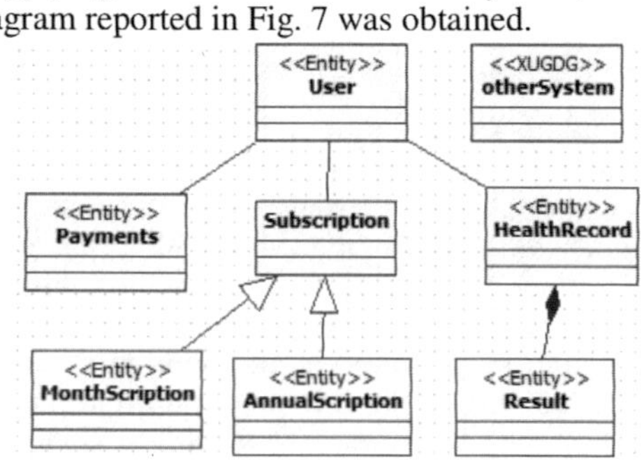

Fig. 7. Extended Class diagram of the Gym IS

C. *Counting and summing*

Here our SiFP counting procedure is redefined with respect to the UML model with the following goals: it must be coherent with the principles reported in SiFP reference manual [13]; it must be precise, without ambiguities, thus leaving no space to the measurer for interpretation; it must require little effort; it must be executable by people without big skill in FP counting and with little knowledge of the requirements.

As mentioned earlier, a UGEP is represented as a use case, but not every use case should be counted as a UGEP. By analyzing the role and the characteristics of each use case belonging to a set of use cases connected by include, extension or generalization relations (see Table IV), and according to SiFP rules, we define rule 9.

TABLE IV. COMMON ELEMENTS FROM GENERAL MODEL AND FPA ORIENTED UML MODEL

Type of UC	Role of UC	Complete	Abstract	for measure unit
Include	Base UC	Yes	No	Yes
	Inclusion	Yes	No	Yes
Extension	Base UC	Yes	No	Yes
	Extension	Yes	No	Yes
Generalization	general UC	No	Yes	No
	Specialized UC	Yes	No	Yes

Rule 9: In general, a use case is counted as a UGEP. A relevant exception is that the use case noted as abstract is not counted as a UGEP.

Rule 10: As defined by the rules 4-8, whether it is a single class or a group of classes, as long as it is defined as a UGDG, it is counted as a UGDG.

Rule 11: A class stereotyped <<XUGDG>> is counted as a UGDG.

Once the UGEP and UGDG lists are complete, the scores are assigned to the individual BFCs and added together as shown below. The scores to assign to each individual BFC are: UGDG = 7.0 SiFP and UGEP = 4.6 SiFP.

So the size of a whole application is:

SiFP=M(UGEP)+M(UGDG)= #UGEP*4.6 + # UGDG*7.0.

Here #X means the number of X.

According to the conversion between SiFP and UFP defined in the SiFP reference manual, we can draw the following equation to calculate the FPA functional size from the SiFP value:

UFP = #SiFP /0.998

D. *Measure Tool for SiFP*

There are several UML modeling tools which support OO modeling, such as Visio, Rational Rose, Power Designs, EA and StarUML. These tools not only provide a graphical modeling function, but also export the model as XMI and/or XML file. Measurement tools can be designed by parsing XMI/XML document and using measurement rules. We designed a measure tool SiFPOOTool to automatically measure the SiFP size of an application by its UML model, precisely use case diagram and class diagram. The high-level structure of the tool is shown in Fig.8.

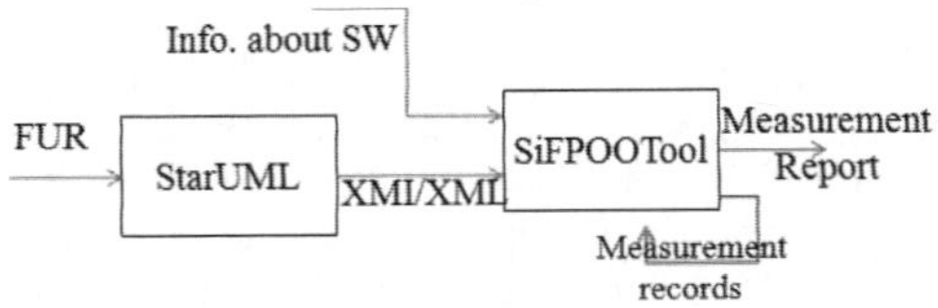

Fig. 8. Theory of SiFPOOTool

The tool provides some functions, such as, reading and parsing XML file derived from UML model, recording and reporting the measure result. Moreover, the related information about the application being measured, the company which holds the application (see Fig. 9), the measurer that carries out the measurement are all recorded by the tool to meet the needs for analysis and inquiries.

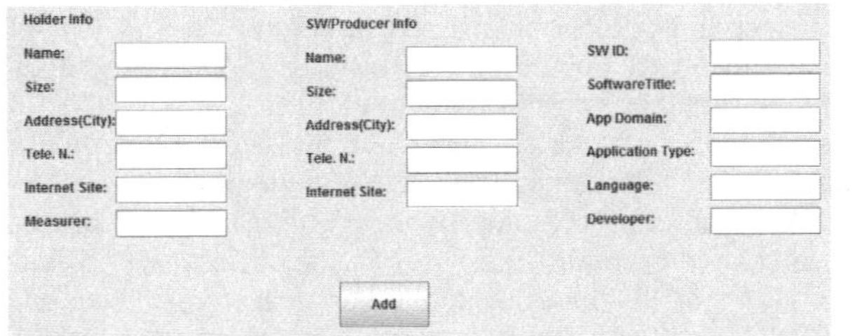

Fig. 9. Information input interface of the tool

We measure the GymIS software application using our tool SiFPOOTool: 5 UGDG and 7 UGEP were identified, thus the total size is 67.2 SiFP.

IV. EMPIRICAL VALIDATION

We aimed to validate the two issues: the first one is whether the tool can be used to replace the manual SiFP measurement, when a UML requirement model is available. The second is to validate whether our SiFP-oriented UML modeling rules are correct. The validation overview is shown in the Fig.10.

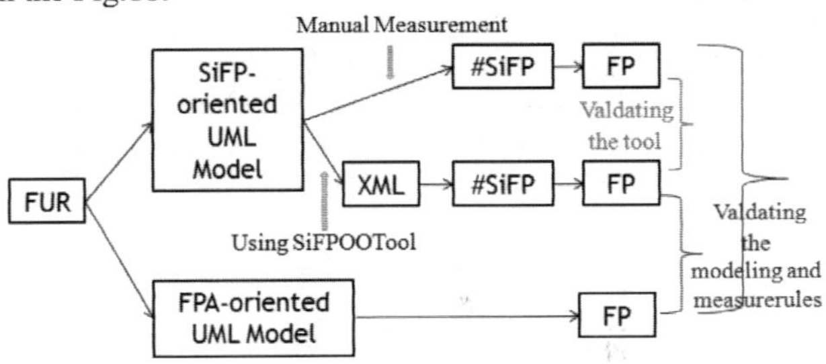

Fig. 10. Validation overview

We used 17 projects' models mainly prepared during previous work [19]. The FURs, UML models (use case diagram, class diagram, components diagram, and sequence diagram) and size measures (in UFP) of those projects are available.

The experimental validation procedure was organized as follows:

–Firstly, for each project, the use case diagrams are reviewed and modified according to the rules 1, 2 and 3 defined in Section III.B.

–Second step: the class diagrams are reviewed and modified according to the rules 4-8 in Section III.B.

–Third step: The activities involved in steps 1 and 2 are repeated until all the projects' use cases and class diagrams comply with the rules 1-8 in Section III.B. Using StarUML, the XMI/XML files are exported from UML model.

– The fourth step: those 17 projects are manually measured using the SiFP method: the results are given in columns 2-4 of Table V. The correspond SiFP and UFP are also calculated automatically and inserted in the 4th and 5th columns of the Table V. The UFP values are computed according to the function SiFP = #UFP*0.998 described in the reference manual [13].

– Then we use our tool SiFPOOTool to measure each model XMI/XML file obtained at step 4. The results and their corresponding UFPs are inserted in columns 6-8 of Table V. To automatically obtain the UFP values, the previous function SiFP=#UFP*0.998 was used in our tool.

– Finally, we copied into Column 10 the functional size measures in UFP manually measured in the previous work.

When all the preparatory work was finished, we performed three paired sample t-Tests on the datasets of manual measurement (Column 5), of the measurement based on SiFPOOTool (Column 9) and of UFP values (Column 10) obtained in the previous work. As usually the level of significance is set as 5%. Test results are as follows: on the datasets of manual measurement (Column 5) and of the measurement based on SiFPOOTool (Column 9), the two-tailed test p-value is approximately 0.104. For the datasets of the manual measurement(Column 5) and the UFP(Column 10), the datasets of measurement based on the tool(Column 9) and UFP(Column 10), both the two-tailed test p-values are approximately 0.001. Then we analyzed the average of absolute value of the ratio of UFP based on the tool(Column 9) and the UFP(Column 10), it is approximately 9.95%, which is less than 10%, so the results obtained based on the tool is acceptable. Our approach (based on UML model) belongs to the third level, detailed measurement level, of the six accuracy levels for software sizing defined in [20][21].

In conclusion, our estimation tool SiFPOOTool can be used to replace manual SiFP measurement in the early phases of the software development cycle, namely domain modeling phase, to measure the functional size of software project. As it turns out, our modeling and measure rules (Rules 1-11 presented in Section III. B, C and D) lead to good experiment results.

TABLE V. DATASETS OF MEASUREMENTS BY HAND, USING SIFPOOTOOL

P.ID	Manual Measurement				Measurement Using SiFPOOTool				UFP	Ratio of 5th/9th column	Ratio of 5th/10th column	Ratio of 9th/10th column
	#UGEP	#UGDG	SiFP	UFP	#UGEP	#UGDG	SiFP	UFP				
1	15	13	160	160.3	15	13	160	160.3	160	0.00%	0.20%	0.20%
2	15	15	174	174.3	15	14	167	167.3	140	4.19%	24.53%	19.52%
3	12	6	97.2	97.4	12	3	76.2	76.4	84	27.56%	15.95%	-9.10%
4	22	10	171.2	171.5	22	11	178	178.6	163	-3.93%	5.24%	9.54%
5	20	6	134	134.3	20	6	134	134.3	128	0.00%	4.90%	4.90%
6	18	8	138.8	139.1	18	9	146	146.1	130	-4.80%	6.98%	12.38%
7	16	3	94.6	94.8	16	3	94.6	94.8	78	0.00%	21.53%	21.53%
8	15	8	125	125.3	15	6	111	111.2	107	12.61%	17.06%	3.95%
9	17	7	127.2	127.5	17	5	113	113.4	102	12.37%	24.96%	11.20%
10	7	8	88.2	88.4	7	8	88.2	88.4	79	0.00%	11.87%	11.87%
11	18	7	131.8	132.1	18	5	118	118.0	105	11.88%	25.78%	12.42%
12	28	4	156.8	157.1	28	4	157	157.1	138	0.00%	13.85%	13.85%
13	22	5	136.2	136.5	22	5	136	136.5	124	0.00%	10.06%	10.06%
14	13	2	73.8	73.9	13	2	73.8	73.9	73	0.00%	1.30%	1.30%
15	20	3	113	113.2	20	3	113	113.2	106	0.00%	6.82%	6.82%
16	27	6	166.2	166.5	27	6	166	166.5	159	0.00%	4.74%	4.74%
17	14	5	99.4	99.6	14	5	99.4	99.6	86	0.00%	15.81%	15.81%

V. RELATED WORK

The generic concepts of FPA were published in the late 1970s. Later, more detailed measurement rules were developed to improve consistency of measurement. Due to lack of good software documentation, it is not always possible to apply all the detailed rules, and measurers must fall back on approximation techniques [22].

In [22] M. Lelli and R. Meli announced this as a paradox: Size estimation is necessary when we do not have enough information (thus, early estimation methods must be used to obtain it). When we can measure with the greatest accuracy, we no longer need that information any more.

In order to figure out whether FPA in the early phases is a realistic option, the committee "FPA" in the early phases" was established in September 1989. The committee investigated whether FPA can be used to perform an indicative size estimate before a complete logical (detailed) design is available [23].

Many techniques for early size estimation have been proposed for FP, such as component sizing technique by Putnam and Myers [24] and the Early and Quick Function Point size estimation techniques by Conte et al. [25]. These methods – such as Estimated NESMA method [8], ISBSG average weights, simplified FP [13], prognosis of CNV AG [11] and so on - do not require the weighting of functions; instead each function is weighted with average values.

Some methods extrapolated the FP counts from the countable components (usually the ILFs) using statistical methods (mostly regression analysis). Some simplified methods – Mark II, NESMA's Indicative FP, Tichenor ILF Model, Prognosis by CNV AG, and ISBSG Benchmark – were constructed according to such technique.

In [15] Lavazza et al. proposed a FPA-oriented UML modeling technique that can make FPA performed in a seamless way, while yielding reliable results. In [26] del Bianco et al. introduced the model-based technique into COSMIC method and suggested a simplified model-based cost estimation models. By using the data from a large popular public dataset Lavazza and Meli confirmed that SiFP can be effectively used in place of IFPUG [14]. However, there has been no measure tool for SiFP so far.

VI. Conclusions and Future Work

Performing Function Point measurement according to the traditional process is expensive and time consuming. The SiFP was proposed as a replacement of FPA. Functional size is mainly used for estimating development costs and project planning. Many software developers use UML, hence they are interested in basing functional size measurement on UML models. In principle, UML-based estimation can be used effectively at the earliest stage of software: our proposal makes this possibility practical and viable. Additional researches (concerning both measurement technology and measurement tools) are necessary to support functional size measurement in different stages of software development.

Acknowledgment

The authors thank Prof. Luigi Antonio Lavazza from the University of Insubria in Varese, Italy, for his constructive suggestions and comments on this research. The authors also thank Jun Wu for his contribution to the implementation of the first version of the tool. The research presented in this paper has been supported by the Start Project Foundation of Hangzhou Dianzi University under Grant No. KYS105614069, by the Defense Industrial Technology Development Program under Grant No. JCKY2013415C001 and Grant No. JSZL2014415B002, and by Weapon Equipment Pre-Research Foundation under Grant No. 9140A15040214DZ04221.

References

[1] A. J. Albrecht, "Measuring Application Development Productivity", Joint SHARE/ GUIDE/IBM Application Development Symposium, pp. 83-92, 1979.

[2] International Function Point Users Group, "Function Point Counting Practices Manual - Release 4.3.1", January 2010.

[3] ISO/IEC 20926: 2003, "Software engineering – IFPUG 4.1 Unadjusted Functional Size Measurement Method – Counting Practices Manual", Geneva: ISO, 2003.

[4] A. J. Albrecht and J.E. Gaffney, "Software function, Source Lines of Code and Development Effort Prediction: a Software Science Validation", IEEE Transactions on Software Engineering, vol. 9(6), pp.639-648,1983.

[5] C. Jones, "A New Business Model for Function Point Metrics", http://www.itmpi.org/assets/base/images/itmpi/privaterooms/capersjones /FunctPtBusModel2008.pdf, retrieved: June, 2016.

[6] Total Metrics, "Methods for Software Sizing – How to Decide which Method to Use", http://www.totalmetrics.com/function-point-resources/downloads/R185_Why-use-Function-Points.pdf, retrieved: June, 2016.

[7] "Early & Quick Function Points for IFPUG Methods v.3.1 Reference Manual 1.1", April 2012.

[8] ISO/IEC 24570: 2004, "Software Engineering-NESMA Functional Size Measurement Method version 2.1 - Definitions and Counting Guidelines for the Application of Function Point Analysis", International Organization for Standardization, Geneva, 2004.

[9] J. Geraci and C. Tichenor, "The IRS Development and Application of the Internal Logical File Model to Estimate Function Point Counts,"1994. Presented at the Fall 2000 IFPUG Conference.

[10] L. Bernstein and C. M. Yuhas, "Trustworthy Systems Through Quantitative Software Engineering", John Wiley & Sons, 2005.

[11] M. Bundschuh, "Function Point Prognosis Revisited", FESMA 99, Amsterdam, The Netherlands, October 4-8, 1999, pp. 287–297. http://www.academia.edu/1024603/FUNCTION_POINT_PROGNOSIS_REVISITED, retrieved:June, 2016.

[12] R. A. Monge, F. S. Marco, F. T. Cervigón,V. G. García, and G. U. Paino, "A Preliminary Study for the Development of an Early Method for the Measurement in Function Points of a Software Product", Eprint Arxiv Cs, 2004.

[13] SiFPA, "Simple Function Point Functional Size Measurement Method - Reference Manual, V. SiFP-01.00-RM-EN-01.01", http://www.sifpa.org/en/index.htm, retrieved: June, 2016.

[14] L. Lavazza and R. Meli, "An Evaluation of Simple Function Point as a Replacement of IFPUG Function Point", in 9th Int. Conf. on Software Process and Product Measurement (Mensura) IWSM-MENSURA 2014, October 6-8, 2014, Rotterdam.

[15] L. Lavazza, V. del Bianco, and C. Garavaglia, "Model-based Functional Size Measurement", 2nd International Symposium on Empirical Software Engineering and Measurement (ESEM 2008), Oct. 9-10, 2008, Kaiserslautern, Germany.

[16] OMG–Object Management Group, "Unified Modeling Language: Superstructure", version 2.1.1, OMG formal/2007-02-05, February 2007. (available from http://www.omg.org)

[17] D. Rosenberg and M. Stephens, "Use Case Driven Object Modeling with UML Theory and Practice", Apress, Berkeley, USA, 2007.

[18] G. Antoniol, C. Lokan, G. Caldiera, and R. Fiutem, "A Function Point-Like Measure for Object-Oriented Software", Empirical Software Engineering , Volume 4, Issue 3, pp 263–287, Sept. 1999.

[19] G. Liu, "Towards Making Function Size Measurement Easily Usable in Practice", PhD thesis, University of Insubria, Varese, Italy, 2014.

[20] P. Hill, "Software early lifecycle- Function sizing", SoftwareTech, June 2006, Vol. 9, No.2.

[21] Total Metrics, "Levels of Function Points, Version 1.3", January 2004, http://www.totalmetrics.com/total-metrics-articles/levels-of-function-point-counting, Total Metrics, 2004.

[22] M. Lelli and R. Meli, "from Narrative User Requirements to Function Point", IN: Proceedings of Software Measurement European Forum-SMEF 2005, Mar. 16-18, 2005, Rome, Italy.

[23] NESMA, "The Application of Function Point Analysis in the Early Phases of the Application Life Cycle - A Practical Manual: Theory And Case Study, V. 2.0", http://www.nesma.nl/download/boeken_NESMA/N20_FPA_in_Early_Phases_(v2.0).pdf, retrieved:June, 2016.

[24] L. H. Putnam and W. Myers, "Measures for Excellence: Reliable Software on Time within Budget", Prentice Hall, UpperSaddle River, 1992.

[25] M. Conte, T. Iorio, R. Meli, and L. Santillo, "E&Q: An Early & Quick Approach to Function Size Measurement Methods", In Proceedings of Software Measurement European Forum-SMEF 2004, January 28-30, 2004, Rome, Italy.

[26] V. del Bianco, L. Lavazza, and S. Morasca, "A Proposal for Simplified Model-Based Cost Estimation Models", In Proceedings of 13th Int. Conf. on Product-Focused Software Development and Process Improvement, pp. 59-73, June 13-15, 2012, Madrid, Spain.

[27] F. Ferrucci, C. Gravino, and L. Lavazza, "Assessing Simple Function Points for Effort Estimation: an Empirical Study", 31st ACM Symposium on Applied Computing, April 4-8, 2016, Pisa, Italy.

Transaction-Aware Aspects with TransJ: An Initial Empirical Study to Demonstrate Improvement in Reusability

Anas M.R. AlSobeh
Computer Information Systems-Yarmouk University
Irbid, Jordan
Email: anas.alsobeh@yu.edu.jo

Stephen W. Clyde
Computer Science-Utah State University
Logan, Utah, USA
Email: stephen.clyde@usu.edu

***Abstract*—TransJ is an extension to AspectJ for encapsulating transaction-related cross-cutting concerns in modular aspects. This paper presents an empirical study to evaluate the reusability and performance cross-cutting concerns implemented with TransJ compare to AspectJ alone. As part this study, we define a reuse and performance quality model as an extension to an existing quality model. We then formalize eight hypotheses that can be tested using metrics from the quality model. Finally, to assess the hypotheses, we compare implementations of different sample applications across two study groups: one for TransJ and another for AspectJ. Results from the study show improvement in reusability when using TransJ, while preserving the performance.**

Keywords-Transaction-related Aspects; Aspect-Oriented Programming (AOPL); Abstractions; Transaction Joinpoint; Dynamic Weaving; Pointcuts; Transaction-related Contexts (TCC's); software reuse; and performance.

I. INTRODUCTION

The implementation of complex applications using Aspect-Oriented Software Development (AOSD) –as a modern modularization technique– results in a better implementation structure relative to essential application qualities, such as maintainability, reusability, modularity, and reduce complexity [1]. One of the recognized strengths of Aspect-Oriented Programming Languages is the separation of concerns (SoC's) through the definition of modular abstractions, called Aspects, that reduce scattering and tangling of crosscutting concerns (CC's) in the application code. By definition, CC's impact multiple components of an application's core code. Common examples include logging, enforcement of real-time constraints, concurrency controls, transaction management, access controls, and so on. Implementing these such concerns directly into a Distributed Transaction Processing System (DTPS) can cause the scattering and tangling of code and, thus, make the code unnecessarily complex and difficult to understand, reuse, maintain, and evolve.

AspectJ is considered the de facto standard and the most widely used Aspect-Oriented Programming (AOP) framework for modeling CC's. It extends Java with mechanisms for supporting logic related to CC's, starting with aspect, which are first-class programming constructs for CC's [2][3]. Aspects encapsulate advice, pointcuts, and type-introduction declarations. An advice is a method that embodies some piece of CC functionality, but it is not called explicitly like class or object methods. Instead the execution of an advice method is woven into the core application according to specifications, called pointcuts. A pointcut is a predicate that defines where to weave advice at compile time and when to execute at runtime. More specifically, it is a pattern that identifies a set of joinpoints, which are best characterized as intervals within the program's execution flow. A joinpoint represents places (intervals or times) in execution on program and advice run before, after, or around these intervals [2].

AspectJ supports many different kinds of joinpoints, such as fields, methods, constructors, and catch blocks in exception handling, but they only related to program-language abstractions and their contexts are limited to single-threaded execution flows. The problem is that AspectJ does not inherently handle higher level abstractions or application-level contexts, like transactions, which may be tied to runtime objects and used by multiple execution threads or processes. Hence, AspectJ cannot directly support the dynamic weaving of advice into transaction abstractions or directly leverage transaction context information.

TransJ is an extension to AspectJ that introduces transaction-aware aspects, independent of any specific transaction-processing framework. With TransJ, developers can weave Transaction-Related Crosscutting Concerns (TCC's) into a DTPS in a modular and reusable way, while preserving core functionality, and obliviousness to those TCC's. (See Section II).

In this paper, we report on a study that investigated the impact of TransJ on the reuse of DTPS code while preserving performance. It does so by evaluating certain desirable characteristics and attributes defined in an extended quality model (see Section III) using a set of computable metrics. Based on an initial theoretically investigation, we hypothesized that developers would see improvement reuse improvements while preserving the software performance when using TransJ. We formalize this notion into eight specific hypotheses (see Section IV). Section V explains our experiment methodology; selection of the sample software application; and identification of interesting TCCs that would provide good coverage. The methodology also included supporting activities such as recruitment and training of the developers as test subjects. After the experiment, we collected and analyzed data from the code, journals, questionnaires, and surveys. From the results (see Section VI) of the study, we conclude that application using TransJ have less coupling (less scattered), less complex, and required less effort and time to enhance. Also, they are more cohesive (less tangling) and oblivious without sacrificing the performance. These preliminary results lead us to believe that further experimentation with TransJ and refinement of its framework could prove to be very beneficial to a wide range of software applications.

II. HIGH-LEVEL OVERVIEW OF TRANSJ

Fig. 1 provides a high-level overview the TransJ's layered design [6], in which each layer embodies reusable functionality and provides services to the layer above it and uses the services of the layer below it.

One component at the lowest layer is the Unified Model for Joinpoints in Distributed Transactions (UMJDT), first introduced in a 2014 ICSEA paper [5]. The UMJDT is a conceptual model for weaving advice into distributed transactions that captures key events and context information, and use that ideas to define interesting joinpoints relative to transaction execution and context data for woven advice.

AspectJ and some transaction-processing framework, like JTA, are two components at the lowest level.

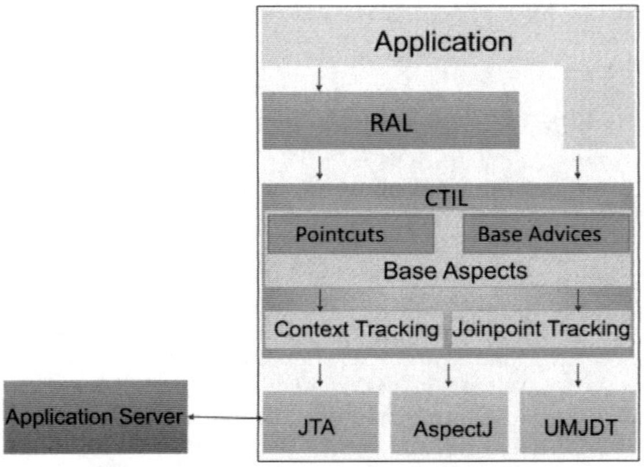

Figure 1. TransJ Architectural Block Diagram.

The Core TransJ Infrastructure Layer (CTIL) is a library that implements a transaction joinpoint model on top of an AspectJ joinpoint model. It defines transaction abstractions, transaction-events joinpoints, a collection of pointcuts for gathering context information that can be used in the advice code, and mechanisms to track transaction contexts and joinpoints. This library allows developers to treat transactions as first-class concepts into which aspects can be woven, promoting greater enhancements, obliviousness, and localization, along with code reusability.

The Reusable Aspect Layer (RAL) is a toolkit-like collection of transaction-related aspects that application programmers should find useful in many different kinds of applications with significant transaction requirements. These reusable aspects can decrease the development time; make CC's more understandable, reusable, and predictable; and ensure that the core application is oblivious to the CC's.

Application-level Aspect Layer is where application developers implement transaction-related aspects using the abstractions provided by TransJ directly or by specializing the aspects from the RAL. These aspects can encapsulate complex TCC behaviors in understandable, predictable and reusable software components, without sacrificing obliviousness or efficiency [6].

III. Extended-Quality Model for Transactional Application (EQMTA)

Many empirical studies have found that different soft-ware factors influence the quality of a software system [7][8][9]. Of these, we picked reusability and performance as important qualities to consider initially because of potential for cost savings that they both represent. To formalize the reuse and performance qualities, we adapt and extend the Extended-Quality Model [9], which was based on the Comparison Quality Metrics (Sant'Anna quality model) [1][7] to include quality factors and internal attributes specific for DTPS's, forming EQMTA.

EQMTA consists of four elements: Qualities, Factors, Quality Attributes, and Metrics. The qualities, i.e., reusability and performance, are the most abstract concepts in the model and represent the ultimate goals of "good" software. Each quality is affected by one or more factors, which are in turn determined by quality attributes (internal attributes). The quality attributes describe the internal view of the system attributes with a set of quality metrics that are de-fined and used to provide a scale and method for measurement.

Fig. 2 shows the specific qualities, quality factors, and quality attributes of the EQMTA's suite, and Fig. 3 shows the metrics. A single star (*) next to an element in either of these figures tags a concept that not exist in the original EQM [8] or Comparison Quality Model [1]. Double stars (**) mark elements that are in the previous

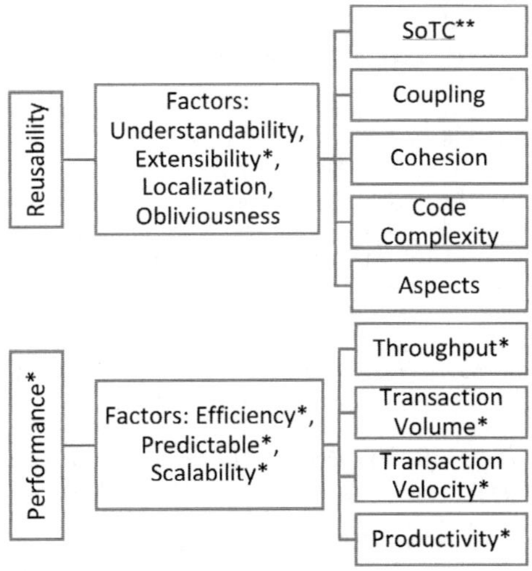

Figure 2. Extended-Quality Model for Transactional Applications (EQMTA)

models, but have been modified to be a measure quality in transaction systems.

The quality factors are the secondary quality attributes that influence the defining primary qualities and associated with well-established internal quality attributes of the soft-ware systems as shown in Fig. 2. Raza [8] proposes three important characteristics of modular code, namely understandable, obliviousness and localization of design decisions. Hence, reasoning reusability in terms of understandability, localization of design decisions, and obliviousness are not complete. Introduction of efficiency, predictability, and scalability are also equally important. At the time Parnas [11] and Coady [12] proposed that the definition of reusable modular code, obliviousness and extensibility has not been documented as fundamental design principles. How-ever, in the context of our research experiment, they are critical to understanding the impact of TransJ.

A. *EQMTA Metrics*

The EQMTA contains 29 design and code metrics for the 9 internal attributes shown in Fig. 3. In some cases, we had to adapt the metrics to better evaluate the attributes in DTPS. Twelve of the metrics can be computed automatically from the code written by the subjects. The others have to be computed by hand. Below are brief descriptions of these metrics, so the reader can better understand the

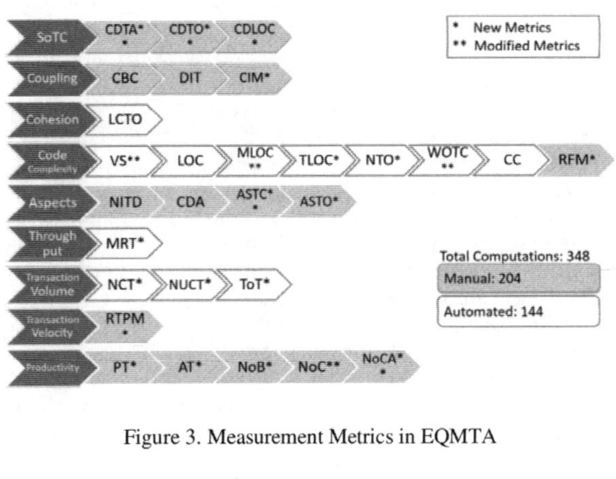

Figure 3. Measurement Metrics in EQMTA

results presented in Section VI. For space considerations, the full definitions of all metrics are not shown.

1) *Separation of Transaction Concern (SoTC)/ Scattering Metrics*

SoTC defines the ability to capture, encapsulate and manipulate unnecessary complexities of transaction system that are relevant to a particular concern [13]. The Concern Diffusion in Transaction Application (CDTA), Concern Diffusion over Transaction Operations (CDTO) and Concern Diffusion over Line of Code (CDLOC) are SoTC metrics. CDTA number of primary transaction components (class or aspect) whose main purpose is to contribute to the implementation of a concern. CDTO counts the number of methods and advices that access any primary transaction component to pull all relevant operation context information by calling their methods or using them in formal parameters, local variables, return types, and throws declarations. Constructors also are counted as operations. CDLOC counts the total lines of primary transaction components whose main purpose is to contribute to the implementation of a single transaction-related concern.

2) *Transaction-related Coupling Metrics*

It is an indication of the strength of interconnections between the transaction components in a DTPS [10][14]. Coupling between Components (CBC), Depth Inheritance Tree (DIT), and Coupling on Intercepted Modules (CIM) are coupling metrics. CIM counts the number of classes, aspects or interfaces explicitly named in pointcuts of a given aspect. High values of these metrics indicate tight coupling, due to high crosscutting.

3) *Transaction-related Cohesion and Tangling Metrics*

The cohesion of a transaction is a measure of the degree fitness between its internal pieces [7]. Lack of Cohesion in Transaction Operations (LCTO) measures the lack of cohesion of a class or aspect in terms of the occurrences of the method and advice pairs that do not access the same context variable and hence should be reasonably separated [15]. High cohesion often correlates with loose coupling, and vice versa [10]. Low coupling is often an indicator of a well-structured DTPS and a good design, and when combined with high cohesion, supports the general goals of high reusability.

4) *Complexity Metrics*

The EQMTA defines metrics that are concerned with the different aspects of the DTPS complexity. It measures how transaction components are structurally interrelated to one another and measures the size of a software system's design and code [1]. In EQMTA, the Vocabulary Size (VS), Line of Code (LOC), Method Lines of Code (MLOC), Transaction Lines of Code (TLOC), Number of Transaction Operations (NTO), and Weighted Operations per Transaction Component (WOTC), McCabe's Cyclomatic Complexity (CC), and Response for Module (RFM) are complexity and size metrics in EQMTA. VS counts the number of classes and aspects into the DTPS. Sant' Anna mentioned that if the number of components increases, it is a clue of more cohesive and less tangled set of abstract datatype concepts [1]. NTO counts the number of transaction-related operations. A transaction contains with more operations are less likely to be reused and assumed to have more complex collaboration with other components. Sometimes LOC is less, but NTO is more, which indicates that the transaction component is more complex. The number of advices and methods and complexity is an indication of how much time and effort is required to develop and maintain the transaction-related components. The larger the value of WOTC, the more complex the program would be [15][16]. CC is intended to measure system complexity by examining the software program's flow graph [17]. In practice, CC amounts to a count of the decision points present in the software system. The high value of CC affects transaction components reuse. RFM counts the number of methods and advices that are executed by a given transaction in response to the request received by another transaction or system. Transactions with a higher RFM value are more complex and complicated.

5) *Aspects/Obliviousness Metrics*

The EQMTA involves metrics on concerns that evolve into concrete pieces of code, i.e., Aspects, and contribute directly to the core functionality of the transaction software system [8]. This model defines the following aspect metrics: Number of Inter-type Declarations (NITD), Crosscutting Degree of an Aspect (CDA), Aspect Scattering over Transaction Components (ASTC), and Aspect Scattering over Transaction Operations (ASTO).

6) *Transaction Throughput Metrics*

Transaction throughput is the rate at which transactions are processed by the system. The EQMTA defines the rate of the Mean Response Time (MRT) to measure the performance of an individual transaction, in milliseconds. MRT represents the amount of time required for transaction completion, i.e., commit or abort. The response time for a transaction tends to decrease as you increase overall throughput.

7) *Transaction Volume Metrics*

Transaction volume is an indication of the efficiency of transaction system to handle huge data volume, which determine the amount of transactions processed by the system over the defined period of time, i.e., second. The EQMTA defines the following transaction volume metrics: Number of the Committed Transactions (NCT), Number of the uncommitted (aborted) Transactions (NUCT), and Timed-out Transaction (ToT).

8) *Transaction Velocity Metrics*

Transaction Velocity gives an indication of the performance of the transaction system. Rate of the Transaction Per Minute (RTPM) is the only velocity metric in EQMTA that measures velocity of a transaction in our model. RTPM is the average number of transactions that are begin completed, either committed, aborted, or timed-out, per minute on the transaction system.

9) *Productivity Metrics*

Productivity is a measure of the amount of effort needed to understand, implement and debug the transaction system components. It considers the amount of bugs, and total development time into active and passive times. Active Time (AT), Passive Times (PT), Number of Bugs (NoB), Number of Changes in Concern at the application level (NoC), and Number of Changes in Concern and its Application (NoCA) are productivity metrics. NoC and NoCA count the number of changes required to reuse the concern for another application, and to maintain the concern, respectively. The difference among them is that the NoC only considers changes in the concern; however, the NoCA considers changes both in the concern and application. A lower value of PT, AT, NoB, NoC and NoCA is more desired to increase the efficiency of the development transaction-related components.

IV. EXPERIMENTAL HYPOTHESES

The theoretical ideas underpinning TransJ lead to the following eight hypotheses. All of these hypotheses have the same premise and are tested using the EQTMA metrics. Let S represent a software system that has TCC's and is implemented in AspectJ. Also, let S' be an implementation of same system using TransJ. The premise is implementation of the TCC in S' make reasonably effective use of TransJ.

A. S' has better encapsulation and Separation of Concerns (SoCs) and less scattering than S.
B. S' has a lower coupling than S.
C. S' has higher cohesion and less tangling than S.
D. S' not significantly larger or complex S.
E. S' is significantly more oblivious to TCC's than S.

F. The runtime of $S'$is no worse than S
G. The implementation TCC's in S' requires a smaller number of changes to reuse compared to S.
H. The total programming hours for S' is less than S, indicating that S' is less complex and more readable than S.

V. EXPERIMENTAL PROCEDURE

The research experiment consisted of the following steps:

1. Experiment Approval: We submitted an application for conducting this Human Research Experiment to the USU IRB and got its approval [4]. Before submitting this application, all the researchers passed the online human research experiment-training course offered through the Collaborative Institutional Training Initiative (CITI) [18].
2. Selection of Applications: we developed three non-trivial software applications that were diverse in the way they implemented transactions; used JTA API, X/Open standards, Jboss Application Server; multithreaded; and therefore provide a good coverage of different types of distributed transactions as shown in Table 1. We used Java 2 Enterprise Edition (J2EE) to build these non-trivial applications. They include classes for distributed resources and make used Enterprise Java Bean (EJB), Java Persistence (JPA), Maven, Hibernate, Jboss, JTA, Arjuna, and MySql database drivers. The current EJB architecture supports flat transactions only, but the Arjuna supports nested transactions in the application. Most of the implementation details are not relevant to the contributions of this paper, and are there omitted for space considerations.
3. Selection of TCC's: we picked three common TCC's for the experience such that they were applied to all the sample applications and the various concepts of transactions, as shown in Table 2. To reduce chaos in our data, we wanted to make sure that these CC's were adequately simple to a novice developer could understand and integrate them into the selected sample applications in less than 15 hours, regardless of whether TransJ or AspectJ is used.
4. Recruitment of Developers: To transparently recruit the developers, we sent invitation letters and then recruited four developers who were experienced OO and AOP software development, Java, transaction, and software-engineering design principles such as reusability and performance. We randomly organized them into two study groups: 1 and 2. Group 1 implemented using an AOP approach and Group 2 used TransJ fashion. Next, the participants completed a survey that assessed their background and skill levels. We also provided JTA, Arjuna library, Jboss, AOP training to developers in Groups, and had them worked through some practice applications. Similarly, we trained Group 2 developers with TransJ, and had them worked through some practice applications. Next, each developer filled a pre-implementation questionnaire, developed the application using initial requirements, recorded hourly journals and completed a post implementation questionnaire.
5. We analyzed the understanding of the requirements, familiarity with the language and tools, and debugging the most prominent challenges. They also recorded hourly journals of productivity. At the end of implementation, each developer filled the post-implementation questionnaire. Observation of this questionnaire indicated that all developers correctly understood the requirements, familiarized with the language, tools, and debugged the challenges.

TABLE 1. CATEGORIES OF SELECTED APPLICATIONS

Applications		Gadget Manufacturing System	Conference Registration System	Local Bank System
1	Distributed	*	*	
	Local			*
2	Flat		*	*
	Nested	*		
3	Few Resources		*	*
	Many Resources	*		
4	Low Concurrency			*
	High Concurrency	*	*	
5	Low Potential for Conflict		*	*
	High Potential for Conflict	*		

TABLE 2. SELECTED TRANSACTION-RELATED CROSSCUTTING CONCERNS (TCC)

#	Aspect Name	Description
1	**Measuring Performance**	It measures some performance-related statistics for transaction-based applications between a client and server, such as turn-around time (i.e., response time).
2	**Data-Sharing Optimization**	It shares context information across hosts only when necessary.
3	**Audit Trail**	It records a history of actions executed by transactions and users in order to monitor transaction activities and provide assurance that meet the predefined minimum requirements.

We measured EQMTA code metrics using both manual-based and automated tool-based methods [19][20]. Total measurements include following: experiment input variables included a total of four developers and three applications with each; experiment generated a total of 12 software systems against which the metrics need to be applied; the 29 code metrics of EQMTA, which will have a total of 348 measurements. Of these, 144 measurements from 12 metrics were generated using tools, and 204 measurements from 17 metrics were calculated manually.

VI. EXPERIMENT RESULTS

This section presents empirical results relevant to the eight hypotheses. We analyzed and evaluated the reusability and performance using the code developed by the student participants, questionnaires, hourly journals, and maintenance history. In the following graphs, the vertical axes represent the measurements, and the horizontal axes represent the three activities of the experiment. For each activity, there are two bars: a blue bar for the results of AspectJ group and an orange bar for the results of TransJ group. For space limitation, we did not show all results.

A. *S' has better encapsulation and Separation of Concerns (SoCs) and less scattering than S*

From the graphs in Fig. 4, we found that the interest average of CDTA, CDTO and CDLOC values for TransJ went to zero in all three activities of the experiment, and the result was significantly different from AspectJ in the all activities. The reason for this phenomenon is that TransJ pointcuts provide total obliviousness between the transaction application and TCC's. AspectJ, transaction

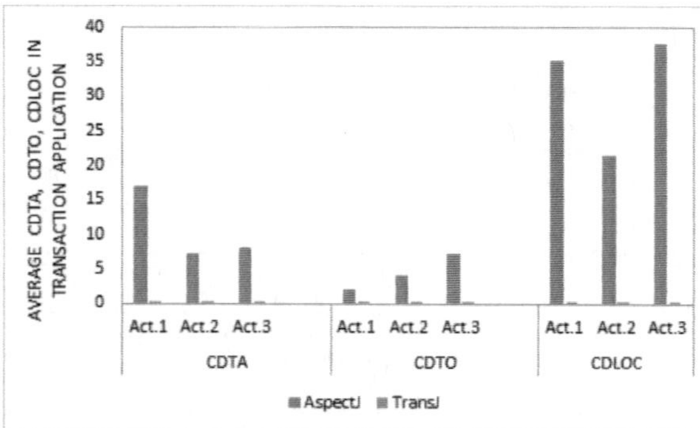

Figure 4. CDTA, CDTO, and CDLOC Coverage over Applications

components and their operations for CC's were significantly more diffused in the transaction application because the pointcuts had to be tied to programming constructs instead of transaction abstractions. From these results, we can conclude that the first hypothesis holds true for better separation of concerns in TransJ than in AspectJ.

B. *S'has a lower coupling than S*

Fig. 5 shows that TransJ implementation decreased the values of CBC, DIT, and CIM in all the three activities of the experiment. TransJ removed dependencies and did not maintain any direct relationship between TCC's and the core transaction application components. In AspectJ, unnecessary coupling of TCC's with the core application components increased CBC, which hindered reuse and code understandability.

On the one hand, wide variations were found in DIT and CIM metrics from TransJ group and AspectJ group. The most significant indicator of the decrease in coupling between aspects and the core code is the impact of TransJ's joinpoints on the CIM metric. This metric counts the number of modules explicitly named in pointcuts. Compared to the AspectJ activities, the TransJ activities have a reduction of 100%, 100% and 100% in CIM (i.e., all of the three activities have an average value of zero for CIM metric). This was caused by providing a comprehensive set of pointcuts, which fully encapsulates the distributed transaction abstractions. This allows participant programmers to reuse the pointcuts directly, so they did not need to override or inherit the aspect components to name in the pointcuts of a given class. In contrast, the AspectJ programmers suffered from a lack of clarity of relationship among TCC's and application components, wherein aspects acquire context information from one of more classes. Thus, they preferred to inherit all of the attributes and operations from parent (superclass) methods in CC's to share context data across aspects and distributed transaction application components.

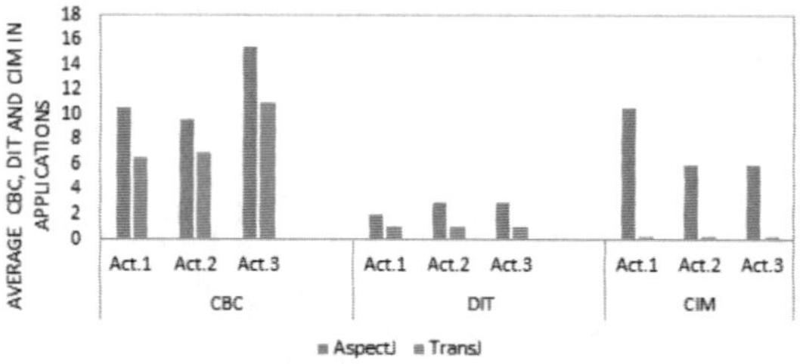

Figure 5. CBC, DIT and CIM Coverage over Applications

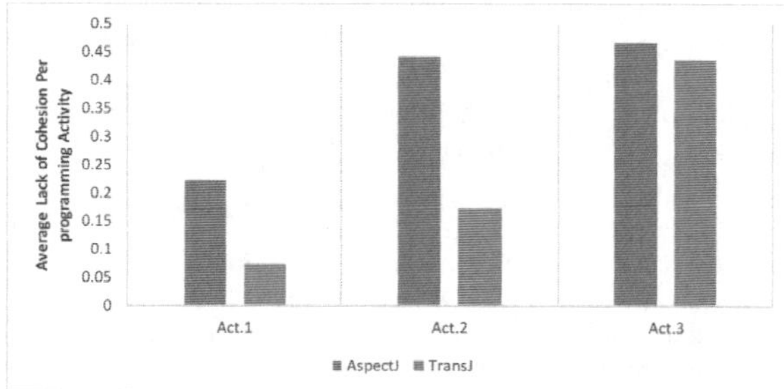

Figure 6. LCTO Coverage over Applications

In consonance with these results, we can confidently conclude that the second hypothesis holds true for reduced coupling in TransJ compared with AspectJ.

C. *S'has higher cohesion and less tangling than S*

In Fig. 6, the result reveals that TransJ maintains a lower value for LCTO than AspectJ in all the three activities of the experiment. Thus, TransJ promoted encapsulation with implementing a more independent component that implements a single logical function (more cohesive) than implemented with AspectJ. Compared to the AspectJ group, the TransJ group improved cohesion in all activities, sometimes significantly (from 8% to 75%). The decrease in the cohesion of the AspectJ activities is caused by the need to extract new methods to expose advisable joinpoints i.e., multiple transaction joinpoints cannot be advised as an atomic unit (e.g., begin – commit, begin – abort, or lock – release). From these results, we conclude that the third hypothesis holds true for increased cohesion in TransJ than in AspectJ.

D. *S' not significantly larger or complex S*

Figures 7 (a) through 7 (e) show that TransJ implementations decreased the metric values for LOC, MLOC, TLOC, NOT, WOTC, CC and RFM and increased VS value in all the three activities of the experiment. In comparison with TransJ, AspectJ programmers found the aspects and application code tends to contain very terse pointcuts, advices and extra code, especially, when combined with transaction constructs, such as transaction demarcations, to pull all relevant context information. In TransJ, two induced factors affect these metrics: the UMJDT model captures various general distributed transaction abstractions in meaningful, reusable joinpoints and a set of base aspects, which help developers implement the TCC's in simpler and logical method bodies, i.e., advice, with no extra lines of codes and less number of operations and advices, thus this reduced the RFM value. Second, TransJ's joinpoints referenced by broad contexts and stable pointcut definitions, therefore, applications did not need additional context information, such as an identifier or lock snapshot. This allowed the reusable and application-level aspects to inherit or reuse pointcuts to apply the logic of TCC' in appropriate transaction places. Hence, TransJ reduced the values of MLOC, TLOC, NTO, WOTC, and RFM. Fig. 7 (d) shows that the value of CC is smaller for TransJ than AspectJ, because TransJ hides complex transaction abstractions, as mentioned, which result in simple conditional statements and less tangled code. As predicted by the above hypothesis, results shown in Fig. 7 (e) give sufficient evidence that the average VS value of all programs was more for TransJ than AspectJ, due to inlined code in transaction scopes being extracted and gathered to inner classes, i.e., contexts and base aspects (caused improvements of 12% to 23%). Although the number of components were more in TransJ implementations, but they were more cohesive. From these results, we can confidently conclude that

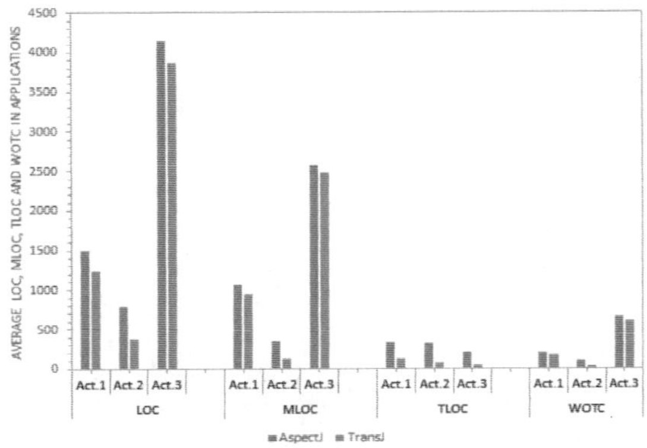

Figure 7 (a) Average LOC, MLOC, TLOC and WOTC over Applications

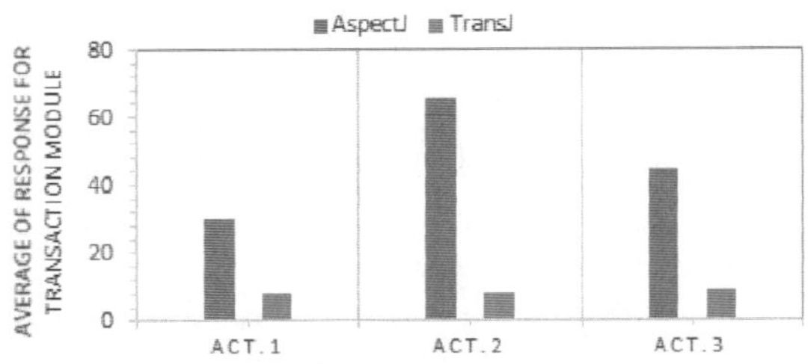

Figure 7 (b) Average RFM over Applications

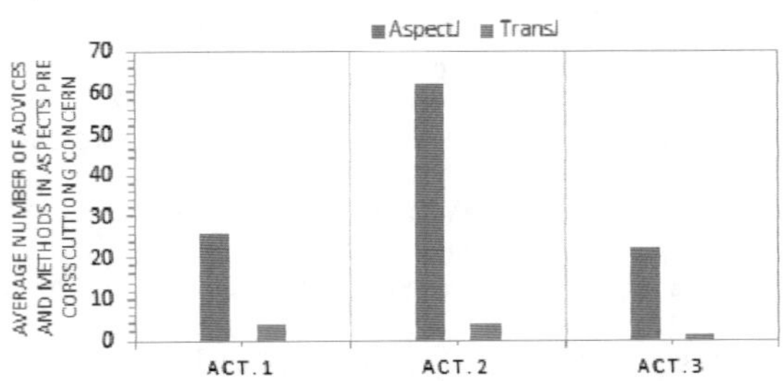

Figure 7 (c) Average NTO over Applications

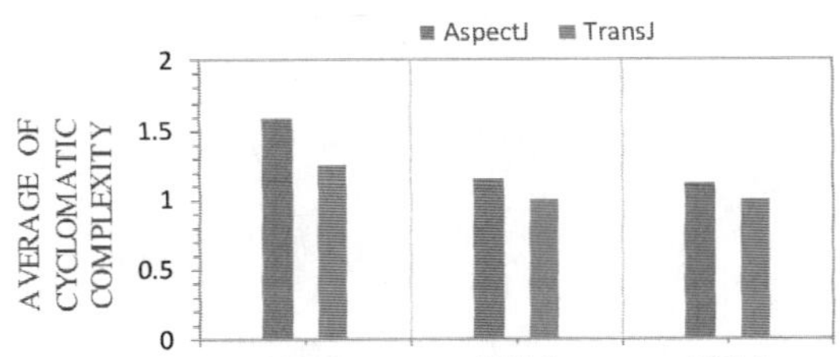

Figure 7 (d) Average CC over Applications

the fourth hypothesis hold true for less complex and a small code size software in TransJ compared with AspectJ.

E. *S′ is significantly more oblivious to TCC's than S*

Fig. 8 shows that TransJ implementations significantly reduced the values of NITD, CDA, ASTC and ASTO metrics. Compared to the AspectJ, NITD and CDA for all TransJ activities differed by 100%. The reason for having this result, i.e., zero value, TransJ programmers directly used transaction abstractions and did not need to use Inter-Type Declarations (ITDs) for sharing of context information between application and aspect components. Significant reduction in ASTC and ASTO was due to the layers of indirections among the transaction application and aspect components, which TransJ provides but are missing in AspectJ. In a nutshell, the improvement of the TransJ activities verse the AspectJ activities was caused by (a) the higher level of reuse of base aspects, and (b) scoped joinpoints, i.e., contexts, eliminating the need to create operations to expose new joinpoints. From these results, we can confidently conclude that the fifth hypothesis hold true for less oblivious software CC's in TransJ compared with AspectJ.

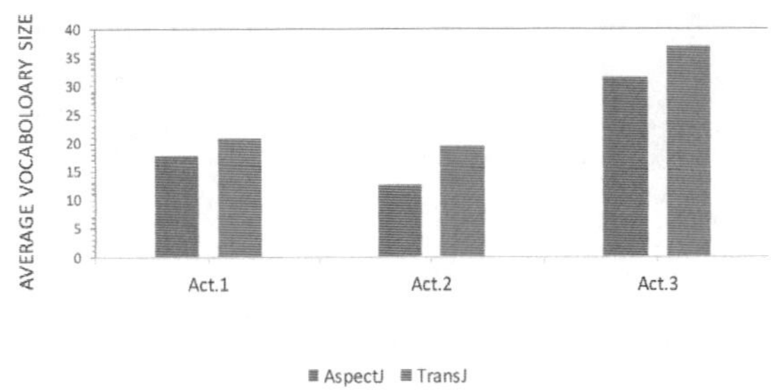

Figure 7 (e) Average VS over Applications

F. *The runtime of S′ is no worse than S*

Figures 9 (a) through 9 (c) show that TransJ implementation slightly decreased the metric values for MRT, NUCT, ToT, and slightly increased NCT with maintaining the RTPM in all three activities of the experiment. TransJ allows dynamic weaving of aspects at run-time by looking up to the contexts instead of needing to programing by hand as done in AspectJ. Figures 9 (a) and 9 (b) indicate that the TransJ group performed very slightly better than the AspectJ group for Act.1 and Act.2 with almost 0% improvement for Act.3. This lack of improvement for Act.3 was caused by the overhead of creating a transaction and transaction operation thread instances, synchronization and the high concurrent potential for conflicts over the shared resource. In other words, there are no major differences between the efficiency of TransJ activities and AspectJ activities.

Fig. 9 (c) shows that the results for the NUCT and ToT metrics remained the same for the Act.1 and Act.2. However, in Act.3 TransJ decreased very slightly the potential of having better ToT and NUCT values. The decrease in NUCT and ToT values in TransJ at Act.3 was caused by exposing advisable joinpoints, i.e., lockingJP and resourceLockedJP and dynamic weaving of aspects on them.

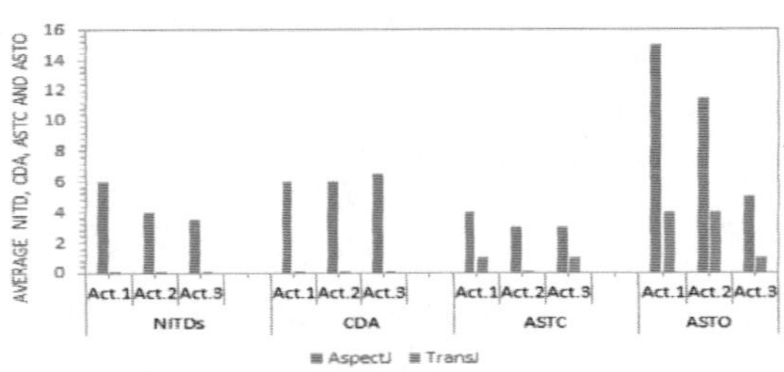

Figure 8. Average NITD, CDA, ASTC and ASTO over Applications

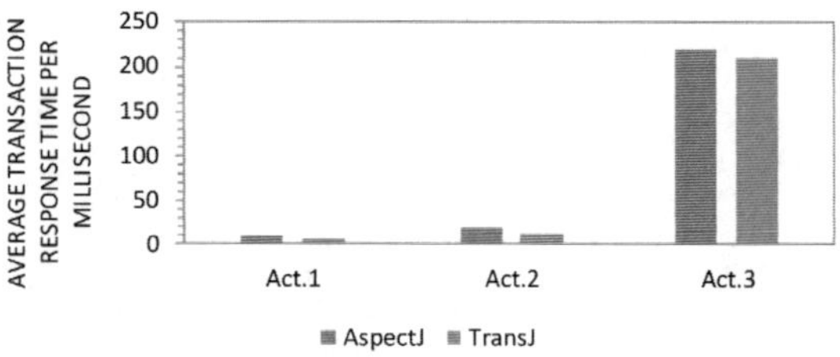

Figure 9 (a) Average MRT over Applications

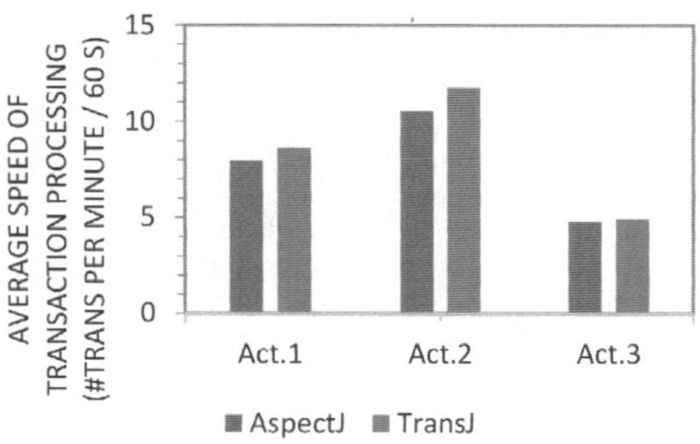

Figure 9 (b) Average Transaction Velocity (RTPM) over Applications

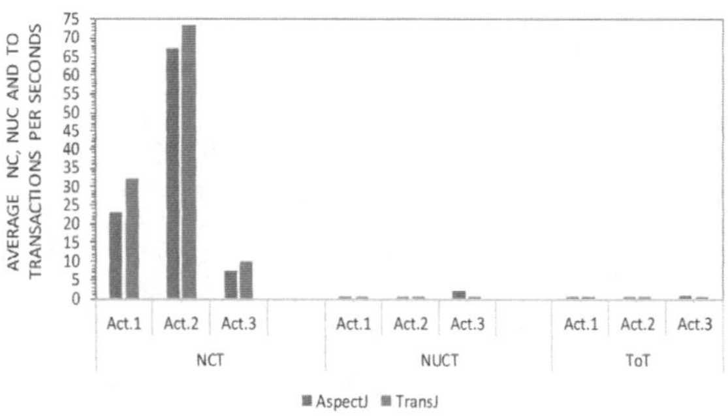

Figure 9 (c) Average NCT, NUCT and ToT over Applications

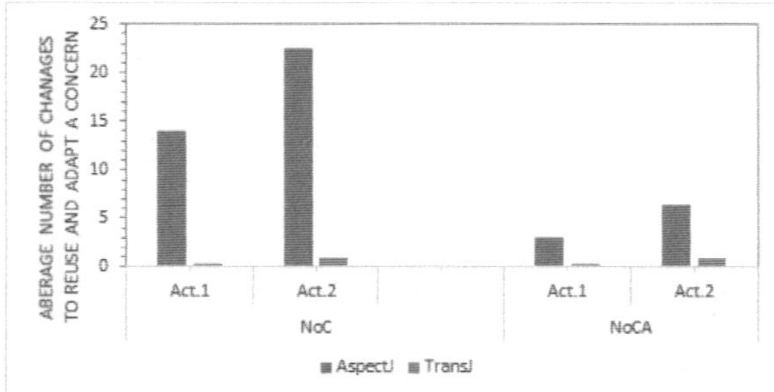

Figure 10 (a) Average Number of Changes of Performance Measurement Concern over Conference Registration System and Bank System Applications

These joinpoints represented an indication of the benefits that can come when concurrent operations access the shared resource. However, there are no major differences between the throughput of TransJ activities and AspectJ activities. In a nutshell, the results of figures do not give sufficient evidence to claim that the benefits of improving software performance. But from these results, we can confidently conclude that the sixth hypothesis holds true: preserving runtime performance in TransJ compared to AspectJ.

G. *The implementation TCC's in S' requires a smaller number of changes to reuse compared to S*

From the results shown in Fig. 10 (a), we can see that TransJ implementation significantly reduced the changes required to reuse the performance measurement concern implementations in Act.1 and Act.2. This means that the application is more amenable to extension.

Compared with AspectJ, the presence of joinpoints in the base aspect of TransJ allows the implementation of the CC' logic in reusable and application-level aspects, which allow contexts and CC's to be explicitly communicated. Fig. 10 (a) presents the percentage of CC's that were implemented by abstract aspects (in base aspect). The data confirm that significant increases in reusability can be gained by applying TransJ's joinpoints where appropriate.

Fig. 10 (b) provides another graphical representation of the analysis of reuse for AspectJ and TransJ. The orange-colored graphs represent scattering in TransJ (aspects only) and the blue-colored graphs represent scattering in AspectJ implementations. The scat-

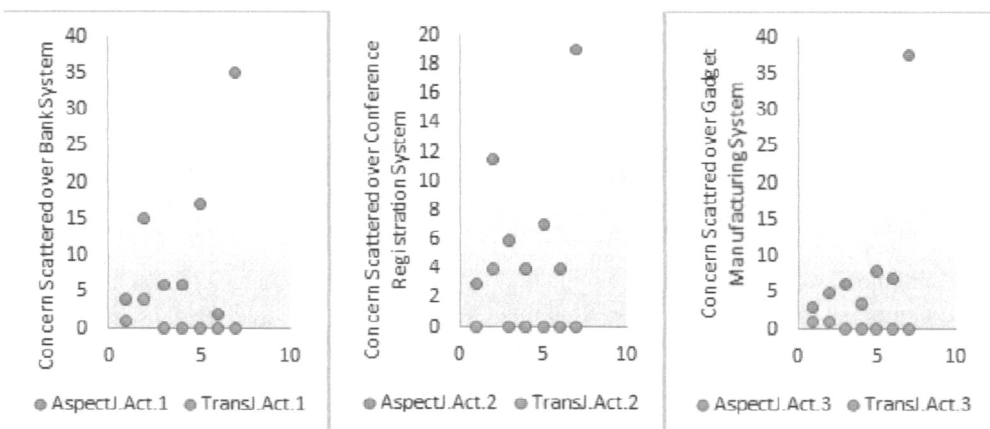

Figure 10 (b) ASTC, ASTO, CDA, NITD, CDTA, CDTO and CDLOC over Applications of AspectJ and TransJ

Figure 11. Average AT, PT and NoBs over Applications

tered points in the graph indicate that the number of changes required for reusing a concern with TransJ and AspectJ in different activities, respectively. The scattered points represent ASTC, ASTO, CDA, NITD, CDTA, CDTO, and CDLOC metrics results. Overall, activities of TransJ (highly reusable and more extensible), but were highly scattered for AspectJ. The reason for less scattering is discussed above. From these results, we can conclude that the seventh hypothesis holds true: more reusability and extensibility in TransJ compared to AspectJ.

H. *The total programming hours for $\mathcal{S}'$ is less than $\mathcal{S}$, indicating that $\mathcal{S}'$ is less complex and more readable than $\mathcal{S}$*

From the results shown in Fig. 11, we can see that TransJ significantly reduced the period that required to read, understand, implement, and debug the implementations of TCC's in all activities of the experiment compared to AspectJ. These results confirm that the applications were more flexible to implement with TransJ and were robust with respect to bugs and error compared to the AspectJ implementation. In addition, this figure indicates that TransJ participants performed significantly better than the AspectJ participants for all activities.

PT represents the amount of time they spent on reading the source code, understanding secondary requirements and looking for bugs. The increases in the PT in the AspectJ activities are caused by the need to study the whole code to find new pointcuts to expose advisable joinpoints and to gather the relevant information to a specific context that is required to weave the CC's of appropriate joinpoints. In contrast, TransJ provides pointcuts that help developers code the CC's obliviously. In addition, they do not need to create shared data structures, i.e., contexts, to have an explicit cooperation between base application code and aspects. This one simple benefit in the mindset of programmers can drastically reduce the number and seriousness of bugs, i.e., NoBs. From these results, we can confidently conclude that the eighth hypothesis hold true: less software development time is required for TransJ than for AspectJ.

VII. Summary

In ICSEA 2014, we presented the new conceptual model, i.e., UMJDT, to define interesting joinpoints relative to transaction execution and context data for woven advice. TransJ is a new abstract framework, which allows developers to encapsulate TCC's in reusable and cohesive modules [6]. This paper presents a preliminary research experiment on hoped-for benefits of TransJ in comparison with AspectJ. It defines an extended-quality model for transactional application, then setup an experiment methodology, involving 8 hypotheses and data collection from 12 applications. Initial findings provide sufficient evidence to conclude that TransJ is capable of encapsulating a wide range of TCC's and that it can provide more modular, reusable distributed transaction software without sacrificing the performance. We hope to gather more empirical evidences of the TransJ's value by increasing the number of aspects in the reusable aspect library and by continuing to expand the number and types of applications that use TransJ. Our future research will include more formal software-engineering productivity experiments to verify the performance belief. TransJ can be extended for distributed remote pointcuts that would simplify the implementation of even more complex crosscutting concerns, such as recovery, or multithreaded in a distributed system.

References

[1] C. Sant'Anna, A. F. Garcia, C. F. G. Chavez, C. J. de Lucena, and A. Staa, "On the Reuse and Maintenance of Aspect-Oriented Software: An Assessment Framework," In Proc. 17th Brazilian Symp. Software Engineering, Manaus, Brazil, pp. 19-34, 2003, doi: PUCRioInf, MCC26/03.

[2] G. Kiczales, J. Lamping, A. Mendhekar, C. Maeda, C. V. Lopes, J.M. Loingter, and J. Irwin, "Aspect-Oriented Programming." Proceedings of ECOOP '97, Springer Verlag, pages 220--242, 1997.

[3] G. Kiczales and M. Mezini, "Aspect-Oriented Programming and Modular Reasoning," in ICSE 2005, pp. 49-58, 2005.

[4] Office of Research and Graduate Studies at Utah State University, Institutional Review Board [Online]. [retrieved: June, 2015], Available: http://rgs.usu.edu/irb/.

[5] A. AlSobeh and S. Clyde, "Unified Conceptual Model for Joinpoints in Distributed Transactions." ICSE'14. The Ninth International Conference on Software Engineering Advances. Nice, France. October, pp. 8-15, 2014, ISBN: 978-1-61208-367-4.

[6] A. AlSobeh, "Improving Reuse of Distributed Transaction Softwares with Transaction-aware Aspects," in Ph.D. Dissertation, Computer Science Department, Utah State University 2015. Paper 4590. http://digitalcommons.usu.edu/etd/4590

[7] C. Nunes, U. Kulesza, C. Sant'Anna, I. Nunes, and C. Lucena, "On the Modularity Assessment of Aspect-Oriented Multiagent Architectures: a Quantitative Study." International Journal of Agent-Oriented Software Engineering, v. 2, pp. 34- 61, 2008.

[8] A. Raza and S. Clyde, "Communication Aspects with CommJ: Initial Experiment Show Promising Improvements in Reusability and Maintainability," ICSEA'14, pp. 48-55, 2014, Nice, France, Oct. 2014.

[9] A. Raza and S. Clyde, "Weaving Crosscutting Concerns into Inter-process Communications (IPC) in AspectJ," ICSEA 2013. Venice, Italy, pp. 234-240, 2013, ISBN: 978-1-61208-304-9.

[10] R. Burrows, A. Garcia and F. Taiani, "Coupling Metrics for Aspect-Oriented Programming: A Systematic Review of Maintainability Studies," In Evaluation of Novel Approaches to Software Engineering, volume 69 of Communications in Computer and Information Science, pp. 277-290, 2010.

[11] L. Parnas, "On the Criteria to be used in Decomposing Systems into Modules," Commun. ACM, vol. 15, no.12, pp. 1053-1058, Dec. 1972.

[12] Y. Coady et al., "Can AOP Support Extensibility in Client-Server Architecture?" In European Conference on Object-Oriented Programming (ECOOP), Aspect-Oriented Programming Workshop, June 2001.

[13] C. Sant'Anna, E. Figueiredo, A. Garcia, and C. J. P. Lucena, "On the Modularity of Software Architectures: A Concern-Driven Measurement Framework." In Proc. ECSA, pp. 24-26, 2007, Madrid, Spain.

[14] J. Zhao, "Measuring Coupling in Aspect-Oriented Systems", Int.Soft. Metrics Symp. 2004.

[15] S.R. Chidamber and C. F. Kemerer, "A Metrics Suite for Object-Oriented Design," IEEE Trans. Softw. Eng., vol. SE-20, no. 6, pp. 476–493, June 1994

[16] T.J. McCabe, "A Complexity Measure," IEEE Trans. Softw. Eng., vol. 2, no. 4, pp. 308-320, Dec. 1976.

[17] G. Jay, J. E. Hale, R. K. Smith, D. Hale, N. A. Kraft, and C. Ward, "Cyclomatic Complexity and Lines of Code: Empirical Evidence of a

Stable Linear Relationship," Journal of Software Engineering and Applications, vol. 3, no. 2, pp. 137-143, 2009.

[18] Collaborative Institutional Training (CIIT), 2014, Social & Behavioral Research Modules [Online], [retrieved: June, 2015], Available: https://www.citiprogram.org.

[19] Narayana, Narayana Transaction Anaylser (NTA) Tool [Online], [retrieved: Septemeper, 2015], Available: http://narayana.jboss.org/

[20] SourceForge, Eclipse Metrics Project 1.3.6 [Online]. [retrieved: Jul, 2015] Available: http://metrics.sourceforge.net.

Modeling and Formal Specification Of Multi-scale Software Architectures

Ilhem Khlif[1,2,3], Mohamed Hadj Kacem[1], Khalil Drira[2,3] and Ahmed Hadj Kacem[1]
[1] University of Sfax, ReDCAD Research Laboratory, Sfax, Tunisia
[2] CNRS, LAAS, 7 avenue du colonel Roche, F-31400 Toulouse, France
[3] Univ de Toulouse, LAAS, F-31400 Toulouse, France
ikhlif@laas.fr, mohamed.hadjkacem@isimsf.rnu.tn, khalil.drira@laas.fr, ahmed.hadjkacem@fsegs.rnu.tn

Abstract—**Modeling correct complex systems architecture is a challenging research direction that can be mastered by providing modeling abstractions. For this purpose, we provide an iterative modeling solution for a multi-scale description of software architectures. We define a step-wise iterative process starting from a coarse-grained description, and leading to a fine-grained description. The refinement process involves both system-independent structural features ensuring the model correctness, and specific features related to the expected behavior of the modeled domain. We provide a visual notation extending the graphical UML (Uniform Modeling Language) notations to represent structural as well as behavioral features of software architectures. The proposed approach mainly consists of two steps. In the first step, the architecture is modeled graphically according to the UML notations. In the second step, the obtained graphical models are formally specified using the Event-B method. We implement the resulting models describing structural and behavioral properties using the Rodin platform and prove their correctness. We apply our approach for a methodological design of a smart home scenario for the homecare monitoring of disabled and elderly persons.**

Keywords–Software; Architecture; multi-scale; iterative; modeling; UML; formal; specification; structural; behavioral; refinement; Event-B.

I. Introduction

Software architecture design has become the key factor for the success of the development of large and complex software systems, for mastering the costs and the quality of their development. The design of a software architecture is a complex task. On the one hand, we have to describe the system with enough details for understanding without ambiguity and implementing in conformance with architects requirements and users expectations. On the other hand, we have to master the complexity induced by the increasing model details both at the human and automated processing levels. Some high level properties can be expressed on informal descriptions with a high level of abstractions and checked on simple formal descriptions. Some other properties need more detailed descriptions to be expressed and deep specifications to be elaborated. Description details may be application-independent and mainly structural such as component decomposition, or system-specific and mainly behavioral, such as message ordering in interaction protocols. An iterative modeling process that helps architects to elaborate complex but yet tractable and appropriate architectural models and specifications can be implemented by successive refinements. Different properties of correctness and traceability have to be maintained between the models and the specifications at the different levels of iterations. Providing Rules for formalizing and conducting such a process is our objective, which we implemented in visual modeling notations and formally specified in a formal description technique. For this purpose, we propose to consider different architecture descriptions with different levels of modeling details called **"the scales"**. We define a step-wise iterative process starting from a coarse-grained description and leading to a fine-grained description. The proposed approach mainly consists of two steps. In the first step, multi-scale architectures are modeled graphically using UML notations. In the second step, the obtained models are formalized with the Event-B method, and validated by its supporting Rodin platform [11]. In order to illustrate our solution, we experiment our approach with a case study dedicated to the smart home system for the homecare monitoring of elderly and disabled persons. The remainder of the paper is organized as follows. We describe the UML modeling approach in Section II. In Section III, we present the generated Event-b specifications. Section IV presents the case study. In Section V, we present a survey of related work. We conclude and outline some perspectives in Section VI.

II. Iterative Modeling

At the level of abstraction, a software architecture is represented as a collection of interconnected components, and it is at this level that the structural and behavioral properties of software systems are addressed. We define multi-scale modeling as an incremental process where we constantly refine software systems descriptions. We propose to illustrate UML notations for describing software architectures at different description levels. In the first iteration, an abstract model is defined. At each iteration, design modifications are made and new details are added. We consider both structural and behavioral descriptions. In model-driven engineering, traceability links are established from the application requirements. The traceability links specify which parts of the design contribute to the satisfaction of each requirement [9].

A. Structural modeling

We propose structural modeling for describing software architectures using a visual notation based on UML. To describe the structure of a multi-scale architecture, we model the first scale by a given coarse-grained description using a UML component diagram. This model is refined until reaching a fine-grained description representing the necessary modeling details. We define a vertical description scale "$S_{v+1.h}$" as a model that provides additional details of the design, that pertain to "$S_{v.h}$" and more abstraction related to "$S_{v+2.h}$". A vertical scale can be further refined into several horizontal description scales ("$S_{v.h}$", "$S_{v.h+1}$",...) thus providing more details. We consider that v, resp. h, represents the vertical and

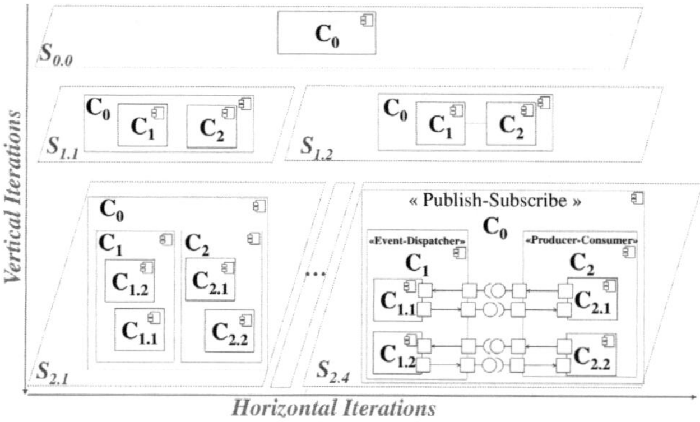

Figure 1. Structural modeling

horizontal iterations (v,h $\geq$ 0). We, first, elaborate an initial abstract architecture description from the user requirements. At the first scale $S_{0.0}$, application requirements are specified (a unique component C_0 is identified). This is the beginning of the traceability. A first vertical iteration from $S_{0.0}$ to $S_{1.1}$ is required in order to provide details on the application, and refine it with several components. In Figure 1, two components named C_1 and C_2 are added. At the same scale, an horizontal iteration is needed to specify the interactions between components. We represent a link between C_1 and C_2 in the scale $S_{1.2}$. A second vertical iteration is helpful for refining components with new sub-components, and checking that at the scale $S_{2.1}$, the components identification is preserved, as we keep traceability of a component from one scale to another. This notation is used for identifying a component: C_m where m represents a cursor on the current component (m $\geq$ 0). It can be decomposed in the next scale. The component C_1, is refined with two sub-components identified as $C_{1.1}$, $C_{1.2}$, etc. The component C_2 is refined with two sub-components ($C_{2.1}$ and $C_{2.2}$). Several horizontal iterations are needed in the second vertical scale to show more specific details (related to the UML description). An horizontal iteration called $S_{2.2}$ adds details on data relating to the components: roles are associated with components such as *"Event-Dispatcher", "Producer", "Consumer", "Producer-Consumer", "Client", "Service", etc.* The scale $S_{2.2}$ is inserting communication ports and more details; the scale $S_{2.3}$ allows the addition of component interfaces. Finally, we obtain the model $S_{2.4}$ where connections are established between components to define the architectural style of the application. In the illustrated example, we are limited on three vertical iterations to show the necessary details. However, the iterative process continues while there are still components to refine. The number of iterations depends on the application requirements. Each new iteration does not only include new sub-components but also adds necessary design details on the information flow between components. In the scale $S_{2.4}$, we propose to refine the interaction (link) between the two components C_1 and C_2 illustrated at the scale $S_{1.2}$ with respect to the following traceability constraints: if the component C_1 performs the role of an "Event-Dispatcher" and the component C_2 is a "Producer-Consumer", the link between C_1 and C_2 in $S_{2.1}$ will be decomposed into a double assembly connection in the scale $S_{2.4}$ connecting ($C_{1.1}$ and $C_{2.1}$). We preserve the model traceability from one scale to another by decomposing links, at the abstract scale, and refining them, at the next scale, to show possible connections established between components. Traceability is a desired characteristic for software management. However, it is not always possible to trace every design (or architectural) component back to requirements. To ensure this property, we check during the iterative process that the interface compatibility is preserved in the multi-scale architecture: First, we verify through added details on component roles that each required interface is associated with a producer component and each provided interface is associated with a consumer component. The main issue is to ensure the well-typed and the well-connected in UML component diagram. For this purpose, we have implemented a tool supporting our approach in visual modeling notation as an Eclipse plug-in to providethe designerwith an editor for UML modeling architecture. Using this editor, we make sure that refined models are correct by design. Second, we check the interface compatibility through constraints on different scales using the OCL (Object Constraint Language) interactive console associated with the Eclipse.

B. Behavioral modeling

To specify behavioral features, we use UML sequence diagram that provides a graphical notation to describe dynamic aspects of software architectures [7]. The application is initialized (at the first scale), and after successive iterations, the sets of components and interactions among them are identified in a way that supports the required behavior of the abstract application level. We describe the specified behavior of an application using the UML sequence diagram in Figure 2. The sequence diagram is helpful for describing the message ordering in interaction protocols during the iterative modeling. In the first scale, the whole application is presented as a black box to illustrate the System Sequence Diagram (SSD) named "C_0". The main issue here is to secure the message transmission and how elements cooperate to ensure correct information propagation. Several events may refine an abstract event: The single message (M_1) between actors in the scale (S_1) is refined with a set of messages ($M_{1.1}$, $M_{1.2}$, $M_{2.1}$, and

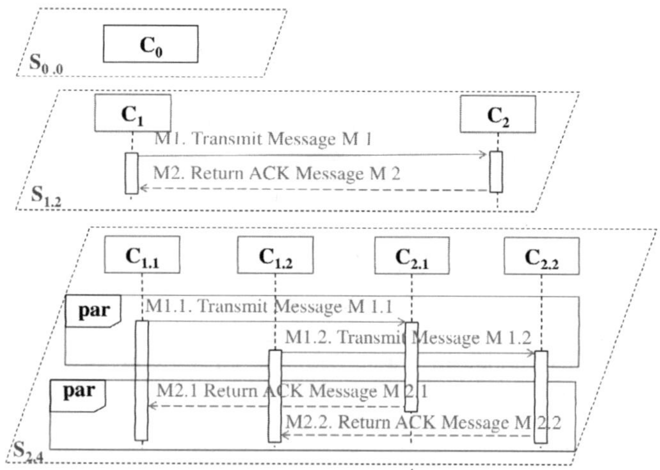

Figure 2. Behavioral modeling

$M_{2.2}$) in the scale (S_2), or the content of translated messages depends on earlier received message. The sequence diagram, represented in Figure 2, specifies the behavioral features of the publish-subscribe architecture. When the Producer-Consumer component C_1 sends a message (M_1) to the Event dispatcher component C_2 at the scale S_1, the Event-dispatcher tracks this message and, it replies to the Event-dispatcher by sending an acknowledgement message (M_2). At the next scale S_2, the two messages will be refined into a parallel sequence of messages while keeping track of the type of message sent or received in the abstract scale.

Our approach is based on a multi-scale modeling that helps to automate the construction of correct design architectures. So, we need to specify the software architecture model that describes the software components and their composition. In fact, each model is represented as a set of scales, and each scale denotes a set of architectures. Following our approach, the designer starts by modeling the first scale architecture which is refined to give one or many architectures for the next scale. Then, these architectures are refined in turn to give the following scale architectures and so on until reaching the last scale. The transition between scales is ensured by applying specific rules defined using the Event-B specifications. After constructing the architectures of software architecture model, we apply the relation between the two models in order to obtain model-based architectures with different description levels.

III. EVENT-B FORMAL SPECIFICATION

The aim of formal modeling is to achieve a precise specification of the intended structures and behaviors in the design [1]. The advantage of such specifications is to determine whether a modeled structure can successfully satisfy a set of given properties derived from the user requirements. We consider here specifying a multi-scale architecture using the refinement-based formal method: the Event-B [11]. We use the Event-B method and its event based definition to formalize UML models. Our approach facilitates layering and mapping the informal requirements to traceable formal models. An Event-B model is made of two types of components: contexts and machines [2]. The obtained UML models are mapped to Event-B specifications: the component diagram constitutes the static part of the architecture, it is specified with the Event-B method in the Context part. The sequence diagram constitutes the dynamic part of the architecture, it is specified with the Event-B method in the Machine part. A context describes the static part of a model, and a machine describes the dynamic behavior of a model. Each context has a name and other clauses like "Extends", "Constants", "Sets" to declare a new data type and "Axioms" that denotes the type of the constants and the various predicates which the constants obey. Machines and contexts can be inter-related: a machine can be refined by another, can see one or several contexts, while a context can be extended by another [8]. A multi-scale software architecture is described with structural features and behavioral features. Structural features are specified with one or several contexts and behavioral features are specified with one or several machines.

A. Structural specifications

In the component diagram we specify components that constitute the architecture, their types and their connections. This diagram constitutes the static part of the defined architecture. It is specified in the Context part. In the first scale S_0, the graphical model is transformed into an Event-B specification called Context0. In the Context0, we specify the whole application with a Component as constants. The component, that composes the architecture at scale $S_{0.0}$, is named C_0. This is specified by using a partition in the AXIOMS clause (C0_partition).

CONTEXT
  $Context0$
SETS
  $Component$
CONSTANTS
  $C0$
AXIOMS
  C0_partition : $partition(Component, \{C0\})$
END

In the next scales, we use the refinement techniques to gradually add details until obtaining the final scale specification. A new context named Context1 extends the Context0 and specifies new components in the application. We define two components C_1 and C_2 as constants and the established link between them. Formally, links are specified with an Event-B relation between two components (Link_partition).

CONTEXT
  $Context1$
EXTENDS
  $Context0$
CONSTANTS
  $C1, C2, Link$
AXIOMS
  C1_partition : $partition(Component, C0, \{C1\}, \{C2\})$
  Link_partition : $Link \in C1 \leftrightarrow C2$
END

A Context2 is extending the previous Context1, and is adding sub-components of each component. We specify the role of each component (producers, consumers and event-dispatcher) as constants. Connectors are specified with an Event-B relation between two components. The set of Connectors is specified formally with two partitions (Ct1_part, Ct2_part).

CONTEXT
  $Context2$
EXTENDS
  $Context1$
SETS
  $Role$
CONSTANTS
  $C1.1, C1.2, C2.1, C2.2, Prod,$
  $Cons, EventDis, Prod1, Prodn,$
  $Cons1, Consn, ED1, EDn, Connector1, Connector2$
AXIOMS
  C2_partition :
  $partition(Component, \{C1.1\}, \{C1.2\}, \{C2.1\}, \{C2.2\})$
  Ct1_part : $Connector1 \in C1.1 \leftrightarrow C2.1$
  Ct2_part : $Connector2 \in C1.2 \leftrightarrow C2.2$
  Role_part :
  $partition(Role, \{Prod\}, \{Cons\}, \{EventDis\})$
  $Cons = \{C1, .., Cn\} \wedge C1 \neq C2 \wedge .. \wedge \neq Cn$
  $EventDis = \{ED1, .., EDn\} \wedge ED1 \neq ED2 \wedge .. \wedge \neq EDn$
  $Prod = \{P1, .., Pn\} \wedge P1 \neq P2 \wedge .. \wedge \neq Pn$
END

B. Behavioral specifications

The Event B machine is used formally, to find structural errors and to verify the semantic of the UML model. To specify behavioral features, we specify the abstract description scale with a machine at a high level of abstraction. Then, we add all necessary details to the first machine by using the refinement process. In the first machine, we only specify the modeled application by extending Context0.

MACHINE
  $Machine0$
SEES
  $Context0$
VARIABLES
  $C0$
INVARIANTS
  inv : $C0 \in BOOL$
EVENTS
  INITIALISATION
    BeginAct
    $act : C0 := TRUE$
    EndAct
END

Machine1 is a refinement of the Machine0, using the context Context1 and adding communication between the components C_1 and C_2. The behavior is described as follows: the component C_1 sends a Message to the component C_2. When the component C_2 becomes available, it receives the Message, processes it and sends the Acknowledgement Message. When the component C_1 becomes available, it receives the ACK-Message. The invariants (Send_Message, Receive_Ack) specifies what is the sent message, who is the sender and the receiver. The Machine1 has a state defined by means of a number of variables and invariants. Some of variables can be general as the variable Send, which denotes the sent message and the variable Receive, which denotes the received message. The variable Send is defined with the invariant (Send_Msg) which specify that Send is a relation between two components so that the sender, the receiver and the message are known.

MACHINE
  $Machine1$
REFINES
  $Machine0$
SEES
  $Context1$
VARIABLES
  $Send, Receive$
INVARIANTS
  Send_Message : $Send \in BOOL$
  Receive_ACK : $Receive \in BOOL$
EVENTS
  INITIALISATION
    BeginAct
    $act1 : Send := FALSE$
    $act2 : Receive := FALSE$
    EndAct
    EVT
    $init1 : Send \in C1 \rightarrow C2$
    $init2 : Receive \in C1 \rightarrow C2$
    $init3 : Transmit := C1 \rightarrow True, C2 \rightarrow False$
END

We follow the same method to specify a second machine named Machine2 which refines Machine1, using the context Context2 and adding communication between the sub-components $C_{1.1}$, $C_{1.2}$, $C_{2.1}$ and $C_{2.2}$. The invariants (SendMsg1.1 , SendMsg1.2 , ReceiveAck2.1 , ReceiveAck2.2) are specified in the INVARIANTS clause to check that each sub-component can't send a message or receive an acknowledgment only if it is authorised.

MACHINE
  $Machine2$
REFINES
  $Machine1$
SEES
  $Context2$
VARIABLES
  $SendMsg1.1, SendMsg1.2, ReceiveAck2.1, ReceiveAck2.2$
INVARIANTS
  Send_Message : $SendMsg1.1, SendMsg1.2 \in BOOL$
  Receive_ACK : $ReceiveAck2.1, ReceiveAck2.2 \in BOOL$
EVENTS
  INITIALISATION
    BeginAct
    $a1 : SendMsg1.1 := FALSE$
    $a2 : SendMsg1.2 := FALSE$
    $a3 : ReceiveAck2.1 := FALSE$
    $a4 : ReceiveAck2.2 := FALSE$
    EndAct
    EVT
    $init1 : SendMsg1.1 \in C1.1 \rightarrow C2.1$
    $init2 : SendMsg1.2 \in C1.2 \rightarrow C2.2$
    $init3 : ReceiveACK2.1 \in C1.1 \rightarrow C2.1$
    $init4 : ReceiveACK2.2 \in C1.2 \rightarrow C2.2$
    $init5 : transmit1 := C1.1 \rightarrow True, C2.1 \rightarrow False$
    $init6 : transmit2 := C1.2 \rightarrow True, C2.2 \rightarrow False$
END

The Event-B machine is used formally, to find structural errors and to verify the semantic of the UML model. Besides, behavioral properties are checked like liveness and reachability. The reachability means that the components are able to capture all exchanged messages. We formulate those properties as predicates (INVARIANTS, AXIOMS). We check that each component only sends a message if it is authorised. This is controlled by the invariants (Send-Msg, Receive-ACK). Reaching the last scale description by using refinement techniques, we guarantee that refined models are not contradictory and we ensure that they are correct by design. The multi-scale modeling helps to automate the construction of correct design architectures. The aim is to derive those UML models by applying correctness preserving transformations, i.e. refinements, that conform to the constraints defined by the application and by the adopted architecture styles. The refinement techniques proposed by this method allow to represent architectures at different abstraction levels and are implemented using the Rodin platform.

IV. Application to the Smart Home

This section focuses on modeling the smart home system for the homecare monitoring of elderly and disabled persons. The main issue is to ensure efficient management of the optimized comfort, and the safety of the elderly and disabled person at home [5]. We illustrate, in Figure 3, the constituent elements of the smart home application. The monitoring center is composed of three systems: the Environment Control and Comfort Management, the Emergency Surveillance Center, and the Medical Surveillance Center. The Home Care Actor interacts with the monitoring center, by setting medical or emergency conditions; the Equipment includes sensors and house devices; the emergency surveillance center controls critical situations using the activity sensors. Activity sensors include fall sensors, presence sensors, video camera and microphone. The medical surveillance center monitors physiological sensors. While there are problems, the center requires the medical assistant intervention (the doctor, the nurse). The comfort management and the environment control system guarantees a comfort life for the users. This center enables communications between users, control the environment sensors (Humidity

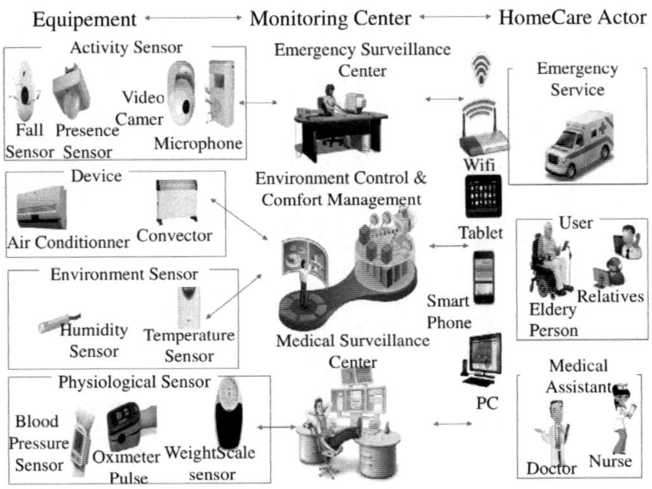

Figure 3. Smart Home application

and Temperature Sensors), and commands the house devices (Convectors, Air conditioners).

A. Smart Home Model

We experiment our approach by applying successive iterations to the smart home application. We obtained then the

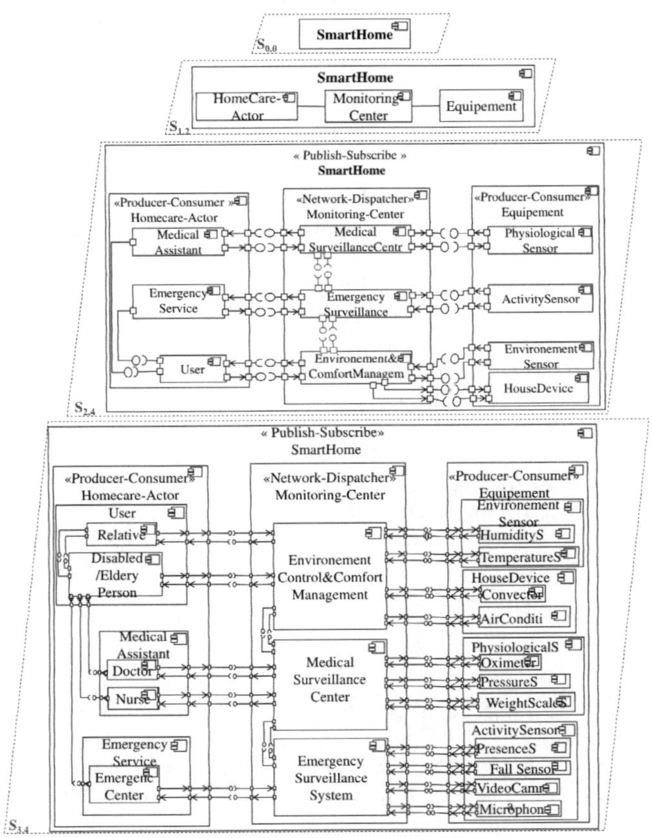

Figure 4. The Smart Home model

following results: In $S_{0.0}$, we define the application named "*SmartHome*". The constituent systems of the smart home are described (in $S_{1.1}$): *HomeCare-Actor*, *Equipment*, and *MonitoringCenter)*. Those systems communicate with each other via the monitoring center. Those relationships are represented (in $S_{1.2}$) as links. In Figure 4, We illustrate the iterative process applied to the smart home system. In the next scale, the three components are refined and specified with an associated role as shown in Figure 4. The *MonitoringCenter* plays the role of an "*EventDispatcher*". The *HomeCare-Actor* and *Equipment* play the role of "*Producer-Consumer*" in the application. We briefly describe the list of required/provided services of the *HomeCare-Actor* component. The *MedicalAssistant* receives information about the patient's situation from the *MedicalSurveillanceCenter*, he manages the patient's medical care (provides) and returns a report after the care. The *EmergencyService* receives information about a critical situation *EmergencySurveillanceCenter*, reacts to save the patient (provides), and returns a report after the intervention. The *User* receives not only emergency and medical services but also comfort services like online communication or house device command provided by the *EnvironementControl And ComfortManagement* component. During the iteration process, we apply the link decomposing rule with respect to the component role: if C_1 plays the role of an "Event-dispatcher" and C_2 acts as a "Producer-Consumer", the link in the scale $S_{1.2}$ between C_2 which is related to "HomeCareActor" or "Equipment" and C_1 in the scale $S_{1.2}$ will be decomposed into a double assembly connection in the scale $S_{2.4}$ between $C_{1.1}$ which is related to "MonitoringCenter" and $C_{2.1}$ which is related to 'HomeCareActor" or "Equipment". While there are still components to refine in the smart home, we move to the third scale to add more design details. We focused on mastering the system complexity description details through including the third scale. This scale has not only included new sub-components but also detailed the information flow between them. Each added sub-component (e.g. the doctor) is important for the design process. It influences the abstract level where smart home requirements are specified. We illustrate the last horizontal scale $S_{3.4}$ adding new sub-components (*Doctor, Emergency Service, Video Camera, etc*), and their connections.

B. Smart Home system-specific properties

In Figure 5, we present one of three fragments of the UML sequence diagram to demonstrate the behavior of constituent elements. The sequence diagram shows the instances participating in the interaction having two dimensions: the vertical dimension represents time; the horizontal dimension represents different objects which is related to the behavior of the smart home components. We illustrate the first scale $S_{0.0}$ using the SSD named "Smart Home" to show the whole system (as a black box). A vertical refinement called $S_{1.2}$ allows to describe the objects *HomeCare-Actor*, *Equipment*, and *MonitoringCenter)* and the exchanged messages in the diagram "Sd Monitoring". An object of class *Equipment* starts the behavior by sending an alert message to an object of class *MonitoringCenter)*. This object responds by an acknowledgment message to the equipment and sets the Sleep mode. The monitoring center sends the information to the object *HomeCare-Actor* that will respond immediately and send return message describing the situation after the care.

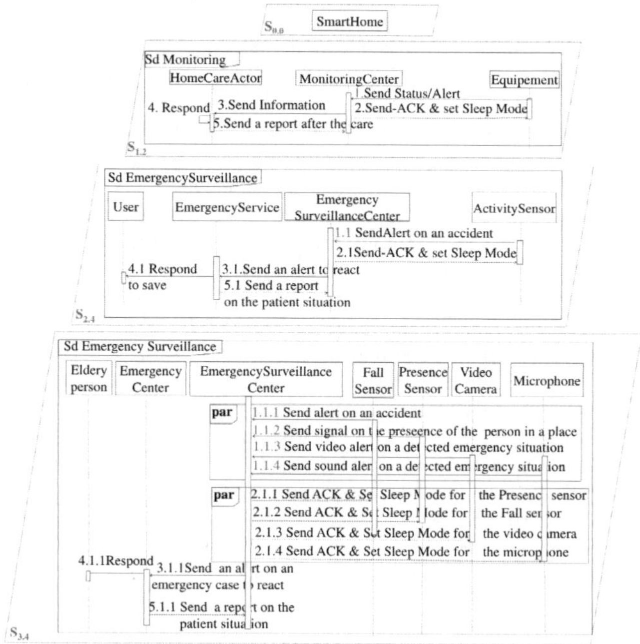

Figure 5. Fragment of the UML Sequence Diagram

C. Event-B specifications

We apply the Event-B refinement techniques to check the correctness of the multi-scale architecture applied to the Smart Home. We illustrate the Context2 that is extending the previous Context1, and is adding all sub-components in the smart home. They are specified with three partitions: equipment-partition, Monitoring-partition and Actor-partition. We specify in the Context2 the components type role (producer-consumers and event-dispatcher) as constants. There are many connections between components. The Connectors are specified with constants in the CONSTANTS clause. The set of Connectors is composed of all Connectors. This is specified formally with a partition (Connector-partition).

CONTEXT
$Context2$
EXTENDS
$Context1$
CONSTANTS
$ActSensor, Device, EnvSensor, PhysSensor, EmerSurvCenter, EnvControl, MedSurvCenter, User, MedAssistant, EmerService, Connector1, ..$
AXIOMS
Eq_partition :
$partition(Component, \{ActSensor\}, \{Device\}, \{EnvSensor\}, \{PhysSensor\})$
Eq_partition :
$partition(Component, \{EmerSurvCenter\ \{EnvControl\}, \{MedSurCenter\})$
$Connector = Connector1, .., Connector15\top$
END

To specify behavioral features, we have two steps. First, we specify the first machine at a high level of abstraction. Second, we add all necessary details by using the refinement technique. We illustrate an example of machines called Machine1 that is refining the Machine0, adding communication between the Smart Home components. The behavior is described as follows: the Monitoring-Center sends a Message to Equipment and then remains released from resources. When the component Equipment becomes available, it receives the Message, process it and sends the Acknowledgement Message. When Monitoring-Center becomes available, it receives the ACK-Message, process it and then becomes deactivated. The invariants (Send_Message, Receive_Ack) specifies what is the sent message, who is the sender and the receiver (The same description for the message from the Monitoring-Center to the HomeCare-Actor Component).

MACHINE
$Machine1$
REFINES
$Machine0$
SEES
$Context1$
VARIABLES
$Send, Receive$
INVARIANTS
Send_Message : $Send \in BOOL$
Receive_ACK : $Receive \in BOOL$
EVENTS
INITIALISATION
EVT
$i1 : Send \in MonitoringCenter \rightarrow Equipment$
$i2 : Receive \in MonitoringCenter \rightarrow Equipment$
$i3 : transmit := MonitoringCenter \rightarrow True, Equipment \rightarrow False$
$i4 : transmit := MonitoringCenter \rightarrow True, HomeCareActor \rightarrow False$
END

During the refinement process, we check the correct transmission of messages between actors and we prove the correctness property using the Event-B specifications. We demonstrate that there is no conflict problem between messages sent and received in parallel sequence which is not possible and correct with UML notations. Dispatchers cooperate together to route information from the producer-consumers to the subscribed event-dispatcher (Monitoring-Center). This interaction is governed by a principle of information dissemination requiring that produced information have to reach all subscribed consumers. This is to check the correct message transmission between dispatchers and producer-consumers.

The Event-b specifications allow to guarantee a correct by construction architectures. This formal method provides three steps. At the first step, the designer describes the necessary information for the software architecture model and the relation between them. Then, the second step consists in generating automatically all the correct design architectures following a multi-scale modeling approach. In fact, for each model, a scale is defined by the designer. Then, it is refined by successively adding smaller scale details. This refinement process is performed by applying specific rules. Finally, the third step is the selection of the efficient architecture according to resource constraints.

V. Related Work

Considerable research studies have been proposed on the description of software architectures. Multi-level modeling approaches [10] have been proposed to represent the different abstraction levels. Baresi et al. [3] presented a UML based approach and proposed formal verification and validation of embedded systems. The approach is implemented using the "CorrettoUML": a formal verification tool for UML models. Other research studies have been proposed for the specification of software systems using formal methods. Model verification activity [12] is performed to ensure the correctness of model. Formal verification means that any errors found in the design of the system should be corrected. Ben Younes et al. [4] proposed a meta-model transformation between UML Activity Diagram and Event B models. A formal framework is defined to ensure the correctness of the proposed transformations, and the event B method is used for the formal verification of applications. Bryans et al. [6] presented a model-based approach to assist in the integration of new or modified constituent systems into a System of Systems. The authors defined two levels for system composition, the high-level structural view that considers the connections within the system, and the low-level behavioral view that deals with the behavior of contractual specifications. They treated an industrial case study for modeling Audio/Video system.

We can note that the research activities [3], [4], [6] deal only with structural features during the design of the architecture. They do not take into account the respect of behavioral featuress to validate the architecture. Whereas, in our work, we deal with both structural and behavioral features.

We analyze that several studies have been performed on the modeling of multi-level architectures based on UML. These semi-formal approaches did not, however, include the concept of refinement. Although formal techniques and, more specifically, works based on graph transformations allow the architecture refinement, they require certain expertise in mathematics for architects. Moreover, only few studies have provided a clearly defined process that takes the compatibility between different description levels into account, a challenging condition for the multi-level description of software architectures. Model-based methods have addressed significant challenges in software Engineering. Semi-formal models are used in the architectural description of complex software systems. This representation has advantages, mainly with regard to comprehension, and can help to clarify areas of incompleteness and ambiguity in specifications.

In this study, we have considered that a given modeling level can be described by both vertical and horizontal scales. Our work will help the architect to design a correct and elaborated solutions for modeling multiple different levels of description of the same modeling level through the scales. Thus, we applied our model-based approach for describing multi-scale architecture , defining both the structure and the behaviour of the complex system and interactions between them. Event-B as a formal method support an interactive and an automatic theorem proving so that the resulted specification after the transformation process can be proved automatically. With the notion of refinement, we can to perform successive refinement to the Event-B model in order to specify different description scales.

VI. CONCLUSION

In this paper, we have presented a multi-scale modeling and specification approach for software architectures. We have proposed UML notations to represent the structure and the behavior for modeling different description scales, and second formally specified the models with the Event-B method. The formalisation phase allows to formally specify both structural and behavioural features of these architectures at a high level of abstraction using Event-B method. We implemented the elaborated specifications under the Rodin platform. We have also presented the application of our approach to the smart home scenario. Finally, we have presented some research studies discussing multi-level modeling for software architectures using semi-formal and formal methods. Currently, we are working on the improvement of the formal verification of architectural properties, and the model transformation from UML to Event-B. In our future work, we expect to apply the multi-scale approach to other use-cases for modeling complex systems architectures (e.g. System of Systems (SoS)) and implement a tool supporting the approach.

REFERENCES

[1] Compatibility and inheritance in software architectures. *Science of Computer Programming*, 41(2):105 – 138, 2001.

[2] J.-R. Abrial. *Modeling in Event-B: System and Software Engineering*. Cambridge University Press, New York, NY, USA, 1st edition, 2010.

[3] L. Baresi, G. Blohm, D. S. Kolovos, N. Matragkas, A. Motta, R. F. Paige, A. Radjenovic, and M. Rossi. Formal verification and validation of embedded systems: The UML-based mades approach. *Softw. Syst. Model.*, 14(1):343–363, Feb. 2015.

[4] A. Ben Younes, Y. Hlaoui, and L. Jemni Ben Ayed. A meta-model transformation from uml activity diagrams to event-b models. In *Computer Software and Applications Conference Workshops (COMPSACW), 2014 IEEE 38th International*, pages 740–745, July 2014.

[5] S. Bonhomme, E. Campo, D. Esteve, and J. Guennec. Methodology and tools for the design and verification of a smart management system for home comfort. In *Intelligent Systems, 2008. IS '08. 4th International IEEE Conference*, volume 3, pages 24–2–24–7, Sept 2008.

[6] J. Bryans, J. Fitzgerald, R. Payne, A. Miyazawa, and K. Kristensen. Sysml contracts for systems of systems. In *System of Systems Engineering (SOSE), 2014 9th International Conference on*, pages 73–78, June 2014.

[7] S. Cîmpan, F. Leymonerie, and F. Oquendo. *Software Architecture: 2nd European Workshop, EWSA 2005, Pisa, Italy, June 13-14, 2005. Proceedings*, chapter Handling Dynamic Behaviour in Software Architectures, pages 77–93. Springer Berlin Heidelberg, Berlin, Heidelberg, 2005.

[8] T. S. Hoang, H. Kuruma, D. Basin, and J.-R. Abrial. *Integrated Formal Methods: 7th International Conference, IFM 2009, Düsseldorf, Germany, February 16-19, 2009. Proceedings*, chapter Developing Topology Discovery in Event-B, pages 1–19. Springer Berlin Heidelberg, Berlin, Heidelberg, 2009.

[9] I. Omoronyia, G. Sindre, S. Biffl, and T. Stålhane. *Relating Software Requirements and Architectures*, chapter Understanding Architectural Elements from Requirements Traceability Networks, pages 61–83. Springer Berlin Heidelberg, Berlin, Heidelberg, 2011.

[10] P. Petrov, U. Buy, and R. Nord. The need for a multilevel context-aware software architecture analysis and design method with enterprise and system architecture concerns as first class entities. In *Software Architecture (WICSA), 2011 9th Working IEEE/IFIP Conference on*, pages 147–156, June 2011.

[11] W. Su, J. Abrial, and H. Zhu. Formalizing hybrid systems with event-b and the rodin platform. *Sci. Comput. Program.*, 94:164–202, 2014.

[12] B. Uchevler and K. Svarstad. Assertion based verification using psl-like properties in haskell. In *Design and Diagnostics of Electronic Circuits Systems (DDECS), 2013 IEEE 16th International Symposium on*, pages 254–257, April 2013.

A Cost-benefit Evaluation of Accessibility Testing in Agile Software Development

Aleksander Bai, Heidi Camilla Mork
Norwegian Computing Center, Oslo, Norway
Email: {aleksander.bai | heidi.mork}@nr.no

Viktoria Stray
University of Oslo, Oslo, Norway
Email: stray@ifi.uio.no

***Abstract*—Accessibility testing in software development is testing the software to ensure that it is usable by as many people as possible, independent of their capabilities. Few guidelines exist on how to include accessibility testing in an agile process, and how to select testing methods from a cost-benefit point of view. The end result is that many development teams do not include accessibility testing, since they do not know how to prioritize the different testing methods within a tight budget. In this paper, we present an evaluation of four accessibility testing methods that fits in an agile software development process. We discuss the cost of each method with regards to resources and knowledge requirements, and based on a cost-benefit analysis, we present the optimal combinations of these methods in terms of cost and issues discovered. Finally, we describe how accessibility testing methods can be incorporated into an agile process by using the agile accessibility spiral.**

Keywords*—*Accessibility testing; Agile software development; Cost-benefit analysis; Usability.

I. Introduction

The past decades have seen an increased interest in integrating usability in the software development process. However, far to little attention has been paid to the field of accessibility. Accessibility focuses on letting people with the widest range of capabilities be able to use a product or service [1]. There is an increased focus on accessibility from governments and the United Nations with "Convention on the Rights of Persons with Disabilities" [2].

Studies show that doing usability testing is costly and can take around 8-13% of the project's total budget [3]. Much of the cost goes to recruiting participants and evaluators in addition to the man-hours required for conducting and evaluating the results [4]. For accessibility testing, the cost can be even higher than usability testing, since recruitment and accommodation of participants usually have more requirements.

However, by not doing accessibility testing at all or by postponing testing until the end of the project, the cost can be extremely high, and it might not even be possible to do accessibility adjustments at a late stage [5] [6]. Many studies show that software that is hard to use, or have features that are hard to understand, make users find better alternatives [7]. There might also be legal requirements to provide accessibility.

We argue that developers and testers in software teams can take more responsibility for accessibility testing, and thus lower the total testing cost of the project and at the same time deliver a better product that is both more usable and accessible. Our approach is targeted towards agile software development, since it has become the mainstream development methodology [8] [9].

During our evaluations, we have investigated different accessibility testing techniques, and we discuss the cost-benefit aspect of these in an agile development process. We argue that accessibility testing does not necessarily require a high cost. We describe where in the process the methods can be used and how they can be combined in optimal ways. Consequently, the impact from accessibility testing towards the end of the project will be minimized, and thus reduce the cost of retrofitting [5]. Our suggested approach is not a substitute for doing user testing, but an addition, incorporated into the agile development process, to reduce the overall cost and increase the usability and accessibility of the software.

The remainder of this paper is organized as follows. Section II summarizes related work, and section III gives an overview of accessibility testing methods. Section IV describes the evaluation approach and the issues that were found during the evaluations. Section V reports our cost-benefit analysis of the accessibility testing methods and Section VI discusses the results. Finally, we summarize and conclude in Section VII.

II. Related Work

Zimmermann and Vanderheiden [10] have proposed a method for integrating accessible design and testing in the development of software applications, both iterative and non-iterative processes. However, the proposed method's main focus is on how to gather accessibility requirements and does not contain much details on how to actual perform testing in an iterative process. There has been some focus on integrating an agile development process with usability testing [11], and in recent years, there has been an increasing interest in Agile UX (User Experience) [12]. Bonacin et al. [13] propose how to incorporate accessibility and usability testing into an agile process, but do not discuss which accessibility testing methods that are optimal to use or how to combine them in an efficient setup.

A recent systematic review of usability testing methods for software development processes [7] request more research into evaluating the different testing methods and how they affect the testing outcome. To the best of our knowledge, there are no evaluations of accessibility testing methods in an agile process, and there are no studies of which accessibility testing methods that are most effective compared to resources and knowledge available in a agile team. We address the latter issue in this paper by showing a cost-benefit approach on how to select accessibility testing methods in an agile process.

III. BACKGROUND

There are several methods for testing usability [7] and accessibility [10] in software development: automated tools, guidelines, expert walkthrough, interviews and user testing to name a few. There are different alternatives of grouping these methods [14], and we have chosen to divide them into five groups based on the resources and knowledge required when using the methods in software development, as shown in Table TableI.

The amount of resources and knowledge required is categorized as either *low*, *medium* or *high*. In terms of resources, *low* means that none or little prerequisites (tools, setup, administration) are required to conduct the method; *medium* means that some prerequisites are required, and they are relatively cheap (under $1000); *high* means that the method requires considerably investments in terms of setup, purchase, administration or maintenance. In terms of knowledge, *low* means that no or very little prior knowledge is required; *medium* require some prior knowledge, either technical (usage, commands) or domain (knowledge or experience with the impairment); *high* means that extensive or expert training is required to conduct the evaluation.

TABLE I. ACCESSIBILITY TESTING GROUPS.

#	Group	Resource requirements	Knowledge requirements
1	Automated tools	Low	Low
2	Checklist and guidelines	Low	Low
3	Simulation using wearables	Medium	Low
4	Expert walkthrough	Low	High
5	User testing	High	Medium

Automated testing tools require fewer resources in terms of time, knowledge and resources, compared to other testing methods. It is quite feasible for a developer or tester to install a tool and run an evaluation, and most of the tools are also free to use. There are numerous alternatives out there, like the NetBeans accessibility module [15] that integrate directly into the developer's tools, but most automated tools only support simulation of visual impairments or a limited variant of other impairments. Overall, the automated testing tools are *low* in resources required to acquire and use them. The automated tools usually explain the evaluation results in great details to the operator, and give suggestions on how to fix or improve the problems that have been found. This means very little prior knowledge is required from the operator, and explains why we have also labeled the automated tools methods with *low* knowledge requirements in Table I.

Checklists and guidelines provide the evaluator with a set of instructions and criteria to evaluate, and the WCAG (Web Content Accessibility Guidelines) 2.0 standard [16] is a common choice. It is easy to find both checklists and guidelines on the Internet, and they have good and detailed documentation on how to perform the evaluation and how to assess the results from the evaluation. This is why we have labeled checklists and guidelines methods with *low* for resource and knowledge requirements. Even though these methods require little resources and knowledge, studies have shown that guidelines are hard to understand and follow, and have not increased accessibility as much as anticipated [17].

There are many different tools or wearables that an able-bodied person can use in a simulation. The motivation is to let a person experience an impairment so the person might be able to gain some insight into the issues that an impairment might have with a certain design or solution [18]. It is important to note that the intention of a simulation kit is not to simulate the disability in itself, which is highly criticized [19]. Simulation kits are fairly cheap to purchase and setup, but it requires some planning; the simulation kits must be evaluated to discover which is most suitable, and the simulation kits must also be purchased. The planning and cost aspect is the reason for labeling the simulation methods as *medium*. However, simulation kits come with good instructions on how to operator them and normally requires no prior knowledge, which is reflected by *low* knowledge requirements in Table I.

Expert walkthrough, also called persona walkthrough or persona testing approach [20], is where an expert simulates or play-acts a persona while carrying out tasks. The more knowledge the expert has about the disability that a particular persona has, the easier it is to do a realistic and credible acting while testing the solution. The approach is informal and relatively quick to do, but is heavily dependent on the selected personas and the experience that the expert has with the particular type of disability. All expert walkthrough methods requires expert knowledge (as the name indicates) and is thus marked with *high* knowledge requirements. However, there are few resource requirements for expert walkthrough methods, and this is why they are labeled with *low* for resource requirements.

The best approach for accessibility testing is user testing, since the actual users are involved and the testers does not have to do any approximation of impairments or mental states [21] [22]. However, it is also an expensive method because it requires much planning, recruitment and management [4]. Examples of user testing involves inquiry, interview, focus group and questionnaire. This means that resource requirements are *high* as indicated in Table I. User testing methods requires some prior knowledge on how to recruit, organize and conduct user testing, and we have indicated this with *medium* knowledge requirements.

IV. ACCESSIBILITY EVALUATIONS

We conducted eight evaluations. The goal of the evaluations was to investigate what kind of issues the different test methods can discover, and how the test methods differ from each other. The findings of the evaluations were then used in a cost-benefit analysis, to suggest where in an agile development process the methods might be most valuable.

The system used for evaluation was a pilot for electronic identification, developed during the EU project FutureID. The pilot uses a software certificate or an ID card with a card reader for the authentication process. The pilot uses both a

Java client and a web front end, and consists of around ten different user interfaces with varying complexity.

A. Selected Methods

We selected methods from the groups in Table I suitable to be performed by a person working in an agile team, i.e., from all groups except user testing and testing with automated tools. Table II shows the selected method types; Simulation kit (group 3), VATlab (group 2), Persona (group 4) and Manual WCAG (group 2).

The four types of methods were selected based on a combination of resources and knowledge required to perform a method. Ideally, in a development cycle, one wants to use as little resources as possible on accessibility testing, but at the same time discover the most critical accessibility issues that exists in the software. Therefore, we focused on testing methods that are relatively inexpensive to conduct in terms of time and resources. This is why user testing was omitted, since it is an expensive method to conduct. Automated tools were also omitted, since they are limited in what they can actually test.

Almost all methods are labelled as *low* with regards to resources. The only method with prerequisites is the simulation kit because some hardware must be purchased ahead of testing. This is usually a one-time purchase, but it must also be stored and assembled before usage, so we think it qualifies as medium resource demanding compared to the others.

Most of the methods require very little prior knowledge. Method 3 involves using a screen reader that requires knowledge on how to operate it, but almost everyone can learn how to use a screen reader in a short amount of time, and therefore we labelled it *medium*. However, our level of using screen readers cannot compare with the expert level of people that use screen readers daily and are dependent of them. The persona testing methods requires much more prior knowledge, both in terms of the method itself, but also on the impairments that is being play-acted. Thus, the persona testing methods are *high* in knowledge demands.

TABLE II. OVERVIEW OF THE EIGHT EVALUATIONS

#	*Method*	*Impairments*	*Resources*	*Knowledge*
1	Simulation kit	Reduced vision	Medium	Low
2	Simulation kit	Reduced dexterity	Medium	Low
3	VATLab	Blindess	Low	Medium
4	VATLab	Light sensitivity	Low	Low
5	VATLab	Multiple	Low	Low
6	Persona	Dyslexia	Low	High
7	Persona	Being old	Low	High
8	Manual WCAG	Multiple	Low	Low

For the simulation kit approach, two impairments were selected that cover both visual and physical dimensions. We used Cambridge inclusive design glasses [23] for simulating reduced vision, and the Cambridge inclusive design gloves [23] to simulate dexterity reduction. These gloves are typically used for testing a physical products, but they were included in our evaluation since there was a card reader involved.

We used a Virtual Assistive Technology Lab (VATLab) to test various assistive technologies [24]. The VATLab contains two different screen readers; NVDA and SuperNova. These tools are used by blind people, and give a good indication of how accessible the solution is for this type of impairment. We also used the built-in high contrast mode in Windows. The VATLab project also includes a checklist for evaluating web pages for screen readers, and we used this checklist in the evaluation [24].

For the persona walkthrough we defined two personas that we had experience with, one being old and one with dyslexia. For each persona there was an expert play-acting the particular persona while performing the predefined test-scenarios. To make it more realistic, the persona testing of being old was also conducted with two layers of Cambridge glasses to simulate reduced vision that often comes with age.

Finally, we conducted a manual testing of the WCAG checklist. The testing was performed with supportive use of available browser plugins to check for instance color contrast.

B. Participants

Six different participants performed the evaluations, where the participants' knowledge on accessibility testing ranged from beginner to expert. All the participants had technological background, their age ranged from 35 to 61, and there were both males and females in the group. Two of the participants where recruited based on their experience with persona testing and their knowledge on dyslexia and aging.

C. Procedures

Before we started the evaluation, we defined whether an issue was critical or cognitive. We defined a *critical issue* as an issue that prevents the participant from continuing or completing a task; e.g. difficult to read images or text because of poor contrast or resolution. A *cognitive issue* was an issue caused by confusing or missing information for the given context; e.g. not understanding the purpose of a screen or not understanding how to operate a controller. A problem can thus belong to both the critical and cognitive category, as it was often the case.

All the evaluations were conducted on the same machine with the same setup to ensure an equal test environment. Each evaluation also had a coordinator who wrote down the issues reported by the tester, and the coordinator also made notes when difficulties, that were not verbally expressed, were observed. All the evaluations were conducted by at least two different participants, and the results were aggregated.

A short initial test was conducted before the evaluations started, in order to verify that the overall setup, the scenarios and the ordering of them were best possible. The goal of all the scenarios was to successfully log into the system. Each participant performed five different scenarios in the same order: 1) Invalid digital certificate 2) Valid digital certificate 3) Invalid smart card 4) Valid smart card, but incorrect PIN code 5) Valid smart card and correct PIN code

The participants were unaware that they were given invalid certificate, invalid smart card and invalid PIN (Personal Identification Number) code. The scenarios were also executed in the listed order to avoid biasing the participants as they should gradually progress a little further in the logging process. Each method took under two hours to complete for a single participant for all the scenarios.

D. Evaluation results

As can be seen from Table III, a high number of critical issues were discovered with most of the methods. It should be noted that a critical issue might only be critical in the context of a given disability. For instance, incorrect HTML tags can be critical for blindness, but may not be relevant for impairments like reduced dexterity. However, for the solution as a whole, all critical issues are equally relevant since an issue might exclude some users if nothing is done to improve the problem.

TABLE III. ISSUES FOUND.

Method	*Issues*	*Critical*	*Cognitive*
1	54	14	9
2	4	0	0
3	33	26	0
4	10	4	0
5	19	17	0
6	34	15	15
7	27	13	9
8	32	7	5
	213	96	38

The simulation kit methods found fewer critical issues than VATLab and persona testing, and this is mostly because most of the issues reported were visual problems that were annoying at best and in most cases problematic, but not marked as critical since it did not hindered further progress. Of the critical issues discovered with simulation kit, almost all were also marked as cognitive. Note that a relative few number of issues were found when simulating reduced dexterity, and we believe this is mainly because the application did not require much motoric precision. This is of course highly related to the software that is evaluated.

WCAG also reported few critical issues, however this was mostly because the WCAG evaluations criteria are high level. For instance did a single criteria in WCAG cause over 17 critical issues to be reported in the VATLab methods since it has a much finer granularity. WCAG also reported few cognitive issues for the same reason.

VATLab methods reported on average the most critical issues, and many of the issues were related to poor compatibility for screen readers. We suspect that more issues could be found if there had not been so many critical problems which made further investigate in many screens impossible.

Persona testing methods found the most cognitive issues, and this is not unexpected since the persona used in the evaluations had focus on usability and understanding the context. Most of the issues reported by persona testing were directly related to the participant not understanding the context of a screen and what was expected from the participant. A high number of the cognitive issues were also marked as critical since it is impossible for the participant to complete his task, and this explains the high number of critical issues discovered by persona testing.

V. RESULTS

Based on the evaluation results in Section IV, we performed an cost-benefit analysis (CBA) of what combinations of accessibility testing methods that discovered most issues with regards to resources and knowledge. The motivation for doing a CBA is to get a more objective evaluation of the different testing methods, so it is easier to evaluate when to include a testing method in the process. CBA is a systematic approach for comparing strengths and weaknesses for different options [25]. It has not been used for comparing accessibility testing methods to our knowledge, but it is a well known technique that is used in many fields [26].

In order to do a CBA, we first defined the cost to be the combination of resources and knowledge where $resources$ and $knowledge \in \{1, 2, 3\}$ where *low* corresponds to 1, *medium* to 2 and *high* to 3. This makes sense since both variables contributes equally to the cost of executing a testing method. We argue that the most beneficial accessibility testing methods are those that find a high number of issues, but also many critical and cognitive issues. We can then define the benefit as the sum of found, critical and cognitive issues. Based on the the definition of cost and benefit we can then define the cost-benefit relationship accordingly:

$$CB = \frac{1}{\sqrt{n}} \frac{total^2 + critical^2 + cognitive^2}{resources \times knowledge} \qquad (1)$$

Where $total$ is the total number of issues for n methods, $cognitive$ is the total number of cognitive issues for n method, $critical$ is the total number of critical issues for n method and n is the number of methods. We have included squared weighting of both cognitive and critical issues since we argue that these issues are more important to discover than minor issues. We used $\sqrt{n}$ instead of n as a penalty for the number of evaluations, since using only n gave a too big penalty when using multiple methods.

We calculated *CB* for all permutations of the different accessibility testing methods to identify the combinations that gives most benefit compared to cost. The top results in addition to some selected results are shown in Table IV ordered by *CB*.

Combining all methods (except method 2) gives a very high coverage (almost 100%), but comes at a high cost, as shown with #20. The *CB* found 19 better alternatives when considering the costs. The optimal combination of methods that maximize benefit compared to cost is using methods 5, 8, 3 and 1 (#1). This combination has a relatively low cost, and discovered almost 65% of all issues in addition to a high number of both critical and cognitive issues (66.7% and 36.8%).

It is not surprising that if more methods are combined then the results are better, but at a higher cost, as for instance shown with combination #5 and #8 in Table IV. However, a combination of two methods (#3) gives reasonable good results of discovering around 40% of the known issues, and a large number of both critical and cognitive issues (21.9% and 36.8%).

TABLE IV. COST BENEFIT RESULTS.

#	Methods	Cost	Issues	Critical	Cognitive
1	5, 8, 3, 1	6	64.8%	66.7%	36.8%
2	8, 3, 1	5	55.9%	49.0%	36.8%
3	8, 1	3	40.4%	21.9%	36.8%
4	5, 8, 1	4	49.3%	39.6%	36.8%
5	5, 8, 6, 3, 1	9	80.8%	82.3%	76.3%
6	8, 6, 3, 1	8	71.8%	64.6%	76.3%
7	5, 8, 4, 3, 1	7	69.4%	70.8%	36.8%
8	5, 8, 7, 6, 3, 1	12	93.4%	95.8%	100%
9	5, 3, 1	5	49.8%	59.4%	23.7%
10	5, 8, 7, 3, 1	9	77.5%	80.0%	60.5%
...					
20	5, 8, 7, 6, 4, 3, 1	13	98.1%	100.0%	100.0%
...					
53	5, 8, 7, 6, 4, 2, 3, 1	15	100.0%	100.0%	100.0%
...					

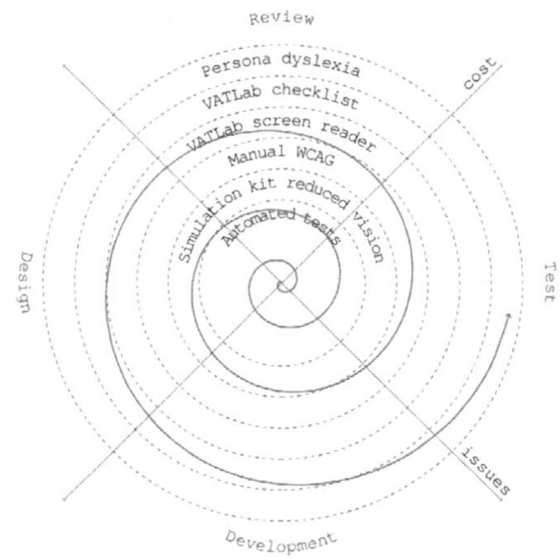

FIGURE 1. AGILE ACCESSIBILITY SPIRAL.

With a small increase in cost using three testing methods, around 50% of all issues were discovered, as shown with combination #2 and #4. Combination #2 finds 55.9% of all issues, and almost half the known critical issues. It is also worth noting that this testing method combination use three different accessibility testing method types (simulation kit, VATLab and Manual WCAG testing) to discovery many different issues.

VI. DISCUSSION

Based on the results in Table IV we found that the combination of several methods provides good results compared to the investment. Our CBA shows that combining the testing methods 5, 8, 3 and 1 is the most profitable combination of methods. The cost is moderate, and yet, the combination of methods discover a large number of the issues with the software we evaluated. However, the results does not say anything about when to apply the different methods during a development process.

Testing accessibility using simulation kit with reduced vision (method 1) is the only method which is always part of top ten results. Manual WCAG (method 8) is part of the combinations a total of 9 times, while testing blindness using VATLab (method 3) is part of top ten a total of 8 times. VATLab with checklist (method 5) is part of the top 10 results 7 times, while dyslexia persona testing (method 6) is part of the top results three times. Based on these results we can make some general recommendations on which methods to include in accessibility testing during an agile process, and the order in which they should be included.

In Figure 1 we have illustrated how to prioritize the different accessibility testing methods in an agile development process, and we call this the *agile accessibility spiral*. The circular layers represents the testing methods, and start from the center with automated tests and expands outwards to show the priority of the testing methods. The red arrow illustrates an agile process that spirals outwards and cover the same activities in different iterations, and the motivation behind the *agile accessibility spiral* is that the different testing methods can be included in all the activities. The total cost increase as more testing methods are included in testing, but the number of issues discovered also increases.

The different process activities are shown at the edge of the circle with blue separations between the different activities. The activities are gradual and not necessarily clearly separated as shown in the illustration, and they often happen in parallel. We have illustrated four common activities (design, development, test, review) that usually occur in agile software development.

Automated tests are always a vital part of any development process and are thus in the center of the spiral, but we argue that the first accessibility testing method that should be added to automated tests is the simulation kit for reduced vision. This is supported by our results in Table IV, and by the knowledge required as shown in Table I. It is a method that can be performed many times without affecting the bias of the tester too much, since it is a wearable gadget that is used by the tester and not so much a mental testing approach.

Other testing methods like persona testing should be performed less often since the cost is quite high, but also because it is a mental process which might be biased if performed too often by the same person. After the simulation kit method with reduced vision the methods follow successive with manual WCAG, VATLab and blindness, VHL checklist, persona dyslexia. We have not illustrated more methods in Figure 1, since these 5 methods cover over 80% of known issues as shown in Table IV. As a minimum at least two different testing method should be included during testing [27].

During the first iterations in an agile development process, a prototype is often developed, and since the motivation behind a prototype is to show a concept and not necessarily think about all possible outcomes or users, it is still beneficial to do some accessibility testing to avoid costly adjustment at a later stage [5]. However, not all accessibility testing methods are suitable for testing against prototypes or even design sketches. The agile accessibility spiral in Figure 1 also incorporate this in the ordering.

Simulating reduced vision with simulation kit can be done

against both prototype and design sketches, and parts of WCAG can also be tested at an early stage. Further out in the agile accessibility spiral layers, when testing blindness with VATLab and screen readers, a more stable software version should be tested instead of design sketches or prototypes. This is because screen readers requires elements to be marked so the screen readers can find the required information.

VII. Conclusion

Based on our results, we recommend to use the *agile accessibility spiral*, as a reference for accessibility testing in agile development. We recommend to start from the center and gradually apply more testing methods as the project progresses. The cost and knowledge of testing methods increase from the center and outwards, but the discovery of issues also increases when moving outwards from the center. Ideally, if the team has access to staff that can perform persona testing, or are willing to invest the resources to train one or more in persona testing, then we strongly recommend to include persona testing as part of the development cycle.

The different testing methods should be adjusted to the software and the expertise of the development, so they fit into the agile process. The more knowledge and experience an agile team gains, the smaller the circles in the *agile accessibility spiral* will become. And as stated before, we strongly recommend to do testing with actual users at some point in the software development. No amount of automated tools, checklist and guidelines, simulation using wearables or expert walkthrough can replace feedback from real users. However, we argue that developers and testers can contribute more with accessibility testing to deliver a better end product.

Our study of accessibility testing methods was limited in number of participants and the size of the evaluated application, hence, future work should explore the different accessibility testing methods for other software solutions. More research on cost benefit evaluation in accessibility testing should be done, and it would be interesting to evaluate more testing methods and place these in the *agile accessibility spiral*.

Acknowledgment

This research was partially funded as part of the FutureID project. The FutureID project is funded by the EU FP7 program (Grant agreement no: 318424).

References

[1] H. Petrie and N. Bevan, "The evaluation of accessibility, usability and user experience," The universal access handbook, 2009, pp. 10–20.

[2] United Nations, "Convention on the Rights of Persons with Disabilities," http://www.un.org/disabilities/convention/conventionfull.shtml.

[3] J. Nielsen, "Return on investment for usability," Jakob Nielsen's Alertbox, January, vol. 7, 2003.

[4] L. C. Cheng and M. Mustafa, "A reference to usability inspection methods," in International Colloquium of Art and Design Education Research (i-CADER 2014). Springer, 2015, pp. 407–419.

[5] M.-L. Sánchez-Gordón and L. Moreno, "Toward an integration of web accessibility into testing processes," Procedia Computer Science, vol. 27, 2014, pp. 281–291.

[6] B. Haskins, B. Dick, J. Stecklein, R. Lovell, G. Moroney, and J. Dabney, "Error Cost Escalation Through the Project Life Cycle," in Incose - Annual Conference Symposium Proceedings- Cd Rom Edition; 2004, 2004.

[7] F. Paz and J. A. Pow-Sang, "A systematic mapping review of usability evaluation methods for software development process," International Journal of Software Engineering and Its Applications, vol. 10, no. 1, 2016, pp. 165–178.

[8] D. Bustard, G. Wilkie, and D. Greer, "The maturation of agile software development principles and practice: observations on successive industrial studies in 2010 and 2012," in Engineering of Computer Based Systems (ECBS), 2013 20th IEEE International Conference and Workshops on the. IEEE, 2013, pp. 139–146.

[9] T. Dingsøyr, S. Nerur, V. Balijepally, and N. B. Moe, "A decade of agile methodologies: Towards explaining agile software development," Journal of Systems and Software, vol. 85, no. 6, 2012, pp. 1213 – 1221.

[10] G. Zimmermann and G. Vanderheiden, "Accessible design and testing in the application development process: considerations for an integrated approach," Universal Access in the Information Society, vol. 7, no. 1-2, 2008, pp. 117–128.

[11] J. C. Lee and D. S. McCrickard, "Towards extreme (ly) usable software: Exploring tensions between usability and agile software development," in Agile Conference (AGILE), 2007. IEEE, 2007, pp. 59–71.

[12] D. Salah, R. F. Paige, and P. Cairns, "A systematic literature review for agile development processes and user centred design integration," in Proceedings of the 18th International Conference on Evaluation and Assessment in Software Engineering, ser. EASE '14. New York, NY, USA: ACM, 2014, pp. 5:1–5:10. [Online]. Available: http://doi.acm.org/10.1145/2601248.2601276 [Accessed: 1. June 2015].

[13] R. Bonacin, M. C. C. Baranauskas, and M. A. Rodrigues, "An agile process model for inclusive software development," in Enterprise information systems. Springer, 2009, pp. 807–818.

[14] K. S. Fuglerud and T. H. Røssvoll, "An evaluation of web-based voting usability and accessibility," Universal Access in the Information Society, vol. 11, no. 4, 2012, pp. 359–373.

[15] NetBeans, "Accessibility Checker," http://plugins.netbeans.org/plugin/7577/accessibility-checker.

[16] W3C, "Web Content Accessibility Guidelines," https://www.w3.org/TR/WCAG20/.

[17] C. Power, A. Freire, H. Petrie, and D. Swallow, "Guidelines are only half of the story: accessibility problems encountered by blind users on the web," in Proceedings of the SIGCHI conference on human factors in computing systems. ACM, 2012, pp. 433–442.

[18] C. Cardoso and P. J. Clarkson, "Simulation in user-centred design: helping designers to empathise with atypical users," Journal of Engineering Design, vol. 23, no. 1, 2012, pp. 1–22.

[19] A. M. Silverman, J. D. Gwinn, and L. Van Boven, "Stumbling in their shoes disability simulations reduce judged capabilities of disabled people," Social Psychological and Personality Science, vol. 6, no. 4, 2015, pp. 464–471.

[20] T. Schulz and K. S. Fuglerud, "Creating Personas with Disabilities," in Computers Helping People with Special Needs, ser. Lecture Notes in Computer Science, K. Miesenberger, A. Karshmer, P. Penaz, and W. Zagler, Eds., vol. 7383. Linz, Austria: Springer Berlin / Heidelberg, 2012, pp. 145–152.

[21] J. S. Dumas and J. Redish, "A practical guide to usability testing". Intellect Books, 1999.

[22] R. G. Bias and D. J. Mayhew, "Cost-justifying usability: An update for the Internet age". Elsevier, 2005.

[23] Cambridge, "Inclusive Design Toolkit," http://www.inclusivedesigntoolkit.com.

[24] K. S. Fuglerud, S. E. Skotkjerra, and T. Halbach, "Håndbok i testing av websider med hjelpe-middel-program-vare, Virtuell hjelpe-middellab," 2015.

[25] M. M. Mantei and T. J. Teorey, "Cost/benefit analysis for incorporating human factors in the software lifecycle," Communications of the ACM, vol. 31, no. 4, 1988, pp. 428–439.

[26] A. E. Boardman, D. H. Greenberg, A. R. Vining, and D. L. Weimer, "Cost-benefit analysis: concepts and practice," 2006.

[27] K. S. Fuglerud, "Inclusive design of ICT: The challenge of diversity". Dissertation for the Degree of PhD, University of Oslo, Faculty of Humanitites, 2014.

Toward Automatic Performance Testing for REST-based Web Applications

Chia Hung Kao
Department of Applied Mathematics
National Taitung University
Taitung, Taiwan
Email: chkao@nttu.edu.tw

Chun Cheng Lin
CloudCube Co., Ltd
Taipei, Taiwan
Email: jimlin@cloudcube.com.tw

Hsin Tse Lu
DATA, Institute for Information Industry
Taipei, Taiwan
Email: oliu@iii.org.tw

***Abstract*—Nowadays, more and more web applications are developed to provide their services over the Internet. In addition to functionalities, performance characteristics, including response time, throughput, latency, stability etc., are key factors when selecting appropriate web applications. However, complex architectures, fast changing requirements, strict quality criteria and time to market pressure all impose difficulties and complexities on testing activities. Therefore, for software testers, how to evaluate and ensure performance characteristics systematically and efficiently becomes a critical challenge. In this paper, an approach for automatic performance testing for Representational State Transfer (REST)-based web applications is introduced. Based on Application Programming Interface (API) document and test cases, the proposed approach employs natural language processing (NLP) to parse, match and generate test scripts for performance testing tool automatically. It not only eases the burden of test scripts design, implementation and maintenance efforts on software testers, but also facilitates the execution of performance testing tasks.**

Keywords–Performance testing; web application; software testing.

I. Introduction

Software companies and service providers develop more and more web applications to provide their services over the Internet. In addition to functionalities, potential users will consider performance characteristics, including response time, throughput, latency, stability, etc. when selecting appropriate web applications for their tasks [1]. Nowadays, in order to fulfill various functional and quality requirements from users, the complexity of web applications is increasing dramatically. Multi-tier considerations, the composition of different software components, architecture concerns, distributed or cluster designs, and data processing mechanisms, all impose design and implementation complexities on web applications. Thus, the difficulties of testing activities arise correspondingly [2]. Furthermore, fast changing requirements and time to market pressure could worsen the situation. In such circumstances, software testers need to frequently create or refine test cases, redesign and implement corresponding test scripts, and execute test scripts to acquire results for further actions. Therefore, how to evaluate and ensure the performance characteristics of web applications systematically and efficiently is a critical issue for software testers [3].

In this paper, an approach for automatic performance testing for REST-based web applications is introduced. It aims to provide software testers with an integrated process from test cases design, automatic test scripts generation, to test execution. Two major software artifacts, including APIs document and test cases, generated from the software development process are used in the proposed approach. APIs document describes information about functionalities provided by specific web application. On the other hand, test cases depict the test scenarios designed by software testers. Through the composition of necessary APIs, the test scenario can be achieved for testing tasks. Based on APIs document and test cases, the proposed approach uses NLP [4] to parse and match corresponding test cases and API, and then generate test scripts for performance testing tool automatically. On the one hand, it eases the burden of test scripts design, implementation and maintenance efforts on software testers. On the other hand, software testers can focus more on the design of test cases and the analysis of test results. Finally, it facilitates the execution of performance testing tasks through automation. Thus, the performance characteristics of web applications can be identified efficiently for further actions on development, operation and maintenance tasks.

The remainder of this paper is organized as follows. Section II reviews related studies. Section III describes the design of the proposed architecture and Section IV presents the usage of the architecture. Finally, Section V presents conclusion and future works.

II. Related Work

In this Section, related studies about automatic test cases generation are introduced. Nébut, Fleurey, Traon, and Jézéquel [5] proposed an approach for automating the generation of test scenarios from use cases. Through the developed transition system, the approach synthesized and generated test cases based on use cases extended with contracts. Jiang and Ding [6] also designed a framework for automatically generating test cases from textual use cases. By using use cases in specific format, the framework built an activity table for constructing EFSM (Extended Finite State Machine), which is the base for test cases generation. Lipka et al. [7] presented a method for semi-automated generation of test scenarios based on textual use cases. The method derived the scenarios from use cases with annotations and then generated the sequence of method invocations for testing. Landhäußer and Genaid [8] proposed the usage of ontology to present the relationship among source code, natural language elements of user stories and test scripts. Through the ontology, the test steps and related artifacts (e.g., APIs and test scripts) can be identified and reused for testing new user stories. Wang et al. [9] proposed an approach that automatically generates executable

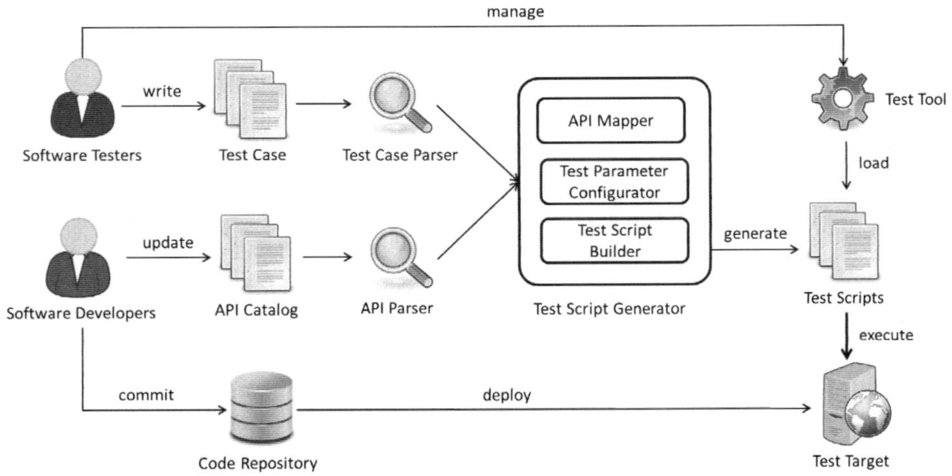

Figure 1. Overview of the automatic performance testing architecture.

system test cases from use case specifications and a domain model. NLP is also used in the approach to extract behavioral information from use cases for test automation. Chen and Miao [10] presented an automatic approach to generate test scripts automatically against JavaScript. The study parsed test cases in XML format and generated Java code for Selenium to execute testing tasks.

To sum up, several studies discussed about the automatic generation of test cases for testing tasks. Based on previous studies, the gap between test scenarios and test scripts is considered in this study through the matching of test cases and APIs document to achieve more automatic testing. In addition, the integrated environment and process for facilitating automatic testing is designed and introduced in this paper.

III. Architecture Design

Fig. 1 depicts the design of the automatic performance testing architecture. Major actors and components are described as follows.

- **Software Testers:** Software testers are responsible for all the testing activities throughout the software development process. Generally, the testing activities include (1) identify test environment, (2) identify performance acceptance criteria, (3) plan and design tests, (4) configure the test environment, (5) implement the test design, (6) execute the test, and (7) analyze results, report and retest [11]. In the proposed approach, software testers can focus on the planning and the design of test cases based on requirements or quality criteria. The implementation and the execution of tests can be achieved automatically.
- **Software Developers:** Based on specific software development process, software developers perform requirement analysis, design, implementation and maintenance tasks to web applications. The implementation will be committed to code repository for version control and continuous delivery. Besides, software developers should update modifications to the API Catalog in the proposed architecture correspondingly.
- **Test Case:** Software testers are responsible for the design, implementation and maintenance of test cases based on requirements and specifications. Generally, test cases include preconditions, test steps, postconditions, and expected results. Test cases can be preserved and managed by test case management systems. In addition, several test case management systems (e.g., Testopia [12]) provide APIs for external access of specific contents within test cases. In the architecture, the test case will be retrieved and analyzed by a test case parser.
- **Test Case Parser:** The test case parser is responsible for analyzing the test steps written in test case. By using NLP, major components can be analyzed and identified, including cardinal number (CD), singular noun (NN), plural noun (NNS), verb (VB), determiner (DT), to (TO), etc. Basically, CD can be considered as the configurations (e.g., number of users and workload) in the performance test case. NN and NNS could be actors, specific objects and the system, respectively. Finally, VB may indicate specific operations of the system. The analysis result can be used to match corresponding APIs and determine configurations in test scripts.
- **API Catalog:** The API catalog helps software developers to create, update, query and maintain API documents for software systems. Famous API catalogs [13] or API management services [14] include Swagger, WSO2 API Management, Apigee, 3Scale, etc. It is anticipated that software developers update API documents to the API catalog once changes happen. Thus, the API information will be kept up to date with the committed code and the deployed test target.
- **API Parser:** The API parser is responsible for analyzing components in an API document. In recent web applications, REST has emerged as the foundation and development principle of the web architecture [15]. A RESTful web service contains three major aspects: the

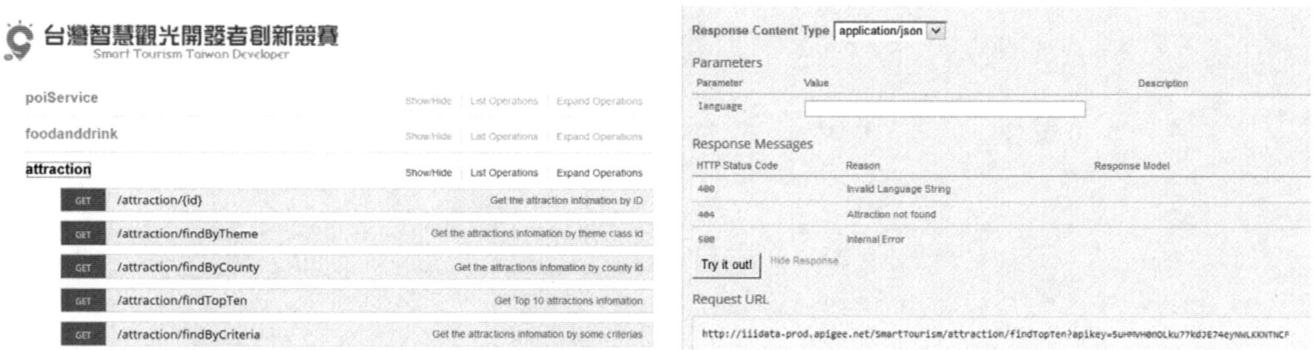

Figure 2. API catalog for web application Smart Tourism Taiwan.

URL of the service, the communication data, and the operations supported by HTTP methods. Through the parsed result, the information about how to invoke the service can be identified.

- **Test Script Generator:** The test script generator is used to generate corresponding test scripts based on test case and API documents. Three major components, the API Mapper, the Test Parameter Configurator and the Test Script Builder, are included in the test script generator. Firstly, the API mapper analyzes the parsed result of test case, searches and maps corresponding APIs based on the information extracted from API catalog. If a specific API is matched, the information described in the API document is parsed and obtained. Secondly, test parameter configurator helps to identify configurations (e.g., number of users and workload) described in test case. Finally, based on the information extracted from test case and API document, the performance test script conformed to specific format of test tool is generated by the test script builder.
- **Test Tool** After the generation of performance test script, the test tool loads and executes the test script to test the target system. In current design, Apache JMeter [16] is selected as the test tool in the performance testing architecture.

IV. Case Demonstration

A web application "Smart Tourism Taiwan" [17] is used to describe the usage of the automatic performance testing architecture. The information of all the APIs are managed by Swagger, and Fig. 2 depicts the screenshot of partial API information. The test case is "1000 users find top ten attractions." Through NLP, "1000" can be identified and used as the input of "ThreadGroup.num_threads" for thread configuration (number of users) in jmx for JMeter. On the other hand, based on the information (API classification, URL and description) from Swagger and NLP result, the API '/attraction/findTopTen' can be identified. Then, the information of "Request URL" can be parsed and used as the input of "HTTPSampler.domain," "HTTPSampler.path," "Argument.name," and "Argument.value" in jmx for JMeter. Based on the content parsed and retrieved from test case and API document, the test script can be built for JMeter for performance testing tasks.

V. Conclusion

Performance characteristics are important factors when users select and use web applications. Due to growing complexity of web applications and the fast changing requirements, efficient and systematic performance evaluation will be the key for further development, operation and maintenance tasks. In this paper, an approach for automatic performance testing for REST-based web applications was introduced. It used NLP to parse and match test cases and API document, and then generate test scripts for the performance testing tool automatically. Through the approach, the burden of software testers can be eased and the performance testing tasks can be facilitated efficiently. A demo case was also introduced to describe the feasibility of the design. Future works include the identification and modeling of test cases to better analyze and realize the purpose of testing tasks. In addition, the API document can be indexed (e.g., by Apache Solr [18]) for better identification, setting and deployment for more flexible and complex test scenarios. Furthermore, the precision of API matching will be analyzed quantitatively and the false positive should be handled. Finally, the overall design will be deployed and evaluated in the development process of various REST-based web applications.

Acknowledgment

This study is supported by the Ministry of Science and Technology of the Republic of China under grant MOST 105-2218-E-143 -001 -.

References

[1] E. J. Weyuker and F. I. Vokolos, "Experience with Performance Testing of Software Systems: Issues, an Approach, and Case Study," IEEE Transactions on Software Engineering, vol. 26, no. 12, Dec. 2000, pp. 1147–1156.

[2] A. Bertolino, "Software Testing Research: Achievements, Challenges, Dreams," Proceedings of the 2007 Future of Software Engineering, May 2007, pp. 85–103.

[3] M. Woodside, G. Franks, and D. C. Petriu, "The Future of Software Performance Engineering," Proceedings of the 2007 Future of Software Engineering, May 2007, pp. 171–187.

[4] S. Bird, E. Klein, and E. Loper, Natural Language Processing with Python. O'Reilly Media, 2009.

[5] C. Nébut, F. Fleurey, Y. L. Traon, and J. M. Jézéquel, "Automatic Test Generation: A Use Case Driven Approach," IEEE Transactions on Software Engineering, vol. 32, no. 3, Mar. 2006, pp. 140–155.

[6] M. Jiang and Z. Ding, "Automation of Test Case Generation From Textual Use Cases," Proceedings of the 4th International Conference on Interaction Sciences, Aug. 2011, pp. 102–107.

[7] R. Lipka, T. Potuák, P. Brada, P. Hnetynka, and J. Vinárek, "A Method for Semi-automated Generation of Test Scenarios based on Use Cases," Proceedings of the 41st Euromicro Conference on Software Engineering and Advanced Applications, Aug. 2015, pp. 241–244.

[8] M. Landhäußer and A. Genaid, "Connecting User Stories and Code for Test Development," Proceedings of the 2012 Third International Workshop on Recommendation Systems for Software Engineering, June 2012, pp. 33–37.

[9] C. Wang, F. Pastore, A. Goknil, L. Briand, and Z. Iqbal, "Automatic Generation of System Test Cases from Use Case Specifications," Proceedings of the 2015 International Symposium on Software Testing and Analysis, July 2015, pp. 385–396.

[10] R. Chen and H. Miao, "A Selenium based Approach to Automatic Test Script Generation for Refactoring JavaScript Code," Proceedings of the 2013 IEEE/ACIS 12th International Conference on Computer and Information Science, June 2013, pp. 341–346.

[11] J. Meier, C. Farre, P. Bansode, S. Barber, and D. Rea, "Performance Testing Guidance for Web Applications," Microsoft Corporation, Tech. Rep., Sept. 2007, URL: https://msdn.microsoft.com/en-us/library/bb924375.aspx[accessed: 2016-06-24].

[12] Testopia, URL: https://wiki.mozilla.org/Testopia [accessed: 2016-06-24].

[13] Swagger, URL: http://swagger.io [accessed: 2016-06-24].

[14] A. Acharya, P. Kodeswaran, P. Dey, S. Sharma, and S. Agrawal, "The Talking Cloud: A Cloud Platform for Enabling Communication Mashups," Proceedings of the 2014 IEEE International Conference on Services Computing, July 2014, pp. 496–503.

[15] R. T. Fielding and R. N. Taylor, "Principled Design of the Modern Web Architecture," ACM Transactions on Internet Technology, vol. 2, no. 2, May 2002, pp. 115–150.

[16] Apache JMeter, URL: http://jmeter.apache.org [accessed: 2016-06-24].

[17] Smart Tourism Taiwan, URL: http://www.vztaiwan.com [accessed: 2016-06-24].

[18] Apache Solr, URL: http://lucene.apache.org/solr [accessed: 2016-06-24].

Reports with TDD and Mock Objects: an Improvement in Unit Tests

Alan S. C. Mazuco
Department of Computer Science
Masters in Applied Computing
University of Brasilia (UnB)
Campus Darcy Ribeiro
Brasilia, DF, Brazil
Email: alanmazuco@hotmail.com

Edna Dias Canedo
Faculdade UnB Gama - FGA
University of Brasilia (UnB)
Brasilia, DF, Brazil
Email: ednacanedo@unb.br

***Abstract*—The construction of reports in software engineering, although considered a simple task, is sometimes extremely difficult for the developer, especially if the report has a rich amount of detail and web software as a backdrop. This article will show how you can reduce the stress of developers using agile methodologies, such as Test Driven Development (TDD) associated with Mock Objects. Software testing is gaining the attention of software scholars because of the huge impact on the quality they produce and of the reduced delivery time. This study was driven by a shortage of literature and comes, as appropriate, to demonstrate how it is possible to reduce the drudgery of creating reports using open source tools like Jaspersoft and their implementers, such as IReport, along with the Eclipse IDE. The study was based on experiments carried out in the Brazilian Army's Performance Management Project, with a team of professionals who used mock objects to save time and improve performance gain speed and which also used performance in conducting their work and also the TDD Methodology as the main reference. From the results, empirical observation showed us the best and worst aspects encountered by participants during their work.**

Keywords*–*TDD, Test Driven Development; Mock Objects; Reports.

I. Introduction

The Brazilian Army's Performance Management project, materialized in a corporate system of the same name, the "SGD", or "PMS" - Performance Management System, came into the world in order to carry out and follow the evaluations of its internal public, whose final destination is the subsidy decision-making of subsidies for several finalistic programs. The project has become a priority in the high command of the Brazilian Army, and there were several factors that led to such a distinction. However, what most drew attention was how quickly it got off the ground and won the web pages in the form of robust and efficient software. The system was completed in six months of development. In the seventh month, the system went into production as planned. The project's success was due to the fact that the project manager had decided to use agile methodologies, such as Test Driven Development (TDD), throughout the project development phase.

This case study will permeate some definitions, guiding and reinforcing the experiences developed along the Brazilian Army's Performance Management project, and showing why the TDD process has been tenaciously important in the software development process.

What caught the eye with the production of reports using mock objects was the increased pace of implementation, as well as the reduced fatigue of programmers. Such improvements led to an increase in the satisfaction of business owners due to the high demand for increasingly rich reports.

The results were obtained by performing an experiment conducted in the General Headquarters of the Brazilian Army, Such experiment followed empirical methodologies, allowing us to observe the best and worst aspects encountered by members of the participating teams.

For a better understanding, this paper is structured as follows: Section 2 presents several concepts on the subject at hand, as well as some major works reported in the community. This is very important because we found basis in the research literature that supports the experiments that were conducted. The Section 3 describes how the experiment was conducted, the subject of this study, the methodologies used and the composition of the teams that performed in it. The Section 4 presents the results, collected in the light of the experiment, using previously selected indicators.

II. Related Works

The utilization of Mock Object simulates the behavior of complex real objects and are therefore very useful when used in conjunction with TDD practices. This section explores some of the literature on the subject.

A. *The Problem of Errors*

A study published by the National Institute of Standards and Technology[1] and also by the United States Department of Commerce reveals that software errors cost around $60 billion to the US economy each year. Much has been said about techniques to minimize the catastrophic effect caused by software errors, as we see in Borges [1]. Such techniques include reusing code that has been widely tested and is trusted, as well as exhaustive verification techniques and validation tests performed by a team of testers.

As reported in Leon and Kochs [2], agile methodologies create ever-growing controversy, having their true effectiveness auestioned and putting their advocates in a heated battle of claims. However, the practice has shown that processes arising from the agile methodology bring many benefits for development, culminating in the satisfaction of clients.

Fig. 1 shows that the use of agile methodologies can systematically reduce the cost of making code changes. Regarding this, Beck [3] believes that the following are key aspects of agile methodologies:

- Effective (fast and adaptive) response to change;
- Effective communication among all stakeholders;
- Drawing the customer onto the team;
- Organizing a team so that it is in control of the work performed; Quick, incremental delivery of software.

According Baumeister and Wirsing [4], there are benefits to an evolutionary approach in which the developer writes the test before they write the functional code needed to satisfy that test.

Below, we can see a graphical representation of this study.

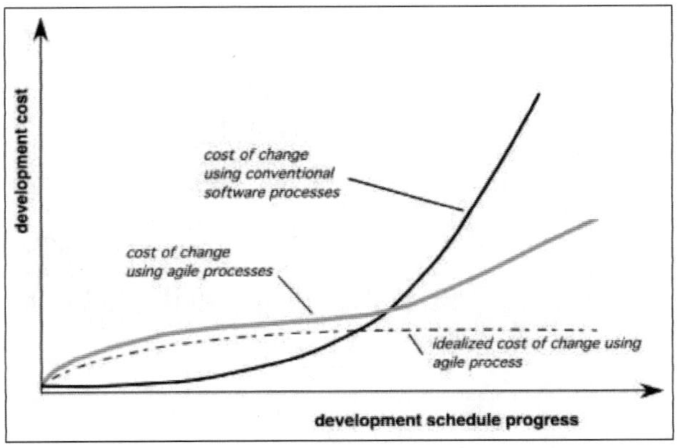

Figure 1. Agility and the Cost of Change [3]

B. The TDD as Tonic

TDD is defined as a set of techniques of Extreme Programming (XP) associated with agile methodologies.

According to Beck [5], an agile method could be compared to driving a car, where the driver has the task of driving the vehicle to his destination safely, without committing traffic offenses.

According Baumeister and Wirsing [6], there are benefits to an evolutionary approach in which the developer writes the test before he writes the functional code needed to satisfy that test.

According to Marrero and Settle [7], TDD is a way to reflect on modeling before writing the code itself. But as reported by Baumeister and Wirsing [6], the testdriven development is a programming technique where the main goal is to write clean functional code from a test that has failed.

According to a manifesto published in 2001 [3], we see that:

> We are uncovering better ways of developing software by doing it and helping others do it. Through this work we have come to value:
>
> - Individuals and interactions over processes and tools;
> - Working software over comprehensive documentation;
> - Customer collaboration over contract negotiation;
> - Responding to change over following a plan That is, while there is value in the items on the right, we value the items on the left more.

As Fowler has shown in [8] developers should worry about performing a refactoring of the code in order to optimize it more and more, and TDD processes are perfectly consonant with this approach.

Fig. 2 illustrates the TDD methodology. Note that, while the traditional approach first encodes the main business rule for later testing, the general idea of the TDD is to mitigate the code through unit testing until it passes the test [9], where frameworks like JUnit (Java) are often used by more savvy developers.

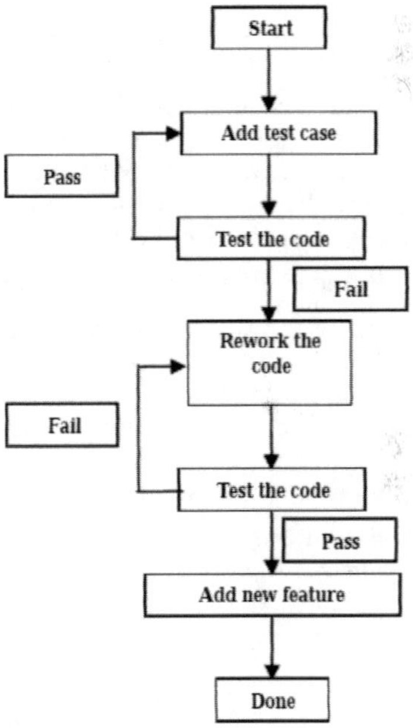

Figure 2. Concept of the TDD, in general lines [10]

C. Mock Objects par Excellence

The main ground of TDD is to use intensive testing, even before coding the main object. Therefore, the concept of Mock Objects fits like a glove, from which false objects could be created and tested with the main code, to obtain the desired result.

A mock object, according Mackinnon et al [11], is a substitute implementation to emulate another domain code. It has to be simpler than the actual code, not a duplicate implementation, and allow you to set your status to help the test.

As seen in Stroustrup and Lenkov [12], it can be difficult to conceive detailed unit testing in scoped languages such as Java, without breaking the scope. To remedy that, the unit testing technique for field packs was created.

Fowler is emphatic when he says [13]:

> "The term *Mock Objects* has become a popular one to describe special case objects that mimic real objects for testing. Most language environments now have frameworks that make it easy to create mock objects. What's often not realized, however, is that mock objects are but one form of special case test object, one that **enables a different style of testing**".

From what we can presume, and as we pointed out in the text above, the use of Mock Objects is not limited to performing unit testing using JUnit or similar frameworks. Rather, Mock Objects are flexible enough to perform tests for various purposes. In the case of our experiment, it was used to build reports. The results were measured and scientifically proven, and have brought many benefits to our team of developers, allowing greater flexibility in the process.

Testing with Mock Objects has been the key to solving problems, as it transfers the actual behavior of the object to a close-to-real fictional situation, being in perfect conformity with the principle of Demeter Law [14]:

> "Code with the encapsulation of ideas and modularity, easily following the object-oriented technique to the programmer... while minimizing code duplication, the number of method arguments, and the number of methods per class."

Nevertheless, Freeman et al. [15] state the following:

> "Mock Objects is an **extension to Test-Driven Development** that supports good Object-Oriented design by guiding the discovery of a coherent system of types within a code base. It turns out to be less interesting as a technique for isolating tests from third-party libraries than is widely thought."

According to Brown and Tapolcsanyi [16], Mock Objects are divided into patterns, as we can see in Table 1:

TABLE I. PATTERNS CATALOG FOR MOCK OBJECTS [16].

Pattern Name	Synopsis
MockObject	Basic mock object pattern that allows for testing a unit in isolation by faking communication with collaborating objects.
Test Stubs	
MockObject via Factory	A way of generating mock objects, utilizing existing factory methods.
Self Shunt	Unit Test code serves as the mock object by passing an instance of itself.
Pass in Mock Collaborator	Pass in a mock object in place of the actual collaborating object.
Mock Object via Delegator	Creates a mock implementation of a collaborating interface in the Test class or mock object.

The following patterns will be added next year for 2004 PLOP:
-Mock Objects via CrossPoints;
-Write Testable Code; and
-Mock Object with Guard.

During the experiments conducted in this study, as seen in the table, we used the Mock Object described below.

III. THE EXPERIENCE

1) The Mock Object used: According to Brown and Tapolcsanyi [16] and Fowler [13] Mock Objects can be used to build repeatable, automated, and highly leveraged Unit Tests. In many cases, setting up Mock Object frameworks that "emulate" the real world objects is necessary. Thus, the pattern used in the experiment was the Self Shunt. This pattern fit like a glove, as the Java report-creation operations are extremely repetitive, bringing some fatigue obstacles and construction time.

Fig. 3 shows the report to be created in the experiment, just to get an idea of the complexity of development. From there, a mock object containing all the data would be used to create form this report using fictitious data.

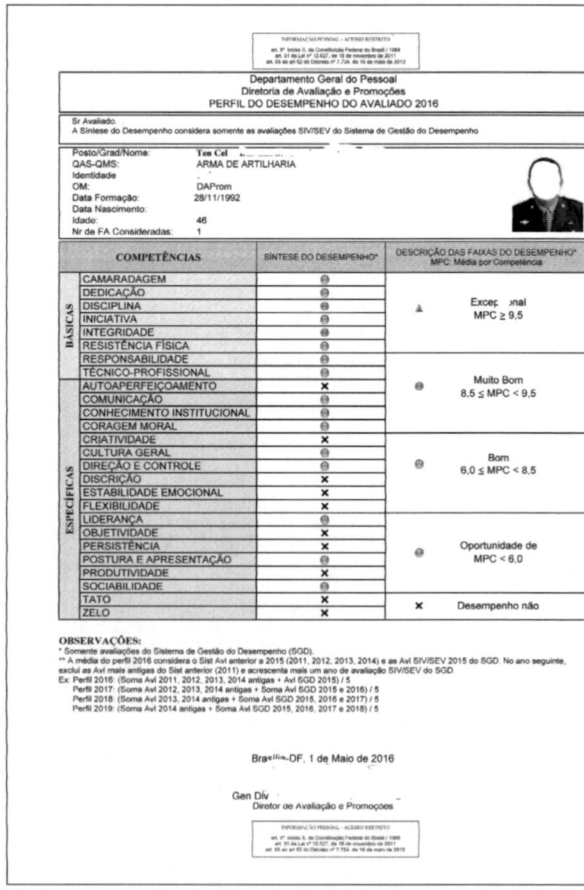

Departamento Geral do Pessoal
Diretoria de Avaliação e Promoções
PERFIL DO DESEMPENHO DO AVALIADO 2016

Sr Avaliado.
A Síntese do Desempenho considera somente as avaliações SIV/SEV do Sistema de Gestão do Desempenho

Posto/Grad/Nome: Ten Cel
QAS-QMS: ARMA DE ARTILHARIA
Identidade
OM: DAProm
Data Formação: 28/11/1992
Data Nascimento:
Idade: 46
Nr de FA Consideradas: 1

COMPETÊNCIAS		SÍNTESE DO DESEMPENHO*	DESCRIÇÃO DAS FAIXAS DO DESEMPENHO* MPC: Média por Competência
BÁSICAS	CAMARADAGEM	●	▲ Excep[illegible]onal MPC ≥ 9,5
	DEDICAÇÃO	●	
	DISCIPLINA	●	
	INICIATIVA	●	
	INTEGRIDADE	●	
	RESISTÊNCIA FÍSICA	●	
	RESPONSABILIDADE	●	● Muito Bom 8,5 ≤ MPC < 9,5
	TÉCNICO-PROFISSIONAL	●	
ESPECÍFICAS	AUTOAPERFEIÇOAMENTO	×	
	COMUNICAÇÃO	●	
	CONHECIMENTO INSTITUCIONAL	●	
	CORAGEM MORAL	●	
	CRIATIVIDADE	×	● Bom 6,0 ≤ MPC < 8,5
	CULTURA GERAL	●	
	DIREÇÃO E CONTROLE	●	
	DISCRIÇÃO	×	
	ESTABILIDADE EMOCIONAL	×	
	FLEXIBILIDADE	×	
	LIDERANÇA	●	● Oportunidade de MPC < 6,0
	OBJETIVIDADE	×	
	PERSISTÊNCIA	×	
	POSTURA E APRESENTAÇÃO	●	
	PRODUTIVIDADE	×	
	SOCIABILIDADE	●	
	TATO	×	× Desempenho não
	ZELO	×	

OBSERVAÇÕES:
* Somente avaliações do Sistema de Gestão do Desempenho (SGD).
** A média do perfil 2016 considera o Sist Avl anterior a 2015 (2011, 2012, 2013, 2014) e as Avl SIV/SEV 2015 do SGD. No ano seguinte, exclui as Avl mais antigas do Sist anterior (2011) e acrescenta mais um ano de avaliação SIV/SEV do SGD.
Ex: Perfil 2016: (Soma Avl 2011, 2012, 2013, 2014 antigas + Avl SGD 2015) / 5
Perfil 2017: (Soma Avl 2012, 2013, 2014 antigas + Soma Avl SGD 2015 e 2016) / 5
Perfil 2018: (Soma Avl 2013, 2014 antigas + Soma Avl SGD 2015, 2016 e 2017) / 5
Perfil 2019: (Soma Avl 2014 antigas + Soma Avl SGD 2015, 2016, 2017 e 2018) / 5

Bras[illegible]-DF, 1 de Maio de 2016

Gen Div
Diretor de Avaliação e Promoções

Figure 3. Report template that served as "guide" to build the report.

Professionals in JasperReports know the difficulty in formatting a report as complex as this, so much so that some prefer not to venture. However, reports provide a lot of function points as a measure to estimate the system size, ensuring larger, more rewarding results from a financial point of view [17]. Therefore, no software factory will ignore this practice.

To aid in the experiment, the stakeholders have provided a psychologist, whose main function would be to analyze the developers over of the more cognitive aspects, such as fatigue, while also monitoring of the interviews.

2) Description of Experiment: The team of the Brazilian Armys Performance Management Project performed the experiment. It was conducted in an isolated room, and carried out by three pairs of certified developers, all of which were timed, in accordance to the following:

TABLE II. DESCRIPTION OF EXPERIENCE.

OBJECT OF THE EXPERIMENT	Create a complex report of one of the system's activities, SGD, containing a relatively heavy image and 45 attributes.
USED TOOLS	Programming language: Java other tools: IDE Eclipse, JUnit and IReport.
METHODOLOGY	Alpha team: Development using TDD only. Beta team: Development using TDD with Mock Object;
TIMING	The stopwatches were linked at the beginning of implementation experiment, but had no finishing time preset.

A. Sequence of Activities

First, we conceived the construction of a report, where the sequence of the activities of developers should rotate around through the steps shown in Fig. 4:

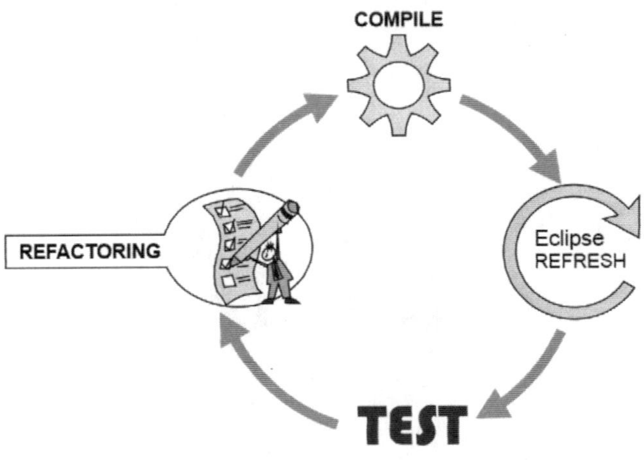

Figure 4. Report construction with TDD

Performing that activity to build reports with the aforementioned tools is extremely strenuous, since the developer uses a lot of manual effort to draw pictures, frames, lines and put texts in places previously defined by the template that serves as a guide, see Fig. 3. The time spent on the activity could harm the progress of timelines, creating frustrations and stress. Because of this, the developer should focus their tasks exactly in this manual effort, not worrying about the collection and processing of data, and thus gaining additional time.

When using Eclipse IDE, developer reports required the execution of a "refresh" in preparation for the report, after refactoring and recompiling the report. Only after that could they call the run-time report. Such process is tiresome and time-consuming. When running a report he needed to go to the database and bring the data to fill the report. This does not seem very productive.

Before connecting the chronometers, each team received the complete description for making the Mock Object and the corresponding business rules, consisting of:

1) **Alpha Team**: The report should present the data from a database, consisting basically of an object with 45 attributes and one more consisting of type byte array - an image. It was delivered to staff together with the business rules for the connection and information, as well as a report template as a guide, Fig. 3.

2) **Beta Team**: The report should present the data from a Mock Object, consisting basically of an object with 45 attributes and one more consisting of type byte array - an image. It was explained also that this object should be an identical copy of the original object. The names of the attributes for making the Mock Object were delivered along with the business rules as well as the report template as a guide, Fig. 3.

IV. RESULTS

For a better understanding, we have grouped the results into two subsections, with the metrics in the first subsection and the analysis in the second.

A. Presentation

Prior to the experiment, we created an index to measure the work of developers around seven items we deem relevant for the study. This index was scaled from 2 to 10 points. To understand it better, Table 3 shows this index in more detail. Fig. 5, along with Table 4, present the final result of the experiment.

TABLE III. DESCRIPTION AND CONTENT OF THE INDEXES.

Index	*Orientation index*
10	Higher than expected.
8	Sometimes higher than expected.
6	Expected.
4	Sometimes lower than expected.
2	Below expected.

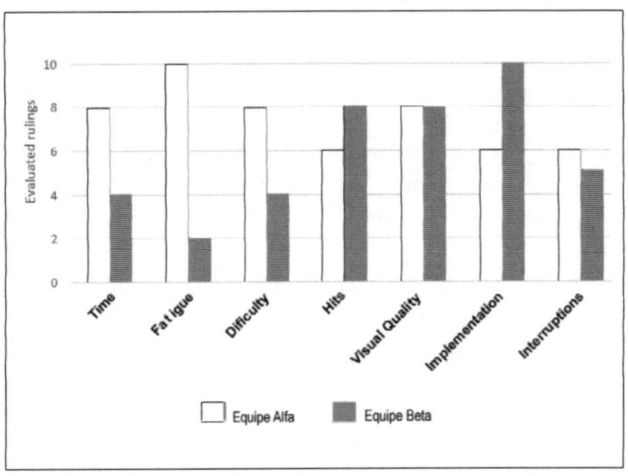

Figure 5. Results with seven variables.

Where:

1) **Time**: Average Results of chronometers after delivery of work, marked to the accuracy of seconds;
2) **Fatigue**: The developer reported extreme tiredness, often interpreted as a painful sensation, result of physical and mental effort;
3) **Difficulty**: The developer reported feeling some difficulty performing the work required;
4) **Hits**: By examining the code, the developer has submitted correct answers;
5) **Visual quality**: On visual inspection, the work presented refinements;
6) **Implementation**: correct implementation of the business rules and alignment with the template which was the implementation guide;
7) **Interruptions**: The developer interrupted the proceedings to ask questions.

Table 4 shows the final result of the experiment, the time spent per each participant to carry out the work, and the number of interruptions of each to the removal of doubts.

TABLE IV. TIMEKEEPING TEAMS.

Team	*Developer*	*Time*	*Interruptions*
A	1	3h 35m 37s	6
	2	3h 15m 08s	5
	3	3h 25m 15s	7
B	4	1h 35m 47s	4
	5	1h 15m 22s	6
	6	1h 40m 57s	4

The Time column displays the time, we measurements for all developers and the Interruptions column shows the stops made to clear doubts from developers in relation to business rules considered by them as confusing. Each participant possessed their corresponding timer, in order not to invalidate the experiment.

B. Analysis

Analyzing the results, we confirmed our suspicions and were not surprised that the Beta Team presented the best performance, both from a qualitative point of view, as well as quantitative. The disparities are more relevant in the following items: **Fatigue**, **Time** and **Difficulty**. Notably, the Fatigue presented by Alpha Team was most notorious.

TIME

In relation to the measured time, we see that no individual participant fulfilled the expectations. However, the Beta Team, which used Mock Objects, spent nearly half the time of the Alpha Team to solve the problem. Fig. 6 shows the data of Table 4 in a chart showing the real-time taken from their stopwatches on the y-axis, where we can see more clearly the disparity. The developer 6 from Beta Team has most experience among the other.

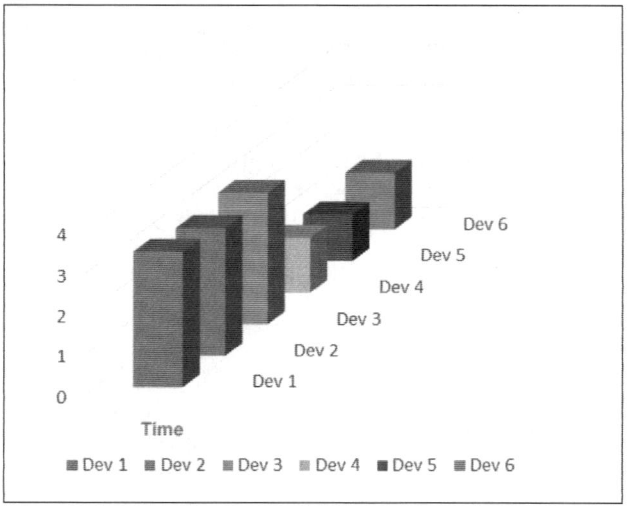

Figure 6. Analysis of time developers.

FATIGUE

Fig. 7 shows the measurement of fatigue. Such measurement was done empirically, by conducting interviews with developers. The score was measured based on reports and on a psychological evaluation. To this regard, a second interview was necessary, this time with a psychologist, to evaluate the general conditions of the participants and greater accuracy of the calculation. The graph below is materializing these indexes.

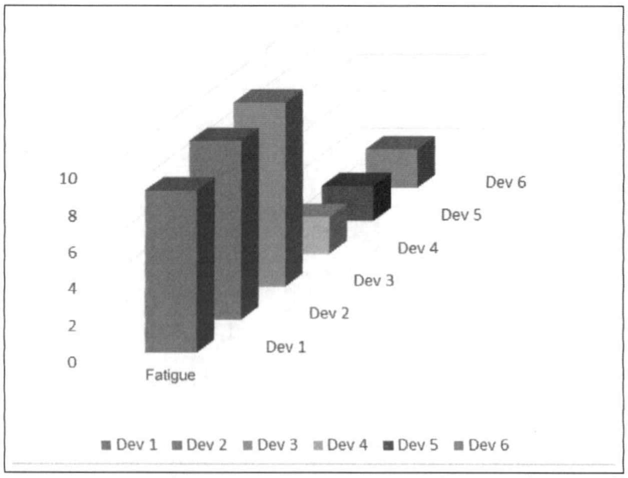

Figure 7. Analysis of fatigue developers.

TIME x FATIGUE

Analyzing fatigue and time, side by side, we can see a huge disparity between the teams. It can be seen quite clearly that the Beta Team, represented by the participants 4, 5 and 6, showed less wear than the Alfa team. It was a result we expected, since the Beta team was the one who was using Mock Object in the experiment. This analysis can be seen in detail in Fig. 8.

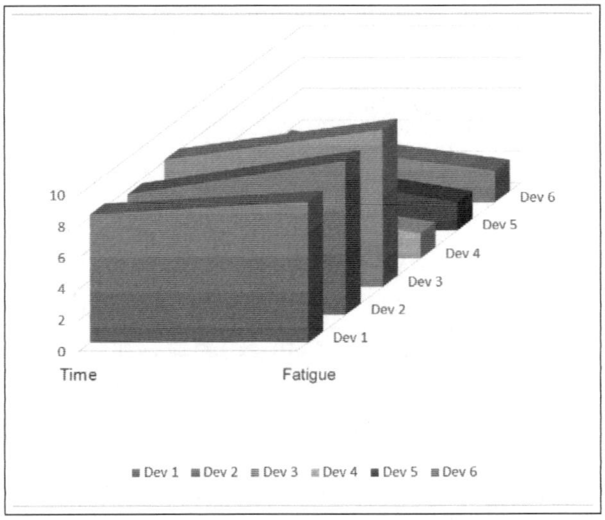

Figure 8. Relationship between time and fatigue.

V. CONCLUSION

In this paper, we present the use of Mock Objects with TDD, a few quotes on the subject and an experiment in the laboratory which demonstrates the practice of this activity. The experiment had two multidisciplinary teams that conducted a study, consisting of the preparation of a report considered quite complex, using the IReport and Eclipse IDE tools, the use of timing and direct observation of the leader.

For the experiment, seven items were submitted for evaluation: elaboration time, fatigue presented by the developers, perception of difficulty reported by the participants, number of hits, visual quality of the work, correct implementation of business rules and the number of interruptions per participant. Each of the items were measured empirically by using a scale of 2 to 10. For the analysis of results, we infer that the adoption of Mock Objects can be a good strategy when work requires great effort from developers. However, one more refined analysis of the situation may provide better subsidies for decision-making.

There is strong evidence for the growth of TDD practice in future. In recent years, the academic community has been conducting various experiments to show empirically that TDD helps the software development process. Some of these studies are done by professors well known in the community, such as prof. Laurie Williams (North Carolina State University) [18] and Prof. David Janzen (California Polytechnic State University) [19].

The Brazilian Army collaborated with researchers providing the means to carry out this work, bringing an important contribution to the science of Software Engineering. Based on the studies in this field, we believe that the TDD process will continue to be of interest to researchers.

REFERENCES

[1] E. N. C. Borges, "Benefits of test driven development," Universit of Rio Grande do Sul/Computer Institute, 2006.

[2] A. Leon and A. S. Koch, Agile software development evaluating the methods for your organization. Artech House, Inc., 2004.

[3] K. Beck et al., "Manifesto for agile software development," 2001.

[4] K. Beck, "Embracing change with extreme programming," Computer, vol. 32, no. 10, 1999, pp. 70–77.

[5] ——, "Extreme programming explained: embrace change," 2000.

[6] H. Baumeister and M. Wirsing, "Applying test-first programming and iterative development in building an e-business application," in International Conference on Advances in Infrastructure for e-Business, e-Education, e-Science, and e-Medicine on the Internet, SSGRR 2002, LAquila, Italy, 2002.

[7] W. Marrero and A. Settle, "Testing first: emphasizing testing in early programming courses," in ACM SIGCSE Bulletin, vol. 37, no. 3. ACM, 2005, pp. 4–8.

[8] M. Fowler, "Refactoring: Improving the design of existing code," in 11th European Conference. Jyväskylä, Finland, 1997.

[9] K. Beck, Test-driven development: by example. Addison-Wesley Professional, 2003.

[10] S. Yenduri and L. A. Perkins, "Impact of using test-driven development: A case study." in Software Engineering Research and Practice, 2006, pp. 126–129.

[11] T. Mackinnon, S. Freeman, and P. Craig, "Endo-testing: unit testing with mock objects," Extreme programming examined, 2001, pp. 287–301.

[12] B. Stroustrup and D. Lenkov, "Run-time type identification for c++(revised yet again)," document X3J16/92-0121, American National Standards Institute Accredited Standards Committee, Tech. Rep., 1992.

[13] M. Fowler, "Mocks arent stubs," 2007.

[14] K. Lieberherr, I. Holland, and A. Riel, "Object-oriented programming: An objective sense of style," in ACM SIGPLAN Notices, vol. 23, no. 11. ACM, 1988, pp. 323–334.

[15] S. Freeman, T. Mackinnon, N. Pryce et al., "Mock roles, objects," in Companion to the 19th annual ACM SIGPLAN conference on Object-oriented programming systems, languages, and applications. ACM, 2004, pp. 236–246.

[16] M. Brown and E. Tapolcsanyi, "Mock object patterns," in The 10th Conference on Pattern Languages of Programs, Monticello, USA, 2003.

[17] G. C. Low and D. R. Jeffery, "Function points in the estimation and evaluation of the software process," Software Engineering, IEEE Transactions on, vol. 16, no. 1, 1990, pp. 64–71.

[18] W. Laurie, "Laurie Williams - profile," http://collaboration.csc.ncsu.edu/laurie/, 2016, [Online; accessed 08-August-2016].

[19] D. Janzen, "David Janzen - profile," http://users.csc.calpoly.edu/~djanzen/, 2016, [Online; accessed 08-August-2016].

FAST: Framework for Automating Software Testing

Ana Paula Furtado[1,2], Silvio Meira
[1]Informatics Centre – CIn
Federal University of Pernambuco
Recife, Brazil
e-mail: {apccf, srlm}@cin.ufpe.br

Carlos Santos, Tereza Novais, Marcelo Ferreira
[2]Recife Centre for Advanced Studies and Systems – CESAR
Recife, Brazil
e-mail: {carlosdombosco,terezanovais, marsantosfer}@gmail.com

Abstract— **The automation of software testing has played an important role in assessing the quality of software prior to delivering the product to the market. Several practices to introduce test automation are found both in the literature and in practice. However, most of these are not directly related to how automation practices could be systematically introduced into a software development context. Therefore, this paper describes a study which is still in progress on the best practices of test automation and how they can be systematically introduced into the software development process. It is in this context that this article presents and describes FAST – Framework for Automating Software Testing and does so by defining automation levels, areas and practice areas. The methodology used for this research is based on a systematic review of the literature, empirical research, a focus group and a case study. The initial general approach of the framework has been defined and will undergo this method of evaluation in order to collect feedback and identify improvements that need to be made in order to produce the complete version of the framework.**

Keywords* - *software testing automation; software testing; process improvement; software quality.

I. Introduction

Test automation is the use of software to support test activities. It is considered an important topic of research and has been intensively studied in the literature [25]. However, despite its wide use, there are still gaps between existing approaches to test automation and its use in the software industry. The process of test automation needs time to mature: the creation of an infrastructure for tests for automation requires time and for automation-related processes to mature [25]. If the strategy for introducing automation in a project were to be inappropriate, this would not allow the company to reap the benefits related to test automation. Moreover, a large amount of time and resources is needed to support testing activities in the software development process [21]. For example, based on the model developed by Kit [17], it is estimated that software testing uses up to 80% of the total cost of software development, while the use of test automation could reduce the software development effort by up to 50%. Fewster [8] states that automating the running of tests is becoming more popular due to the need to improve the quality of software, whilst the complexity of software systems is becoming greater.

Despite the need to provide test automation techniques, there is still a lack of approaches and guidelines to assist with the design, implementation, and maintenance of test automation approaches [33]. Based on the gaps derived from observations in the software industry and on academic research, the problem related to this study can be stated as: **How should software test automation be introduced in the software development process?**

The main goal of this research is to produce a framework for software testing that could be used by the software industry to support the systematic introduction of test automation in the software development process. More specifically, we propose a test automation framework to reduce costs and improve product quality during the life-cycle of software development.

The rest of this paper is organized as follows. Section 2 gives a review of the literature followed, in Section 3, by a description of the research methodology. Section 4 introduces the technical approach and how it has been assessed so far. Finally, Section 5 contains some concluding remarks and offers suggestions for future studies.

II. Literature Background

This study is based on the concepts and theory associated with testing in the software engineering domain, more precisely in the area of test automation. Many of the tasks and activities of tests can be automated, as can aspects of testing techniques. Many additional test tasks and activities can be supported by software-based tools, such as test case management; test monitoring and control; test data generation; static analysis; test case generation; test case execution; test environment implementation and maintenance; and session-based testing [14].

With a view to improving software quality, some studies present technical approaches to introduce testing within the software development context, by defining maturity models. Over the years, some maturity models and approaches have been developed, including models specifically related to the software testing area (those related to this study), as well as generic ones.

The first model to appear was the Software Capability Maturity Model – CMM-SW [23]. From that point on, some models appeared in order to present maturity models in the test process, such as MMAST [20], TAP [29], TMM [30], TCMM [2], TIM [7], TPI [19], TOM [32], TSM [11], TMMI [31], MPT.Br [10], and TAIM [6]. Besides these, some maturity models mention best practices for software development processes, without specifically focusing on testing discipline, such as CMM-SW [23], CMMI [28] and MPS.Br [27]. However, most of the test automation-related studies are defined as maturity models. These require levels of implementation and maturity assessment and this is one of the differences between these models and the one set out in this article.

In addition, except for Test Automation Improvement Model (TAIM), these models do not directly address techniques to introduce test automation into software development and therefore they do not answer the research question that this paper poses. On the other hand, TAIM presents a model based on measurement to support automation and the steps for improvement to be followed in 10 key areas and 1 general area. This approach is defined as a maturity model but it does not show what steps towards maturity must be taken in order to introduce automation.

Another approach related to this is the Maturity Model for Automated Software Testing (MMAST). This is a model that was developed for manufacturers of computerized medical equipment and its purpose is to define the appropriate level of automation into which an equipment manufacturer fits. It has four maturity levels: Level 1 - accidental automation, level 2 - beginning automation, level 3 - intentional automation and Level 4 - advanced automation. Despite being a maturity model, it has neither key areas nor process areas and its description is very broad and does not include matters as to how test automation can, in fact, be performed.

The Testing Assessment Program (TAP) is a maturity model which consists of 5 maturity levels, namely: initial and ad hoc (chaotic); repeatable and intuitive; defined qualitative; quantitative managed; and optimizing continuous improvement. Maturity is evaluated based on four key areas, namely: goals, people, management and techniques. however, the literature has only superficial descriptions of the model that impede it from making a more detailed analysis.

Test Maturity Model (TMM) is a model with 5 maturity levels: Level 1 - initial, Level 2 - phase definition, Level 3 - integration, Level 4 - management and measurement and Level 5 - optimization/ defect prevention and quality control. However, TMM does not discuss any issue directly related to test automation.

Testing Capability Maturity Model (TCMM) consists of 5 maturity levels: initial, repeatable, defined, managed and optimizing. The model includes key areas for each maturity level. However, the little information available does not describe TCCM appropriately so that what automation issues are present in the model can be analyzed.

Testability Support Model (TSM) was developed with a view to identifying actions that can improve the ability that a system has to be testable. This has three levels of maturity and 6 Key Support Areas, namely: Software Engineering Infrastructure, Project plans, Product information, Software design, Testware and Test environments. However, there is little information available on the model that enables it to be analyzed in greater depth.

Test Improvement Model (TIM) is a model intended to guide testing functions in their improvement work which has a four-step improvement ladder. The initial level has been given the number zero, as it is a non-compliance level and the other levels are numbered from 1 to 4, namely: Level 1 – optimizing, Level 2 – risk-lowering, Level 3 – cost-effectiveness and Level 4 – baseline. It has 5 key areas, namely: organization; planning and tracking; test case, testware and reviews. In its scope, testware deals with the actual testing procedures that are run, the support software, the data sets that are used to run the tests, and the supporting documentation. It includes managing the configuration of testware and the use of testware and tools. The model also mentions that tools can assist in performing non-creative and repetitive tasks, such as running the same test cases several times and automating testing activities. However, no guidelines are presented to support them

The Test Process Improvement Model (TPI) has 3 levels and 14 scales. Each level consists of a number of scales and these indicate which key areas need to be improved. The levels are: controlled, efficient and optimizing. The model also has 20 key areas, 1 of which is testware management. The model states that testing products (testware) should be maintainable and reusable and so they must be managed. Yet, test automation itself is absent in the model.

The objective of the Organization Testing Maturity Model (TOM) is to identify and prioritize organizational bottlenecks and generate solutions to these problems. A questionnaire is used to identify and prioritize both the symptoms and suggestions for improvement. Despite its name, it is not characterized as maturity model, as its focus is to solve problems and not improve testing in the organization, and there is no information on test automation.

The Test Maturity Model Integration (TMMi) is a model for improving the testing process developed as a guide and reference framework. It follows the staged version of CMMI, and also uses the concepts of maturity levels for evaluating and improving the testing process. TMMi consists of 5 maturity levels, namely: Level 1 - initial; Level 2 - managed; Level 3 - defined; Level 4 - measured; and Level 5 - optimization. Each level of maturity presents a set of process areas that must maturity at that level, in which each level of maturity is the starting point for the next level.

Despite being a maturity model specifically for the test area and its having systematic ways to enter the practice of software testing in the context of projects under development, it does not have a process area specifically dedicated to tools and/or test automation, nor does it include systematic suggestions for improving testing automation.

The Brazilian Maturity Model for Testing (MPT.BR) is a reference model that defines, implements and improves testing processes based on its being continuously improved. It also tackles the same approach to improving the testing process by using process areas that include the best practices of testing activities throughout the testing life cycle of the product. The model has 5 maturity levels, namely: Level 1 - partially managed; Level 2 - managed; Level 3 - defined; Level 4 - prevention of defects and Level 5 - automation and optimization.

Within the ambit of test automation, the model shows the process area of Automation of Executing the Test (AET), the purpose of which is to develop and maintain a strategy to automate the running of the test. This process area comprises the following list of specific practices:

- Defining the objectives of the automation regime;
- Defining criteria for selecting test cases for automation;
- Defining a framework for automating testing;
- Managing automated testing incidents;
- Ensuring adherence to the objectives of automation; and
- Analyzing the return on investment in automation.

Although the specific practices have a systematic way for introducing testing, they are still vague as to identifying the moment at which automation is to be performed. There is no specific information on introducing automation into the software development process, besides its not saying which testing levels can be automated. The written format is generic and comprehensive, into which every type of automation can fit. However, it does not help choosing where automation should start and what benefits can be achieved.

Therefore, this article puts forward a framework that can fill this gap in current research and aids taking a more flexible approach, for which there are no strict steps for introducing practices as this is in a maturity model. In this context, the next section will detail the research methodology associated with this study.

III. Research Methodology

The research methodology planned for this study has three phases. The first is a **Bibliographical Review**, which comprises an exploratory review and a systematic review and the second is that of defining the **Proposal.** The latter is developed, underpinned by an empirical research including conducting interviews in the industry. The third phase is **Evaluation**, which will be conducted by using a focus group and a case study. Fig. 1 illustrates this approach.

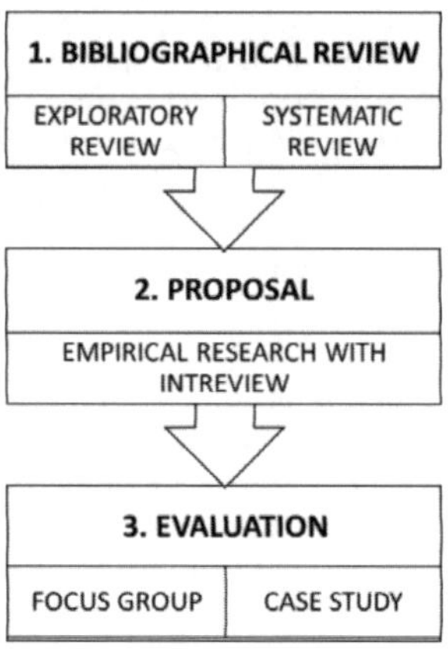

Figure 1. The design of the research activities | Source: author.

A. Exploratory Review

An exploratory review, or a bibliographical review, is a critical, meticulous and comprehensive analysis of current publications in a given field of knowledge. It is an important step in the research, since it supports understanding the subject of research and assessment, if this is worth studying, and provides insights into how a researcher can define the scope for a particular area of interest [4]. The literature review correlates the research to the ongoing dialogue in the extensive literature, thereby filling in gaps and extending prior studies [22].

The main objective of this research instrument is to identify and explore publications related to the area being studied in order to learn how this problem has been approached and analyzed in previous studies with a view to reaching a better understanding of the research problem being investigated.

An ad-hoc bibliographical review has been undertaken by conducting searches of the scientific libraries available, such as IEEE Explorer, Engineering Village (including Inspec and Compendex), Scopus, ACM, Google Scholar and Springer.

B. Systematic Review

According to Kitchenham [18], a systematic review of the literature is a way to identify, assess and interpret all relevant research available on a specific research question, or related phenomena of interest.

In order to achieve these benefits, a systematic review is under development which will be used to help assess the benefits and limitations of software testing automation and to analyze how the cost and quality of software is affected as a result of introducing automation practices.

In this research, an analysis is made of material published between 2005 and 2015, based on the main libraries such as IEEE Explorer, Engineering Village (including Inspec and Compendex), Scopus, ACM, Google Scholar and Springer. In addition, several relevant journals and conference proceedings are examined under the manual method. This is work-in-progress, during which data are being extracted by automatic searches. These data will be used to synthesize this study and report the results.

This systematic review is very important because it will ensure that all relevant studies in the literature are mapped. This will underpin how best to define the strategy needed to introduce test automation and guarantee that all related work is known and assessed in this research.

C. Empirical Research with Interview

The empirical research with interview, based on experts' opinion, was one of the methods chosen to support this study. This consists of a comprehensive system for collecting information to describe, compare or explain knowledge, attitudes and behavior [24].

A group of experts in software testing automation was selected in order to collect their opinions, attitudes and expectations about the research questions for this study.

The survey was organized in three parts. The objective of **Part 1** was to gather personal information and information on the professional background. The goal of **Part 2** was to validate the problems of test automation, and this included analyzing the challenges, problems, benefits of the testing automation area and determining what gaps there are. **Part 3** focused on analyzing the automation strategy used in the companies, and included questions about the test strategy, levels of automation and technologies used. Finally, the aim of **Part 4** was to evaluate what opinions experts have as to the hypothesis of this study.

This survey was applied to 4 experts on testing, 2 of whom work in England and the other 2 in Brazil. They work directly on test activities in their companies and each of them has had more than ten years' experience in testing.

The results from **Part 2** mainly showed that there is a shortage of qualified professional who can engage on test automation and this makes it harder to introduce automation practices into a project. Moreover, the lack of senior management support also makes it more difficult to include automation practices in a project. Moreover, the difficulties faced in setting up an automation environment is also an impediment, as is the need for rework on tests assets due to changes made in requirements.

In **Part 2**, the benefits gained from test automation were: an increase in the team's velocity; more frequent delivery of working software; code continuous integration; fast execution of a group of test cases; parallel work can be done while tests are running; better visibility of code test coverage; and increasing the likelihood of finding new errors before delivering software to the market.

In **Part 3**, the intention was to collect experiences on how test automation was first introduced into a project. No results could be reached from this question, which re-emphasized the hypothesis of this study that there are no systematic ways to introduce test automation in a project that has not implemented this practice when that project was under development.

D. Focus Group

Using a focus group is an approach in which a group of people gather to evaluate concepts and/or problems [3], and consists of a survey to obtain qualitative insights and feedback from experts in certain subjects. A focus group meeting involves semi-structured group interviews, in which the interactions in the group are explicitly used to generate data. Participants offer personal opinions but can also interact based on the response of other participants while the interviewer acts as moderator so that the interview remains focused on its objectives [9].

The objective of the focus group in the context of this paper is to evaluate the proposal of this thesis with a view to collecting suggestions for improving and developing the proposal prior to conducting the case study.

E. Case Study

A case study can be defined as a research strategy on understanding the dynamics present in a given environment, in accordance with the view of Eisenhardt [5]. A case study is an empirical method that targets analyzing a phenomenon in a given context. The purpose of the case study is to seek pieces of formal evidence by using variables that can be measured and to draw inferences coming from the example for a given population.

Case studies are appropriate when the boundaries between the phenomenon and the context are not clearly defined, and the type of evidence is considered to be very rich and contextualized [9].

In this context, a case study should be used as a tool to validate the solution proposed, and will be conducted as proposed by Runeson and Höst [26], based on the following steps:

- Designing the case study;
- Preparing for data collection;
- Collecting evidence;
- Analyzing the data collected; and
- Writing a Report.

The case to be applied will be in a software development company that has an academic management product that integrates all areas of the educational institution. The data collection method will start from the principle that the researcher will have direct contact with the data and collect them in real-time (first degree data), by using interviews and focus groups.

Data analysis shall be conducted quantitatively, using correlation analysis, which describes how a given measurement of a process activity is related to the same measurement in a previous process, and thus compare them. The measurement being compared is the cost of testing, by assessing whether it decreases when automated testing is introduced into the software development process. In addition, the quality of the software shall also be analyzed from when automated testing was introduced in the software development process.

Based on all observations so far gathered, in line with the steps defined in the research methodology, the technical approach has been developed and will be detailed in the following Section.

IV. Technical Approach

The approach developed to support the objective of this study and to answer the research questions is the **Framework for Automating Software Testing (FAST)**.

According to ISO/IEC/IEEE [16], a framework can be defined as "a reusable design (models and/or code) that can be refined (specialized) and extended to provide some portion of the overall functionality of many applications".

Although conceptually, the term 'framework' is more related to the technical component of a software, this study uses this term in order to make it clearer how a group of best practices can be adapted to a project in accordance with its specific needs so as to reap the best benefits of software testing automation. FAST differs from a maturity model in that the practice areas are not mandatory and there is no need to certify a company in the framework; and in accordance with the needs of a specific environment, each process area can be applied to a project.

Therefore, FAST is defined in accordance with the components shown in Fig. 2 and described as follows:

- **Automation level.** Determining this is a separate test effort that has its own documentation and resources [15]. This represents the scope within which automation activities will be welcomed in a project;

- **Area** is a general range of interest in which FAST is divided into two parts, Technical and Support, as shown in Fig. 3. It includes what is needed to introduce testing automation techniques into a project and consists of process areas;
- **Process Area** This is a group of related practices in an area that, when implemented collectively, satisfies a set of goals considered important for enhancing that area [28]. Each process area is assigned a specific **purpose**, has **guidelines** that must be implemented, and suggested **work products** that must be produced by engaging on such practices.

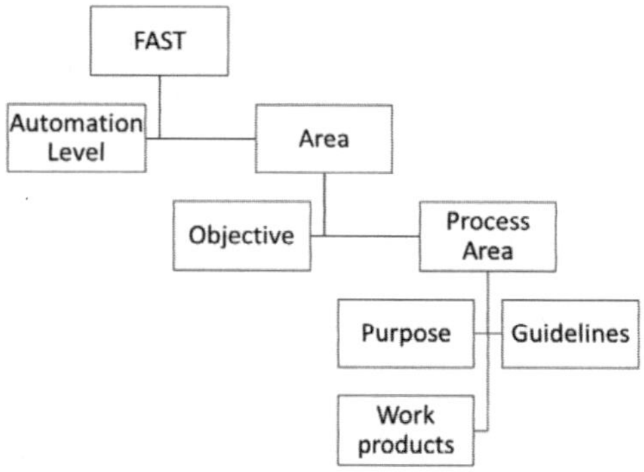

Figure 2. FAST components | Source: author.

The relationship between the areas were defined in accordance with CMMI-DEV [28], where the support process areas address processes that are used in the context of performing other processes. In this case, the Support Area comprises a fundamental support function and relies on the processes of the Technical Area for input. For example, the process area for Project Planning will plan the test strategy for the Process Area of Unit Testing.

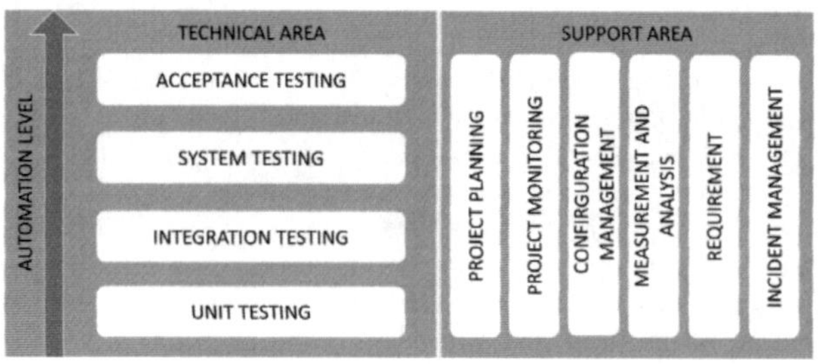

Figure 3. FAST areas | Source: author.

Fig. 3 presents the overall structure of FAST, together with the process areas for each area. The framework can be applied by instantiating it in a project context, where the process areas can be adapted to best fit the environment where it will be applied. The objectives and process areas will be described in the following section.

A. *FAST Support Area*

The objective of the FAST Support area is to cover essential mechanisms to support establishing and maintaining the automation environment. It was developed based on the reference model of both CMMI-DEV, which covers a generic view of best practices for software development projects, and TMMI, which has a group of guidelines specific to test projects. The objective of process is to undertake practices that are fundamental to systematically introducing automation practices but are not specifically directed towards automation practices. The objective and guidelines of the process areas from the support area are given below.

Project Planning

The purpose of Project Planning is to define a plan to support setting up an automated test project for which the **guidelines** are as follows:

- Plan test project;
- Define test strategy;
- Make estimates;
- Analyze project and product risks; and
- Obtain commitment to the plan.

The **work products** related to this process area can be a test plan which has the information required by the guidelines.

Project monitoring

The purpose of Project Monitoring is to provide an understanding of the project's progress so that appropriate corrective actions can be taken when the project's performance significantly diverges from the plan [28].

It has the following **guidelines**:

- Monitor progress against the plan;
- Monitor product quality;
- Conduct corrective actions as per the demand; and
- Manage corrective actions to closure.

The **work products** related to this process area can be defined as project monitoring sheets, together with systems to track adherence to the project schedule and issues from start to closure.

Configuration management

One reason maintainability is so important is that without it tests cannot be accumulated. Therefore, the purpose of Configuration Management is to establish and maintain the integrity of testware by defining the management system for the configuration, for which there are the following **guidelines**:

Establish project baselines;

- Control and track changes; and
- Establish the integrity of the project.

The main **work products** related to this process area are the configuration management system together with its plan.

Measurement and analysis

The purpose of this process area is to define, collect, analyze and apply measurements to support an organization in objectively evaluating the effectiveness and efficiency of the test process [31]. In this case, all indicators defined are specifically aligned to the automation strategy, in order to best achieve its desired objectives. The **guidelines** for this are as follows:

- Define test indicators for the project;
- Specify test measures in terms of data collection and storage procedures;

- Specify analysis procedures;
- Collect test measurement data;
- Analyze test measurement data;
- Communicate results; and
- Store data and results.

The main **work product** here is the measurement and analysis plan, together with the data collected and formally analyzed.

Requirement

The purpose of this process area is to clearly define the test automation requirements and the following **guidelines** area associated with this process area:

- Define what products need to be automated;
- Prioritize requirements; and
- Maintain the traceability of requirements.

The **work products** in this case are those on the list of requirements, for which tests will be automated in the software development process.

Incident management

The purpose of this is process area is to objectively define the mechanism and procedures to formally monitor all product incidents derived from test automation activities. It supports testers in the investigation and documentation of test incident reports and the retesting of defects when required [10].

In order to achieve this, the following **guidelines** are suggested:

- Establish incident management system;
- Register, classify and prioritize incidents;
- Solve and track incident upon its closure; and
- Escalate non-solved incidents.

The main **work product** related to this process area is the incident management system.

B. FAST Technical Area

The objective of the FAST Technical area is to establish and maintain automated mechanisms for testing software applications throughout test levels in order to produce test environments that can be developed, managed and maintained efficiently. The technical area consists of four process areas, in accordance with the automation levels that a software can undergo, and its objective is to describe practices to support automation activity. The details of the processes areas of the technical area re given below.

Unit Testing

The objective of this process area is to provide mechanisms so that unit tests are implemented in a systematic and documented way in order to maximize the benefits of automation in the test project. This area has the following **guidelines**:

- Design the test suite;
- Implement the refined plan and test design;
- Measure the test unit;
- Run the test procedures;
- Evaluate test completion; and
- Evaluate the effort and test unit.

The **work products** related to this process area are the test items, the design of the test specification [15], test summary report [15], and reporting the failures found.

Integration Testing

The purpose of the Integration Testing process area is to evaluate the integration between software components, to ensure that the architectural design of the system is implemented correctly [13][13]. It tests the interface between components and interactions in different parts of the system, such as operating system, the file system and the interface between the systems [1]

This process area has the following **guidelines**:

- Design the integration approach (bottom-up or top-down), in accordance with the system's requirements;
- Design the set of integration tests;
- Implement the design of the integration tests:
- Run the test procedures;
- Assess whether the tests have been completed and whether they have achieved the required coverage of the requirements; and
- Formally record and direct the non-conformities and restrictions arising from the integration actions.

The **work products** related to this process area are the set of integration tests and formally reported results.

System Testing

The purpose of the System Testing process is to test the integrated and complete systems so as to assess its ability to communicate with each other and validate whether the systems are in accordance with the specifications of the requirements [15].

The objective of this process area is to test the finalized system and analyze the behavior of the system as a whole in order to analyze compatibility with the specified requirements, and can be performed in line with the testing approach selected, such as risk-based products, business processes or other description of the behavior of a high-level system [1].

This process area has the following **guidelines**:

- Establish the testing approach of the system;
- Select the testing techniques of the system;
- Design the set of system tests;
- Implement the system tests;
- Run the system tests;
- Assess whether the test was completed; and
- Register, formally, and direct non-conformities.

This process area needs to address questions about the selection of requirements so as to generate a group of test cases to be automated and run in the context of a project. The related **work products** are the set of test cases, and the formal record in a specific tool of the results.

Acceptance Testing

The objective of the Acceptance Testing process area is to ensure that the product is working and that it can be presented for acceptance, in which the customer and/or user is expected to be involved [12]. At this level of automation, the object to be tested is the complete system and this must address activities in order to demonstrate the customer's acceptance regarding the final system.

The objective of this process area is to ensure that the suite of acceptance tests, planned in accordance with the strategy and needs of the end user, is implemented so that it can run automatically. To this end, this process area has the following **guidelines**:

- Define acceptance criteria;
- Define the acceptance plan;
- Prepare the testing acceptance environment;
- Assess the conditions of acceptance; and
- Conduct the closure of acceptance.

The **work products** related to this process area are the acceptance plan, the acceptance environment, the suite of acceptance tests, the due register of the test results and incidents recorded and followed upon until closure on the appropriate tool.

In this context, this section presented the FAST way to include the theoretical structure and its process areas. The following section presents the conclusions and future studies planned for this research.

V. CONCLUSIONS

This paper proposes a framework to support the systematic introduction of test automation in the context of software development. The approach was defined by describing automation levels, technical and support areas, and practice areas.

In order to evaluate this general approach, a plan was drawn to conduct a focus group and a case study, in accordance with the descriptions given in the methodology Section, in order to gather feedback on the value of FAST being feasible, complete and adequate. After this phase, it was expected that the description of the framework would be enhanced in order to finalize how to define the framework.

Some threats to this study were identified and are being dealt with in order to minimize side effects to the expected results. The first threat is the possibility of bias while analyzing data from the case studies, since the results of introducing FAST may vary according to the domain of application. In order to minimize this threat, three different scenarios and domains were planned to be part of the scope of the case study, in which the absence of information in a specific context can be complemented by having it in another.

Another threat would be to focus the definition of the framework upon the perspective of the very few authors found in the literature review. Hence, to diminish this possible problem, a systematic review of the literature is being developed to guarantee that all research studies are taken into consideration when developing this project.

Therefore, this work-in-progress offers contributions to research on test automation and its practice, whereby a framework is compiled from a combination of experience, practice and a systematic review of the literature in the form of best practices, which can be applied when running tests in software development.

ACKNOWLEDGMENT

This research work was supported by the Brazilian National Research Council (CNPq) of the Ministry of Science, Technology and Innovation of Brazil, process #206328/2014-1. The international cooperation with the Open University was part of the Science without Borders program (http://www.cienciasemfronteiras.gov.br/web/csf).

REFERENCES

[1] R. Black, E. Veenendaal and D. Graham, Foundations of Software Testing ISTQB Certification. 3rd Edition, Reino Unido, January 2012.

[2] S. M. Burgess and R. D. Drabick, "The I.T.B.G.testing capability maturity model (TCMM)", 1996, available from https://wwwbruegge.informatik.tu-muenchen.de/lehrstuhl_1/files/teaching/ws0708/ManagementSoftwareTesting/12-4-1-FPdef.pdf, retrieved: July, 2016.

[3] S. Caplan, "Using focus group methodology for ergonomic design. Ergonomics", v. 33, n. 5, p. 527-33, 1990.

[4] J. Creswell, Research design: qualitative, quantitative and mixed methods approaches, 4th Edition, Washington D.C., 2014.

[5] K, Eisenhardt, Building theories from case study research. The Academy of Management Review, October 1989.

[6] S. Eldh, K. Andersson, A. Ermedahl and K. Wiklund, "Towards a test automation improvement model (TAIM)", in 014 IEEE Seventh International Conference on Software Testing, Verification and Validation Workshops (ICSTW), Cleveland, pp. 337-342, April 2014.

[7] T. Ericson, A. Subotic and S. Ursing, "TIM - A test improvement", Software Testing Verification and Reliability 7(4), pp. 229-246, December 1998.

[8] M. Fewster, Common Mistakes in Test Automation, Grove Consultant, 2011.

[9] S. Fincher and M. Petre, Computer Science Education Research. Taylor and Francis, January 2004.

[10] A. P. Furtado, M. Gomes, E. Andrade and I. Farias, "MPT.BR: A Brazilian maturity model for testing", in The 12th International Conference on Quality Software (QSIC), Xi'an, pp. 220-229, August 2012.

[11] D. Gelperin, "A testability support model (TSM)", in the fifth International Conference On Software Testing, Analysis & Review, Orlando, Florida, pp. 13-17, May 1996.

[12] A. M. Hass, Guide To Advanced Software Testing, Artech House, London, 2008.

[13] IEEE 610.12 Standard Glossary of Software Engineering Terminology, IEEE Computer Society, 1990.

[14] IEEE 29119-1: Software and Systems Engineering – Software Testing – part 1: Concepts and Definitions, IEEE Computer Society, 2013.

[15] IEEE 829 Standard for Software and System Test Documentation, IEEE Computer Society, 2008.

[16] ISO/IEC/IEEE 24765 International Standard, Systems and Software Engineering Vocabulary, 2010.

[17] E. Kit and S. Finzi, Software testing in the real world: improving the process, Addison-Wesley Publishing Co., New York, 1995.

[18] B. Kitchenham and S. Charters, Guidelines for Performing Systematic Literature Reviews in Software Engineering, Software Engineering Group, School of Computer Science and Mathematics, Keele University, Tech. Rep. EBSE-2007-01, July 2007.

[19] T. Koomen and M. Pol, Test Process Improvement (TPI), A Practical Step-by-step Guide to Structured Testing, Addison-Wesley, 1999.

[20] M. E. Krause, "A maturity model for automated software testing", in Medical Device & Diagnostic Industry Magazine, December 1994, available from https://wwwbruegge.informatik.tu-muenchen.de/lehrstuhl_1/files/teaching/ws0708/ManagementSoftwareTesting/12-4-1-FPdef.pdf, retrieved: July, 2016.

[21] H. K. Leung and L. White, "A cost model to compare regression test strategies," in 1991 Conference on Software Maintenance, Sorrento, pp. 201-208, October 1991.

[22] C. Marshall and G. Rossman, Designing Qualitative Research, SAGE Publications, Washington, DC, USA, 2011.

[23] M. Paulk, C. Weber, S. Garcia, M. Chrissis and B. Bush, "The Capability Maturity", version 1.1., IEEE Software 10, no3 pp. 18-27, 1993.

[24] S. L. Pfleeger and B. A. Kitchenham, "Principles of survey research: part 1: turning lemons into lemonade", ACM SIGSOFT Software Engineering Notes, 26(6), pp. 16-18, 2001.

[25] D. M. Rafi, K. R. K. Moses, K. Petersen and M. V. Mäntylä, "Benefits and limitations of automated software testing: systematic literature review and practitioner survey", in 2012 7th International Workshop on Automation of Software Test (AST), Zurich, p.p. 36-42, June 2012.

[26] P. Runeson and M. Höst, "Guidelines for conducting and reporting case study research in software engineering", In: Empirical Software Engineering Journal, Volume 14, Issue 2, pp. 131-164, April 2009.

[27] Softex, "MPS.BR – Brazilian software process improvement", General Guide, V1.2., Rio de Janeiro, Softex, 2007.

[28] Software Engineering Institute (SEI). CMMI for Software Development, version 1.3, staged representation, Pittsburgh, PA, 2010. Available from: www.sei.cmu.edu/reports/10tr033.pdf, CMU/SEI-2010-TR-033, retrieved: July, 2016.

[29] TAP, Testing Assessment Program (TAP), Software Futures Ltd and IE Testing Consultancy LTD, 1995.

[30] TMM, Test Maturity Model, Illinois Institute of Technology. , Available from http://science.iit.edu/computer-science/research/testing-maturity-model-tmm 2014.08.11 retrieved: July 2016.

[31] TMMI, Test Maturity Model Integration, Release 1.0, TMMi Foundation, Ireland, 2012, Available from http://www.tmmi.org/pdf/TMMi.Framework.pdf 2014.08.11, retrieved: July 2016.

[32] TOM apud R. Swinkels, A Comparison of TMM and Other Test Process Improvement Models, Project Report 12-3-1-FP, 2000.

[33] K. Wiklund, S. Eldh, D. Sundmark and K. Lundqvist , "Technical debt in test automation", in 2012 IEEE Fith International Conference on Software Testing, Verification and Validation (ICST), Montreal, pp. 887-892, April 2012.

Configuration Management to Tests Automatics in a Software Factory

Marcelo dos Santos Ferreira
C.E.S.A.R - Educational
Recife Center for Advanced Studies and Systems
Recife, Brazil
e-mail: marsantosfer@gmail.com

Ana Paula Cavalcanti Furtado
Informatics Center – C.I.n
Federal University of Pernambuco
Recife, Brazil
E-mail: anapaula.cavalcanti@gmail.com

Abstract—**Artifact traceability during software development allows reusability and increases quality and productivity. Software requirements should be traceable because they represent the needs of a certain product. In several processes during software development cycle, requirements are related to other artifacts such as test suites and automation scripts. Configuration management assures the usage of an input file version corresponding to a software requirements version during automated tests. This research proposes an integrated process for software development, using configuration management from requirements up to test suites for automated tests. This article describes the effect of absence of configuration management on the control over software artifacts versions.**

Keywords-configuration management; reuse; tests automations; traceability; sotware requirements;

I. INTRODUCTION

The increasing demand for high quality products, made in shorter time, and at lower cost, requires from both academic world and industry innovative strategies and actions. Because software production is an industry of intangible goods, it has strong challenges in its production line as compared to conventional industry, which has fixed process input, tools, techniques and defined output [1]. Software production is tailor-made work, to fit client needs, with demands on functional and non- functional requirements. These requirements form input artifacts to several processes in a software factory.

During software development, the requirements might change due to variable market needs or legal regulation. Therefore artifacts traceability is necessary during the software building process [1].Configuration management assures artifacts traceability and keeps it in storage to control artifacts versions.

This article describes the impact of lack of configuration management on tools for test automation, and therefore legitimating the research on integrated process applied to software production.

This article has 5 sections, wherein the first section is an introduction. The motivation and problem definition are described in the second section. The third section addresses the methodology and its phases, and the proposed integrated process is discussed in the fourth section. Finally, in the fifth section, we have conclusion and future works.

II. LITERATURE REVIEW

Rework, low-quality products, demotivated teams, high software production and delays are symptoms caused by the absence of configuration management during software development, which directly affect users and development team [2]. This absence of configuration management creates the possibility for a software product does not meet the requirements.

The lack of version control of test suits and/or automatic test script to for the software requirements automation tests tools [1], reduces the reliability of such tools. In this way, software products can present nonconformities affecting directly the product acceptance by the client.

Configuration management (CM) should be active during whole software development, from infrastructure definition to information generation and maintenance. CM will support requirements changes during the development process resulting in flexibility during development. In addition to information and content of software requirements [3], the development process in software factories should perform requirements validations in all process sub-phases in order to guarantee continuous information and its understanding. Isolation of requirements after initiation phase can lead to wrong validation of content and its changes, consequently affecting the product that will be create.

The reusability of artifacts originated from software requirements, as well as source codes, tests suits and/or automatized scripts [4], is impaired by lack of relationship dependence between artifacts. This generates uncertainty concerning completeness of available artifacts, versions, and compatibility to project characteristics [5]. In this way, at each new automated test cycle, a new tests suite and/or automated scripts should be create to validate the most actual software requirements

Configurations management has only as unit control the configuration items [6] that are identified, controlled and kept, according the configurations management plan. The control realized in order to manage configurations does not include dependences and relationships between artifacts, in other words, are isolated unit controls, without dependence relationship with other software artifacts. This configurations management approach has only a data and code reposition function.

The software tests that have as input software requirements to created test plans and tests projects are impaired by the lack of requirements traceability if requested changes are accepted included in requirements during development phase and the information is discontinued [2]. In this case, we might have scenarios where we will obtain software products having old versions of requirements. This affects products certification, as it does not meet their specifications. The tests automation tests when used in software process development [7], has as main function the coverage of regression tests and test suit. At one side, this will open the opportunity for the tests analysts to follow and test new features or to perform exploratory tests. On the other side, the use of automation test tools becomes a risk when tests suites and/or automatized scripts do not correspond to the actual version of software requirements. This will lead to loss of computation and human resources, which should be used to repair the missing update due to lack on artifacts traceability. The losses of computational and human resources reflect on delays in the product delivery and quality.

Based on these scenarios, we formulated the following research question: How to introduce a product-guided configuration management for automation tests in the development process of software factories?

Software requirements traceability was subject of study for Gotel [5] and Antoniol [3]. They realized interviews and surveys to identify support to requirements traceability. In addition, they identified problems related to providers or users of the software requirements. However, the research focus was limited to the requirement creation phase. Our research has the objective show how use configuration management [3] of software requirements and test suites for tests automatization tools will be able to solve several problems found in software factories.

III. RESEARCH METODOLOGY

The research approach was divided in four phases, as shown in Figure 2. The first phase corresponds to a literature review, that comprising bibliographical review and systematic review. In the second phase, we will postulate a proposal. Afterwards, we will evaluate the proposal with a case study and survey research. Finally, phase four should lead to suggestions for improvement.

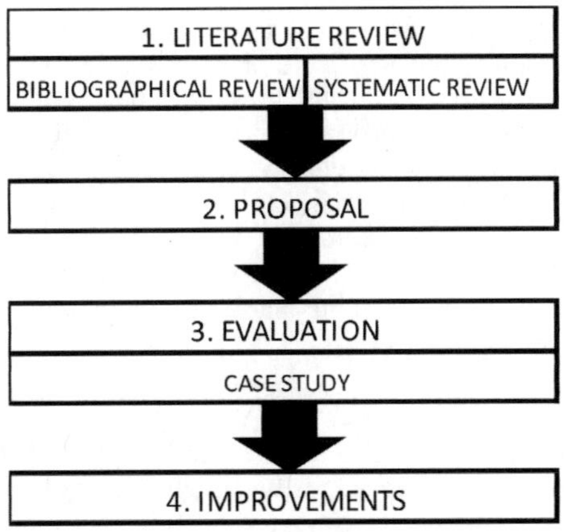

Figure 1. Schematic flow research activities.

A. *Bibliographical Review*

The review has as main objective the identification and exploration of scientific publications related to this study area. It will give an analysis of the previous studies in the field.

This review will be based on articles in the period of 2010 and 2015 available at IEEE digital libraries, ACM, Scopus, and Science Direct.

B. *Systematic Review*

The systematic review provides interpretation of relevant research in the field [8], followed by structure analysis [9] leading to gaps identification which might guide future new investigations in the field [10].

C. *Case study*

The case study has as main objective the analysis of a phenomenon within its context. The experimentations is an attempt to replication the phenomenon, taking into account factors, which affect software engineering results [11].

Software engineering involves development, operation, and maintenance of software and related artifacts [12]. The case study applies the research proposal and experimentation to determine the applicability of proposed solution, and to solve issues that prior application to process were not possible to predict.

D. *Improvements*

The activities performed in this phase are evaluation of current process in the software factory, development of a configuration management plan, implementation and validation. This will be followed by a process of continuous improvements. In short:

- Process implementation, identification of deviations and followed by continuous improvement
- Finally, analysis of proposed process impact.

This process has a requirements information update flow directly affecting the test suits and automated scripts as its differential. In other words, changes realized in software requirements will be able available during the whole software development cycle, and consequently having an efficient management of automation tests.

The research approach presented here will result in a structured research process, which allows more control over activities and as scientific research process, will be applicable to new researches.

In the next session, we will present a proposal of integrated process to insert configuration management in automation tests, including phases, input and output artifacts, roles and responsibilities.

IV. PROPOSAL

The proposal presented here is partially a process of configuration management that might be implemented in a software development company in such way that it includes configurations items updates related to automatic tests. The proposed process objective is to maintain integrity, traceability of artifacts that affects automatic tests, and reuse of software components.

The process presented here was divided in two steps: The first step consists in evaluating the actual process of configuration management of a software factory; this will be used as study case resulting in the identification and analysis of gaps in the process. In the second step, we have a creation of integrated process of configuration management with the purpose to maintain integrity of artifacts during the whole software development cycle, developing the capacity to incorporate project scope changes. Bellow, we have a more detailed description of these two steps.

A. *Actual configurations management process evaluation in a software factory*

An analysis is performed to identify gaps related to items configuration control, and their impact in the utilization of automation tests tools; this step has two phases:

- Actual configuration management evaluation in a software factory chosen as study case. During this phase, we will use quality assurance such as process analysis and quality audits.
- Software development process evaluation. During this phase, we will use quality controls such as root cause diagrams, Pareto diagram, management of change revision and evaluation

B. *Preparation of an integrated configuration management process*

After the first step, we will create an integrated configuration management process to maintain integrity of the software requirements and automatic tests employed during the software development process. As part of the proposed process, we will define activities, roles, artifacts and tools, according description in Figure 2.

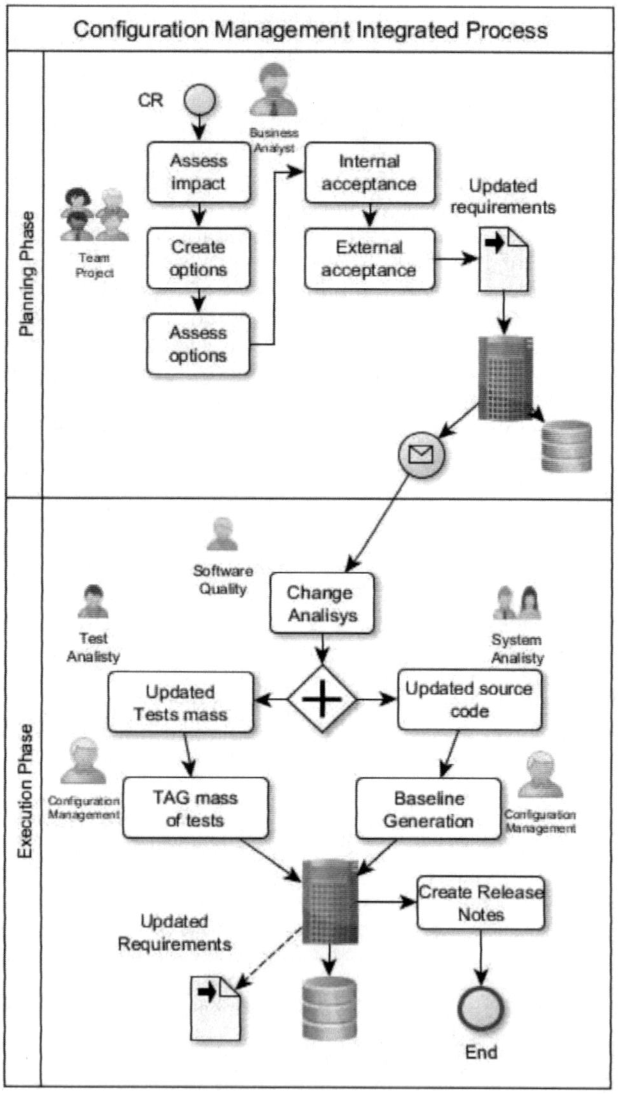

Figure 2. Integrated process flow chart. Source: Autor.

The integrated process is explained bellow

- The process is divided in between the two phases in a software development cycle, known as Planning and Execution Phase.
- During planning phase, we have as start point the changes request. The changes request might be initiated due to market reasons or regulation. The business analyst is responsible for the translation of the changes request into artifacts requirements. The change control is recorded in a bug tacker tool, making it possible to follow its evolution.
- Impact evaluation activities are performed by the project management that uses techniques such as learned lesson and expert opinion, as a technical evaluation of the changes request impact is needed. The changes request will be updated in a bug tracker tool.

- The options creation activity has as goal to generate many scenarios to fulfill the changes request, taking into consideration risk mitigation and impact into the product and finally project objectives. This activity is realized with the whole project team.
- Options validation has as purpose to simulate the implementation results obtained by the different proposed scenarios. After that, an unbiased selection process is possible, discarding the options that do not fit to the boundaries of project. The whole project team will realize this activity.
- After options validation, the next step is the internal acceptance, where consensus and finally approval and consensus of team on the solution to be applied to the changes request is obtained. The project management looks for consensus within project team.
- External acceptance is the final control activity in the integrated process; this activity has the purpose to obtain approval of project sponsor. The Project management is responsible to present and get approval from project sponsor.
- After the external acceptance of the integrated process for changes control is obtained, the software requirements will be updated. The System Analyst will be responsible for modification in software requirements. The approved change request is used as input for this activity, and as output, the software requirements updated should be available for the team in a repository. To finalize this activity, an automatic communication will be send to quality administration, reporting the requirements that were updated, and the modifications applied.
- The execution phase of project will be start when the communication on the software requirements update arrives.
- The software quality administration should analyze the changes, in order to guarantee the quality of the software development process. As responsible for this activity, we have a Quality Analyst. This activity has the updated software requirements as input. The analyst uses inspection and validation techniques. The updated software requirements keep a pendent status, as it reference sessions will have to wait for the new product version and new version to scripts designation to perform automatic tests.
- After Quality analysis, Systems Analysts modify the applications source code conform the updated software requirements. For this activity, we have the updated and QA verified software requirements as input. As output for this activity, we have a new software component for a new product baseline generation to be performed by the configuration management.
- In parallel to the changes implementation activity, the tests analysts will build the test suits and scripts for automatic tests. This activity has as input the updated software requirements, and previous versions test suits and scripts for automatic tests.
- The baseline generation activity, which has a configuration management as responsible, should update in the software requirements documents the product version that fulfills the requirements. , In addition, he should make the new package available as repository. In case of Release, it is necessary to send a package to distribution.
- The Tag creation activity for test suites and scripts used for automatic tests will be realized by Configuration Management, who should updated in software requirements document the artefacts version used for tests suites and scripts for automatic tests that attend this software requirements, in addition to verify, this item configuration in the repository.
- The Release notes creation activity, has as input the updated software requirements, test suites and scripts for automatic tests, product version, as well as components necessary to demonstrate it. The responsible to build this note is configuration management this activity finalizes the proposed process.

V. Conclusion and Future Works

This article presented a process proposal to support configuration management in automated software tests environments. The main objective was to provide better specific items configuration management between software requirements and automatic tests. Besides that, we aimed to improve artifacts traceability artifacts throughout software development cycle. The literature review has been finalized and we are working on the proposal implementation.

As this is a work in progress, we planned the proposal validation through a case study and survey, in order to evaluate the adherence and applicability this process. This will be combined with the identification of possible adjustment points in in view of its application to software development process.

The main obstacle in this proposal is the resistance against changes to the current software development process, and the absence of tools that support infrastructure of the proposed process. We used as constraints the minimization of the changes that impact the software development cycle inside the software factory used for case study. Other phases in the software development cycles are out of the scope of this research, e.g. project closure, business and software implementation processes.

The next step in this research is the implementation and evaluation of the proposed process in a software factory that builds payment applications and has a safe software development cycle.

References

[1] M. Ferreira, C. Santos, T. Novais, and C. Albuquerque, "Gerência de Configuração para Testes Automatizados em uma Fábrica de

Software : Um estudo de caso Configuration Management to Tests Automations in a Software Factory : A case study.

[2] U. Ali and C. Kidd, "Barriers to effective configuration management application in a project context: An empirical investigation," Int. J. Proj. Manag., vol. 32, no. 3, pp. 508–518, 2014.

[3] G. Antoniol, G. Canfora, G. Casazza, A. De Lucia, and E. Merlo, "Recovering traceability links between code and documentation," IEEE Trans. Softw. Eng., vol. 28, no. 10, pp. 970–983, 2002.

[4] W. B. Frakes and S. Isoda, "Success factors of systematic reuse," Software, IEEE, vol. 11, no. 5, pp. 14–19, 1994.

[5] O. C. Gotel, A. C. W. Finkelstein, and L. Sw, "An Analysis of the Requirements Traceability Problem Imperial College of Science , Technology & Medicine Department of Computing , 180 Queen ' s Gate," pp. 94–101, 1994.

[6] T. View, C. M. Plans, and T. View, "IEEE Standard for Software Configuration Management Plans," IEEE Std, vol. 2005, no. August, pp. 0{_}1–19, 2005.

[7] K. Petersen and M. V. Mantyla, "Benefits and limitations of automated software testing: Systematic literature review and practitioner survey," 2012 7th Int. Work. Autom. Softw. Test, pp. 36–42, 2012.

[8] O. C. Gotel, A. C. W. Finkelstein, and L. Sw, "An Analysis of the Requirements Traceability Problem Imperial College of Science , Technology & Medicine Department of Computing , 180 Queen ' s Gate," pp. 94–101, 1994.

[9] B. Kitchenham and S. Charters, "Guidelines for performing Systematic Literature Reviews in Software Engineering," Engineering, vol. 2, p. 1051, 2007.

[10] P. Jamshidi, A. Ahmad, and C. Pahl, "Cloud Migration Research: A Systematic Review," IEEE Trans. Cloud Comput., vol. 1, no. 2, pp. 142–157, 2013.

[11] F. Selleri Silva, F. S. F. Soares, A. L. Peres, I. M. De Azevedo, A. P. L. F. Vasconcelos, F. K. Kamei, and S. R. D. L. Meira, "Using CMMI together with agile software development: A systematic review," Inf. Softw. Technol., vol. 58, pp. 20–43, 2015.

[12] P. Runeson and M. Höst, "Guidelines for conducting and reporting case study research in software engineering," Empir. Softw. Eng., vol. 14, no. 2, pp. 131–164, 2009.

[13] A. Jedlitschka, M. Ciolkowski, and D. Pfahl, "Reporting experiments in software engineering," Guid. to Adv. Empir. Softw. Eng., pp. 201–228, 2008.

[14] D. Tofan, M. Galster, P. Avgeriou, and D. Weyns, "Software engineering researchers' attitudes on case studies and experiments: An exploratory survey," Eval. Assess. Softw. Eng. (EASE 2011), 15th Annu. Conf., no. 638, pp. 91–95, 2011.

An Exploratory Study of DevOps
Extending the Dimensions of DevOps with Practices

Lucy Ellen Lwakatare, Pasi Kuvaja, Markku Oivo,

M3S, Faculty of Information and Electrical Engineering
University of Oulu,
P.O. Box 3000, 90014 Oulu, Finland
Email: firstname.lastname@oulu.fi

***Abstract*—Software-intensive companies constantly try to improve their software development process for better software quality and a faster time to market. The DevOps phenomenon emerged with the promise of easing the process of putting new software changes to production at a fast rate whilst also increasing the learning and innovation cycles of their products. However, the DevOps phenomenon lacks clear definition and practices, and this makes it difficult for both researchers and practitioners to understand the phenomenon. In this paper, we focus on consolidating the understanding of DevOps and its practices as described by practitioners using multivocal literature and interviews. The study contributes to a scientific definition of DevOps and patterns of DevOps practices to help identify and adopt the phenomenon.**

Keywords–DevOps; Continuous Deployment; Agile.

I. INTRODUCTION

Innovative online companies, such as Amazon, Google and Facebook, have fuelled customers expectations for great services at fast speed due to their quick response times to customer demands. Consequently, more companies from most fields are learning and emulating their capabilities in order to cope with competition and technological changes in the field of IT [1]. Today's technology landscape and advances, such as cloud computing, have changed the ways in which software products are developed and delivered to customers. For instance, in the cloud environment, providers of Software-as-a Service (SaaS) applications are expected to update software frequently and in much faster release cycles to customers.

The recent paradigm shift towards fast and frequent delivery of software updates to customers is referred to as continuous deployment (CD) [2]. CD has been described as an evolutionary step after Agile and continuous integration (CI) practices [2] [3]. CD is a practice whereby software features and updates are rapidly rolled out to production as soon as they are developed, whilst also rapidly learn from real-time customer usage of software [2] [3]. The advantage is that companies can proactively identify and validate assumptions of customer needs by applying practices, such as feature experimentation, that tightly integrate runtime-monitored data fromEmphsi production into the software development activities [4].

Responsiveness to customer needs achieved through CD can put a strain on functional teams within an organisation [2]. Consequently, the DevOps phenomenon emerged with the aim of breaking down organisational silos and encouraging cross-functional collaboration among stakeholders involved in software development and delivery processes–especially development and IT operations. The DevOps phenomenon, despite its growing interest in software industry, faces several challenges such as the lack of a clear definition [5]. This lack of clear a definition has resulted to a number of problems and criticisms, including tensions as to whether DevOps is about culture, technical solution or, alternatively, an entirely new role within a software development organisation [6].

The goal of this research is to consolidate the understanding of DevOps phenomenon as described by practitioners. We use an exploratory case study technique that involves a review of multivocal 'grey' literature and interviews. Our work extends other previous studies that have tried to characterise the DevOps phenomenon. Multivocal literature review and interviews were selected as appropriate approaches for this study because DevOps is very much driven by practitioners, and as such, contribution from non-scientific community are worthwhile. The contribution of this paper is twofolds. First, to validate and improve the scientific definition of DevOps proposed by Penners and Dyck [7]. Second, to extend our work on the dimensions of DevOps [8] with a set of examplary practices and patterns of DevOps. The following research questions are addressed in this study:

- RQ1: How do practitioners describe DevOps as a phenomenon?
- RQ2: What are the DevOps practices according to software practitioners?

This paper is organized as follows: Background and related work, including a scientific definition of DevOps, are presented in the next section. Section 3 presents our research methodology. The results of the study are presented in Section 4, which is followed by a discussion and conclusions in Section 5 and 7, respectively. Section 6 presents validity threats including limitations of the study.

II. BACKGROUND AND RELATED WORK

According to Humble and Molesky [9], DevOps– a blend of two words Development and Operations– is about aligning incentives of everybody involved in delivering software, with particular emphasis on developers, testers and operations personnel. The problems resulting from misalignment between development and operations are not new, though their appearance in the literature is scarce [10]. Prior studies investigating cooperation between developers and operations personnel in real contexts have revealed that very often development and operational activities are not tightly integrated [10] [11]. The latter, according to Iden, Tessem and Päivärinta [11], results to a number of problems, including IT operations not being involved in requirements specification, poor communication and information flow between the two groups, unsatisfactory test environments, lack of knowledge transfer between the two groups, systems put into production before they are complete and operational routines not established prior to deployment. These problems were identified from a delphi study consisting of 42 experts grouped in three panels representing the roles of developers, operations personnel and systems owners. In the latter study, the authors [11] concluded that operations personnel are to be regarded as important stakeholders throughout system development activities, especially in systems requirement, testing and deployment.

The closest similar work, though different in terms of the studied phenomenon, is by Tom, Aurum and Vidgen [12]. Using a multivocal literature review (MLR) approach supplemented by interviews, the authors of the latter study [12] examined and consolidated the understanding on an unclear phenomenon i.e., technical debt. The approach was used by the authors to develop a theoretical framework that gives a holistic view of the phenomenon comprising of dimensions, attributes, precedents and outcomes. In this study we apply similar approach used by Tom, Aurum and Vidgen [12] to consolidate the understanding of DevOps phenomenon whilst also compare and complement other related works of DevOps particularly those done by Kerzazi and Adams [6] and Penners and Dyck [7].

A. DevOps Definition and Practices

DevOps is a phenomenon that has often been said to a lack clear and precise definition [5] [7] [8] [13]. Its ambiguity and lack of clarity often hinders its adoption [5]. To address this problem, a scientific definition of DevOps is proposed by Penners and Dyck [7]. The definition was derived from comparing and contrasting various descriptions of DevOps and release engineering as the two terms seemed to have a big overlap [7]. According to the authors, DevOps and release engineering share the same goal of providing high-quality software as fast as possible. However, DevOps tries to achieve the goal by improving the collaboration aspect, whereas release engineering addresses the goal in a holistic way i.e., covers all aspects that impact or influence the delivery process of software product to customer [7]. The authors [7] define DevOps as:

> "*a mindset, encouraging cross-functional collaboration between teams - especially development and IT operations - within a software development organization, in order to operate resilient systems and accelerate delivery of changes* ".

This definition of DevOps was developed through discussion with some experts, but the feedback of its description from practitioners was not as consistent as that of release engineering. Based on this, the authors recommended additional inquiry from more practitioners for a more precise definition of DevOps. This study explores how different practitioners have described DevOps and in addition compare our findings of such descriptions with the definition provided by Penners and Dyck [7] [13].

In addition to the definition of DevOps, different aspects and dimensions characterising the DevOps phenomenon such as culture, sharing, automation, collaboration and measurement have been presented in other works [8] [9] [14]. However, the various aspects or dimensions of DevOps seem to lack a consolidated overview to a set of practices and patterns attributed to DevOps [15] [16] [17]. The latter is largely due to the limited number of scientific studies reporting the DevOps phenomenon in practice, although this is changing as there is presently an increasing number of studies of DevOps e.g., studies from IEEE Software special issue on DevOps [18] [19] [20].

III. METHODOLOGY

We report an exploratory case study [21] on the DevOps phenomenon conducted between September 2015 and April 2016. Exploratory case studies are useful in finding out what is happening on a phenomenon whilst also seek new insights and generate ideas for new research.

A. Data Collection

This study uses qualitative data–both primary and secondary data– collected from practitioners in two phases. Phase 1 involved collecting primary data using semi-structured interviews with software practitioners from one case company. Secondary data, consisting of readily accessible writings from the Internet, such as blogs, white papers, trade journals and articles, were collected in phase 2 of the study using Google search. The documents gathered during Phase 2 are collectively referred to as multivocal literature (ML) [22]. The multivocal literature review provides a method for exploring a common, often a contemporary topic of interest [22]. ML embodies views and voices of diverse set of authors expressed in variety of forms [12] [22].

1) Phase-1 Interviews: Three interviews with software practitioners were conducted in one company (Company A), that provides consultancy and product engineering services to its customers. In the latter company, we focused our study on one project, that involved the development of cloud-based road maintenance reporting tool. The company was developing the tool for a customer in the public sector. Convenience sampling was used to select suitable companies based on their participation in the Need for Speed (N4S) project (http://www.n4s.fi/en/), which the present study is part of. A contact person from company A was asked to select a project team that was applying DevOps practices. All interviews were recorded and later transcribed for analysis. The roles of the interviewed practitioners are summarized in Table I .

TABLE I. SUMMARY OF INTERVIEWEES.

Company	*A*
Number of Employees	< 350
Studied Project	Road maintenance tool.
Team Size	7 (co-located).
Number of Interviews (role)	2 (senior developers) 1 (project manager)

A semi-structured interview guide was used during the interviews and had questions that inquired about the (1) current way of working in software development and deployment, (2) strengths and weaknesses in ways of working and (3) definitions, practices, benefits and challenges of DevOps and CD. DevOps questions were guided by the results of our previous work that analysed and synthesized the DevOps phenomenon as described in academic literature [7].

2) Phase-2 review of multivocal literature: In phase 2, we conducted MLR in the beginning of March 2016. In this study, we selected the MLR as an appropriate method because DevOps is a phenomenon that is largely driven and discussed by practitioners in non-academic circles, and as such it requests the review of the largely available information in non-scietific forums, as seen also in a study done by Kerzazi and Adams [5]. Despite the apparent issues of rigor associated with MLR approach [22], the contemporary nature of DevOps phenomenon suggests some value in reviewing ML that cannot be overlooked. As noted by Ogawa [22], the information presented in ML cannot be assessed in the same way as that of academic literature. We therefore considered various recommended procedures by Ogawa [22] in order to minimize bias and error that can be transferred to, and incorporated in the review of ML. The latter included focusing our study on presenting a thicker picture of the DevOps phenomenon that would serve as input for more sophisticated examination in future research. We carried out the MLR in the following three stages:

a) Data sources and search strategy: Google web search engine (http://www.google.com) was used to source ML from the World Wide Web. The query used to retrieve results from the search engine was what is DevOps. From the retrieved results, we went through the links provided, page by page, saving the outputs of each link as a PDF file until the page where job adverts started and at this point, the review was stopped. A total of 230 records were collected as data sources and included in subsequent steps.

b) Inclusion and exclusion: A total of 230 documents were imported to NVivo (www.qsrinternational.com/product) for analysis. The inclusion and exclusion of the records were done simultaneously with the initial coding of these records. The process also involved classifying the sources with different attributes, such as author information, e.g. name, role and place of work; and source information, e.g. publication year, forum and link. After reviewing all 230 documents, 201 sources were included as relevant documents and excluded 29 documents as they were either duplicates, video links, pointers to catalogues, course adverts, certification adverts or presentation slides.

c) Quality assessment: Quality assessment was mostly done when classifying the sources with metadata, e.g. author name, role, place of work/affiliation, year of publication, view point. This process offered minimal assessment of position, certainty and clarity of source or alignment with research goal i.e., to consolidate the understanding of DevOps phenomenon as determined by the research questions.

B. Data Analysis

Interview transcripts and results from the MLR (list of ML at http://tinyurl.com/z3jpu5v) were coded in NVivo. At first, codes were assigned inductively to the following categories: (1) Definition (with referred as and description as subcategories) and (2) Practices. Other emerging themes found within and across the sources were also coded (e.g., Motivations for DevOps, DevOps in relation to Agile and CD, Problems addressed by DevOps). Following the inductive coding of raw data into the main categories, i.e., Definition and Practices, a second iteration of inductive coding was performed to form other subcategories. The latter proceeded in multiple iterations until similar patterns in the practices and definition were identified and saturation reached. Interestingly, the practices could be grouped into the dimensions of DevOps identified in previous work [8]; however, a new dimension was also added.

IV. FINDINGS

In this section, we present the findings with respect to the two research questions. Fig. 1 gives a summary of the findings from MLR. For MLR, Internet blogs made up the largest source with 53.2% (107) of all sources. Compared to personal blogs, most of the blogs were affiliated with companies. The MLR showed a growing number of sources writing about DevOps over the past 5 years since its conception in 2009.

From the case company, the project team in company A uses Scrum– agile software development method, with a 3-week sprint cycle. The development team has three environments to which software changes are deployed, i.e., development, test and staging. The production environment was not in use at the time of the interviews because the project was phased and the deliverables as well as the schedule of each phase was determined by the customer. The development team automatically deployed software changes from the test to staging environment using Ansible playbooks. The infrastructure team located in another city supported the development team by provisioning the virtual servers used to create the environments.

A. How do practitioners describe DevOps as a phenomenon? (RQ1)

Most practitioners acknowledge that DevOps is a concept that is difficult to define with accuracy. However, many of them still used different terms and descriptions to describe the DevOps phenomenon as elaborated below:

1) DevOps referred to as: A large number of MLR sources have referred to DevOps as a cultural and professional movement (52). Other terms used to describe the DevOps phenomenon in MLR sources include practices (41), culture (38), approach (38), philosophy, mindset, ideology (37), tool (36), a set of values and principles (30), software methodology (24), role, team or engineer (19) and strategy (8). Fig. 2 summarizes the prevalence of the terms in MLR sources. It should be noted that a single source of MLR can use more than one term to describe the DevOps phenomenon.

2) DevOps descriptions: There is an agreement that the term is a combination of development and operations, that encourages collaboration between software development and operations activities. However, when describing the concept further, practitioners often diverge their descriptions depending on whether they place the emphasis more on the goal or more on the means of achieving collaboration. The most common goals that were described include the following: to reduce response time and fast deployment of high quality and reliable software products and services, to allow instant interactions, to unify workflows for transparency and collaboration. On the other hand, those that emphasise means include: through advanced automation and, by evolving traditional roles of

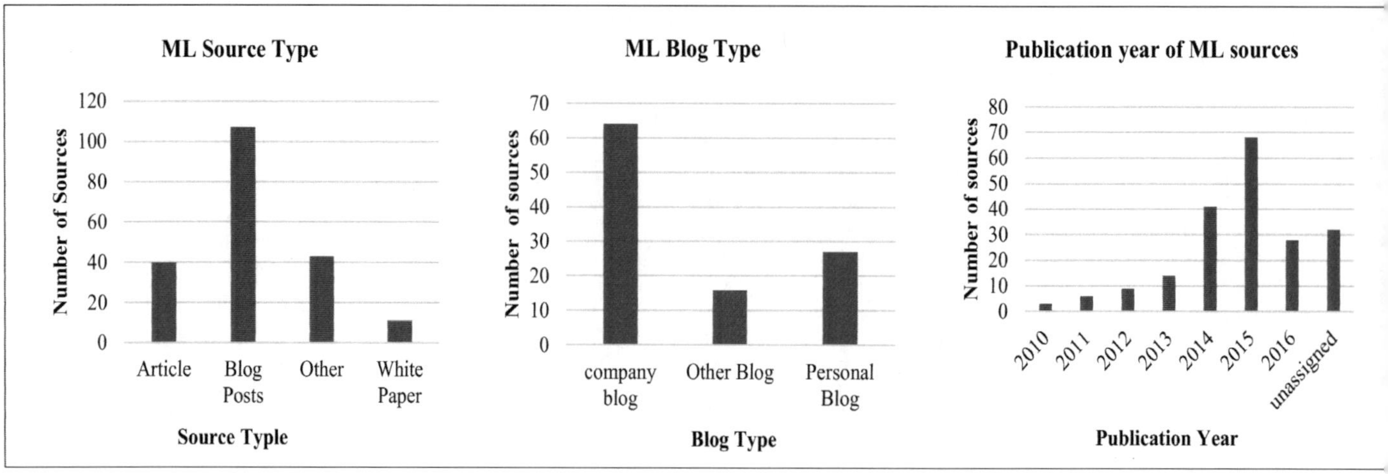

Figure 1. ML Sources.

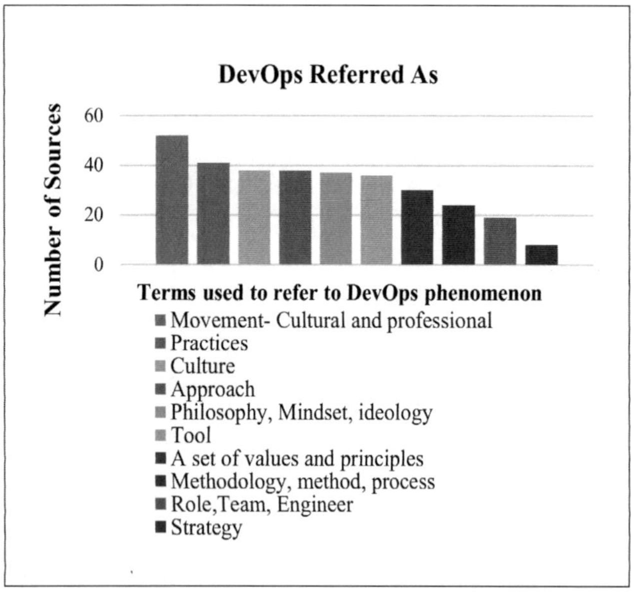

Figure 2. Terms referring to DevOps and their prevalance in ML.

development and operations. In company A, two out of three interviewed practitioners had an understanding of DevOps. One person, the project manager, had no prior understanding of the concept and had learned about it through our study. The following descriptions are extracts from interviewed practitioners in company A when asked how they understood DevOps. The first developer described DevOps as

> *a set of practices to govern everything that is related to installing the software, maintaining it, making sure that all these connections work, i.e. firewalls, version management, etc. It is kind of a little bit of what happens, right after the actual development.*

Another description given by the second developer was:

> *DevOps is mostly about the organisation of work, tearing down the walls that separate typical development organisation from the operational organisation...like instead of provisioning new systems with a ticket, automation projects are modifying the servers and developer can make or commit changes to them by themselves when needed. If you have a separate ops team, then you need to have a very good practice in place for documenting changes and transferring knowledge about the system. A DevOps person will know how to run their own system .*

B. What are the DevOps practices according to software practitioners? (RQ2)

DevOps practices can be crystalized into five dimensions that characterize DevOps. The five dimensions are further elaborated with examplary DevOps practices and patterns to the practices below. Table 2 summarizes some of the DevOps practices in each of the dimensions.

1) Collaboration: rethinking and reorientation of roles and teams in development and operations activities: The issue of role is one of the most widely discussed topics by practitioners in ML. On the otherhand, DevOps phenomenon offers no blue print of how companies can reorganize those roles. A common pattern that was observed is that, companies are forced to rethink and reorient roles, whether new or existing, around the performance of the entire system or service, as opposed to the performance of a specific silo of department or an individual module. Practices in collaboration are often seen as empowerment to team members, especially for the developer since in some cases they gain more control over system operability. This in turn helps to broaden their skillset and knowledge. According to some practitioners, such control allows a single team to be responsible for all aspects, i.e. development and operations of the entire software product or service. Some criticism to this was also observed, including coding time for developers is reduced and the fact that developers need to find ways to effectively balance the support and operations tasks alongside development tasks. Others agree that, companies will need to pick right technology and methodologies to be able to empower developers, as advocated by DevOps. We identified the following two common practices in the collaborative aspect of DevOps.

TABLE II. DEVOPS DIMENSIONS, PATTERNS AND PRACTICES

DevOps Dimension	Patterns of DevOps practices	Examples of practices found in ML
Collaboration	Rethinking and reorientation of roles and teams in development and operations activities	Increasing the scope of responsibilities • Developers paying closer attention to deployment scripts, configuration files, load and performance testing and other activities usually associated with operations groups • Developers learning from operations about resilience, monitoring and diagnosing distributed systems • Developers leverage the support enabled through virtualization, microservice architecture and automation in deployment pipeline to do less operations work, e.g., Docker to remove the need for specifying environments specifications • Development has access and can make changes to critical environments, e.g. production Intensifying cooperation and involvement in each others daily work • Development rotates roles with operations teams, operations attend developer stand-ups and showcases • Operations involved earlier in development to understand what project environments are required to support the application. Also, regular meetings, e.g. weekly to discuss cross-team priorities • In circumstances in which production incidents occur, development and operations come together to troubleshoot and resolve problems as one team • Setting-up shared (virtual and physical) workspace
Automation	Infrastructure and deployment process automation	Infrastructure-as-code • Automate and maintain infrastructure configurations and files using tools such as Chef, Puppet • Developers are shielded from infrastructure issues and are able to create virtual development, test and production environments as well as deploy application using tools like Vagrant and Docker • Scripts used to handle infrastructure are versioned, testable and repeatable • Immutable infrastructure, i.e. artifacts, in their production environments are not updated, rather the infrastructure is always replaced Deployment process automation • Production-like environments are used by development teams for development and testing • Developers self-service environments and deployments • Consistent, reliable and repeatable deployment mechanism across different environments • Configuration changes across environments are automated
Culture	Empathy, support and good working environment between development and operations	• Both developers and operations wear pagers as responsible persons to handle incidents • Integrating development into blameless production post-mortems • Making communication between development and operations non-adversarial and less formal • Mutual respect, support and willingness to work together and share responsibilities
Monitoring	Instrumenting application and aggregating monitored data into insights	• Developers and operations are both involved in determining and implementing monitoring parameters of a system • Set-up monitoring on the production environment for development teams visible through radiators • Development team, including QA, use small subset of high-priority test cases to be executed in production to actively monitor the environment • Effective instrumentation of software by development in collaboration with operations to give information about its health and performance. Also, developers are able to quickly recover code failures in production using aids, such as feature flags
Measurement	Useful Metrics	• Both operations team and development team are incentivized and rewarded by the same metrics • Both development and operations focus on business value as the essential unit of measurement • Progress in development is measured in terms of a working system in production environment • Developers use production feedback to drive decisions, improvements, and changes to the system

a) Increasing the scope of responsibilities: This practice is particularly prominent in the developer role and is the most common implementation of DevOps phenomenon. According to practitioners, developers are responsible for other tasks in addition to designing, coding and testing. Increasing the scope of responsibilities involves pro-activeness of team members in learning the new tasks or alternatively leverage on the automation done to the technical infrastructure of the project. This was also evident from the interviewed practitioners as expressed by the developer from company A: *Shared access to change things, so not just that there's collaboration within the ops teamand ask should you even have an ops team and a development team. If something is broken on the production machine, why do you need an ops team to fix it? It should be possible for anyone in the dev team or any other team to just fix things that are broken.*

b) Intensifying cooperation and involvement in each others daily work: DevOps requires both groups to recognise their key skills in order to share and learn from each other. This aspect may not necessarily mean retraining or crossskilling but encourages providing feedback and visibility across the teams in order to improve. Involving members from each others teams, development and operations teams can provide valuable information outside individuals areas of expertise. As such, practices such as early involvement of operations in development are emphasized. The following interview extract is a response given by an interviewed practitioner from company A when asked to elaborate how the development team interacts with the infrastructure team:

> *We interact with them through HipChat, which is like an IRC channel. We have a project channel and a member of infrastructure team; [name] has been allocated to support our project. We are basically just sending a message to [name]if we need some help, e.g., we want two more servers to run Java virtual machine and Jenkins, and then he waves some magic and we get what we want. It's pretty instant even if we are technically in a different team i.e., virtual team element, in it.*

2) Automation: infrastructure and deployment process automation: Automation underlies most of the practices that constitute DevOps. Two common practices include automation of deployment process and infrastructure-as-code (IaC). The two practices help to eliminate error-prone manual processes associated with deployments and configuration settings for improved traceability and repeatable workflows. For instance, the use of IaC practice to standardize development, test and production environments.

a) Deployment process automation: as evident in deployment pipeline that views the entire development to operations lifecycle as one coherent end-to-end process rather than numerous multiple and diverse steps. The deployment pipeline is an integrated flow that puts great emphasis on the automation of build, test and deployment processes. It involves continuous development whereby code written and committed to version control is built, tested and installed (deployed) in the production environment. An automated deployment process takes into account and ensures the management of dependencies, versions and configurations of application and infrastructure, which is often challenging. The following interview extract is a response given by an interviewed practitioner from company A when asked to give an example of a DevOps practice they have had in their team:

> *The actual building of the CI pipeline has been done collaborative with ops team, who basically just provisions machines for us. They have a library of useful profiles that can be helpful, e.g., our servers have Java 8, database servers have PostgreSQL installed, etc. So, we've been pretty active in building and modifying our own CI pipeline, and we have had within ourselves actual tangible tasks to deploy our stuff to production.*

In addition to the development team interacting with the operations team to implement the deployment pipeline, the teams collaboratively work together to improve the pipeline in order to improve their processes. This is described by an interviewed practitioner when asked to give an example of a problem that the development team encountered and needed help from the infrastructure team:

> *We are using Jenkins in CI, and whenever we want to update software, we push the newest version to Jenkins and it runs unit tests. If everything goes fine, it automatically installs the new version to the test environment. At some point, we started using Selenium for automated end-to-end functional tests. We have had quite a lot of random failures with Selenium tests, for example, we did not know if the software or just the test tool was broken. Quite often, either of these were true, and sometimes I think we also run out of space in CI machines and the Jenkins build would fail because there is no space left. So we have used [name of the assigned person from Infrastructure team] to debug and have a look at what's going on when we have encountered failure that we shouldn't have.*

b) Infrastructure-as-code: This practice is central to automation dimension and entails treating infrastructure the same way developers treat code. This includes making the process of infrastructure provisioning, orchestration and application deployment reproducible and programmatic. Application code has a defined format and syntax that follows the rules of the programming language in order to be created. Typically, the code is stored in a version-management system that logs a history of code development, changes and fixes. When code is compiled (built) into an application, the expectation is that a consistent application is created. When the latter occurs, the build process is said to be repeatable and reliable. Practicing IaC means applying the same rigor of application code development to infrastructure provisioning, orchestration and deployment. All configurations should be defined in a declarative way and stored in a version management system, just like application code. With IaC, it becomes possible to quickly provision application environments and deploy application automatically and at scale as needed. The following interview extract is a response given by an interviewed practitioner from company A about how the team handles their infrastructure:

> *We use Ansible for all server automation, so we have Ansible tasks and playbooks for the infrastructure, i.e. we use Ansible projects for setting up the machines and installing. When a new machine comes, we just automatically run that and it sets up everything. Then we have other playbooks for deploying our software on top of the page.*

3) Culture: empathy, support and good working evironment for teams especially development and operations: Many of DevOps practices also involve changing culture and mindset to the one that encourages empathy, support and a good working environment for those involved in software development and delivery processes.

a) Empathy: According to majority of ML authors, development and operations need to empathize with each other and more importantly also with users of software product or service. For operations engineers, empathy helps them to understand the needs as well as to appreciate the importance of being able to push code quickly and frequently, without problems. To developers, it also allows them to recognise the problems resulting from writing code that is erroneous, unstable or insecure. Generally, empathy in DevOps culture allows software developers and operators to help each other deliver the best software possible. Information exchanges require (and can contribute to) mutual understanding. As an example to this pattern includes having both developers and operations, personnel wear pagers as responsible persons to handle incidents.

b) support and a good working environment for teams: The need for mindset change and cross-discipline learning associated with DevOps necessitates the support from members within and across development and operations teams, as well as of those outside the two functions or roles. A good working environment that welcomes innovation, experimenting and stops finger pointing when mistakes are done as long as they constantly improve learning, helps to facilitate and embrace DevOps phenomenon amongst others.

4) Monitoring: Instrumenting application and aggregating monitored data into insights: This pattern involves having a continuous feedback loop that runs from the production environment to the start of the development cycle, including a complete timeline of development and operations events. It involves proactive detection and awareness of events in critical environments, such as test and production, in order to expose (know the state of) issues before they cause failures. According to practitioners, the latter is important especially for SaaS application because development teams are increasingly placing more reliance on detection and recovery than standard QA testing practices. Since the cost and time of fixing defects in production for SaaS are less than packaged software, teams tend to reduce reliance of extensive testing and instead rely more on production monitoring to detect defects as long as they can be quickly fixed. On the other hand, monitoring of advanced architectures with highly distributed systems and nodes that appear and disappear pose challenging tasks that should not only involve operations engineers. Two common patterns in monitoring include emphasis on instrumentation of application and increased use of modern tools for monitoring purposes.

a) Instrumenting application: A well-instrumented software system can provide rich data and insights about its health and performance that can be used in bug reporting, troubleshooting, feature suggestion or general finetuning of the system. Effective instrumentation of an application tries to minimize problems associated with the aggregation of large amounts of data from a variety of sources by capturing feedback as part of the application. Reliance on monitoring, developers can quickly recovery from code failures by the use of feature flags that enable or disable code functionality through configuration settings. Additionally, instrumentation can help to extend features of monitoring tools with domain knowledge. To implement this, a broad set of skills are required amongst developers that involve mainly scripting and knowledge of performance-monitoring practices, often a responsibility of operations. The following interview extract is a response given by an interviewed practitioner from company A when asked to give an example of a DevOps practice experienced by their team:

> *When we do not know how to do something, the ops team, i.e. the infrastructure team, has shared services that I use, like log aggregation services and monitoring services. We have asked them to set these up for us.*

b) Aggregation of monitoring data into insights: For comprehensive system monitoring, several tools at different system levels are used, and different tools are used to monitor application and infrastructure. Although modern tools try to provide insight into almost every aspect of system behaviour, the biggest challenge facing the tools is developing data analytics that predict problems before they become outages. Some practitioners also argue that it is impossible to catch all the issues using the out-of-the box features of such tools.

5) Measurement: different metrics are used to monitor and assess the performance of processes in development and operations activities, e.g., developers on system quality and operations on system stability. As such, instead of using proxy metrics, DevOps, according to practitioners, emphasizes the use of common metrics that are often business focused to assess and give incentive to both development and operations teams. Additionally, developers, operations and other stakeholders can use production feedback to drive decisions, improvements and changes to the systemnot just problem reports and user suggestions, but measurable data collected on how the system is working according to the conversion rate or whatever metric that the business uses to determine success.

V. DISCUSSION

Our findings show that often practitioners vary their description of DevOps depending on whether they put their emphasis on either the goal or the means for achieving collaboration between development and operations. The most common goal according to practitioners was to reduce response time and provide fast deployment of high-quality and reliable software products and services. This finding supports the second part of the definition proposed by Penners and Dyck [7]. Evidence from how practitioners referred to the DevOps phenomenon also supports that DevOps is a mindset as stated in the proposed definition. However, the results showed that, in addition to being a mindset, DevOps constitutes practices attributed to it. We therefore argue that both mindset and practices be included in the definition and that the first part of the definition should not exclude the results. By doing this, we improve the definition to be *DevOps is a mind-set substantiated with a set of practices to encourage cross-functional collaboration between teams - especially development and IT operations - within a software development organization, in order to operate resilient systems and accelerate delivery of change.*

On the other hand, the DevOps phenomenon has no explicit one-size-fits-all set of practices that guide its adoption and implementation, but that common patterns can be identified from its diverse set of practices. For each pattern of DevOps, practitioners can choose different ways to implement it even though it was possible to identify similar implementation. Patterns to the DevOps practices are more useful than one-fits-all set of practices that will not suffice due to contextual limitations in organisations, e.g., team members skill and scenarios vary among companies. As an example, we can observe the reorientation of roles and teams in development and operations activities pattern in studies reported by Balalaie, Heydarnoori, and Jamshidi [19]. In the latter study, the authors depict the formation of small and autonomous teams consisting of multi-skilled persons of both development and operations activities as a DevOps practice. According to the authors, the practice helps to minimize development and operations inter-team coordination, which is important for Microservices.

Callanan and Spillane give empirical evidence to infrastructure and deployment automation pattern [18]. Continuous monitoring of both infrastructure and application, as a DevOps practice helping to bridge development including quality assurance and operations are described as lesson learned and experiences by authors of these studies [15] [16] [17] [18] [19] [20].

Generally, the results of our study signify the importance of considering context when describing DevOps practices. In our case study, even though most practitioners elaborated the practices in the context of cloud and web development, other contextual information, such as size and maturity, influenced the ways in which some practices are implemented. This is an important consideration that needs to be taken into account when discussing DevOps practices, i.e., to understand the context in which the practices are described.

VI. Threats to Validity

This study has a number of validity threats that need to be taken into account. We considered three categories of validity threats– construct validity, reliability, and external validity [21]– and used different countermeasures to minimize the threats. The countermeasures included: (a) consulting multiple sources in MLR (b) maintaining chain of evidence, and (c) incorporating practitioners reviews. In addition, particulary to MLR approach, three minimal standards for enhancing rigor in ML suggested by Ogawa [22] were considered.

To ensure construct validity, we only included one out of three contacted and interviewed case companies. The latter is due to not having the two other companies implement DevOps as well as the lack of DevOps understanding thereof. As a result of the selection process, our study faced some limitation with regards to the few number of interviews included in this study. This limitation serves as an opportunity for further inquiry in future works. On the otherhand, the interviews were conducted with at least two researchers to minimize researcher bias. A document describing the background and objective of the study was sent to practitioners prior to the interviews. With regards to the MLR, a threat to construct validity comes from different constraints, e.g., the selected search term as well as the inclusion and exclusion criteria of ML. To ensure construct validity and minimal rigor, prior to MLR, the objective of the study was clearly defined which served as the primary criterion for seeking and selecting ML.

To ensure the reliability of results, initial results were made available for discussion to practitioners and other researchers prior to the writing of this report. One meeting (with company representatives of the interviewed company) and a workshop with practitioners of the N4S research program were also conducted to solicit feedback from practitioners. Both events were useful for collecting feedback. We also ensured an audit trail, i.e., maintain all records and analysis in NVivo. With regards to ML, the reliability of the study would have improved further with contact and additional discussion with the authors of the ML. However, due to the large number of ML sources and diverse set of authors, at the time of writing the report, this was not feasible due to limited time.

External validity and the generalization of the findings is threatened by the small number of interviewees as described earlier as well as our reliance on ML sources as data sources for analysis. For this reason we acknowlede this limitation and , the results serve as a basis for empirical evaluations.

VII. Conclusion and Future Work

The analysis of multivocal literature and interviews with software practitioners showed software practitioners use different terms and variety of practices when describing the DevOps phenomenon. We used findings from our analysis to provide more evidence that supports and builds upon the scientific definition of DevOps proposed by Penners and Dyck [6]. Our findings showed that DevOps as a phenomenon is not just a mind-set but rather some patterns of DevOps practices described by the practitioners can be identified. This study presents the identified patterns in relation to the five dimensions of DevOps, i.e. collaboration, automation, culture, monitoring and measurement. Our findings show that DevOps phenomenon is more prominent in organisations providing services over the Internet. It would be beneficial for future research to focus on further empirical evidence of DevOps practices and patterns in companies that claim to have implemented it. More important will be a research that not only identifies the practices but also for which kinds of system, organisations and domains are DevOps practices applicable.

Acknowledgment

This work was supported by TEKES (Finnish Funding Agency for Innovation) as part of the Need for Speed project (http://www.n4s.fi/) of DIGILE (Finnish Strategic Centre for Science, Technology and Innovation in the field of ICT and digital business).

References

[1] M. Leppanen et al., "The Highways and Country Roads to Continuous Deployment," IEEE Software, vol. 32, no. 2, mar 2015, pp. 64–72.

[2] P. Rodríguez et al., "Continuous Deployment of Software Intensive Products and Services: A Systematic Mapping Study," Journal of Systems and Software, jan 2016. [Online]. Available: http://www.sciencedirect.com/science/article/pii/S0164121215002812

[3] H. H. Olsson, H. Alahyari, and J. Bosch, "Climbing the "Stairway to Heaven" – A Mulitiple-Case Study Exploring Barriers in the Transition from Agile Development towards Continuous Deployment of Software," in 38th Euromicro Conference on Software Engineering and Advanced Applications. IEEE, sep 2012, pp. 392–399.

[4] T. Karvonen, L. E. Lwakatare, T. Sauvola, J. Bosch, H. H. Olsson, P. Kuvaja, and M. Oivo, "Hitting the Target: Practices for Moving Toward Innovation Experiment Systems," in 6th International Conference on Software Business. Springer International Publishing, 2015, pp. 117–131.

[5] J. Smeds, K. Nybom, and I. Porres, "DevOps: A Definition and Perceived Adoption Impediments," in 16th International Conference on Agile Software Development (XP). Springer International Publishing, 2015, pp. 166–177.

[6] N. Kerzazi and B. Adams, "Who Needs Release and DevOps Engineers, and Why?" in International Workshop on Continuous Software Evolution and Delivery. ACM Press, 2016, pp. 77–83.

[7] R. Penners and A. Dyck, "Release Engineering vs. DevOps-An Approach to Define Both Terms," Full-scale Software Engineering, 2015. [Online]. Available: https://www2.swc.rwth-aachen.de/docs/teaching/seminar2015/FsSE2015papers.pdf#page=53

[8] L. E. Lwakatare, P. Kuvaja, and M. Oivo, "Dimensions of DevOps," in 16th International Conference on Agile Software Development (XP). Springer International Publishing, 2015, pp. 212–217.

[9] J. Humble and J. Molesky, "Why enterprises must adopt DevOps to enable continuous delivery," Cutter IT Journal, vol. 24, no. 8, 2011, pp. 6–12.

[10] B. Tessem and J. Iden, "Cooperation between developers and operations in software engineering projects," in In Proceedings of the 2008 international workshop on Cooperative and human aspects of software engineering. ACM, 2008, pp. 105–108.

[11] J. Iden, B. Tessem, and T. Päivärinta, "Problems in the interplay of development and IT operations in system development projects: A Delphi study of Norwegian IT experts," Information and Software Technology, vol. 53, no. 4, apr 2011, pp. 394–406.

[12] E. Tom, A. Aurum, and R. Vidgen, "An exploration of technical debt," Journal of Systems and Software, vol. 86, no. 6, jun 2013, pp. 1498–1516.

[13] A. Dyck, R. Penners, and H. Lichter, "Towards definitions for release engineering and DevOps," 2015.

[14] F. Erich, C. Amrit, and M. Daneva, "Cooperation between information system development and operations: a literature review," p. Article No.69, 2014.

[15] J. Roche, "Adopting DevOps practices in quality assurance," Communications of the ACM, 2013, pp. 1–8.

[16] D. Cukier, "DevOps patterns to scale web applications using cloud services," in In Proceedings of the 2013 conference on Systems, programming, & applications: software for humanity. ACM, 2013, pp. 143–152.

[17] L. Bass, I. Weber, and L. Zhu, DevOps: A Software Architect's Perspective. Addison-Wesley Professional, 2015.

[18] C. Ebert, G. Gallardo, J. Hernantes, and N. Serrano, "DevOps," IEEE Software, vol. 33, no. 3, may 2016, pp. 94–100.

[19] M. Callanan and A. Spillane, "DevOps: Making It Easy to Do the Right Thing," IEEE Software, vol. 33, no. 3, may 2016, pp. 53–59.

[20] A. Balalaie, A. Heydarnoori, and P. Jamshidi, "Microservices Architecture Enables DevOps: Migration to a Cloud-Native Architecture," IEEE Software, vol. 33, no. 3, may 2016, pp. 42–52.

[21] P. Runeson and M. Höst, "Guidelines for conducting and reporting case study research in software engineering," Empirical software engineering, vol. 14, no. 131, 2009, pp. 131–164.

[22] R. Ogawa and B. Malen, "Towards rigor in reviews of multivocal literatures: Applying the exploratory case study method," Review of Educational Research, vol. 61, no. 3, 1991, pp. 299–305.

The Daily Crash:
A Reflection on Continuous Performance Testing

Gururaj Maddodi*, Slinger Jansen*, Jan Pieter Guelen† and Rolf de Jong†
* Utrecht University, Princetonplein 5, 3584 CC Utrecht, Netherlands
Email: g.maddodi@uu.nl, slinger.jansen@uu.nl
†AFAS Software, Philipsstraat 9, 3833 LC Leusden, Netherlands
Email: j.guelen@afas.nl, r.dejong@afas.nl

***Abstract*—Software architects base their design tasks on experience mostly, when developing new architectures. The requirements that are placed on these architectures, such as high-availability and minimum performance requirements, are becoming more demanding continuously. In this paper, we reflect on a method for continuous performance testing, to provide architects with feedback on their design/implementation and prevent problems before they affect the users or other systems. If architects employ the method, they are no longer flying blind, and can continuously evaluate and improve their application. We illustrate the use of the method at a large software company and report on the outcomes of using continuous performance testing in the development of their upcoming enterprise resource planning application release that is going to be used by over a million users.**

Keywords–Workload Generation; Performance Testing; Software Architecture.

I. INTRODUCTION

Performance demands placed upon modern software systems are constantly increasing. Systems ranging from simple websites to large business solutions need to support concurrent access by large numbers of users [1][2]. Both conventional wisdom and several studies [3][4] indicate that many software projects have performance problems. Catching these performance problems before they affect users of a system in production is becoming a focal point in the development of software systems.

To gain insight into performance variations of a software system, it has to be monitored before and after changes are made to the system. This can be done through testing the system with a test workload. Workload generation is a process of simulating usage load that the software system is expected to handle in a production environment. Performance testing of a software application involves measuring the resource usage or throughput, by giving a set of inputs to the system by means of generated workload. In performance testing, a realistic workload is simulated/generated and thrown at the working system, while different monitoring mechanisms are being used to evaluate system behavior. One of the most common problems in performance testing is that an unrepresentative workload is used, which gives misleading results [5]. The selected workload used for testing has a major influence on the eventual performance results [6]. Hence, an outline of workload generation techniques and tests is a helpful tool in testing software performance.

Also as most software producing organizations continuously upgrade software products, either with new features or bug fixes, these systems must be continuously tested for their performance. Continuous Performance Testing (CPT) is a methodology of testing the performance of a software system every time a change is made to it. This term stems from the continuous software improvement movement, which prefers guided incremental improvement over discontinuous burst of unreliable major software releases and updates [7].

The contributions of this paper are: (1) an outline of available workload generation techniques is provided, and (2) a reflection on a method of CPT in practice at a large software organization. We structure the work as follows. First, the research method is described in Section II. Secondly, an overview is provided of the topic of workload generation with a structured literature review in Section III. Thirdly, a literature review on continuous performance testing is described in Section IV. In Section V, the CPT method is presented, based on the literature study. In Section VI, a case study is presented at a software company describing a practical implementation and results of the method. The case is evaluated with practitioners, who share their experience using CPT and insights it has given to their development process. We describe analysis and discussions in Section VII. Conclusions are described in Section VIII, where we illustrate that CPT, when based on realistic workloads, is an essential tool for any software architect.

II. RESEARCH METHOD

The research was conducted in two phases. First, a literature study was performed to establish the available methods for CPT. Secondly, through design research, a new method for CPT has been created. Thirdly, a case study is conducted to evaluate the practical aspects of CPT.

A. Literature Study

This section details the literature study protocol created to find papers discussing workload generation methods and performance testing. We used the following keywords to find publications on workload generation and continuous performance testing:

"Testing workload generation" OR "Workload generator" OR "Deriving workload" OR "Test user generation" OR "Performance profiling" OR "software performance testing" OR "Workload characterization" OR "Continuous integration testing"

A literature protocol is established based on the recommendations of Webster and Watson [8], and Kitchenham and Charters [9]. Our data collection strategy consisted of using three scientific search engines: Google Scholar, CiteSeerX, and ieeexplore. Besides the mentioned keywords, references to papers were also looked at, a technique Webster and Watson [8] calls "going backward". This method was also taken in the opposite direction ("going forward") as the references of important papers were also considered.

B. The Case-study Method

The case-study was conducted at AFAS Software. AFAS is a Dutch vendor of Enterprise Resource Planning (ERP) software. The privately held company currently employs over 350 people and annually generates €100 million in revenue. AFAS currently delivers a fully integrated ERP suite, which is used daily by more than 1.000.000 professional users from more than 10.000 customers. The NEXT version of AFAS' ERP software is completely generated, cloud-based, and tailored for a particular enterprise, based on an ontological model of that enterprise. The ontological enterprise model will be expressive enough to fully describe the real-world enterprise of virtually any customer, and as well form the main foundation for generating an entire software suite on a cloud infrastructure platform of choice: AFAS NEXT is entirely platform and database-independent. AFAS NEXT will enable rapid model-driven application development and will drastically increase customization flexibility for AFAS' partners and customers, based on a software generation platform that is future proof for any upcoming technologies. AFAS is continuously evaluating NEXT for its performance, hence they are an attractive choice for the case-study. The case company was also chosen pragmatically, as a long term relationship exists between the company and Utrecht University.

The case study comprised of interviewing four experts from AFAS Software, including software architects and project managers with years of experience in software architecture design. The interviews conducted as part of the case-study were semi-structured. An interview protocol was defined with questions pertaining to: benefits of CPT that AFAS are seeing, tools and frameworks used for testing, workload generation, alert mechanisms, and organizational aspects of decision making. The interviews were recorded and then later transcribed to extract findings regarding the CPT process at AFAS. One of the co-authors of this paper is also the person who implemented some of the basic principles of CPT. He is now working at AFAS and his previous work is being continued and worked on by his colleagues.

Threats to validity can be internal or external. To counter internal validity threats, one of the co-authors, who has in-depth knowledge of the process of CPT at the company, was asked to validate the findings. Also, a company representative was asked to review the findings. External threats we foresee is how the findings can be applicable to other organizations. Further validation can be done by involving more organizations, which we see as future work.

III. Workload Generation

Workload generators have been around since the early 90s, both as academic and commercial tooling. In order to generate for specific scenarios, the generators generally allow for a number of input parameters to be set. Workload generation techniques can have a number of different characteristics associated with them, and can generally can be classified into two types: static (do not depend on earlier of future actions) and dynamic (based on temporal correlations or other outside sources). Early tools were designed for specific circumstances, mostly generating HTTP requests for static environments, such as Webjamma [10] and S-clients [11]. Other tools generate dynamic behavior, such as TPCW [12], SPEC WEB99 [13], Webload [14], and JMeter [15].

Some workload generation methods target non-existent systems and in these cases the generated load is tested against a performance model of the system. In those cases, both the workload and the system are simulated. This does require detailed performance measurements from the original workload. This helps to know the effects of a task on the system (or similar measurements), so the basis of the model has corresponding link to a performance measurement. Burstiness is a commonly overlooked factor when generating workload [16]. The usage of a software system is not evenly distributed across time, but has bursts and lulls. Applying a smaller degree of burstiness to a workload can give the workload more realistic behavior.

Finally, workload generators vary in the workload they output. In the empirical approach, sampling is done of existing data (data recorded from live sessions). In contrast, analytic approaches use mathematical modeling to generate synthetic workload. The empirical approach is easiest to implement, however it lacks the flexibility as the recorded traces are only representative of one specific configuration and software version. A workable analytic model has the shortcoming that it does not accurately exhibit the large number of unique possible characteristics.

A. Workload Characterization and Generation Techniques

In this section, we describe some of the commonly used workload generation and characterization techniques available in literature.

Descriptive Generation [6][17][18][19] is a technique frequently associated with simple statistical methods: averaging, variances, standard deviation, correlations, distributions, and their corresponding visualization such as histograms or scatter plots. These statistic generation methods are meant to generate workload characteristics such as active users, user think time, actions per sec, etc.

Clustering [19][20] is a workload generation technique that groups similar actions as a unit, making generalizations possible. The selected clusters can be made based on other workload generation methods such as correlations, or by making a selection manually based on functionality within the chosen system. Antonatos [21] describes a method, in which the available network traffic is clustered based on protocol and message type, dividing the traffic into 5 clusters: HTTP request, HTTP Images, HTTP Text, HTTPapp data, and so on.

Markov chains [18][22][23][24] use the temporal characteristics of a workload. A Markov chain consists of series of different states a target system can exist in and the transitions between those states. Transitions are given probabilities of occurrence with several states being active at once, for e.g., many users can use a system at once and their actions are not affected by each-other but only by their own previous actions.

Stochastic form charts [19][20][25] are similar to Markov chains, in that, in addition to states and transitions between those states, actions can also be present. A state can only have transitions towards actions with a corresponding probability, while an action can have one transition towards a state. An example could be a series of web-pages as states and user actions such as logging in or saving as the actions to transition to different or same web pages.

Reactivity [26] is a technique of workload generation which takes output of the target system into account, such as response time of the system to earlier tasks. Response time is a critical factor to the user in an interactive system. Also findings from [27] show that, user think time i.e., the time between subsequent user tasks, is affected by the time it takes for the system to respond. Short response times (0.1 sec) keep the user in the flow improving think time, while longer (10 secs) response times disrupt the user's attention and results in longer think times and different tasks.

Layering is a technique used to model workload from multiple layers instead of only a single layer responsible for the actual workload. This follows the reasoning that, not only the current and preceding task but also the complete state of its parent service/applications affects the total workload.

Regression based modeling [28] is an analytical approach of predicting performance of a target system. By collecting performance test results at different workloads and performing a regression analysis on the results, predictions can be made about the performance for any workload. Hence, only a subset can be used to predict their performance data by extrapolation.

It is important to note that these techniques can be combined to have required characteristics in the generated workloads. With all these techniques, it is important that one should already have the most important characteristics of the workload in mind to generate an appropriate workload. For e.g., if the ideal workload contains a large variability over time, then considering burstiness is necessary. Also the target system and its limitations are important. For instance, should the user only perform certain actions from a given state, then using state diagrams is necessary.

B. Workload Generation Techniques in Practice

There have been many research works to improve realism of the generated workload as well as variability. Many approaches from code analysis to Domain-specific Languages (DSLs) have been adopted. In this section, we describe some of the recent works on workload generation that use combinations of the techniques described above.

Ittershagen et al. [29], proposes a simulation based approach to estimate application's observable shared resource usage. It uses a combined approach of extracting embedded software's processor usage and memory access patterns to get an abstract workload model. This model can then be used in host-based simulation or on a target specific architecture. A compiler infrastructure based system is used, through which the application is processed, which gives the CPU usage and memory access patterns that are used to create an abstracted workload model.

Busch et al. [30] describes an automated workload characterization approach to estimate the performance behavior of I/O intensive software applications in cloud a platform. The proposed algorithm extracts workload characterization models by a non-invasive and lightweight monitoring to get performance metrics such as, request size, read/write ratio, etc. The approach works by dividing high-level operations into several low-level ones corresponding to a workload metric.

In Casaliccio et al. [31], a workload characterization for Desktop-as-a-service (DaaS) is presented. The study was conducted over three months on actual user traffic by measuring resource usage on a DaaS provider's servers. The aim was to study the resource usage and develop a statistical performance model. Several observations were reported from this study: the session length could be modeled with an exponential distribution, and the CPU Load as well as the Disk load (r/w rate) had a long-tail distribution. It was also observed that the peaks in CPU Load or disk read/write rate exceeds the average value by two (or more) orders of magnitude.

Zakay et al. [32] proposes a workload generation method by combining realism of workload tracing (through sampling) and flexibility of workload modeling. The workload traces were divided into sub-traces, which represent activity of real users. New workloads with varying characteristics can then be created by combining the sub-traces in various ways. In order to keep the reconstructed workload close to a real one, re-sampling is done at the user level also taking into account daily and weekly user activity for added realism.

In Van Hoorn et al. [33], a framework for performance testing of session-based applications is proposed using analytical modeling and automatic workload generation. A DSL based approach is used to generate workload specifications, which are then used by workload generation tools to generate workloads. The proposed DSL, WESSBAS-DSL, uses the Markov4JMeter workload modeling formalism for behavior modeling of user session (session duration and 'think' times). The generated WESSBAS-DSL instances are then transformed into corresponding JMeter test plans.

Vogele et al. [34] extend the WESSBAS-DSL approach of [33] by transforming of WESSBAS instances into workload specifications of Palladio Component Model [35], representing architecture-level performance models. The approach enables layered modeling and automatic extraction of workloads. Using WESSBAS-DSL several aspects of session-based system's workload can be modeled such as, Workload Intensity, Application Model, Behavior Models, and Behavior Mix.

Table I shows the workload generation techniques described in III-A used in the literature described above. From Table I, it can be seen that several workload generation techniques can be used depending on the requirement of the test and workload specification.

IV. Performance Testing Methods

In Brunnert et al. [36], a continuous performance evaluation scheme is proposed for new releases or updates for enterprise applications. The main contribution is that architectural information is considered, while defining a resource profile for an application. A model is defined for content and structure to describe performance modeling for an application. A continuous delivery mechanism is also described with steps: create resource usage profile for current version and put it into a repository, predict performance for current version and compare with previous, and if change is detected send notification to development team.

Bezemer et al. [37] describes performance maintenance and improvement of software application in cloud platform after their deployment. The authors argue that continuously detecting Performance Improvement Opportunities (PIOs), which

TABLE I. COMPARISON OF WORKLOAD GENERATION METHODS.

Literature	Proposed Method	Description	Workload Generation Techniques Used
Ittershagen et al. [29]	Code analysis	Generate abstract workload model by analysis code and observing resource usage pattern	Simulation of system and workload
Busch at al. [30]	Usage tracing	I/O Workload characterization by using lightweight monitoring cloud usage	Descriptive (statistics means for file size, workload intensity etc.)
Casaliccio et al. [31]	Usage tracing	Mathematical performance model generation for workload characterization by tracing usage of Daas server	Layering, Descriptive (statistical properties of CPU, read/write loads), Burstiness
Zakay et al. [32]	Usage tracing and modeling	Generating workload by tracing real usage load and resampling parts of it to generate workloads with variability and realism	clustering (users), Burstiness, Regression modeling (resampling workload trace parts)
van Hoorn et al. [33]	Domain-specific Language	Generation of performance test plan with workload by using DSL to model workload specifications	Layering (session and protocol), Clustering (behavior mix), Markov chains
Vogele et al. [34]	Domain-specific Language	Using DSL model and transforming it into a PCM model to include architecture-level performance metrics	Markov chains and Layering (similar to [33])

are defined as situations during which performance can be improved, can assist in performing perfective maintenance (the goal of which is improving performance and therefore perfecting a software system after delivery) of deployed software. An algorithm is proposed to detect PIOs based on response times. From analyzing the PIOs an association rule set can be defined which can be used for detecting bottlenecks.

Rasal et al. [38] proposed a reactive-based framework for performance testing of web applications. In the work, reactivity is described as the way users behave for a provided quality of service. In the proposed scheme web log data is captured from the server-side (from a website set up by the experimenters for a company). A usage pattern is derived in terms of execution time (time taken to process a request) and think time (time user takes to send the next request) from both the server-side and the client-side. A usage pattern model is derived and then it is used to generate automated test cases.

Arcelli et al. [39] proposes a framework for automated generation of software models subject to continuous performance analysis and refactoring. The aim is to detect potential performance anti-patterns (PA), which are mistakes induced during design phase, using the principles of model-driven engineering. The algorithm consists of identifying specific metrics which could degrade performance and associate threshold to them. PA are evaluated by comparing metrics to their threshold. Then, the PA and its solution are identified and refactoring is applied to get the new software model. With the PA knowledge base built, framework can process software models automatically.

In Horkỳ et al. [40], performance unit tests are used to generate performance documentation to help developers make informed decisions (i.e. keeping performance in mind) during software development. In the setup phase, workload for the system is determined, the system is subjected to the workload, and performance is measured. The observed results are evaluated against test criteria using statistical hypothesis testing. Performance documentation is presented for methods in the software framework which would help make choices between different software libraries.

Lou et al. [41] proposes an approach (FOREPOST - Feedback-ORiEnted PerfOrmance Software Testing) to automatically identify input combinations or specific workload to find performance bottlenecks. It uses an adaptive feedback-directed learning system using application execution traces. If-then rules are used to automatically select input values for testing. Initially, a small number of random input values are selected, and then using clustering, execution profiles are grouped into performance categories. The categorized data are then classified using machine learning to obtain rules. The learned rules are used to generate test-cases.

Danciu et al. [42] proposes an approach of analyzing performance of Java 2 Platform, Enterprise Edition applications and providing feedback related to performance in the Integrated Development Environment (IDE) itself. The source code is parsed and converted into a Palladio component model. This is then used to predict the response time of the application. The predicted performance results is presented within the IDE, making developers performance aware during development.

The literature study presented above, encompasses different phases of performance testing of software applications; from testing performance during development/modeling application [39], application upgrading [36], to maintaining deployed software [37]. It also shows reactive approaches [38], and proactive approaches where application development choices are influenced by performance [40][42]. The literature described takes focus on resource usage, throughput, response time, or a combination of them. Various workload generation method were used: real production loads for approaches that use reactive mechanism or deployed application [37][38], predicted workloads [41][42], workloads generated from the software model [36][39], or just stress test specific parts (as only limited functionality is available) of the application by iteratively calling them [40].

In the next section, we extract steps and process phases from the methods and frameworks above, to create an abstract method that can be deployed by practitioners.

V. THE CONTINUOUS PERFORMANCE TESTING METHOD

In Table II, an overview of the steps of CPT that are found in literature is described. It is important to choose the purpose of performance tests and hence the criteria being measured. Table II shows that each work has a specific criterion, such as resource usage [36][37][41] or response time [37][38].

The processes and frameworks found in the literature, all have a workload generation phase as part of the test. For example, Brunnert et al. [36] use usage models that help in predicting resource usage while Lou et al. [41] and Danciu et al. [42] use predicted workloads. Furthermore, Bezemer et al. [37] and Rasal et al. [38] use real production workload, and Horky et al. [40] iteratively call parts of an application to stress test the system. Monitoring points are defined in the test setup, be it logs or the software model itself. Following up, there is a test that involves either performance prediction for analytical approaches or measuring parameters, such as response time. The obtained results are compared either to

TABLE II. COMPARISON OF (CONTINUOUS) PERFORMANCE TESTING METHODS.

Paper	Perf. criteria	Workload	Monitoring	Testing	Alert mechanism
Brunnert et al. [36]	Resource usage	Synthetic workload (usage modeling, think times)	Resource prediction from performance model	Performance prediction	Comparison b/w current and previous version
Bezemer et al. [37]	Throughput, response time and resource usage	Live production workload	Logs	Build ruleset and compare	Provides performance improvement opportunities through bottleneck identification
Rasal et al. [38]	Execution time	Live production workload	Logs	Build usage pattern	Implicit, not stated
Arcelli et al. [39]	Over-used S/W components and resource usage	None, deduced from software model	S/W model annotated with performace indices	Model transformation and threshold comparison	Automated model refactorisation
Horky et al. [40]	Resource usage	Iteratively call a piece of code	Measure resource usage on local system	Run the piece of code and measure response	Performance documentation
Lou et al. [41]	Resource usage	Workload predicted	Measure resource usage on local system	Tracing execution of methods	Identified bottlenecks as methods
Danciu et al. [42]	Response time	Synthetic Workload using modeling	Resource Prediction using performance model	Tracing execution of methods	Identified bottlenecks as methods presented in IDE

previous values or to a threshold. At the last stage, an alert mechanism is used to notify the results to the stakeholders of performance tests. Several ways of alert mechanisms can be observed in the literature, such as, through PIOs [37], performance documentation, or presenting results on the IDE during development.

Based on these observations, an abstract method for CPT is presented with the following steps:

1) **Assess critical performance criteria -** In this step performance metrics to be measured are selected. This is important as this determines the type of test to be performed and the workload parameters.
2) **Decide on workload generation technique to use** - This step is very important as a representative workload is necessary to get reasonable results for the purpose of the test. As stated earlier, this step depends on the type of performance to be performed. Section III gives more information on selecting an appropriate technique.
3) **Identify monitoring points and build in monitoring -** In this step, the points where the application performance in relation to identified metrics is to be located.
4) **Decide on performance testing method and tools to use -** This depends on the performance criteria and stage of development cycle of application. It can be simulation based approach for software under development to monitoring application under use. Section IV describes some of the methods.
5) **Set up alert mechanisms and describe actions -** Setup system to send performance results to concerned personnel for the next course of action.

Using the steps described above, the proposed method for CPT is shown in Fig. 1. By introducing a feedback loop from the testing phase, comprising of alert mechanism and decision making step back to testing, performance evaluation can be done on a continuous basis. In the next section, we validate this method by means of a case-study at AFAS, where a similar CPT method is used. We compare the proposed method with the tools and mechanism used at AFAS, and present the usefulness of CPT being performed in development of NEXT.

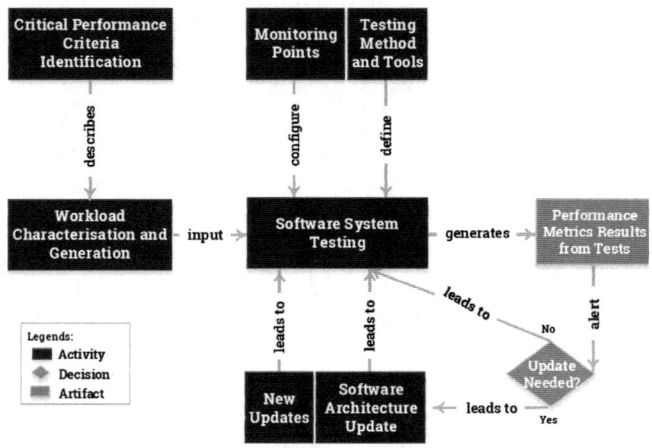

FIGURE 1. CONTINUOUS PERFORMANCE TESTING WORKFLOW.

VI. CASE STUDY AND EXPERT EVALUATION

Currently, AFAS Software is using CPT to evaluate performance changes for NEXT on a regular basis. One of the key design drivers of this redesign is the focus on Command Query Responsibility Segregation (CQRS) [43][44] distributed architecture. CQRS is an architectural pattern developed to support scalability, and provides a practical solution to Brewer's theorem [45] in a distributed system architecture. This pattern prescribes separation in client-server communication between commands and queries, commands being actions which can modify the data while queries are the request to access the said data. This strict separation allows architects to make different architectural choices on command and query side of the system. CPT has become a major tool in the design and validation of architectural choices on both the command and the query side of the CQRS architecture for NEXT.

A. *Implementation at the Case Company*

The case study was performed with an intention to find out how, in an organization and in real software production setup, performing CPT has lead to improvement in software quality and development process. To this end, the case-study included interviewing experts from AFAS on the process of performance testing of NEXT. The interview protocol was designed with several sections each discussing different aspects of CPT as described in Section V. The questions were designed to extract the process and tools used at AFAS in each aspect of the CPT. In the Table III, we describe the AFAS context at each aspect of CPT and the tools used by AFAS in their CPT implementation.

B. Case Findings

From transcribing the interviews of the case-study and comparing it with the CPT method described, the following observations were made:

First, the performance criteria that are important for the selected performance test and the purpose of the test are identified. At AFAS, the performance testing is more stress testing the system. The metrics that are measured are: the number of user operations which correspond to commands/queries and events projected per second on their designed CQRS architecture choices. The aim of the tests is to see the trends on the selected data stores and eventually make a choice of selection for stores on command and query side.

A workload generation mechanism is used to suit the test, for instance to do stress tests, concurrent commands and queries are generated, as the tests are mainly focused on measuring throughput of the data stores. The workload is generated by a custom-built application which uses a template for commands and queries to generate workload. The workload generator generates the required number of commands or queries. It is known beforehand the number of events which are to be projected. This helps comprehensively test the designed architecture for its performance.

Monitoring points are identified in the architecture for the selected test. At AFAS the monitoring points are introduced at the command, query and event projection. Plugins are introduced at monitoring points which have performance counters that measure the number of operations (commands, queries, and events) per second. This selection of monitoring points helps to measure the number of commands/queries handled per second as well as the time it takes for the whole process chain to execute.

Currently performance testing is done mainly for the selection of data stores. Testing is done on many different database options (MongoDB, MySQL, MSSQL and PostgreSQL) and are repeated for every database choice. The application is hosted on a server and input with the generated workload. The tests are run with different stores and the said performance metrics are registered at the monitoring points. Since CQRS architecture allows separate choices to be made on command and query side, parts of the system can be optimized independently. one software architect stated :*"It (CPT) helps with the way we want to choose stores or changes we made were right or wrong in terms of performance"*. Another software architect stated: *"From the testing it is noted that PostgreSQL performs better on the query side for transactions"*.

Alert mechanism works by sending emails to the stakeholders after the tests each day. Also, the recorded results are published on the company's intranet and can be accessed by anyone within the organization. The plotted results show metrics from last few weeks, and can be useful to see trends in performance of the application as it evolves. The concerned team monitors the results and makes decisions when it is necessary to investigate the cause. A software architect stated: *"The performance test results become very important when changes are implemented and some variation in performance is expected"*. If the results obtained after changes differ very much than expected, then it is inspected as one of the architects mentioned: *"If the change can be explained, after some new feature was implemented and some drop was expected then it might be fine. But if the change cannot be explained then it will be investigated"*.

In the case-study, a performance testing scenario was created with the goals of comparing database options and operating systems for NEXT. The configurations consisted of MSSQL and MongoDB on Windows and Linux operating systems. As described earlier, the critical performance criteria were defined to be measured, i.e., throughput, response time, CPU, and disk I/O. The workload characterization was done with the metrics in mind to test individual components of CQRS architecture. Hence, the workload consisted of database operations (in large numbers) on a work item, such as Insert (create commands), InsertQMB (create events), Update (update commands), UpdateQMB (update events), Query, Query40 (40 simultaneous queries at a time). Several interesting observations were noted: SQL offered most throughput in inserts, MongoDB showed higher average throughput but gaps were observed (as it processes writes in large batches), MongoDB on Linux showed lower throughput for inserts and queries, etc. This testing configuration gave a basis for performance testing NEXT on a daily basis as new options (in database, event bus, etc.) are tested and the new features are added to the software model NEXT.

The NEXT platform currently exists in a pre-release phase, but parts of it are already being used within the company. The platform is evolving rigorously (*"We make massive architecture changes almost daily (as model-driven development is used and model evolves everyday and thus leads to many changes in implementation)"*) and CPT is helping to evaluate changes from a performance point of view. The company benefits from continuous insight into the platform's performance evolution, especially because the platform is in such an early phase of development. That said, employees in the company states that CPT is useful in any maturity phase of the platform, because at a later stage they expect that CPT can help them identify small changes with large impact on the performance.

C. Expert Evaluation

In the case study, the interviewees indicate that CPT has been essential in the development process of NEXT in the areas of architecture, implementation, and software quality.

With regards to **architecture**, one senior software architect at AFAS, when asked about how CPT has influenced architectural choices for NEXT, stated: *"Performance testing has given cause to rethink [...] things, what you think helps to improve performance but doesn't actually"*. This flexibility is seen by others as well: *"Doing performance testing during design/implementation phase is important because the impact of changes can be seen can and work on it rather than during production"*. He also stated that the selection of test is important based on state of the application: *"But it is important to select the type of test as it is not known about production load during development"*. One instance was cited where performance test had helped to identify a bottleneck and prompted a change in architecture - *"A bottleneck was*

TABLE III. PERFORMANCE TESTING TOOLS.

Process	Case-study Method	Tools
Assess critical performance criteria	Requests handled per second and time taken to process each request, it can be just the commands or queries or the whole process measuring commands and no. of events it generates or queries and execution of all the projected evens, future: resource usage CPU, memory, IO	This is a choice made based on current state of the product
Workload generation	Commands and/or queries are generated containing user information and in order to stress the system either on command side or query side or both and measure how many requests can be handled	Workload generator which uses a CSV file containing random user information and a template specifying no. of commands and/or queries
Identify monitoring points	monitoring points are inserted on command, query side, and event handler to measure no. of commands	Custom-built plugins at command, query, and event bus side
Performance testing method	Stress test system with concurrent user load (commands or queries or both) and on different data stores and compare the identified performance criteria	RabbitMQ, Event Tracing for Windows, ELK stack, and datastores such as MongoDB, MySQL, MSSQL, and PostgreSQL
Setup alert mechanism and describe action	Email, intranet, and coffee room dashboard, the results can be monitored for trends	Custom tools for transforming events into graphs and publishing it through email and web

detected in initial testing of ServiceFabric [46] in event dispatching. One component of the ServiceFabric was detected as producing the bottleneck. As a result a new component was planned to replace the existing one to alleviate the problem". Also, in selections of stores, one of the trend that was reported was that PostGreSQL was seen to perform better on query side.

CPT has helped in making **design decisions** as well as validating the designed changes. Project manager at AFAS gave an example: *"it (CPT) has helped us make decision whether to use of dynamic commands vs typed commands in the backend architecture. We expected some performance issues, but through performance testing we observed that no significant degradation in performance occured. Hence it (CPT) helped us validate changes".*

CPT has furthermore helped in making decisions about where to deploy the application and what kinds of **resources will be used**. Currently, the most important reason to use CPT at AFAS is to create an overview of resource usage on each database platform and find the most performant database for the development of NEXT.

The representatives at the company indicate that **quality** problems that would normally be caught in production are now caught earlier. *"CPT has helped in finding bugs we don't find in normal usage. It also help with deciding whether changes were right or wrong in terms of performance. It has helped now and will help in future if the application monitored properly (after changes) and we get more informative results".*

VII. ANALYSIS AND DISCUSSION

Continuous performance testing is the best way to provide architects with continuous insight into the implementation of their designs. There are other ways of reporting on architecture patterns, such as empirical qualitative evaluations, but these report on a particular implementation of a pattern, and are thus less usable by other architects. One of the most powerful features of CPT is that it requires architects to provide an upfront expectation of what the performance will be, providing them benchmarks and targets to constantly adjust their design by. The case study is but one observation, but its results can be generalized to other large and long-lived systems.

Frequent exchange of knowledge is required by architects in different working sessions. Their design decisions have long lasting effects on developer productivity, flexibility, variability, and performance of a system. Architects need experience and frequent interactions with other architects in cross-organization expert groups. In the future, we suggest that other authors too report case studies, such that synthesis becomes possible and the CPT framework can be perfected. In particular, academia still need to develop and evaluate tools for CPT.

VIII. CONCLUSION

This paper functions as a call to action for practitioners and researchers to employ CPT in practice and report on their results. The case study illustrates how an organization has benefited from CPT in an early-stage development project. The main advantages are found in software architecture, design decisions, resource usage, and software quality.

We present directions for future research. Firstly, workload generation techniques can be combined, to create more realistic workloads. In the case-study, random data was used to generate template-driven workload, that was based on the model underlying the application. Secondly, it would be interesting to create realistic workloads based on the devices that are used to access the application. Once a change in end-user behavior is detected, switching from mainly web application to mainly mobile, for instance, could change the workloads that are used for testing accordingly. Thirdly, in case of an ERP application, the user category can dictate the kind of functionality used more often in each category and time of day the application is used most often. This, however, we leave to future research.

ACKNOWLEDGMENT

This is an AMUSE Paper. This research was supported by the NWO AMUSE project (628.006.001): a collaboration between Vrije Universiteit Amsterdam, Utrecht University, and AFAS Software in the Netherlands. The NEXT Platform is developed and maintained by AFAS Software. See amuse-project.org for more information.

REFERENCES

[1] K. Wiegers and J. Beatty, Software requirements. Pearson Education, 2013.

[2] T. F. Abdelzaher, K. G. Shin, and N. Bhatti, "Performance guarantees for web server end-systems: A control-theoretical approach," IEEE Transactions on Parallel and Distributed Systems, vol. 13, no. 1, 2002, pp. 80–96.

[3] E. J. Weyuker and F. I. Vokolos, "Experience with performance testing of software systems: issues, an approach, and case study," IEEE transactions on software engineering, vol. 26, no. 12, 2000, pp. 1147–1156.

[4] Compuware, "Applied Performance Management Survey," 2006.

[5] R. Jain, The art of computer systems performance analysis. John Wiley & Sons, 2008.

[6] S. Elnaffar and P. Martin, "Characterizing computer systems workloads," Tr. 2002-461, School of Computing, Queen University. Ontario, Canada, 2002.

[7] H. H. Olsson and J. Bosch, "Towards continuous customer validation: A conceptual model for combining qualitative customer feedback with quantitative customer observation," in Proc. of 6th International Conference of Software Business (ICSOB) June 10-12, 2015, Braga, Portugal. Springer International Publishing, Jun. 2015, pp. 154–166.

[8] J. Webster and R. T. Watson, "Analyzing the past to prepare for the future: Writing a literature review," MIS quarterly, vol. 26, no. 2, 2002, pp. 13–23.

[9] B. A. Kitchenham, "Systematic review in software engineering: Where we are and where we should be going," in Proc. of the 2nd International Workshop on Evidential Assessment of Software Technologies Sep 22, 2012, Lund, Sweden. ACM, 2012, pp. 1–2.

[10] T. Johnson, "Webjamma," 1998.

[11] G. Banga and P. Druschel, "Measuring the capacity of a web server." in USENIX Symposium on Internet Technologies and Systems, Dec. 1997, pp. 61–72.

[12] D. A. Menascé, "Tpc-w: A benchmark for e-commerce," IEEE Internet Computing, vol. 6, no. 3, 2002, pp. 83–87.

[13] A. G. Saidi, N. L. Binkert, L. R. Hsu, and S. K. Reinhardt, "Performance validation of network-intensive workloads on a full-system simulator," Ann Arbor, vol. 1001, 2005, pp. 48 109–2122.

[14] Y. Sherman, U. Hare, and I. Kinreich, "Method of load testing web applications based on performance goal," Aug. 13 2002, uS Patent 6,434,513.

[15] E. H. Halili, Apache JMeter: A practical beginner's guide to automated testing and performance measurement for your websites, Jun. 2008.

[16] N. Mi, G. Casale, L. Cherkasova, and E. Smirni, "Injecting realistic burstiness to a traditional client-server benchmark," in Proc. of the 6th international conference on Autonomic computing, Jun. 2009, pp. 149–158.

[17] M. Wang, K. Au, A. Ailamaki, A. Brockwell, C. Faloutsos, and G. R. Ganger, "Storage device performance prediction with cart models," in Proc. The IEEE Computer Society's 12th Annual International Symposium on Modeling, Analysis, and Simulation of Computer and Telecommunications Systems (MASCOTS), Oct. 2004, pp. 588–595.

[18] A. Van Hoorn, M. Rohr, and W. Hasselbring, "Generating probabilistic and intensity-varying workload for web-based software systems," in SPEC International Performance Evaluation Workshop, Jun. 2008, pp. 124–143.

[19] M. Calzarossa, L. Massari, and D. Tessera, "Workload characterization - issues and methodologies," in Performance Evaluation: Origins and Directions. Springer, 2000, pp. 459–482.

[20] I. S. Moreno, P. Garraghan, P. Townend, and J. Xu, "An approach for characterizing workloads in google cloud to derive realistic resource utilization models," in IEEE 7th International Symposium on Service Oriented System Engineering (SOSE), Mar. 2013, pp. 49–60.

[21] M. Yuksel, B. Sikdar, K. Vastola, and B. Szymanski, "Workload generation for ns simulations of wide area networks and the internet," in Proc. of Communication Networks and Distributed Systems Modeling and Simulation Conference, 2000, pp. 93–98.

[22] A. Bahga and V. K. Madisetti, "Synthetic workload generation for cloud computing applications," Journal of Software Engineering and Applications, vol. 4, no. 07, 2011, pp. 396–410.

[23] H. Hlavacs, E. Hotop, and G. Kotsis, "Workload generation by modeling user behavior," Proc. OPNETWORKS, 2000.

[24] W. Sobel, S. Subramanyam, A. Sucharitakul, J. Nguyen, H. Wong, A. Klepchukov, S. Patil, A. Fox, and D. Patterson, "Cloudstone: Multi-platform, multi-language benchmark and measurement tools for web 2.0," in Proc. of CCA, vol. 8, 2008.

[25] C. Lutteroth and G. Weber, "Modeling a realistic workload for performance testing," in Enterprise Distributed Object Computing Conference, 2008. EDOC'08. 12th International IEEE. IEEE, 2008, pp. 149–158.

[26] A. Pereira, L. Silva, W. Meira, and W. Santos, "Assessing the impact of reactive workloads on the performance of web applications," in IEEE International Symposium on Performance Analysis of Systems and Software, Mar. 2006, pp. 211–220.

[27] D. A. Menasce, V. A. Almeida, L. W. Dowdy, and L. Dowdy, Performance by design: computer capacity planning by example. Prentice Hall Professional, 2004.

[28] Q. Zhang, L. Cherkasova, and E. Smirni, "A regression-based analytic model for dynamic resource provisioning of multi-tier applications," in 4th International Conference on Autonomic Computing (ICAC'07), Jun. 2007, pp. 27–27.

[29] P. Ittershagen, P. A. Hartmann, K. Grüttner, and W. Nebel, "A workload extraction framework for software performance model generation," in Proc. of the Workshop on Rapid Simulation and Performance Evaluation: Methods and Tools (RAPIDO), Jan. 2015, pp. 3:1–3:6.

[30] A. Busch, Q. Noorshams, S. Kounev, A. Koziolek, R. Reussner, and E. Amrehn, "Automated workload characterization for i/o performance analysis in virtualized environments," in Proc. of the 6th ACM/SPEC International Conference on Performance Engineering, Jan. 2015, pp. 265–276.

[31] E. Casalicchio, S. Iannucci, and L. Silvestri, "Cloud desktop workload: A characterization study," in IEEE International Conference on Cloud Engineering (IC2E). IEEE, Mar. 2015, pp. 66–75.

[32] N. Zakay and D. G. Feitelson, "Workload resampling for performance evaluation of parallel job schedulers," Concurrency and Computation: Practice and Experience, vol. 26, no. 12, 2014, pp. 2079–2105.

[33] A. van Hoorn, C. Vögele, E. Schulz, W. Hasselbring, and H. Krcmar, "Automatic extraction of probabilistic workload specifications for load testing session-based application systems," in Proc. of the 8th International Conference on Performance Evaluation Methodologies and Tools, Dec. 2014, pp. 139–146.

[34] C. Vögele, A. van Hoorn, and H. Krcmar, "Automatic extraction of session-based workload specifications for architecture-level performance models," in Proc. of the 4th International Workshop on Large-Scale Testing, Feb. 2015, pp. 5–8.

[35] S. Becker, H. Koziolek, and R. Reussner, "The palladio component model for model-driven performance prediction," Journal of Systems and Software, vol. 82, no. 1, 2009, pp. 3–22.

[36] A. Brunnert and H. Krcmar, "Continuous performance evaluation and capacity planning using resource profiles for enterprise applications," Journal of Systems and Software, 2015.

[37] C.-P. Bezemer and A. Zaidman, "Performance optimization of deployed software-as-a-service applications," Journal of Systems and Software, vol. 87, 2014, pp. 87–103.

[38] Y. M. Rasal and S. Nagpure, "Web application: Performance testing using reactive based framework," IJRCCT, vol. 4, no. 2, 2015, pp. 114–118.

[39] D. Arcelli and V. Cortellessa, "Assisting software designers to identify and solve performance problems," in Proc. of the 1st International Workshop on Future of Software Architecture Design Assistants, May 2015, pp. 1–6.

[40] V. Horký, P. Libič, L. Marek, A. Steinhauser, and P. Tuuma, "Utilizing performance unit tests to increase performance awareness," in Proc. of the 6th ACM/SPEC International Conference on Performance Engineering, Jan. 2015, pp. 289–300.

[41] Q. Luo, A. Nair, M. Grechanik, and D. Poshyvanyk, "Forepost: finding performance problems automatically with feedback-directed learning software testing," Empirical Software Engineering, 2016, pp. 1–51.

[42] A. Danciu, A. Brunnert, and H. Krcmar, "Towards performance awareness in java ee development environments," in Proc. of the Symposium on Software Performance: Descartes/Kieker/Palladio Days, Nov. 2014, pp. 152–159.

[43] G. Young, "Cqrs and event sourcing. feb. 2010," URl: http://codebetter.com/gregy oung/2010/02/13/cqrs-and-event-sourcing.

[44] J. Kabbedijk, S. Jansen, and S. Brinkkemper, "A case study of the variability consequences of the cqrs pattern in online business software," in Proc. of the 17th European Conference on Pattern Languages of Programs, Jul. 2012, pp. 2:1–2:10.

[45] S. Gilbert and N. Lynch, "Brewer's conjecture and the feasibility of consistent, available, partition-tolerant web services," ACM SIGACT News, vol. 33, no. 2, 2002, pp. 51–59.

[46] "MS Azure ServiceFabric," 2016, URL: https://azure.microsoft.com/en-us/documentation/articles/service-fabric-overview/.

Formalization of Ergonomic Knowledge For Designing Context-Aware Human-Computer Interfaces

Dorra Zaibi
Cristal Laboratory
National School of Computer Sciences
University of Manouba
Manouba, Tunisia
e-mail: zaibi.dorra@gmail.com

Meriem Riahi
Higher National School of engineering of Tunis
University of Tunis
Montfleury, Tunis, Tunisia
e-mail: meriem.riahi2013@gmail.com

Faouzi Moussa
Cristal Laboratory
National School of Computer Sciences
University of Manouba
Manouba, Tunisia
e-mail: faouzimoussa@gmail.com

Abstract—**During the last three decades, different methodologies and tools were developed for the design and the evaluation of Human-Computer Interaction. However, ergonomic knowledge is often informal and lacks - for the utmost part any structure to be directly exploited by designers. Ergonomists still find it hard to use the ergonomic requirements in practice. This paper presents an ergonomic approach for designing Human-Computer Interfaces considering context information. We are particularly interested in formalizing the ergonomic knowledge. To validate our approach, we propose the application of a Computerized Maintenance Management System, dedicated to the management of intervention requests and dashboard monitoring.**

Keywords- Ergonomic knowledge; expert system; Human computer Interaction (HCI), Model Driven Architecture (MDA); context-aware design.

I. INTRODUCTION

Nowadays, interactive systems are continuously evolving. They are pervasive in all areas and fields [1]. Additional functionalities further increase the complexity of these systems making them less suitable to use [2]. Thus, the Human-Computer Interaction (HCI) community is facing a growing challenge to obtain high quality User Interfaces (UI) [3][4]. To this aim, several novel methodologies and techniques were presented and explored during the last three decades [5][6][7]. However, as stated in Scapin, Reynard and Pollier [8], ergonomic knowledge is usually rather informal and lacks - for the utmost part - structuration to be directly applied by designers. It still remains a difficult task to ergonomists for the ergonomic recommendation practice.

Many directions were explored. They differ by means of interactive system life cycle phase (specification, design, development, testing, validating, etc.). Different quality factors were used, over which the evaluation process can be established. The most frequently used one for interactive system evaluation are essentially the utility and the usability [9][10]. As reported by Charfi et al. [11], "the utility determines if the system allows the user to perform his task and if he is able to achieve what is necessary to meet his expectations from the system. It corresponds to the functional capabilities, system performance, and the technical assistance quality given to the user by the system". According to ISO 9241-18, the term usability has been defined as "the extent to which a product can be used by specified users to achieve specified goals with effectiveness, efficiency and satisfaction in a specified context of use" [12]. The utility and usability are important issues to validate ergonomic UI and assure optimal functioning of Human-Computer systems.

Model-Driven Architecture (MDA) [13] has been revealed to be an appropriate approach for the design and the development of software system and their user interfaces. Following this trend, the HCI community has highlighted the benefits of its technology and used MDA approaches.

In this paper, we propose an ergonomic approach for designing context-aware UI based on MDA. We are interested in ergonomic evaluation process since early design stages. This work aims to formalize ergonomic knowledge for the specification of context-aware Human-Computer interfaces.

The remainder of the paper is organized in the following way: Section II surveys the related work. Section III introduces our contribution for ergonomic knowledge formalization and integration in the design process. Section IV presents an overview of our current implementation prototype as well as a case study. Finally, we conclude and discuss our research perspectives in Section V.

II. RELATED WORK

Ergonomic approaches motivated many publications.

Tarby et al. [14] based their approach on traces to conduct design phase evaluation, which include Aspect Oriented Programming (with aspects that are devoted to evaluation).

Trabelsi et al. [15] present the evaluation of agent-based interactive systems. They propose an evaluation approach based on three complementary techniques: assistance evaluation tool, questionnaire, and verbalization.

User Interface evaluation framework (RITA) [16] is an evaluation tool. It is composed by software applications structured in a modular architecture way. This framework uses three different evaluation techniques: the electronic informer, the ergonomic quality inspection and the questionnaire. It has a modular architecture that can be configured to evaluate different kinds of user interfaces.

Destine [17][18] is a tool, which allows the UI evaluation using a language of ergonomic rules definition. It permits to integrate or change intended rules for the evaluation without altering the source code of the evaluation tool.

EISEval [19] is an environment dedicated to the evaluation of interactive systems having agent-based architecture. The authors presented an electronic informer using Petri Nets.

These approaches vary in several ways. Their applications differ with the system lifecycle. Some tools and approaches are proposed to be used during design phases [14][16]. Others are designed to evaluate UI during the last phase of the development life-cycle [15][17][18][19], without considering the design and implementation process of the UI. In fact, we noticed that the UI evaluation phase is skipped in most cases of the development. It may be neglected for different reasons such as time and budget constraints. In addition, the evaluation can be expensive when applying it to the final stage of the lifecycle of a system. According to Nielsen [10], it is a hundred times cheaper to evaluate the UI during the early stages than in the final ones. Thus, it is more appropriate to consider the UI evaluation early in the development cycle. Some existing techniques propose to incorporate ergonomic guidelines in UI design process. Unfortunately, they do not take into consideration context changes. Thus, interactive systems face mostly the challenge of their ergonomic inconsistencies due to context requirements.

The novelty of this work is how to consider the ergonomic guidelines properly with eventually possible changes in the context of interactive systems for obtaining successful UI. We present in the next section our methodology for designing context-aware UI.

III. Human-Comuter Interface Design Methodology : Overview

Since our focus is to provide ergonomic knowledge, we include some ideas to consider ergonomic specifications since early design stage. In this way, it is necessary to first conduct a formalization of ergonomic knowledge, then to provide the appropriate ergonomic guidelines considering context information, and finally to integrate these guidelines in context-aware specifications.

Our approach is summarized in Fig. 1. The system is developed by performing two main steps. We consider that we are given regularly context information. In this sense, a specific system is held, at runtime, updating continuously context changes. During the design phase of the system, we consider this information when designing the UI. The main steps of our approach are explained in the sequel.

A. *Expert System for Reasoning Ergonomic Knowledge*

Ergonomic knowledge is generally informal. For this purpose, we aim to formalize ergonomic knowledge for integrating them in the context-aware specifications. To be used in such approach, an ergonomic knowledge base is supplied. Our methodology is based on Artificial Intelligence techniques. In fact, our solution can be thought of as an expert system. As Fig. 1 shows, we have followed three sub-stages:

1) Structuring of ergonomic knowledge: The ergonomic knowledge that we used is mainly derived from [11][12][20][21].

It addresses more particularly the ergonomist to provide specific structural definition. This organization is important to ease the management of rules database. In this phase, we use the structuration of User Interface Markup Language (UIML) [22], since it allows the description of user interfaces in an abstract way. UIML, as defined in [22], separates the elements of the interface. It contains two main components: *interface* and *peers*. The interface component represents the description of the user interface according to four parts: *structure*, which describes the organization and the hierarchies of all the parts constituting the UI; *content*, which represents the application's information to be shown; *behavior*, which defines the behavior of the application during the interaction with the user, and *style,* which describes all the particular properties for each element of the UI. The peers' component contains two parts: *presentation*, which links the generic elements of the UI to a particular platform and *logic*, which defines the calling conventions for external methods in application logic that the UI raises.

Building on the organization of UIML elements, this stage promotes the semantic description of ergonomic knowledge. At the end of this phase, the knowledge base is shared in "knowledge sub-bases" (*KD Sub-Base*), each sub-base is related to a semantics of the ergonomics: *Structure, Style, Contents, Behavior, Logic and Presentation.*

2) Formalization of ergonomic knowledge: After the structuring phase, the ergonomic knowledge is formalized in form of productions rules. The set of production rules is related to particular context information. The production rules' formalism is of the following type:

IF $(C_1 * C_2 * \text{---} * C_i)$ *THEN E.*

The contextual conditions of a rule are a logic arrangement of premises *Ci*. The operator "*" may be the one of the logical operator "AND" or "OR". The ergonomic guidelines *E* represent the set of appropriate conclusions of a rule.

3) Rule-based Inference System: We are based on a Rule-based system, which is designed to resolve problems by reasoning knowledge, represented initially as if-then rules. The rule-based system uses a working memory that initially comprises the input data for a particular run, and an inference engine.

The set of context instance *Ci* is stored in facts. It is exploited by the inference engine. The context information is defined, initially, in a Context Model (detailed in Section B) and is then explored. The rules deduction is accomplished by the inference of a set of rules contained in the knowledge sub-bases. The ergonomic rules are fulfilled by a first order inference engine that is based on forward chaining inference.

Forward chaining inference engine is an automated reasoning system, working from a current state by evaluating the premises of the inference rules (IF-part), performing pertinent rules, and then asserting new knowledge.

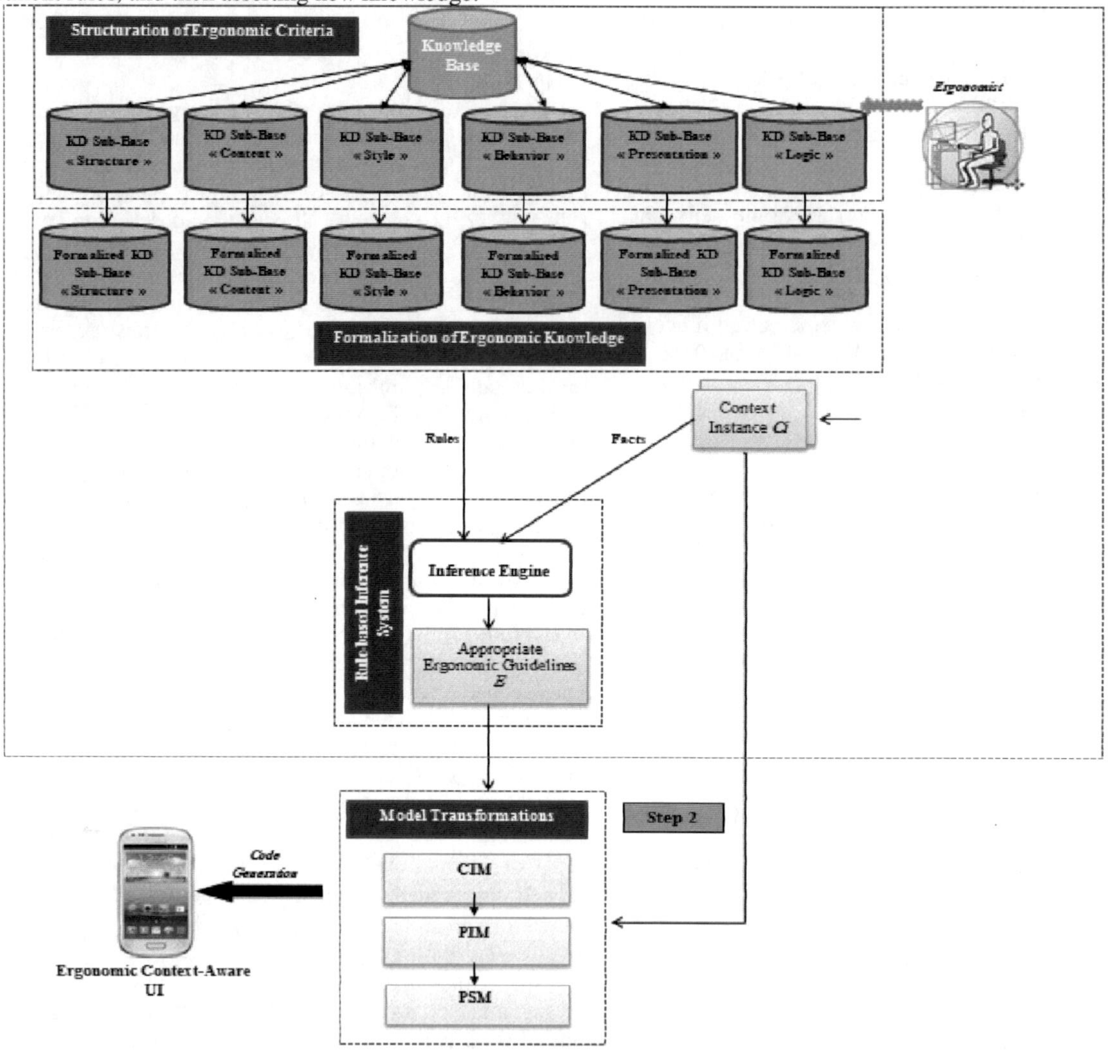

Figure 1. Our Approach overview.

The inference engine draws knowledge based on given facts Ci and production rules. This knowledge presents the set of appropriate ergonomic guidelines for a given context information. The Rule-based system is implemented with DROOLS rule engine [23] using an enhanced implementation of the Rete algorithm [24] for pattern matching, adapted for object oriented languages, and for Java in particular. Rules are stored in the production memory, whereas facts are preserved in the working memory. The Rete algorithm generates a network from rule conditions. Each single rule condition is a node in the Rete network. We use a conflict resolution strategy, if there are multiple selected rules, by managing execution order via the Agenda.

In order to be included on the next step, we have modeled the set of appropriate ergonomic guidelines in an ergonomic model instance (detailed in Section B) using a specific algorithm (i.e., algorithm for converting from a set of appropriate guidelines to a corresponding ergonomic model instance in the Ergonomic Model).

B. Integration of Ergonomic Guidelines in Model-Driven Development

MDA [13] is an approach that allows specifying the system independently of any platform that supports it by transforming the specification into a software system, for a specific platform. A set of guidelines is provided by its approach for the structuring of specifications. It uses three types of models: computation independent model (CIM) that allows describing the context of the system and the requirements without consideration for its structure or treatment; platform independent model (PIM) that allows describing only those parts of a complete specification that can be abstracted without any specific platforms; and, platform specific model (PSM) that associates PIM specification with specific information for a specific platform.

Following the MDA structure, we distinguish four main models (Fig. 2): The Business Process Model (as CIM), Platform Independent Model 1 (as PIM), Platform Independent Model 2 (as PIM), and Platform Specific Model (as PSM).

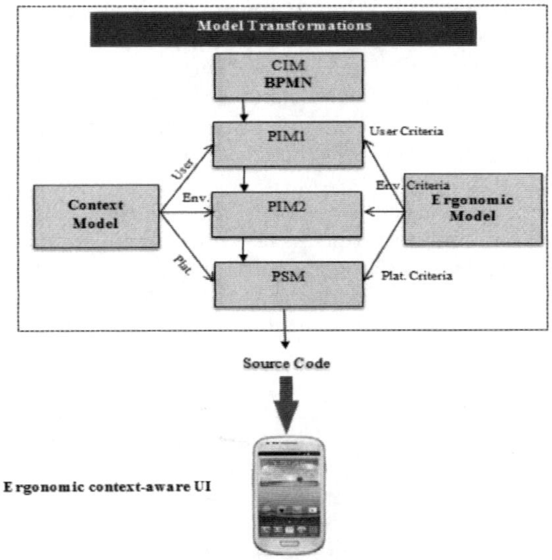

Figure 2. Model-Driven Development .

As described in Fig. 2, this step is composed of six models:

- Business Process Model (BPM): To describe the CIM model, we used Business Process Modeling Notation (BPMN) [25], which is able to define tasks. for the specification of the business goal (interactive tasks, non-interactive tasks and manual tasks) and the information flow among tasks, since we are interested in providing ergonomic guidelines into user interaction. Each BPMN element has been defined in the BPMN model with a specific type (i.e., interaction element type) in order to describe the nature of the interaction with the user, such as: types of input information (e.g., *UIFieldInMultipleChoice*), output information (e.g., *UIFieldInAction*) or grouping information (e.g., *UIUnit*). (Table I);
- Context Model: We have used a defined Context Model all along the MDA model definition and transformations. It is composed of a description about user, environment and platform;

TABLE I. SOME INTERACTION ELEMENTS

BPMN Element	Associated Interaction Element
Pool	UIGroup
Lane	UIUnit
UserTask	UIFieldAction
UserTask	UIFieldInManual

- Ergonomic Model: Fig. 3, below, defines the Ergonomic Model. It is composed of two major parts: *Antecedent*, which is the first half of the hypothetical proposition and contains context information; and *Consequent,* which describes the ergonomic guidelines;
- Platform Independent Model 1 (PIM1): To specify the user interaction by introducing the user requirements and ergonomic guidelines according to the user independently of any platform. It is specified using the User Interface Markup Language UIML [22], specially the *structure* and *style* parts;
- Platform Independent Model 2 (PIM2): To specify the user interaction by taking into account environment constraints and appropriate ergonomic guidelines according to the environment and independently of any specific platform. It is also defined by UIML language [22], which specifies the *style* parts;

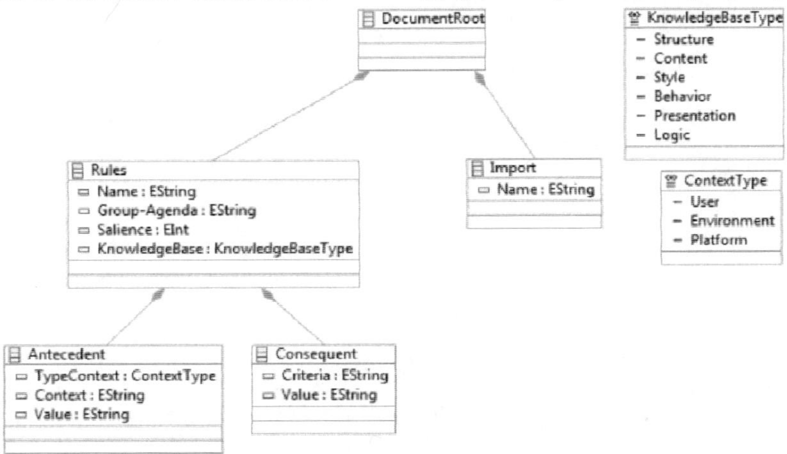

Figure 3. Ergonomic Model

- Platform Specific Model (PSM): To specify the user interaction for a particular platform, integrating ergonomic guidelines related to platform dimensions (e.g., displays information). Moreover, it is described by the use of User Interface Markup Language UIML [22], and allows specifying the *presentation*, *logic* and *style* parts.

By applying Model-To-Model transformations, we generate the first transformation, PIM1 model, based on two UIML parts (*structure* and *style*), which are independent of the platform and integrate the specific information of the user context and its ergonomic guidelines. The second transformation from PIM1 to PIM2 includes environment information and its ergonomic guidelines and generates the *style* part. The third transformation from PIM2 to PSM is generated based on three UIML parts (*presentation*, *logic* and *style*) by including the platform's specific characteristics and its ergonomic guidelines (i.e., according to the platform context). Finally, the last transformation from PSM to the source code is performed, to generate the final UI, supported by existing tools supporting the code generation from UIML (e.g., Acceleo [26]).

IV. CASE STUDY

We have developed our methodology for a simplified case study that implements a Computerized Maintenance Management System (CMMS) application dedicated to the management of intervention requests and dashboard monitoring. In such system, production agent, technician and administrator must be taken into consideration to represent the context of the application. After signing up, a user having technical problem needs to send a request for a new intervention. Therefore, the system shows a detailed form with the required information: *Intervention N°, Sender, Receiver, Desired Date, Intervention Type, Priority, State, Equipment and Observations*. Fig. 4 presents a part of Business Process Model related to this scenario of the process.

Ergonomic knowledge are, initially, stored in a database. We formalized these knowledge considering user, environment and platform dimensions. Since CMMS applications focus on industrial sectors, the user may be localized in a factory. We consider that an industrial environment is typically too noisy. The noise of running machinery is prevalent. In consequence, the system should increase the volume for the notification sound. In the contrary, we want a low sound volume, when a user is having a meeting. Moreover, in order to ensure more visibility for users who have visual problems, the system provides the background with white color theme (i.e., by default, the background is a dark color theme), font size 18 (i.e., the default size is 'medium' or size 12), bold font and activates the zooming options. A beep is emitted when a user has simultaneously a visual problem and is in a meeting. In addition, we consider different platforms with either wide or restricted screens (e.g., in the case of a small screen space, we only display the relevant information, such as Intervention N°, Sender, Receiver, Desired Date, Equipment and Observation).

We consider a sample scenario that describes a user using the CMMS application. As an administrator profile, we chose one that is visually impaired, using the application through a smartphone during a meeting. Using an inference engine (i.e., DROOLS Engine), we inferred a set of appropriate ergonomic guidelines. Fig. 5 presents the appropriate ergonomic guidelines resulted.

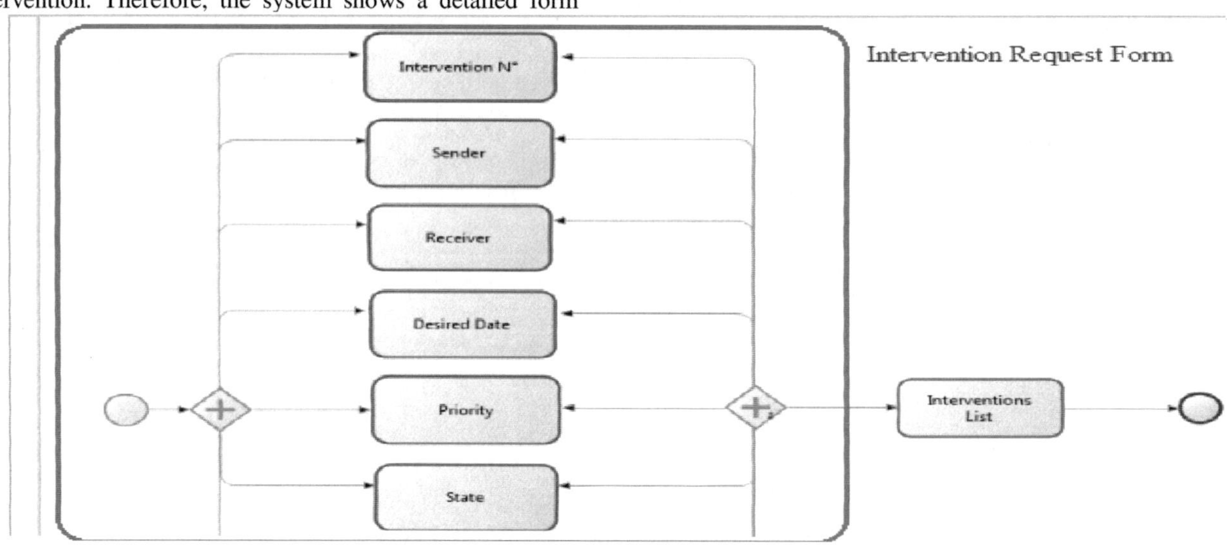

Figure 4. A Part of Business Process Model related to the Intervention request

```
background= WhiteColorTheme
font_size= 18
font_weight= Bold
Zooming_option= true
Volume_control= beep
```

Figure 5. Example of the generated ergonomic guidelines.

After generating appropriate ergonomic guidelines with the consideration of specified context information, the designer should integrate these guidelines within the transformation models. We have implemented model transformation with ATLAS Transformation Language (ATL) [27]. Fig. 6 describes the structure part of PIM1, generated by the ATL transformation rule. Fig. 7 shows the style part of PIM2, generated for both user and environment context. The style contains a list of properties and values. The properties are associated with parts within the UIML document through part-name elements. For example, for the "Intervention_Request_Form" form defined in the <part> element (G:Area class part in Fig. 6), we have defined the background of the form with "WhiteColorTheme" attribute in the property element of Style part. We also specified the "Intervention_N°", "Sender", "Receiver" labels, with font size 18 and bold font style.

The generated ergonomic context-aware UI for dashboard monitoring is illustrated in Fig. 8. The UI provides the current user with a rich set of indicators and charts. In Fig. 8, one chart per line is displayed, for enhancing the visibility. Moreover, the zooming option is activated, when selecting the chart for more information.

```
<Structure>

  <part class="G:Area" name="Intervention_Request_Form ">
  ..
   <part class="G:Label" name="Intervention_N°"/>
   <part class="G:TextField" name="Sender"/>
   <part class="G:TextField" name="Receiver"/>
   <part class="G:TextField" name="Desired Date"/>
   ..
  <part class="G:Button" name="Submit"/>
   ..
</Structure>
```

Figure 6. Generated PIM1: Structure Part

```
<style>
  <property name="Background" value="WhiteColorTheme" part-name="Intervention_Request_Form"/>
  <property name="Font-Size" value="18" part-name="Intervention_N°"/>
  <property name="Font-Size" value="18" part-name="Sender"/>
  ..
  <property name="Font-Weight" value="Bold" part-name="Intervention_N°"/>
  <property name="Font-Weight" value="Bold" part-name="Sender"/>
  ..
</style>
```

Figure 7. Generated PIM2: Style Part

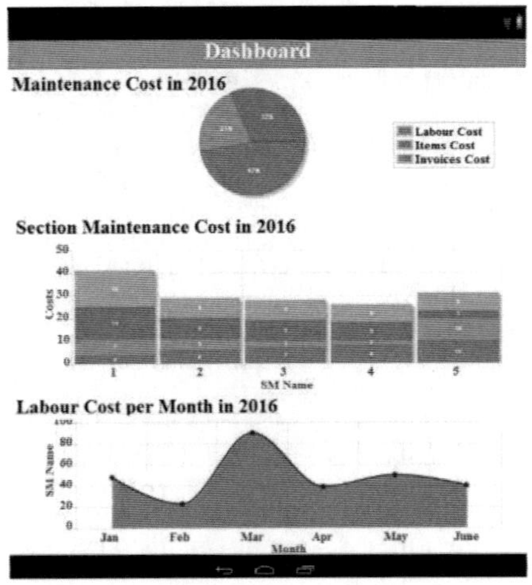

Figure 8. The generated Human-Computer interface

V. CONCLUSION AND FUTURE WORKS

In this paper, we presented a new ergonomic approach for designing context-aware Human-Computer interfaces. To model its ergonomic methodology, we used Artificial Intelligence techniques to design such systems. Finally, through the transformation rules, we have specified UI and produced UIML code that could be rendered in order to generate final interfaces for specific platforms. Ongoing and future works include the development of our approach with more case studies for ergonomic context-aware pervasive systems.

ACKNOWLEDGMENT

This project has been developed in the scope of a MOBIDOC doctoral thesis of the PASRI program sponsored by the European Union and administered by the ANPR. The authors would like to thank Mohammed Fouad Mansour Alzuhiry, who has also been active contributor during the implementation tasks and the company BMI (Tunisia) for financial and technical support.

REFERENCES

[1] J. Karat and C. M. Karat, "The evolution of user-centered focus in the human-computer interaction field," IBM Syst. J. vol. 42(4), pp. 532-541, 2003.

[2] R. Yvonne, H. Sharp, and J. Preece, "Interaction Design: Beyond HumanComputer Interaction", Wiley Publishing, 2011.

[3] C. Stephanidis, "Towards An information Society for All and Human Factors and Ergonomics," Universal Access in HCI, vol. 3(1), Press, C.R.C, 2001.

[4] B. A. Myers, "Interface Software Technology," chapter 72 of CRC Handbook of Computer Science and Engineering. Allen B. Tucker, editor in chief. Boca Raton, FL: CRC Press, Inc. pp. 1571-1595, 1997.

[5] M. Helander, Handbook of Human Computer Interaction, M. Helander (ed.), Elsevier Science Publishers B.V., North Holland, 1988.

[6] W.E. Gilmore, D.I. Gertman and H.S. Blackman, User-Computer Interface in Process Control, A Human Factors Engineering Handbook, Academic Press, 1989.

[7] M. Tendjaoui, C. Kolski and P. Millot, "An approach t owards the design of intelligent man-machine interfaces

[8] D.L. Scapin, P. Reynard and A. Pollier, "La conception ergonomique d'interfaces : problèmes de méthode, " Rapport de recherche n° 957, INRIA, Décembre 1988. used in process control," International Journal of Industrial Ergonomics, 8, 1991, pp. 345-361.

[9] J. Lazar, "Universal Usability: Designing Computer Interfaces for Diverse User Populations," Chichester, UK: John Wiley and Sons, 2009.

[10] J. Nielsen, "Usability Engineering, Morgan Kaufmann Publishers Inc, San Francisco, CA, USA, 1993.

[11] S. Charfi, A. Trabelsi, H. Ezzedine, and C. Kolski, "Towards ergonomic guidelines integration within graphical interface controls for the evaluation of the interactive system Application to a transport network Information Support System," In: Logistics (LOGISTIQUA), pp. 76-82, 2011.

[12] ISO, ISO/IEC 9126-1: Software engineering, Product quality, 2003, Part 1,2,3 and 4, (JIS X 0129).

[13] OMG, MDA Guide Version 1.0., http://omg.org/mda/mda_files/MDA_Guide_Version1-0.pdf, 2003, [retrieved: October, 2015].

[14] J. Tarby, H. Ezzedine, and C. Kolski, "Prevision of evaluation by traces during the software design of interactive systems: two approaches compared," In A. Seffah, J. Vanderdonckt, and M. Desmarais (Eds.), Human-Centered Software Engineering: Architectures and Models-Driven Integration, Springer HCI Series, pp. 257-276, 2009.

[15] A. Trabelsi and H. Ezzedine, "Evaluation of an Information Assistance System based on an agent-based architecture in transportation domain: first results," International Journal of Computers, Communications and Control 8: 2, pp. 320-333, 2013.

[16] S. Charfi, H. Ezzedine, and C. Kolski, "RITA: a useR Interface evaluaTion frAmework," Journal of Universal Computer Science, pp. 526-560, 2015.

[17] A. Beirekdar, J. Vanderdonckt, and M. Noirhomme-Fraiture, "A Framework and a Language for Usability Automatic Evaluation of Web Sites by Static Analysis of HTML Source Code," Computer-Aided Design of User Interfaces III, Proceedings of the Fourth International Conference on Computer-Aided Design of User Interfaces, Valenciennes, France, pp. 337-348, 2002.

[18] C. Mariage, J. Vanderdonckt, A. Beirekdar, and M. Noirhomme, "DESTINE: Outil d'aide à l'évaluation de L'ergonomie des sites web," Proceedings of the 16 Conference on Association Francophone d'Interaction Homme-Machine, ACM, pp. 117-124, 2004.

[19] C. Tran, H. Ezzedine, and C. Kolski, "Evaluation of Agent-based Interactive Systems: Proposal of an Electronic Informer Using Petri Nets," Journal of Universal Computer Science (J.UCS), 14(19), pp. 3202-3216, 2008.

[20] D. L. Scapin and J. M. C. Bastien, "Ergonomic criteria for evaluating the ergonomic quality of interactive systems," Behaviour & Information Technology, pp. 220-231, 1997.

[21] J. Nielsen and R. Budiu, "Mobile Usability", New Riders Press, ISBN 0-321-88448-5, 2012

[22] User Interface Markup Language (UIML), Version 4.0. Oasis, http://docs.oasisopen.org/uiml/v4.0/cd01/uiml4.0- cd01.html, 2008, [retrieved: October, 2015].

[23] JBoss Drools, http://www.jboss.org/drools/, [retrieved: March, 2016]

[24] C. Forgy, "On the efficient implementation of production systems," PhD Thésis, Carnegie-Mellon University, 1979.

[25] OMG, BPMN – Business Process Modeling Notation Specification version 1.0. OMG Available Specification, 2006.

[26] Acceleo, https://eclipse.org/acceleo/, [retrieved: March, 2016].

[27] ATLAS group LINA & INRIA, ATL, "Atlas Transformation Language. ATL User Manual," version 0.7, 2006.

COTS Adaptation Method – A Lifecycle Perspective

Waldemar Britts
Accenture Digital
Stockholm, Sweden
waldemar.britts@accenture.com

Mira Kajko-Mattsson
School of Information and Communication Technology
KTH Royal Institute of Technology
Stockholm, Sweden
mekm2@kth.se

***Abstract*— More and more organizations customize Commercial-Off-The-Shelf (COTS) standard systems instead of developing the bespoke ones. Despite this, there are still few methods that support adaptations of COTS standard systems. The ones that exist are either outdated or they only focus on some specific steps. None of the currently defined methods cover standard system adaptation from the lifecycle perspective and none of them provide concrete guidance for how to adapt COTS systems to the customers' needs. As a result, many organizations have to develop their own adaptation methods in a trial and error manner. This paper suggests COTS Adaptation Method (COTSAM) including steps and guidelines providing advice for how to develop and evolve COTS-based systems during their lifecycle. The method has been explored and evaluated within one company that has used COTS for supporting the company's business processes for more than a decade.**

Keywords-standard systems; reuse; lifecycle; business process.

I. INTRODUCTION

Standard systems have become very popular in the software industry. More and more organizations go over from developing bespoke systems to re-using complete standard systems instead [2][11]. This is because standard systems are considered to be more cost and resource effective than the bespoke ones. They have been reused many times in many different contexts by many different customer groups. For this reason, they are regarded to be of higher quality, reliability and maintainability. [7] [9]

Standard systems cannot always be used in their original form. Since they are created for a larger client base, they are very complex in their structure and can include elements that are not always needed by some clients. Therefore, they must be adapted to specific customers and their businesses. Some of their components must be removed, some may be retained in their current form and some other need undergo various types of adaptations. [3]

Adaption work can be very complex [1]. It does not only require knowledge of the standard system and of the customer's business but also knowledge of how to adapt standard systems to the needs of particular customers [7]. Methods supporting adaptation work are often called COTS (Commercial-Off-The-Shelf) adaptation methods or simply standard adaptation or customization methods.

COTS adaptation methods are extremely important for succeeding with the creation of standard-based software systems [10]. Lack of them may cost companies many failures in form of malfunctioning software, missed deliveries, failed projects, or at its worst, failed businesses. Despite this, there are still very few methods that support adaptations of COTS systems. The ones that exist are either too general, or they focus on a limited part of COTS adaptation process, often dealing only with COTS selection step. Most of them are also old. Their average age is more than ten years [4][6][12][13]. To the knowledge of the authors of this paper, no published standard adaptation method focuses on the lifecycle of the standard-based systems.

To succeed with the adaptation efforts, many organizations are forced to use their own adaptation methods, which they have developed in a trial and error manner. Kliento is one of such organizations. They have customized one standard system for building their software applications for supporting their business operation. They used commercial-off-the-shelf (COTS) component package, which they then adapted to their own needs by mainly reconfiguring its components, writing glue code, by making various settings and by writing new own components. In the absence of such a method, Kliento was forced to develop their own COTS adaptation method. It has taken them more than one decade to develop it and it has cost Kliento both time and money in form of initial project problems and obstacles. Recently, the method has been successfully applied within ten sub-projects. Still however, it has not been formalized and documented within the company.

This paper suggests a **COTS Adaptation Method** (COTSAM) including steps and guidelines providing advice for how to manage COTS-based systems during their lifecycle. The method has been explored and evaluated within Kliento that has used COTS for more than a decade. So far, no research proposal has covered a complete adaptation method that manages the entire software lifecycle. Therefore, we regard COTSAM a unique and innovative method suggestion.

Our work was commissioned by Kliento. It included exploring the structure of their adaptation method, identifying problems with the method and providing suggestions for improving it. The company's name, Kliento, is a fictitious name. The company wishes to remain anonymous. We are not allowed to mention any information that can be used for identifying the company, project, or even the standard system used. The only thing we are allowed to reveal is that the application managed information about the organization's business and its very complex equipment.

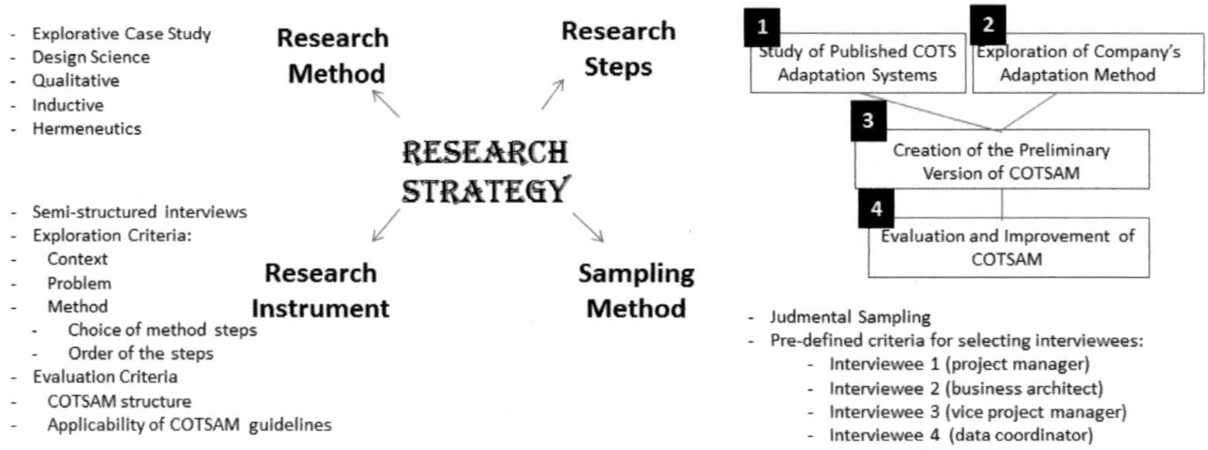

Figure 1. Our research strategy

The remainder of this paper is as follows. Section II describes the research method taken in this study and the criteria for exploring and evaluating the adaptation method. Section III presents the explored method at the company studied whereas Section IV describes COTSAM method. Finally, Sections V and VI evaluate COTSAM and make suggestions for future work.

II. RESEARCH METHOD

This study focused on an area that was relatively unexplored. The literature proved to be very limited and there were few methods dealing with the lifecycle perspective of COTS-based systems. Apart from literature limitations, it turned out that the method was not well established within Kliento. In Swedish parlance, the method sat in the walls, everybody knew it, however, understood it from his/her individual perspectives. The method was simply not well established within the company studied.

The status within Kliento has strongly impacted the design of our research strategy. As shown in Fig. 1, we conducted explorative case study to extract the design of standard adaptation method and elicit experiences related to the adaptation effort. The research was of a design science paradigm where the theory was extracted using the hermeneutic method [8].

A. Research Phases

Our study was divided into four research steps. As shown on the top right handside of Fig. 1, these were (1) *Study of Published COTS Adaptation Systems*, (2) *Exploration of Company's Adaptation Method*, (3) *Creation of the Preliminary Version of COTSAM*, and (4) *Evaluation and Improvement of COTSAM*. The first two steps were conducted in parallel. Here, we studied publications about standard adaptation methods and problems related to them. To our surprise, there were very few publications dealing with the subject. Although we found thousands of articles in various scientific databases, only five publications were of interest. Their focus was however restricted to only selection of standard systems.

In the next parallel step, we first studied Kliento's organization, products, adaptation method and problems related to the method. The step was conducted in form of explorative interviews with four different interviewees. Here we made four interviews with four different interviewees possessing the roles of project manager, business architect, vice project manager and data coordinator. We used Questionnaire 1 to be discussed in Section II.B. Explorative interview with Interviewee 1 was made for the purpose of understanding the company and its contexts. The explorative interviews with Interviewees 2-4 were made for the purpose of exploring the standard adaptation method.

In the third step, we created a preliminary version of COTSAM. Here, we studied all the interview answers using a hermeneutic method [5]. The interview results were interpreted in the context of the organization studied and its background and compared to published scientific results as achieved in the first research phase. The COTSAM preliminary version was then evaluated during our fourth step. Here, we had an evaluative interview together with Interviewee 4. We used Questionnaire 2 to be discussed in Section II.B. The purpose was to determine the soundness and applicability of COTSAM method within Kliento.

B. Research Instruments

The research instruments used in this study were two interview questionnaires based on explorative and evaluative research criteria. Using the explorative interviews, we examined Kliento's organization, its structure, adaptation method and its problems and consequences. Using the evaluative interviews, we established the soundness and applicability of COTSAM at Kliento.

Explorative interviews were conducted using the explorative questionnaire. Its purpose was to get acquainted with the activities within the organization, its standard adaptation method and problems. Questionnaire 1 was based on the following explorative criteria:

- ***Context*** standing for the development context in which Kliento's standard adaptation method was used. This

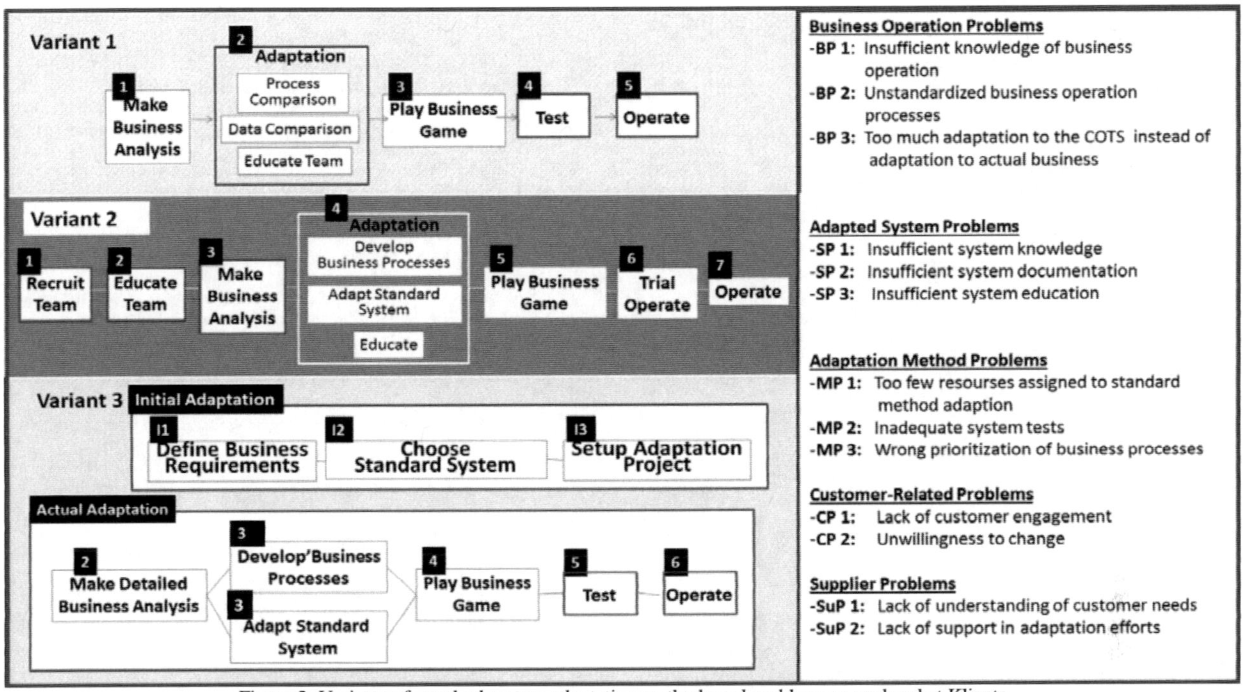

Figure 2. Variants of standard system adaptation methods and problems as explored at Kliento

criterion was used for acquiring basic knowledge of Kliento and for understanding its main activities.

- ***Method*** standing for a set of activities, rules and criteria aiding in adapting standard systems to a functioning information system.
- ***Problems*** standing for difficulties and consequences that Klinto has experienced within standard adaptation work. Identification of problems is an important prerequisite for drawing lessons learned, for relating them to lack of or insufficient process steps, and for designing method solutions that may avoid them.
- ***Method ownership*** standing for the role possessing end-to-end responsibility for developing, establishing and improving the standard adaptation method and for assuring its quality across the whole organization. The role's ultimate responsibility is to ensure that the method is consistent throughout the whole organization and that it is understood in a uniform manner.

Questionnaire 2 was of evaluative nature focusing on evaluating the applicability and soundness of the preliminary version of COTSAM. It was designed according to the following evaluation criteria:

- *COTSAM structure* evaluating the choice of standard method steps and the order among them.
- *Applicability of COTSAM guidelines* finding out whether the guidelines were realistic, whether they were robust in preventing the problems as identified at Kliento and whether they were applicable at Kliento.

C. Sampling

The choice of the interviewees was not done through randomization but through *judgmental sampling* [5][11]. The interviewees were chosen according to their ability to contribute to our research results. They had to fulfill the three following criteria: (1) they should have extensive experience of the company studied, (2) they should have experience in adaptation work, and (3) they should both represent user and development sites.

III. EXPLORATION RESULTS

The exploration step (Step 2 in Fig. 1) has resulted in three different method variants. This implies that three different interviewees has three different opinions of the standard adaptation method. The variants are all presented in Fig. 2 and briefly describe below. To facilitate the follow up of Fig. 2, we mark each activity with a numeric identifier both in the figure and the text describing it.

Variant I has been explored by interviewing *Interviewee* 2. In its first step (1), Kliento makes business analysis and analyzes a specific business operation by studying its documentation and by identifying its needs. The step results in a summary of the business operation and a list of requirements for the improvements of business operation under consideration. This provides input to the next step (2), during which the standard system gets adapted according to the business requirements. Here, one compares the current business process and the data used by the process to the business requirements. In parallel, one educates in the new improved business operation. In Step 3, Kliento performs a serious business game focusing on making initial tests of the adapted system. During the game, Kliento reviews the overall business workflow and makes sure that it works as

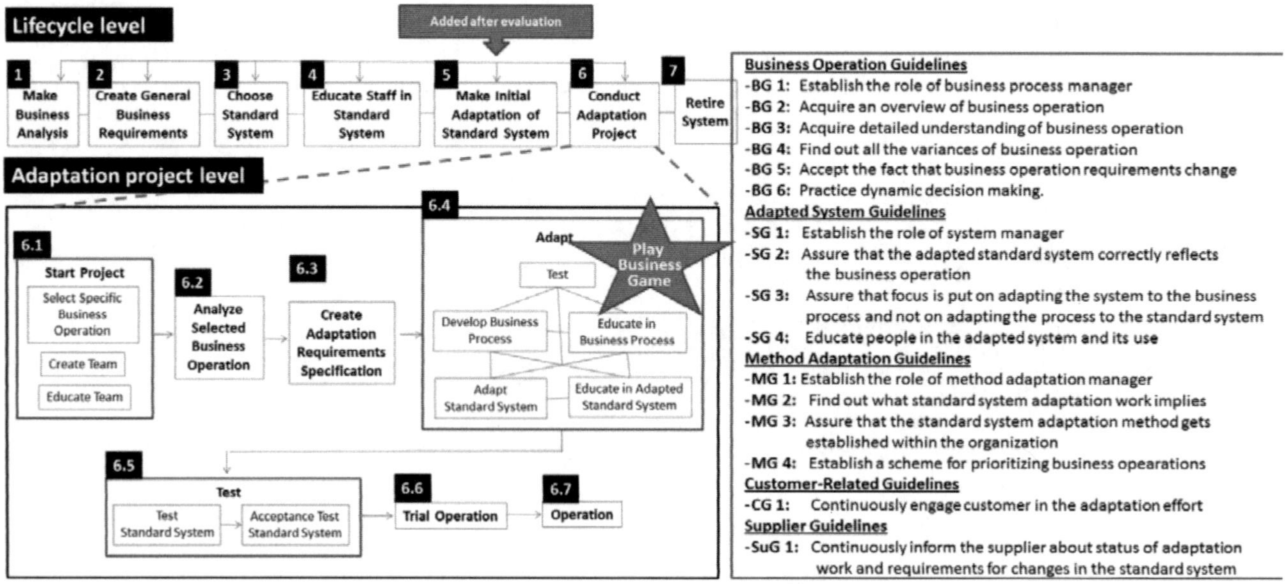

Figure 3. COTSAM steps and guidelines

requested. Finally, Kliento conducts system and acceptance tests (4) before deploying the system for operation (5).

Variant II has been explored by interviewing *Interviewee 3*. As shown in the middle part of Fig. 5.3, the adaptation process starts with recruiting a team (1). The step ensures that Kliento has enough staff with the right skills who can conduct the work. The team is then educated and trained (2). Afterwards, the team members conduct business analysis with the aim of laying out the status of the part of business under consideration (3). This provides input to Step 4, that is, input for developing business processes, adapting the standard system to the newly defined business processes and for educating the end users in the new business process and the system supporting the process. The three parallel adaptation steps converge in the business game step (5) testing the changes made. Finally, Kliento deploys the system in two consecutive steps: for trial operation (6) and for final operation (7).

Variant 3 has been explored with Interviewee 4. The process consists of two stages: *initial adaptation* and *actual adaptation*. The initial adaptation includes activities required for starting the adaptation project. These imply definition of business requirements (I1), choice of a standard system (I2) and setup of the adaptation project (I3). As soon as those activities are finalized, the actual adaptation of the standard system starts.

The actual adaptation is realized in a number of sub-projects, each dedicated to a particular business operation. Here, Kliento makes a detailed analysis of the business process under study (2), develops or improves the business process (3) and then adapts the standard system (3). The system process is then tested with the serious business game (4), to be then system and acceptance tested (5), and finally, to be deployed for operation (6).

Our reader does not need to be very astute to see the differences of the perceptions of the standard system adaptation method at Kliento. The reason is that the process was not standardized and established within the whole organizations. As shown on the righthand side of Fig. 2, this has led to many problems which we classify as follows:

- *Business operation problems* dealing with insufficient knowledge of business operation, lack of standard business operation process and too much focus on adapting the business process to the standard system instead of adapting the system to the process.
- *Adapted system problems* dealing with insufficient system knowledge due to problems, such as insufficient system education and system documentation.
- *Adaptation method problems* dealing with putting too few resources into the adaptation projects, inadequate tests and improper prioritization of business processes to be implemented.
- *Customer-related problems* implying lack of customer engagement and unwillingness to change the business processes.
- *Supplier problems* implying lack of understanding of customer needs when developing and evolving standard systems which is the result of supplier's absence in assisting the client companies in their adaptation efforts.

IV. COTSAM

COTSAM is a method that has been explored within the adaptation projects at Kliento. It is been extended with issues elicited within the literature and evaluated though the interview with Interviewee 4. As shown in Fig. 6.1 COTSAM consists of two parts. These are *Method Steps* and *Guidelines*. The method steps list the main steps in the adaptation work and guidelines provide guidance for how to optimally implement the steps.

A. COTSAM Method Steps

COTSAM method steps are presented on two levels (1) on the lifecycle level and (2) on the adaptation project level. The overall lifecycle steps range from making initial general business analysis, to defining business requirements, to choosing a standard system, starting adaptation projects, to finally, retiring the system. The steps on adaptation project level focus on selecting a particular business process and adapting the system to the requirements of the selected business process. Below, we describe the two levels in detail. To facilitate the follow up of Fig. 3, we mark each activity with a numeric identifier both in the figure and the text below.

On the lifecycle level, the following takes place. First a general business analysis is made (1) and general business requirements are specified (2). Here, one does not need to go into all the details of the business and requirements. What is important is to create an overview of the business operation on such a level of detail that it enables informed standard system selection (3).

After having selected the standard system and before starting the adaptation projects, key people must be educated in the standard system (4). Education is then followed by an initial adaptation of the standard system (5). Here, one makes general adjustments of the standard system to the overall business needs. This step is then followed by a series of adaptation projects (6). Adaptation projects are carried out iteratively where focus is put on a particular business operation. Finally, the system gets retired if it no longer is able to support business operation.

Each adaptation project includes a number of sub-steps (5). Projects start with the selection of a specific business operation (5.1), creation of the team dealing with the adaptation of the standard system to the business operation under consideration and education of its members. The team then analyzes the business operation (5.2) and creates adaptation requirements specification describing what parts of the standard system need to be adjusted to fit the business operation.

As a next step, the standard system gets adapted (5.4). The adaptation step is not simple. It consists of several steps and the order among the steps may vary from case to case. Overall, the steps are conducted almost simultaneously. While developing the business process, one adapts the standard system to the business needs and educates people both in the business process and the adapted standard system. All this provides feedback to testing. The newly defined business process is being tested at the same time as the standard system gets adapted and as the people are educated in business processes and in the adapted standard systems. The same applies to the adapted standard system. As soon as its fully or partially workable solution has been implemented, it is tested by playing a serious business game simulating the newly defined business operation.

If the outcome of the business game is satisfying, the adapted standard system undergoes system and acceptance tests (6.5) to be then forwarded for trial operation (6.6). During the trial operation, the new system part is operated on together with the old system part. Only after one is certain that the new system correctly supports the business operation, it gets deployed for operation (6.7). The old system part gets retired.

Our reader may probably react that COTSAM presents and suggests the order among its activities. The order however is not compulsory. Users of COTSAM may conduct activities in any order that they feel comfortable with. However, some order is natural and if it is not followed, then the adaptation endeavor may encounter problems, and thereby, endanger the adaption work. For example, you have to define the entire business first, at least on a coarse level, before setting up a system to support it.

B. COTSAM Guidelines

COTSAM guidelines provide guidance for how to optimally carry out the method steps and avoid problems that may be encountered within standard method adaptation efforts. COTSAM suggest six groups of guidelines. As listed on the righthand side of Fig. 3, these are *(1) Business Operation Guidelines, (2) System Guidelines (3) Method Adaptation Guidelines, (4) Customer-Related Guidelines* and *(5) Supplier Guidelines.* Their choice depends on the problems that have been encountered within Klento. Their purpose is to remedy these problems.

Business Operation Guidelines deal with business process understanding, ownership and decision making with regard to business processes. Guidelines ***BG 2-4*** deal with acquiring understanding of the business process on both general and detailed levels. Organizations should put enough resources into assuring that the business process is correctly understood. One should also have a good understanding of all the variants of business operation so that they get considered when adapting the standard system. All this constitutes a basis for defining the system support for the business process.

To assure uniform understanding of business operation, one should define a role responsible for it. For this reason, we suggest Guideline ***BG 1***. Here, we suggest establish the role of business process manager who should define business operation and establish it within the organization. Lack of such a role implies a risk that the business process will be implemented in different ways by different individuals and that the adapted system supporting the process will not reflect it properly.

The last two business operation guidelines, ***BG 5-6***, deal with decision making. Organizations should accept the fact that business processes change as late as during the adaptation process. While adjusting the standard system to the business process, one may acquire a better understanding of the business process and its defects. This should not prevent organizations from changing their business processes even that late in the adaptation project work. To enable this, organizations should practice dynamic decision making allowing them to change or improve their decisions based on what is known now and based on the new expected or unexpected events that motivate decision changes.

Adapted System Guidelines focus on assuring that the system correctly reflects business operation (*SG 2*). For this, organizations should define the role of system manager (*SG 1*) who makes sure that while adapting the standard system, focus is put on assuring that the system gets adapted to the business process and not vice versa (*SG3*). Finally, system manager should make sure that people are educated in the adapted system and its use (*SG 4*).

Method Adaptation Guidelines focus on assuring that companies establish an organization-wide standard system adaptation method (*MG 3*). Companies should make sure that they have an appropriate prioritization scheme of business operations that should be chosen for implementation (*MG 4*). Before starting any adaptation project, they should find out what standard system adaptation work implies (*MG 2*). Is it better to use a standard system or is it better to develop a customized system? All this should be managed by a method adaptation manager (*MG 1*), the role ensuring that everyone in the organization is using the adaptation method in a uniform manner.

The last two guidelines deal with customers and suppliers. *Customer-Related Guideline (CG 1)* remedies the problem of lack of customer engagement in the adaptation work whereas the *Supplier Guideline (SuG 1)* aids in assuring that the supplier gets insight into the status of the adaptation work of their customers, and thereby, become better in adapting their standard systems to the needs of their customers.

V. DISCUSSION

The preliminary version of COTSAM was evaluated during the fourth interview using two evaluation criteria (1) *the structure of COTSAM* and (2) *the applicability of its guidelines*. Here, Interviewee 4 was presented the COTSAM draft, three variants of the adaptation method as perceived by our three interviewees and the COTSAM guidelines. Below, we briefly describe the evaluation results.

A. COTSAM Structure

Interviewee 4 was of the opinion that COTSAM was sound and out of the four variants (three initial variants plus the COTSAM draft), the COTSAM draft was the best reflection of the standard adaptation work at Kliento. Since Kliento did not have time to formalize and generalize their method, COTSAM would serve as a basis for improving the company's method.

According to Interviewee 4, the method was satisfactory and all its steps were relevant. The method was complete from a lifecycle perspective, and none of its steps were superfluous. However, after a closer analysis of the three method variants, Interviewee 4 pointed out that COTSAM missed a very important step, Step I3 in Variant 3 dealing with a setup of an adaptation project. According to him, this step constitutes a basis for all further adaptation projects and it should be clearly distinguished in the model. This step is important for achieving a stable foundation for continuing with the adaptation efforts. To remedy this, we extended COTSAM with Step 5 which we call *Initially adapt the standard system*.

The interviewee pointed out that even if the overall design of COTSAM looked simple, its steps were very complex. For example Step 3 dealing with standard selection is very complex, difficult and costly. Also Step 4 and the newly added Step 5 dealing with the education in the standard system and its initial adaptation are very heavy and extensive. Here, one must understand the system's processes, understand business processes, customize business processes and system processes, find out how the data from the system to be replaced can be transferred to the new customized system and how to build interfaces between the two systems. All this cannot be done on first attempt. A number of retakes is normally required before everything falls on place.

The contents of Step 5 almost corresponds to Step 6 (*Conduct Adaptation Project*). The difference lies in the fact that the initial project is the first adaptation project (5) in a series of adaptation projects (6). It should however be distinguished as a separate step due to the fact that its success is crucial for the next-coming projects. On purpose, the initial project should neither be too large nor too small. It should be of such a size so that the organization may begin to find its own feet in the adaptation work.

With the addition of Step 5, the interviewee was of the opinion that the choice and the order of COTSAM steps were relevant. The sequence of steps assured that the method could be conducted in a systematic and controlled manner. An incorrect sequence has already led to some large efficiency problems at Kliento. For instance, Kliento neglected Step 4 dealing with the education in the selected standard system. This created problems in Step 5.The initial adaptation project took extra long time. This is because the adaptation team had to learn the standard system while doing the actual adaptation work.

Although our interviewee agreed that the order was relevant and important, he pointed out that the performance of COTSAM steps could differ from case to case. For example, one could perform the first two steps (Step 1 and Step 2) in a number of iterations before one went over to Step 3.

Interviewee 4 was of the opinion that the order of the COTSAM steps constituted an excellent roadmap of what main steps are to be carried out and where they belong to in the standard system adaptation lifecycle. There should be a general business analysis before creating a general specification which should be done before choosing a standard system. You should not choose a standard system first and do a business analysis and create specifications then. Nor should you create requirements before you have made a business analysis.

The order between the substeps in Step 6 dealing with the actual performance of the adaptation projects was found relevant as well. According to our interviewee, these activities could be performed either sequentially or in parallel. The grade of parallelism could vary from case to case and it often depended on the complexity of and understanding of the business process to be implemented. The simplest case was when business process users mastered the business process well. Here, the adaptation steps could be conducted sequentially implying that a complete solution got produced for a particular business operation which was then tested and deployed. Only minor training was required.

More complex cases take place when one defines a new business operation and implements it in the standard system. Here, each business process step gets implemented in an iterative manner. One develops business functionality for only the first step, tests it, educates in it while implementing and testing the next step and so forth. Next iterations may not always imply implementations of the next business operation steps. They may imply adjustments of the implemented business process steps before going over to the next step.

B. COTSAM Guidelines

The applicability of the COTSAM guidelines was evaluated against the problems as experienced by Kliento. Our interviewee agreed that the guidelines were appropriate and that most of them have already been implemented at Kliento. Only four guidelines have not yet been implemented. These are going to be discussed below.

Our interviewee was of the opinion that all the business guidelines were relevant. Kliento has implemented them all except for **BG 1** dealing with the definition of a business process manager role. Although Kliento was aware of its importance, they have not managed to fully implement it. They have defined the role of business process manager. This role however did not conduct his/her responsibilities in a satisfactory manner.

Regarding Business Guidelines 5 and 6 (**BG 5 and BG 6**), our interviewee found them especially important and crucial for the successful implementation of business processes. The guidelines suggest that companies should accept the fact that business operation requirements change, and therefore, companies should practice dynamic decision making. It took Kliento several years to understand that they could not practice the traditional decision-making pattern. This resulted in substantial project delays, enormous costs and other serious productivity problems.

Guidelines **BG2-4** are extremely important according to our interviewee. They deal with acquiring understanding of business operation on both coarse-grained and detailed levels and identifying all their variances. Without them, it is practically impossible to run standard system adaptations. Because of their negligence, Kliento has experienced most of the problems as listed in this paper.

Kliento has implemented all the system guidelines. Despite this, they had problems in understanding the system. The system was very complex and as our interview expressed it, it was too big for one person to grasp it. More people need to have the role of the system manager where each system manager is responsible for a specific part of the system.

Out of four method guidelines, Kliento has not implemented three of them. These are **MG1** suggesting the establishment of the role of the method adaptation manager, **MG 2** dealing with finding out what standard system adaptation work implies before starting adaptation projects and **MG 4** dealing with establishing a prioritization scheme for business operations. Kliento is now in the process of implementing them. All of them are important for succeeding with the adaptation projects and they should be implemented from the very beginning. For instance, by not finding out what standard adaptation method implied, Kliento failed in balancing the allocation of resources to the different adaptation method steps. The organization had a wrong understanding of what a standard adaptation meant with regard to time resource consumption in different process steps. Insufficient resources were allocated to planning and testing.

Last but not least, all the customer and supplier guidelines (**CG1** and **SuG1**) have been implemented, however, too late. Kliento has not been successful in continuously engaging the end user in the business process development. Neither have they been successful in communicating their needs to the standard system supplier. Unfortunately, it took several years for Kliento to realize that these guidelines were very crucial for the success of current and future adaptation efforts. Especially the supplier guideline (**SuG 1**) is crucial for the organization's survival. If the supplier lacks understanding of the needs of its clients, the clients may become supplier-less, and thereby, system-less in the future.

VI. FINAL REMARKS

Despite the fact that more and more organizations procure standard systems, there are still few methods that support their adaptation and implementation. The ones that are available are either out of date or they focus on only the initial adaptation stages. This paper suggests a method for customizing standard systems. The method is called COTSAM (COTS Adaptation Method) and it was developed at Kliento. The work was carried out in form of a qualitative and explorative study [8]. The study was based on five interviews. Overall, one interviewee was involved in

COTSAM STEPS	COTSAM	CBA Framework
1. Make Business Analysis	+	– (Implicit)
2. Create General Requirements Specification	+	+
3. Choose Standard System	+	+
4. Educate Staff in Standard System	+	–
5. Make Initial Adaptation of Standard System	+	–
6. Conduct Adaptation Project	+	P
6.1a. Select Specific Business Operation	+	– (Implicit)
6.1b. Create Team	+	–
6.1c. Educate Team	+	–
6.2. Analyze Selected Business Operation	+	– (Implicit)
6.3. Creat Requirements Specification Selected Business Operation	+	– (Implicit)
6.4. Adapt	+	+ (General)
6.5. Test	+	+
6.6. Trial Operate	+	+
6.7. Operate	+	+
7. Retire System	+	–

Figure 4. Comparing COTSAM to CBA Framework

providing a context for our study, three interviewees were involved in the exploration of standard adaptation method as defined at Kliento. One of these three interviewees was also involved in the evaluation of COTSAM.

The exploration showed that Kliento's employees had a slightly varying picture of the company's adaptation method. Therefore, our work resulted in three variant method descriptions. The reason was the fact that Kliento's method had not been defined and properly established within the company. The exploration also resulted in a list of problems that were the actual consequences of lack of a defined and established standard adaptation method.

The three variants and the explored problems constituted a good basis for defining COTSAM consisting of a number of steps and guidelines that will guide the implementation of the COTSAM steps. COTSAM method covers the entire lifecycle, and therefore, it may be considered to be unique and innovative in its design. It provides a new and original perspective on a standard adaptation method which has no counterpart in the existing methods today. The only method that was reasonably related to this study was the Framework for Value-based CBA process decisions suggested by [13].

To evaluate the innovative contribution of this study, we compare the COTSAM constituents to the constituents of the Framework Value-based CBA decision process. As shown in Fig. 4, CBA framework does not take into account the important steps, such as training in the standard system, the initial adaptation of standard systems, creation of adaptation team, training team and training in the system. Finally, the main difference is that COTSAM covers the entire life cycle whereas CBA is not explicit about it.

VII. Conclusion

COTSAM is defined on a general level and has only been evaluated within one organization. Its structure and guidelines need be further evaluated in other organizations. COTSAM needs be further expanded with more detailed activities and more guidelines. Last but not least, it should be expanded with more roles and responsibilities. Hopefully, the results of this study will contribute to, and accelerate, development of adaptation methods for standard systems.

References

[1] L. D. Alford Jr, "The problem with aviation COTS," Proceedings of AUTOTESTCON, IEEE, pp. 519-524, 2000.

[2] B. Boehm and C. Abts, "COTS integration: Plug and Pray?" Computer, vol. 32, no. 1, pp. 135-138, 1999.

[3] D. Carney, S. A. Hissam, and D. Plakosh, "Complex COTS-based software systems: practical steps for their maintenance," Journal of Software Maintenance: Research and Practice, vol. 12, no. 6, pp. 357-376, 2000.

[4] I. Crnkovic, M. Chaudron, and S. Larsson, "Component-based development process and component lifecycle," Proceedings of International Conference on Software Engineering Advances, IEEE, pp. 44-44, 2006.

[5] N. K. Denzin and Y. S. Lincoln, "The Sage handbook of qualitative research," Sage Publications, Incorporated, 2005.

[6] X. Franch and M. Torchiano, "Towards a reference framework for COTS-based development: a proposal," In ACM SIGSOFT Software Engineering Notes, ACM, vol. 30, no. 4, pp. 1-4, 2005.

[7] S. Gilbert, "The emergence of the system configurator," IT professional, vol. 7, no. 2, pp. 64-62, 2005.

[8] A. R. Hevner, S. T. March, J. Park, and S. Ram, "Design science in information systems research," MIS quarterly, vol. 28, no. 1, pp. 75-105, 2004.

[9] M. Keil, and A. Tiwana, "Beyond cost: the drivers of COTS application value," Software, IEEE, vol. 22, no. 3, pp. 64-69, 2005.

[10] L. Mariani, and M. Pezzè, "Dynamic detection of COTS component incompatibility," Software, IEEE, vol. 24, no. 5, pp. 76-85, 2007.

[11] M. N. Marshall, "Sampling for qualitative research," Family practice, vol. 13, no. 6, pp. 522-526, 1996.

[12] M. Morisio, et al., "COTS-based software development: Processes and open issues," Journal of Systems and Software, vol. 61, no. 3, pp. 189-199, 2002.

[13] Y. Yang, J. Bhuta, B. Boehm, and D. N. Port, "Value-based processes for COTS-based applications," Software, IEEE, vol. 22, no. 4, pp. 54-62, 2005.

Towards Easier Implementation of Design Patterns

Ruslan Batdalov and Oksana Nikiforova

Department of Applied Computer Science
Riga Technical University
Riga, Latvia
Email: Ruslan.Batdalov@edu.rtu.lv, Oksana.Nikiforova@rtu.lv

Abstract—**Design patterns help in managing complexity of software systems, but in many cases their implementation may entail even greater complexity. We argue that this complexity is caused, at least partially, by the lack of expressiveness of the mainstream programming languages. In order to support this hypothesis, we propose a set of potential language-level features that might make implementation of design patterns easier, identified by dissecting some widely used design patterns.**

Keywords–design patterns; design patterns implementation.

I. INTRODUCTION

At present, design patterns are widely used in development of software systems. Erich Gamma et al. defined the role of patterns as follows: 'A pattern gives a solution to a recurring problem and allows developers not to invent a design from scratch. [1]' As Frank Buschmann et al. pointed out, '[a]ny significant design will inevitably draw on many patterns, whether consciously or otherwise. [2]'

At the same time, introducing design patterns into a software system may increase the level of its complexity. This danger was anticipated yet by Erich Gamma et al.: 'Design patterns should not be applied indiscriminately. Often they achieve flexibility and variability by introducing additional levels of indirection and that can complicate a design and/or cost you some performance. [1]' Frank Buschmann et al. in the first book of the series 'Pattern-oriented Software Architecture' saw one of the goals of the patterns in helping developers to manage software complexity [3], but in the fifth one admitted: 'There are also many tales of failure to relate: stories about systems in which patterns were used intentionally and explicitly in design, but whose architectures were penalized by unnecessary and accidental complexity. [2]' Peter Sommerlad, an author of many design patterns and a co-author of the same series, went even further and bluntly argued that design patterns are bad for software design because of unnecessary complexity [4].

We argue that the excessive complexity introduced by the design patterns stems, at least partially, not from the patterns, but from insufficient expressiveness of the existing programming languages. The languages have trouble expressing the ideas, on which the patterns are built, and that is a reason why the implementation of the patterns is too complex. To support this hypothesis, we propose an approach to coping with the mentioned complexity by means of including necessary constructs into the programming languages.

The goal of the study is to identify a set of language-level features that could facilitate implementation of the common design patterns. This result, as well as our approach in general, could be used by the designers of programming languages to identify new features that might be useful for reducing systems complexity.

The remainder of this paper is organised as follows: Section II briefly describes the background of the study related to the common design patterns and their implementation. Section III presents our approach and illustrates it with a detailed example. Section IV contains the proposed set of language-level features, their motivation and drawbacks. Related work is covered in Section V, and Section VI concludes the paper.

II. BACKGROUND OF THE STUDY

There exist a lot of design patterns appearing again and again in different systems. They are described in a huge number of books and papers. The seminal work by Erich Gamma et al. [1] popularised the idea of a pattern in software design and gave an impetus to studying, discovering and applying new and new design patterns. Among other work, we should mention the series 'Pattern-oriented software architecture', which gives not only a catalog of patterns, but also many useful insights into purposes of design patterns and relationships between them.

These books are by no means the comprehensive description of the field. In 2007, Grady Booch mentioned that he had catalogued almost 2,000 design patterns found in the literature [5]. By now, this number is obviously much greater since the process of detection of new patterns has not been standing still. Nevertheless, the mentioned works describe perhaps the most commonly used and verified patterns, so it is logical to refer to them in the first place. In this paper, we work with the design patterns described by Erich Gamma et al. in 'Design patterns' [1] and by Frank Buschmann et al. in the first volume of 'Pattern-oriented software architecture' [3].

The books describing implementation of design patterns in the existing programming languages are numerous too. In general, they are less relevant to our study, but we can get some helpful insight from them. In particular, it is quite clear from such descriptions that the process of extending programming languages for the needs of the design patterns users is already going on. For example, enumerators and for-each loop in C# facilitate implementation of the Iterator pattern, and query expressions provide the interface of this pattern to the results of database queries [6]. These features were not supported in the first version of the language. Our study is to support this direction of programming languages development by providing some ideas on what features could be included.

III. Approach to Identification of Necessary Language-level Features

The simplest way to support design patterns that comes to mind is direct inclusion of the known design patterns into a programming language. In a sense, that is what happened with the Iterator pattern in the example given above. Joseph Gil and David H. Lorenz described the general characteristics and the typical steps of this process in 1998 [7]. In our opinion, this approach is fruitful, but not universal. In the late 1990s, just a few dozens of patterns were documented well enough, but there are thousands of them at present. The enormous number of the patterns and the pace of their emergence clearly do not allow to make them all language constructs. However, the fact that patterns are so numerous suggests that there should be recurring themes in them. So, we can try to find common elements of different design patterns and discuss whether they are able to become language-level features.

Another reason not to include a design pattern into a language directly is that many patterns are rather instructive than formal constructs and allow too high variation. Frank Buschmann et al. give the example of the Observer pattern, whose particular implementation may depend on the model of interaction between the subject and the observer (push or pull), on the presence of a middleware for the exchange of messages, on the chosen data structures, etc. They conclude that design patterns are not generic, but *generative* [2]. In our opinion, decomposition of patterns may allow to implement variation in patterns semantics by means of combining primitive elements having strictly defined semantics. These elements are better candidates for becoming language-level features than the patterns themselves.

According to the goal of our study, we are interested in the elements that are logically similar to the existing language-level constructs, but are not supported currently. The motivation here is that introduction of design patterns into a software system or getting rid of them may require substitution of such elements in place of standard language-level constructs or vice versa. If the required syntactical constructs are significantly different, these operations may require complex co-ordinated changes in different parts of the system, which is undesirable. Examples of such differences may be seen below.

Eliminating design patterns from a working system as a source of complexity was mentioned by Peter Sommerlad, who stated that it is (somewhat counter-intuitively) more difficult than their introduction [4]. On the basis of this observation, he argued against using design patterns too frequently, but, in our opinion, facilitating of such transitions is a more fruitful approach.

So, we can try to use the following approach to identification of potential language constructs:

- dissect a design pattern and decompose it into logical elements at level with language constructs (in the sense of the level of abstraction): elementary operations, simple relationships, etc.,
- find elements that are similar to the existing language constructs and/or recur in different patterns,
- analyse the extent to which the discovered elements are supported in the existing languages (they may be partially supported) and similarities between the elements and the existing language constructs,
- describe semantics of the discovered elements,
- analyse consequences of introduction of the potential language features.

As an example, we try to dissect the Abstract Factory pattern, described by Erich Gamma et al. [1], and identify the language-level features that would make its usage easier.

According to the original description, Abstract Factory is intended to provide an interface for creating families of related or dependent objects without specifying their concrete classes. Its application includes the following steps:

1) Declare an interface for creation of abstract objects (**AbstractFactory** creating **AbstractProduct**).
2) Implement the operations for creation of concrete objects (**ConcreteFactory** creating **ConcreteProduct**).
3) Choose a concrete implementation of the family of objects, depending on either compile-time or run-time conditions (i.e., choose a **ConcreteFactory** that will be used).
4) Instantiate required objects by means of methods declared in the **AbstractFactory** and implemented in the **ConcreteFactory** (usually implemented using the Factory Method or Prototype pattern) [1].

A point in this description that can attract our attention is that the last step is performed by auxiliary methods instead of the standard instantiation operator (`new` or whatever a particular programming language uses). That means that introduction of the pattern or getting rid of it requires changes in every client that instantiates the objects. It does not cause problems in the languages where factory methods are the primary means of objects instantiation (e.g., Perl), but in the languages with a separate instantiation operator it might be difficult. The problem is that such languages do not allow to use the instantiation operator with an abstract class since its concrete implementation that should be instantiated is not known in advance. The cause of this 'ignorance', in turn, is that the third step (choosing a concrete implementation) is not supported at the level of the programming language and needs to be implemented in the application itself. We may suppose that turning this step into a language-level operation can make implementation simpler.

We can turn to other patterns as well and see that the same idea of choosing an implementation is utilised, for example, in Builder, Bridge, Command and Strategy. So, this operation is a recurring theme in design patterns and probably deserves support at the language level.

The idea is to introduce an operator that would set a default implementation for an abstract class. It could be used either at the compile time or at the run time. If the choice has been made by the compile time, the compiler should substitute the constructor of the concrete class for the one of the abstract class. If the choice is delayed until the run time, the compiler should create an internal (hidden from the developer) Abstract Factory and redirect all requests for instantiation of an object of the abstract class to this factory.

We can foresee at least two problems related to this approach. First, the choice of an implementation is a form of binding, and its scope should be clearly defined. On the one hand, the scope should not be restricted to a single class (otherwise, we still need to change each and every client class to change the used implementation). On the other hand, a change of the binding from a class that would affect all other classes in the program may lead to unpredictable results. The second problem is that this binding is a shared state, so it should be carefully treated in a concurrent environment.

The mentioned problems can make one conclude that this feature should *not* be introduced, and such an argument would be reasoned. Nevertheless, we believe that what we see here is not a weakness, but a strength of the proposed approach. The problems of the scope and the global state belong to the pattern itself, not to its language-level support. An ad-hoc implementation of the pattern still needs to deal with the same issues. A native language-level support may provide a developer with a ready solution of the potential problems (inevitably limited, but suitable for most cases).

In a similar manner, we can see that responsibility delegation appears really often in various design patterns and clearly deserves its place in a programming language. The Builder, Command and Command Processor patterns generalise common ideas of object initialisation, function and executor respectively. A number of patterns (Blackboard, Pipes and Filters, etc.) provide alternatives to standard synchronous calls between objects. The State pattern abandons the assumption that a binding between an object and its class should remain the same throughout the whole life time of the object. The Template Method pattern involves switching between portions of code implemented in a class and its superclass (in both directions), which causes problems described below. We are not going to describe analysis of these patterns at the same level of detail as with the Abstract Factory pattern since the argument is very similar. Instead, the next section presents concrete language features that might be based on these observations.

IV. Proposed Features

This section contains the results of the analysis of the patterns described in [1][3]. For each feature, we give a context, in which it might be needed, and briefly describe the current situation, our proposal, and the negative consequences or issues that should be considered if the proposal is accepted.

The current state differs between programming languages, but we do not have a goal to observe all existing languages in this paper. Therefore, the description of the current situation is generally limited to a few mainstream object-oriented languages (C++, Java, C#). Occasionally, other languages are mentioned when it can give useful insight.

Limiting the scope of observed languages means that some proposed features may be already supported in other languages. Nevertheless, we believe that even in this case motivation from the design patterns angle might be useful. It may be illustrated by the example of for-each loop, iterating through collection-like data. It has been in use in Unix shell since the late 1970s, later it was added to some other languages (e.g., Pascal, Perl), but the mainstream languages ignored this feature for a long time, and incorporated it only after the rise of the patterns (the Iterator pattern in particular).

Table I lists all proposed features and the patterns, implementation of which they might facilitate. The table also includes a classification, inspired by the classification of design patterns according to their purpose by Erich Gamma et al. [1]. The features are classified according to whether they relate to the object lifecycle (creation, initialisation, association to the class), object behaviour (object's actions between its creation and destruction), or structural aspects (class hierarchy). It does not mean that if a particular feature is described as related to, for example, the lifecycle, then it is associated with creational patterns only. Behavioural patterns may also include elements related to the lifecycle or structure, etc.

A. Default Implementation

Context: An object may be declared to have an abstract class and instantiated with a concrete subclass.

Current situation: The concrete subclass is defined by the instantiation statement. If we need to change the used implementation, we have to change every instantiation statement. The concrete implementation is fixed at the compile time and cannot be changed at the run time.

Proposal: Introduce an operator that would choose the default implementation of an abstract class. If the default implementation has been defined (either at the compile time or at the run time), an instantiation statement may refer to the abstract class.

Known drawbacks: It is not clear what scope the binding of a class to its default implementation should have. If the scope is not local, the binding will be a shared state and require extra care in concurrent environments.

B. Extended Initialisation

Context: Some languages make difference between phases of the object lifecycle. For example, an object may be declared constant, so that it is initialised once only and cannot change its state later.

TABLE I. SUMMARY OF THE PROPOSED FEATURES

Feature	Type	Related patterns: *GoF [1]*	Related patterns: *POSA1 [3]*
Default implementation	Lifecycle	Abstract Factory, Builder, Bridge, Command, Strategy	
Extended initialisation	Lifecycle	Builder, Factory Method	
Chameleon objects	Lifecycle	State, Factory Method	
Generalised functions and executors	Behaviour	Command, Strategy	Command Processor
Object interaction styles	Behaviour	Façade, Proxy, Observer	Blackboard, Broker, Forwarder-Receiver, Master-Slave, Pipes and Filters, Proxy, Publisher-Subscriber
Responsibility delegation	Behaviour	Adapter, Bridge, Chain of Responsibility, Composite, Decorator, Façade, Flyweight, Mediator, Proxy	Broker, Layers, Master-Slave, Microkernel, Proxy, Whole-Part
Subclassing members in a subclass	Structure	Template Method, Visitor	

Current situation: An object declared as constant must be fully initialised with a single instantiation statement. At the same time, the Builder pattern constructs a complex object in a few operations. This prohibits using constant declaration for such objects even if they are never changed later.

Proposal: Treat single-line and multi-line initialisation uniformly. Allow the initialisation phase to consist of a few operations, requiring it to have a definite boundary nevertheless. After the boundary has passed, a constant object cannot be changed anymore.

Known drawbacks: Separation of initialisation phase will require careful definition for work in concurrent environments.

C. Chameleon Objects

Context: The State pattern is used when an object needs to change its behaviour at the run time (according to the original definition, the object *appears* to change its class [1]).

Current situation: Usually the class of an object is fixed at its creation. Some languages (e.g., Perl) allow to change objects' classes later, but it is uncommon.

Proposal: Allow to change an object's class at the run time.

This feature is also related to the Factory Method pattern. A factory method may decide on the concrete class of an object depending on its parameters. Being able to change class, we could implement the same logic in a class constructor.

Known drawbacks: It is not obvious how to ensure at least two natural requirements. First, the change should not involve data conversion (i.e., the classes should differ in behaviour only, not in their data structure). Second, in order to avoid unexpected behaviour, both the client and the object itself should 'know' the limits within which the class may be changed. For example, the client might expect that all possible classes of the object are descendants of one abstract class. If the state is changed by the state object itself (which is allowed by the original description [1]), it should declare that the class will never be changed to something else. Then the client may rely on the interface defined in the base class.

D. Generalised Functions and Executors

Context: The Command pattern describes a generalisation of conventional functions, which has the following features: is a first-class object, uses inheritance, may store internal state, supports undo, redo and logging. Some of this functionality may be implemented in a Command Processor instead.

Current situation: The existing languages have different forms of generalised functions (lambda-expression, functors, generators, etc.) that have some of these features, but not all. These forms are summarised in Table II.

Proposal: Replace conventional functions with a generalisation having the power of the Command pattern. Implement classes responsible for functions execution (threads, executors, debugging environments) according to the Command Processor pattern.

Known drawbacks: Such generalisation may be too complicated for simple functions. On the other hand, the proposal does not require implementing all mentioned operations for each and every function. The essence of the proposal is the opportunity to add them as smoothly as possible when they *are* needed. Moreover, these operations may be needed even for simple functions. For example, Online Python Tutor supports undoing and redoing of every executed statement for the purposes of studying and debugging [8] (in terms of the design patterns, it means implementing undo and redo in the Command Processor).

Another problem is that it may be hard to find a design that is simple enough and suitable for the general case. The proper distribution of responsibilities between functions and executors is not obvious as well.

TABLE II. GENERALISED FUNCTIONS

	First-class objects	**May inherit**	**May store state**	**Undo, redo, logging**
Conventional functions	Yes/No[a]	No	No	No
Lambda-expressions (Java, Python, etc.) Delegates (C#)	Yes	No	No	No
Functors (C++)	Yes	Yes	Yes	Yes/No[b]
Generators (Python) Enumerators (C#)	Yes	No	Yes	No

[a] Depending on the language.
[b] May be implemented, but syntactically differ from conventional function calls.

E. Object Interaction Styles

Context: Using the Façade or Proxy patterns, a single class may represent a whole component, a subsystem or an external system. With the Broker pattern, such a system may be even distributed.

Current situation: There are different ways how components may interact: synchronous request-response, asynchronous request-response, pipe&filter, broadcast, blackboard, publish-subscribe [9]. Nevertheless, synchronous call is the predominant interaction style between objects in the existing languages. Other styles are usually implemented with a complex sequence of synchronous calls.

The need for a simpler approach may be illustrated by the existence of interface definition languages for concurrent and distributed systems. These languages describe interaction between systems using richer sets of interaction mechanisms (at least, including asynchronous requests and responses).

Proposal: Introduce constructs that would represent different interaction styles at the language level. They may better represent the way how developers think about components. Interface definition languages would not be needed any more since we would be able to define the required interactions directly.

Known drawbacks: The resulting syntax may be difficult to learn.

F. Responsibility Delegation

Context: A class may delegate its responsibility to another class. Usually, this delegation involves some changes in the call, but sometimes a request is simply forwarded.

Current situation: Delegation adds an extra level of indirection, even if it is unnecessary. Long chains of delegation may be resource-consuming. Peter Sommerland mentioned delegation as one of the main sources of excessive complexity introduced if we use design patterns carelessly [4].

Another problem is that once the request is forwarded, the reference to the object originally receiving the request is no longer available (*self* problem) [10].

Proposal: Allow a method to be explicitly marked as delegated. There may be different types of delegation, for example, keeping the original reference or not. A starting point in identifying which types of delegation should be supported may be the types identified by Jan Bosch in [10].

Provided that the delegate is known in advance and the method signatures are the same, the compiler or the run-time environment may get rid of the extra level of indirection. Even if this optimisation is impossible, delegation may be supported in integrated development environments. It would facilitate grasping code that uses delegation extensively.

Known drawbacks: Conditions of when the optimisation is possible may happen to be very restrictive. Probably, most delegations will not allow it. Furthermore, in our opinion, the self problem often should *not* be solved, since keeping the original reference may easily lead to violation of Demetra's law. Nevertheless, sometimes the original receiver of the call is really needed.

G. Subclassing Members in a Subclass

Context: A class may use a member declared in its superclass, but restrict the set of possible values (for example, choose a concrete implementation of an abstract class). The behaviour of the subclass may rely on this restriction since the subclass never assigns an illegal value to this member.

Current situation: A member defined in the superclass keeps its declaration in all subclasses. A subclass that have decided to use a particular subclass for this member must perform run-time casts, which is error-prone. It is especially important when the behaviour is distributed between the class and its superclass (e.g., using the Template Method or Visitor patterns).

For example, programming a user interface for Android requires to subclass standard classes, such as `Activity`, `Fragment`, etc. The application may know that a fragment of class `MyFragment` can be attached only to an activity of class `MyActivity`. Methods of class `MyFragment` may need to refer to methods and data defined in class `MyActivity`. Nevertheless, method `MyFragment.getActivity()` returns an object of class `Activity`, since it is defined in the superclass `Fragment`. The result of every such call should be dynamically casted to class `MyActivity`.

Proposal: Allow to redeclare a member in a subclass, restricting the member's class. It is known as depth subtyping in the type theory [11] and may be generalised to predicate subclassing, proposed earlier by Ruslan Batdalov [12].

Known drawbacks: To be useful, the change of class should be propagated to getters and setters, which is difficult in languages without a language-level association between fields and getters/setters (C++, Java).

Another problem to solve is the issue of variance. Although the proposal itself does not violate variance rules, its propagation to a setter would mean covariance of a method argument, which is considered unsafe [13].

V. Related Work

A number of approaches to incorporation of design patterns into programming languages were proposed. The number of attempts itself shows the desire to have a better support of design patterns at the language level (even though the work in this area is mostly rather old).

Joseph Gil and David H. Lorenz described gradual percolation of design patterns into languages [7]. Unfortunately, they did not provide a systematic approach to how to perform this process and make related decisions.

Jan Bosch described design patterns in terms of layers and delegations and proposed an implementation using so called Layered Object Model [10]. Effectively, the approach involves using a completely new language to solve their tasks. Some ideas of this work are used in ours, but in general, the approach does not solve the problem of identifying separate language-level features.

Perhaps, the most notable are implementations of the design patterns in aspect-oriented languages. Jan Hannemann and Gregor Kiczales described an implementation of the design patterns described by Erich Gamma et al. [1] in Java and AspectJ [14]. Miguel P. Monteiro and João Gomes did the same in Object Teams [15]. Pavol Bača and Valentino Vranić developed the idea further and proposed to replace the commonly known object-oriented design patterns with aspect-oriented ones [16].

Frank Buschmann et al. proposed the hypothesis that it is possible to provide configurable generic implementations for patterns that cover their whole design space, but refuted it in just ten pages [2].

Our approach differs from the mentioned ones in that it provides an insight on *how* we could find new language-level features for easier implementation of design patterns. The proposed features are also supposed to be suitable for object-oriented languages and not require a less common programming paradigm. At the same time, they may in principle be used in aspect-oriented or other extensions as well. So, these approaches can be considered rather complementary than competing.

Another field of study related to our approach is decomposition of design patterns. Uwe Zdun and Paris Avgeriou tried to identify primitives of which architectural patterns consist [17]. These primitives are of the architectural nature and not directly related to programming languages features. Francesca Arcelli Fontana et al. performed a detailed analysis of micro-structures comprising common design patterns [18][19]. Their primary goal was to facilitate design patterns detection, so the found micro-structures are not necessarily at level with language features either. In our opinion, the observation by Frank Buschmann et al. that design patterns are not generic, but generative [2] refers to many of these micro-structures as well.

VI. Conclusion and Future Work

Our study addressed the problem of excessive complexity, often introduced by application of design patterns. The developed approach allowed to identify a set of language-level features supporting the patterns described in [1][3]. We can conclude that the problem of implementation complexity may, at least in principle, be tackled by extending programming languages, so that the design patterns would be easier to apply. A sample set of such features is the main contribution of this study. At the same time, these features have their drawbacks, and their introduction requires to solve a number of problems.

The work may be continued in order to cover more patterns from different sources. At the same time, we do not expect finding a big number of new features in the course of this work. Although some new discoverings are inevitable, the viability of the system will be best justified if Table I grows more rightwards than downwards. A language should not grow infinitely with the number of expressions in this language.

Another direction of the future research is looking for the ways how the proposed features can be implemented in real programming languages and whether they can be implemented at all. If they can, it will raise, perhaps, the most important question of further study – the practical testing of our hypothesis that introduction of the proposed features allows to reduce complexity of the patterns usage in real software systems.

References

[1] E. Gamma, R. Helm, R. Johnson, and J. Vlissides, Design Patterns: Elements of Reusable Object-Oriented Software. Addison-Wesley Publishing Company, 1995.

[2] F. Buschmann, K. Henney, and D. C. Schmidt, Pattern-Oriented Software Architecture, On Patterns and Pattern Languages, ser. Pattern-Oriented Software Architecture. Wiley, 2007.

[3] F. Buschmann, R. Meunier, H. Rohnert, P. Sommerlad, and M. Stal, Pattern-Oriented Software Architecture, A System of Patterns, ser. Pattern-Oriented Software Architecture. Wiley, 2013.

[4] P. Sommerlad, "Design patterns are bad for software design," IEEE Software, vol. 24, no. 4, pp. 68–71, 2007.

[5] G. Booch, "The well-tempered architecture," IEEE Software, vol. 24, no. 4, pp. 24–25, 2007.

[6] J. Bishop, C# 3.0 Design Patterns. O'Reilly Media, 2008.

[7] J. Gil and D. H. Lorenz, "Design patterns and language design," Computer, vol. 31, no. 3, pp. 118–120, 1998.

[8] P. J. Guo, "Online Python Tutor: Embeddable web-based program visualization for CS education," in Proceedings of the 44th ACM Technical Symposium on Computer Science Education, ser. SIGCSE '13. New York, NY, USA: ACM, 2013, pp. 579–584.

[9] I. Crnković, S. Séntilles, A. Vulgarakis, and M. R. V. Chaudron, "A classification framework for software component models," IEEE Transactions on Software Engineering, vol. 37, no. 5, pp. 593–615, 2011.

[10] J. Bosch, "Design patterns as language constructs," Journal of Object-Oriented Programming, vol. 11, no. 2, pp. 18–32, 1998.

[11] B. C. Pierce, Types and programming languages. MIT press, 2002.

[12] R. Batdalov, "Inheritance and class structure," in Proceedings of the First International Scientific-Practical Conference Object Systems — 2010, P. P. Oleynik, Ed., 2010, pp. 92–95. [Online]. Available: http://cyberleninka.ru/article/n/inheritance-and-class-structure.pdf 2016.07.11

[13] F. S. Løkke, "Scala & design patterns," Master's thesis, University of Aarhus, March 2009.

[14] J. Hannemann and G. Kiczales, "Design pattern implementation in Java and AspectJ," ACM Sigplan Notices, vol. 37, no. 11, pp. 161–173, 2002.

[15] M. P. Monteiro and J. Gomes, "Implementing design patterns in Object Teams," Software: Practice and Experience, vol. 43, no. 12, pp. 1519–1551, 2013.

[16] P. Bača and V. Vranić, "Replacing object-oriented design patterns with intrinsic aspect-oriented design patterns," in Proceedings of the 2nd Eastern European Regional Conference on the Engineering of Computer Based Systems (ECBS-EERC). IEEE, 2011, pp. 19–26.

[17] U. Zdun and P. Avgeriou, "A catalog of architectural primitives for modeling architectural patterns," Information and Software Technology, vol. 50, no. 9-10, pp. 1003–1034, 2008.

[18] F. A. Fontana, S. Maggioni, and C. Raibulet, "Understanding the relevance of micro-structures for design patterns detection," Journal of Systems and Software, vol. 84, no. 12, pp. 2334–2347, 2011.

[19] ——, "Design patterns: a survey on their micro-structures," Journal of Software-Evolution and Process, vol. 25, no. 1, pp. 27–52, 2013.

Spider-DAR: A Tool to Support the Implementation of Decision Analysis and Resolution Process based on CMMI-DEV and MR-MPS-SW Models

Luiz Otávio Danin de Lima, Sandro Ronaldo Bezerra Oliveira
Graduate Program in Computer Science
Federal University of Pará
Belém, Pará, Brazil
e-mail:otaviodanin@gmail.com, srbo@ufpa.br

Bleno Wilson Franklin Vale da Silva, Géssica Pinheiro da Silva, Iuri Igonez Silva Raiol
Faculty of Computing
Federal University of Pará
Belém, Pará, Brazil
e-mail: {blenofvale, gesspinhero, iuriraiol}@gmail.com

Abstract—**This paper presents a software tool called Spider-DAR, which is a desktop solution that operates in a client-server system and seeks to help the implementation of decision analysis and resolution process in adherence to CMMI-DEV (Capability Maturity Model Integration for Development) model. This involves the following: laying down the guidelines for decision analysis and the evaluation criteria, identifying alternative solutions, selecting evaluation methods, evaluating alternatives and selecting solutions. The software conforms to all the specific practices of the DAR (Decision Analysis and Resolution) process area included in CMMI-DEV. We expect that this tool will be readily adopted by software organizations because it is based on models and standards that are generally accepted. Furthermore, this tool adopts free (non-proprietary) technologies as a means of reducing costs. This tool was used in a software company that implemented its processes on the basis of CMMI-DEV Maturity Level 3, and the employees of this company evaluated its efficiency and effectiveness.**

Keywords-software engineering; software quality; decision analysis and resolution; process improvement; software tool.

I. INTRODUCTION

Within the domain of the knowledge and information society and the administrative scope of Information Systems (IS), there have been a number of significant changes in the social, technical and business domains. According to Evans *et al.* [1], the competition and cooperation that accompany the different stages of production have led to a growing trend: a desire to enhance it by automating the manual process and to make future improvements in a general way. Thus, in software engineering, as in several areas of knowledge, special skills are required to analyze different decisions made throughout the IS development and evolution process.

It is essential to analyze key issues, such as types of technology, the selection of personnel, and the acquisition of resources or tools, the value of which can be substantiated by means of a systematic process, so that rational choices can be made about what should be required from products or services. As defined in the Capability Maturity Model Integration for Development (CMMI-DEV) [2] the decision analysis establishes guidelines to determine which issues should be the objects of a formal evaluation process on the basis of defined criteria. This process involves adopting a structured approach to evaluate alternative solutions. Thus, the most appropriate choice about the real circumstances of a project or organization, significantly affects all the stages of its lifecycle. The decision-making processes and systems are of crucial importance to improve the efficiency, quality and cost / benefit ratio of the organizations.

Moreover, it is also worth underlining that the decision-making support is a new paradigm for organizations that seek to introduce continuous learning in all the processes carried out by its various sectors, because, according to Association for Promotion of Brazilian Software Excellence (SOFTEX) [3]:

- It facilitates the structuring of problems within a specific research study,
- It leads to an understanding of the information required to make effective decisions,
- It provides access to data, which would not otherwise be available or would be difficult to obtain,
- It generates and assesses alternative solutions,
- It prioritizes alternatives through explicit models,
- It prioritizes alternatives through a method that is supported by a formal and objective process and thus avoids making poor choices that are entirely based on subjective factors.

In this way, the Decision Management (GDE) process is included in the Brazilian Reference Model of Process Improvement for Software (MR-MPS-SW) [4] and the Decision Analysis and Resolution (DAR) process area is included in the CMMI-DEV [2] model. According to Pizzoleto [5], this makes it possible to generate indicators and form perspectives that can supplement and facilitate a better way of undertaking an activity; this involves setting these components within these improvement programs. Thus, this paper is driven by a desire to assist in defining and deploying a decision management strategy in organizations involved in software development. Moreover, it is guided by the essential activities and tasks, which are the expected results and specific practices included in the processes of these quality models that support the decision-making.

The area of decision-making for software development companies is very important, because today, most of these companies create spreadsheets to implement the practices included in the quality models. However, this does not allow the history of the company's decision-making to be maintained and does not assist any formal evaluation of the problem that needs to be analyzed. For this reason, the development of a systematic tool, which centralizes the information obtained during the formal evaluation process, might benefit the future decision-making that is based on an analysis of the historical background; it might also guide the implementation of the decision management process in a systemic way.

Hence, the aim of this paper is to adopt an approach (workflow and tool) for the Decision Analysis and Resolution process area that is aligned with CMMI-DEV and MR-MPS-SW quality models. This approach is based on the specification and implementation of tools, which consist of: (1) a process workflow that takes account of the constant assets in quality models, and (2) a systemic support, with a free tool, to carry out activities defined in the workflow. On the basis of this approach, it is expected that it will be possible to simplify the implementation of the decision analysis and resolution process in organizations seeking the improvement, standardization and institutionalization of their development process, with an emphasis on the application of resources in software projects. This tool is based on free standards and technologies and is the outcome of research on the Software Process Improvement: Development and Research (SPIDER) project [6], carried out at the Federal University of Pará.

Following this introduction, Section II discusses the stages of the decision analysis and resolution stages in software process, and also reviews some related works in the literature. Section III outlines the approach adopted for the decision analysis and resolution, and the tool that supports its implementation. Section IV conducts an analysis of the application tool in industry and its adherence to the CMMI-DEV and MR-MPS-SW models. Section V examines the results obtained in this research study in both the academic world and industry. Finally, Section VI summarizes the conclusions.

II. Background and Related Works

This section provides an overview of the concepts of decision-making in the CMMI-DEV model and some related works.

A. Concepts and Definitions

A decision-making system is not just a sequence of instructions, but rather an organized team of people and set of procedures, software, information databases and devices used to support specific decisions that are made to tackle a problem. In a review of decision-making, Keeney [7] defines it in technical terms as reflecting different levels of a philosophy or methodology, that are articulated by a set of auxiliary axioms, that can be employed to address the complexity of the problems during the decision-making.

Decisions can be classified in terms of the time it takes to make them. They can be divided into two basic types: scheduled and unscheduled. Scheduled decisions are routine and repetitive, and the organization usually finds specific ways to deal with them. Unscheduled decisions are usually made once, which means they are generally less structured than the scheduled ones.

A model of the decision-making process that is recommended for management use includes the following: (1) identifying an existing problem, (2) listing possible alternative ways to solve the problem, (3) selecting the most promising alternatives and implementing the one that is chosen, (4) obtaining feedback to find out if the implemented alternative is able to solve the identified problem. However, this means that it is impossible for people who make decisions to know exactly what the future implications of implementing an alternative might be. This is because the dynamics of organizations and their environments are constantly changing and the future implications of the decisions that are implemented are not entirely predictable.

The quality models that guide this paper have equivalent processes that are the driving-force behind the review and support the decision management. Both models (CMMI-DEV and MR-MPS-SW) include specific practices and show the results of decision analysis and resolution. In a similar way, they employ objective criteria to explore, the resolutions of problems related to the decision-making, and these can be employed for the evaluation of alternative solutions, by means of a formal process. Table I shows the correspondence between the assets of both models (CMMI-DEV and MR-MPS-SW) with regard to their specific practices or expected results [4].

TABLE I. The Correspondence of Practices and Expected Results in the CMMI-DEV and MR-MPS-SW Models

Specific Practices of DAR process area - CMMI-DEV	**Expected Results of GDE process - MR-MPS.BR**
SP 1.1 Establish Guidelines for Decision Analysis	GDE1 - Organizational Guidelines to decisions management are established and maintained
-	GDE2 - The problem or issue is defined as the object of a formal process of decision-making
SP 1.2 Establish Evaluation Criteria	GDE3 - Criteria for the assessment of the alternative solutions are established and maintained in order of importance, so that the most important criteria exert more influence on the assessment
SP 1.3 Identifiy Alternative Solutions	GDE4 - Acceptable alternative solutions to the problem or issue are identified
SP 1.4 Select Evaluation Methods	GDE5 - The evaluation methods of the alternatives solutions are selected in accordance with their application viability
SP 1.5 Evaluate Alternative Solutions	GDE6 - Alternative solutions are evaluated by means of the criteria and established methods
SP 1.6 Select Solutions	GDE7 - Decisions are made on the basis of an evaluation of the alternatives based on the evaluation criteria that are laid down

B. Related Works

Assistance in defining a strategy and implementing a decision management in software development organizations is provided by the CMMI-DEV and MR-MPS-SW Implementation Guides where activities and key tasks are described, together with the expected results and specific practices that are included in the process to support decision-making. However, despite the availability of these guides, most organizations that attempt to deploy an analytical decision-making process experience obstacles, which prevent or delay their implementation. Among the main difficulties that have been encountered periodically, is the problem of defining a non-intrusive strategy, i.e. ensuring that it does not have an impact on people's daily activities in the organizational unit and can easily be integrated with other processes. As well as this, there is the question of choosing appropriate tools to support and facilitate the use of the practices required by a Decision Management process. Thus, the choice of tools to be adopted can be regarded as a crucial factor in employing a defined strategy that can implement the decision support in organizations.

Thus, the choice of free software tools is justified by the economic self-sufficiency and freedom that a certain product in this category can give. According to Campos [8] one of the freedoms provided is that it improves the software so that it can be used in either a personal or public way in organizations. However, on the basis of research carried out in the specialized literature, no free and completed tools were found that support and facilitate the decision management, and have an adherence to the MR-MPS-SW and the CMMI-DEV models. The tools and models researched do not have the characteristics mentioned, although they were of significance in the area of decision management, (whether academic or marketing). These tools are discussed below.

The DPMTool [9] supports decision management in software projects, in the domain of global development. Thus, the description of this tool states that it allows the creation, storage, recovery and transmission of decisions made by a software design, and performed in a distributed way. In addition, the tool allows the project managers to control the information about software projects, since the value and importance of project development is that it also provides techniques that can allow the decision-making carried out in previous projects to be re-used for new projects, which have similar features.

The main purpose of this tool is that it allows information from previous decisions to be used again; to support the decision-making in future projects. However, there is no evidence that this information is, in fact, useful. In addition, the management of roles or the way criteria is laid down is not clear in the DPMTool, or even if there is a systematic process involved. Hence, the reuse of knowledge for project management is something that is not trivial, and it is being used by distributed teams in an even more challenging way. However, understanding and carrying out project management, in an efficient way, has become the greatest challenge for distributed teams.

It is known that the information sharing is restricted to certain professionals (e.g. managers). Likewise, in this kind of work, i.e. in a single project that is undertaken by many professionals (managers) spread around the globe, only a few of them will obtain crucial information for the correct decision-making, and most of those who take part in projects, will not necessarily know all the solutions adopted by the other participants in the same project. In addition, from the standpoint of decision-making, this kind of work does not seems to be as productive, as a continuous process in which the team reaches an agreement, about what criteria should be employed and the alternative solutions that can be found.

Another study on simulation models [10] describes the results of a project, which aimed at investigating specific aspects of decision-making in personnel management, which involved software projects and development teams and took account of dynamic variables, such as stress, conflicts, motivation and performance. The simulation was adopted that employs system dynamics models as a powerful technique to deal with the problem. In this study, decision-making is regarded as a means of giving support to personnel management through an evaluation model applied to other useful projects. However, it includes features that allow a high degree of subjectivity in personnel management. Moreover, the project can even be influenced by other variables that are not taken into account - for instance, the variable about motivation is not included in the survey. In the decision management processes governed by the CMMI-DEV and MR-MPS-SW models, it seeks to reduce subjectivity to a minimum in the process so that the decision-making is not biased.

From the works reviewed, it is clear that the authors were not concerned about implementing decision management in a systematic way. They did not adopt the traditional practices set out in the quality models that guide the implementation of a decision-making process. Moreover, they have failed to design support tools that could adopt all the concepts and fundamental principles of a formal evaluation. It was also noted that the works did not apply the evaluations obtained from their approaches to the academic world or industry; nor did they provide an analysis of the efficiency and effectiveness of the solutions that support decision-making.

III. A Tool that supports Decision Analysis and Resolution

The support concept adopted in this paper defines a set of technologies that can be integrated to assist in the decision analysis and resolution process. This domain includes the following: tools, techniques, procedures, processes, roles, methodologies, frameworks, languages, standards, patterns, and so on.

A. The Spider-DAR Workflow

The aim of this section is to describe the Spider-DAR workflow for the Decision Analysis and Resolution process. The workflow can be split into seven tasks that cover all the requirements and expected results from MR-MPS-SW [4] and specific practices from CMMI-DEV [2]. Fig. 1 illustrates the process workflow.

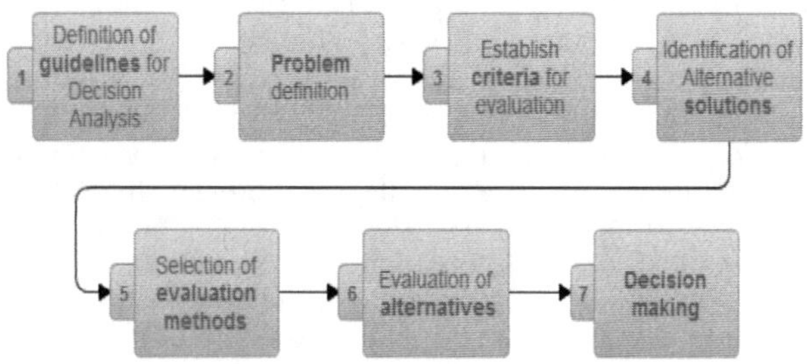

Figure 1. A Flowchart for Decision Analysis and Resolution

The first task consists of defining the guidelines for the decision analysis process, and basically involves setting out institutional guidelines for formally selecting the problem to be solved. According to Table I, this task involves DAR SP 1.1 in CMMI-DEV and GDE1 in MR-MPS-SW.

Following this, the second task of the main process is the formal definition of the problem or issue to be solved, which can enable an objective analysis of the problem to be conducted. This task is required for the GDE2 in MR-MPS-SW.

After the two tasks have been carried out, the next one takes place after the problem definition. It consists of the definition and prioritization of all the listed criteria for the problem, so that they can be evaluated later. The SP 1.2 in CMMI-DEV and the GDE3 in MR-MPS-SW are attained on completion of the third task.

The fourth task is carried out after all the possible criteria needed to evaluate the problem have been defined and involves examining all the possible alternative means of solving it. Furthermore, this task requires discussing all the possible alternatives and, additionally, it is necessary to assess the risks associated with the alternative solutions for future evaluations. Thus, this task covers the SP 1.3 in CMMI-DEV and the GDE4 in MR-MPS-SW.

With the aid of both the criteria and alternative solutions, the next task is to define the methods for evaluating the alternative solutions, and select which method is more appropriate for evaluating each alternative. This task covers the SP 1.4 in CMMI-DEV and the GDE5 in MR-MPS-SW.

The alternative evaluation process is the core of the DAR process. The aim of this task is to make an evaluation of all the alternative solutions by using all the defined criteria in the process; the selected method is then employed to rank the best solutions to the problem. This phase involves analysis, discussion and a review. Thus, the SP 1.5 in CMMI-DEV and the GDE6 in MR-MPS-SW are covered in this process.

The final task involves choosing the most appropriate solution for the problem or issue being analysed, and hence, registering and documenting all the experiences for future usage. This task covers the SP.1.6 in CMMI-DEV and the GDE7 in MR-MPS-SW.

B. The Spider-DAR Tool

The Spider-DAR is a General Public License (GPL) tool that is specifically concerned with Decision Management, and adhering to the good practices recommended by the CMMI-DEV and the MR-MPS-SW models. The requirements that guided the development of the tool were extracted from the workflow presented in this paper.

This tool was developed as a desktop environment using Java and was based on the use of free technologies, such as Netbeans 8.0.2 IDE, MySQL 6.3 DBMS and the iText, a library for creating and manipulating PDF files.

The architecture of Spider-DAR was based in the three-layer model called Model-View-Controller (MVC). Thus, the actions that occurred are managed by controllers, which make the intermediation between the interface with the user and the entities modeled in the database. The main benefit of its use is its ease of maintenance and the fact that any new components that might arise can be added, like a change of interfaces or the native database.

The development team had a standardized method to facilitate the encoding system, as well as to optimize computing resources. The FACADE and SINGLETON [11] design patterns were also used for uncoupling the business layer from the persistence layer and thus, providing a better management of the instantiated objects. The architecture is visualized in Fig. 2.

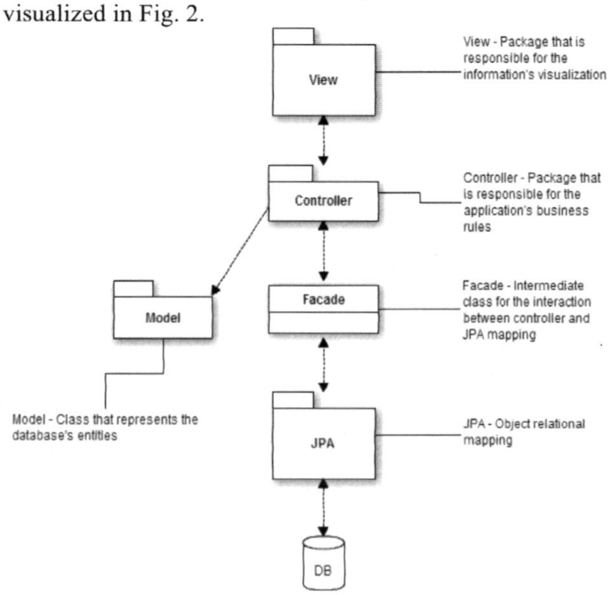

Figure 2. The Architectural Components of Spider-DAR

The Spider-DAR tool was designed for use in organizations and academic environments, to support multiusers. Each unit of the organization has an area in the tool to register and evaluate problems. The tool allows the storage of a Decision Management Guide in a text format, and also attaches an existing document, for future searches. The Decision Management Guide is used to define how a process should be implemented within the organization. The centralization of information streamlines the planning and monitoring, and reduces the effort required for the execution of the project.

The tool allows the registering of problems that will be objects of the decision-making process, and also the allocation of participants for its execution. Each participant has a profile that determines which modules of the tool the participant has access to. Fig. 3 shows the details of the problems to be registered.

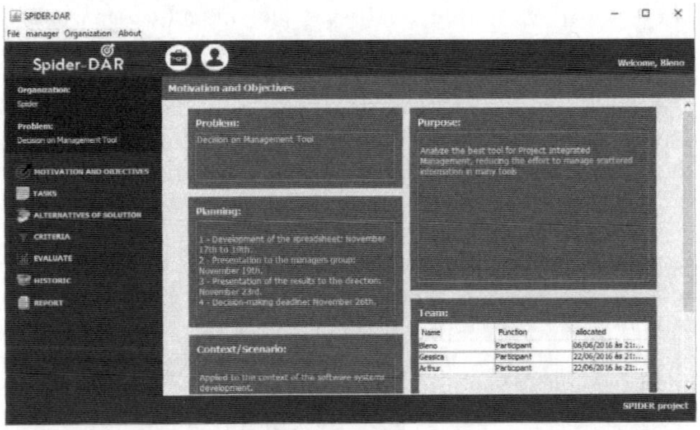

Figure 3. Motivation and objectives of a problem registered in spider-DAR

After the problem has been defined, it is permissible to define alternative solutions and the features that will be applied to evaluate the viability of these alternatives. The tool also allows the evaluation criteria in each problem, to be defined; these are variables that will influence the choice of alternative solutions.

The Spider-DAR has a module to evaluate the alternatives, as shown in the Fig. 4. The rate of satisfaction is calculated in accordance with the established criteria and, a ranking is generated in a visual way to determine which alternative is the best for the resolution of the problem. The tool just indicates which alternative is more viable, however, and because of the peculiarities of each problem, the decision-making is the responsibility of the user.

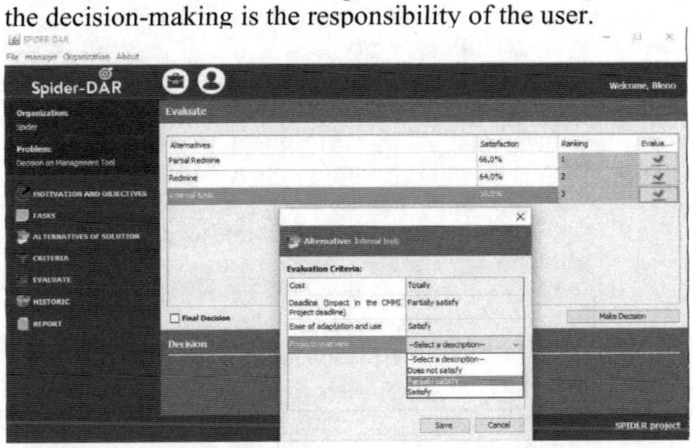

Figure 4. Evaluation of alternatives solutions in Spider-DAR tool

During the management process or after it has been completed, the tool can at any moment allow, the user to generate a report in a PDF file with all the entries of the data tools. Thus, after the end of the decision management process, a generated report will contain the data of the Problem, Alternatives Solutions, Evaluation Criteria, Evaluation and Decision, and this will facilitate the analysis of the whole process until the result has been obtained.

IV. Software Tool Evaluation

This section describes the tool evaluation in the software industry and their adherence to CMMI-DEV.

A. Application in the Software Industry

The tool was used during the implementation of CMMI-DEV Maturity Level 3 in a software development organization in Brazil, called EMPREL, in 2015 and 2016, and supports constant practices in the Decision Analysis and Resolution (DAR) process area. The organization was assessed at this level and obtained a certificate issued by the CMMI Institute.

The tool's users reported that its use made it possible for the organization to carry out a historic decision-making in all the software development projects. It also undertook a mapping of the problems and decision-making to facilitate the knowledge management, and thus provide a more efficient and effective means of managing the implementation of the DAR process area.

The EMPREL employees evaluated the Spider-DAR tool as efficient and effective to support for decision management. The main obtained results were:

- The use of the tool allows a decentralization of employees responsibilities during the execution of tool features, because all employees can perform together the formal evaluation process,
- Because the workflow implemented in the tool presents sequenced activities and tasks, this tool allows a systematic implementation of the Decision Analysis and Resolution process,
- The continuous maintenance of the historical basis in the tool allows the analysis of information generated from a problem or issue resolution during the decision-making of another problem or issue;
- By execution of features the tool facilitates the structuring of problems or issues, leads to an understanding of the information required to make effective decisions, generates and assesses solutions and prioritizes alternatives through a method that is supported by a formal and objective process.

The official CMMI assessment confirmed that the use of the tool had been successful. It should be emphasized that this company was chosen because it meant that the authors of this paper were able to conduct the implementation of the organizational process improvement program in its organizational units.

B. Adherence to CMMI-DEV

The Adherence concept analysis of the proposed tool is conducted through the mapping of the features outlined in Section III with the specific practices (SP) contained in the DAR process area in CMMI-DEV and the expected results (ER) in the GDE process included in MR-MPS-SW. Specific practice can be defined as "the description of an activity that is considered important in achieving the associated specific goal, i.e. it describes the activities that are expected to result in the achievement of the specific goals of the CMMI process area" [2] and expected results is "an observable result anticipated from the successful performance of the process" [12]. The description of the specific practices and the expected results were shown in Table I. This analysis can be observed in Table II.

TABLE II. ADHERENCE BETWEEN THE SPIDER-DAR FEATURES TO CMMI-DEV AND MR-MPS-SW

SP	ER	RequiredTasks	Tool Features
SP1.1	GDE1	• Set out a formal decision guide, • Evaluate the questions of high to medium impact risk for the organization.	Definition of Guidelines for Decision Analysis
-	GDE2	• Definition of the problem or issue which will be the object of a formal decision-making process, • Definition of the scope of the problem or issue.	Problem Definition
SP1.2	GDE3	• Define the criteria for the evaluation of alternative solutions, • Define the range and scale for ranking the evaluation criteria, • Rank the evaluation criteria.	Establish the Criteria for Evaluation
SP1.3	GDE4	• Identify alternative solutions.	Identification of Alternative Solutions
SP1.4	GDE5	• Select evaluation methods based on their ability to focus on the issues and problems that are not being influenced by them, • Determine the measures needed to support the evaluation method.	Selection of Evaluation Methods
SP1.5	GDE6	• Evaluate alternative solutions proposed using the evaluation criteria established and the methods selected, • Obtain and record the results of the evaluation.	Evaluation of Alternatives
SP1.6	GDE7	• Recommended solutions to address significant issues, • Register and communicate the results and rationale for the recommended solution to the appropriate stakeholders.	Decision-making

To view the details of each of the recommendations of the specific practices and expected results listed in the first and second columns of Table II, it is necessary to consult the official guides of the CMMI-DEV [2] and MR-MPS-SW [4].

V. OBTAINED RESULTS

This section describes the results of this work that were obtained for the academic world and industry.

A. *The Academic World*

This research study included two graduate students and two undergraduates who are studying this subject and monitoring process improvement in a software development organization as research assistants. The research can be characterized as a subproject of the SPIDER Project, and was accepted for the 2011/2012 cycle of the PBQP-SW (Brazilian Program of Software Quality and Productivity). The Workflow and the Tool were the subject of a master's dissertation that was defended at the Federal University of Pará (Graduate Program in Computer Science). Thus, a workflow process and a tool to support the decision management were obtained, and an investigation was conducted to verify how these results (described in Section IV) could be implemented in a software company.

In academic world, the tool presented in this paper can help with the teaching of decision analysis and resolution because it has a systematic step by step of the activities that compose this knowledge area. This tool can also be used to simulate the learning of implementation of process improvement program through the use of concepts of decision analysis and resolution. Students involved in this work have been trained in the area of decision analysis and resolution through this tool and today they help the software companies in the implementation of good practices included in this area and in the quality models.

B. *In Industry*

The authors used the technology described in this paper for consultation projects related to process improvement. First, the tool was used by software development organizations that are partners of the SPIDER project, such as the EMPREL, which is located in Recife city. Basically, the tool assisted in the different stages of the decision analysis and resolution by defining and monitoring the projects. On the other hand, the activities of the Workflow are widely adopted in the implementation of Maturity Level 3 of CMMI-DEV in organizations in which the authors act as consultants, located at Porto Digital (Recife city) and Farol Digital (João Pessoa city).

The tool helped efficiently and effectively the Emprel reach the CMMI-DEV Maturity Level 3 because it has a workflow that meets all specific practices included in the decision analysis and resolution process area. Thus, the strenghts for the Emprel employees were:

- The employees perform a formal evaluation of the problems or issues through the tool's features, performing together this evaluation because they do not work with spreadsheets that were under the control of a single person. Thus, the employees feel part of decision-making,
- Through the information maintained in the tool database and used to obtain the results in previous decisions, the employees can identify insights that can help in current decisions. It can help in the knowledge management,
- The employees know which information should be filled to the implementation of a formal evaluation

because the tool displays all the fields required for this one. Thus, the decision process becomes less complex,

- The final decisions of the employees are founded on a formal method that prioritizes the alternatives according to the evaluation criteria. Thus, it makes the evaluation more formal and objective.

VI. CONCLUSION

The development of the decision analysis and resolution tool is intended to support the activities about decision analysis and resolution in software process which are based on the good practices defined by the quality models and standards. Hence, the Spider-DAR systemic approach is designed to facilitate the adoption of these models and standards by the software development organizations that use this tool.

In the face of many possible systemic and business solutions, our approach addresses the challenge of becoming a solution that can be employed in multiple scenaries. It is not linked to commercial interests, and is a viable candidate for consideration when compared with the private solutions that are marketed.

Of the lessons learned from this project, we would like to list the following: the importance of systematic processes for the implementation of a decision-making process, and the development of a support tool for this process. The main challenge of this work was to implement the results in a software company that is keen to adopt good practices within a quality model.

It should be noted, as a strong point of this research project, that the tool is opensource, and can thus enable the academic community and / or industry to contribute to the development and evolution of this solution. The use of the tool is also of value since it helps the software organization to achieve more satisfactory levels of discipline through the combination of techniques and methods that assist in the decision analysis and resolution of its processes.

As a future study, that is already in development, we are seeking to integrate this tool with other tools available in the SPIDER project by focusing on a joint venture which involves the implementation of the other process areas included in CMMI-DEV and MR-MPS-SW, such as risk management, project planning, configuration management, and product and process quality assurance.

ACKNOWLEDGMENTS

The authors would like to thank Coordination for the Improvement of Higher Education Personnel (CAPES) for granting a Master's degree scholarship to the Postgraduate Program in Computer Science at the Federal University of Pará (PPGCC/UFPA). We are also grateful to the Institutional Scientific Initiation Scholarship Program (PIBIC-UFPA) for granting a scientific initiation scholarship. Both programs are sponsored by the Brazilian Government. The authors would also like to thank the Dean of Research and Postgraduate Studies at the Federal University of Pará (PROPESP/UFPA) for providing financial support through the Qualified Publication Support Program (PAPQ). This subproject is part of the SPIDER Project (*www.spider.ufpa.br*), institutionalized at the Federal University of Pará.

REFERENCES

[1] D. S. Evans, A. Hagiu, and R. Schmalensee, 2006, "Invisible Engines: How Software Platforms Drive Innovation and Transform Industries", Cambridge, MA: The MIT Press, 2006.

[2] SEI – Software Engineering Institute, "CMMI for Development – V 1.3", 2010, Available: http://www.sei.cmu.edu/reports/10tr033.pdf. Retrieved: march, 2016.

[3] SOFTEX – Associação para Promoção da Excelência do Software Brasileiro "Implementation guide Level C of MR-MPS-SW", 2015, Available: www.softex.br/mpsbr.Retrieved: march, 2016.

[4] SOFTEX – Associação para Promoção da Excelência do Software Brasileiro, "General Guide of MPS Software: 2012", 2012, Available: http://www.softex.br/mpsbr.Retrieved: march, 2016.

[5] A. V. Pizzoleto, "Business Ontology of the reference Model Mps for software (Mr-Mps-Sw) with focus on G E FLevels", Dissertação de Mestrado, São José do Rio Preto - Universidade Estadual Paulista, 2013.

[6] S. Oliveira, M. Souza, W. Lira, E. Yoshidome, and J. Furtado, "A System Solution Proposal of a Free Software Tools SUITE to Support the Implementation of MPS.BR Model", Revista do Programa Brasileiro de Qualidade e Produtividade em Software, pp. 103-107, 2011.

[7] R. L. Keeney, "Decision Analysis: An Overview", Operations Research, Vol. 30, N. 5, 1982, pp. 803-838.

[8] A. Campos, "What is Free Software", BR-LINUX, 2006, Available: http://br-linux.org/linux/faq-softwarelivre. Retrieved: april, 2016.

[9] P. J. Garrido, A. Vizcaino, J. Andrada, M. J. Monasor, and M. Piattini, "DPMTool: a tool for decisions management in distributed software projects", in: Proceedings in the 7th International Conference on Global Software Engineering, ICGSE, Workshops, Porto Alegre, Brazil, 27–30, 2012.

[10] S. D. Costa, J. L. Braga, L. A. Abrantes, and B. G. Ambrósio, "Suppport in decision making in people management software process based on simulation models", RESI: Revista Eletrônica de Sistemas de Informação, v. 12, p. 1-27, 2013.

[11] E. Gamma, R. Helm, R. Johnson, and J. Vlissides, "Design Patterns: Elements of Reusable Object-Oriented Software", Bookman, 2010.

[12] ISO/IEC – the International Organization for Standardization / International ElectrotechnicalComission, "ISO/IEC 15504-1: Information Technology - Process Assessment - Part 1: Concepts and Vocabulary", Geneve, 2004.

Challenges of the Digital Transformation in Software Engineering

Michael Gebhart
iteratec GmbH
Stuttgart, Germany
e-mail: michael.gebhart@iteratec.de

Pascal Giessler, Sebastian Abeck
Cooperation & Management
Karlsruhe Institute of Technology (KIT)
Karlsruhe, Germany
e-mail: pascal.giessler@kit.edu, abeck@kit.edu

Abstract—**Digital transformation describes the changes that the increased digitization within society causes or influences in all aspects of human life. The digital business transformation can be understood as the impact of the increased digitization on the business domain. Companies are challenged to transform, i.e., to create new business models that consider and leverage the increased digitization. As a result, from a software engineering perspective, the digital transformation changes the way how software is developed. Current trends are the development of applications for mobile devices and Internet of Things (IoT) applications. However, with these new application fields, new challenges for software engineering arise that have to be met to successfully conduct software projects in a digitized world. It is necessary for software companies to solve these challenges if they want to be successful on the market. In this article, these challenges are worked out. Furthermore, solution approaches, such as Application Programming Interface (API) strategy and an appropriate team culture, are derived to help software developers and companies to prepare for future software projects and to remain competitive.**

Keywords-digital transformation; digitization; software engineering; challenge

I. INTRODUCTION

Digital transformation can be understood as the changes that the digital technology causes or influences in all aspects of human life [1]. From a business perspective, companies are required to react on the increased digitization and to adapt accordingly. The resulting digital business transformation represents the idea of creating new or adapting existing business models based on the increased digitization within society, such as the usage of mobile devices, social media, and Internet of Things (IoT) [2].

As software systems are meant for supporting human life, the digitization influences the way how software should be developed. For example, more and more software projects are conducted that focus on the development of applications for mobile devices, such as smart phones and tablets, or the IoT. According to current studies, such as the one conducted by EC SPRIDE in collaboration with the University of Darmstadt and Fraunhofer Institute for Secure Information Technology (SIT) [3], this trend will continue and apps and rather small special purpose software predominantly in use on smart phones and tablets will further propagate.

These new application fields of software systems bear new challenges for the software engineering discipline. For example, in the last years, several new technologies and frameworks have evolved that are especially meant for the upcoming new devices and technologies. Instead of developing the entire functionality from scratch, more and more web services are available that are integrated into the developed solution [3]. Furthermore, software systems become increasingly omnipresent [1], which requires software developers to consider the consumer of software. The attractiveness of the software for the consumer, i.e., its user experience, has become one of the most important success factors for software systems.

To be successful on the market, software companies have to solve these challenges. However, in most cases, companies try to respond on the digitization with changes of the development methodology. For example, agile development is wide-spread today. But, the increased digitization requires more than focusing on the development methodology. It is more about the attitude when developing software and the necessary mindset and environment. It is about the roles and their responsibilities during the development. The digitization requires to deal with the upcoming changes, such as the increasing technology heterogeneity, instead of trying to avoid them.

This article examines the challenges caused by the digitization in society. The challenges are systematically worked out and described. Purpose of this article is to support software developers and companies to prepare for these challenges the digitization and the resulting digital transformation bring with them. For that reason, in addition, after introducing the challenges, possible solution approaches are presented in this article. The challenges and solutions are not limited to technological aspects. Instead, they focus both technological and organizational respectively human-oriented aspects. For that reason, this paper is meant for software developers and business managers who want to prepare themselves or their company for the future.

The article is organized as follows: Section II examines existing work in the context of digital transformation and its impact on software engineering. The resulting challenges of the digital transformation on software engineering are summarized in Section III. Section IV introduces solution approaches to overcome the challenges managed in Section III. Section V concludes this article and introduces future research work.

II. Background

This section analyzes existing work in the context of digital transformation and possible impacts on software engineering. Based on this work, in the following section, the future challenges for software engineering and solution approaches are derived and summarized.

In [1], Stolterman and Fors introduce the term digital transformation as the changes that the digital technology causes or influences in all aspects of human life. They state that the most crucial challenge for Information System Research is the study of the overall effects of the ongoing digital transformation of society. This is, why we focus on the effects of digital transformation on software engineering from a holistic view. We do not focus on software development methodologies like Scrum. Instead, we describe challenges on software engineering as a whole with the involved people in mind.

Opportunities to create new business models based on the results of the increased digitization in society are described by Berman in [2]. Even though Berman focuses on the business perspective and does not describe concrete recommendations for the software engineering, the work gives some important hints about how the business will evolve. This allows to derive the impact on software engineering. For example, according to Berman, the focus should be on digital products and services with better customer experience. This shows the importance of considering the customer experience as developer as part of the software engineering.

In [3], Ochs presents a study about emerging trends in software development. The study is conducted by EC SPRIDE in collaboration with the University of Darmstadt and Fraunhofer Institute for Secure Information Technology (SIT) sponsored by the German Federal Ministry of Education and Research. The study shows essential characteristics for future software systems. We reuse these software characteristics, adapt them to software engineering with focus on digital business transformation and combine them with challenges mentioned in other work.

A list of challenges and methodologies to master the digital transformation is introduced by Hanna in [4]. The aspects described by Hanna are business-driven and consider companies as a whole. For example, Hanna describes how to develop the human resources, leadership and institutions, policies and regulations. Even though it is not focusing Information Technology (IT), we use this work to derive challenges that relate to software engineering.

The importance of solutions being consumer-oriented is emphasized by Leimeister et al. [5]. They describe that "in digital societies, companies must understand that the digital customers and their preferences are key and at the center stage for developing innovative solutions". This work shows that it is necessary to rethink about the way solutions are developed today.

The analysis of existing work shows that the digitization within society influences the software engineering. With the digital transformation, new challenges arise that have to be considered by software companies. Some work also describes certain challenges and trends for software engineering that have to be solved. However, a list of challenges of the digital transformation in software engineering with concrete advices how to solve these challenges is missing. This is the motivation to investigate this aspect in more detail.

III. Challenges of the Digital Transformation in Software Engineering

In this section, the challenges of the digital transformation in software engineering described. The challenges are derived from existing work and experiences. The challenges consider both technical and organizational, i.e., human-oriented aspects as both are important for successful software projects. They constitute the basis for the solution approaches introduced in Section IV.

A. Reduced Time-To-Market

More than ever, new innovations are expected by the customers to be available as soon as possible [4]. Especially due to the increasing digitization in society and thus, due to the focus on private customers, the time to market has to be further reduced. This applies to completely new products and new features for existing products.

As a result, software developers and companies have to prepare their development process in way that allows to deploy new functionality continuously.

B. Flexibility and Agility

The reduced time to market requires software systems to be flexible enough to consider new requirements afterwards. Furthermore, the high competitive pressure requires to replace originally planned features by other ones. Thus, if not already done, the development process has to be agile to react on changing requirements.

Wherever useful, software developers and companies have to avoid waterfall development models and work in an agile way to be flexible enough to consider new and just needed functionality.

C. New Disciplines

In the last few years, a high number of new business words have been established with partially new concepts. Terms like Big Data, Internet of Things (IoT), Industry 4.0, and Machine Learning comprise complex topics that might be understood to create competitive products.

Thus, software developers and companies have to understand these new terms and concepts. As described by Hanna in [4], technological change creates new demand for learning. This requires enough time and freedom and efficient trainings for developers.

D. New Devices and Technologies

With the increased digitization, new devices are used by the customers [4]: mobile devices, virtual reality glasses, smart watches, intelligent in-ear headphones, and all the intelligent devices in a smart home [3]. They all create a completely new device environment with partially completely new technologies. The number of programming languages, partially device-specific frameworks increases.

Thus, software developers and companies have to prepare for completely new devices and technologies. This means that companies have to establish trainings and give developers the necessary freedom that allows them to learn new concepts. The training of developers is an important success factor as the new devices and technologies bring new possibilities with them that are necessary to stay competitive in the market.

E. High Degree of Technology Heterogeneity

The high number of devices and technologies results in another challenge: The rapid time to market does not allow to wait for a homogenization of the technology portfolio. As a result, software developers and companies are challenged to deal with a high number of devices and technologies in parallel. Within one project, several different technologies might be used with all their specifics.

For that reason, developers and companies have to find a solution to deal with this high degree of heterogeneity. Possible solutions are on the one side to standardize the interfaces between these technologies and on the other side to enable a continuous integration that considers different technologies.

F. Stronger Networking

Software systems developed today are mostly connected to other already existing software systems. This kind of networking can be the classical usage of programming interfaces to exchange data (e.g., by means of web services [6]) or the integration with social networks for authentication. In every case, software systems are less often isolated components. Instead, customers want them to interact with a bunch of existing components [2][3].

For that reason, for developers, it is necessary to know the requirements customers have on the networking aspect of software.

G. Extended Service Market

Today, we find more and more services providers that offer infrastructure, platform, and software as a service [2]. Compared to traditional software development, the trend is to reuse existing functionality instead of developing it from scratch [3]. Even though, using software from within the cloud includes operational costs, the development speed and the quality of the results can be much higher when reusing provided services.

Thus, the way how to develop software systems changes from coding the required functionality to assembling existing solutions. Software developers and companies have to understand the opportunities this way brings with it. As a result, the new service market has to be overseen. Software developers and companies have to inform about services that are currently available on the market.

H. Consumer-/ Customer-Orientation

Today, more and more software systems are used by ordinary people. Especially with the advent of smart phones and tablets, there is a new understanding about how software systems are expected to be used. The opportunity to enhance products and services for a better customer experience is mentioned by Berman in [2]. Also, Leimeister et al. emphasize the necessity to create solutions that are consumer-oriented [5].

This means that software developers and companies have to focus more than ever on the user of the system. An appealing user interface with a clear user experience has become one central success factor for consumer applications. Thus, developers and companies have to consider this aspect in their development process and to increase their competence in this area if not already done.

I. Business-Awareness

One central idea of the digital business transformation is to consider and leverage the increased digitization within society to create new business models. According to Hanna [4], product innovation has become crucial for sustained growth, competitiveness, and moving up the value ladder. As innovations require technological knowledge, the creation of business models is not a pure business task any longer. More than ever, developers themselves are invited to communicate new business ideas and models to the management.

For that reason, the developers within a company are required to think more business-oriented and to think outside the box. On the other side, the management is required to support developers in this task. This requires on the one hand freedom to give new ideas a trial and on the other side to open up to new ideas from developers.

J. Combination with Legacy IT

The increased speed with which new devices and technologies arise results in a faster aging of existing IT [3]. Especially in grown landscapes as they exist in bigger companies, the existing IT cannot be replaced rapidly. For that reason, developers and companies will be more often challenged to combine their new and modern software systems with IT that can be considered as legacy in the meanwhile. In [4], Hanna states that "adjusting the social and institutional environment to take advantage of a technological revolution and its associated techno-economic paradigm involves painful adjustments, often disruptions to, and even destruction of, legacy systems, institutions, practices, and processes". For example, in some cases, the new intelligent solutions have to exchange data with existing systems. In other cases, the new solution has to be deployable in an infrastructure that is not as modern as the new software system.

Thus, software developers and companies have to keep in mind where the software system is expected to be executed. Possibly, it is necessary to work out a more complex integration and deployment process to combine the new and modern software system with existing legacy IT.

IV. SOLUTION APPROACHES

In Section III, challenges of the digital transformation in software engineering were introduced. To overcome these challenges, next, solution approaches are described. These approaches are meant to help software developers and companies to prepare for future software projects and to remain competitive.

A. Microservices

Microservices can be seen as "small and autonomous services that work together" [8] via well-defined web interfaces. The size of a microservice is usually given by bounded contexts derived from business boundaries [8][9]. Therefore, the business has direct influence on the resulting system design which is also known as Conway's Law. But, there is also an influencing factor towards the opposite direction especially when evolving the service landscape [8].

The concept behind microservices results in a large number of benefits that address the mentioned challenges in Section III: First, reduced time to market when developing new functionalities through service autonomy. Each service can be developed and deployed separately without a central release coordination between different development teams. If this is not possible, the bounded context of the microservice should be usually revised and adapted to fit current needs.

Second, the support of technology heterogeneity when designing service landscapes especially microservice landscapes. We can decide to use different technologies inside each microservice based on our needs instead of using a company-wide standardized one [8]. For example, one service can be written in Java, another one in C#. It is not necessary to have company-wide unification. The communication between microservices with different technological setup is ensured by the service interface. This service interface must follow a technology-independent approach, such as the architectural style Representational State Transfer (REST) introduced by Fielding [7].

Third, the reuse aspect that is the core idea behind service landscapes [10]. Each service can expose different functionality via a well-defined service interface so that other services can benefit from that offer. For discovering existing services in a service landscape, a service discovery solution, such as Consul or Eureka, is usually set up.

B. API Design and Strategy

An Application Programming Interface (API) can be seen as a contract prescribing how to interact with the underlying system. In the context of a service landscape, the system can be an operable service that exposes business functionality via an API.

Today, APIs are a big deal and the growth of public APIs regarding their activity measured in requests is still unbroken [11]. Popular examples for public APIs are Facebook with the Graph API or Google with several APIs, such as YouTube Data API or Cloud Vision for image recognition.

There are several reasons for serving an API, such as offering business functionality for a mobile application, more flexibility in providing content, and allowing external developers or partners to transform new use cases in reality [11].

When designing an API, it is very important to have clear vision and business objective. In addition to the business view, it also crucial to comply with some design principles and best practices to simplify the usage of the API. For instance, in [13], several best practices for RESTful Web APIs are identified, collected, and explained.

C. Automation

Automation can be a key factor in the success of a company since it can drastically reduce the time and effort incurred by recurring tasks. This in turn increases the team productivity because the team does not have to deal with these tasks anymore.

For instance, deploying new applications or services should be as easy and fast as possible to reduce the time-to-market. At best, there is only one command for the deployment. That is why, Platform as a Services (PaaS) solutions, such as Heroku, DigitalOcean, or Amazon Web Services (AWS), are particularly popular among companies since it simplifies and reduces the necessary effort for deployment or infrastructure configuration.

But, deployment is just one of many examples, such as application monitoring or log analysis. It should be clear that an initial invest has to be taken, but it will pay off.

D. Technical Governance

The technical governance provides corporate-wide guidelines that have to be respected by all development teams to keep the heterogeneity within limits. Although, it is desirable when development teams take individual design or technological decisions, it makes, for example, no sense to choose a different coding style or to use a distinct deployment workflow. Sometimes, some technological decisions taken by team are not appropriate within the company due to bad experience in the past or other business related reasons.

Particularly important are corporate-wide guidelines when composing software components or services since the guidelines lay the foundation of the API that forms a contract for communication (see Section IV.B). For instance, the usage of different naming styles of exposed functionality can impede the reusability. Or in the worst case, when choosing a technology-dependent API, it can even prevent the reuse entirely.

In our opinion, any decision that affects the whole system should be covered by one or more guidelines and governed by a technical committee.

E. Accepting and Dealing with Heterogeneity

As mentioned, the technical governance tries to limit the heterogeneity in case of, for example, API design, but it does not want to avoid it when it comes to technological decisions. The company has to get used to the fact that several different technologies are applied. This is not a weakness but a strength because the new technologies offer new possibilities. Furthermore, a heterogeneous technology landscape avoids that too many people get used to a technology that becomes outdated one day. Developers are challenged to learn new technologies. As a result, developers remain attractive for the labor market. Finally, also, the company remains attractive for developers and young applicants that prefer to work and learn new and modern technologies.

Thus, heterogeneity is nothing that should be avoided. Instead, the company should learn to deal with and get used to it. The attempt to homogenize the IT at any price will result in a reduced adoption of new technologies, thus less innovative software projects and business models. It is more important to accept the coming changes and to make it part of the company philosophy.

F. Critical Analysis of new Trends

Every day, new technical solutions in form of libraries, frameworks, and tools appear on the internet. Some of them offer a comparable solution to a recurring problem or use case. Then again, others offer a completely new approach to solve the same problem.

The rapid growth of new technologies, the necessary learning and training effort as well as the lack of detailed and objective comparison between technologies in the same domain make it difficult to choose one technology over the other. In many cases, the taken decision has also to be reasoned especially when some people or the whole company must be convinced to rely on this technology for upcoming projects. There is no silver-bullet on how to choose the right technology since there are several factors that have to be considered. Furthermore, it is often an illusion to choose one technology for the next ten or more years since at some point a new technology or new approach will arise and form a community around it. Then, the cycle starts from the beginning.

We recommend to be open for new technologies or approaches and not hang on prior decisions based on the motto "It still works and will also be a suitable solution for the next years. We do not need a new technology". In our opinion, new technology should be analyzed as soon as possible to get a clear picture if it makes sense to follow the further development and how this approach can improve the already used technology in a specific application field. Thereby, it is important to look behind the scenes and get an idea of how the technology works and how it is build up since this is crucial for a proper and reasoned decision.

G. Design

A lot of great services and (digital) products pop up every day on the market. The design is the first impression that a potential customer will get from a product. It is often a misunderstanding that the design is only the user interface of an application. Instead, we should see the design as a method for problem solving that can be applied on different contexts, such as the user interface of an application but also on an API of a service. For instance, if the API design is not easy to understand or easy to try and use, it can have a negative impact on the adoption rate. Similar to this, if the frontend of an application looks confusing, customers could look after the opponent's solution. The design is therefore an essential ingredient of a product that decides if a potential customer is interested or not.

When developing new products, the whole development team should concentrate on a good design for the target user group instead of only focusing on the functionality aspect of the product.

H. Team Culture

The team culture of the development team can have a positive impact on the productivity and the self-awareness of each member. It can be difficult to form a good team culture since there are several factors that have to be considered, such as the identification of each member with the company or how proud someone is about shipped or developed products. Nevertheless, there are some key points that should be achieved within a company.

First, you should give each member of the development team the feeling that (s)he is unreplaceable and essential for the success for the product.

Second, each manager should be open for discussions and ideas since innovation comes from ideas. Each developer should be encouraged to be more business-oriented and think outside the box.

This leads to the third important key point: The employees are the most important asset of a company and should be treated accordingly. For development teams, you should give them the opportunity to learn and teach as much as possible to keep up with the industry leaders since no developer wants to work with "old" technologies for the rest of his working life. If this is not possible in current projects, then the company should find a compensation for the developers, perhaps by starting an open source project that allows to study new technologies. Thus, the management is responsible to give the necessary freedom and to provide trainings wherever possible.

V. CONCLUSION AND OUTLOOK

Digital business transformation can be understood as the idea of creating new or adapting existing business models based on the increasing digitization within society. As these new business models influence the way software systems have to be developed, software developers and companies have to adapt to these changes. For that reason, in this article, we derived and described challenges for software engineering the digital business transformation brings with it. Furthermore, we listed solution approaches for software developers and companies for overcoming these challenges.

Our list of challenges and solution approaches is expected to help software developers and business managers of software companies to remain competitive in times of digital transformation. Furthermore, more than ever, it is important to remain attractive for the labor market. Competitiveness requires companies to be attractive for talents. For that reason, the challenges and solution approaches are not limited to technological aspects. Instead, we considered aspects that are both technological and organizational, i.e., human-oriented.

For the future, we plan to refine the solution approaches. In the past we started with methodologies for designing services in service-oriented architectures [12]. We extended this work for API design and strategy including best practices for RESTful web services [13] and approaches to measure the compliance regarding these best practices [14]. We will continue this technological work to provide guidelines for designing a clear and maintainable API. In addition, we will focus on the non-technological, the human-oriented aspects. We will investigate solution approaches for being attractive for talents as this is significant for remaining competitive on the market. Furthermore, we will investigate how to adjust the mindset within companies so that new innovative and competitive business models can be created. This will help companies to benefit from the increased digitization and to prepare for the future.

REFERENCES

[1] E. Stolterman and A. C. Fors, "Information technology and the good life," in Information Systems Research: Relevant Theory and Informed Practice, pp. 687-692, 2004.

[2] S. J. Berman, "Digital transformation: opportunities to create new business models," Strateg. Leadersh., vol. 40, no. 2, pp. 16–24, 2012.

[3] C. Ochs, "Emerging trends in software development & implications for IT security: an explorative study", EC SPRIDE, 06/2014.

[4] N. K. Hanna, Mastering Digital Transformation: Towards a Smarter Society, Economy, City and Nation. Emerald Group Publishing Limited, 2015.

[5] J. M. Leimeister, H. Österle, and S. Alter, "Digital services for consumers," Electron. Mark., vol. 24, no. 4, pp. 255-258, 2014.

[6] S. Varghese, "Web Development with Go: Building Scalable Web Apps and RESTful Services," Berkeley, CA: Apress, pp. 159–209, 2015.

[7] R. Fielding, "Architectural styles and the design of network-based software architectures," University of California, Irvine, 2000.

[8] S. Newman, "Building Microservices – Designing fine-grained systems," O'Reilly, 2015, ISBN 9781491950357.

[9] E. Evans, "Domain-Driven Design: Tacking Complexity In the Heart of Software," Addison-Wesley Longman Publishing Co., Inc., 2003, ISBN 0321125215.

[10] T. Erl, SOA – Design Patterns, Prentice Hall, 2008. ISBN 978-0-13-613516-6.

[11] D. Jacobsen, G. Brail, and D. Woods, "APIs – A Strategy Guide," O'Reilly, 2012, ISBN 9781449308926.

[12] M. Gebhart and S. Abeck, "Metrics for evaluating service designs based on soaml," International Journal on Advances in Software, 4(1&2), pp. 61-75, 2011.

[13] P. Giessler, M. Gebhart, D. Sarancin, R. Steinegger, and S. Abeck, "Best Practices for the Design of RESTful web Services," International Conferences of Software Advances (ICSEA), pp. 392-397, 2015.

[14] M. Gebhart, "Query-based static analysis of web services in service-oriented architectures," International Journal on Advances in Software, 7(1&2), pp. 136-147, 2014.

An Approach to Generation of the UML Sequence Diagram from the Two-Hemisphere Model

Oksana Nikiforova, Konstantins Gusarovs
Riga Technical University
Riga, Latvia
konstantins.gusarovs@rtu.lv,
oksana.nikiforova@rtu.lv

Anatoly Ressin
SIA AssistUnion
Riga, Latvia
anatoly@assistunion.com

Abstract – Modelling for model-based development of software concerns the representation of both system structure and behavior. To this end, in order to satisfy this requirement Unified Modelling Language (UML) provides a range of static and dynamic diagram types; of these class and sequence diagrams are most frequently used. In contrast to the UML class diagrams, which are well researched and discussed in the literature, sequence diagrams are a 'dark horse' especially in regard layout and transformation. This paper proposes an approach to the generation of UML sequence from two-hemisphere model with the main attention to a dynamic aspect of the system.

Keywords – two-hemisphere model; UML sequence diagram, model transformation; finite-state machines; regular expressions.

I. Introduction

One of the trends for software developments, namely Model-Driven Software Development (MDSD) [1], is being widely introduced in order to support both the business analysis of the system being built as well as its implementation. According to MDSD, the development process is started with the modelling of the problem domain in order to produce the software domain model and to achieve once developed system model reuse [2].

The primary benefit of MDSD is an ability to provide a big-picture view of the architecture of the entire system. Usage of MDSD requires a common modelling notation and a system that can be used on all the stages of the development. Object Management Group (OMG) proposes its standard – Unified Modelling Language (UML) [3] that nowadays is being widely adopted. UML defines a notation for a set of the diagrams used for modelling the different aspects of the system – both static and dynamic. According to the research provided by Scott Ambler [4], the most popular UML diagrams in software development projects are the UML class and sequence diagrams. Static modelling is mainly done using UML class diagram that defines the general structure of the system and can be used as a basis for the implementation. The UML sequence diagram serves to define dynamic aspect presenting object interactions in the system. The UML sequence diagram includes both classes inside of the system as well as its environments represented as a set of the actors. These elements are exchanging the messages that are being placed on the lifelines that allow defining both the interaction patterns as well as the sequence of the interactions.

The UML class diagrams have been quite well studied in the MDSD-related researches and several methods exist for producing the UML class diagrams from the different types of the notations representing the problem domain. However, situation with the methodological modelling of the system dynamic is worse – only a few MDSD approaches focus on this question. As a result, issues associated with the transformations of the system dynamics are one of the main reasons why MDSD adoption is quite slow nowadays.

Since 2004, the research group lead by Oksana Nikiforova has been working on the applications of two-hemisphere model for the generation of different sets of the UML elements. This paper focuses on the UML sequence diagram, especially, its timing aspect. In this paper authors propose an approach that allows a way of transforming a two-hemisphere model into the UML sequence diagram based on the sequence diagram topology and using finite state machine (FSM) [5][6] as an auxiliary model within the series of model transformations. In addition, authors are going to analyze current limitations of the notational conventions proposed for the two-hemisphere model and argue the ideas of improving it in order to be able to receive results that are more precise.

The rest of the paper is structured as follows. Section 2 contains a short description of the two-hemisphere model. Section 3 describes related researches in the MDSD context providing an insight to similar existing methods and techniques. Section 4 provides a short description of the UML sequence diagram that is selected as a target model for the proposed transformation. The transformation method itself is described in the section 5 and a simple example is being analyzed in the section 6. In Section 7, method application results, as well as current limitations, are being analyzed and the possible solutions, in order to lift these limitations are being offered. Finally, the section 8 contains authors' conclusions and plans for the future work in this area.

II. Two-Hemisphere Model at a Glance

The two-hemisphere model-driven approach first published in 2004 [8] introduces an idea of joining elements both from the static and dynamic presentation of problem domain in the source model that consists of two diagram types (see Figure 1):

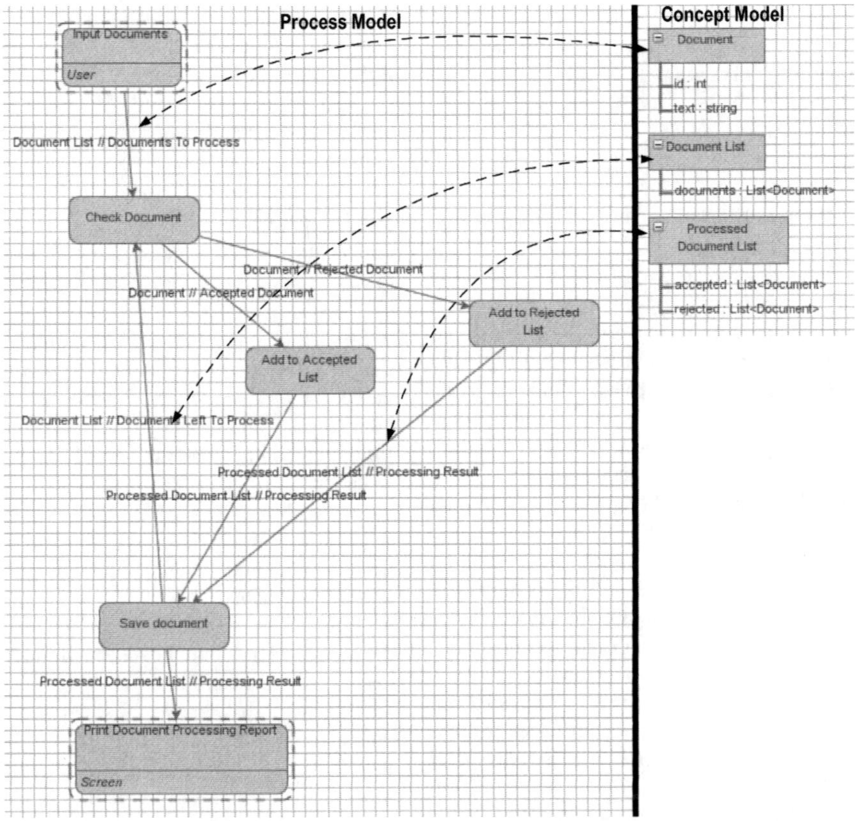

Figure 1. Two-hemisphere model for document processing created by BrainTool [7]

1) Concept model describes objects (or data types) used in the analyzed system presenting those in a form of concepts. Each concept has its attributes that are describing its inner structure. An attribute may be of the primitive type – such as an integer or string as a well as refer to another concept in the concept model.

2) Process model describes interactions performed inside the system. It consists of the processes connected with the data flows. Processes describe activities in the system and are divided into internal and external – external processes are defining system's interaction points with its environment and should only produce or consume the data flows whilst internal processes are defining activities inside the system and should both consume and produce the data. Data flows are used for the process interconnection and are describing the data migration inside the system. Each data flow is assigned to a concept of a given type thus linking both models.

A valid two-hemisphere model contains a single concept diagram as well as several process diagrams each of which might be describing a single activity inside the system, for example, it is possible to construct the process diagram for each of the use cases (or user stories) defined in the system requirements.

Currently, there exist several methods (and tools) for converting the two-hemisphere model into the UML class and sequence diagrams that are described in the papers [8]-[12]. Similarly to the situation in the MDSD area, transformations targeting the UML class diagram are a well-studied area.

III. RELATED WORK

A two-hemisphere model-driven approach can be described as one of the branches in the UML-DFD method family tree. UML-DFD methods are based on the usage of the dataflow diagram (that is being called process diagram in the two-hemisphere model-driven approach). Original transformation method that allows dataflow diagram (DFD) conversion into the UML class diagram is described in 2004 in the paper [13]. It involved composite transformation from the system requirements into the UML class diagram that consists of the 9 steps:

1. System requirement identification.
2. Use case diagram creation.
3. Composition of the textual scenario for the each of the use cases.
4. A transformation of the use case diagram into the initial object diagram.
5. Reducing of the initial object diagram by analyzing object functional features and

grouping, dividing and removing some of the initial objects.
6. Constructing the data flow diagram using reduced initial object set.
7. Identification of the data flows and data vocabulary creation.
8. Modelling of the system behavior using the activity diagram.
9. Data flow transformation into the resulting UML class diagram.

After the initial publication of the UML-DFD approach, several ways of improving it have been offering by the different authors in 2004-2012 [14]-[17].

The main difference between the UML-DFD approach and the two-hemisphere mode-driven approach is an initial presentation of the system and a resulting data model type that has been produced. UML-DFD based methods create so-called anaemic data model [18][19]. The main principle covered in the anaemic data model design can be stated with a single phrase: "data are data", which means that domain classes should contain no business logic, which in turn should be contained in the appropriate services processing the data. Two-hemisphere model-driven approach in turn, produces so-called rich data model in which domain classes share the part of the system functional features. While it may seem that the anaemic data model breaks the idea of the Object-Oriented Programming (OOP), in practice it is widely used [20] due to the fact it well suits the commonly used Model-View-Controller (MVC) pattern [21].

UML-DFD family methods are producing an activity diagram that can be later translated into the UML sequence diagram. In turn, in 2013, a method for transforming the two-hemisphere model into the UML sequence diagram was offered by O. Nikiforova, L. Kozacenko and D. Ahilcenoka [12][22]. The transformation used in the proposed approach was similar to the transformation used for generating the UML class diagram from the two-hemisphere model [22].

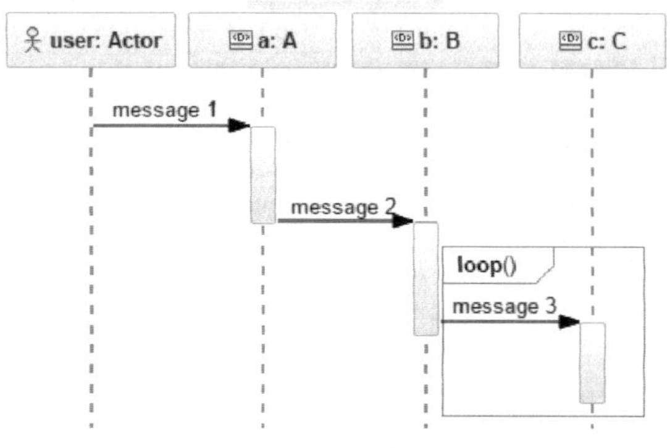

Figure 2. An example of the UML sequence diagram

The main idea behind the two-hemisphere model-driven approach was always a responsibility sharing, which in turn means, that the approach tends to find the most appropriate class for hosting one of the processes in process model as a method. As a result, both UML class and UML sequence diagrams generated from the two-hemisphere model will utilize the rich data model.

IV. UML SEQUENCE DIAGRAM AT A GLANCE

The UML sequence diagram is one of the well-known UML artefacts used for the representation of a modeled system's dynamical features. It focuses on the definition of the object interaction in the correct sequence. The diagram's vertical axis is used to display the time. It is being directed downwards with the beginning of the interaction in the model's top. It is possible to define the following components of the UML sequence diagram:

- Object – is an instance of a class that reflects real system's object.
- Lifeline – represents the time of object existence and the participation in the interactions with the other diagram elements.
- Actor – is a specific type of object. It is not the part of the analyzed system; however, it interacts with it and represents the part of the system's environment.
- Message – represents a single communication fact between actors/objects. Message connects its sender and its receiver and can have additional arguments.
- Fragment – is used to combine several messages into the block. Fragments can represent different multi-message interaction patterns: parallel interaction, alternate interaction as well as loop (repeated) interaction etc.

An example of the simple UML sequence diagram is given in Figure 2. It consists of "user" actor, objects A, B and C and their appropriate lifelines, messages 1, 2 and 3 and a loop fragment that contains the third message.

V. PROPOSED TRANSFORMATION METHOD

The two-hemisphere model uses the process diagram that should contain performers for the external processes (ones that determine system's integration with its environment). These performers are then transformed into the actors of the UML sequence diagram. Another diagram that is a part of the two-hemisphere model is a concept diagram holding the concepts that are transformed into objects of the UML sequence diagram.

As a result, all of the actors and the objects of a target UML sequence diagram are created. Next part of the transformation method involves the creation of the messages and the identification of the fragments in order to finalize the UML sequence diagram creation. This can be achieved by representing the process diagram in a different way and applying a transformation to a changed process diagram.

It is possible to transform the process model into a FSM [5][6] by transforming both the processes and the data flows into the transitions and inserting the state nodes between them. During this transformation, an additional change applies to the diagram's topology. The first change involves the creation of an initial node that is connected to all the external processes that only produce data flows and do not consume them. The second topology change is the creation of the final node that is connected to all the external processes that only consume and do not produce any of the data flows. In this case, the connection is made via special empty transition that is not in any way connected to the original model and is only used for the processing of an intermediate model. Former transformation can be described using the following pseudocode:

```
let de = Process Diagram Element
let parents = {de → [de]}
let children = {de → [de]}
let fsm = new Finite-State Machine

for each data flow d in data flows:
    let t = d.target
    let s = d.source

    children += {d → t}
    children += {s → d}

    parents += {t → d}
    parents += {d → s}

let initialProcesses = []
for each process p in processes:
    if not parents contains p:
      initialProcesses += p
let stateId = 1
let is = new State with stateId
let ts = new State with maximal
    allowed id
let nodeMap = {de → State}

fsm.addState(initialState)
fsm.addState(terminalState)

for each process p in initialProcesses:
    let n = new State with stateId
    nodeMap += {p → n}
    fsm.addState(n)
    let e = new Transition with p
    fsm.addTransition(e, is → n)
    stateId += 1

let open = [initialProcesses]
let closed = []

while open is not empty:
    let next = first entry from open
    let childs = children[next]
    let node = nodeMap[next]

    if childs is empty:
        let edge = fsm.findTransition(
            node → ts)

        if edge == null:
            let e = new Empty Transition
            fsm.addTransition(e, node → ts)

    for each child in children:
        let n = nodeMap[child]

        if n == null:
            n = new State with stateId
            stateId += 1

        nodeMap += {child → n}
        fsm.addState(n)

        let e = new Transition with child
        fsm.addTransition(e, node → n)

        if not closed contains child:
            open += child

        closed += next
```

In order to demonstrate the process model to the FSM transformation, a simple example is provided in Figure 3 and Figure 4. In this example, a process model containing two external and one internal processes interconnected with two data flows is transformed into the FSM .

After the initial FSM has been created from the process diagram, it is possible to minimize it and convert into the regular expression. In order to perform those operations, authors define the following formulas for the transition manipulation:

- `conj` – combines two transitions `a` and `b`, if transition b follows transition a (Formula 1):

$$conj(a,b) = \begin{cases} \emptyset, if\ a = \emptyset\ and\ b = \emptyset \\ b, if\ a = \varepsilon \\ a, if\ b = \varepsilon \\ a\ b, otherwise \end{cases} \quad (1)$$

- `disj` – combines two transitions `a` and `b`, if transition a is an alternative for transition `b` (Formula 2):

$$disj(a,b) = \begin{cases} \emptyset, if\ a = \emptyset\ and\ b = \emptyset \\ b, if\ a = \emptyset\ or\ a = \varepsilon \\ a, if\ b = \emptyset\ or\ b = \varepsilon \\ a, if\ a = b \\ (a)\Theta(b), otherwise \end{cases} \quad (2)$$

- `star` – marks a repeating transition `a` (Formula 3):

$$star(a) = \begin{cases} \emptyset, if\ a = \emptyset \\ \varepsilon, if\ a = \varepsilon \\ (a)*, otherwise \end{cases} \quad (3)$$

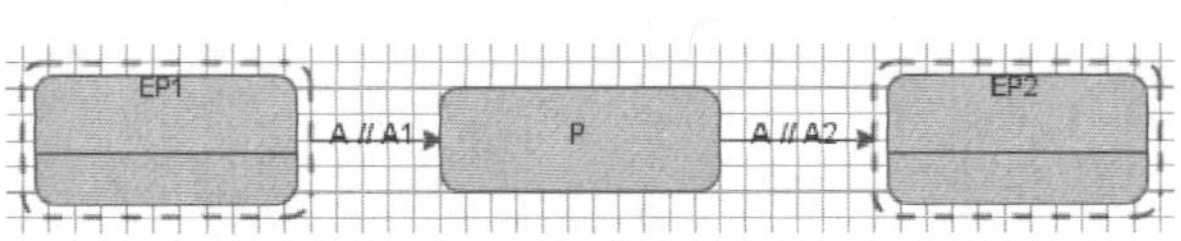

Figure 3. A source process diagram

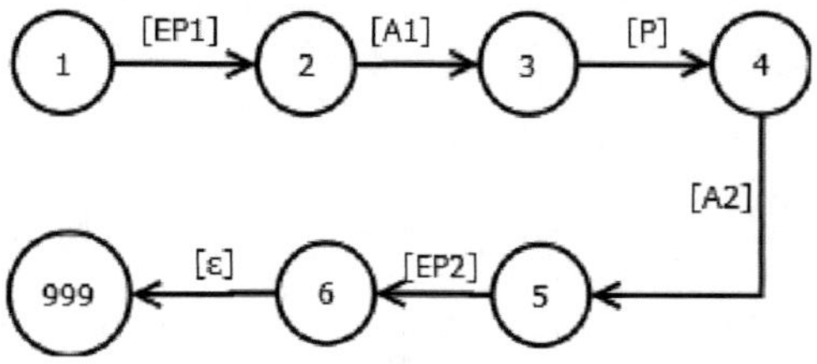

Figure 4. A finite state machine for the source process diagram

Using these formulas, it is possible to perform the FSM minimization using the following rules (where `ie` is incoming transition, `oe` is outgoing transition and $c_1 ... c_n$ are circles in a FSM graph):

- If a state has only one incoming and only one outgoing transition, it is possible to eliminate this state and merge those transitions into the single one (Formula 4):

$$newTransition = conj(ie, oe) \quad (4)$$

- If there are several transitions between two states, it is possible to merge these transitions into a single one (Formula 5):

$$newTransition = disj(ie, oe) \quad (5)$$

- If a state has only one incoming and only one outgoing transition and also has circles from itself to itself, it is possible to remove this state and create a new transition (Formula 6):

$$cDsij = \emptyset$$
$$for\ c\ in\ c_1, c_2, \dots, c_n: cDisj = disj(cDisj, star(c)) \quad (6)$$
$$newTransition = conj(ie, conj(cDisj, oe))$$

After the minimization of the initial FSM is done, resulting the minimized FSM can be converted into the regular expression using the transitive closure method [23]:

```
let m = Finite-State Machine state count

for i = 0 to m - 1:
    for j = 0 to m - 1:
        if i == j:
            R[i, j, 0] = ε
        else:
            R[i, j, 0] = ∅

        for a in transitions:
            if a is transition from i to j:
                R[i, j, 0] = disj(R[i, j, 0],
                    a)

for k = 1 to m - 1:
    for i = 0 to m - 1:
        for j = 0 to m:
            let s = star(R[k][k][k - 1])
            let c1 = conj(s, R[k, j, k - 1])
            let c2 = conj(R[i, k, k - 1], c1)
            R[i, j, k] = disj(R[i, j, k - 1],
                c2)
let regex = ∅
for i = 0 to m - 1:
    if i is final state:
        regex = disj(regex, R[0, i, m - 1])
```

After the FSM has been transformed into the regular expression, all the empty transitions (ε) are being removed from it. Resulting regular expression in turn can be transformed into the UML sequence diagram by performing its tokenization and tokens one by one using the following algorithm:

```
let ci = null
let sequenceModel = new Sequence Model
let lastConcept = null

function checkCurrentInteraction(token):
    if token == null:
        return

    if token is not data flow:
        return

    if ci != null:
        let df = token.dataFlow
        ci += Receiver(df.concept)
        sequenceModel += ci
        ci = null

while there are tokens to process:
    let token = next token to process
    let nextToken = token after token

    match token:
        case '(':
            checkCurrentInteraction(
             nextToken)
            ci = null
            open new interaction fragment

        case ')':
            checkCurrentInteraction(
             lastConcept)
            ci = null
            close last opened
             interaction fragment

        case '*':
            mark last closed interaction
            fragment as 'repeat'

        case 'Θ':
            mark last closed interaction
            fragment as 'alternate'
            and attach next opened
            interaction fragment to it
            as a part of alternate execution

        case DataFlow df:
            checkCurrentInteraction(
             df.concept)
            ci = Sender(df.concept)
            lastConcept = df.concept

        case ExternalProcess with only
          outgoing data flows p:
            ci = Sender(p.performer) +
                Message(p)

        case ExternalProcess with only
          incoming data flows p:
```

```
        ci += Message(p) +
             Receiver(p.performer)
        sequenceModel += ci
        ci = null

    case InternalProcess p:
        ci += Message(p)
```

As a result, the UML sequence diagram, which corresponds to the appropriate process model, is generated. The resulting diagram contains actors, objects and messages as well as parallel and loop interaction fragments.

VI. AN EXAMPLE FOR A TRANSFORMATION

In order to demonstrate the proposed transformation execution, authors have created a simple two-hemisphere model for an abstract use case describing document processing (shown in Figure 1). The user inputs a list of documents to be processed, the system in turn splits the document into the accepted and the rejected thus forming a processed document list that later is being outputted on the screen. The model itself consists of a three concepts: Document, Document List, and Processed Document List as well as two external processes that are responsible for the document input and the processing result output, four internal processes: Check Document, Add to Accepted List, Add to Rejected List and Save Document. Former processes are interconnected with data flows carrying the necessary information.

In order to be able to present both the FSM and the regular expression for the given two-hemisphere model, its elements are being marked with numbers that are presented in Table 1 and will be used in later descriptions.

TABLE I. EXAMPLE MODEL ELEMENT IDENTIFIERS

Identifier	Element
1	Input Documents (External Process)
2	Documents To Process (Data Flow)
3	Check Document (Internal Process)
4	Rejected Document (Data Flow)
5	Add to Rejected List (Internal Process)
6	Processing Result (Data Flow)
7	Save Document (Internal Process)
8	Accepted Document (Data Flow)
9	Add to Accepted List (Internal Process)
10	Processing Result (Data Flow)
11	Documents Left To Process (Data Flow)
12	Processing Result (Data Flow)
13	Print Document Processing Report (External Process)

The first constructed FSM for the given model is not shown here due to its size; however, Figure 5 presents its minimized form before applying the transitive closure algorithm.

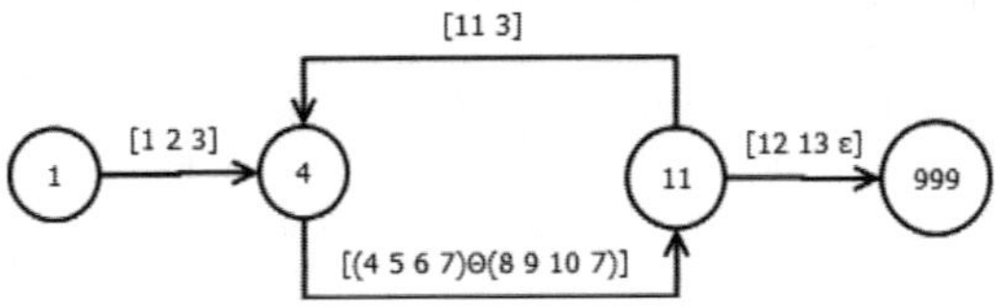

Figure 5. A minimized finite-state machine

The resulting regular expression that is obtained from this finite state machine is:

```
1 2 3 (4 5 6 7)Θ(8 9 10 7)(11 3 (4 5
6 7)Θ(8 9 10 7 ))* 12 13
```

This regular expression in turn can be transformed into the UML sequence diagram presented in Figure 6.

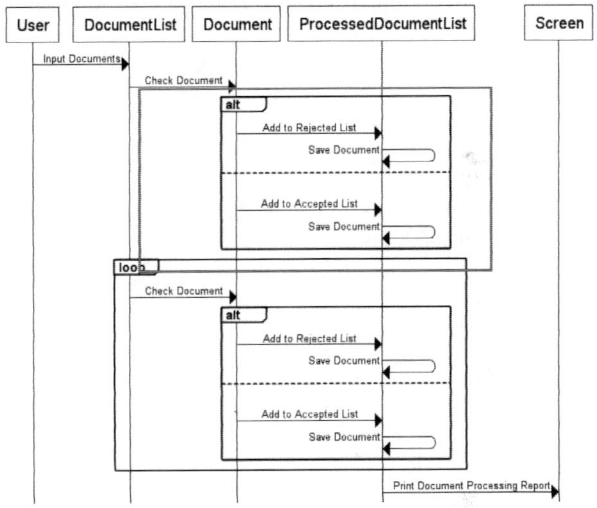

Figure 6. Resulting UML sequence diagram

VII. ANALYSIS OF PROPOSAL

The proposed transformation method allows the generation of the UML sequence diagram from the two-hemisphere model by using finite-state machines that in turn are being converted into the regular expressions. However, authors would like to note some limitations of this approach that will become the main targets for the further improvements:

1. While resulting regular expression is correctly representing the source process model, it could be redundant. In the example shown in the previous section, it is not necessary to have the part marked with the red rectangle – since it will be repeated within the following loop frame. The post processing of the regular expression after applying the transitive closure is one of the further research directions that authors are planning to work on.

2. Currently, only the alternate interaction fragments are being generated. In the example above, it is fine

since the document processing in the source model has the alternative meaning – the document can only be added to the accepted or to the rejected list. However, there could be models where the several outgoing data flows are actually being sent in the parallel. It is necessary to improve the two-hemisphere model's process diagram notation in order to be able to distinguish between those cases.

VIII. CONCLUSIONS AND FUTURE WORK

In this paper, a method of generating the UML sequence diagram from the two-hemisphere model is described. Authors have studied the related work and have proposed the transformation algorithm that uses the finite-state machines and regular expressions in order to achieve the result.

The proposed transformation is able to generate the UML sequence diagram that is correctly representing the source process model in terms of interaction. However there are still some issues that require additional work and are described in the previous section. These improvements mark the first direction of the future work to be done by the paper authors.

Another direction of future research is the development of a produced regular expression interpretation algorithm that will allow to generate the UML sequence diagram for the anaemic data model based system. As it was mentioned before, the anaemic data model approach is currently being widely used in the industry and its adoption in terms of the two-hemisphere model could help in introducing the two-hemisphere model-driven approach to the target audience, i.e., enterprise system developers.

Finally, the last direction of future research is a study of different applications of the generated regular expression, e.g., using it directly for the code generation or producing UML diagrams.

ACKNOWLEDGEMENTS

The research presented in the paper is partly supported by Grant of Latvian Council of Science No. 12.0342 "Development of Models and Methods Based on Distributed Artificial Intelligence, Knowledge Management and Advanced Web Technologies for Applied Intelligent Software".

REFERENCES

[1] D. C. Schmidt, Model-Driven Engineering, http://www.cs.wustl.edu/~schmidt/PDF/GEI.pdf [retrieved 03/2016]

[2] A. Kleppe, J. Warmer and W. Ba, MDA Explained: The Model Driven Architecture™: Practice and Promise USA: Addison-Wesley Longman Publishing Co., Inc., 2003.

[3] Unified Modelling Language superstructure v.2.2, OMG Available: http://www.omg.org/spec/UML/2.2/Superstructure [retrieved 02/2016]

[4] Ambler, S. Modeling and Documentation 2013 Mini-Survey Results, Ambysoft, 2013,http://www.ambysoft.com/surveys/modelingDocumentation2013.html [retrieved 03/2016]

[5] D. R. Wright, "Finite State Machines" (CSC215 Class Notes), http://heim.ifi.uio.no/~trygver/themes/mvc/mvc-index.html [retrieved 03/2016]

[6] S. S. Skiena, The Algorithm Design Manual, Springer, 1988, ISBN 978-0387948607

[7] O. Nikiforova et al., "BrainTool for Software Modeling in UML", Scientific Journal of RTU: Applied Computer Systems, Grundspenkis J. et al. (Eds), Vol.16, pp. 33-42, 2014.

[8] O. Nikiforova and M. Kirikova, "Two-hemisphere model Driven Approach: Engineering Based Software Development", Scientific Proceedings of CAiSE 2004 (the 16th International Conference on Advanced Information Systems Engineering), pp. 219-233, 2004.

[9] O. Nikiforova and N. Pavlova, "Development of the Tool for Generation of UML Class Diagram from Two-hemisphere model", Proceedings of The Third International Conference on Software Engineering Advances (ICSEA), International Workshop on Enterprise Information Systems (ENTISY). Mannaert H., Dini C., Ohta T., Pellerin R. (Eds.), Published by IEEE Computer Society, Conference Proceedings Services (CPS), pp. 105-112, 2008.

[10] O Nikiforova and N. Pavlova, "Open Work of Two-Hemisphere Model Transformation Definition into UML Class Diagram in the Context of MDA" In: Software Engineering Techniques: Lecture Notes in Computer Science. Vol.4980. Berlin: Springer Berlin Heidelberg, pp.118-130, 2011. ISBN 9783642223853

[11] O. Nikiforova, K. Gusarovs, O. Gorbiks and N. Pavlova, "BrainTool. A Tool for Generation of the UML Class Diagrams", Proceedings of the Seventh International Conference on Software Engineering Advances, Mannaert H. et 26 al. (Eds), IARIA ©, Lisbon, Portugal, November 18-23, pp. 60-69 (Scopus), 2012.

[12] O. Nikiforova, L. Kozacenko and D. Ahilcenoka, "UML Sequence Diagram: Transformation from the Two-Hemisphere Model and Layout", Applied Computer Systems. Vol.14, pp.31-41, 2013.

[13] D. Truscan, J. M. Fernandes and J. Lilius, "Tool Support for DFD-UML based transformation." In: Proceedings of the IEEE International Conference and workshop on the engineering of Computer-Based Systems (ECBS'04) (Brno, Czech Republic, May 24-27, 2004), pp 378-397, 2004. IEEE Press, New York.

[14] T. N. Tran, K. M. Khan and Y. C. Lan, "A framework for transforming artifacts from Data Flow Diagrams to UML". In: Proceedings of the 2004 IASTED International Conference on Software Engineering (Innsbruck, Austria, Feb. 17-19, 2004). ACTA Press, Calgary, AB,

[15] F. Meng, D. Chu and D. Zhan, "Transformation from Data Flow Diagram to UML2.0 Activity Diagram",1/10, 2010 IEEE Journal.

[16] A. A. Jilani, M. Usman, A. Nadeem, I. M. Zafar and M. Halim, "Comparitive Study on DFD to UML diagrams Transformations", journal of WCSIT, vol. 1,no. 1,10-16,2011.

[17] K. Tiwari, A. Tripathi, S. Sharma and V. Dubey, "Merging of Data Flow Diagram with Unified Modeling Language." International Journal of Scientific and Research Publications, Volume 2, Issue 8, August 2012, ISSN 2250-3153

[18] E. Evans, Domain-driven design: tackling complexity in the heart of software. Addison-Wesley Professional, 2004.

[19] M. Fowler, Anaemic Domain Model, http://www.martinfowler.com/bliki/AnemicDomainModel.html [retrieved 03/2016]

[20] The Anaemic Domain Model is no Anti-Pattern, it's a SOLID design | SAPM: Course Blog, https://blog.inf.ed.ac.uk/sapm/2014/02/04/the-anaemic-domain-model-is-no-anti-pattern-its-a-solid-design/ [retrieved 03/2016]

[21] Trygve MVC, http://heim.ifi.uio.no/~trygver/themes/mvc/mvc-index.html [retrieved 03/2016]

[22] O. Nikiforova, L. Kozacenko, and D. Ahilcenoka, "Two-Hemisphere Model Based Approach to Modelling of Object Interaction", ICSEA 2013 : The Eighth International Conference on Software Engineering Advances, pp. 605-611, 2013.

[23] T. Koshy, Discrete Mathematics With Applications, Academic Press, 2004, ISBN 0-12-421180-1

ReUse: A Recommendation System for Implementing User Stories

Heidar Pirzadeh, Andre de Santi Oliveira, Sara Shanian
SAP SE, SAP Hybris
Montreal, Quebec, Canada
email: {heidar.pirzadeh, andre.de.santi.oliveira, sara.shanian}@sap.com

Abstract— **In agile software development, user stories contain feature descriptions that are used as the entry points of discussions about the design, specification, requirements, and estimation of the software features. The first step in implementing a user story is to find proper files in the code base to make changes. To help the developers, in this paper, we describe a new approach that automatically recommends the files where a feature will most likely be implemented based on a given user story that describes the feature.**

Keywords—Recommendation System; Text Mining; Program Comprehension; Information Retrieval; Agile Software Development

I. INTRODUCTION

Since 2010 more than 200 big software companies have adopted Agile software development methodology [1]. Important motivations behind the widespeard adoption of Agile software development are fast delivery to the market, efficient handling of new requirements, and increased overall productivity of development teams.

The development team in an Agile setting typically receives the new requirements in the form of a user story (hereinafter interchangeably referred to as story). A user story is a very high-level definition of a requirement, which contains enough information so that the developers can produce a reasonable estimate of the effort to implement it. Given a story, developers go through three basic steps of 1) identification of code locations as starting points, 2) finding and applying a solution, and 3) testing and validating the implemented change.

Any delay in one of the above-mentioned steps will result in a delayed implementation of the story and undermines the important goal of fast delivery. In fact, it has been shown that developers could get stuck in the first step of finding the right location to start making their changes to implement the request [2], [3]. While experienced developers are usually faster in identifying and understanding the subset of the code relevant to the intended change, studies have shown that developers spend up to 50 percent of their time searching for information [4], [5] to answer their questions about the system under development.

The reason that experienced developers are faster in their identification step is because of their higher familiarity with the system and with the previously implemented similar requirements. Their knowledge and experience makes them a valuable source for answering others' questions during their program comprehension [6]. If an experienced developer leaves the team, usually, part of that knowledge will also go with him. We think that externalizing this knowledge and how it is gained could enable everybody in the team to speed up and improve their deliveries and, in turn, make the team less prone to personnel changes. A recommendation system that could provide team members with suggestions to help with identification of changes locations seems like a perfect fit for this scenario.

Once implemented, a user story could be usually mapped to the creation or modification of one or more classes in the code base. Many companies use ticket management (e.g., JIRA [12]) and code management (e.g., Bitbucket [13]) ecosystems to respectively maintain and store the stories, the code and the mapping between them. For example, each story in JIRA has a ticket number. When committing the code that implements a story to Bitbucket, the developer could include the story's ticket number in the commit message so that JIRA creates a link between the story and the committed code. The information accumulated in ticket/code management systems could be leveraged by the recommendation system in creating insightful recommendations that could help developers in faster and more reliable deliveries.

In this paper, we propose ReUse a recommendation system that employs techniques from information retrieval, text mining, and the field of recommender systems to automatically suggest a list of files where a story will most likely be implemented. We evaluated the effectiveness of our recommendation system in an industrial setting on the Order Management System (OMS) product at SAP Hybris. The results show that our recommendations are of 71% precision.

We start by reviewing a few related works in Section II. In Section III, we describe the proposed approach. Section IV discusses the results of our case study on OMS. In Section V, we discuss the threats to validity. We conclude the paper and describe future avenues in Section VI.

II. RELATED WORK

To the best of our knowledge, no other work has been reported on a recommendation system for user stories in Agile software development. However, a few works have been done on recommendation systems for bug localization during software maintenance. Kim et al. [11] propose a prediction model to recommend files to be fixed. In their model, the features are created from textual information of already existing bug reports, then Naive Bayes algorithm is applied to train the model using previously fixed files as classification labels, and then use the trained model to assign multiple source files to a given new bug report. Our evaluation of the effectiveness of a recommendation is also quite different. They "consider the prediction results to be *correct* if at least one of the recommended files matches one of the actual patch files for a given bug report". We think for a developer to go through the recommended files he needs to be assured about the precision of the list. Zhou et al. [3] proposed a revised Vector Space Model approach for improving the performance for bug

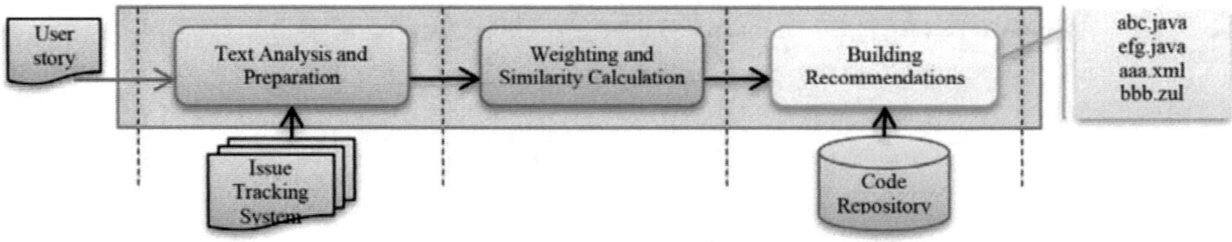

Figure 1. Overview of the ReUse recommendation system

localization. They measure the lexical similarity between a new bug report and every source file and also give more weight to larger size files and files that have been fixed before for similar bug reports. Their approach relies on good programming practices in naming variables, methods and classes. In comparison, our approach is independent of file names or the content of the files.

III. The Proposed Approach

The idea behind our approach is based on the assumption that there are naturally occurring groups of user stories in any project that can be identified by looking at their description. By using such information, our system could provide recommendations for a new user story by first finding the group of user stories it belongs to by computing its similarity to existing user stories. Thus, a user story could have a set of nearest neighbors that can be used to make recommendations about the files needed to implement that user story based on the files that were modified during the implementation of similar user stories.

As shown in Fig. 1, our recommendation system performs its task through three main steps:

- Analyzing the textual content of the new story to prepare it for next steps by tagging the content with meta information,
- Creating a weighted vector of the new story and use it in finding other stories that are closely similar to it, and
- Preparing a recommendation for the new story by providing a precise set of recommended files to be used by developers.

A. Text Analysis and Preparation

A common pre-processing step in many information retrieval approaches is one that removes stop-words - The words that add little value to the process of finding relevant information. Stop-word identification, which is the process of identifying these words, makes use of domain and global information. For example, in the domain of English literature, stop-words include auxiliary verbs (e.g., have, be), pronouns (he, it), or prepositions (to, for).

In our text analysis and preparation, our stop-word remover component uses Lucene's StandardAnalyzer to remove the terms in a user story that are listed in a set of common English stop-words dictionary. Another pre-processing step in our approach is *Stemming*. A stemmer maps different forms of a term to a single form. A stemmer, for example, could strip the "s" from plural nouns, the "ing" from verbs, and so on to extract the stem of the term. That way, a stem could act as a natural group of terms with a similar meaning. Our stemmer component uses Lucene's EnglishStemming to find the stems; the English stemmer is an updated version of the famous Porter Stemmer [9].

Whether it is in a query or in a document some terms can represent different meaning depending on the role that they take. The role is even more important when there are processes like *Stemming* that changes a term to an alternative (usually simpler) that could result in an unjustifiable similarity while the original form of the term had a different meaning because of the role it had. For example, the term "dogs" has a different meaning in the sentence "The sailor walked the dogs" in comparison to the meaning that it has in "The sailor dogs the hatch" because of its roles that are correspondingly *noun* in the first sentence and *verb* in the second one. This role is also referred to as the part-of-speech (POS) for that term. The similarity between two similar looking terms should increase only if their roles are the same in the places that the word has appeared in. That is why we perform a POS tagging on a user story before we pass it to our stemming component. Our current POS tagger component is implemented using Maxent part-of-speech tagger from the Stanford NLP group.

B. Weighting and Similarity Calculation

We use a weighting process for finding representative terms in each user story and add them to a corresponding *terms vector* that is weighted based on the representativeness of each term for that user story. Our weighting function is implemented as a Term Frequency, Inverse Document Frequency (TF-IDF) [10] schema. The goal of TF-IDF term weighting is to obtain high weights for terms that are representative of a document's content and lower weights for terms that are less representative.

In our case, the weight of a term depends both on how often it appears in the given story (term frequency, or *tf*) and on how often it appears in all the stories (document frequency, or *df*) of the ticket management system. In general, a high frequency of a term (high *tf*) in one story shows the importance of that term while if a term is scattered between different stories (high *df*), then it is considered less important. Therefore, if a term has high *tf* and low *df* (or high *idf* -inverse document frequency) it will have a higher weight. Since the importance of a term does not increase proportionally with the term's frequency, the weight of term *i* in story *k* is calculated as shown in (1):

$$w_{i,k} = \frac{(log(tf_{i,k}) + 1) * \log(^{N}/_{n_i})}{\sqrt{\sum_{j=1}^{e} \left[(\log(tf_{j,k}) + 1) * \log\left(\frac{N}{n_j}\right) \right]^2}} \quad (1)$$

where term frequency $tf_{i,k}$ of term *i* in story *k* is the number of times that *i* occurs in *k*, *N* is the total number of stories, n_i is the number of stories where the term *i* has appeared in and *e* is the total number of terms. The factor $\log(^{N}/_{n_i})$ is the "*idf*" factor that decreases as the terms are used widely in all user stories. The denominator in the equation is used for weight normalization. This factor is used to adjust the terms vector of the story to its norm, so all the stories have the same modulus and can be compared no matter the size of the story.

Once we have the terms vector of each story ready, we need to measure the similarity between stories. The similarity between two objects is in general regarded as how much they share in common. In the domain of text mining, the most commonly used measure for evaluating the similarity between two documents is the cosine of the angle between term vectors representing the documents. In the same way, as shown in (2), we calculate the similarity between two stories x and y by measuring the cosine similarity between their terms vectors V_x and V_y:

$$S(V_x, V_y) = \frac{\sum_{i=1}^{n} w_{i,x} * w_{i,y}}{\sqrt{\sum_{i=1}^{n}(w_{i,x})^2} * \sqrt{\sum_{i=1}^{n}(w_{i,y})^2}} \quad (2)$$

where $w_{i,x}$ and $w_{i,y}$ are respectively the weight of term i in vectors V_x and V_y, and the denominator of the fraction is for normalization. The weights cannot be negative and, thus, the similarity between two vectors ranges from 0 to 1, where 0 indicates independence, 1 means exactly the same, and in-between values indicate intermediate similarity.

C. Building Recommendations

Recommendation systems are now part of many applications in our daily life. These systems provide the user with a list of recommended items and help them to find the preferred items in the bigger list of available items [7], [8]. Our recommendation system is based on collaborative filtering. In collaborative filtering, the items are recommended to the users based on the previously rated items by the other users. Mapping the idea back to our case, our recommendation system should recommend files for a new user story based on the previously modified files by other user stories. More formally, as shown in (3), the usefulness of file f for implementing story s noted as the utility $u(s,f)$ of file f for story s has the following form

$$u(s,f)\text{: Func}(u(s_i,f)) \qquad \forall s_i \in C_s \quad (3)$$

where $u(s_i,f)$ is the utility assigned to the file f for story s_i in C_s the set of stories that are similar to story s. Different utility functions could be plugged into our recommendation system to be used in creating recommendations. When building the recommendation, our goal is to provide the user with a highly precise list of recommended files that our recommendation system deems necessary to implement the user story.

The recommendation can help developers in building their mental model in a quicker and more accurate way. If the developer is already familiar with the code base, she could use the recommendation as a potential checklist to increase her confidence in the changes that are planned. The basic idea in creating a precise recommendation is to find the files that are associated with similar stories and are frequently changed to implement those stories. More formally, as presented in (4), to build the recommendation, we calculate the utility u_F of file f for a given story s as follows

$$u_F(s,f) = \begin{cases} \sum_{i=1}^{n} u(s_i,f) * S(V_s, V_{s_i}) & \text{if } S(V_s, V_{s_i}) > t \\ 0 & \text{otherwise} \end{cases} \quad (4)$$

where $S(V_s, V_{s_i})$ is the calculated similarity between the given story s and a similar story s_i, t is a certain cut-off threshold, n is the maximum number of similar stories to be considered, and $u(s_i,f)$ is the utility of file f for story s_i which is defined as $u(s_i,f) = c_{i,f}$ where $c_{i,f}$ is the number of commits in which the file f has appeared for implementing story s_i.

IV. Evaluation

To evaluate the effectiveness of the ReUse recommendation system, we use it in an industrial setting on the OMS project at SAP Hybris. The OMS enables customers to flexibly pick and choose from a set of omni-channel order management and fulfillment functionalities. We use release 5.7 of OMS in 2015. This version of OMS contains 3018 files in 928 packages. The total number of tickets (excluding bugs) for this release was 176. All 176 tickets were already implanted at the time of evaluation and each ticket was linked to the modified files in the Git repository management system Bitbucket. The tickets were extracted from JIRA as a CSV file. Although the exported file contained many attributes for each ticket we only kept *Summary* (the name of the ticket), *Description*, *Issue Type*, *Ticket ID*, *Sub-task ID*, *Parent ID* for the experiment.

Technically, the goal in our evaluation is to find out how effectively our recommendation system can predict the set of files that need to be changed for each story and compare the recommended set with the actual set of files that were modified for that story. This way, our recommendation problem could be seen as a classification problem where our recommendation algorithm tries to classify the source code files into two class of relevant and irrelevant for each story. The effectiveness of classification in this case would be the rate of true and false predictions that the algorithm makes. These rates can be arranged in a contingency table that is called the confusion matrix (see Table I).

TABLE I. CONFUSION MATRIX

	Relevant	Irrelevant	
Recommended	TP	FP	TP + FP
Not recommended	FN	TN	FN +TN
	TP + FN	FP + TN	

As seen in Table II, True Positive (TP) is the number of correctly predicted the relevant files. False Positive (FP) is the number of incorrectly predicted relevant files. False Negative (FN) is the number of incorrectly predicted irrelevant files. True Negative (TN) is the number of correctly predicted irrelevant files.

As shown in (5), *Precision* or true positive accuracy is calculated as the ratio of recommended files that are relevant to the total number of recommended files:

$$precision = \frac{TP}{TP + FP} \quad (5)$$

Recall or true positive rate, as presented in (6), is calculated as the ratio of recommended files that are relevant to the total number of relevant files:

$$recall = \frac{TP}{TP + FN} \quad (6)$$

Specificity or true negative accuracy is calculated as the ratio of not recommended files that are irrelevant to the total number of irrelevant files as shown in (7):

$$specificity = \frac{TN}{TN + FP} \quad (7)$$

Then as presented in (8) *Accuracy* is calculated as the ratio of correct predictions:

$$accuracy = \frac{TP + TN}{TP + TN + FP + FN} \quad (8)$$

In our evaluation, we needed to have a portion of our tickets as a training set for the recommendation system to use them to build recommendation and a second portion as our test set (set of stories that we want to feed to the recommendation system and evaluate the suggestions that the system provides for each of those stories). To avoid any bias in the selection of the training and the test set we use k-Folds Cross Validation. In k-Folds cross validation, sometimes called rotation estimation, the data set D is randomly spilt into k mutually exclusive subsets (the folds) $D_1, D_2, \ldots, D_k$ of approximately equal size. The algorithm is trained and tested k times; each time $t \in \{1, 2, \ldots, k\}$, it is trained on $D \backslash D_t$ (i.e., D minus D_t) and tested on D_t.

The result presented in this section uses the following configuration: we fold the data by splitting our set of 176 stories randomly into 18 sets (roughly 10 stories per set). On each iteration, we use 17 sets as our training set and 1 set as the test set. That is, a cross validation (k = 18). In our experiment we only consider the most similar story (n = 1) and the cutoff threshold is (t = 0.5). The number of files that will be recommended in this case is equal to the number of files modified files for the most similar story. The following table shows the result of our evaluation as the average of 18 iterations.

TABLE II. EVALUATION RESULTS

Metric	Value
Precision	0.7125751
Recall	0.4658216
Accuracy	0.9178191
Specificity	0.9363258

Execution of the experiment on a typical developer machine (Intel Core i7 2.5 GHz processor of 4 cores and 16 GB of Ram) took less than 30 seconds. This time includes the time for training and the time to run the test of each iteration. As shown in the Table I, the files that our recommendation system suggests to the developers in the recommendation are 71% of the time the files that they certainly needed to make a change to implement the user story. At the same time, our recommendation system scores a very high specificity and accuracy. Our system, is successful in avoiding the recommendation of irrelevant files 93% of the time while in general makes a correct prediction 91% of the time in its recommendation.

We also performed a case by case analysis for the stories for which our recommendation system scored lower than 50% precision. One of such stories was OMSE-31, for which the precision of the recommended files was only 4%.

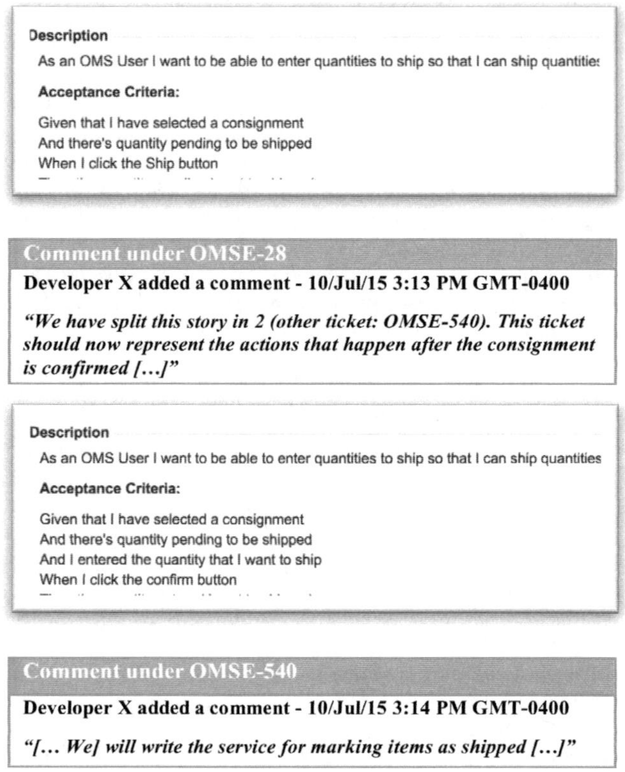

Figure 2. OMSE-28 and its comment (top), OMSE-540 and its comment (bottom)

Our investigation showed that, the story description was updated during a sprint but the previous content was not deleted (the content was rather formatted with ~~strikethrough~~). The csv parser in our system ignores all text formatting and could not detect such situations and as a result recommended files associated to a story that was similar to OMSE-31 considering the content that should have not been considered.

Another case was for story OMSE-540 with only 8% of precision. The recommendation system detected OMSE-28 as highly similar story and recommended the modified files accordingly. However, the list of files that was actually modified was significantly different than the predicted one. Further investigation showed that OMSE-28 was describing a feature from the end user perspective. While, as shown in Fig. 2, later on, the story was split into two smaller stories one to implement the user interface and the second one to implement the services in the backend that will be used by the user interface to implement the feature. For this, the developer cloned the original user story (OMSE-28) and created OMSE-540 and made a minimal change to the description. However, he left two comments, one for each story. The current version of our recommendation system does not take comments into account.

V. THREATS TO VALIDITY

There are potential threats to the validity of our work. The effectiveness of our recommendation system is highly dependent on the quality of the stories that the members of the Agile team maintain for their project. Although our recommendation system showed an impressive effectiveness on the commercial project of OMS at SAP Hybris, not all teams or companies have similar level of standards when it comes to creating and maintaining their backlog of the stories. TF-IDF alone is prone to misspellings and multi-word verbs and expressions. To have a resilient approach we need to check the frequency of those cases and remove them.

VI. Conclusion And Future Work

In this paper we proposed an approach to help developers in during their implementation tasks by taking benefit from the suggestions that our recommendation system provides them on where to make code changes. Our recommendation system called ReUse, builds a precise recommendation list of files that are need to be changed with high probability. We evaluated our recommendation system on the OMS at SAP Hybris and the results show 71% precision in recommending the files that need to be changed.

For our future work, we would like to look into automatic fine tuning of parameters in our recommendation builder along with plugging in new utility functions to increase the recall and take advantage of our recommendation system on other projects at SAP. Taking other sources of information such as comments or the links to other tickets (the hierarchy of tickets) into account could help us take advantage of relations other than the textual and conceptual relation between stories to improve the results.

Handling the rich texts by the parser in our work, as shown in our case study, could potentially reduce the chances of inaccurate similarities and result in better recommendations. Also, adding components to our system to deal with misspelled words and expressions could also potentially be beneficial in detecting the similarities between stories.

References

[1] J. Little, "The List of Firms Using Scrum", [Online]. Available from: http://scrumcommunity.pbworks.com/w/page/10148930/Firms Using Scrum 2016.07.12

[2] A. T. Nguyen, T. T. Nguyen, J. Al-Kofahi, H. V. Nguyen, and T. Nguyen, "A Topic-Based Approach for Narrowing the Search Space of Buggy Files from a Bug Report," Proc. IEEE/ACM 26th Int'l Conf. Automated Software Eng., pp. 263-272, 2011.

[3] J. Zhou, H. Zhang, and D. Lo, "Where Should the Bugs Be Fixed?—More Accurate Information Retrieval-Based Bug Localization Based on Bug Reports," Proc. 34th Int'l Conf. Software Eng., pp. 14-24, 2012.

[4] A. J. Ko, R. DeLine, and G. Venolia "Information Needs in Collocated Software Development Teams", In Proceedings of the 29th International Conference on Software Engineering, ICSE'07. IEEE, 2007.

[5] G. C. Murphy, M. Kersten, and L. Findlater "How Are Java Software Developers Using the Eclipse IDE?" IEEE Software pp. 76–83, 2006.

[6] Th. D. LaToza, G. Venolia, and R. DeLine "Maintaining mental models: a study of developer work habits". In ICSE '06: Proceeding of the 28th international conference on Software engineering. ACM, New York, NY, USA, 492–501, 2006.

[7] Y. Koren, R. Bell, "Advances in Collaborative Filtering", ch. 5. Springer,. Recommender Systems Handbook, 2011.

[8] L. Baltrunas, and F. Ricci. "Experimental evaluation of context-dependent collaborative filtering using item splitting" User Modeling and User-Adapted Interaction 24, no. 1-2: 7-34, 2014.

[9] M. F. Porter, "An algorithm for suffix stripping". Program, 14(3):130–137, 1980.

[10] T. Joachims. "Text Categorization with Support Vector Machines: Learning with Many Relevant Features". In Proc. of ECML98, 137-142, 1998.

[11] K. Dongsun, Y. Tao, S. Kim, and A. Zeller. "Where should we fix this bug? a two-phase recommendation model" Software Engineering, IEEE Trans. on 39, no. 11: 1597-1610, 2013.

[12] JIRA, [Online]. Available from: https://www.atlassian.com/software/jira 2016.07.12

[13] Bitbucket, [Online]. Available from: https://bitbucket.org/ 2016.07.12

Combining Logistic Regression Analysis and Association Rule Mining via MLR Algorithm

Ozge Yucel Kasap
Nevzat Ekmekci
Utku Gorkem Ketenci

Cybersoft R&D Center
Istanbul, Turkey
Email: ozge.kasap@cs.com.tr

***Abstract*—One of the keys in marketing is to recommend the right products to the right customers. This paper proposes a solution to this problem as a part of the development of a new data mining tool PROPCA (Proximus Optimum Canistro). The aim is to use logistic regression analysis and association rule mining together to make recommendations in marketing. An innovative approach in which combination of these two algorithms provides better results than algorithms used stand-alone is presented. While association rule mining searches all rules in the data set, logistic regression predicts a purchase probability of a product for customers. The combination of these two approaches are tested on a real-life banking data set. The results of combination are shown and their suitability in general is discussed.**

Keywords–Logistic Regression; Logit; Association Rule Mining; Apriori; Ensemble Learning; Stacking; MLR.

I. Introduction

People are facing the challenge of choosing the right service or product due to wide range of choices. On the other hand in marketing, it is important to know which customers might be interested in a specific product or which customers could be annoyed by receiving the campaign mails or messages about uninteresting products.

This is a major problem in the finance and banking sector. According to a survey conducted in 2014 by IBM Silverpop [1], the unique open rate and click-through rates of e-mails are %22.4 and %3.3 respectively for the finance sector in the United States. Given these statistics, if the potential purchasers of each product are determined properly, this may increase the company profit as well as decrease unnecessary expense concerning messages, calls, mails etc. Considering the growth of wide range of products, for a marketing expert, it is inevitable to turn into statistical models or machine learning algorithms to understand and explain the customer behaviors.

In recent years, logistic regression models (logit) have been used prevalently in several domains to make predictions [2]. To be more specific, Akinci et al. examined the application domains of logistic regression models in marketing researches such as consumer behavior modelling, international marketing, branding, societal marketing, promotion, retailing, health services marketing [3].

Similarly, mining for association rules (AR) is one of the well-studied issues in data mining for marketing [4]. AR aim to discover patterns, such as two or more products that are often purchased together.

The main purpose is to build a more reliable model to predict a large number of customers who are likely to purchase specific products. Considering how big marketing data can be, it is not suitable to perform data mining algorithms in the whole data set. Instead, a sample can be selected to apply data mining algorithm and the results can be generalized for whole set of customers. However, for a better predictive force, it is inevitable to use multiple data mining algorithms together.

This research suggests and examines an approach by combining two prediction models used widely in marketing in order to obtain better results: logistic regression and association rules. These two models are implemented as a part of a new data mining tool PROPCA, the way they work is completely different from each other. Logit uses customer and product features to make predictions whereas association rule mining uses only the ownership information of product families. Combining these two complementary models by Ensemble Learning and placing a new model will be an innovative approach in consumer behavior modeling.

The outline of this paper is as follows. Section II briefly explains general concepts and related works about Logistic Regression Analysis, Association Rule Mining, Ensemble Learning. Section III describes the proposed model. Results of this research in addition to the implementations and tests are given in Section IV. Finally, Section V gives conclusions and recommendations for further researches.

II. Related Work

As aforementioned, this research's aim is to combine logit and AR with Ensemble Learning methods in order to obtain better prediction (classification) results. In this section, firstly the researches about Association Rule Mining will be introduced. Then, the works on Logistic Regression models will be examined. Last but not least, the researches about Ensemble Learning will be briefly presented.

A. Association Rule Mining

AR mining was first proposed by Agrawal et al in 1993 [5]. After the first AR algorithm, named AIS (Agrawal, Imielinski, Swami), was discovered [5], a very known algorithm, Apriori, was introduced [6]. Although Apriori is the most used algorithm, there are many other algorithms in this field such as Eclat [7] and FP-Growth [8].

AR mining is one of the most important fields of data mining [9]. AR are generated by finding frequent patterns from the data simply by using if/then conditions and identifying the most significant relationships.

AR may be used for analyzing and predicting customer behaviors [10]. They were initially adopted for "Market Basket Analysis" to find which items purchased with which items.

Given a set of customers' transactions (i.e., logs of products purchased together by different customers), the aim of AR is to find frequently purchased products or items in these transactions. On the other hand, they are useful for product clustering and catalog design.

An itemset is the subset of all products in the database and transactions are product groups that a customer has purchased together. $X \Rightarrow Y$ is an example expression of an association rule, where X and Y are sets of items. The meaning of such a rule is that transactions which contain X tend to contain Y. There are two important parameters of AR algorithms: *support* and *confidence*. Support of any itemset is defined as the number of transactions in which products appear together in all transactions. Confidence is defined as the ratio of support value of $X \cup Y$ to the support value of X itemset.

This research uses AR mining algorithm to identify the mostly purchased product families in finance and banking sectors and to generate rules according to these products. Apriori is the best known algorithm to mine association rules [11], and it is adopted in this research.

B. Logistic Regression

Usage of statistical models for explaining categorical choices is a common approach [12]. These choices are generally denoted with qualitative values and logit models are appropriate for such analysis [13]. Logit models are frequently used in medical and social sciences researches because they are easily applied and easily understood. In addition to these areas, logit models have also been used in biology, psychology, economics and transportation [14]. Since 1977, logit models are being used effectively in marketing [15]. Several usages of logit models for different marketing situations are studied in [16–21].

The main aim of logit analysis is the same as other techniques used for modeling in statistics such as Least Square Regression, Curve Fitting or Generalized Linear Model. They represent the relationship between dependent and independent variables and find the best fit among them. The relationship can be represented with a simple function, $y = f(x)$, where y and x are the dependent and the independent variables respectively. Considering statistical relationships, if the value of x is known, the value of y can be estimated with a specific error term.

The following formula is used to define the logistic cumulative distribution function [12].

$$y = f(x) = \frac{1}{1 + e^{-z}} \tag{1}$$

z is called the "utility function" and can be represented as

$$z = \beta_0 + \beta_1 x_1 + \beta_2 x_2 + \ldots + \beta_n x_n + \varepsilon \tag{2}$$

where β_0 is the intercept and $\beta_1 x_1, \beta_2 x_2, \ldots, \beta_n x_n$ are the regression coefficients multiplied by some values of the predictor, n is the number of independent variables in the data set and ε is the error term.

Logit can be classified as binomial, ordinal or multinomial. If the observed values for the dependent variable has only two types such as "yes" vs. "no" or "success" vs. "failure", binomial (or binary) logistic regression can be used. If the dependent variable has the number of types equal or more than three and types are not ordered, multinomial logistic regression can be used. If types are ordered ordinal logistic regression can be used. Because of the configuration of products and existing data in banking sector (Detailed in Section III), in this paper, product choices of customers are modeled using binomial logit.

Generally, in binomial logit, "0" or "1" is used to represent the types of dependent variable [22], e.g., 1 being purchased, 0 being not purchased. Based on one or more continuous or categorical independent variables (such as demographic or socioeconomic), binomial logit predicts the probability that an observation falls into one of two types of a dependent variable [23].

When logit is used to estimate the probability of a certain event occurring (e.g., purchasing or not), Maximum Likelihood (ML) approach provides a basis to find the smallest possible deviance between the observed and predicted values by trying different solutions through multiple iterations. ML gives the values of regression coefficient which maximizes the probability of obtaining the observed values [24]. According to the established model and learned coefficients, it will be determined whether to recommend or not a modeled product to the bank customers who do not own this product yet.

C. Ensemble Learning

Ensemble Learning aims to create a better predictive model based on the combination of multiple classification results instead of single one. Early studies about this methodology has been seen in late seventies [25]. Schapire mentioned the Boosting algorithm in 1990 [26]. Boosting tries to create a strong classifier from weak classifiers. Thus, it combines the prediction of each weak classifier using weighted average. Tumer and Ghosh studied on combining neural networks in 1996 [27]. Schapire developed a new boosting algorithm with Freund and Adaboost [28]. Bagging was introduced by Breimann [29] and Random Subspace method was discovered by Ho [30]. Skurichina compared the popular algorithms such as Bagging, Boosting and Random Subspace and mentioned optimal working conditions [31]. Zhang and Zhang proposed resampling version of Adaboost [32].

Stacking was first introduced by Wolpert [33]. According to the study of Dzeroski and Zenko, stacking is the best method for combining heterogeneous classifiers [34].

Up until today, Ensemble Learning is used by researchers from different disciplines, especially pattern recognition, statistics and machine learning [35]. Based on this method, this paper's aim is to combine results of logit and AR.

In general, combining methods in Ensemble Learning are examined in two categories [36]:

- Weighting Methods: If the classifiers are working for the same tasks and the results are comparable, it is convenient to use this approach [37].
- Meta-Learning Methods: In this approach, there are several base classifiers and one meta classifier. Firstly, base classifiers make predictions, then according to these results learning is performed and meta-classifier is created. Meta-classifier's results are the system's results at the same time. Stacking is the most popular technique used in this domain [34].

Results of classifiers cannot be evaluated directly because logit and AR give numerical values in separate scales. Given these conditions, this study was shifted to meta-learning (Stacking). Stacking has two stages, base classifiers and meta classifier, as shown in Figure 1 of Philip Chan's study [38]. Even though there are many studies on how to combine different classifier outputs, there is no specific study about the combination of logit and AR results. From the literature review of stacking, it has been seen that StackingC algorithm, which uses multi-response linear regression (MLR) method in meta learning stage [39][40], is suitable for this study since it tries to combine the probability values calculated by heterogeneous classifiers.

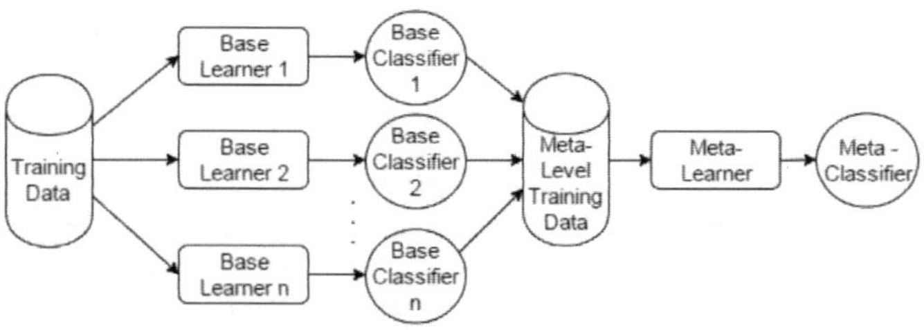

Figure 1: Meta Learning System.

Logit and AR calculate the probabilities of purchasing each product for each customer separately. MLR takes these probabilities produced by different algorithms as input. It runs linear regression and generates outputs for each product (1 if this product is bought, 0 otherwise).

Consequently, the models are formed separately for each product. Later on, when asked to predict for a new instance (new customer), all product models (AR-logit) are executed for this instance and the results of separated models are combined by MLR coefficients that are determined during the learning phase. In the end, one customer can be classified as purchaser of zero or multiple products.

The result of binomial logit model does not require any special regulation since it produces different probabilities for each product. These results can be used directly in MLR. However, determination of the probability value produced by AR is problematic. As a first approximation, probability of each product predicted by AR is identified by the confidence value of the related association rule. If the product appears in multiple rules and more than one rule is applicable for a specific customer, the confidence value of association rule with the highest confidence is selected as a probability value.

III. Model

As stated in Section II, logit and AR mining are widely used approaches in the marketing literature for estimating the probability of a customer purchasing an item. Considering the real-life industrial data set from a medium sized bank in Turkey, which includes features of customers and ownership information for four different retail banking product families; these approaches are applied. 1 presents owners and 0 shows non-owners of the products.

As shown in Figure 2, the training data set was prepared for the algorithms by feature selection (See Figure 2(a)) and sampling (See Figure 2(b)) steps (Detailed in Section IV). Sampling steps were taken into consideration due to decrease memory consumption and increase performance. While modeling with logit, ownership values are used as dependent and demographic informations are used as independent variables. Since the product families are not equivalent to each other and do not represent alternatives to each other, the results are calculated separately for each product family in the training data set with a separate binomial logit model. The same data set, except the demographic part, is used to mine the association rules using the Apriori algorithm. According to the ownership information of all product families for all customers, frequent itemsets are created and association rules are mined accordingly for each training data set.

While the logit model is performed separately for each product family in the training data set, it is possible to apply AR for each product family at once. Hence, the results of the binomial logit model cannot be merged directly for any customer because the results for each product are in different scale and not directly comparable. Therefore, the results from both the logit model and AR must be considered separately for each product because of the output format. This is why it is needed to combine logit and AR mining results with MLR.

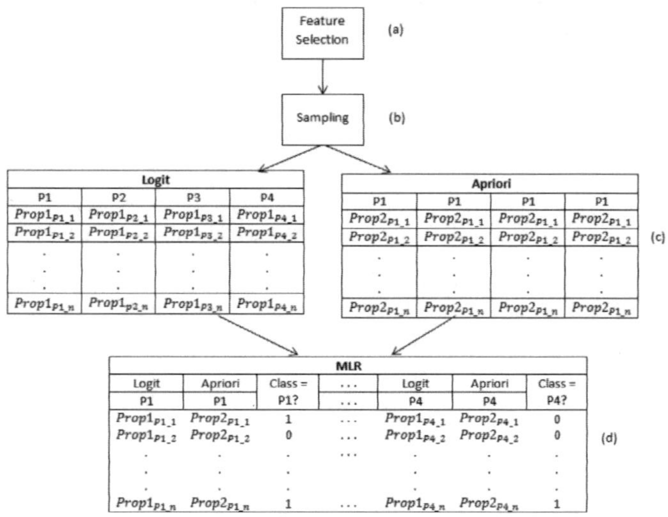

Figure 2: Illustration of MLR Algorithm with Logit and AR

In Figure 2, illustration of MLR algorithm on a data set with four classes (P1, P2, P3 and P4), n observations and two (logit and AR) base classifiers are given. $Propi_{j\_k}$ refers to the probability given by base classifier i for product j on observation number k. Figure 2(c) shows the predicted probabilities of both logit and AR separetely and Figure 2(d) shows the meta training set for MLR which will be used to learn a linear regression function to predict the ownerships of each product (class). Basically, MLR learns a linear regression function for each classifier and the calculated coefficients are used on the relevant test sets to predict the ownerships.

Coefficients for logit, association rules and coefficients for MLR are obtained at the end of this learning step. Using this learned parameters, the ownership (or purchasing) probability for each product for each customer in the test data set is calculated.

In general, MLR is used to combine two or more multiclass classifiers that have equal number of classes. Therefore, the sum of each observations's probability for each classifier is equal to one in the meta training set. In this research, there is no such restriction as logit models generate probabilities for each product independently because of the product families being not equivalent to each other.

IV. Implementation and Tests

Implementation and tests have been done via Java as part of the development of a new data mining tool PROPCA.

PROPCA includes every necessary data mining component such as feature selection, sampling, etc. Moreover, PROPCA contains two parallel offer production models: association rules and the logistic regression. These two models have different requirements in terms of data.

As aforementioned, logit models the relation between the demographical properties of customers and the purchase action. Banking data sets contain hundreds of demographical attributes. The usage of all these attributes in modeling is time consuming and it will be an error prone approach. Therefore, the identification of relevant ones in the whole set of attributes is commonly done before the modeling task. Strong predictors are selected using the Information Value (IV) algorithm implemented in PROPCA among frequently referenced attributes in banking domain. These attributes have both categorical and numerical values.

Final banking data set contains 19818 customers' data having 5 demographic features (3 numerical and 2 categorical) chosen by IV and ownerships of 4 product families. The names of the used features and products cannot be mentioned in this work because of privacy of banking customers' data. In order to apply logistic regression, categorical attributes are represented with dummy values and all of the selected attributes are standardized.

TABLE I. OWNERSHIP RATIO (≈)

	P1	*P2*	*P3*	*P4*
Ownership	32.2 %	25.3 %	62.2 %	63 %

In Table I, all product families and ratio of number of these products' owners to number of all customers are presented. Some customers own more than one of these products at the same time. Association algorithms examine the relation between these products ownership and detect customers who may purchase a new product. To perform this, AR algorithms need minimum support and minimum confidence values. These values are fixed as 0.01 and 0.20 respectivelly. While the minimum support threshold is used to find frequent itemsets, the minimum confidence threshold is used to generate rules from frequent itemsets.

The data set has splitted into three equal parts by the stratified sampling mechanism implemented in PROPCA and each part is used as training set and the rest of the data is used as test set iteratively. Therefore, effects of distinct training set on general results was observed. Each data set contains 6606 different customers' data and having slightly different ownership ratio for each product (See Table II).

TABLE II. OWNERSHIP RATIO IN DISTINCT TRAINING SETS (≈)

	P1	*P2*	*P3*	*P4*
Training Set 1	32.3 %	25.7 %	62.1 %	63.0 %
Training Set 2	32.1 %	24.8 %	61.6 %	63.2 %
Training Set 3	32.1 %	25.3 %	63.0 %	62.8 %

In each iteration, the model learns from one data set and it is tested with the remaining two. The predicted probabilities of algorithms are evaluated by a cut-off point (i.e., 0.5) to obtain "1" or "0" for the class value. The true positive rate (TPR), true negative rate (TNR) and accuracy (Acc) are calculated for each product family on distinct test sets. The aim of these tests is to show the benefit of combining different algorithms with MLR.

A. *TPR and TNR*

TPR and TNR are two complementary indicators. While TPR measures the ratio of correctly identified positives (e.g., purchaser of a product), TNR measures the ratio of correctly identified negatives (e.g., non-purchaser of a product). In Figure 3, the TPRs and TNRs for each product (Product 1, 2, 3 and 4) obtained from each test (Test Data 1, 2 and 3) set with different algorithms (Logit, Association and MLR) are shown.

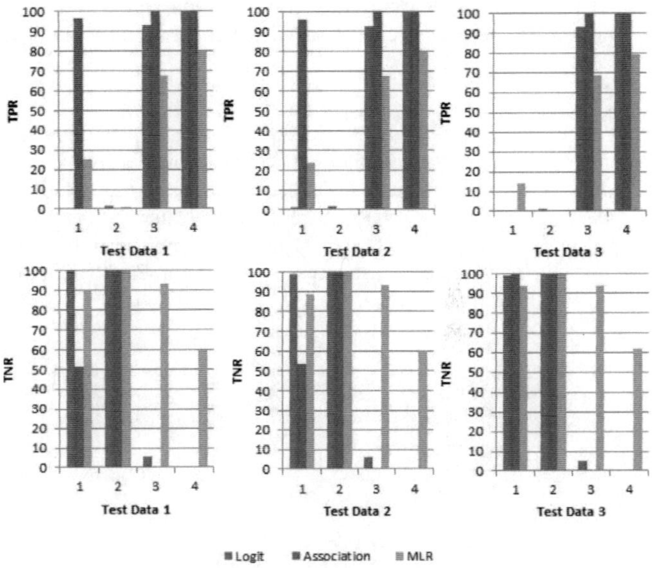

Figure 3: TPR and TNR

TPRs and TNRs of logit are respectively about 0 % and 100 % in all tests, for Product 1. Logit cannot distinguish purchaser of Product 1 from non-purchaser and it tends to classify a negligible part of customers as purchaser. One reason of these unsuccessful results may be low ownership ratio of Product 1 (less than 50 %) in whole data set (see Table I and II). In Test Data 1 and 2, association rules' TPRs and TNRs are respectively about 95 % and 50 %. However, in Test Data 3, it tends to classify none of customers as purchaser. Therefore, TPR is 0 % and TNR is 100 % in this last test. In first two tests, MLR's results are between logit's and AR's results. In the last test, MLR's TPR (≈ 14 %) is greater than and TNR (≈ 94 %) is less than both of the base classifiers. Thus, with a little loss in terms of TNR, MLR makes 14 % gain in terms of TPR.

None or a very little number of customers are classified correctly as purchaser of Product 2. Thus, poor TPRs for this product are obtained from all test data. Neither logit nor association algorithm can model the purchase action of Product 2. One reason of this fact can be the poor ownership rate of this product in whole data set (25 %). Conversely, TNRs of Product 2 equals approximately 100 % in each test. In this case, MLR does not add any gain on these results.

In all of the tests, all of the customers are classified as purchaser of Product 3 and 4 by association algorithm. Therefore,

TPRs of association algorithm are always 100 % and TNRs are 0 %. Association algorithms cannot distinguish purchaser and non-purchaser. On the other hand, performance of logit is not significantly different from association algorithms. TPRs rate are greater than 90 % and TNRs are less than 10 %. MLR algorithm equalizes TPRs and TNRs. With a loss about between 10 % and 35 % on TPRs, it makes gain about between 60 % and 90 % on TNRS for Product 3 and Product 4 in different test sets.

In a nutshell, MLR takes the output of two poor classifiers' results as input and it increases the equilibrium between TNRs and TPRs. In some case, like in Test Data 3 for Product 1, MLR obtain a TPR more than both base classifiers' results. In the next section, accuracies and MLR's impact on this indicator will be examined.

B. Accuracy

Accuracy measures how well the classifiers predict positive and negative class together. As shown in Figure 4, using MLR algorithm increases the accuracy of both Logit and Association Rules. To be more specific, except for Product 2, MLR provides an increase in accuracy by approximately 2 % for Product 1 and even more ($\approx$ 8 %) for Product 3 and 4 for each test data set.

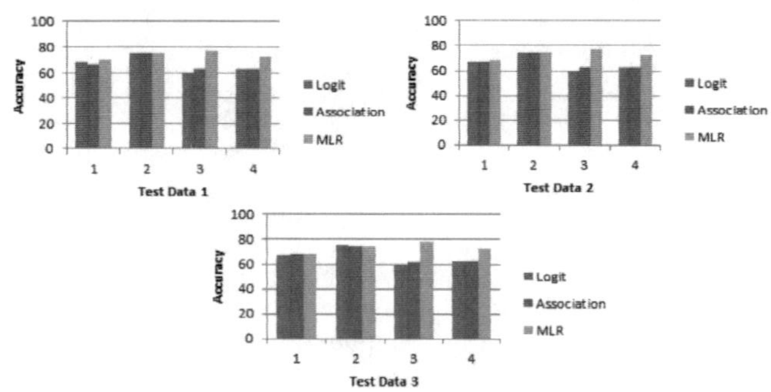

Figure 4: Accuracy

The reason that accuracy rates are around 60% for each product family can be interpreted by simply saying user behavior is complex. It is particularly more complex when the issue is recommending something to a customer. The retrieval of what is known before is not the same thing as suggesting something to a customer that he has never seen or heard before. Therefore, accuracy rates being not that high is something that can be acceptable in social sciences.

In the light of Figure 4, it can be said that MLR separates the purchaser customers from non-purchaser customers more successfully than both of Logit and Association algorithms in almost every test data set.

V. Conclusion and Future Works

In this research, it is aimed to obtain a model that combines the outputs of two seperate algorithms, logit and AR mining developed as a part of PROPCA, which have difficulties to work effectively with large data sets and also have different operation principles. The results are promising and show that this model works more efficiently and has a higher accuracy than logit or AR mining used standalone. It can be considered as a model that develops and strengthens the power of prediction of these two algorithms. However, the authors are aware of the fact that the tests have to be extended with a data containing more products and more customers and also other evaluation metrics like precision and recall can be used in order to validate the model and also camparison of the proposed approach with other ensemble techniques could also be performed.

It is known that logit works better when learning data set is balanced in terms of the number of positive and negative cases. It is possible to improve accuracy of the model by carrying attention to sampling models. If for each product, balanced training set (approximately 50 % negative, 50 % positive observations) is created, the performance of logit could be increased comparing to current sampling. Hence, this increase in performance will give better predictive probabilities as logit output and this could also positively affect the overall model's success.

In addition to balanced traning set, selection of diffrent strong attributes and various cut-off points for each product separately could also result in increasing the success of both logit and consequently the MLR model.

As a future work, to increase the efficiency of the proposed model some primarily work can be performed. Before applying association rule mining to the data set, some additional steps might be taken into consideration such as clustering (e.g., k-means or expectation maximization (EM) [41]) in order to gather customers having similar demographic features together. For each cluster of customers, AR algorithms could be executed separately.

Similarly, Latent Class (LC) approach can be used with logit. Choosing the correct number of classes in LC analysis is an important issue. A likelihood criteria such as Akaike Information Criterion (AIC) [42] and Bayesian Information Criterion (BIC) [43] could be used to compare models with different numbers of classes. Customers in the sample could be separated into segments based on customer characteristics and product preferences. Then, characterized values for each segment could be calculated using the attributes of customers in them. Using the selected attributes of each customer in the universe, the distance to each segment can be calculated and customers can be assigned to the segment having the minimum distance and the predicted probabilities can be calculated using the related segments propeties.

Acknowledgment

It is worth mentioning that this research has been carried out based on a mutual team work cooperation between the authors of this paper. The authors would like to thank to the other members of the research and development department at Cybersoft for their help throughout this work and also it should be stated that this study is conducted under the scope of PROPCA which is supported by the Scientific and Technological Research Council of Turkey (TUBITAK).

References

[1] Silverpop, "Silverpop email marketing metrics benchmark study," 2014.

[2] J. Tanguma and R. Saldivar, "Interpretation of logistic regression models in marketing journals," in The Sustainable Global Marketplace. Springer, 2015, pp. 2–2.

[3] S. Akinci, E. Kaynak, E. Atilgan, and S. Aksoy, "Where does the logistic regression analysis stand in marketing literature? a comparison of the market positioning of prominent marketing journals," European Journal of Marketing, vol. 41, no. 5/6, 2007, pp. 537–567.

[4] S. Brin, R. Motwani, and C. Silverstein, "Beyond market baskets: Generalizing association rules to correlations," in ACM SIGMOD Record, vol. 26, no. 2. ACM, 1997, pp. 265–276.

[5] R. Agrawal, T. Imieliński, and A. Swami, "Mining association rules between sets of items in large databases," ACM SIGMOD Record, vol. 22, no. 2, 1993, pp. 207–216.

[6] R. Agrawal, R. Srikant et al., "Fast algorithms for mining association rules," in Proc. 20th int. conf. very large data bases, VLDB, vol. 1215, 1994, pp. 487–499.

[7] M. J. Zaki, "Scalable algorithms for association mining," Knowledge and Data Engineering, IEEE Transactions on, vol. 12, no. 3, 2000, pp. 372–390.

[8] J. Han, J. Pei, and Y. Yin, "Mining frequent patterns without candidate generation," in ACM Sigmod Record, vol. 29, no. 2. ACM, 2000, pp. 1–12.

[9] S. Kotsiantis and D. Kanellopoulos, "Association rules mining: A recent overview," GESTS International Transactions on Computer Science and Engineering, vol. 32, no. 1, 2006, pp. 71–82.

[10] R. Srikant and R. Agrawal, Mining generalized association rules. IBM Research Division, 1995.

[11] M. Hegland, "Algorithms for association rules," in Advanced lectures on machine learning. Springer, 2003, pp. 226–234.

[12] D. Flath and E. Leonard, "A comparison of two logit models in the analysis of qualitative marketing data," Journal of Marketing Research, 1979, pp. 533–538.

[13] J. Berkson, "Maximum likelihood and minimum x 2 estimates of the logistic function," Journal of the American Statistical Association, vol. 50, no. 269, 1955, pp. 130–162.

[14] N. K. Malhotra, "The use of linear logit models in marketing research," Journal of Marketing research, 1984, pp. 20–31.

[15] P. E. Green, F. J. Carmone, and D. P. Wachspress, "On the analysis of qualitative data in marketing research," Journal of Marketing Research, 1977, pp. 52–59.

[16] J. R. Hauser and G. L. Urban, "A normative methodology for modeling consumer response to innovation," Operations Research, vol. 25, no. 4, 1977, pp. 579–619.

[17] A. J. Silk and G. L. Urban, "Pre-test-market evaluation of new packaged goods: A model and measurement methodology," Journal of marketing Research, 1978, pp. 171–191.

[18] R. R. Batsell, "Consumer resource allocation models at the individual level," Journal of Consumer Research, 1980, pp. 78–87.

[19] R. G. Chapman and R. Staelin, "Exploiting rank ordered choice set data within the stochastic utility model," Journal of marketing research, 1982, pp. 288–301.

[20] D. H. Gensch and W. W. Recker, "The multinomial, multiattribute logit choice model," Journal of Marketing Research, 1979, pp. 124–132.

[21] N. K. Malhotra, A. K. Jain, and S. W. Lagakos, "The information overload controversy: An alternative viewpoint," The Journal of Marketing, 1982, pp. 27–37.

[22] S. Hosmer, David W.; Lemeshow, Log-linear models. Springer-Verlag, 1990, ISBN:0-471-35632-8.

[23] L. De La Viña and J. Ford, "Logistic regression analysis of cruise vacation market potential: Demographic and trip attribute perception factors," Journal of Travel Research, vol. 39, no. 4, 2001, pp. 406–410.

[24] P. McCullagh and J. A. Nelder, Generalized linear models. CRC press, 1989, vol. 37.

[25] J. W. Tukey, "Exploratory data analysis," 1977.

[26] R. E. Schapire, "The strength of weak learnability," Machine learning, vol. 5, no. 2, 1990, pp. 197–227.

[27] K. Tumer and J. Ghosh, "Analysis of decision boundaries in linearly combined neural classifiers," Pattern Recognition, vol. 29, no. 2, 1996, pp. 341–348.

[28] Y. Freund, R. E. Schapire et al., "Experiments with a new boosting algorithm," in ICML, vol. 96, 1996, pp. 148–156.

[29] L. Breiman, "Stacked regressions," Machine learning, vol. 24, no. 1, 1996, pp. 49–64.

[30] T. K. Ho, "The random subspace method for constructing decision forests," Pattern Analysis and Machine Intelligence, IEEE Transactions on, vol. 20, no. 8, 1998, pp. 832–844.

[31] M. Skurichina and R. P. Duin, "Bagging, boosting and the random subspace method for linear classifiers," Pattern Analysis & Applications, vol. 5, no. 2, 2002, pp. 121–135.

[32] C.-X. Zhang and J.-S. Zhang, "A local boosting algorithm for solving classification problems," Computational Statistics & Data Analysis, vol. 52, no. 4, 2008, pp. 1928–1941.

[33] D. H. Wolpert, "Stacked generalization," Neural networks, vol. 5, no. 2, 1992, pp. 241–259.

[34] S. Džeroski and B. Ženko, "Is combining classifiers with stacking better than selecting the best one?" Machine learning, vol. 54, no. 3, 2004, pp. 255–273.

[35] M. Sewell, "Ensemble learning," RN, vol. 11, no. 02, 2008.

[36] L. Rokach, "Ensemble-based classifiers," Artificial Intelligence Review, vol. 33, no. 1-2, 2010, pp. 1–39.

[37] G. Sigletos, G. Paliouras, C. D. Spyropoulos, and M. Hatzopoulos, "Combining information extraction systems using voting and stacked generalization," The Journal of Machine Learning Research, vol. 6, 2005, pp. 1751–1782.

[38] D. W. Fan, P. K. Chan, and S. J. Stolfo, "A comparative evaluation of combiner and stacked generalization," in Proceedings of AAAI-96 workshop on Integrating Multiple Learned Models, 1996, pp. 40–46.

[39] A. K. Seewald, "How to make stacking better and faster while also taking care of an unknown weakness," in Proceedings of the nineteenth international conference on machine learning. Morgan Kaufmann Publishers Inc., 2002, pp. 554–561.

[40] K. M. Ting and I. H. Witten, "Issues in stacked generalization," J. Artif. Intell. Res.(JAIR), vol. 10, 1999, pp. 271–289.

[41] L. Bottou and Y. Bengio, "Convergence properties of the k-means algorithms," in Advances in Neural Information Processing Systems 7. Citeseer, 1995.

[42] H. Akaike, "Factor analysis and aic," Psychometrika, vol. 52, no. 3, 1987, pp. 317–332.

[43] G. Schwarz et al., "Estimating the dimension of a model," The annals of statistics, vol. 6, no. 2, 1978, pp. 461–464.

Modeling System Requirements Using Use Cases and Petri Nets

Radek Kočí and Vladimír Janoušek

Brno University of Technology, Faculty of Information Technology,
IT4Innovations Centre of Excellence
Czech Republic
email: {koci,janousek}@fit.vutbr.cz

***Abstract*—The fundamental problem associated with software development is a correct identification, specification and subsequent implementation of the system requirements. To specify requirement, designers often create use case diagrams from Unified Modeling Language (UML). These models are then developed by further UML models. To validate requirements, its executable form has to be obtained or the prototype has to be developed. It can conclude in wrong requirement implementations and incorrect validation process. The approach presented in this work focuses on formal requirement modeling combining the classic models for requirements specification (use case diagrams) with models having a formal basis (Petri Nets). Created models can be used in all development stages including requirements specification, verification, and implementation. All design and validation steps are carries on the same models, which avoids mistakes caused by model implementation.**

Keywords–Object Oriented Petri Nets; Use Cases; requirement specification; requirement implementation.

I. Introduction

This paper is part of the *System in Simulation Development* (SiS) work [1] based on the formalism of Object Oriented Petri Nets (OOPN) [2]. One of the fundamental problems associated with software development is an identification, specification and subsequent implementation of the system requirements [3]. The use case diagram from UML is often used for requirements specification, which is then developed by further UML models [4]. The disadvantage is the inability to validate a specification modeled by that method and it is usually necessary to develop a prototype, which is no longer used after fulfilling its purpose.

Utilization of OOPN enables the simulation (i.e., execute the model), as well as direct integration into a real surroundings, which solves mentioned disadvantage. All changes in the validation process are entered directly into the model, and it is therefore not necessary to implement or transform models. The approach presented in this paper is based on the use cases that are specified by the OOPN formalism. This approach can therefore be mapped to commonly used modeling techniques.

There are methods working with modified UML models that can be executed and, therefore, validated by simulation. An example is the Model Driven Architecture (MDA) methodology [5], language Executable UML (xUML) [6], or Foundational Subset for xUML [7]. These methods are faced with a problem of model transformations. It is complicated to validate proposed requirements through models in real conditions. They either have to implement a prototype or transform models into executable form, which can then be tested and debugged. All changes that result from validation process are hard to transfer back into the models. It is a problem because the models become useless over the development time.

Similar work based on ideas of model-driven development deals with gaps between different development stages and focuses on the usage of conceptual models during the simulation model development process—these techniques are called *model continuity* [8]. While it works with simulation models during design stages, the approach proposed in this paper focuses on *live models* that can be used in the deployed system.

The paper is organized as follows. Section II summarizes concepts of modeling requirements using use cases from UML and describes our extension to one special relationship. Section III deals with use case specification using OOPN. Modeling use case relationships is discussed in Section IV and the way of actor modeling is described in Section V. The summary and future work is described in Section VI.

II. Use Case Diagrams

Use case diagrams (UCDs) are used in the process of software system design for modeling functional requirements. The system is considered as a black-box, where only external features are taken into account. The objective of UCDs is identify system users, user requirements, and how the user interacts with the system. The model consists of *actors* and *use cases*.

A. Actor

Actor is an external entity working with the software system, so that actor is not part of the system, but it is a generator of input stimulus and data for the system. Actor models a group of real users, whereas all members of the group work with the system by the same way. Therefore, actor represents *a role* of the user in the system. A real user can play multiple roles. Let us consider the example of conference system with actors *author* and *reviewer*. These actors model two roles, each of them defines a set of functions (use cases) the user can initiate or can participate on. The real user can either be author or reviewer, or can work with the system in both roles.

Now, let us consider the example of a system of garage gate handling. The system consists of actuators (garage gate), sensors (driving sensor, card scanner), and control software. It is closed autonomous system with which two groups of real users can work—*driver* and *reception clerk*. The driver comes to the garage gate, applies a card to the scanner, and the system opens the gate. If the user does not have a card, he can ask reception clerk, who opens the gate. From system point of view, actuators, sensors, and control software are internal parts of the system. From the software engineering point of view, actuators and sensors are *external* items the system can handle.

So, if actuators and sensors are not internal parts, could we model them using actor concept? Actors represent human users in many information systems (*human actors*), but they can also be used to model other subsystems such as sensors or devices (*system actors*). The system has to communicate to such subsystems, nevertheless they need not to be parts of the modeled software system.

B. Use Case

An important part of functional requirements analysis is to identify sequences of interaction between actors and modeled system. Each such a sequence covers different functional requirement on the system. The sequence of interactions is modeled by *a use case*. The use case describes a main sequence of interactions and is invoked (its execution starts) by input stimulus from the *actor*. The main sequence can be supplemented by alternative sequences describing less commonly used interactions. Their invocation depends on specified conditions, e.g., wrong information input or abnormal system conditions. Each sequence (the main or alternative one) is called *scenario*. Scenario is complete implementation of a specific sequence of interactions within the use case.

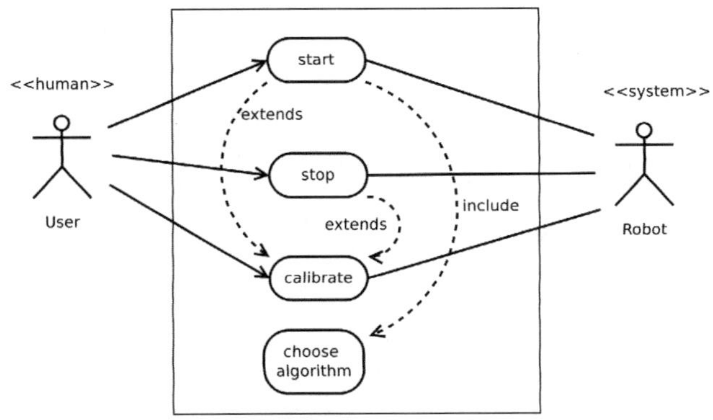

Figure 1. First Use Case Diagram for the robotic system.

We will demonstrate basic principles and problems of use case modeling on the simplified example of robotic system. The example works with a robot, which is controlled by the algorithm. Users can handle algorithms for controlling the robot (he/she can start or stop an algorithm or choose one of them for handling). The first use case diagram is shown in Fig. 1. Model contains two actors, an *User* (human actor) and a *Robot* (system actor). We can also see the software system boundary and basic use cases arising from specification, *start*, *stop*, *calibrate* the basic settings, and *choose algorithm* for execution. *Robot* is viewed as another system with which modeled system works.

C. Relationships Between Use Cases

Among the different use cases you can use two defined relationships, *include* and *extend*. The aim of these relations is to maximize extensibility and reusability of use cases if the model becomes too complex. A secondary effect of using of these relationships is to emphasize the dependence of the individual use case scenarios, structuring too long scenarios to more lower level use cases, or highlighting selected activities.

1) Relationship extend: Relationship *extend* reflects alternative scenarios for basic use case. In cases where the specification of a use case is too complicated and contains many different scenarios, it is possible to model a chosen alternative for new use case, which is called *extension use case*. This use case then extends the basic use case that defines a location (point of extension) in the sequence of interactions and conditions under which the extension use case is invoked. The relationship *extend* is illustrated in Fig. 1. The use case *calibrate* has to stop the running algorithm first, then to calibrate the system and, finally, to start it. Use cases *start* and *stop* can thus expand the base case scenario *calibrate*.

2) Relationship include: Relationship *include* reflects the scenarios that can be shared by more than one use case. Common sequence can be extracted from the original use cases and modeled by a new use case, which we will call *inclusion use case*. Such use case can then be used in various basic use cases that determine the location (point of insertion) in the sequence of interactions for inclusion. The relationship *include* is illustrated in Fig. 1. Now, we adjust the original sequence of interactions with the use case *start*, which will need to select the algorithm to be executed first. Use case *start* thus includes the use case *choose algorithm*.

D. Generalization use cases

The activities related to interactions between the software system and a robot were not highlighted yet. One possibility is to define *inclusion use case* describing these interactions, i.e., the algorithm. However, this method supposes only one algorithm, which contradicts the specified option to choose algorithm. Second possibility is to define *extension use cases*, everyone for various algorithms. The disadvantage of this solution is its ambiguity; there is no obvious the problem and the appropriate solution.

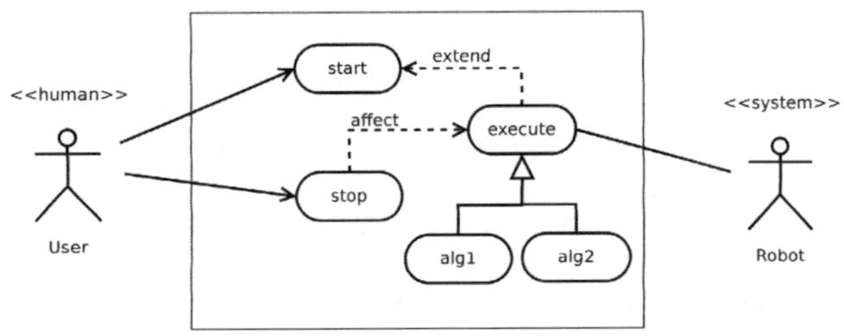

Figure 2. Specialization of the use case *execute* and the relationship affect.

Use case diagram offers the possibility to generalize cases. This feature is similar to the generalization (inheritance) in an object-oriented environment. In the context of the use case diagrams, generalization primarily reflects the interchangeability of the base-case for derived cases. Although there are methods that consider generalization as abstruse [9] and recommend replacing it with relation *extend*, generalization has a unique importance in interpreting the use case diagram. Relation *extend* allows to invoke more extension use cases, whereas generalization clearly expresses the idea that case *start* works with one of cases *execute* (the model is shown in Fig. 2). The model can also be easily extended without having to modify already existing cases.

E. Use Case Diagram Extension

The present example shows one situation that is not captured in the diagram and use case diagrams do not provide resources for its proper modeling. This is the case *stop*, which affects the use case *execute* (or possibly derived cases), but does not form its basis (the case *execute* is neither part of it nor its extension). Nevertheless, its execution affects the sequence of interactions, which is modeled by use case *execute* (it stops its activity). In the classical chart this situation would only be described in the specification of individual cases, however, we introduce a simple extension *affect*, as shown in Fig. 2. Relation *affect* represents a situation, where the base use case execution has a direct impact on other, dependent use case. This relation is useful to model synchronization between cases in such a system, which suppose autonomous activities modeled by use cases.

III. USE CASE SPECIFICATION USING PETRI NETS

Use case specification format is not prescribed and can have a variety of expressive and modeling means, e.g., plain text, structured text, or any of the models. UML offers an activity diagram, a state diagram, etc. These charts allow precise description based on modeling elements with clear semantics, but their validation can be problematic because of impossibility to check models either by formal means or by simulation. Of course, there are tools and methods [6][10] that allow to simulate modified UML diagrams. Nevertheless, there is still a strict border between *design* and *implementation* phases. Another way is to use some of the formal models. In this section, we introduce Object Oriented Petri Nets (OOPN) for specifying *use case*, i.e., interactions between the system and the actors. Let's walk through the previous example of use case *alg1* shown in Fig. 3.

A. States and Transitions Declaration

The system state is represented by places in the OOPN formalism. System is in a particular state if an appropriate place contains a *token*. Actions taken in a particular state is modeled as part of the transition whose execution is conditioned by a presence of tokens in that state. The transition is modeled as an element that moves the tokens between places. Except the input places, the transition firing is conditioned by a *guard*. The guard contains conditions or synchronous ports. The transition can be fired only if the guard is evaluated as true. If the transition fires, it executes the guard, which can have a side effect, e.g., the executed synchronous port can change a state of the other case.

B. Common Net and Common Places

For modeling the workflow that includes multiple separate synchronized nets may need to share a single network to other networks. For this purpose, the synchronous ports are used. Nevertheless, it can be difficult to read the basic model of the flow of events, because of the need for explicit modeling synchronous ports for data manipulation. Therefore, we introduce the concept of *common net* and *common place*. It is not a new concept, only the syntactic coating certain patterns using synchronous ports. For each model, we introduce one common net represented by the class *CommonNet* that for each running model has exactly one instance identified by the name *common*. The object net of *CommonNet* may contain *common places*, i.e., place whose content is available through standard mechanisms (e.g., synchronous ports). Difference to the ordinary usage lies in the fact that access mechanisms are hidden and access to the common places from other nets is modeled by *mapping*—the place marked as common in the other net is mapped onto common place defined in the common net.

C. Modeling of Interaction Sequences

The states *testing*, *walking*, and *turnRight* are represented by places. State *turnRight* is only temporal and the activity goes through these ones to the one of stable states (e.g., *walking*).

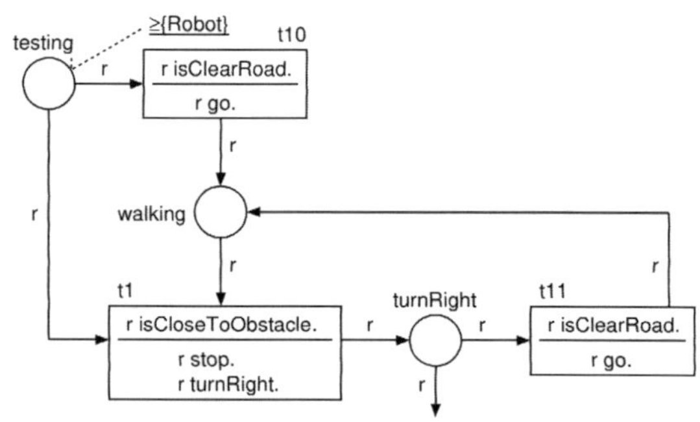

Figure 3. Petri net modeling the use case *Algorithm1* (*alg1*).

Control flow is modeled by the sequence of transitions, where each transition execution is conditioned by events representing the state of the robot. Let us take one example for all, the state *testing* and linked transitions *t10* and *t1*. The transition *t1* is fireable, if the condition (modeled by the synchronous port) *isCloseToObstacle* is met. When firing this transition, actions to stop the robot (*stop*) and to turn right (*turnRight*) are performed and the system moves to the state of *turnRight*. The transition *t10* is fireable, if the condition (synchronous port) *isClearRoad* is met. When firing this transition, the action to go straight (*go*) is performed and the system moves into the state *walking*.

Both testing condition and messaging represent the interaction of the system with the robot. The robot moves the control flow as *token*, which allows interaction at the appropriate point of control flow and at the same time defines the state of its location in one of the places. To achieve correct behavior, it is useful to define type constraints on tokens (see $\geq \{Robot\}$;

it means the token should be of a type *Robot*). Even as, it clearly shows *which* actor (and derived actors) interacts in those scenarios.

D. Alternative Scenarios Modeling

Alternative scenarios, i.e., scenarios that supplement the basic scenario, is modeled by synchronous ports (perhaps even methods) to handle a response to an external event. We show a variant of the suspension of the algorithm, i.e., removal of the token from the current state and restoring algorithm, i.e., return the token back to the correct place. We introduce a new state (place) *paused* representing suspended algorithm. Because the formalism of OOPN does not have a mechanism for working with composite states, we should declare auxiliary transitions or ports for each state we want to manipulate with.

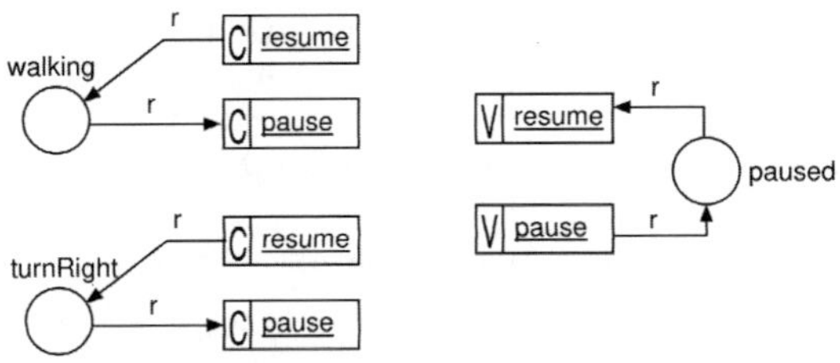

Figure 4. Composite state manipulation in OOPN.

This way of modeling is clear, however, confusing for readability. Furthermore, to work with a larger set of states is almost unusable. Nevertheless, there is the same pattern for each state, so that the concept of collective work with the states is introduced. It wraps the syntax of the original net. This will improve the readability of the model, while preserving the exactness of modeling by Petri nets including testing models. The example is shown in Fig. 4. The synchronous port is divided into two parts—the *common* part (*C-part*) and the *variable-join* part (*V-part*). The *C-part* represents all synchronous ports, that should be called from the composite port. The *V-part* represents a way how to work with the *C-part*—it is fireable, if at least one item of the *C-part* is fireable.

IV. Relationships Modeling

We turn now to a method of modeling the relationships between use cases. As we have already defined, we distinguish relations *include*, *extend*, *affect*, and *generalization*.

A. Modeling of the relation include

We will continue our example and create models of use cases *start* and *choose algorithm*, which is *inclusion case* to the case *start*. Case *start* is activated by actor *user*, connected by a mutual interaction. Actor *user* is the primary actor, so it generates stimulus to that the case has to respond. It implies a method of modeling events in the sequence of interactions. Responses to actor's requirements have to be modeled as an external event, i.e., using a synchronous port. Another significant issue is a place of inclusion into the basic sequence of interactions and invocation activities of the integrated case.

The model of use case *start* is shown in Fig. 5. The inclusion use case is stored in a place *inclusion* and the insertion

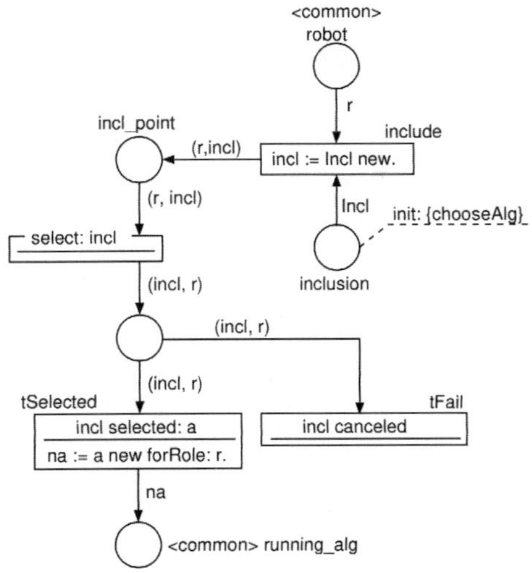

Figure 5. Petri net specification of the use case *start*.

point is modeled by internal event (transition) *include* with a link to a place *incl_point*. Invoking the use case corresponds to instantiate the appropriate net (see the calling *new* in the transition *include*). The following external event (synchronous port) *select:* initiates the interaction of the actor *user* with integrated activity. The event binds the inclusion case to the free variable *incl*, and simultaneously stores it to an auxiliary place. Conditional branching is modeled by internal activities (transitions) *tSelected* and *tFail*. Their execution is subject to a state of inclusion case, which is tested by synchronous ports in guards. In case of success (transition *tSelected*), the synchronous port *selected:* binds the selected algorithm to the free variable *a* and stores it to the common place *running_alg*.

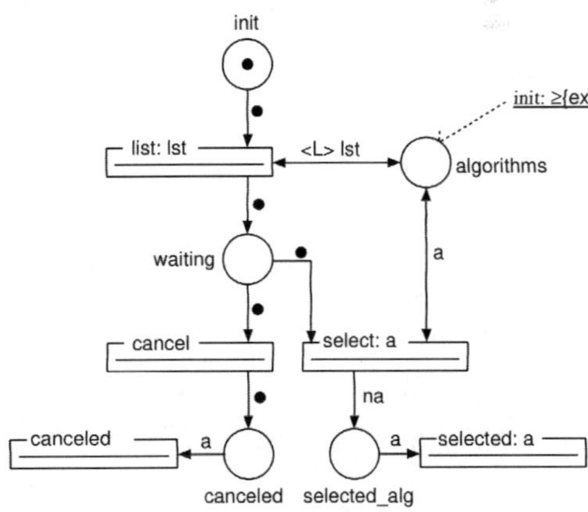

Figure 6. Petri net specification of the use case *choose algorithm*.

The use case *choose algorithm* specification is shown in Fig. 6. The basic sequence (to obtain algorithm list and select one of them) is supplemented with an alternative sequence (the user does not select any algorithm) and a condition (empty list corresponds to the situation when a user selects no algorithm). Inclusion case is viewed from stimuli generation point of view as secondary element; its activities are synchronized by basic case or actor, which works to the base case. Synchronization points are therefore modeled as external events, i.e., using synchronous ports. The case does not work with any secondary actor, so that to define the status of the net is sufficient type-free token (modeled as dot). The first external event is to obtain a list of algorithms (synchronous port *list:*); the variable *lst* binds the entire content of the place *algorithms*. This place is initialized by a set of cases (nets) derived from the case (net) *execute*. Now, the case waits for actor decision, which may be two. A user selects either no algorithm (external event *cancel*), or select a specific algorithm from the list, which has to match the algorithm from the place *algorithms* (external event *select:*). Token location into one of the places *canceled* or *selected_alg* represents possible states after a sequence of interactions. These conditions can be tested by synchronous ports *unselected* and *selected:*.

B. Modeling of the relation extend

Relation *extend* exists between cases *start* and *execute*, where *execute* is the extension use case. This relationship expresses the possibility of execution of the algorithm, provided that some algorithm was chosen. Since this is an alternative, it is expressed by branches beginning transition *tSelected*, as we can see in Fig. 5. The transition *tSelected* represents the insertion point of the extension of the basic sequence of interactions.

C. Modeling of the relation affect

Relationship *affect* exists between cases *stop* and *execute*, where *stop* influences the sequence of interactions of the case *execute*, respectively any inherited cases. Petri nets model for this use case is shown in Fig. 7. The activity begins from the common place *running_alg* and branches in three variants (transitions *t1*, *t2*, and *t3*). Branch *t1* says *no algorithm is running*; common place *running_alg* is empty. Because OOPN do not have inhibitors, the negative predicate *empty* is used to test conditions, which is feasible, if it is impossible to bind any object to the variable *a*.

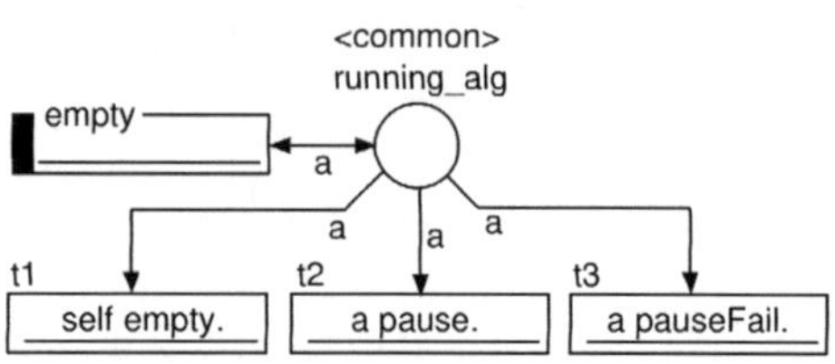

Figure 7. Petri net specification of the use case *stop*.

Branch *t2* says *an algorithm is invocated and run*; the common place *running_alg* contains an active algorithm. Synchronous port *pause* (see Fig. 4) called on the running algorithm is evaluated as true and when performed, it moves the algorithm into *stopped* state. Branch *t3* says *an algorithm is invocated and not running*; the common place *running_alg* contains an active algorithm. Synchronous port *pauseFail* called on the running algorithm is evaluated as true and when perform, it has no side effect.

This model is purely declarative. We declare three possible variants that may arise, and simultaneously declare target individual options to be done. Only one variant can be performed at a time. We can define other activities related to these variants. We can see that it does not invoke the use case *execute*, i.e., there is no instantiating a net, but this activity is affected. It is therefore not appropriate to model this situation with the relations *include* or *extend*. After all, it is appropriate to model that relationship.

D. Modeling of the relation generalization

This relationship demonstrates, that it is possible to use any inherited case instead of the base case. If there is a point defining the relationship *include* or *extend* to a base case *c*, we can work with any case inherited from the base case *c*. In our example, this situation is shown on the use case model *choose algorithm* (Fig. 6). The place *algorithm* contains all possible algorithms that can be provided, i.e., nets inherited from base use case *execute*. Wherever the case *executed* is used in the model, it is possible to use any inherited case.

V. Actor Specification

Until now we have neglected the essence of the token that provides interaction with the actors and defines the system state by its position. As mentioned, actor represents *role* of the user or device (i.e., a real actor), which can hold in the system. One real actor may hold multiple roles, can thus be modeled by various actors. Actor defines a subset of use cases allowed for such a role. For instance, the *robot* is not allowed to choose algorithm to execute, so its model does not contain any interaction to that use case.

A. Modeling Roles

An actor is modeled as a use case, i.e., by Petri nets. Interactions between use cases and actors are synchronized through *synchronous ports* that test conditions, convey the necessary data and can initiate an alternative scenario for both sides. Use case can then send instructions through messages too.

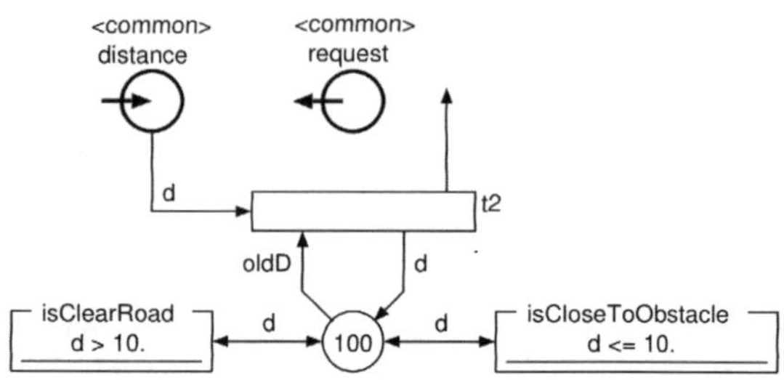

Figure 8. Petri net specification of the actor *Robot*.

In our example, we will model the secondary actor *Robot*, whose basic model is shown in Fig. 8. Scenarios of the *execute* use cases are synchronized using synchronous ports *isCloseToObstacle* and *isClearRoad* whose definition is simple—to test the distance to the nearest obstacle, which is stored in the place *distanceToObstacle*. Its content is periodically refreshed with a new value coming through the common place *distance*. The net can define methods for controlling a real actor too.

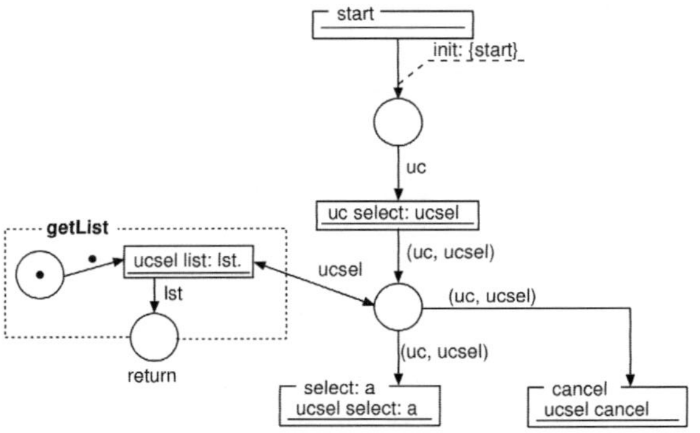

Figure 9. Petri net specification of the use case *User*.

Model of the next actor *User* is shown in Fig. 9. The primary actor defines stimuli (modeled as synchronous ports and methods) that can perform a real actor. Their execution is always conditioned by an actor workflow and a net of currently synchronized use case. Model shows the workflow of the use case *start*, which starts by calling a synchronous port *start*. It invocates the use case *start* (the syntactically simpler notation is used, it is semantically identical to invocation shown in Fig. 5). Using the method *getList* is possible to obtain a list of algorithms. Allowed actions can be executed by one of the defined synchronous ports *select:* and *cancel*.

B. Modeling Real Actors

Real actor can hold many roles that are modeled by actors in the system. Each of these roles always has a common base, that is a representation of the real actor, whether a user, system, or device. The model has to capture this fact. For terminological reasons, in order to remove potential confusion of terms *actor* and *real actor*, we denote a real actor by the term *subject*. The subject is basically an interface to a real form of the actor or to stored data. Therefore, it can be modeled in different ways that can be synchronized with Petri nets. Due to the nature of the used nets, there can be used Petri nets, other kind of formalism (e.g., DEVS), or programming language (Smalltalk until now).

For instance, the subject of the actor *Robot* can be modeled as an external component, which is linked with the actor through the *component interface* consisting of one input port *distance* and one output port *request* (shown in Fig. 8). These ports are modeled as common place, so that the common net can serve for component interfacing [11]. The subject of the actor *User* can be modeled as a Smalltalk class, whose object can access OOPN objects directly [12]. The following pseudo-code shows a simple example of accessing model from the subject implemented in programming language. First, it asks a common net to get a role of user, then invokes synchronous port *start*, a method *getList*, and finally select first algorithm from the list.

$usr \leftarrow common.newUser();$
$usr.asPort.start();$
$lst \leftarrow usr.getList();$
$usr.asPort.select(lst.at(1));$

VI. Conclusion

The paper presented the concept of modeling software system requirements, which combines commonly used use case diagrams with not so commonly used Petri nets. The relationship between actors, use cases, and Petri nets has been introduced. Use case diagram is used for the initial specification of functional requirements while Petri nets serve for use case scenario descriptions allowing to model and validate requirement specifications in real surroundings. This approach does not need to transform models or implement requirements in a programming language and prevents the validation process from mistakes caused by model transformations.

At present, we have developed the tool supporting presented approach. In the future, we will focus on the tool completion, a possibility to interconnect model with other formalisms and languages, and feasibility study for different kinds of usage.

Acknowledgment

This work was supported by the internal BUT project FIT-S-14-2486 and The Ministry of Education, Youth and Sports of the Czech Republic from the National Programme of Sustainability (NPU II); project IT4Innovations excellence in science - LQ1602.

References

[1] R. Kočí and V. Janoušek, "Modeling and Simulation-Based Design Using Object-Oriented Petri Nets: A Case Study," in Proceeding of the International Workshop on Petri Nets and Software Engineering 2012, vol. 851. CEUR, 2012, pp. 253–266.

[2] M. Češka, V. Janoušek, and T. Vojnar, PNtalk — a computerized tool for Object oriented Petri nets modelling, ser. Lecture Notes in Computer Science. Springer Verlag, 1997, vol. 1333, pp. 591–610.

[3] K. Wiegers and J. Beatty, Software Requirements. Microsoft Press, 2014.

[4] N. Daoust, Requirements Modeling for Bussiness Analysts. Technics Publications, LLC, 2012.

[5] R. France and B. Rumpe, "Model-driven development of complex software: A research roadmap," in Proc. of Future of Software Engineering, FOSE, 2007, pp. 37–54.

[6] C. Raistrick, P. Francis, J. Wright, C. Carter, and I. Wilkie, Model Driven Architecture with Executable UML. Cambridge University Press, 2004.

[7] S. Mijatov, P. Langer, T. Mayerhofer, and G. Kappel, "A framework for testing uml activities based on fuml," in Proc. of 10th Int. Workshop on Model Driven Engineering, Verification, and Validation, vol. 1069, 2013, pp. 1–10.

[8] D. Cetinkaya, A. V. Dai, and M. D. Seck, "Model continuity in discrete event simulation: A framework for model-driven development of simulation models," ACM Transactions on Modeling and Computer Simulation, vol. 25, no. 3, 2015, pp. 1–15.

[9] H. Gomma, Designing Software Product Lines with UML: From Use Cases to Pattern-Based Software Architecture. Addison-Wesley Professional, 2004.

[10] D. S. Frankel, Model Driven Architecture: Applying MDA to Enterprise Computing, ser. 17 (MS-17). John Wiley & Sons, 2003.

[11] R. Kočí and V. Janoušek, "The Object Oriented Petri Net Component Model," in The Tenth International Conference on Software Engineering Advances. Xpert Publishing Services, 2015, pp. 309–315.

[12] R. Kočí and V. Janoušek, "Formal Models in Software Development and Deployment: A Case Study," International Journal on Advances in Software, vol. 7, no. 1, 2014, pp. 266–276.

A Strategy for Statistical Process Control Education in Computer Science

Julio Cezar Costa Furtado
Departament of Exact and Technological Sciences
Federal University of Amapá
Macapá, Amapá, Brazil
e-mail: furtado@unifap.br

Sandro Ronaldo Bezerra Oliveira
Graduate Program in Computer Science
Federal University of Pará
Belém, Pará, Brazil
e-mail: srbo@ufpa.br

***Abstract*—SPC (Statistical Process Control) was originally developed in the area of manufacturing, to support the implementation of continuous improvement programs in production lines. The use of SPC in process improvement is not new to the industry in general. In the context of software organizations, statistical control can be regarded as a relatively recent subject-area, although there are still many doubts about its application. Thus, this paper focuses on drawing up a curriculum for Statistical Process Control within a Computer Science course. The aim of this initiative is to provide software development organizations with computer science professionals who are fully able to perform this task.**

Keywords-software engineering; measurement and analysis; statistical process control; software process improvement; software quality; education.

I. INTRODUCTION

According to Lantzy [1], Statistical Process Control (SPC) was originally carried out in the area of manufacturing, to support the implementation of continuous improvement programs in production lines. The underlying principles of SPC are based on the works of Sherwar [2] in the Bell Telephone Laboratories. A process considered for statistical control must be stable and repeatable [3]. Thus, the SPC comprises a set of techniques that can achieve this goal.

Despite the fact that the use of SPC in process improvement is not new to the industry, in the context of software organizations, statistical control can be regarded as something that is relatively recent [4], although there are still many doubts about its application [5][6][7]. However, the importance of SPC for the software industry has grown in recent years, mainly owing to its use of internationally recognized quality models [8]. The Capability Maturity Model Integration (CMMI) [9] maturity level 4 requires an organization to manage the execution of its processes quantitatively and seek its continuous optimization.

In addition to this introductory section, which covers aspects of the justification and identification of the issue under study, this paper is structured as follows: Section II will formulate the problem statement of this PhD and examine the related work, together with its limitations, in Section III, a number of research questions and hypotheses will be raised. Section IV will outline the research methods employed to answer the research questions and test the hypothesis, and the contribution made by this paper and expected results are discussed in Section V.

A. *A Gap in the Area*

The reason why the use of SPC in software development organizations has proved to be complex is that these techniques exist in a context that does not take account of the particular features that currently exist in a software development process [8]. As a result, many software organizations tend to seek the assistance of outside professionals in the area of Computer Science to assist in the execution of statistical process control. It thus fails to draw on the expertise of Computer Science professionals who form a part of the hierarchy of an organization. Owing to their position in the software development organization, these professionals are real experts who have a full understanding of the processes and the reality of an organization, as well as being active agents in them.

This difficulty in finding Computer Science professionals may be due to the type of training these professionals are given, and the approach that is adopted for teaching SPC during their graduation course. The studies by Soare [9], Castro *et al.* [10] and Hazzan and Dubinsky [11] have shown that there are situations where there is too much content to teach in a short time. This leads to low motivation among the students and makes it difficult for teachers to prepare students to engage in professional practices within the academic environment.

B. *Scope of the Research*

With regard to the quality of the development process and the CMMI reference model [12], in the early levels of these improvement programs, organizations employ the measurement techniques that simply consist of collecting data from the execution of the project and comparing them with the planned values. Although this may seem a reasonable approach, it is not suitable for organizations that seek high maturity, to evaluate and evolve their processes. In these organizations, it is necessary to perform statistical control of software processes to find out about their behavior, determine their performance in previous executions and predict their performance in current and future projects. At the same time, it is necessary to make sure that they are able to achieve their established goals and take corrective measures and make improvements when appropriate [13].

Thus, this quantitative management of the organizational process involves a process that should lead to a controlled and predictable performance [12]. In this context, this PhD research study will:

- examine the Statistical Process Control practices

that are relevant to the software industry. This involves conducting an analysis to determine what knowledge about SPC is required for professionals in this area to carry out their activities with maximum performance,

- identify the existing SPC practices in computer courses. The results of this analysis will be used to define a new approach for the teaching of SPC in computer courses, which will be aligned with the recommendations of CMMI [12] and the needs of the software industry.

C. *Identification of the Issue*

The great difficulty of employing these professionals for statistical process control is the fact that most of them do not have the necessary knowledge and skills for such an undertaking. This leads to a paradoxical situation when assessing the performance of computer professionals, since their basic education often covers the discipline of Probability and Statistics. Moreover, the many disciplines of Software Engineering (SE) / Software Quality should provide a solid basis that is enough to allow this professional to act with more confidence in the market when there is a need for statistical process control in an organization. The industry complains that undergraduate courses do not teach the necessary skills that can enable students to undertake their jobs efficiently [14]. In the case of most companies, up to 80% of their employment opportunities are taken up by incoming students (freshmen), and up to 80% of the training budget is spent on them [37].

In general, the software industry suffers from a lack of qualified professionals who are able to work in activities involving the software development process [15][38][39]. Thus, although this may not be a global problem, it is, at least, a problem in developing countries. In addition, both Association for Computing Machinery (ACM) / Institute of Electrical and Electronics Engineers (IEEE) Curricula [18] and Brazilian Computer Society (SBC) Reference Curricula [22] fail to address specific aspects of Statistical Software Process. This difficulty is particularly accentuated when dealing with the activities of an organization that have a high maturity level in their processes.

D. *Statement of the Position*

The Brazilian software industry has widely adopted the use of quality models, such as CMMI for Development (CMMI-DEV) [12] and the Brazilian Reference Model for Software Process Improvement (MR-MPS-SW) [16], which normally takes place through the Process Improvement Software (SPI) programs implemented by consultancy firms.

The consultants adopt several training strategies for the transfer of the knowledge that is needed to the specific practices or expected results included in the process area, specifically in Statistical Process Control. The purpose of this is to develop the skills and competencies needed in the technical team of the organization.

The consultants noticed that so much time and resources were spent on training programs for effective teamwork, that many of these professionals do not have adequate knowledge in areas of Software Engineering [17].

On the basis of these observations and our professional experience as SPI consultants and SE lecturers, we believe that if the Software Engineering discipline adopted training approaches to Statistical Process Control, the students would be better prepared for the high maturity software industry and have more appropriate skills than those provided by the current teaching approaches.

II. Problem Statement and Related Works

The research problems of this PhD thesis can be categorized into two groups, which are as follows:

- The need to analyze the SPC practices used in the software industry, i.e. to determine which activities are really relevant to the training of a software engineering professional,
- The need to analyze the reference curricula and teaching approaches used by teachers in the area, to identify which SPC activities are covered.

A. *The Background of Software Engineering Teaching*

According to the ACM / IEEE [18], SE is a discipline that is concerned with the application of theory, knowledge and practice to the effective and efficient development of software systems that meet user requirements. The SE professionals must have the ability to understand software development as a process and to ensure deadlines are met, costs are reduced, and the quality of the product is maintained [19].

A survey was conducted by Wangenheim and Silva [14] to gauge the opinion of professionals in the Software Engineering area about the relevance of the topics covered in the Computer Science courses. As a result, it was found that some SE topics are neglected. In certain topics, there was clearly a complete lack of attention paid by the lecturers and students. For example, there was limitied interest in "Software Configuration Management", which in practice is considered to be an essential basis not only for software engineers, but also for any professional software [14].

On the other hand, despite the importance of this knowledge with regard to the activities of SE, in [20], it was found that professionals learn more about these activities during their work than from their university courses / education. This may be due to the simple question of the study schedule. Assuming that out of a total of at least 280 hours for a Computer Science course [21], about 36 hours are allocated to SE, this does not correspond to the general recognition of the importance of these subject-areas and thus not enough time can be spent on areas of real importance.

There are studies in the literature on project-based learning within computer courses as a means of learning soft skills and complex technical competencies. A teaching approach has been put forward as a means of integrating contextualized project experiences with the basic concepts of Software Engineering. This approach, called the Software Enterprise, tends to represent the most common system that is employed to teach these skills and competencies during an undergraduate course and is a software development practice in SE disciplines. This approach makes it more possible to be aware of the fruits of one's labor than when working within student teams as they attempt to "put it all together" and produce a real software product [22].

Gary *et al.* [22] propose a pedagogical model for the teaching of SE in undergraduate courses in computing. This involves the students attending lectures and practising the learned concepts in lab sessions performed in each week of the course. This proposal combines traditional classroom activities with Problem-Based Learning (PBL). In this approach, the professor plays the role of a coach and the "veteran" students perform the role of a mentor. We believe that Gary's pedagogical model [22] provides the main supporting evidence for this research.

B. Problems Area

SE professionals working in the industry have expressed dissatisfaction with the level of preparedness of recently graduated students entering the job market [23][24]. Software companies find they have to complement the knowledge of recent graduates with training and have to provide technical and non-technical skills related to the software development process [25].

According to Lethbridge *et al.* [23], this failing in the training of graduates in the SE area is the result of an inadequate education. This finding is corroborated by the research carried out by Sargent [26], which reveals that: (i) only 40% of Information Technology (IT) professionals in the United States have training in this area, (ii) 40% of those are aware of the main fields of SE, such as requirements, architecture, testing, human factors, and project management.

Although we did not find statistical data with regard to SPC, we believe that the reality of SE professionals in this specific area is no different, from the situation observed by the authors of this paper on numerous consulting assignments involving the implementation of CMMI high levels.

C. Limitations of Related Works

Studies such as [22][25][27] propose teaching approaches to software engineering. However, these approaches restrict the scope of the evaluation to the content of the course or the process and the resulting product of carrying out a practical discipline of Software Engineering. This means that these approaches do not adequately prepare students for working in organizations of software development.

In [25], a game is designed that simulates real-world environments in the software industry to support the learning of SE. Although the game really succeeds in empowering students, it restricts this learning to cover only certain curricular areas. The approach of [25] does not properly explore the topics of Software Engineering, and thus fails to cover the area of statistical process control. By adopting an overly complex approach, it misses the point of the game which is the teaching and learning process.

A multidisciplinary approach is proposed in [27], which offers a set of guidelines that can be applied in the teaching of many disciplines of Computer Science. However, this approach is of limited value because its only concern is with the application and teaching of curriculum topics of Computer courses. It does not bother to find out what are the real professional skills that students must acquire to be able to perform their tasks efficiently in a real software project.

We also evaluated the [28][29][30][31] courses with regard to their instructional strategies for teaching the SE topics. As a result, we were able to observe the effects of combining traditional lectures with indirect instruction through academic projects. We also found evidence of the use of other instruments that could be used for experimental learning by means of simulations and interactive instruction by peer group learning. However, the focus of all these studies is on their approaches to teaching Software Process Modeling (SPM), without offering proven instrumental alternatives that can be used in SPC teaching.

Finally, Gary *et al.* [22] propose a pedagogical model for SE teaching in undergraduate courses in computing.

III. Questions, Hypotheses and Discussion

The main goal of our research is to propose a teaching approach to Statistical Process Control in computer courses, and this approach is based on quality standards and the recognized market practices.

Although we did not find many references, apart from [8] that support our innitiative, it is based on our field observations as SPI consultants and lecturers on SE, (as described in section I.D), and we strongly believe that a better approach to training SPC will improve the preparation of students and enable them to work in high maturity software companies.

To this end, the following research questions (RQ) should be addressed:

- **RQ1.** *What are the Statistical Process Control practices that are most widely used by the software industry?*
- **RQ2.** *What are the Statistical Process Control topics covered in the curriculum guidelines of computer courses?*
- **RQ3.** *What are the Statistical Process Control topics covered in the curricula of computer courses?*
- **RQ4.** *What are the Statistical Process Control topics that are effectively learned by computer students?*
- **RQ5.** *What are the Statistical Process Control skills required by the software industry and which of them were acquired in the computer courses?*

These research questions were defined in an attempt to refute the following null hypothesis:

- **H0.** *The current approach to teaching Statistical Process Control meets needs of the the software industry.*

If the null hypothesis is refuted, we intend to test our alternative hypothesis:

- **H1.** *The current approach adopted to teach Statistical Process Control does not meet the needs of the software industry owing to the lack of an alignment between the Software Engineering curriculum and the real needs of industry.*

IV. Research Method and Progress

The research methods employed to answer the research questions and to test the hypothesis will be outlined in this section.

A. Identifying SPC Practices Relevant to the Software Industry

To answer our RQ1 and help RQ5, there will be a systematic review with the aim of determining which SPC practices used by the software industry, can be regarded as following these guidelines [40][41]. This will allow us to create a catalog based on the main practices selected from this review. This catalog will form a part of the analysis that will either support or refute hypothesis H0, by providing the necessary information about the real needs of the software industry. We are currently working on this systematic review.

B. Identifying SPC Practices Included in Computer Courses

To answer RQ2, we will conduct a literature review of the the curriculum guidelines from ACM / IEEE [18] and SBC [21] with the aim of establishing which Software Process topics are covered by them. The results of this review will either support or refute hypothesis H0, by giving us evidence that the process activities suggested in the curriculum guidelines meet the requirements of the software industry.

To answer RQ3, a survey will be conducted with the lecturers of undergraduate Computer courses. The purpose of this survey is to analyze which SPC activities found in the literature review are included in the SE syllabus. These results may validate the H0 hypothesis.

With regard to RQ4, another survey will be conducted with students that completed their Software Engineering courses. This survey aims to assess whether the students are learning SPC activities, and if these are covered in SE syllabus. The results might validate H0 too, if they provide evidence that the problem may be in the teaching approach adopted in the classrooms.

Both surveys will be applied to undergraduate Computer Science courses in both public and private universities in Brazil and will follow the guidelines of Kitchenham and Pfleeger [42].

C. Defining an Approach to SPC Teaching in Computer Courses

After the five research questions had been answered, they yielded the following results:

- The catalog of SPC practices used by the software industry,
- The recommendations for the guidelines of the SPC curriculum,
- The existing teaching approaches to SPC in computer courses,
- Which topics are considered important by industry.

These results will guide the development of our SPC teaching approach. The approach will adopt Problem Based Learning as a teaching method [25]. The application of PBL in engineering education is increasing [32], and has been recognized as one of the most effective ways for students to become active participants in design learning [33]. PBL is combined with lectures, and focuses on the application and integration of knowledge that has been acquired previously [34].

On the basis of the results obtained in [19], it is clear that the students are more interested in carrying out practical activities, such as development projects in laboratories that simulate situations close to those that will be found in the market. It is believed that this is due to the fact that software engineering has many topics (83 in total), which ultimately make it less attractive to students who do not have an affinity with the area. The practical approach allows these students to grasp the concepts more easily from their application.

D. Performing Case Studies to Evaluate the Teaching Approach

Our proposal of a teaching approach can be evaluated and validated by conducting a controlled experiment in an area of software engineering in a Computer Science undergraduate course. Initially, we plan to carry out this experiment in two computer science classes in two Brazilian public universities.

This experiment will follow the guidelines proposed by Wohlin [37].

V. Conclusion and Future Works

This paper has shown the importance of statistical process control in software development, focusing on a PhD research project that aims to study on drawing up the curriculum for Statistical Process Control within the Computer Science course. This initiative is to provide development organizations software with computer science professionals who are fully able to perform this task. Thus, this paper showed the discussions about the gap in this area, the problems of statistic process control in computer science, some related works, the research questions and hypotheses, and the method used to conduct this research.

The aim of this PhD research study is to identify practices of Statistical Process Control and their relevance to the current software industry, by taking note of possible problems in the teaching approach to software engineering, in particular in SPC. This can be achieved through the implementation of the curriculum guidelines and a new educational approach that ensures that undergraduate students of computer courses will be given a background training in SPC, as required by the market.

The current educational scene shows that certain topics are regarded as less important by teachers and thus students have a low learning levelin these areas. It turns out that these topics impose a heavy workload on software engineering, while some topics considered to be more important, have a low learning priority. Perhaps this is due to the fact that there is not enough time to teach all these units effectively.

Finally, we intend to allow free access to the results that have been obtained in this research, so that the experiments and results obtained can be replicated. This should ensure that more gaps in our knowledge are filled and problems solved and clarified, since the teaching of Software Engineering is of the utmost importance in computer courses [36].

ACKNOWLEDGMENT

The authors would like to thank the Dean of Research and Postgraduate Studies at the Federal University of Pará (PROPESP/UFPA) by the Qualified Publication Support Program (PAPQ) for the financial support.

REFERENCES

[1] M. A. Lantzy, "Application of Statistical Process Control to the Software Process", In: Proceedings of the 9th Washington Ada Symposium on Empowering Software Users and Developers, ACM Press, pp. 113-123, 1992.

[2] W. Shewhart, "Economic Quality Control of Manufactured Product", Bell System Technical Journal, vol. 9, pp. 364-389, 1930.

[3] D. C. Montgomery, "Introduction to Statistical Quality Control". John Wiley & Sons, 2007.

[4] M. A. Alhassan and D. N. Jawawi, "Sequential Strategy for Software Process Measurement that Uses Statistical Process Control", in: 8th Malaysian Software Engineering Conference (MySEC), pp. 37-42, 2014.

[5] F. García, M. Serrano, J. Cruz-Lemos, F. Ruiz, and M. Piattini, "Managing Software Process Measurement: A Metamodel-Based Approach", Information Sciences, v. 177, n. 12, pp. 2570-2586, 2007.

[6] N. Boffoli, G. Bruno, D. Caiavano, and G. Mastelloni, "Statistical Process Control for Software: a Systematic Approach", Proceedings of the Ninth European Conference on Software Maintenance and Reengineering, pp. 288-293, 2008.

[7] A. Tarhan and O. Demirors, "Assessment of Software Process and Metrics to Support Quantitative Understanding", Lecture Notes in Computer Science, v. 4895, pp. 102-113, 2008.

[8] C. Fernández-Corrales, M. Jenkins, and J. Villegas, "Application of Statistical Process Control to Software Defect Metrics: an Industry Experience Report", in: 2013 ACM/IEEE International Symposium on Empirical Software Engineering and Measurement, pp. 323-331, 2013.

[9] M. Soares, "An experience in teaching software engineering oriented practical work", I Workshop on Computer Education, Vitória / Rio das Ostras, Brazil, 2004.

[10] J. Castro, I. Gimenes, and J. Maldonado, "A proposal for pedagogical plan for the Software Engineering discipline", II quality course of undergraduate of Computing and Informatics area, Curitiba, Brazil, pp. 251-270, 2000.

[11] O. Hazzan and Y. Dubinsky, "Teaching a software development methodology: The case of Extreme Programming", 16th Conference on Software Engineering Education and Training, Madrid, Spain, pp. 176-184, 2003.

[12] Software Engineering Institute, "CMMI® for Development, Version 1.3, Improving processes for developing better products and services", No.CMU/SEI-2010-TR-033. Carnegie Mellon University, Pittsburgh, PA, 2010.

[13] M. P. Barcellos, R. A. Falbo, and A. R. Rocha, "Establishing a Well-Founded Conceptualization about Software Measurement and High Maturity Levels", in: 2010 7th International Conference on the Quality of Information and Communication Technology, pp. 467-472, 2010.

[14] C. Wangenheim and D. Silva, "What software engineering knowledge is important for the professional software", in Proceedings of II Forum on Education in Software Engineering, Fortaleza, Brazil, 2009.

[15] ABES, "Brazilian software market: scenario and trends", in Brazilian Software Market and Services 2014, 1st ed. São Paulo, Brazil: Brazilian Association of Software Companies, 2014.

[16] Association for Promotion of Brazilian Software Excellence, "SPI Reference Model for Software, version 2012", SOFTEX, General Guide SPI for Software, Dec. 2012.

[17] G. Leal, P. Stadzisz, C. Almeida, M. Perez, S. Reinehr, A. Malucelli, "Empirical study about the evaluation of the implantation of MPS.Br in enterprises of Paraná", In Proceedings of XXXVIII Conferencia Latinoamericana en Informatica, pp. 1-9, 2012.

[18] ACM/IEEE. Computer science curricula 2013. Curriculum guidelines for undergraduate degree programs in Computer Science. December 20, 2013.

[19] C. S. Portela, A. M. L. Vasconcelos, and S. R. B. Oliveira, "How to Develop Competencies and Abilities Professional in Software Engineering in Undergraduate Students?", in Int'l Conf. Frontiers in Education: CS and CE - FECS'15, pp. 91-94, 2015.

[20] T. LethBridge, "What knowledge is important to a software professional?", Journal Computer, 33(5), IEEE Computer Society Press, Los Alamitos, CA, USA, pp 44-50, 2000.

[21] SBC. Reference curriculum for undergraduate courses in Bachelor in Computer Science and Computer Engineering, 2005.

[22] K. Gary, T. Lindquist, S. Bansal, and A. Ghazarian, "A Project Spine for Software Engineering Curricular Design", In Proceedings of 26th Conference on Software Engineering Education and Training (CSEET), pp. 299-303, 2013.

[23] T. Lethbridge, J. Diaz-Herrera, R. LeBlanc, and J. Thompson, "Improving software practice through education: Challenges and future trends", Conference Future of Software Engineering, Minneapolis, MN, pp.12-28, 2007.

[24] T. B. Hilburn, and M. Towhidnejad, "A case for software engineering", 20h Conference on Software Engineering Education and Training, Dublin, Ireland, pp. 107-114, 2007.

[25] B. Bessa, M. Cunha, and F. Furtado, "ENGSOFT: Simulation tool for real environments to support the Problem Based Learning (PBL) in teaching Software Engineering", XX Workshop on Computer Education, Curitiba, Brazil, 2012.

[26] J. Sargent, "An overview of past and projected employment changes in the professional IT occupations", Computing Research News, vol. 16, no. 3, pp. 1-21, 2004.

[27] J. Braga, "Guidelines for the interdisciplinary teaching of Software Engineering", in Proceedings of II Forum on Education in Software Engineering, Fortaleza, Brazil, 2009.

[28] M. L. Jaccheri and P. Lago, "Applying Software Process Modeling and Improvement in Academic Setting", Proceedings of the 10th Conference on Software Engineering Education & Training, Virginia Beach, Virginia, IEEE Computer Society Press, pp 13-27, 1997.

[29] D. Groth and E. Robertson, "It's All About Process: Project-Oriented Teaching of Software Engineering", in Proceedings of the Fourteenth Conference on Software Engineering Education and Training. Charlotte, USA, pp 7-17, 2001.

[30] J. Hawker, "A Software Process Engineering Course", Proceedings of the 2009 American Society for Engineering Education Annual Conference. Austin, TX, 2009.

[31] C. Wangenheim and J. Hauck, "Teaching Software Process Improvement and Assessment", Proceedings of 17th European Systems & Software Process (EuroSPI'2010). Grenoble, France, 2010.

[32] H. Hadim and S. Esche, "Enhancing the engineering curriculum through project-based learning", Proceedings of 32nd Frontiers in Education Conference. Boston, USA, Section F3F, pp 1-6, 2002.

[33] C. Dym, A. Agogino, O. Eris, D. Frey, and L. Leifer, "Engineering Design Thinking", Teaching, and Learning. Journal of Engineering Education, 94(1), pp 103–120, 2005.

[34] J. Mills and D. Treagust, "Engineering education: is problem-based or project-based learning the answer?", Australasian Journal of Engineering Education, pp. 2-16, 2004.

[35] C. Wohlin et al., "Experimentation in software engineering: an introduction", in Kluwer Academic Publishers, Norwell, MA, 2000.

[36] IEEE Computer Society, Guide to the Software Engineering Body of Knowledge – SWEBOK, Version 3.0, 2014, Available: www.swebok.org, retrivied: 06/2016.

[37] K. Garg andV Varma. "Software Engineering Education in India: Issues and Challenges", Proceedings of 21st Conference on Software Engineering Education and Training, Charleston, pp., 110-117, 2008.

[38] C. O'Leary, D. Lawless, D. Gordon, L. Haifeng, and K. Bechkoum, "Developing a Software Engineering Curriculum for the Emerging Software Industry in China", 19th Conference on Software Engineering Education & Training(CSEET'06), pp. 115-122, 2006.

[39] G. Taran and M. Rosso-Llopart, "Software Engineering Education in Russia: A Comparative Study of People, Process and Technology: a Four Year Perspective", 20th Conference on Software Engineering Education & Training (CSEET'07), 2007.

[40] B. Kitchenham, Guidelines for performing Systematic Literature Reviews in Software Engineering, Technical Report EBSE - 2007-01, Departament of Computer Science Keele University, Keele, pp. 19-28, 2007.

[41] T. Dyba, T. Dingsoyr, and G. Hanssen, "Applying Systematic Reviews to Diverse Study Types: An Experience Report", First International Sysmposion on Empirical Software Engineering and Measurement, pp. 225-234, 2007.

[42] B. Kitchenham and S. Pfleeger, Personal Opinion Surveys, in Guide to Advanced Empirical Software Engineering, Springer, 2008.

Towards Applying Normalized Systems Theory to Create Evolvable Enterprise Resource Planning Software

A Case Study

Ornchanok Chongsombut, Jan Verelst, Peter De Bruyn, Herwig Mannaert and Philip Huysmans
Department of Management Information Systems
University of Antwerp
Antwerp, Belgium
e-mail: {ornchanok.chongsombut, jan.verelst, perter.debruyn, herwig.mannaert, philip.huysmans} @uantwerp.be

Abstract— **Evolvability is widely considered to be an important concern for the design and development of software architectures, particularly in the area of information systems (IS). Current IS continue to struggle to provide evolvability, especially Enterprise Resource Planning (ERP) software. Complexity in ERP packages leads to a limit on changeable software. Normalized Systems (NS) theory has been proposed with the purpose of incorporate evolvability of IS. In this paper, an existing ERP package was subjected to reverse engineering in order to analyze and explore in terms of combinatorial effects (CEs), of which NS theory prescribes that they are harmful for evolvability. The results indicate that it is possible to redesign a data model for an existing ERP, adhering to NS theory. We also identified some issues and limitations with the current version of the ERP package.**

Keywords- Normalized Systems theory; evolvability; software architecture.

I. INTRODUCTION

IS have played an increasingly visible role over the past few years in improving the competitiveness of businesses. Organizations realize that ERP software is a crucial tool for organizational perfection because it enables flawless transactions and production runs, and can improve business performances and profitability through implementation of Business Intelligence [1][2]. An ERP system is a departmental integration software system that allows a company to have a unified enterprise view of the business and to manage enterprise data in one database [2][3]. ERP systems offer significant benefits to an enterprise through improving strategic planning and operational efficiency.

Notwithstanding the significant benefits, however, ERP systems have been criticized, since they are prone to extreme complexities and are often difficult to implement [4]. This complexity is mostly due to the fact that the system has to integrate all functions and data of a company. This contributes to development and maintenance costs, being important barriers to realize the potential gains which can be achieved through IS. Therefore, IS should exhibit a certain amount of simplicity to result in the anticipated gains.

Moreover, IS should be evolvable as well. The business environment is dramatically changing and the ability to easily change software therefore becomes crucial [7]. In this context, we consider software evolvability as the capability of software to be easily changed (i.e., with a reasonable effort). Current IS continue to struggle to provide such evolvability, especially ERP software. The significant complexity in these packages leads to a serious limit being placed on their ability to change.

In particular, evolvability can be considered as a criterion to evaluate and analyze the quality and usefulness of ERP packages for several reasons. First, the main objective of ERP is to support various organizations to achieve their business goals. Therefore, ERP should be adaptable to the specificities of organizations, for example, by means of configuration. Second, as stated before, business environments dramatically change. The evolvability of ERP systems becomes an increasingly crucial condition to enable changes for an enterprise as a whole and their increasing complexity.

The design of IS which are evolvable has been addressed in NS theory. For this purpose, the theory uses the stability concept (i.e., requiring that a bounded set of functional changes to the system should have a bounded impact within the system). The theory argues that CEs are the main obstruction to software evolvability. A CE occurs when the size of the impact of a change depends on the size of the information system [6]. In other words, NS states that the evolvability and flexibility is largely determined by (the absence of) CEs [8] and software without the CEs lead to evolvable software [5]. The theory proposes a set of theorems eliminating CEs.

The aim of this research is to identify CEs within existing ERP packages and to rebuild them based on NS theory. To this end, existing ERP packages are subjected to reverse engineering in order to explore the existence of CEs and their potential for other improvements. We describe how part of the existing ERP package is designed and developed based on the NS theory. Therefore, this paper tackles the evolvability of existing ERP software by designing a set of ERP guidelines to design and to develop existing ERP software according to the aforementioned theory. The main research question addressed by this paper is:

How to improve the existing ERP package based on NS theory?

Consequently, the proposed research mainly deals with the modularization of the data model of existing ERP packages. The modularity of an information system is important for the degree to which it exhibits evolvability [11]. The design science research approach, focusing on the creation and evaluation of IT artifacts and their surrounding organizational preconditions in order to solve organizational problems [7], is chosen as the methodology for the research.

This paper is structured as follows. Section II describes the essence of NS theory. Section III provides the design method of the paper. Afterwards, a partial analysis of the ERP application's data models is discussed in Section IV. Finally, Section V presents some final conclusions, limitations and suggestions for future research.

II. NORMALIZED SYSTEMS THEORY

NS theory is developed from the concept of stability which implies that a bounded set of input changes (i.e., changes in requirements) should result in bounded amount of output changes or impacts to the software (i.e., changes in software). In other words, stability demands that the impact of changes should only depend on the nature of the change itself. The size of the impact of changes should therefore not be related to the size of the system. If the size of the impact of a change is related to the overall size of the system, this is called a CE [9].

A CE is one of the biggest barriers to creating evolvable software according to NS. The theory states that the evolvability of software should be a characteristic embedded at the level of the software architecture. This implies that the software architecture should not only allow the realization of current requirements but also facilitate the incorporation of future ones. NS theory assumes an unlimited software evolution (i.e., ever growing software throughout time). This means that even the smallest change of which the impact is dependent on the size of the system (i.e., CE) will become troublesome over time and should therefore be removed. In fact, if the CEs occur mainly in software architectures, the software will become more difficult to cope with and the software's evolvability tents to increase.

A set of four theorems and five expandable elements has been suggested by NS theory to prevent CEs and to develop evolvable software.

The four theorems are the following [10][11][12][13]:

- Separation of Concerns: each change driver (concern) should be separated from other change drivers (concerns) in distinct modules;
- Data Version Transparency: the modification (insert, update, delete) of data entities should not impact other entities.
- Action Version Transparency: the modification (insert, update, delete) of data entities should not impact other entities.
- Separation of States: each step in a workflow should be separated from other steps in time by keeping state after every action or step.

Consequently, the systematic application of the theorems results in a very fine-grained modular structure in which each change driver has to become separated. Building software which systematically adheres to the NS theorems should result in software which is highly evolvable software. Moreover, the theory emphasizing the CEs identification will help to build IS that contain the smallest in amount of the CEs.

Furthermore, the NS theory provided evidence of the number of the CEs are the cause of a complex software and difficultness of software maintenance [10]. The NS theory is a modular structure that is free from the CEs. The CEs should not be present at compile time, deployment time, and run time in modular structures in order to constitute an achievement in this [10].

Software architectures without the CEs can be constructed as a set of highly structured instantiations and loosely coupled design patterns that are called elements [10]. For this reason, five elements have been proposed to facilitate the achievement of these aims. There are the NS elements:

- a data element, representing an encapsulated data entity with its set and get methods to access information in a version transparency way [14]. Then cross-cutting concerns should be added to the element in separate constructs;
- an action element, executing a core action or algorithm.
- a workflow element for the execution of the sequence of action elements;
- a trigger element, controlling the states and checking (time or status based) whether an action element has to be triggered;
- a connector element, providing the possibility for external systems to interact with the NS system without calling the elements in a stateless way.

III. APPLYING DESIGN SCIENCE RESEARCH

A. *The Research Design*

The conceptual framework of this research adheres to the IS research framework [15] shown in Fig. 1. The technology problem has been defined in the problem space: the requirement for ERP systems to exhibit evolvability. The research addresses technology which needs to achieve a higher degree of evolvability. The concepts of modularity and stability from NS theory will be applied as the foundation of the research. The NS theory will be used to create artifacts at the software level. The theory will also be used to develop a set of relevant measures or validation criteria in order to ensure that the proposed artifacts can be evaluated by appropriate evaluations. This should further support the rigor within the considered IS research. Finally, as can be seem in the middle of the conceptual framework, we will explore and build an artifact which will be presented in the method term to construct increasingly evolvable in ERP systems. Also, we will create a working system (instantiation) and explore a suitable method to evaluate the artifact.

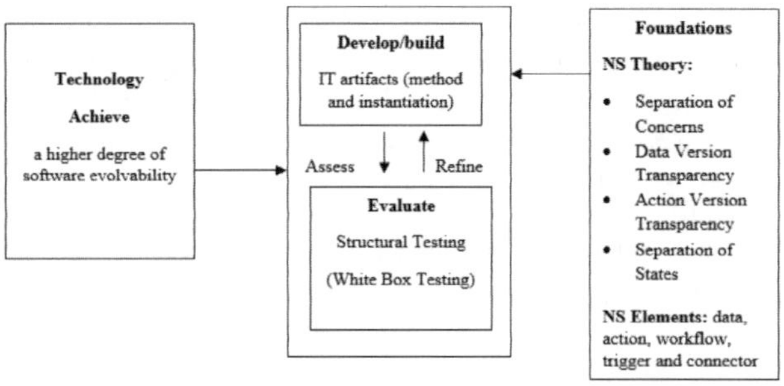

Figure 1. The research framework

Table I illustrates the appropriate evaluation methods which assess the utility, quality, and reliability of our designed artifact. Therefore, the evaluation activity is a crucial process of the research process [15]. Five evaluation methods have been proposed by [15]. In this research, we will combine several types of evaluation to ensure that our designed artifact is rigorously demonstrated via suitable evaluation methods:

TABLE I. THE RESEARCH DESIGN EVALUATION METHOD

The research design evaluation methods	Description	Application
testing evaluation	Executing coverage testing of some metric in the artifact implementation: Structural (White Box) Testing	Number of Change Impacts

B. Desing Science Research in the Research

The behavioral sciences and design science are two paradigms that characterize much of the research in the IS discipline, having a different purpose. Whereas behavioral science seeks to develop and verify theories that explain or predict human or organizational behavior, design science seeks to extend the human boundaries and organizational capabilities by creating new and innovative artifacts [15]. In the design science paradigm, artifacts are studied and created in order to solve a practical problem of general interest [15][16]. A practical problem is a gap between the current situation and a desirable situation that is observed in practice [16]. Therefore, this research was conducted using the design science methodology in order to address the research question.

Design science research includes six main activities according to [17] identify problem and motivation, define objectives of a solution, design and development artifact, demonstration, evaluation, and communication. The methodology allows the researcher to do the research in multiple research iterations to ensure and to improve the qualities of the artifact. The research design was aligned with this iterative process to end up with the research findings.

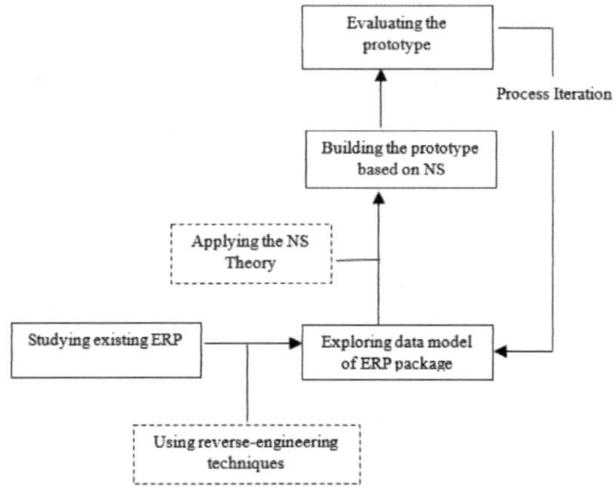

Figure 2. Design Science Process Model

An ERP application is a large and complicated system which often contains customized functions to fit the requirements of organizations. This is why such systems should be designed for evolvability so that maintenance costs remain under control. The paper aims to explore this issue. The processes of the research are demonstrated in Fig. 2. First, a research problem has been sketched by studying the architecture of an existing open source ERP package. Then we have defined a specific objective for the research which is to achieve a higher degree of ERP evolvability. We have solved the problem by using the reverse-engineering technique and applying it to an open source EPR system apart to see how it works. Second, CEs have been identified in the data model of the open source ERP package, which is an output of the reverse-engineering process. Third, we have redesigned the data model and built a prototype using the NS theory to improve the evolvability of the ERP software. The final stage of the design science process is white-box testing was used to evaluate the CEs of the redesigned data model and prototype that measure the number of change impacts.

IV. ANALYZING A PARTIAL OPEN SOURCE ERP MODULE: A SALES MODULE

In this section, we discuss some implications of using NS theory for developing evolvable ERPs in practice. An open source ERP, Odoo, was analyzed. This paper was due to several reasons. First, being open source, we have access to the source code and can analyze the architecture of the software in depth. Second, within the open source ERP market, Odoo is a very popular package. Furthermore, Odoo is an integrated suite of applications that includes modules for project management, billing, accounting, inventory management, manufacturing, and purchasing. However, we only focus on a partial module of the ERP package in this paper.

Fig. 3 illustrates a part of the data model of the sales module of the chosen ERP package which comprises three tables:

- res_partner for storing details of customer data
- sale_order for storing sales orders of customers
- sale_order_line for storing details of sales orders

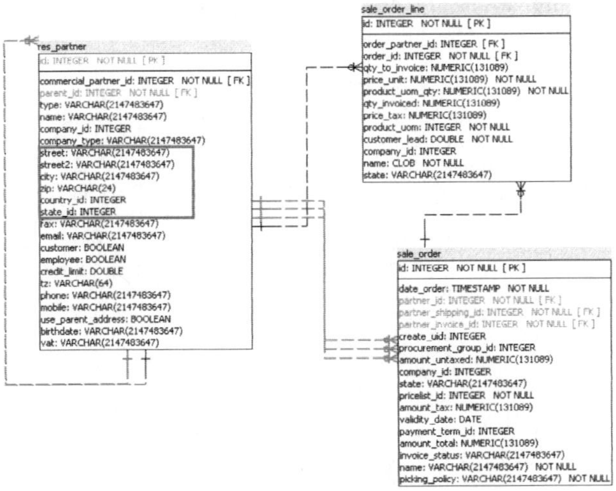

Figure 3. A partial data model of Sale module

Next, we analyzed the entity relationships of the data model. The res_partner table has a recursive relationship by using the parant_id field as a foreign key (FK). The parant_id filed save data to show partners is belonging to which a partner. For instance, Fig. 4 describes that id 46 is a parent of data of id 47, 48, 46. What's more, all of them are the same person.

The sales order table comprises the following foreign keys: partner_id, partner_shipping_id and partner_inovoic_id to join with the res_partner table as presented in Fig. 3. From sales order, employees can know where they have to send invoices and products to their customers.

id	name	parent_id	street	street2	city	zip	state_id	country_id	type
49		46	23 Korning		Antwerp	2000	61	21	contact
48		46	999 Oudan		Antwerp	2000	61	21	delivery
47		46	55 Prinesee		Antwerp	2000	61	21	invoice
46	Ornchanok		23 Korning		Antwerp	2000	61	21	contact

Figure 4. The example of res_partner data

A. *Implementation of the Evolvable ERP Application with regard to NS Fundamentals*

Previously, we described the existing ERP data model from our case study. In this model, only one address is used and it is incorporated in the res_partner table. However, the model can be redesigned in other ways as well. For instance, the sales order data might not want to use only invoice address and shipping address but also other address types. For instance, the organization might want to use different addresses for invoicing and shipment. Moreover, customers might want the company to send sales invoices to more than one address. Initially, we aim to examine how the high evolvable ERP software is designed. Then we have proposed on alternative design explanation for evolvable ERP software development.

Normally, practical requirement of Sale module should be able to serve multiple customer addresses. We developed new approach to meeting the requirements of the evolvability of ERP software.

In order to attain the objective, the following data elements are defined. Address data have been separated from partner data in order to support the requirement. According to the previous model, the tables have been split up into six tables as illustrated in Fig. 5.

- Partner for storing only general data of customers such as name, birthday, status of partner (active, inactive), etc.
- Address_type for storing types of address. Hence, the changing requirement for address type can be supported.
- Address for saving all addresses' details of partners.
- Sale_order_address_line to save details of customers' sale order addresses.
- Sale_order to represent sale order data of customers.
- Sale_order_line to keep sale order details.

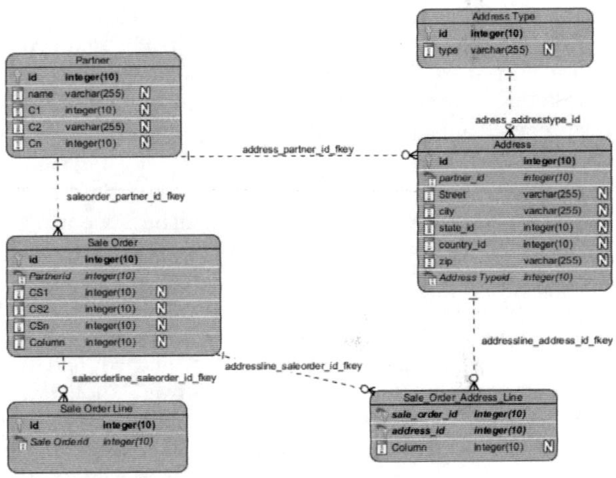

Figure 5. A redesinged data model of Sale module

In this model, address fields are divided into two tables: address and address type. Furthermore, the sale_order_address_line table is created to support the idea about multiple address in sales order data. Furthermore, the foreign keys partner_shipping_id and partner_invocie_id, in the sale_order table were removed.

Consequently, it was made possible to incorporate the new requirement of having different addresses. For example, if organizations can have other types of addresses by adding a new address type into the address_type table. When they want to record more types of customer address in sale order, they can only add more address data details into sale_order_address_line.

In NS theory, the objective of the theory is to design software in an evolvable way. In case a new version of a data model is designed, a new skeleton of the application can be generated by applying the expanders on the defined model [13].

In this study, a prototype of the new designed data model has been created using these NS expanders. Accordingly, the prototype has been developed without the CEs to increase evolvability of software.

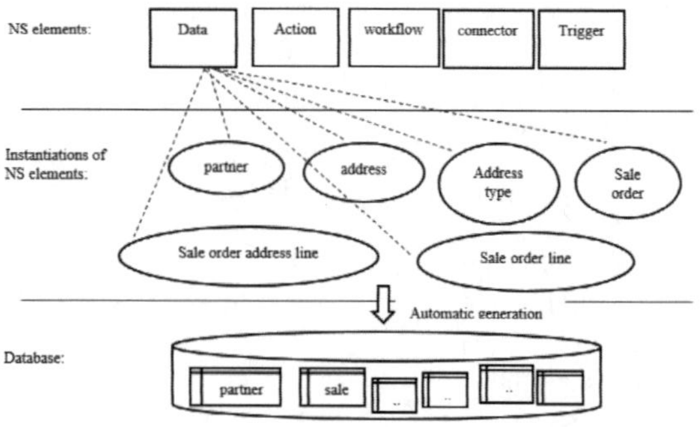

Figure 6. The prototype structure based on NS elements

According to NS theory, an evolvable application could be implemented by using a set of five elements which are already free of many CEs. For the case study that we describe, six data element instances have been generated as illustrated in Fig. 6. For each of these data elements, a set of cross-cutting concerns (persistency, security, graphical user interface, etc.) are automatically generated as well.

V. DISCUSSION

In this paper, we discussed how an existing open source ERP package can be analyzed based on NS theory. The paper raises some significant points. First, designing data models and developing a software application should be done in a modular way to enable the reusability of that software. For example, by using address and address type entities in a sales module. Second, the software should have highly cohesive modules so that the impact of a user requirement change on the actual application, remains limited. In the case, we separated the address data of a partner into two parts: address and address type entities. This represents an attempt to decrease the amount of effect of changes and increase software maintainability. Lastly, this study confirms that NS software will have less ripple effects in its system. For example, adding an address type into the prototype. To record additional address data, a user should now only add the data of the new address type. The change does not affect the partner, sale order and address elements.

This paper made a considerable contribution towards presenting the advantages of developing and maintaining software as stated by NS theory. These advantages can normally be commonly observed in amount of software development life cycle time. The new designed data model and prototype, which are designed using the NS theory, have the smaller number of change impacts. Furthermore, the software prototype can be created in a few days. Additionally, this paper contributes to the redesigning approach of building evolvable ERP software.

The limitations of our exploratory study need to be acknowledged. First, we only analyzed a partial data model of one ERP package. We could not perform reverse-engineering and explore commercial ERP software packages such as SAP, Oracle, etc. As part of future research, analyzing and rebuilding all modules of an existing ERP software package based on NS theory can be considered.

REFERENCES

[1] L. Shaul and D. Tauber, "Critical success factors in enterprise resource planning systems: Review of the last decade," ACM Comput. Surv., 45(4): pp. 1-39, 2013.

[2] K. K. Hong, and Y. G. Kim, "The critical success factors for ERP implementation: an organizational fit perspective. Information & Management," 40(1): pp. 25-40, 2002.

[3] E. J. Umble, R. R. Haft, and M. M. Umble, "Enterprise resource planning: Implementation procedures and critical success factors," European Journal of Operational Research, 146(2): pp. 241-257, 2003.

[4] Y. Xue, H. Liang, W. R. Boulton, and C. A. Snyder, "ERP implementation failures in China: Case studies with implications for ERP vendors," International Journal of Production Economics, 97(3): pp. 279-295, 2005.

[5] G. Oorts, K. Ahmadpour, H. Mannaert, J. Verelst, and A. Oost, "Easily Evolving Software Using Normalized System Theory A Case Study," The Ninth International Conference on Software Engineering Advances, pp. 322-327, 2014.

[6] K. Ven, D. V. Nuffel, P. Huysmans, D. Bellens, and H. Mannaert, "Experiences with the automatic discovery of violations to the normalized systems design theorems," International journal on advances in software, 4:1/2(2011): pp. 46-60, 2011.

[7] P. De Bruyn, "Generalizing Normalized Systems Theory: Towards a Foundational Theory for Enterprise Engineering," in Faculty of Applied Economics. 2014, University of Antwerp: University of Antwerp.

[8] J. Verelst, A. R. Silva, H. Mannaert, D. A. Ferreira, and P. Huysmans, "Identifying Combinatorial Effects in Requirements Engineering," in Advances in Enterprise Engineering VII: Third Enterprise Engineering Working Conference, EEWC 2013, Luxembourg, Proceedings, H.A. Proper, D. Aveiro, and K. Gaaloul, Editors. 2013, Springer Berlin Heidelberg: Berlin, Heidelberg. pp. 88-102, May 13-14, 2013.

[9] P. De Bruyn, P. Huysmans, G. Oorts, D. van Nuffel, H. Mannaert, J. Verelst, and A. Oost, "Incorporating design knowledge into the software development process using normalized systems theory," International journal on advances in software, 6(1-2): pp. 181-195, 2013.

[10] J. Verelst, H. Mannaert, and P. Huysmans, "IT isn't different after all: Implications of Normalized Systems for the Industrialization of Software Development," IEEE International Conference on Business Informatics, pp. 357-357, 2013.

[11] H. Mannaert, J. Verelst, and K. Ven, "Towards evolvable software architectures based on systems theoretic stability. Software: Practice and Experience," 42(1): pp. 89-116, 2012.

[12] D. V. Nuffel, "Towards Designing Modular and Evolvable Business Process," in Department of Applied Economics. 2011, University of Antwerp.

[13] G. Oorts, P Huysmans, P. De Bruyn, H. Mannaert, J. Verelst, and A. Oost, "Building Evolvable Software Using Normalized Systems Theory: A Case Study," 2014 47th Hawaii International Conference on System Sciences, pp. 4760-4769, 2014.

[14] K. D. Ven, D. V. Nuffel, P. Huysmans, D. Bellens, and H. Mannaert, "Experiences with the automatic discovery of violations to the normalized systems design theorems," International journal on advances in software, 4(1/2): pp. 46-60, 2011.

[15] Alan Hevner, "Design Research in Information System Theory and Pratice," 2010: Springer.

[16] Paul Johannesson "An Introduction to Design Science," 2014: Springer.

[17] K. Peffers, T. Tuunanen, M. Rothenberger, and S. Chatterjee, "A Design Science Research Methodology for Information Systems Research.," J. Manage. Inf. Syst., 24(3): pp. 45-77, 2007.

A Three-Level Versioning Model for Component-Based Software Architectures

Abderrahman Mokni*, Marianne Huchard†, Christelle Urtado* and Sylvain Vauttier*
*LGI2P, Ecole Nationale Supérieure des Mînes Alès, Nîmes - France
Email: {abderrahman.mokni, christelle.urtado, sylvain.vauttier}@mines-ales.fr
†LIRMM, CNRS and Université de Montpellier, Montpellier, France
Email: huchard@lirmm.fr

***Abstract*—Software versioning is intrinsic to software evolution. It keeps history of previous software states (versions) and traces all the changes that updates a software to its latest stable version. A lot of work has been dedicated to software versioning and many version control mechanisms are proposed to store and track software versions for different software artifacts (code, objects, models, etc.). This paper addresses in particular component-based software architecture versioning, considering three abstraction levels: specification, implementation and deployment. In previous work, we proposed an approach that generates evolution plans for such software architecture models. The generated plans deal with changes initiated on one of the three abstraction levels and propagate them to the other levels in order to keep architecture descriptions consistent and coherent. As an extension to these mechanisms, a versioning model is proposed in this paper to keep history of architecture definition versions. This versioning model soundly handles the co-evolution of the three abstraction levels by tracking both versions of each abstraction levels and versions of global architecture definitions.**

Keywords–architecture evolution; abstraction levels; versioning; component reuse.

I. Introduction

Versioning is central to software evolution management [1]. In order to ensure the continuity of a software product, it is necessary to keep track of its changes and previous versions after each evolution. Versioning is both essential for users and developers. For users, versioning helps to maintain their installed software up-to-date or at least warn them if their current software version becomes obsolete. For developers, versioning helps select / use the adequate versions of reusable software components, packages or libraries (considering, for instance, compatibility issues) and contributes to collaborative work by developing several versions in parallel or merging them [2].

Many version control mechanisms are currently proposed to store and track software versions for different software forms (code, models, objects, etc.) [3].

While software architectures have become central to software development [4], little work was dedicated to architectural versioning. Existing work on architectural versioning [5][6][7] proposes basic versioning mechanisms that do not take into account the whole software lifecycle. Evolving a software architecture should not only focus on tracking the different versions of software system as a whole. Indeed, the different steps of the software development process generates many artifacts (*e.g.*, documentation, implementation model, deployment models, etc.). It is valuable to keep separate version histories for each artifact and to build a global version history for the whole software from them. It fosters the reuse of artifacts in forward engineering processes (*e.g.*, the implementation of a given specification on different technical platforms or the deployment of a given implementation in different execution contexts). It also enables to trace every design decisions and their impacts (required co-evolution). For instance, when evolving a software architecture, the architect needs mechanisms to know the latest version of its specification and also all the related implementations that will be affected by this evolution.

In this work, we address such versioning issues by proposing a version model that considers the three main steps of component-based software lifecycle: specification, implementation and deployment. The remainder of this paper is outlined as follows: Section II presents the background of this work namely the Dedal three-level architectural model and its evolution management process [8]. Section III presents the contribution of this paper consisting in a three-level versioning model for software architectures and its different versioning strategies to support co-evolution on these three levels. Section IV discusses related work and finally Section V concludes the paper and presents future work directions.

II. Background and Motivation

This work addresses the versioning of component-based software architectures at three abstraction levels. First, we introduce the three-level architectural model Dedal and then we briefly explain how architecture evolution is managed in Dedal.

A. Dedal: the three-level architectural model

Reuse is central to Component-Based Software Development (CBSD) [9]. In CBSD, software is constructed by assembling pre-existing (developed) entities called components. Dedal [8] proposes a novel approach to foster the reuse of software components in CBSD and cover all the three main steps of software development: specification, implementation and deployment. The idea is to build a concrete software architecture (called configuration) from suitable software components stored in indexed repositories. Candidate components are selected according to an intended architecture (called architecture specification) that represents an abstract and ideal view of the software. The implemented architecture can then be instantiated (the instantiation is called architecture assembly) and deployed in multiple execution contexts.

A Dedal architecture model is then constituted of three descriptions that correspond to the three abstraction levels:

The architecture specification corresponds to the highest abstraction level. It is composed of component roles and their connections. Component roles define the required functionalities of the future software.

The architecture configuration corresponds to the second abstraction level. It is composed of concrete component classes, selected from repositories, that realize the identified component roles in the architecture specification.

The architecture assembly corresponds to the third and lowest abstraction level. It is composed of component instances that instantiate the component classes of the architecture configuration. An architecture assembly description represents a deployment model of the software (customized component instances fitting given execution contexts).

Fig. 1 illustrates the three architecture levels of Dedal and represents the running example of this paper. It consists of a Home Automation Software that controls the building's light during specific hours. Its architecture specification is composed of an orchestrator (*Orchestrator* component role) linked to device control functionalities – turning on / off the light (*Light* component role), controlling its intensity (*Luminosity* component role) and getting information about the time (*Time* component role). These component roles are respectively implemented by the *AndroidOrchestrator*, *AdjustableLamp* and *Clock* component classes. This architecture implementation can then be instantiated to describe specific architecture deployments. For instance, the architecture assembly in Fig. 1 is composed of two *AdjustableLamp* component instances that control the lighting of a Sitting room (*SittingLamp*) and a Desk (*DeskLamp*).

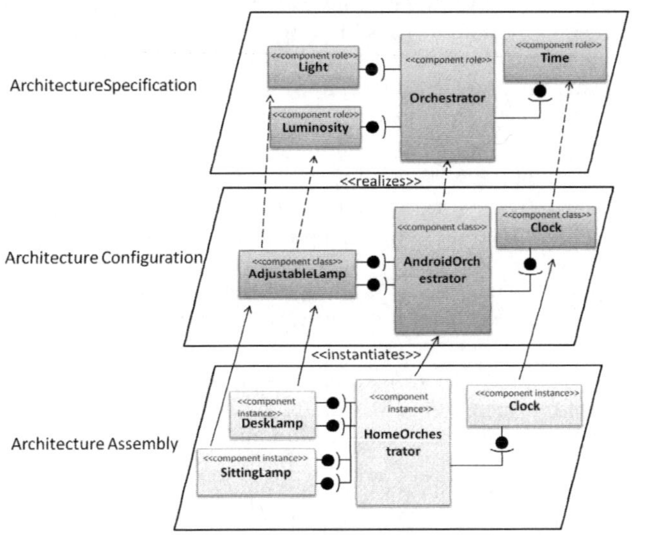

Figure 1. Running example

B. *Evolution management in Dedal*

Software architectures are subject to change at any abstraction level to meet new requirements, improve software quality, or cope with component failure. In previous work [10][11], we proposed an evolution management process that deals with architectural change based on Dedal and the B formal language [12]. Using a customized B solver, the evolution manager captures change at any abstraction level, controls its impact on the affected architecture and propagates it to the other abstraction levels to keep architecture descriptions coherent, both locally (each architecture description level separately) and globally (the whole architecture definition). This results in generating sequences of change operations that evolve the affected architecture to a new consistent state. The generated sequences (called evolution plans) represent the delta between two software architecture versions in an operation-based manner.

C. *Motivation*

Versioning component-based software architectures at multiple abstraction levels is an important issue. Indeed, evolving an architecture description at one abstraction level may impact its other descriptions at the other abstraction levels. For instance, evolving a software specification may require evolving all its implementations. The same way, evolving an implementation may entail evolving not only all its instantiations but also its corresponding specification (to prevent inter-level definition mismatches known as drift and erosion [13]). In the remainder, we set up a version model for three-level software architectures inspired by Conradi's taxonomy [3] and propose three strategies to manage multi-level versioning. The interest of this version model is twofold: (1) To capture information about evolution history by storing the change operation lists that transform architecture definitions into new versions and more importantly (2) to capture information about the co-evolution history by maintaining links between corresponding versions on the different abstraction levels to define versions of the whole architecture definition.

III. Versioning Component-Based Software Architectures

The design of our version model is inspired from Conradi's taxonomy [3] that distinguishes between two graphs representing two dimensions of software: the product space, where each node is a part of the product and edges represent composition relationships, and the version space, where nodes represent versions and edges derivations between them. Depending on the versioning model, the version space can be a linear, arborescent or direct acyclic graph. A version is called a *revision* when it is intended to replace its predecessors and is called a *variant* when it can coexist with other versions. In our model, we distinguish the *architectural space*, which represents software architecture descriptions at the three abstraction levels we consider (*i.e.*, specification, configuration and assembly), from the *version space*, which represents the versions of an architecture at a given abstraction level. In the remainder, we detail the representation of each space.

A. *The architectural space*

The architectural space consists in a set of trees that provide software architecture definitions at three abstraction levels (*cf.* Fig. 2). Nodes represent architecture definitions while edges denote realization relations between nodes at different abstraction levels. The root node of each tree corresponds thus to the specification of an architecture (*e.g.*, Home Automation Software architecture specification). The second level nodes represent all the variant implementations of that specification (*e.g.*, Android OS, Windows system architecture configurations). Finally, the third level nodes represent the variant instantiations that are used to deploy architectures configurations in different execution contexts (*e.g.*, HAS Office architecture assembly, Sitting room architecture assembly, etc.).

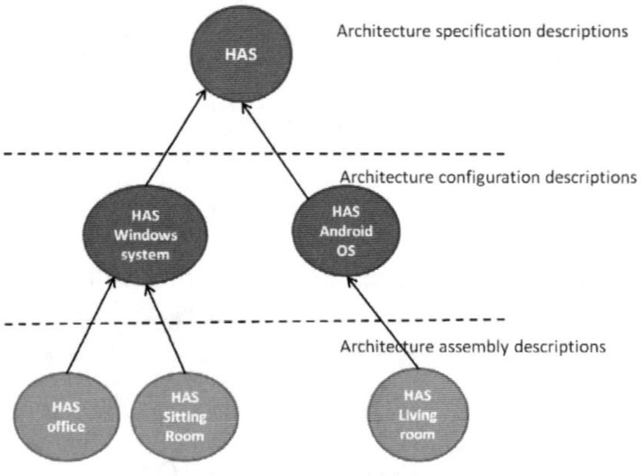

Figure 2. The three-level graph

The architectural space graph supports multiple granularity levels. Indeed, each node points to another graph representing the architecture structure in terms of components and their connections (*cf.* Fig. 1). Composite components embed an inner architecture as well.

The architectural space provides thus a comprehensive set of architecture definitions, including all their existing variants. It can be used to structure and then browse architecture model repositories, as part of a Model-Based Software Engineering environment. Its point of view is intentionally static (the historic derivation relations between architecture definition elements are omitted), in order to separate evolution concerns in the version space.

B. The version space

The architecture version space is composed of a set of version graphs. Each version graph (Fig. 3) is a representation of the version set, called V, related to a given architecture. Each node defines a unique version of the architecture (identified by a unique version identifier) while edges represent derivation relations between versions (the source version is obtained by an evolution of the target version). Our version model covers all the three architecture definition levels. Versioned entities may thus be architecture specifications, architecture configurations or architecture assemblies.

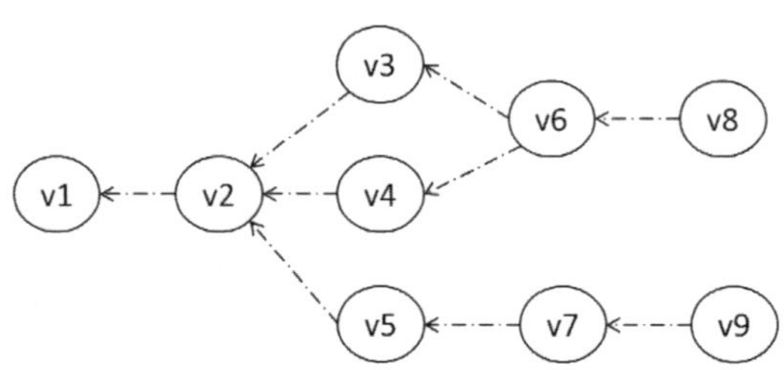

Figure 3. The version graph

The version model is change-based since the delta between two versions is expressed in terms of change operations rather than states. A derivation is the change sequence enabling to construct a version v_2 from its predecessor v_1. Formally, a derivation is a function of type $d : V \rightarrow V$ where V is the version space and $d = op_1 \circ op2 \circ \ldots \circ op_n$ where op_i is an elementary change operation. If v_1 is a version of the software architecture, then successors of v_1 are the set of all the versions resulting from the derivations applied on v_1: $succ(v_1) = \{v | v = d(v_1)\}$.

The architecture version identifier contains information corresponding to the abstraction level and the operation list that lead to the current version. At specification level, recorded information consists of a version ID and the change operation list. At configuration level, these information are a version ID, the ID of the implemented specification and the change operation list. Finally, at assembly level, the recorded information are accordingly a version identifier, the instantiated configuration identifier and the change operations list. The change operation list may be empty when the architecture description is created from scratch (for instance the specification of a new architecture or an implementation variant for a new platform).

C. Relations between the architectural and the version spaces

As aforementioned, the version space is intended to record all the versions of all the architecture definitions that are created by development and evolution processes. It provides a comprehensive and historic vision of architecture definitions, that is suitable to design architectures by the reuse and the evolution of exiting ones. However, as it does not distinguish revisions from variants, the version space does not provides a synthetic vision of the actual architectures definitions, *i.e.*, the up-to-date architecture definitions (based on the latest revisions), with its possible variants. This is the purpose of the architectural space, which can be extracted from the version space to provide architects with a clear view of the usable architecture definitions.

Every node in the architectural space corresponds thus to a node in the version space. Given a three-level graph G and a new derivation d of an architecture definition a in G, we aim to find the resulting three-level graph G' related to $a' = d(a)$. To do so, we need to evaluate the impact of d on the whole graph G. Indeed, d may trigger a change propagation to the other nodes linked to a, what may in turn recursively imply to derive other nodes.

In most cases, this task requires human assistance to decide which derivations are really necessary (*e.g.*, correcting bugs, security enforcement, etc.) and which are optional (*e.g.*, functional extensions, improvements, etc.). To automate this process, we propose versioning strategies that can be selected and activated as required by architects to manage architecture model repositories.

D. Versioning strategies

We propose three versioning strategies:

a) Minimum derivation strategy: The minimum derivation strategy aims to minimize the number of derivations to be applied on the architectural space graph. The principle of this strategy is to version only the active impacted nodes without considering the propagation to all the other nodes. Active nodes consist in a tuple of three nodes (s, c, a) where s, c and a respectively denote an architecture specification, an architecture configuration and an architecture assembly.

For instance, let us consider the three-level graph shown in Fig. 4-a. $d(c_1)$ triggers a change on the specification s_1 and a change on a_{12}. The active nodes are then $(s.v_1, c_1.v_1, a_{12}.v_1)$.

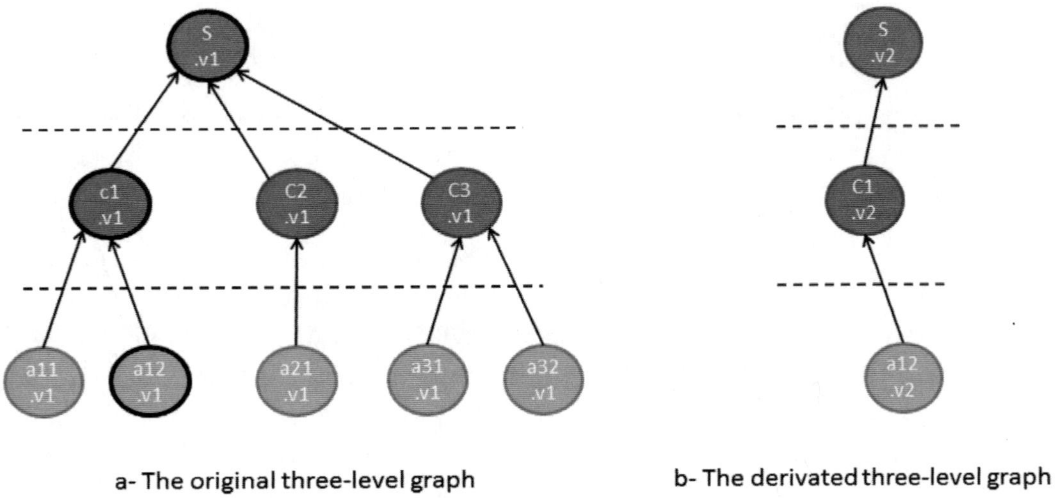

Figure 4. Example of minimum derivation

The minimum derivation strategy creates a new three-level graph with the new versions $(s.v_2, c_1.v_2, a_{12}.v_2)$ (*cf.* Fig. 4-b).

The minimum derivation strategy is suitable when the change purpose is not to correct some version of an architecture definition, resulting in the derivation of a revision, but to create a variant that can coexist with previous versions. Fig. 4 illustrates a special case where the derived architecture definition shares finally no element with its source architecture definition. These architectures definitions could be identified as variants belonging to a software product line [14]. This is a perspective of this work.

b) Full derivation strategy.: In contrast to the minimum derivation strategy, the full derivation strategy aims to version (directly and recursively) all the impacted architecture descriptions. It should be applied when the rationale of evolution (for instance a security fault detected in a component used by all architecture implementations) implies the creation of revisions that are intended to replace previous versions. Firstly, derivation is applied to the active node and then change is propagated recursively to the other nodes (*cf.* Fig. 5). For instance, the revision of node $c1.v1$ (configuration level) is propagated to the other nodes as follows:

- derivation of a new specification revision $s.v2$ from $s.v1$,
- merging of $c2.v1$ and $c3.v1$ nodes into the new $c3.v2$ node (both evolution of $c2.v1$ and $c3.v1$ leads to $c3.v2$) and,
- revisions of all nodes at assembly levels, notably $a21.v2$ derived from $a21.v1$ becomes associated to $c3.v2$ configuration revision.

c) Custom derivation strategy.: This strategy is guided by the architect that has to specify which architecture definitions are kept and which ones are replaced by new versions. Custom derivation strategy is used after a default application of the minimum derivation strategy so that minimum necessary versions, that ensure coherent global architecture definitions, are always created.

IV. RELATED WORK

Software versioning has been studied for many years with the the objective to provide a Software Configuration Management (SCM) systems [3], handling various kinds of entities and different granularities (source code lines, objects, libraries, etc.). Early work targeted mainly source code versioning. Several collaborative source code versioning systems were more recently proposed and have become industrial standards such as SVN [15], CVS [16] and Git [17].

To overcome the limitation of version management based on source code, [18] propose to generate from meta-models version control systems that are aware the corresponding modeling language concepts, in order to trace the evolution of significant logical units.

With the emergence of component-based software development, more recent work addressed component versioning rather than source code [2]. Examples include JAVA [19], and COM .Net. More recent approaches treated as well the issue of component substitutability like the work of Brada *et al.* (SOFA) [20] and the issue of compatibility like the work of Stuckenholz *et al.* [21].

Regarding architectural versioning, only little work was dedicated. The SOFA 2.0 ADL [5] enables to version composite components and therefore entire architectures (which are used to define composite component implementations). Other existing ADLs like MAE [6] and xADL 2.0 [7] also enable architecture versioning. However, all these architectural versioning models neither handle detailed information about evolution (rationale, change operations list that result in new architecture versions) nor maintain the trace of architecture evolutions throughout the whole software lifecycle (what requires to handle the co-evolution of multiple definitions for every architecture).

Another closely related work addressed architectural versioning at multiple abstraction levels [22]. The proposed approach is based on the SAEV model [23] that defines three abstraction levels of software architectures: the meta level, the architecture level and the application level. However, this taxonomy is different from Dedal since the meta level

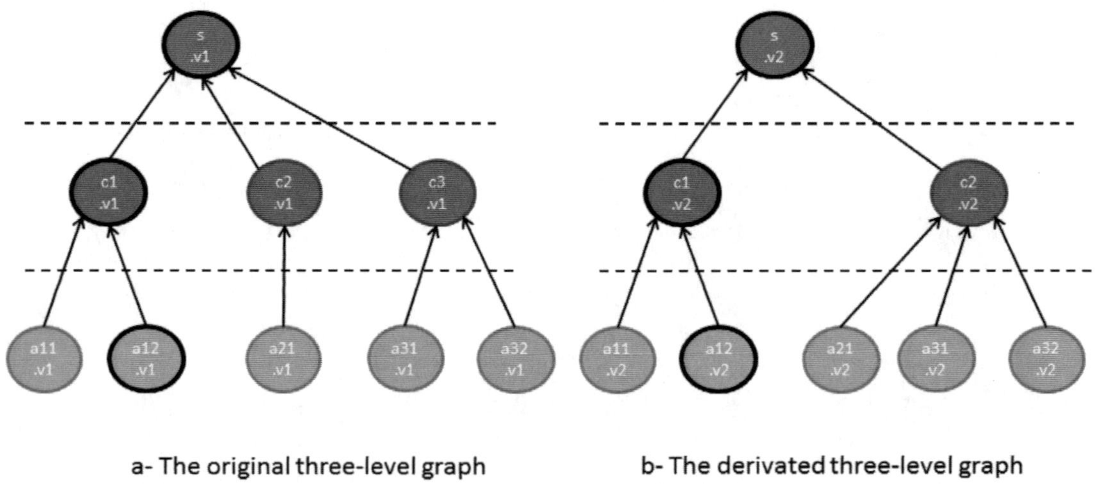

Figure 5. Example of full derivation

encompasses the definition of architectural concepts to be used at the lower level.

V. Conclusion and Future Work

This work proposes a version model for our software architecture description language Dedal. It considers version management at three abstraction levels in order to support the co-evolution of architecture definitions throughout the whole software lifecycle. It captures information about evolution (change operation list) and enables to distinguish its rationale (revisions and variants). Moreover, versioning strategies are proposed to automate the version derivation propagation that may or must result from the co-evolution of the different definition levels of architectures.

Future work consists in studying component versioning and its impact on architectural versioning considering compatibility issues, to detect automatically revisions and variants. Another perspective is to extend our version model in order to support product line engineering. From a practical perspective, ongoing work is to automate further versioning mechanisms and integrate them into DedalStudio, our eclipse-based tool that automatically manages the architecture evolution process [11].

References

[1] J. Estubier et al., "Impact of software engineering research on the practice of software configuration management," ACM Trans. Softw. Eng. Methodol., vol. 14, no. 4, Oct. 2005, pp. 383–430. [Online]. Available: http://doi.acm.org/10.1145/1101815.1101817

[2] C. Urtado and C. Oussalah, "Complex entity versioning at two granularity levels," Information Systems, vol. 23, no. 2/3, 1998, pp. 197–216.

[3] R. Conradi and B. Westfechtel, "Version models for software configuration management," ACM Comput. Surv., vol. 30, no. 2, Jun. 1998, pp. 232–282. [Online]. Available: http://doi.acm.org/10.1145/280277.280280

[4] P. Clements and M. Shaw, ""the golden age of software architecture" revisited," IEEE Software, vol. 26, no. 4, July 2009, pp. 70–72.

[5] T. Bures, P. Hnetynka, and F. Plasil, "Sofa 2.0: Balancing advanced features in a hierarchical component model," in Software Engineering Research, Management and Applications, 2006. Fourth International Conference on, Aug 2006, pp. 40–48.

[6] R. Roshandel, A. V. D. Hoek, M. Mikic-Rakic, and N. Medvidovic, "Mae—a system model and environment for managing architectural evolution," ACM Trans. Softw. Eng. Methodol., vol. 13, no. 2, Apr. 2004, pp. 240–276. [Online]. Available: http://doi.acm.org/10.1145/1018210.1018213

[7] E. M. Dashofy, A. v. d. Hoek, and R. N. Taylor, "A comprehensive approach for the development of modular software architecture description languages," ACM Trans. Softw. Eng. Methodol., vol. 14, no. 2, Apr. 2005, pp. 199–245. [Online]. Available: http://doi.acm.org/10.1145/1061254.1061258

[8] H. Y. Zhang, C. Urtado, and S. Vauttier, "Architecture-centric component-based development needs a three-level ADL," in Proc. of the 4th ECSA conf., ser. LNCS, vol. 6285. Copenhagen, Denmark: Springer, August 2010, pp. 295–310.

[9] I. Sommerville, Software engineering (9th edition). Addison-Wesley, 2010.

[10] A. Mokni, M. Huchard, C. Urtado, S. Vauttier, and H. Y. Zhang, "An evolution management model for multi-level component-based software architectures," in The 27th International Conference on Software Engineering and Knowledge Engineering, SEKE 2015, Wyndham Pittsburgh University Center, Pittsburgh, PA, USA, July 6-8, 2015, 2015, pp. 674–679. [Online]. Available: http://dx.doi.org/10.18293/SEKE2015-172

[11] ——, "A formal approach for managing component-based architecture evolution," To appear in Science of Computer Programming, 2016.

[12] J.-R. Abrial, The B-book: Assigning Programs to Meanings. Cambridge University Press, 1996.

[13] R. Taylor, N. Medvidovic, and E. Dashofy, Software architecture: Foundations, Theory, and Practice. Wiley, 2009.

[14] K. Pohl, G. Bckle, and F. van der Linden, Software Product Line Engineering. Springer, 2005.

[15] M. Pilato, Version Control With Subversion. Sebastopol, CA, USA: O'Reilly & Associates, Inc., 2004.

[16] K. F. Fogel, Open Source Development with CVS. Scottsdale, AZ, USA: Coriolis Group Books, 1999.

[17] J. Loeliger and M. Matthew, Version Control with Git. Sebastopol, CA, USA: O'Reilly & Associates, Inc., 2012.

[18] T. Oda and M. Saeki, "Generative technique of version control systems for software diagrams," in Proceedings of the 21st IEEE International Conference on Software Maintenance, ser. ICSM '05. Washington, DC, USA: IEEE Computer Society, 2005, pp. 515–524. [Online]. Available: http://dx.doi.org/10.1109/ICSM.2005.49

[19] R. Englander, Developing Java Beans. Sebastopol, CA, USA: O'Reilly & Associates, Inc., 1997.

[20] P. Brada, "Component revision identification based on idl/adl

component specification," SIGSOFT Software Engineering Notes, vol. 26, no. 5, Sep. 2001, pp. 297–298. [Online]. Available: http://doi.acm.org/10.1145/503271.503250

[21] A. Stuckenholz, "Component updates as a boolean optimization problem," Electronic Notes in Theoretical Computer Science, vol. 182, 2007, pp. 187 – 200, proceedings of the Third International Workshop on Formal Aspects of Component Software (FACS 2006). [Online]. Available: http://www.sciencedirect.com/science/article/pii/S1571066107003945

[22] T. N. Nguyen, "Multi-level architectural evolution management," in System Sciences, 2007. HICSS 2007. 40th Annual Hawaii International Conference on, Jan 2007, pp. 258a–258a.

[23] M. Oussalah, N. Sadou, and D. Tamzalit, "A generic model for managing software architecture evolution," in Proceedings of the 9th WSEAS International Conference on Systems, ser. ICS'05. Stevens Point, Wisconsin, USA: World Scientific and Engineering Academy and Society (WSEAS), 2005, pp. 35:1–35:6. [Online]. Available: http://dl.acm.org/citation.cfm?id=1373716.1373751

Services for Legacy Software Rejuvenation: A Systematic Mapping Study

Manuel Gonçalves da Silva Neto, Walquiria Castelo Branco Lins, Eric B. Perazzo Mariz
Recife Center for Advanced Studies and Systems (CESAR)
Recife – PE, Brazil
Emails: { manuel.neto, wcbl, eric.perazzo}@cesar.edu.br

***Abstract*— One of the promises of Service-Orientation and Service-Oriented Architecture (SOA) is the ability to revitalize legacy systems and gain a significant return of efforts and investments. SOA has gained significant attention from academic and industry as a promising architectural style enabling legacy applications to expose and reuse their functionalities. When a research area matures, there is a sharp increase in the number of searches and results available and it is important to summarize and provide a more comprehensive overview of this area. The goal of this work is to investigate the use of services in the modernization of legacy software, gathering information of rejuvenation techniques and technologies adopted. To achieve this goal, a systematic mapping study was performed covering papers recently published in journals, conferences, and workshops, available at relevant electronic databases. This study also presents the characteristics of the selected research divided into six research questions. As a result, 47 studies were selected presenting strategies and solutions for legacy rejuvenation. The results indicate that Java or Object-Oriented systems represent a significant number of legacy systems in operation today, which are adopted migration techniques to become more service oriented. The study also showed a growing number of validations with real use cases in enterprise environment.**

Keywords- Systematic Mapping; SOA; Legacy Systems.

I. INTRODUCTION

Nowadays, many companies have systems that have been implemented for some time. These systems must interact with those that are developed nowadays requiring constant adjustment and maintenance to meet new needs and remain aligned with business rules [1].

One of the challenges faced by information technology today is the continuous adaptation and migration of legacy systems to more flexible and modern platforms [2]. With the fast development of business logic and information technology, today´s best solutions are tomorrow´s legacy systems [3].

The legacy systems or existing working systems of enterprise usually contain a mixture of different techniques and protocols which is hard to maintain and update. However, Legacy systems carry out the enterprise's most crucial business information together with business processes and many organizations have leveraged the value of their legacy systems by exposing parts of it as services [4]. Rapid changes in hardware and software technologies combined with the changing requirements require the use of new methods that enable the evolution of these systems efficiently [5].

Service-Orientations and Service-Oriented-Architecture (SOA) are presented as alternatives to the modernization of legacy systems, recovering investments applied in these systems over the years. Almonaies *et al* [6] list some of the features that ease modernization of these systems, including loose coupling, the implementation of logical abstraction, agility, flexibility and reusability. Migrating legacy systems to services enables the reuse of software components already established, as well as its integration with new services to support changing business needs [1]. Modernizing legacy systems using Services may be accomplished in several ways which vary from the creation of intermediate layers for insertion of new features to the development of a completely new system [7]–[9].

When a research area matures there is a sharp increase in the number of search results available and thus it is important to summarize and provide a more comprehensive overview of this area [10]. Secondary studies as the Systematic Reviews and Mappings have been proposed and defended as the main methods of conducting reviews at primary studies and have become pillars in the practice of evidence-based research [11]. Based on this premise, in order to better understand the area and to identify the shortcomings on it, this paper presents a systematic mapping study of the use of Services to modernize legacy software.

The Mapping Study (MS) reported here follows the guidelines from Kitchenham [12], Petersen [10] and the process proposed by Biolchini *et al.* [13], in which the work was divided into three phases, namely, *i)* Planning, *ii)* Conducting, and *iii)* Reporting results. Its main focus is to identify and classify the techniques and legacy systems that are currently rejuvenated with SOA use. For that, it collects evidence on how research are structured according to modernization strategy, implementation technology, legacy system features, feasibility analysis and the main contribution of each study.

This paper is organized as follows: Section 2 presents the systematic mapping process undertaken in this study; Section 3 presents the main findings and analyzes them; Section 4 presents related works relevant to this research; Section 5 presents the conclusions as well as threats to validity of this research and directions for future works.

II. SYSTEMATIC MAPPING STUDY PLANNING

This section presents how the mapping study methodology has been planned, including the research questions, search strategy, inclusion, exclusion and classification criteria used to provide a structure of the primary studies. Additional process details can be found at Silva Neto [14].

A. Research Questions

The goal of this study is to identify and classify primary research addressing the use of Service-orientation in legacy modernization by the following main question: "What are the approaches used in the adoption of Services to modernize legacy systems and how these approaches differ from each other?"

In [15], they recommend that as a research question has different focuses, it must be divided into sub questions in order to facilitate the mapping process. The overall goal and question are divided into the following research questions (RQ):

- **RQ1** - What modernization strategy is adopted? The main purpose of this question is to identify the modernization strategies used to choose SOA for legacy modernization.
- **RQ2** - What Service-orientation implementation technology is used? The purpose of this question is to identify which Service implementation technologies are used for the modernization of legacy software.
- **RQ3** – What is the type of modernized legacy system? This question has as objective to identify the type of legacy system modernized through Services.
- **RQ4** – Were there feasibility analysis? This question has as main objective to identify how feasibility analysis was carried out when selecting the use of Services to modernize legacy software. We intended to map the methodologies and techniques used in the feasibility analysis or the complete lack of this kind of activity.
- **RQ5** - What was the proposed contribution? This question has as objective to identify the type of contribution left by primary research, through which possible gaps and research areas still open on the subject can be mapped out.
- **RQ6** - How was the proposal validated? This question is intended to identify how primary research is being validated, the topics of interest are the research populations where the experiments were applied qualitatively and quantitatively.

B. Search Strategy

Considering the search questions, therea set of keywords was identified. The main keywords for search expression are *legacy*, *modernization* and *SOA* with the following related terms:

- **Service-Orientation and SOA:** Service-Oriented Architecture , Webservice, Web Service, RESTful.
- **Modernization:** Migration, Reengineering, re-engineering, evolution
- **Legacy System:** Legacy Software, Legacy Information

Thus, the following search expression was obtained after refinements:

((legacy AND (system OR software OR information)) AND (migration OR modernization OR evolution OR reegineering OR {re-engineering}) AND (SOA OR webservice OR {web service} OR {Service-Oriented Architecture} OR RESTful))

In addition to research questions and search strategy, we stablished the search sources to find primary studies. In [15]–[20], relevant research bases in the areas of architecture and software engineering in general were found, so we used these works to choose the sources of research in this systematic mapping. Kitchenham[21] recommends including alternative sources of research manually to avoid biasing the research including, among others, a list of search results of the primary research and the Internet itself. Thus they added secondary research bases to perform manual search. Follow the databases chosen:

TABLE I. SELECTED SOURCES

Source	Address
IEEE Xplore	www.ieeexplore.ieee.org
Compendex	www.engineeringvillage.com
Web of Science	www.isiknowledge.com
Scopus	www.scopus.com
Public Domain	www.dominiopublico.gov.br
References	Reference List of primary Studies

The last two rows of Table 1, are secondary research bases to perform manual search.

C. Inclusion/Exclusion criteria

Criteria should be defined to exclude primary research that have no relevance to the research question, as well as ensuring that the relevant work is analyzed [10]. The search of primary studies was divided into three phases or stages, where only selection criteria for excluding non-relevant primary study to the research questions were adopted. The publications that do not fit in any of the exclusion criteria are automatically inserted in the next stages of evaluation.

We named each step and applied the selection criteria as follows on Table II:

- Step one (E1);
- Step two (E2);
- Step three (E3).

TABLE II. INCLUSION/EXCLUSION CRITERIA

Inclusion Criteria
1) Articles published in English from January 2010 to February 2014 for searches in primary research bases
2) Articles in English and Portuguese published from January 2006 to February 2014 for manual searches in the secondary research bases
3) Articles that focus on legacy modernization with services or SOA.
Exclusion Criteria
CS1: repeated publications or already cataloged.
CS2: Very short papers, less than 4 pages.
CS3: Publications that have no direct relation to the main research question and at least one (1) of the sub questions.
CS4: Secondary Studies
CS5: Folders, Books and Catalogues

It was also used the Kitchenham's [21] recommendation that in case of the existence of the same publication in more than one event,the latest one is cataloged.

Quality assessment criteria were defined for the selected studies after the application of exclusion and inclusion criteria. We followed the recommendations in [22], which the evaluation of quality was not used for purposes of exclusion or inclusion, quality assessment was carried out to enhance the quality of the assessed studies.

III. SEARCH CONDUCTION AND CLASSIFICATION: OVERVIEW OF THE RESULTS

This section presents details of search conduction and classification of the studies.

A. *Procedure Selection*

As shown, the conduct of research was carried out in three steps :

Step one (E1): Selection and preliminary registration of publications using primary research bases with the application of the search expression.

Step two (E2): Selection of relevant publications based on the title and summary and application of the first filtering based on exclusion criteria.

Step three (E3): Selection of relevant publications based on their full text and application of the second filtering based on exclusion criteria.

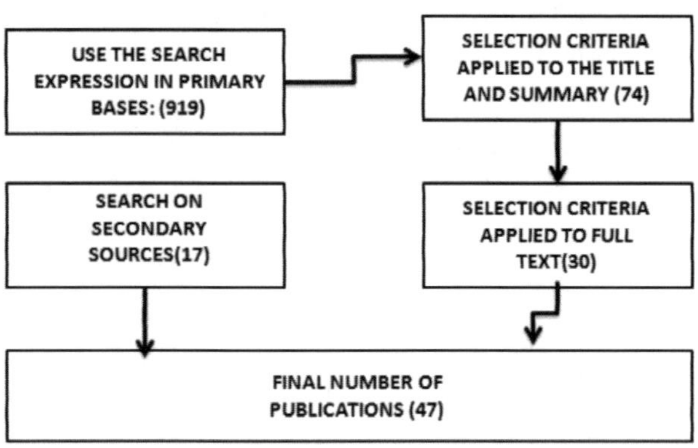

Figure 1. Conduction summary

Initially the search was executed expression in primary search bases selected publications passed through filters as E1, E2 and E3, finally, the search was performed on the secondary databases following the possible exclusion criteria for each base. In [14] there is the complete list of publications. The Appendix A presents Table IX with items chosen after the selection steps.

B. *Overview of the results*

The completion of the search gives an overview of the subject importance, the publications were classified according to each research question, we also obtained relevant data on authors, events and temporal distribution of publications.

The authors with highest number of selected publications are respectively: Khadka, Patricia Lago and Harry Sneed. We used the Scholar to survey the number of citations received by each publication selected. The most cited publication was the *S38: SOMA:A method for developing service-oriented solutions.*

In order to answer the research questions, there was the classification of selected publications for each research question separately.

RQ1: This research question investigates what strategy or modernization approach was used and heavily mentioned in the selected research. They used the classifications in [9] to group publications in three (3) main types of strategies: Redevelopment (i), Wrapping (ii) and Migration (iii).

The first category, Redevelopment, comprises a complete rewrite of the system in a new technology or language. The second category, encapsulation or Wrapping, also known as the integration is to maintain the legacy system with minimal changes to the source code where a new software layer is added to express the functionality through services. The third category, migration, operates in the restructuring and transformation of legacy systems to more flexible platforms keeping its data and key features, it resembles the first category but there is a less extreme character compared to the level of structural changes.

Table III summarizes the publications according to Q1.1, it used the classifier N/A (No Answer) to identify publications that lacked connection with this research question.

TABLE III. Q1.1 CLASSIFICATION

APPROACH	%	SELECTED PUB
REDEVELOPMENT	6,38%	S17;S30;S40
MIGRATION/ENCAPSULATION	2,12%	S15
MIGRATION ONLY	48,94%	S2;S5;S6;S7;S8;S10;S19;S25;S26;S35;S47;S23;S12;S22;S42;S1;S18;S29;S32;S34;S36;S39;S45
ENCAPSULATION ONLY	23,41%	S3;S14;S21;S31;S33;S37;S41;S11;S16;S20;S27
N/A	19.15%	S4;S9;S24;S44;S46;S43;S28;S13;S38

RQ2: This research question investigates which SOA implementation technology was used or heavily mentioned in research. Although SOA and the term "Services Oriented" are initially agnostic about the technology, they tried to sort through the analysis of primary studies the technology that

allowed the realization of SOA concepts and the modernization of legacy systems through service orientation.

Table IV summarizes the publications according to Q1.2, it used the classifier "N/A" (No Answer) to identify publications that lacked connection with this research question.

TABLE IV. Q1.2 CLASSIFICATION

TECHNOLOGY	%	SELECTED PUB
OSGi	2,12%	S1
SOAP	46,81 %	S2;S3;S14;S5;S6;S7;S10;S15; S24;S33;S37;S41;S47;S42;S1 1;S16;S18;S20;S27;S30;S32; S45
RESTFul	4,26%	S19;S36
N/A	46,81 %	S4;S8;S9;S17;S21;S25;S26;S 31;S35;S44;S46;S23;S12;S22; S43;S28;S13;S29;S34;S38;S3 9;S40

Regarding publications not receiving classification from the point of view of this question of search, they had focused on general aspects of legacy modernization SOA ranging from indication to migration aid of processes (S4), by comparing the level of maintainability between two approaches (S17), these publications did not address any implementation techniques and received for this reason the classification N / a (no Answer) for this research question.

RQ3: This research question investigates the main features of the legacy system that has undergone modernization, this information is relatively useful in decision making for new projects with similar characteristics to those presented here.

The main features of the rejuvenated systems were grouped according to the programming language when the author stressed to this feature, regarding the type of system in which such languages are grouped, for example: Web Applications (WEBAPP). We also used the general characteristic of the system when the author took black-box methods and language used in the original system was not addressed.

TABLE V. Q1.3 CLASSIFICATION

LEGACY FEATURE	%	SELECTED PUB
JAVA	23,41 %	S14;S8;S9;S10;S33;S41;S23; S1;S18;S29;S45
ITERACTIVE/FORM BASED	2,12%	S27
FORTRAN	2,12%	S47
COBOL	21,28 %	S5;S15;S24;S25;S26;S42;S16 ;S20;S30;S40
C++	4,26%	S11;S13
WEBAPP	17,02 %	S2;S6;S19;S35;S37;S12;S22; S32
N/A	29,79 %	S3;S4;S7;S17;S21;S46;S31;S 44;S43;S28;S34; S36;S38;S39

Regarding publications classified as N/A (No Answer) in Table V, they addressed these processes or methodologies in general or the type of system have not made clear who would be modernized, receiving so this classification.

RQ4: This research question investigates the feasibility analysis performed in the SOA option for legacy system modernization. The goal here was to determine whether the projects or research that addressed legacy modernization SOA presented some technical or business justification. Justifying a project that involves major changes to existing software is an important task that usually involves the analysis of the software, the maintenance process and the business value that the application adds [23].

In Table VI, the studies were classified and grouped according to the practice or approach used to justify the project or indicative of an absence in any case. This research question has the particularity to make explicit that the absence of criteria or feasibility reasons for this fact in itself is relevant to this issue.

TABLE VI. Q1.4 CLASSIFICATION

METHODOLOGY	%	SELECTED PUB
SOMA	6,38%	S21;S33;S38
OWN METHOD	23,41 %	S3;S14;S5;S8;S9;S10;S25;S3 5;S44;S1;S40
SAAM	2,12%	S17
INTERNAL COMITE	2,12%	S26
SMART	2,12%	S13
CODE INSPECTION	2,12%	S16
NOT USED	61,70 %	S2;S4;S6;S7;S15;S19;S24;S3 1;S37;S41;S46;S47;S23;S12; S22;S43;S42;S28;S11;S18;S2 0;S27; S29;S30;S32;S34;S36;S39;S4 5

Publications that have proposed some kind of process in which there were steps or activities responsible for determining the feasibility received the rating OWN. Publications that showed no indications of feasibility analysis, whether technical or business, were classified as NOT USED. Approximately 61.7% of the publications fit into this category.

RQ5: This question is intended to identify and quantify the contributions provided by selected studies in order to provide information to those who wish to expand or contribute to them. For classification purposes, the works were grouped according to the characteristic that the authors have given greater emphasis to describe the contributions of their research.

TABLE VII. Q1.5 CLASSIFICATION

CONTRIBUITION	%	SELECTED PUB
OVERVIEW	6,38%	S15;S17;S43
PROCESS	40,43 %	S2;S3;S4;S5;S6;S8;S9;S10;S2 5;S26;S35;S37; S44;S22;S1;S13;S36;S38;S40
ARCHITECTURE	6,38%	S14;S31;S47
METHODOLOGY	42,55 %	S7;S19;S21;S24;S33;S41;S46 ;S23;S12;S42;S28;S18;S20;S 27;S29;S30;S32;S34;S39;S45
TOOL	4,26%	S11;S16

In the analysis of publications that contributed to some kind of methodology on table VIII, (S12 and S24) there are proposed methodologies for business rules extraction through legacy code (S41 and S42) they have proposed methodologies for generation or improvement of the extracted services. In (S7 and S39), the focus of the methodology was the extraction of information that would help the process of modernization. In (S32, S34, S45, S29, S18, S28, S46 and S19) they have proposed methodologies to identify services from legacy systems, and (S28) emphasized the need to identify the "right" services that actually represent value for Business. Finally, still in relation to methodologies, in publications (S30, S27, S20, S23, S33 and S21), methods or techniques that help the legacy modernization processes have been proposed.

RQ6: This question is intended to identify how the publications were validated and where the study was applied. These ratings on Table VIII are useful to researchers who wish to extend the study area to new research.

TABLE VIII. Q1.6 CLASSIFICATION

VALIDATION	%	SELECTED PUB
BUSINESS ENVIRONMENT	51,06 %	S1;S3;S14;S7;S9;S15;S17;S25;S26;S35;S37;S41;S44;S47; S23;S12;S42;S13;S16;S20;S30;S34; S38;S40
ACADEMIC	36,17 %	S2;S4;S5;S6;S8;S10;S19;S24; S33;S46;S22;S11;S18;S27;S29;S32;S45
THEORETICAL	12,77 %	S21;S31;S43;S28;S36;S39

For classification purposes, the names "business environment" and "academic environment" where adopted for primary studies that used cases studies. The first term was used in studies that validated their experiments in companies or through business experiences. The second term joins studies that were validated in academic environments, through simulation or implementation in a highly controlled environment. Studies that confirmed its assumptions based on literature with no explicit use of cases of use were classified as theoretical.

IV. RELATED WORK

There are others researches addressing the modernization of legacy systems using SOA or services. In a domain where a number of systematic reviews exist already it may be possible to conduct a tertiary review, in order to answer wider research questions [21]. Although this is not the focus of this paper, this section briefly introduces some of these works.

Laguna *et al* [18], conducted a systematic mapping addressing the evolution of software product lines ranging from legacy systems to reengineer product line. The work was conducted in three stages and conducted by two experts. The first step occurred in 2010, the second and third in 2011 and 2012 respectively. At the end of the research they got 74 selected primary studies which were classified regarding the following perspectives: Focus of research, type of contribution and type of validation. These classifications assisted in the formulation of research questions used in the systematic mapping subject of current research.

Razavian and Lago [24], conducted a systematic review addressing the migration of legacy systems to service-oriented systems. The main objective of the review was the classification of the main migration strategies existing in this area , which they called *SOA Migration Families*.

Khadka *et al* [25], also conducted a systematic review addressing the evolution of legacy systems through SOA. They investigate primary studies produced from 2000 to 2011 getting 121 selected primary studies for classification. The focus of the research took place in the identification and classification methodologies, techniques and approaches relevant to the evolution of legacy to SOA. A framework to guide the rejuvenation process was also developed and used as a guide in their review.

Comparing the work proposed here with the ones already conducted, they were driven around the validation or proposal of a migration process or order to classify the approaches in general. The approach proposed in this systematic mapping aims to present an updated classification based on academic and technological aspects. To achieve this purpose the research questions were adapted to encompass both aspects. A more detailed comparison can be made in a tertiary study.

V. CONCLUSIONS AND FUTURE WORK

The aim of this study was to classify and give an overview of SOA use in the rejuvenation of legacy software. 919 primary studies obtained in search databases widely used in the field of Software Engineering were analyzed. 17 other publications were obtained through manual searches on a reference list in conjunction with conducting searches on Brazilian Public Domain Portal.

From 936 publications found, 47 were selected for analysis which were classified according to six research questions to establish technical and scientific overview updated of the use of SOA in legacy modernization.

The results indicate that migration strategies are the most commonly used, followed by encapsulation techniques. The results also showed that in studies that addressed migration the predominant theme in the studies is to propose processes or methodologies that support or guide the migration projects.

Regarding the type of system or language in which the modernized system was developed, most publications that presented this information were related to systems developed in the Java programming language, the second largest representation was developed in COBOL systems, followed by legacy web. This may indicate the difficulty in disposing of old COBOL systems, justifying the investment in its rejuvenation.

On the feasibility analysis in research involving rejuvenating legacy systems using SOA, it was found that approximately 23.4% of publications used a process or method owned by the author to perform feasibility studies indicating a concern with these activities. However, a critical result is that approximately 61.70% of the total publications made no reference to analysis or feasibility study to choose SOA to modernize legacy software.

On the analysis of each contribution, the results show that the publications that contributed to some kind of process, prioritized guides for modernization tasks, being followed by publications to assist in decision-making on technical feasibility and the identification of services from legacy systems, while publications that contributed methodologies have mostly focused on identifying services.

Regarding the validation of each study, the results showed that those who used the business environment to implement the use cases, chose majoritary banking and financial sectors while the experimental validations dominates the use cases on open source projects in general.

The results showed that the applications in Java or object-oriented already represent a significant number of legacy systems in operation. Migration techniques are easily applied to make this systems service oriented.

The following itens are the main threats to the validity of the results of this study:

(i) Although recommended, manual searches depend on too the opinion of mapping drivers and may lead to biased results.

(ii) A decrement factor in the validity of the research lies in the limitations imposed by the search engines of digital research sources that limiting the replication for future work.

The related studies have shown the presence of other secondary studies on similar topics. Thus, it is proposed for future work, to conduct a tertiary review to take a more global result of the use of services in the rejuvenation of legacy systems.

REFERENCES

[1] A. Fuhr, T. Horn, V. Riediger, and A. Winter, "Model-driven software migration into service-oriented architectures," *Comput. Sci. ...*, vol. 49, no. 261, pp. 65–84, Jun. 2013.

[2] M. Book, S. Grapenthin, and V. Gruhn, "Risk-aware Migration of Legacy Data Structures," *2013 39th Euromicro Conf. Softw. Eng. Adv. Appl.*, pp. 53–56, Sep. 2013.

[3] Z. Zhang, D.-D. Zhou, H.-J. Yang, and S.-C. Zhong, "A service composition approach based on sequence mining for migrating e-learning legacy system to SOA," *Int. J. Autom. Comput.*, vol. 7, no. 4, pp. 584–595, Nov. 2010.

[4] Y. Liu, Q. Wang, M. Zhuang, and Y. Zhu, "Reengineering Legacy Systems with RESTful Web Service," *2008 32nd Annu. IEEE Int. Comput. Softw. Appl. Conf.*, no. 2100219007, pp. 785–790, 2008.

[5] J. Guo, "Software reuse through re-engineering the legacy systems," *Inf. Softw. Technol.*, vol. 45, no. 9, pp. 597–609, Jun. 2003.

[6] A. A. Almonaies, J. R. Cordy, and T. R. Dean, "Legacy system evolution towards service-oriented architecture," in *International Workshop on SOA Migration and Evolution*, 2010, pp. 53–62.

[7] R. Khadka, A. Saeidi, S. Jansen, and J. Hage, "A structured legacy to SOA migration process and its evaluation in practice," *2013 IEEE 7th Int. Symp. Maint. Evol. Serv. Cloud-Based Syst.*, pp. 2–11, Sep. 2013.

[8] M. Razavian and P. Lago, "A lean and mean strategy for migration to services," *Proc. WICSA/ECSA 2012 Companion Vol. - WICSA/ECSA '12*, p. 61, 2012.

[9] S. Ali and S. Abdelhak-Djamel, "Evolution approaches towards a Service oriented architecture," *2012 Int. Conf. Multimed. Comput. Syst.*, pp. 687–692, May 2012.

[10] K. Petersen, R. Feldt, S. Mujtaba, and M. Mattsson, "Systematic mapping studies in software engineering," *12th Int. Conf. Eval. Assess. Softw. Eng.*, pp. 71–80, 2008.

[11] F. da Silva, A. Santos, and S. Soares, "A critical appraisal of systematic reviews in software engineering from the perspective of the research questions asked in the reviews," *Proc. 2010 ACM-IEEE Int. Symp. Empir. Softw. Eng. Meas. - ESEM '10*, p. 1, 2010.

[12] B. Kitchenham, T. Dybå, and M. Jørgensen, "Evidence-based software engineering," *Int. Conf. Softw. Eng.*, vol. 26, 2004.

[13] J. Biolchini, P. G. Mian, Ana Candida Cruz Natali, and G. H. Travassos, *Systematic Review in Software Engineering*, no. May. Technical Report RT - ES 679/05: COPPE/UFRJ/Programa de Engenharia de Sistemas e Computação/Rio de Janeiro-RJ, 2005.

[14] M. G. D. S. Neto, *SOA on Legacy Software Modernization: A Systematic Mapping Study*. CESAR-edu/MPES/Recife-PE: Master Thesis, 2014.

[15] R. L. Novais, A. Torres, T. S. Mendes, M. Mendonça, and N. Zazworka, "Software evolution visualization: A systematic mapping study," *Inf. Softw. Technol.*, vol. 55, no. 11, pp. 1860–1883, Nov. 2013.

[16] A. Shahrokni and R. Feldt, "A systematic review of software robustness," *Inf. Softw. Technol.*, vol. 55, no. 1, pp. 1–17, Jan. 2013.

[17] H. P. Breivold, I. Crnkovic, and M. Larsson, "A systematic review of software architecture evolution research," *Inf. Softw. Technol.*, vol. 54, no. 1, pp. 16–40, Jan. 2012.

[18] M. a. Laguna and Y. Crespo, "A systematic mapping study on software product line evolution: From legacy system reengineering to product line refactoring," *Sci. Comput. Program.*, vol. 78, no. 8, pp. 1010–1034, Aug. 2013.

[19] M. P. Barcelos, "A strategy for software measurement and evaluation of base measures to control statistical software processes in high-maturity organizations," Doctoral Dissertation, UFRJ/COPPE/Systems Engineering and Computing Program, Rio de Janeiro - RJ, 2009.

[20] M. A. Montoni, "An investigation on the critical success factors in software process improvement initiatives," Doctoral Dissertation, UFRJ/COPPE/ Systems Engineering and Computing Program, Rio de Janeiro - RJ, 2010.

[21] B. Kitchenham, *Guidelines for performing systematic*

literature reviews in software engineering. Technical Report RT - EBSE-2007-01: Keele University and Durham University Joint Report, 2007.

[22] F. Q. B. da Silva, M. Suassuna, a. C. C. França, A. M. Grubb, T. B. Gouveia, C. V. F. Monteiro, and I. E. dos Santos, "Replication of empirical studies in software engineering research: a systematic mapping study," *Empir. Softw. Eng.*, vol. 19, no. 3, pp. 501–557, Sep. 2012.

[23] H. Sneed, "Planning the reengineering of legacy systems," *Software, IEEE*, no. January, 1995.

[24] M. Razavian and P. Lago, "A frame of reference for SOA migration," *Towar. a Serv. internet*, pp. 150–162, 2010.

[25] R. Khadka, A. Saeidi, and A. Idu, "Legacy to SOA Evolution: A Systematic Literature Review," *Migrating to SOA ...*, 2012.

APPENDIX A. PRIMARY STUDY

TABLE IX. SELECTED PAPERS

ID	PUBLICATION
S1	Cuadrado, Félix, et al. "A case study on software evolution towards service-oriented architecture." *Advanced Information Networking and Applications-Workshops, 2008. AINAW 2008. 22nd International Conference on*. IEEE, 2008.
S2	Almonaies, Asil A., et al. *A framework for migrating web applications to web services*. Springer Berlin Heidelberg, 2013.
S3	Baghdadi, Youcef, and Wisal Al-Bulushi. "A guidance process to modernize legacy applications for SOA." *Service Oriented Computing and Applications*9.1 (2015): 41-58.
S4	Razavian, Maryam, and Patricia Lago. "A lean and mean strategy for migration to services." *Proceedings of the WICSA/ECSA 2012 Companion Volume*. ACM, 2012.
S5	Khadka, Ravi, et al. "A method engineering based legacy to SOA migration method." *Software Maintenance (ICSM), 2011 27th IEEE International Conference on*. IEEE, 2011.
S6	Sosa, Encarna, et al. "A model-driven process to modernize legacy web applications based on service oriented architectures." *Web Systems Evolution (WSE), 2013 15th IEEE International Symposium on*. IEEE, 2013.
S7	Zhang, Zhuo, et al. "A service composition approach based on sequence mining for migrating e-learning legacy system to SOA." International Journal of Automation and Computing 7.4 (2010): 584-595.
S8	Alahmari, Saad, Ed Zaluska, and David De Roure. "A service identification framework for legacy system migration into SOA." *Services Computing (SCC), 2010 IEEE International Conference on*. IEEE, 2010.
S9	Zhang, Zhuo, et al. "A soa based approach to user-oriented system migration." Computer and Information Technology (CIT), 2010 IEEE 10th International Conference on. IEEE, 2010.
S10	Khadka, Ravi, et al. "A structured legacy to SOA migration process and its evaluation in practice." *Maintenance and Evolution of Service-Oriented and Cloud-Based Systems (MESOCA), 2013 IEEE 7th International Symposium on the*. IEEE, 2013.
S11	Chenghao, Guo, Wang Min, and Zhou Xiaoming. "A wrapping approach and tool for migrating legacy components to web services." Networking and Distributed Computing (ICNDC), 2010 First International Conference on. IEEE, 2010.
S12	Li, Han, et al. "AN EVOLUTION SCHEME FOR BUSINESS RULE BASED LEGACY SYSTEMS." *Journal of Theoretical & Applied Information Technology* 47.1 (2013).
S13	Lewis, Grace, Edwin Morris, and Dennis Smith. "Analyzing the reuse potential of migrating legacy components to a service-oriented architecture.*l*. IEEE, 2006.
S14	LARENTIS, Andrêsa Vargas. *Aruba: Uma Arquitetura para Geração de Serviços a partir de Sistemas Legados de forma não intrusiva*. 2007. 135 f. Universidade do Vale do Rio dos Sinos, 2007.
S15	Rodriguez, Juan Manuel, et al. "Bottom-up and top-down Cobol system migration to web services." *Internet Computing, IEEE* 17.2 (2013): 44-51.
S16	Sneed, Harry M. "COB2WEB a toolset for migrating to web services." *Web Site Evolution, 2008. WSE 2008. 10th International Symposium on*. IEEE, 2008.
S17	Leotta, Maurizio, et al. "Comparing the Maintainability of two Alternative Architectures of a Postal System: SOA vs. non-SOA." *Software Maintenance and Reengineering (CSMR), 2011 15th European Conference on*. IEEE, 2011.
S18	Zhang, Zhuopeng, Hongji Yang, and William C. Chu. "Extracting reusable object-oriented legacy code segments with combined formal concept analysis and slicing techniques for service integration." *Quality Software, 2006. QSIC 2006. Sixth International Conference on*. IEEE, 2006.
S19	Athanasopoulos, Michael, and Kostas Kontogiannis. "Identification of rest-like resources from legacy service descriptions." *Reverse Engineering (WCRE), 2010 17th Working Conference on*. IEEE, 2010.
S20	Sneed, Harry M. "Integrating legacy software into a service oriented architecture." *Software Maintenance and Reengineering, 2006. CSMR 2006. Proceedings of the 10th European Conference on*. IEEE, 2006.
S21	Zhou, Nianjun, et al. "Legacy asset analysis and integration in model-driven soa solution." *Services Computing (SCC), 2010 IEEE International Conference on*. IEEE, 2010.
S22	Huang, Yen-Chieh, and Chih-Ping Chu. "Legacy System User Interface Reengineering Based on the Agile Model Driven Approach." Recent Advances in Computer Science and Information Engineering. Springer Berlin Heidelberg, 2012. 309-314.
S23	Matos, Carlos, and Reiko Heckel. "Legacy transformations for extracting service components." *Rigorous software engineering for service-oriented systems*. Springer Berlin Heidelberg, 2011. 604-621.
S24	Sneed, Harry M., Stefan Schedl, and Stephan H. Sneed. "Linking legacy services to the business process model." *Maintenance and Evolution of Service-Oriented and Cloud-Based Systems (MESOCA), 2012 IEEE 6th International Workshop on the*. IEEE, 2012.
S25	Gedela, Ravi Kumar, et al. "Maximizing the business value from silos: Service based transformation with service data models." *India Conference (INDICON), 2011 Annual IEEE*. IEEE, 2011.
S26	Khadka, Ravi, et al. "Migrating a large scale legacy application to SOA: Challenges and lessons learned." *Reverse Engineering (WCRE), 2013 20th Working Conference on*. IEEE, 2013.
S27	Canfora, Gerardo, et al. "Migrating interactive legacy systems to web services." *Software Maintenance and Reengineering, 2006. CSMR 2006. Proceedings of the 10th European Conference on*. IEEE, 2006.
S28	Alahmari, Saad, Ed Zaluska, and David De Roure. "Migrating Legacy Systems to a Service-Oriented Architecture with Optimal Granularity." (2010).
S29	Matos, Carlos, and Reiko Heckel. "Migrating legacy systems to service-oriented architectures." *Electronic Communications of the EASST* 16 (2009).
S30	Millham, Richard. "Migration of a legacy procedural system to service-oriented computing using feature analysis." *2010 International Conference on Complex, Intelligent and Software Intensive Systems*. IEEE, 2010.
S31	Sheikh, M. A. A., Hatim A. Aboalsamh, and Ahmed Albarrak. "Migration of legacy applications and services to Service-Oriented Architecture (SOA)." Current Trends in Information Technology (CTIT), 2011 International Conference and Workshop on. IEEE, 2011.
S32	Aversano, Lerina, Luigi Cerulo, and Ciro Palumbo. "Mining candidate web services from legacy code." Web Site Evolution, 2008. WSE 2008. 10th International Symposium on. IEEE, 2008.
S33	Fuhr, Andreas, et al. "Model-driven software migration into service-oriented architectures." Computer Science-Research and Development 28.1 (2013): 65-84.
S34	Vemuri, Prasad. "IEEE TENCON-2008 Modernizing a legacy system to SOA-Feature analysis approach." *TENCON 2008-2008 IEEE Region 10 Conference*. IEEE, 2008.
S35	Knight, Daniel P. "Overhauling legacy enterprise software applications with a Concept Refinement Process Model." (2013).
S36	Liu, Yan, et al. "Reengineering legacy systems with RESTful web service."*Computer Software and Applications, 2008. COMPSAC'08. 32nd Annual IEEE International*. IEEE, 2008.
S37	Pérez-Castillo, Ricardo, et al. "Software modernization by recovering Web services from legacy databases." *Journal of Software: Evolution and Process*25.5 (2013): 507-533.
S38	Arsanjani, Ali, et al. "SOMA: A method for developing service-oriented solutions." *IBM systems Journal* 47.3 (2008): 377-396.
S39	Razavian, Maryam, et al. "The SAPIENSA approach for service-enabling pre-existing legacy assets." *SOAME* 2010 (2010): 21-30.
S40	Zillmann, Christian, et al. "The SOAMIG Process Model in Industrial Applications." *CSMR*. 2011.
S41	Bellini, Alexandre, Antonio Francisco do Prado, and Luciana Aparecida Martinez Zaina. "Top-down approach for web services development." *Internet and Web Applications and Services (ICIW), 2010 Fifth International Conference on*. IEEE, 2010.
S42	Salvatierra, Gonzalo, et al. "Towards a computer assisted approach for migrating legacy systems to SOA." *Computational Science and Its Applications–ICCSA 2012*. Springer Berlin Heidelberg, 2012. 484-497.
S43	Razavian, Maryam, and Patricia Lago. "Towards a conceptual framework for legacy to soa migration." *Service-Oriented Computing. ICSOC/ServiceWave 2009 Workshops*. Springer Berlin Heidelberg, 2010.
S44	Kijas, Szymon, and Andrzej Zalewski. "Towards Evolution Methodology for Service-Oriented Systems." *New Results in Dependability and Computer Systems*. Springer International Publishing, 2013. 255-273.
S45	Marchetto, Alessandro, and Filippo Ricca. "Transforming a java application in an equivalent web-services based application: toward a tool supported stepwise approach." *2008 10th International Symposium on Web Site Evolution*. 2008.
S46	Fuhr, Andreas, Tassilo Horn, and Volker Riediger. "Using dynamic analysis and clustering for implementing services by reusing legacy code." *Reverse Engineering (WCRE), 2011 18th Working Conference on*. IEEE, 2011.
S47	Sonntag, Mirko, et al. "Using services and service compositions to enable the distributed execution of legacy simulation applications." *Towards a Service-Based Internet*. Springer Berlin Heidelberg, 2011. 242-253.

A Framework with Agile Practices for Implementation of Project Portfolio Management Process

Lílian Santos Ferreira da Silva, Sandro Ronaldo Bezerra Oliveira
Graduate Program in Computer Science
Federal University of Pará
Belém, Pará, Brazil
e-mail:lilianferreira.ti@gmail.com, srbo@ufpa.br

***Abstract*—There has been an increase in the importance of portfolio management process since its inclusion in quality models and standards. This is shown by the growing number of organizations that are attempting to implement this process effectively and efficiently. This research seeks to assist in the implementation of portfolio management in small and medium-sized companies, by reducing the difficulties and excessive documentation required in traditional processes. This involved carrying out a mapping between the framework for the portfolio management process and the agile practices that were carried out. The result was a set of guidelines that defined how to implement this process framework with agile practices that could be employed for interaction between people.**

Keywords-software quality; process improvement; portfolio management; agile practices.

I. Introduction

Quality is defined by the International Organization for Standardization (ISO) 9000:2000 as "the degree to which a set of inherent characteristics fulfills the requirements" [1]. On the other hand, ISO 10006 adopts a slightly different approach from the previous standard. It states that the scope of quality is the responsibility of management and requires the commitment of everyone involved in the project. Finally, the Project Management Body of Knowledge (PMBOK) defines quality in a similar way to the ISO 9000:2000. According to the Project Management Institute (PMI), "a project with quality is completed in accordance with the requirements, specifications and suitability for use" [2]. It is noteworthy that the aim of these and other concepts of quality is to meet customer requirements and expectations. However, it should be remembered that quality is not only linked to the product but also the process; metrics are defined to ensure the processes comply with applicable quality standards.

In the area of process quality, there have been some improvements in the projects. With regard to software development in particular, there is the Brazilian Software Process Improvement Program (MPS.BR), which is based on the concepts of process maturity and capability. This was set up for the evaluation and improvement of quality and productivity in software and related services. The MPS.BR has maturity levels ranging from A (optimization) to G (partially managed).

This project focuses on the project portfolio management process that is at the maturity level F (Managed) of the respective model. The aim of the process is to "initiate and maintain projects that are necessary, sufficient and sustainable in order to meet the strategic objectives of the organization" [3].

The portfolio management area has become increasingly important, and is included in several other models, such as: (i) Project Portfolio Management Maturity Model (PPMMM) [4], (ii) Portfolio, Programme and Project Management Maturity Model (P3M3) [5], (iii) Programme, and Portfolio Management Maturity Model (P2M3) [6], (iv) Standard for PMI Portfolio Management [7], (v) Organizational Project Management Maturity Model (OPM3) [8], (vi) ISO 12207:2008 [9], and (vii) MPS.BR [3]. As a result of this diversity, software organizations have struggled to implement an efficient portfolio management.

Since 1996, the Association for Promotion of Brazilian Software Excellence (SOFTEX) has carried out initiatives to support the development, promotion and development of the Brazilian Software and IT Services, one of the largest in the world, and renowned for its creativity, competence and source of talent. SOFTEX has been designated by the Ministry of Science, Technology and Innovation (MCTI) to act as the program manager for the Brazilian Promotion of Software Excellence Program. This program benefits more than 2000 companies around the country through a network of 20 regional agents. It is a system ensures that assistance is provided to SOFTEX through the operational and financial training of associated companies by a broad and solid joint partner in the private, government and academic sectors.

According to the website of SOFTEX [10], from 2013 to 2015, there were 286 official assessments of MPS.BR nationwide. Of these, only 10 were held in the North of Brazil, and only 5 included the maturity level F, which is in the project portfolio management process. This shows a low adherence level to maturity models for software process in small and medium-sized companies located in the region.

On the basis of these data, it is clear that of small and medium-sized companies have difficulty in implementing a portfolio management process by following the guidelines and practices described in the MPS.BR model. Thus, the goal of this work is to propose a flexible approach to portfolio management, which involves holding faster and more dynamic meetings that are mainly concerned with the interaction and commitment of those involved in the process. The project portfolio management process was chosen because according to Pinto *et al.* [11], its objectives are to optimize the portfolios of organizations and link projects to strategies. In other words, it is an essential process for successful businesses, because it is aligned to the organizational strategy, business, mission and values.

The Agile Manifesto is a set of practices that aims to guide the actions of agile teams, by keeping them focused on what really adds value to both the project and the client. Based on 12 principles, this manifesto is used as a guide for the agile activities of the projects teams, to maximize results. Its principles are as follows: value, flexibility, frequency, unity, motivation, communication, functionality, sustainability, review strategies, simplicity, organization and self-assessment. In general, the manifesto values are: its ability to allow people to interact with processes and tools, its working software for comprehensive documentation, customer collaboration in negotiating contracts, and its ability to respond to change by following a plan. On this basis, it was decided to work with agile methods, so that the project portfolio management process could be more interactive, and allow the staff to be more involved with the process. This was a means of ensuring faster and tangible results, and the team itself encouraged to execute the defined process. This required employing the process framework proposed in [12]. Thus, it was possible to carry out a mapping between this framework and the agile practices of the software project development and management. The agile methods used in the mapping were: Scrum, eXtreme Programming (XP) and Adaptive Software Development (ASD).

This paper is structured in the following way: Section 2 examines the related work and outlines the background of this work. Section 3 describes the approach that is adopted to implement the project portfolio management with agile practices. Section 4 analyzes the expected results of this research, and Section 5 concludes the study with some final considerations.

II. Background and Related Work

This section provides an overview of the project portfolio management in MR-MPS-SW and some related works.

A. Project Portfolio Management in MR-MPS-SW

The importance of project portfolio management (GPP) for decision-making is underlined by the inclusion of this process in ISO / IEC 12207:2008 [9] and MPS.BR [10], which is particularly designed for the software lifecycle.

Together with the reference model for software included in MPS.BR, which is called the Reference Model for the Software Process Improvement (MR-MPS-SW), the project portfolio management process has two goals: selecting the projects that will be carried out, and monitoring / evaluating these projects to ensure that they remain viable and adhere to the criteria for which they were approved. In addition, it is essential to "initiate and maintain projects that are necessary, sufficient and sustainable in order to meet the strategic objectives of the organization" [3].

This process has obtained investment and the appropriate organizational resources and has the authority to carry out the selected projects. It performs a continuous assessment of the projects to determine whether they justify continued investment, or should be redirected [10]. To achieve these goals, the process assumes there will be eight expected results:

- GPP1 – The business opportunities, needs and investment are identified, qualified, prioritized and selected by objective criteria with regard to the strategic objectives of the organization,
- GPP2 – The resources and budgets for each project are identified and allocated,
- GPP3 - The responsibilities and authority for managing the projects are set out,
- GPP4 - The portfolio is monitored with regard to the criteria, which were used for prioritization,
- GPP5 - Actions to correct deviations in the portfolio and to prevent the detected problems from recurring are fully established, implemented and monitored,
- GPP6 - Conflicts over resources between projects are handled and solved, in accordance with the criteria used for prioritization,
- GPP7 – The projects that meet the requirements are kept together with the agreements that led to their approval and those that do not meet the requirements are redirected or canceled,
- GPP8 - The situation with regard to the project portfolio is communicated to the stakeholders, at defined intervals or whenever the portfolio is changed.

B. Related Work

While carrying out this research a non-systematic literature review was conducted to find previous studies that have related themes to this work but none was found that discusses the question of whether practices by agile methods can be employed to implement portfolio management. However, these studies were analyzed to determine what support can be given by this research to the implementation of portfolio management.

The main work, which was used as a reference-point for this research, was [12], which defined a process framework for software project portfolio management in accordance with the guidelines provided by the MPS.BR Implementation Guide, the ISO / IEC 12207 and the standard for PMI Portfolio Management. In addition, the author supplements this framework with recommendations drawn from the used models and technical literature regarding approaches to the implementation of their activities and tasks.

Another work related to this area is the paper [13], which proposes RisAgi, an agile methodology that supports risk management in software development projects; in the context of the processes, PMBOK is included in the area of risk assessment. Some of the activities within the portfolio management include the identification and analysis of portfolio risks. Thus, this approach was adopted to support the implementation of these practices.

Another work that was analyzed and that makes a contribution to the subject of this research is the work presented in [14]. This paper based on the development of new products and in the case of software engineering literature, a case study that took place in three companies. This adopts an approach to the implementation of portfolio management in small product-oriented software companies, which involves analyzing their early experiences.

The approach integrates the basic assets of portfolio management, such as strategic alignment, portfolio balancing and "to go or not" decisions, in accordance with the pace of modern software development in small companies. This work was very useful because it showed the reality of that happens in small companies, which is the focus of this work.

Finally we studied the work of Sbrocco and Macedo [15], which carries out a comparative study of features, applications and examples of the main paradigms, such as Scrum, XP, Feature Driven Development (FDD), ASD and Crystal methodologies, among other agile methods. This work provided a macro view of the most widely used current agile methods, to ensure that the best practices were chosen to assist in the implementation of agile portfolio management in small companies.

One of the weaknesses of these studies is that they fail to deal with the project portfolio management in an integrated way or consider the benefits offered by agile methods. They do not demonstrate how agile principles can be applied within the portfolio management in a way that can facilitate the implementation of the process in organizations.

On the positive side, the analysis of these works was used to support the construction of a solid knowledge base for this study. First, the portfolio management process was well understood, and then the agile methods were studied; a relationship was forged between them, resulting in the achievement of the goal of this research, which is to propose an agile portfolio management.

III. An Approach to the Implementation Of Portfolio Management by means of Agile Practices

In the context of agile methods, several models have been proposed, but the ones that will be used in this work are as follows: XP, ASD and Scrum [16]. These methods were chosen because their practices are compatible with the activities of project portfolio management.

The XP is one of the best known and most widely used methods. It discusses iterative development and customer engagement at extreme levels. It advocates a number of good practices, such as the use of metaphors that have the power to convey complex ideas simply and clearly. In addition, it includes ideas of refactoring, release delivery, pair programming and the use of stories that are small cards where the customer writes the features that are required by the system.

Another agile method used in this work was Scrum [16], which is also widely used in organizations that employ agile project management. In general, Scrum has three main parts in its model: roles, events and artifacts. It also has the following events: sprint, sprint planning meeting, daily meeting, sprint meeting and sprint retrospective and review meeting [17].

Each Sprint is divided into phases that use roles, events and artifacts to reach their ultimate goal, which was set for the customer.

Finally, ASD practices were used, which are concerned with communication. Sprint also uses the code review to improve its quality and make more progress in learning. In addition, preliminary workshops are run to raise the high-level requirements for the project; these requirements are outlined in detail along with the iterations.

A. *A Workflow for the Portfolio Management*

A portfolio management framework was used for this project as proposed in [12]; the main phases of this are described in Fig. 1.

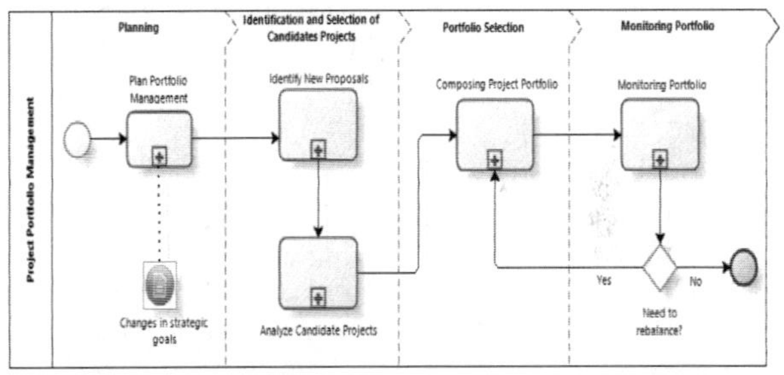

Figure 1. A Macro-workflow for the Portfolio Management

The process framework includes activities, tasks and recommendations to define a process for software project portfolio management in accordance with the recommendations of the Project Portfolio Management process of ISO / IEC 12207 and the expected results of the Project Portfolio Management process included in the MR-MPS-SW model. The framework is divided into phases, activities and tasks, which are defined as a set of good practices, and are arranged in a flowchart as proposed in Fig.1. The following phases are defined:

- **Planning:** this is the stage for defining the guidelines of the project portfolio management process. It consists of the "Plan Portfolio Management" activity. Within this activity, the procedures and techniques used within the portfolio management process were defined, and range from using boards to defining the categories of the projects and the organization has resources,
- **Identification and Selection of Candidates Projects:** the purpose of this phase is to attract new project opportunities for the "pre-selection" of projects with greater strategic potential for the organization. It consists of the "Identify New Proposals" and "Analyze Candidate Projects" activities. In this phase, projects are categorized, evaluated and selected. The projects are written on cards and placed in the CANVAS,
- **Portfolio Selection:** this phase includes the project portfolio composition stage, which makes use of the

information from the "Identification and Selection of Candidates Projects" and "Monitoring the Portfolio Project" phases. It consists of the "Composing a Portfolio Project". The activity of composing the portfolio project includes the following: prioritization and portfolio balancing, identification of expected results, identification and analysis of portfolio risks, approval of the portfolio and starting projects,

- **Monitoring the Portfolio:** this phase is carried out constantly and involves monitoring the portfolio; in addition, it produces some information about the situation of the portfolio and its components for decision-making, balancing and the allocation of organizational resources. It involves the "Monitoring Portfolio" activity. In this activity, the burndown and burnup chart tools monitor the performance, by means of assessment indicators such as: risk probability, delivery, costs and development work.

B. An Agile Approach

The proposal of a framework for agile project portfolio management was based on the results obtained by mapping the 5 activities identified in the macro workflow and the agile practices that can be used in these activities. This required checking the compatibility of the agile practices for all the activities present in the macro workflow - a total of 34 tasks for the project portfolio management. Some of the agile practices that can be used in each activity of the macro workflow are outlined in the subsection below.

1) Activity 1: Planning and Portfolio Management

In this activity, employed practices are that used in Scrum method; for example, the Planning Meeting used in Scrum. A preliminary workshop is run, which employs the ASD method to identify organizational goals and plan the portfolio management.

2) Activity 2: Identifying New Proposals

In this activity an example of agile practice that can be applied is derived from the Scrum and XP. The practice of writing "User Stories" is similar, because it was adopted in this approach to write projects on cards and to compose the portfolio. The stories and features are written with the aid of these methods.

3) Activity 3: Analysis of Candidate Projects

In this activity the Scrum practice of "Meeting the Product Owner" was used, as it will make it possible to evaluate the projects written on cards that will be carried out along with the portfolio management.

4) Activity 4: Composing the Project Portfolio

A technique was employed for carrying out this activity that involved writing "user stories" in Scrum. This practice was used to prioritize the projects and select the projects that make up the company's portfolio.

In addition to this practice, the "Review Meeting" will also be adopted. In Scrum, this meeting is held for the approval of each sprint (iteration) that is completed in the projects. In this research it can be adapted so that not only the modules can be approved but also the portfolio as a whole.

Finally, the "Retrospective Meeting" practice in Scrum is used to record the lessons learned when developing the portfolio, and showing the strengths, weaknesses and improvements needed for the project portfolio.

5) Activity5: Monitoring the Portfolio

The practice of using the Burndown chart is recommended for monitoring the portfolio and tracking the progress of the projects. The graph shows that there was a deviation from the plan and this deviation can be detected in the practice of the "Daily Meeting". If any deviation from the plan is found, the "treatment actions" are turned into cards and are estimated like the others. The portfolio performance can be reported by images from the burndown chart or photos of periods in the project task board.

C. The Evaluation of the Approach

The evaluation of this work was initially carried out to check whether the activities that form the project portfolio management framework are compatible with the agile practices. This involved sending an expert in Software Quality and Process Improvement areas to obtain feedback about its evaluation and to give opinions or make suggestions about improvements.

After the improvements have been made in the mapping on the basis of the appraiser's experience, a set of guidelines was prepared on how to implement the improvements with agile practices was drawn up. The artifacts, events and roles were defined. As a result, the process of agile project portfolio management in an organization could be implemented and a case study will be conducted to determine its effectiveness and efficiency. This case study is underway in a Brazilian software development organization, and some metrics are being collected to assess how far these goals have been achieved. In the case study, we have already identified some factors such as the need to adjust the order of some of the framework activities to provide more mobility for the Process Portfolio Management. In addition, it is clear that there are benefits in using cards and putting a list of the activities carried out on the wall, to provide more transparency to the process.

IV. Expected Results

This paper sets out a model of project portfolio management to support small and medium-sized companies. By means of this model, we intend to offer a new alternative for organizations interested in process improvement or looking for an official evaluation of MPS.BR that can speed up and reduce the costs and time needed for process implementation.

At the end of this work, we hope to make a contribution to this area of studies by means of the following: (1) a mapping of project portfolio management practices underpinned by a framework based on models of quality standards and agile practices, (2) a proposal on how to implement the framework activities in an agile way, and (3) suggestions about the events, artifacts and roles involved in this process.

The main distinguishing feature of this work is to propose a solution for the agile portfolio management based on the activities of a Brazilian region characterized by a limited adoption of quality models. Thus, the work provides knowledge and resources to help improve the local software process and also other small and medium-sized companies not located in this Brazilian region.

V. CONCLUSION

This study shows the importance of improving the process quality within organizations and how the portfolio management process has gained prominence in terms of quality models and standards.

A mapping of the portfolio management framework based on the expected results of the MR-MPS-SW and agile practices that are most widely used was carried out to assist organizations to implement this process. In addition to this mapping, a set of guidelines was recommended on how to implement all the agile portfolio management processes.

Future work in this research area could involve carrying out an experiment through the use of an agile framework in a case study. This could be conducted in a software development organization to make comparisons about the situation of this organization before and after the implementation of the practices. This will be evaluate by us together with the members of the organization to ensure the necessary improvements are made in the framework so that it can be adapted to real situations faced by the organization.

ACKNOWLEDGMENT

The authors would like to thank the Dean of Research and Postgraduate Studies at the Federal University of Pará (PROPESP/UFPA) by the Qualified Publication Support Program (PAPQ) for the financial support.

REFERENCES

[1] ABNT – Associação Brasileira de Normas Técnicas, "NBR ISO 9000:2000 – Quality Management Systems – Fundamentals and Vocabulary", Rio de Janeiro: ABNT, Brazil, 2000.

[2] PMI - Project Management Institute, "A Guide to the Project Management Body of Knowledge - PMBOK™", Syba: PMI Publishing Division, 2008, Available: - www.pmi.org, retrieved: July 2016.

[3] SOFTEX –Associação para a Promoção da Excelêcia do Software Brasileiro, "MPS.BR – Software General Guide MPS: 2016", Brazil, 2016, Available: www.softex.br, retrieved: July 2016.

[4] J. S. Pennypacker, "Project Portfolio Management Maturity Model", Center for Business Practices, Havertown, Pennsylvania, USA, 2005.

[5] OGC - Office of Government Commerce, "Portfolio, Programme and Project Management Maturity Model", Office of Government Commerce, London, UK, 2006.

[6] Gartner, "Programme and Portfolio Management Maturity Model", Gartner RAS Core Research Note G00141742, 2007.

[7] PMI - Project Management Institute, "The Standard for Portfolio Management", Syba: PMI Publishing Division, 2008, Available: www.pmi.org, retrieved: July 2016.

[8] PMI - Project Management Institute, "Organizational ProjectManagement Maturity Model – OPM3", Second Edition, Syba: PMI Publishing Division, 2008, Available: www.pmi.org, retrieved: July 2016.

[9] ABNT – Associação Brasileira de Normas Técnicas, "NBR ISO/IEC 12207:2009 – Software Systems Engineering – Software Life Cycle Processes", Rio de Janeiro: ABNT, Brazil, 2009.

[10] SOFTEX – Associação para Promoção da Excelência do Software Brasileiro, "MPS.BR – General Guide Software: 2012", Brazil, 2012.

[11] J. K. Pinto, D. I. Cleland, and D. P. Slevin, "The Frontiers of Project Management Research", Philadelphia: Project Management Institute, 2003.

[12] M. Souza, "A process framework for software Project portfolio management based on quality standards", Dssertação de Mestrado, PPGCC/UFPA, Brazil, 2013.

[13] J. B. M. C. Neto, K. B. C. Santos, P. V. R. Cardoso, and S. R. B. Oliveira, "RisAgi: An Agile Methodology for Risk Management in Software Development Projects", Trabalho de Especialização em Gerência de Projetos, PPGCC/UFPA, Brazil, 2013.

[14] J. Vähäniitty and K. Rautiainen, "Towards an Approach for Managing the Development Portfolio in Small Product-Oriented Software Companies", Software Business and Engineering Institute, Helsinki University of Technology, Finland, 2005.

[15] J. H. T. C. Sbrocco and P. C. Macedo, "Agile–Software Engineering under measure", Brazil, 2012.

[16] K. Schwaber and J. Sutherland, "The Scrum Guide", 2013, Available: http://www.scrumguides.org, retrieved: July 2016.

[17] S. R. Kennety, "Essential Scrum: A Practical Guide to The Most Popular Agile Process", Addison-Wesley, 2012.

Software Evolution Visualization Tools Functional Requirements: a Comprehensive Understanding

Hani Bani-Salameh
Department of Software Engineering
The Hashemite University, Jordan
Email: hani@hu.edu.jo

Ayat Ahmad
Department of Software Engineering
The Hashemite University, Jordan
Email: ayat_ahmad1991@yahoo.com

Dua'a Bani-Salameh
Department of Computer Science
JUST, Jordan
Email: duaabs@gmail.com

***Abstract*—Software is usually going under many changes during its life time cycle. Following up software changes and enhancements is an essential process for many reasons: it increases the complexity of software projects, and affects the software structure and quality. Software visualization is considered as one of the comprehensive techniques that developers make use of daily in order to analyze and understand how the software evolves and changes over time. To achieve this, developers use software evolution visualization (SEV) tools, and face difficulties finding/identifying the most suitable tool. The goal of this study is to identify generic functional requirements for software visualization tools, in order to help developers choose their tools based on the supported features/requirements. The main focus is on tools that target softwares' evolution. The research methodology is based on a systematic review that aims to summarize the current research on software SEVs and to answer a question on "what are the main functional requirements for software evolution visualization tools that have been identified in the literature?" The most common functional requirements and activities that have been identified in this study are views, detailed-on-demand, filter, select, re-arrange, and comparison.**

Keywords–Evolution; Software Evolution Visualization; Tools.

I. Introduction

Software evolution is an essential topic in software engineering and maintenance [1]. Software continually changes in response to any changes in (1) the requirement, (2) environment to adapt new technology, and (3) to repair errors. With increasing the size and complexity of the software systems, following up the continual software changes is not an easy task. Software engineers need to understand how software evolves over time to keep the software operational with a high quality. Also, this is necessary to present its state and to predict its future development.

Software visualization is a powerful technique for software comprehension by mapping different software aspects with visual properties such as position, size, shape, and color [2][3]. It is shown that it can be effective to understand and analyze software evolution. There are many SEV tools. Such tools aim to visualize the version history of software systems by visualizing history of the software artifact such as - source code changes, test files, and documentation. No matter what is the source of visualization or in what level (source code, documentation, or other) it is implemented . These tools have common requirements and functionalities, and have been studied to extract a set of common functional requirements for SEV tools.

Requirements identification is the base and the start point for building any software project [4]. Also, it is important for the construction of SEV tools. Each tool uses a different technique to represent different types of changes, have particular advantages, and is facing different problems and challenges.

SEV tools usually deal with and process a huge amount of data that is needed to visualize in order to follow software changes and the impact of these changes [5]. A good user interface design for SEV tools involves multiple user interaction techniques which give users the ability to interact with and represent data such as multiple views, select, filter and other features, that can help to overcome challenges and increase user's satisfaction. Also, interaction techniques can affect the quality of SEV tools by allowing higher flexibility and extensibility [6]. Studying such tools allows us to specify more important features and functional requirements that increase the users' satisfaction, and humans' understanding for software evolution in specific.

The main goal of this study is to identify a list of generic functional requirements for SEV tools. Defining requirements for such tools can be used as an indicator to ensure if these tools meet the quality attributes, enhance human perception, and meet user's expectations. Also, this study presents the current state of such tools which represents the first step when building a new SEV tool, and in defining the requirements for the future.

The remaining part of this paper is organized as follow. Section II describes the research approach that have been followed when conducting the review. Section III discusses the functional requirements uncovered by this study. Section IV provides a brief discussion. Finally, Section V presents the future work and concludes the paper.

II. Method

To identify the functional requirements for the SEV tools, we started our study by identifying a research question as follows.

"What are the main functional requirements for the software evolution visualization tools that have been identified in the literature?"

Then, we started to collect papers that have clear demonstration for the used features and interaction techniques. The total of all surveyed papers is 39.

A list of all interaction techniques is introduced, then we started to analyze the papers and summarize most common set of techniques used.

Next, similar features are grouped (categorized) based on what tasks they perform, and what are the goals from those operations. Different interactions/features techniques are used to perform similar tasks and similar goals.

During the analysis of the SEV tools, the focus was on *what important features that help developers to better understand the software evolution process*. For this reason, we focused on what users achieve by using such operations rather than how.

III. Functional Requirements

Following is a list of six functional requirements that have been found common in most SEV tools (see Table I):

- **Views:** show different representation.
- **Details-on demand:** show more information/details.
- **Filter and Search:** show something conditionally.
- **Select:** marks something as point of interest.
- **Re-arrangement:** shows different arrangements of the data sets (e.g. sort, cluster, and aggregate).
- **Comparison:** shows the differences between different data sets.

TABLE I. MOST COMMON FUNCTIONAL REQUIREMENTS.

Method/Functionality	Ways to Visualize
Views	• Different Granularity Levels • Increase Abstraction Level • Dependencies & Relationships • Others
Details-on-Demand	• Zoom • Expand • Mouse Cursor Hovers
Filter & Search	• Uses checkbox • Change color, and change representation
Select	Select and highlight data sets.
Re-arrange	Analyze changes in different ways such as aggregate, cluster and sort.
Comparison	Comparing changes that occur from time to time, and between different software versions.

A. Views: to show different representation

SEV tools provide different visual representations of the target software history (e.g. different colors, size, and shapes with animation). Multiple views is an effective technique that helps software engineers to understand how different parts of the software evolved and changed in different perspectives. It provides flexibility to analyst to directly find views that fit their goals.

Multiple views are used in SEV tools to show how changes occur in different ways as the following:

- **In different granularity levels of the system:** an example of multiple views is provided by Xie et al. who define multiple views of the data history changes at different granularity levels (e.g. system level, file(class) level, method level, and line level) by supporting navigation within views [7].
- **To increase abstraction level:** the DEVis [8] tool uses multiple windows/views to increase the abstraction level. When a part or icon is selected a more detailed window appears.
- **Clear insight about dependencies and relationships:** using different representations which provide the user with a clear insight about dependencies and relationships between software artifacts, and to identify which parts of the project are changed together (see ChronoTwigger [9]).
- **Different types of visualization (chart with histogram):** multiple views can be used to represent how data changed (e.g. charts with histogram), in order to give insight into evolutionary trends and phenomena governing software growth (see SEANet tools [10], AniMatrix [11]). They help to give users with the ability to navigate/travel/fly within views by selecting or clicking a specific node.

B. Details-on-Demand: Show More Information and Details.

Most SEV tools provide users with the ability to get more details when needed about the presented data such as: number of revisions in a specific date, type of changes occurred, and number of nodes in a specific version. User interaction techniques used to get more details are (1)*Zooming* (Zoom-in, Zoom-out), (2)*Expand*, and (3)*Mouse Cursor Hovers* over a data item. Using zoom-out users can change scale of data overview for large data sets, or decrease it using zoom-in to get detailed view for small data sets [12]. Examples such as (AniMatri [11], SEANet [10], and DEVis [8]).

C. Filter and Search: Show Something Conditionally.

Filter used in SEV tools which allows users to control the displayed data based on a specific condition (query), where users specify conditions or ranges (e.g. based on type, range of specific duration time, or another criteria). Only the data that satisfy the condition is presented and the other data is hidden from the view or shown in a different way or different color. ClonEvol [13] uses checkbox to filter by node's type (attribute, class, and file), and by type of operation (add, delete, modified). ChronoTwigger [9] allows to show only the node(file) that have co-change/changed within selected timespan, and hides nodes that do not have any change event. Filter is used in AniMatrix [11], that allows users to control data presented in history navigator, is using filter by interface name or by type of coupling in order to show classes that have been changed over time, and to show different types of coupling. From the above, it appears that user interaction techniques implemented in most of the SEV tools are: *checkbox, change color, and change representation.*

D. Select: Mark Something as Point of Interest.

SEV tools which provide users with the ability to select data sets and highlight them, to facilitate, follow up, and track how large data changed and evolved over time, and to identify locations of more important data that have co-change or most impact change. ChronoTwigger [9] allows users to select a node or set of nodes on the 2D visualization to highlight the set of corresponding/related nodes in 3D view.

E. Re-arrangement: Show Different Arrangement of Data Sets.

SEV tools which provide users with the ability to change the way of representation of software entities in new arrangements, and group it in different perspectives. Re-arrangement allow developers to analyze changes in different ways such as *aggregate, cluster, and sort*. Storyline tool allows users to aggregate developer in one large clusters, and connects everyone to everyone else [14]. iVIS [15] allows to re-arrange the entity layout of the visualizations by selecting software entities and dragging them around. This allows the developers to analyze co-changes between selected entities in different groups, and can give more attentions for a specific entity by the developer.

F. Comparison: Show the Differences Between Different Data Sets.

Comparing changes that occur from time to time, and between different software versions is an essential requirement in the SEV tools, that helps developers to analyze the differences between software versions and to identify the state of the system. Some tools provide comprehensive techniques in the single view using color and animation.

Comparison mode used in eCITY tool [16] which allows to compare between two different dates by using animation, and sequentially insert the new components. This allows users to compare the states of specific dates side by side. Salamanca et al. [17] present a tools that provides a software structures view, and allows a side-by-side comparison of the evolving package or class hierarchy structures from the selected project revisions in circular timeline. Other examples appear in [18] and [19].

G. Other Requirements

Following is a list of requirements mentioned by researchers but not commonly used.

- Source code presentation: which gives users the ability to access the underling source code [11][17][21].
- Panning [11]22], Brushing, Collapse [22][23], manipulate [9][22], move up and down [8][18][24].

The SEV tools can be divided into two categories. The categorization is based on the (1)**type** of visualization that is used (at which level such as Artifacts and Structure Evolution), and (2)**method** to represent the techniques used to visualize the software evolution (See Figure 1). Figure 1 shows that the visualization tools are categorized either based on the type of visualization they support (eg. visualizing software artifacts and structure) or the methods of visualization (eg. views, filters, comparison, etc.).

This study does not pay attention to what are the used types of SEV tools. The main focus is on getting generic functional requirement to guide all users either researchers, developers, or maintainers to better understand software's evolution process.

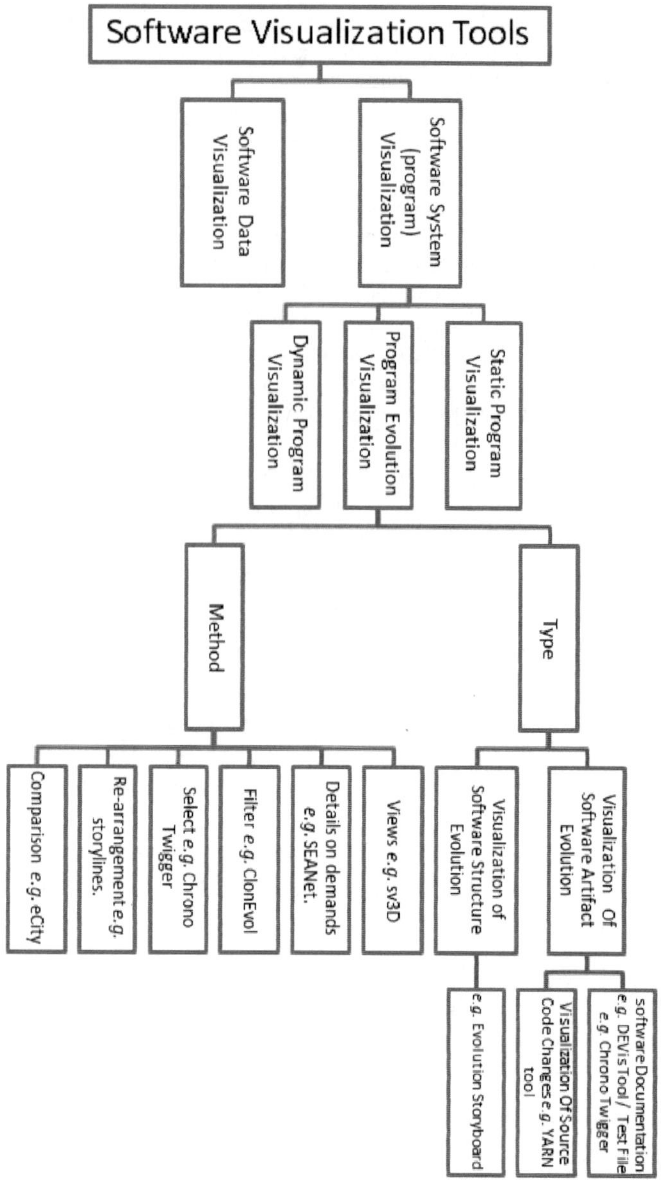

Figure 1. Classification of SEV Tools.

IV. Discussion

It is difficult to find all interaction technique used in the SEV tools. The proposed functional requirements for the SEV tools are defined based on features supported in most of the existing tools. The supported features can help users to better understand software changes and evolution. This section discusses more issues about the proposed functional requirements.

Interactive facilities provided to the user are essential to the quality of the SEV tools. They support higher flexibility and extensibility [6], where users not only can see information but also can interact with it to reduce the effort needed for better understanding, and supports the ability to faster change context of information as needed in powerful ways.

Different visual attributes such as color, animation and

different shape "way of representation" are used by SEV tools requirements to enrich user interface and increase user satisfaction. Also, animation is used to enable to analyze large information in a usable way. It allows to compare instances sequentially, show dependencies between software artifacts. Also, it illustrates dynamic behaviors for software evolution.

Some interaction techniques are used in the SEV tools to fulfill the user's multiple intents, and it is possible to fit more than one requirement/feature in the tool. For example, comparison features are intended to show differences between specific data sets; filters feature helps users to compare their data sets, the re-arrange feature allows to compare two groups, and the multiple views feature allows users to compare between different views of the software. Also, multiple views are used to increase the abstraction level in order to give users the ability to get more details as needed.

We believe that the proposed generic functional requirements for SEV tools is useful and has several advantages. First, they can be used as a first step when building new SEV tools, and in order to examine whether they meet users' needs. Second, they can be used to understand what are the user's needs, and help to find new techniques that might help to better understand the software evolution process.

V. Conclusion and Future Work

This research project identifies generic functional requirements for the software evolution visualization tool by studying the existing literature. The main goal for identified requirement for software evolution visualization tool is to find more essential requirements that help all stockholder to better understand the software evolution process. The six reported functional requirements are: *views*, which provide multiple representations for changes in different granularity level, different version, for different type of artifact; *detailed-on demand* requirements provide the user with more information than needed such as number of revisions, number of nodes in a specific version, and so on, by mouse hover and zoom-in, zoom-out operation; *filter and search* which has the ability to change data presented based on specific condition(e.g. a developer that wants to analyze changes that occur in a specific time stamp and hide the other changes). *Select* requirements give the user the ability to mark specific things as needed. *Re-arrange* feature is considered as a good way to group presented data in different perspectives by sorting or clustering. Finally, *Comparison* is the last suggested requirement in this study. It gives the user the ability to make comparisons, and allows them to notice differences between software versions for different types of entities in different level.

Further study can be performed in the future in order to expand our list of functional requirements. Also, the study can be extended to gather feedback from developers, and domain experts which helps to identify a list of non-functional requirements for the SEV tools. This can help developers and designers to build a generic software quality model for such tools.

References

[1] R. Lima, A. Torres, T. Souto, M. Mendona, and N. Zazworka, "Software evolution visualization: A systematic mapping study", Information Software Technology, vol. 55, no. 11, pp. 1860–1883, 2013.

[2] D. Gracanin, K. Matkovic, and M. Eltoweissy, "Software visualization," Innovations in Systems and Software Engineering, vol. 1, no. 2, pp. 221-230, 2005.

[3] J. Heer, B. Shneiderman, and C. Park, "Interactive Dynamics for Visual Analysis: A Taxonomy of Tools that Support the Fluent and Flexible Use of Visualizations," Queue - Micoprocessors, vol. 10, no. 2, pp. 30-55, 2012.

[4] H. M. Kienle and H. A. Muiller, "Requirements of Software Visualization Tools: A Literature Survey," In Proceedings of the 4th IEEE International Workshop on Visualizing Software for Understanding and Analysis (VISSOFT), Canada, 2007, pp. 2–9.

[5] S.-L. Voinea. "Software Evolution Visualization," PhD thesis, Technische Universiteit Eindhoven, 2007.

[6] M. Lanza, "CodeCrawler-Lessons Learned in Building a Software Visualization Tool," In Proceedings of the European Conference on Software Maintenance and Reengineering, pp. 409–418, 2003, IEEE Press.

[7] X. Xie, D. Poshyvanyk, and A. Marcus, "Visualization of CVS Repository Information," In Proceedings of the 13th Working Conference Reverse Engineering., 2006, pp. 231-242.

[8] J. Zhi and G. Ruhe, "DEVis: A Tool for Visualizing Software Document Evolution," In Proceedings of the First IEEE Working Conference on Software Visualization, Eindhoven, Netherlands, 2013, pp. 1-4.

[9] B. Ens, D. Rea, R. Shpaner, H. Hemmati, J. E. Young, and P. Irani, "ChronoTwigger: A Visual Analytics Tool for Understanding Source and Test Co-Evolution," In Proceedings of the 2nd IEEE Working Conference on Software Visualization (VISSOFT). Victoria, Canada. 2014, pp. 117–126.

[10] T. Chaikalis, G. Melas, and A. Chatzigeorgiou, "SEANets: Software Evolution Analysis with Networks," In Proceedings of the 28th IEEE International Conference on Software Maintenance (ICSM), Trento, Italy, 2012, pp. 634-637.

[11] G. Melanc, "AniMatrix: A Matrix-Based Visualization of Software Evolution," In Proceedings of the Second IEEE Working Conference on Software Visualization (VISSOFT), 2014, pp. 1–10.

[12] J. S. Yi, Y. Kang, J. T. Stasko, and J. A. Jacko, "Toward a Deeper Understanding of the Role of Interaction in Information Visualization," IEEE Transactions on Visualization and Computer Graphics (TVCG), vol. 13, no. 6. Presented in InfoVis 2007, Sacramento, California, October 28 - November 1, pp. 1224–1231.

[13] A. Hanjali, "ClonEvol: Visualizing Software Evolution with Code Clones," In Proceedings of the First IEEE Working Conference on Software Visualization (VISSOFT), 2013, pp. 1-4.

[14] M. Ogawa, "Software Evolution Storylines," 2010, URL:http://www.michaelogawa.com/research/storylines/, [accessed: 13–07–2016].

[15] A. Vanya, R. Premraj, and H. van Vliet, "Interactive Exploration of Co-evolving Software Entities," In Proceedings of the 14th European Conference on Software Maintenance and Reengineering (CSMR), 2010, pp. 260-263.

[16] T. Khan, H. Barthel, A. Ebert, and P. Liggesmeyer, "eCITY: A Tool to Track Software Structural Changes using an Evolving City," In Proceedings of the 29th IEEE International Conference on Software Maintenance (ICSM), 2013, pp. 492–495.

[17] A. Gonzalez, R. Theron, A. Telea, and F. J. Garcia, "Combined Visualization of Structural and Metric Information for Software Evolution Analysis," In Proceedings of the joint international and annual ERCIM workshops on Principles of software evolution (IWPSE) and software evolution (Evol) workshops, ACM, 2009, pp. 25-30.

[18] O. Benomar and P. Poulin, "Visualizing Software Dynamicities with Heat Maps," In Proceedings of the First IEEE Working Conference on Software Visualization (VISSOFT), 2013, pp. 1-10.

[19] Q. Tu and M. W. Godfrey, "An integrated approach for studying architectural evolution," In Proceedings of the 10th International Workshop on Program Comprehension, 2002, pp. 127-136

[20] M. Burch, C. Vehlow, F. Beck, S. Diehl, D. Weiskopf, and I. C. Society, "Parallel Edge Splatting for Scalable Dynamic Graph Visualization, IEEE Transactions on Visualization and Computer Graphics, vol. 17, no. 12, 2011, pp. 2344–2353.

[21] M. Lungu and M. Lanza, "Exploring Inter-Module Relationships in Evolving Software Systems," In Proceedings of the 11th European Conference on Software Maintenance and Reengineering, Amsterdam, 2007, pp. 91–102.

[22] S. Boccuzzo and H. C. Gall, "Multi-Touch Collaboration for Software Exploration," International Conference on Program Comprehension, Portugal, 2010, pp. 30–33.

[23] M. D. Ambros and M. Lanza, "A Flexible Framework to Support Collaborative Software Evolution Analysis," In Proceedings of the 12th IEEE European Conference on Software Maintenance and Reengineering, 2008, IEEE CS Press, pp. 3-12.

[24] M. D. Ambros and M. Lanza, "BugCrawler: Visualizing Evolving Software Systems," In Proceedings of the 11th European Conference on Software Maintenance and Reengineeringpp, Amsterdam, 2007, pp. 333–334.

Development of Network System Based on Fiber-To-The-Desktop (FTTD) in a National University Hospital

Osamu Takaki, Kota Torikai, Shinichi Tsujimura, Ryoji Suzuki, Yuichiro Saito
System Integration Center
Gunma University Hospital
Maebashi, Japan
email: {takaki, torikai, tsujimura, ryoji-s, saitoyui}@gunma-u.ac.jp

Takashi Aoki
Division of Medical Information
Gunma University Hospital
Maebashi, Japan
email: taoki@lemon.plala.or.jp

Kenta Maeda
1st Solution Department
NEC Networks & System Integration Corporation
Tokyo, Japan
email: maeda@z5.nesic.com

Ichiroh Suzuta
Eastern Japan Sales Department
Alaxala Networks Corporation
Kawasaki, Japan
email: ichiroh.suzuta@alaxala.com

Nobukuni Hamamoto
Library and Information Technology Center
Gunma University
Maebashi, Japan
email: n.hamamoto@gunma-u.ac.jp

***Abstract*— The authors have developed a network system in a national university hospital based on Fiber-To-The-Desktop (FTTD), which is a network architecture that has a star network topology. This paper describes backgrounds from which the hospital required the FTTD-based network system and issues that the authors faced in development of the network system. Moreover, this paper evaluates effects of their FTTD-based system and discusses advantages and disadvantages of FTTD, based on the authors' experiences of both development and administration of the network system.**

Keywords-FTTD; network system; national university hospital.

I. Introduction

Recently, a lot of large hospitals including university hospitals introduce various information systems to assist medical care services ranging from administration of patients' healthcare records to accounting service [1][2]. Consequently, network systems, which are base of the hospital information systems, have become large and complex. The reason why the network systems have grown is not only the growth of the server systems of hospital informations systems but also diversification of devices that medical staffs employ. Today medical staffs use multiple information terminal devices ranging from desktop computers to smart phone everywhere in hospitals to input and view information for medical services. Since this tendency continues for the foreseeable future, network systems of hospitals will grow increasingly large.

The growth of scale and complexity of a network system increases in not only the cost of the system development, but also the burden of both operation and maintenance of the system. Therefore, it is important to keep performance of the network system without making the system complex.

Fiber-To-The-Desktop (FTTD) is known as a network system architecture to reduce risks and costs of maintenance by simplifying the structure of the network system itself by eliminating intermediate network switches. However, it seems that FTTD has seldom been publicly evaluated its advantages and disadvantages from practical viewpoints, with real development of FTTD-based network systems. Therefore, this paper describes backgrounds from which a university hospital required a FTTD-based network system, issues that the authors faced in development of the network system, effects of the FTTD-based system, and advantages and disadvantages of FTTD from practical viewpoints, based on the authors' experiences of development and administration of the FTTD-based large scale network system in the university hospital.

In order to develop the FTTD-based network system, the authors employed the standard development framework of information systems in software engineering. The framework consists of (i) requirements analysis for the FTTD-based system, (ii) specification of the system based on the requirements, (iii) implementation of the system based on the specification and (iv) evaluation of the system based on the original requirements.

The remainder of this paper is structured as follows. Section II briefly explains FTTD. Section III takes for example a university hospital, and describes backgrounds from which the hospital required FTTD. Section IV takes the development of a FTTD-based large-scale network system in the university hospital, and describes issues that the authors faced in the development of the network system and how they addressed the issues. Section V evaluates effects of the FTTD-based network system and describes advantages and disadvantages of FTTD based on both development and administration of the system. The last section presents conclusions.

II. Brief Explanation of FTTD

Fiber-To-The-Desktop (FTTD) is a network system architecture that has a star network topology [3][4] (Fig. 1). A star network topology has the central part that controls data (packets or datagrams) and multiple terminals which are attached to servers, client computers and so forth. In this paper, the central part above is called "the central control part", and the terminals above are called "terminal parts". In FTTD, each terminal part is connected to the central control part by a fiber cable (in many cases, an optical fiber cable).

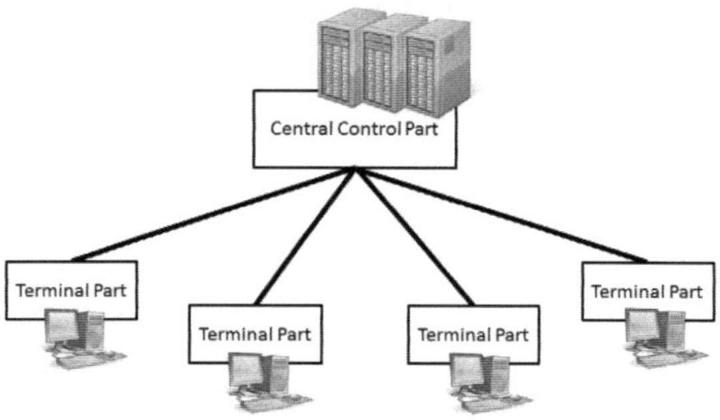

Figure 1. Network topology of FTTD

The main feature of FTTD is that an FTTD-based network system has no network switch that relays data between the central control part and a terminal part, and hence, the structure of FTTD is very simple. Typical advantages of FTTD by virtue of its simple structure are reliability and expandability. The feature that FTTD has no intermediate switches and simple structure reduces opportunities where failure risks occur in the network system. This enhances reliability of an FTTD-based network system. On the other hand, in many cases, the fiber cable between the central control part and each terminal part is made to have not lower than 1Gbps data rate, which makes it possible to connect computers or devices which require more traffic data to the network system. This indicates that FTTD has high expandability.

As a typical disadvantage of FTTD, this network architecture requires higher development costs [4]. The issue will be again described in Section IV.

III. Background from Which a University Hospital Requires FTTD

One of the authors' missions is development and administration of the network system in a national university hospital at which the authors work. When the authors designed a network system of the hospital that became fully operational on September 2015, they chose FTTD as the network architecture of the main part of the network system. In this section, in order to clarify significance of FTTD, the objectives that should be accomplished by developing the network system are described, as follows.

Integration of diversified network systems in the hospital: A university hospital consists of a lot of departments. Each department has a certain level of self-government or process which the staff in the department perform tasks according to. Moreover, each department has its own budget by which its own information systems are independently introduced, and some of which require additional network systems. Therefore, some small network systems are independently developed for a particular department in the hospital. However, when such small network systems are connected to the main network system of the whole hospital remaining the small systems not controlled by the administrators of the main network, various problems including network failure and decline of network performance sometimes happen. Therefore, such small network systems should be developed and operated in accordance with the guideline or governance of the whole hospital. To this ends, the main network should provide unified network environment to each department, on which the staffs in the department can develop their information systems.

Strengthening of fault tolerance: With increasing network devices to that client computers, instruments that need the network system, other network devices including small network hubs and so forth can be connected, the risk of network failure also increases by wrong connecting to the network devices. Moreover, as a network system becomes large, it becomes harder to specify the failure point and to address the point when a failure occurs. Therefore, it needs to develop the network system in that a failure seldom occurs and even if such a failure occurs one can specify the failure point and cope with it easily.

Strengthening of usability: In recent years, there have been increased opportunities that medical staffs use various devices and computers to input and/or view patients' healthcare records including vital data and ordering data for patients everywhere in the hospital. Thus, there is a growing need to assist users to access network systems from wherever in the hospital they need for their tasks.

In the following sections, the authors describe how the objectives are accomplished by FTTD.

IV. Development of FTTD-Based Network System in a University Hospital

In 2015, the authors developed a large-scale network system in our university hospital. The network system consists of three sub-network systems: the first sub-network system is the main part of the whole network system, which is based on FTTD-architecture; the second and third sub-network systems are developed on traditional tree architecture. The three sub-network systems are connected by a big L3-layer switch that we call the "core-switch" (Fig. 2).

This paper focuses on the first sub-network system, which the authors call "FTTD-system". In the following sub-sections, this paper describes main issues that the authors faced when they developed the sub-network system and how they addressed the issues.

A. Development of a Large-Scale FTTD-Based Network System

The FTTD-system is required to have about 1200 terminal parts and considerably large. Thus, from a financial viewpoint, it is not easy to develop the central control part of the FTTD-system by employing a single network switch directly. Therefore, the authors focused on a box-type network switch from Alaxala Networks Corporation, which is one of AX3800S series network switches. Here, the authors call it an "FTTD-switch".

This switch has advantages that it has 40 ports to which optical fiber cable can be attached despite its height with only 1U size, and it has sufficient switching capacity. Moreover, these switches can be connected to each other by 10Gbps cables that are called "directly attached cables" and that are relatively reasonable. The authors procured 35 FTTD-switches, and grouped them into 5 groups. Each group of FTTD-switches, which consists of 7 FTTD-switches, has a ring network topology in which each FTTD-switch connected to each other by four or two 10Gbps directly attached cables (Fig. 2). Moreover, each group of FTTD-switches is connected to the core-switch by four SR-cables that are 10Gbps optical fiber cables (Fig. 2). Thus, the authors constructed a large scale central control part that has 1260 downlink ports.

Moreover, the authors aggregated each pair of the 10Gpbs cables above and duplicated all parts of the core-switch. Thus, the central control part is constructed not to stop even if every part breaks down as far as the failure point is single.

B. Reduction of Development Cost and Space

It is a typical issue that the cost to develop a FTTD-based network system often becomes expensive. In the authors' case too, the issue to reduce the cost was not negligible. The cost issue of FTTD can be classified into the following three issues: (i) the cost of the central control part, (ii) the costs of parts and (iii) the cost of cable wiring. Here, a "part" above mainly denotes a media convertor, that is used to connect an optical fiber cable with a copper (metal) cable, or a small form-factor pluggable (SFP) transceiver, that is a module attached to a port in a network switch to connect fiber cable with the network switch. Moreover, the authors realized that it was also a considerable issue to reduce the size of the central control part. For example, if the authors chose media convertors to connect 1200 optical fiber cables with the central control part, they would need a space to set 1200 media convertors and their electric power supplies.

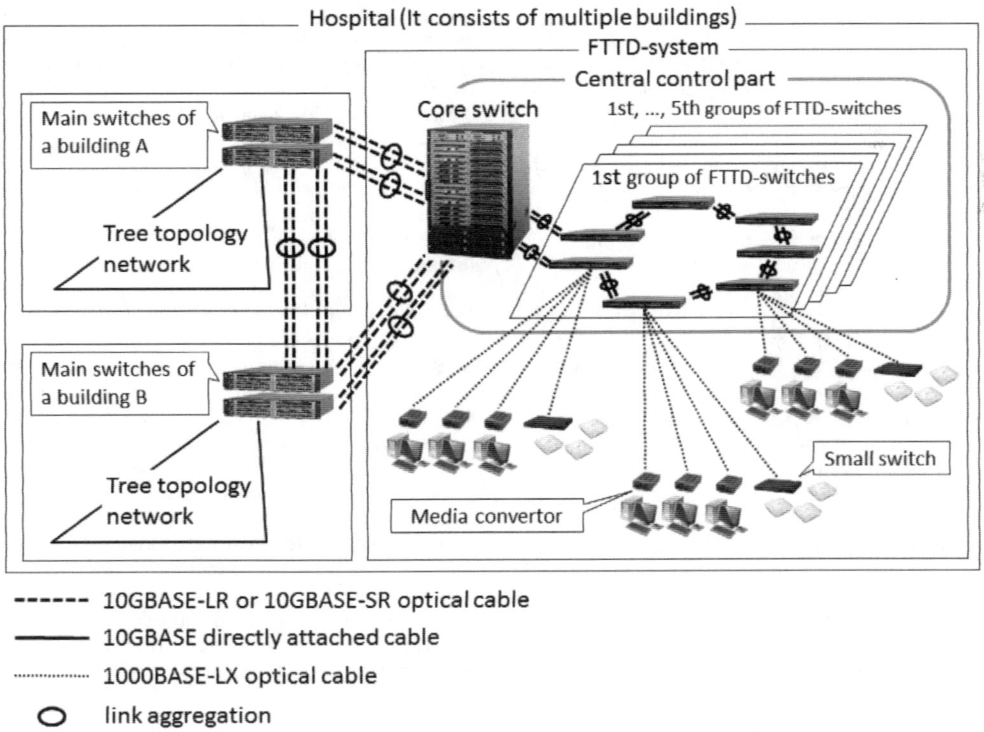

Figure 2. Architecture of FTTD-system

To reduce the cost of network switches that compose the central control part and to reduce the size of it, the authors chose network switches of AX3800S series from Alaxala network Corporation as FTTD-switches. The FTTD-switches have 40 ports to which optical fiber cables can be attached via SFP transceivers per 1U. Moreover, they are relatively reasonable, compared with chassis-type network switches that have the same density of ports as the FTTD-switches.

On the other hand, the authors could not reduce the costs of (ii) and (iii) in the first paragraph of this subsection. Especially, it took considerable cost to have optical fiber cables installed. However, it is partly legitimate that the cost of cable wiring is expensive, since optical fiber cables are longer-term resources than network equipments, and since sooner or later many hospitals will need fiber cables in the near future.

C. Development of Authentication Infrastructure

To realize integrated network systems, it is incomplete only to improve the network topology. That is, the network system also should have the capability to prevent users from adding their own network systems without permission or from attaching unexpected equipments to the network system. Therefore, the authors developed an authorization infrastructure in their FTTD-system. More specifically, they constructed a server that administers mac addresses of equipments that are admitted to be connected to the FTTD-system and VLAN identification numbers (VLAN-IDs) corresponding to the mac addresses. This server prevents any equipment with mac address unregistered from being connected to the FTTD-system. Moreover, when an equipment with mac address registered in the server is connected to the FTTD-system, the server configures the setting for VLAN for the equipment in accordance with the VLAN-ID corresponding to the mac address. Thus, the user of the equipment above can use it wherever in the area that is indicated by the VLAN-ID.

To ensure information security, it is quite insufficient to restrict equipments to connect to the network system only by their mac addresses. In fact, the way to collect mac addresses that are registered in the server and to fake them is well known (for example, see [5]). However, just for preventing staffs in the hospital from connecting non-admitted equipments with the network system, the restriction based on mac addresses is effective at least partly, since staffs should hesitate in explicitly violating information security guideline as well as faking mac addresses.

V. Evaluation of FTTD

This section describes effects of FTTD architecture from two viewpoints, and discusses advantages and disadvantages of FTTD based on the authors' experiences of development and administration of their FTTD-based network system.

A. Evaluation of The FTTD-System Through Observing Its Structure

Before developing the FTTD-system, several departments that have their own information systems constructed their own network systems independently and often connected them to the main network system. When the authors developed the new FTTD-based network system, they clarified and integrated the small network systems as many as possible. They broadened the unified network system and simplified the structure based on FTTD architecture. As a result, they obtained a network system that has considerably good visibility.

Visibility of a network system is useful not only in learning the structure of the system, but also in determining the cause of the failure when a failure occurs in the network system. For example, the authors faced a network failure due to a malfunction of a control device of access points. Since any equipment did not present its malfunction explicitly, it was not easy to completely determine the cause of the failure though they predicted a malfunction of one of the control devises in an early stage. However, due to simplification of the network system, it did not take long time for the authors to eliminate the possibility of other equipments' malfunctions. As a result, they could focus on the control device and begin checking it in detail early on.

B. Evaluation Through Observing Log Data

One of the main objectives from which the authors developed the FTTD-system was to reduce the number of network failures due to connecting a non-admitted equipment to the network system. A typical problem of the failures above was a network loop problem, which is also called a switching loop problem. Thus, the authors looked at log data that FTTD-switches have output since the starting day of operating the FTTD-system. More specifically, they first inspected the number of records of network loop problems among log data of FTTD-switches for 242 days between the starting day of operating the FTTD-system and today. As a result, 4 loop problems were detected.

The authors next inspected how the problems were resolved. By inspecting log data, it was confirmed that, in every case in the four problems, the terminal part that contained the failure point of the loop was cut off by the FTTD-switch immediately after detecting the loop problem. Each terminal part is attached by a media convertor that is attached by a computer or a small switch that is attached by several access points (cf. Fig. 2). Every terminal part attached by a media convertor is set at a location that is easy for network administrators to check, while every terminal part attached by access points is isolated from users. Moreover, network administrators can immediately identify the location of every terminal part. Therefore, even if a user raises a loop problem, network administrators can detect the problem point and remove it immediately by checking log data from FTTD-switches. In fact, in any case in the four loop problems, it did not take long time to resolve the problem. Thus, it can be concluded that it enhanced fault tolerance of the network system to introduce FTTD as the base architecture of the system.

C. *Advantages and disadvantages of FTTD*

In this subsection, the authors discuss advantages and disadvantages of FTTD based on their experiences described in the previous sections. In Section II, they described reliability and expandability as typical advantages of FTTD. For reliability, the authors explained it as fault tolerance against network failures in Section IV. On the other hand, in the case of the authors' FTTD-system, every terminal part to which a user can attach his/her equipment is located at the place near the working place so that both of users and network administrators can easily check what is attached to the terminal part. Moreover, by administering mac addresses of equipments that are admitted to connect to the network system and VLAN-IDs corresponding to the mac addresses, the FTTD-system provides each admitted equipment an adequate network. Thus, while both of users and administrators recognizing conditions of the network system, they can connect their equipments to it. This implies that the FTTD-system enhances expandability as well as reliability.

As a typical disadvantage of FTTD, one can consider the development cost of an FTTD-based network system. Actually, as described in Section III.B, the FTTD-system required considerable costs of FTTD-switches, parts (media convertors and SFP modules) and wiring cables.

The authors learned another issue of FTTD from their experience of administration of the FTTD-switch. That is that SFP modules in FTTD-switches have malfunctions frequently. This is partly understandable because the central control part consists of a lot of FTTD-switches which have a lot of SFP modules in high density which are considerably accurate. Therefore, it will be required to develop a framework that includes a know-how or a guideline to effectively and promptly cope with a failure due to a malfunction of a parts in the FTTD-system.

VI. Conclusion and Future Work

This paper described backgrounds from which a national university hospital required a large scale network system based on a network architecture called "Fiber-To-The-Desktop (FTTD)", and issues that the authors faced in development of a FTTD-based network system. Moreover, to evaluate the FTTD-based system, this paper inspected records of network loop problems in log data in the FTTD-system and how the authors resolved failures including the loop problems above, and discussed advantages and disadvantages of FTTD architecture based on the authors' experiences of both development and administration of the FTTD-based system. The evaluation shows that the FTTD-system partly enhanced reliability and expandability of the network system.

On the other hand, this paper described issues that the FTTD-system required high costs in development and maintenance of it. It will need to develop a framework to maintenance a lot of parts in the FTTD-system.

All data in a FTTD-based network system go through the central control part. It is useful to analyze such log data for investigation into the causes of network failure and security problem and for preparation for addressing such problems. Thus, the authors' next objective will be to develop a mechanism for the maintenance all log data collectively at the central control part.

Acknowledgment

This work was partly supported by JSPS KAKENHI Grant Number 15K00297 and a grant-in-aid for education of healthcare informatics for medical professionals.

References.

[1] L. Nguyen, E. Bellucci, and L. T. Nguyen, "Electronic health records implementation": An evaluation of information system impact and contingency factors, International Journal of Medical Informatics, Vol. 83, Issue 11, pp.779-796, 2014.

[2] B. Hadji, G. Martin, I. Dupuis, E. Campoy, and P. Degoulet, "14 Years longitudinal evaluation of clinical information systems acceptance: The HEGP case", International Journal of Medical Informatics, Vol. 86, pp.20-29, 2016.

[3] H. Ueda et al., "A renovation of campus IT infrastructure with fiber to the desk network", Journal for Academic Computing and Networking, Vol. 14, pp.56-63, 2010, (in Japanese).

[4] J. L. Stong-Michas, "FTTD: Bring the Future to Your Desk", Electrical Contractor, http://www.ecmag.com/print/section/fttd-bring-future-your-desk, Accessed 18 May 2016.

[5] M. Ciampa, "CompTIA Security+ Guide to Network Security Fundamentals (5th Edition)", Course Technology, 2014.

A CASE Tool for Modeling Healthcare Applications with Archetypes and Analysis Patterns

André Magno Costa de Araújo[1,*], Valéria Cesário Times[1] and Marcus Urbano da Silva[1]
[1] Center for Informatics, Federal University of Pernambuco, Recife, Brazil
e-mail:{amca,vct,mus}@cin.ufpe.br

Carlos Andrew Costa Bezerra[2]
CESAR – Recife Center for Advanced Studies and Systems[2]
Recife, Brazil
e-mail: andrew@r2asistemas.com.br

Abstract— **Development of Health Information Systems (HIS) based on dual models allows modifications and extensions to be conducted in the layer of archetypes, reducing dependencies on software developers and on system development tools. However, the literature on HIS has paid little attention to modeling tools that build conceptual data schemes based on dual models and archetypes. This paper proposes a metamodel to represent healthcare concepts and their relationships whose instance is seen as a set of analysis patterns because they are useful to more than a single domain and is a dual conceptual schema based on reusable archetypes. The development of a novel Computer-Aided Software Engineering (CASE) modeling tool is discussed, which is called ArcheERCASE, is based on the metamodel proposed, helps Database (DB) designers in the modeling of HIS applications and enables the reuse of archetypes and the reuse of ArcheERCASE conceptual data schemas. Finally, to illustrate the key features and advantages of the proposed model, an ArcheER conceptual schema built for a real legacy system is discussed.**

Keywords-Archetypes; Database related software; conceptual data modeling; E-health related software.

I. Introduction

The software architecture for HIS proposed by the Open Electronic Health Record (openEHR) foundation aims at developing an open and interoperable computational platform for the health domain [1]. This architecture separates the demographic characteristics of patients and information from the Electronic Health Records (EHR) (called *information level*) from the constraints and standards associated with the clinical data of a specific domain (called *knowledge level*). The dual modeling is the separation between information and knowledge of the openEHR architecture for HIS.

Currently, traditional database modeling techniques, in which both information and knowledge are represented together in a single level schema, are used in the development of many HIS applications [2]. However, HIS must handle a large number of concepts that often change or are specialized after a short period of time and consequently, HIS based on such techniques are expensive to maintain and usually have to be quickly replaced. Therefore, dual modeling approaches to provide conceptual schemas of two-level data (i.e., information and knowledge) are essential. At the first level of the dual modeling, data have no semantics, i.e., their meanings are unknown, and only the data types chosen to represent them are known. The second level consists of domain-driven definitions represented as archetypes and provided by domain specialists at runtime.

Several studies aimed at validating the use of openEHR specifications in the building of EHR of healthcare applications have been described in the literature [3][4]. However, we identified the lack of appropriate computer tools for supporting the dual modeling of conceptual database schemas to provide an understanding about the problem domain through the concepts of archetypes. This is useful to DB designers in the selection of which archetypes of a given repository satisfy the application needs. Also, the importance of building conceptual data schemas for database applications has been acknowledged for several decades because conceptual schemas provide an abstraction of data requirements and help in the validation of user requirements by facilitating the communication between users and DB designers.

In this paper, we propose a metamodel that describes a set of EHR concepts useful for the design of conceptual schemas of HIS applications. This metamodel contains a set of abstract classes that represent clinical care, knowledge data, patient demographic information and administrative data of a health service provider organization. The instances of these classes are seen as a set of analysis patterns because they may be useful to more than a single healthcare domain and compose conceptual data schemas of HIS applications.

Another contribution of this paper is a CASE modeling tool, called ArcheERCASE, for helping DB designers in the modeling of HIS applications. This tool is based on the ArcheER metamodel proposed here and aimed at: (i) providing users with dual modeling constructors to ensure the modeling of unique EHR, (ii) exploiting the advantages of archetypes of the openEHR specifications to facilitate interoperability among HIS, (iii) using concepts of analysis patterns to enable the reuse of archetyped conceptual schemas in different healthcare applications and (iv) providing graphic interface features to guarantee the sharing of archetypes by importing them from the openEHR public repository and exporting them in Extensible Markup Language (XML) format.

This paper is organized as follows. Section II lists the basic concepts used throughout the article. Section III contains a metamodel for the specification of archetyped and reusable conceptual schemas, the main features of our ArcheERCASE modeling tool and examples of application of this tool to illustrate how archetypes and analysis patterns are reused and shared among different healthcare applications. Section IV describes the main difficulties encountered in modeling HIS with the use of traditional approaches and the advantages of modeling HIS using the ArcheER. Finally, Section V concludes the paper and highlights future work.

II. THE DUAL MODELING AND ARCHETYPES

In this section, we describe the main concepts that are essential to understand our ArcheERCASE proposal. In Section A, the definition of archetypes is given, while Section B outlines the main issues related to analysis patterns. Finally, Section C describes the related works.

A. Archetypes

The main feature of a dual model is the representation of data based on archetypes. Archetypes denote a formal model and a reusable domain concept [5]. Thus, if information is represented as archetypes, it can be shared and extended to be used in many different application areas. Archetypes allow HIS to be built based on specific formalisms of health area, promote semantic interoperability of data and adapt to changes and developments in the health field.

The development of computer systems based on dual models allows modifications and extensions (evolution of clinical concepts) to be conducted in the layer of archetypes, reducing dependencies on software developers and on development tools for computer systems. Alterations and extensions are carried out by means of templates. Templates represent user interaction models to group and extend archetypes [6]. The archetypes can be described in Archetype Definition Language (ADL) [7] or XML.

B. Analysis Patterns

Reuse mechanisms may help less experienced DB designers through the reuse of software components by patterns definitions. Analysis patterns is a pattern category, which is seen as a reuse mechanism in the requirement analysis and conceptual modelling areas [8]. In fact, according to [8], analysis patterns is defined as a group of concepts applied to the modeling of domains of problems, i.e., to a single domain or multiple domains, being useful to the reuse of knowledge specified by another designer.

In this paper, analysis pattern is used for obtaining the reuse of part of a conceptual data schema or of the entire conceptual scheme of data. Also, the concept of analysis patterns is applied to our work to enable the reuse of a specific modeling constructor of a given conceptual schema or the reuse of openEHR archetypes stored in public domain repositories. To the best of our knowledge, the literature on CASE modeling tools and studies about the development of healthcare systems have paid little attention to these issues.

C. Related Works and Motivation

As indicated in [4], an archetype minimizes the problems of modeling heterogeneity of EHR data and facilitates the standardization of terminologies and constraints for a given health care sector. Several research projects and many applications have been developed from the concept of archetypes [1][3]. However, some authors exposed the lack of tools and methodologies that would have helped in modeling archetypes in a database [5][9]. This paper points out that the difficulty in applying the openEHR concepts to a given problem domain for enabling the two-level data modeling is due to the lack of a methodology to express which are the data requirements requested by users and how these might be modeled.

The main goal of such tool is to provide application designers with computer support to assist in the database modeling activities of healthcare applications based on Archetypes and analysis patterns.

III. THE ARCHEER CASE TOOL

ArcheERCASE is a computational modeling tool that builds conceptual data schemes based on the dual modeling [9]. For the development of this tool, concepts concerning three-layered architectures, analysis patterns and reverse engineering were used. The first concept allowed the separation among the presentation, business and data layers, while analysis patterns was used in the provision of the ArcheERCASE functionality that allows the reuse of an entire conceptual scheme or of the instance of a specific modeling constructor chosen by the DB designer at runtime. Finally, the concept of reverse engineering [10] was applied to interpret the openEHR archetypes specified in XML language, by drawing their main features and converting them into instances of valid modeling constructors of the ArcheERCASE tool.

A. The ArcheER Metamodel

The ArcheERCASE tool enables the creation of diagrams containing the constructors and stereotypes suggested by the openEHR specifications. From this diagram the user can create its conceptual schema, which supports the class types shown in Fig. 1.

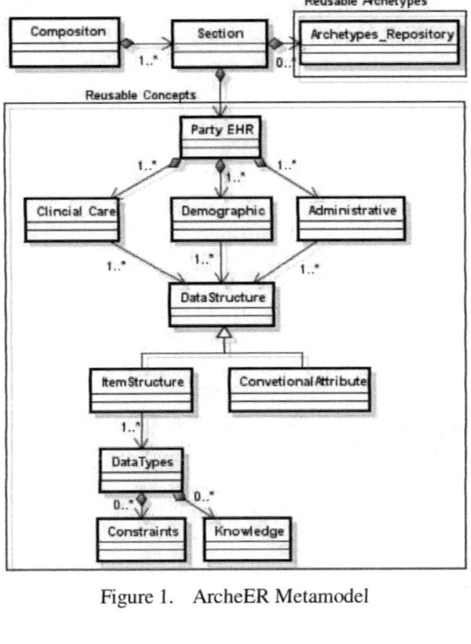

Figure 1. ArcheER Metamodel

Fig. 1 illustrates the ArcheER metamodel specified in the Unified Modeling Language (UML) notation [11]. The *Composition* class represents the metadata of a conceptual schema created by ArcheERCASE and is composed of several sections. A *Section* is the context (e.g., Emergency, Urgency) of a given health field being modeled. ArcheERCASE organizes the modeling constructors of each section in hierarchical structures. The class *EHR Party* expresses the types of information found in EHR and modeled by ArcheERCASE, which are comprised of modeling constructors of the classes *Clinical Care*, *Demographic* and *Administrative*. The *Clinical Care* class denotes all information related to types of assistance and to clinical care given to the patient. The *Demographic* class models information about individuals, groups, organizations or software agents, while the class *Administrative* represents administrative and operational data of a hospital organization.

In addition to constructors for the modeling of EHR, ArcheERCASE has a support for reuse to enable the further use of an archetype specified previously by another designer. The class *Archetypes_Repository* represents archetypes of public domain repositories that are available and can be incorporated into a conceptual scheme of ArcheERCASE. Note that any redesigned archetype is embedded into a section created a priori by the DB designer.

The class *Data Structure* represents the types of attributes used by ArcheERCASE to specify the information of EHR, and is specialized by the classes *ItemStructure* and *convetionalAttribute*. The first class expresses the attributes (called generic data structures) of archetyped entities (called archetypes), i.e., entities that model clinical care records of patients (e.g., *Clinical Care*, *Demographic* and *Knowledge* entities). The class *ConvetionalAttribute* denotes attributes of the type of entity *Administrative*, i.e., operational information of a service organization in health. For each attribute of an archetyped entity, a data type must be given together with the corresponding terminology and constraints, if any. Thus, the class *Data Type* models the data types specified for each attribute, while the classes *Constraints* and *Knowledge* represent respectively, the constraints and knowledge associated with each attribute of an EHR being modeled. Note that knowledge data is given by a domain specialist and can be a health terminology, an internal vocabulary code or any information of free knowledge.

B. The System Prototype Architecture

The architecture of a software must have the following components [10]: (i) a layer of user interface, (ii) a management layer for handling objects and business rules, and (iii) a data storage layer. Fig. 2 illustrates the software architecture proposed for ArcheERCASE.

The application layer is responsible for all the functionality of user interaction, providing a set of libraries designed to standardize any graphic environment, and giving the user a better usability.

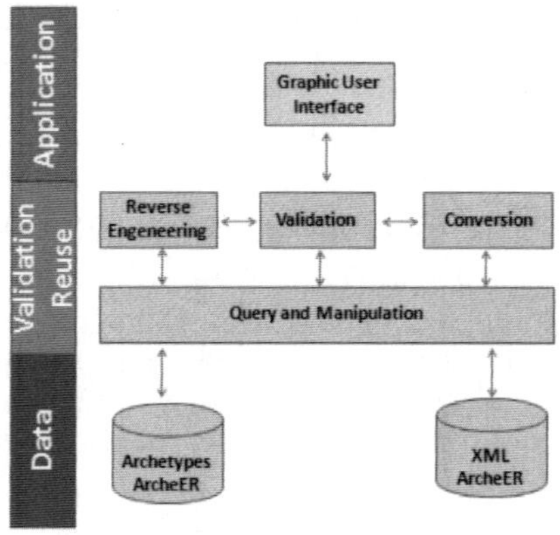

Figure 2. ArcheER Case Architecture

The layer of validation and reuse is responsible for validating all constraints of the ArcheER data model, and is in charge of checking all control structures of the source code and of authenticating all access information to the data layer. Also, the intermediate layer is responsible for providing conversion mechanisms from the openEHR archetypes to conceptual schemas of ArcheERCASE. The data layer provides all the storage structure for the conceptual schema elaborated using our CASE tool.

C. The Graphic Module of ArcheERCASE

The presentation layer of the software architecture described in Section B corresponds to all components and user interface libraries available in the graphic environment of ArcheERCASE.

As shown in Fig. 3, the graphic environment of this tool provides the following features to the DB designer: i) Commands Menu, ii) Area for building and editing conceptual schemes, iii) Solution Explorer, iv) Properties window and v) Toolbox. All of them are described as follows.

Commands Menu: Includes functionality for creating, editing, storing and querying data schemes created with ArcheERCASE.

- Main Form: Represents the central area used for displaying, building and editing conceptual schemes, to which modeling components are added.
- Solution Explorer: Organizes all components of an ArcheERCASE conceptual scheme by displaying them in a hierarchical structure to facilitate the visualization and handling of all elements of such schema.
- Properties window: Allows the designer to describe, edit and view properties of each component.
- Toolbox: Provides modeling components for the creation of conceptual schemas, and organizes them according to their respective categories.

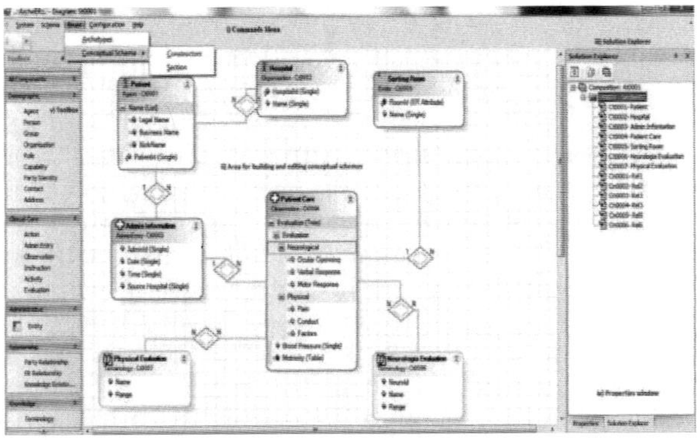

Figure 3. The ArcheERCASE Tool

ArcheERCASE is a graphic drawing software that aims at helping the database designer in his daily data modeling activities by offering him a set of features through a graphic and integrated environment. The main functionality of this tool is detailed as follows.

- Creation of Conceptual Schemas: allows a conceptual schema to be created By default, after the creation of the conceptual scheme, the tool adds the components *Composition* and *Section* to the solution explorer window. If needed, another section may be added to the conceptual schema by the designer.
- Reuse of Conceptual Schemas: allows the reuse of one or all instantiated constructors of a particular *Section* of an ArcheERCASE conceptual scheme.
- Reuse of Archetypes: allows the reuse of archetypes specified in XML that are in public domain repositories. To reuse these archetypes, users, must select an archetype specified in XML. Then, this archetype is inserted into the conceptual scheme previously opened by the designer to reuse its main characteristics, i.e., type and attributes.
- Exportation of Conceptual Schemas: enables the conceptual schema built by ArcheERCASE be exported in two formats. (i) XML format and (ii) an image format (e.g., jpg).
- Generation of Logical Schemas: It generates the logical data schema from the ArcheER conceptual schema.

D. The Reuse mechanisms of ArcheER CASE

The first reuse mechanism of ArcheERCASE converts a openEHR archetype into an instance of a modeling constructor of ArcheERCASE, and this instance is always tied to a Section previously created by the DB designer, while the second mechanism of reuse allows all instances of ArcheERCASE constructors used in the modeling of a particular section be reused in another context of the application (i.e., another section).

To reuse archetypes specified according to the openEHR definitions, ArcheERCASE adopts the concept of reverse software engineering and XML. Fig. 4 gives part of an example of an openEHR archetype written in XML. To validate the XML document and check if it contains an openEHR archetype, ArcheERCASE reads the XML document and verifies if the tag *xmlns: xsd* of line 2 of Fig. 4 has the signature of openEHR. After validation of the XML document, ArcheERCASE converts the referred archetype into an instance of a valid ArcheER modeling constructor by using the type of the archetype and the data structures that compose it, which are listed in the XML document read previously. To define which ArcheER modeling constructor will be instantiated, ArcheERCASE uses the archetype type definition as shown in line 15 of Fig. 4. Thus, the archetype of the XML document is converted to the notation used by the ArcheERCASE and for the example given in Fig. 4, an instance of the clinical care modeling constructor of type *Admin_Entry* would be created.

According to the structure of a XML document specified by the openEHR, the definition of data structures that compose an archetype is given by the tag *ontology* as shown in line 16 of Fig. 4. In lines 18 and 23, this figure illustrates that the first two attributes identified by *at0000* and *at0001*, defines the type of the archetype (i.e., Admin_Entry) and the type of generic data structure (i.e., item_TREE), respectively. In lines 28, 33 and 38, the other attributes represent the elements of the item_TREE structures which are imported by ArcheERCASE. Thus, the instance of the *Admin_Entry* modeling constructor created by ArcheERCASE would have three attributes: Date, Hour and Source.

```
1 <?xml version="1.0" encoding="utf-8"?>
2 <archetype xmlns:xsi="http://www.w3.org/2001/XMLSchema-instance"
3  <original_language>
4  <terminology_id>
5     <value>ISO_639-1</value>
6   </terminology_id>
7   <code_string>pt</code_string>
8  </original_language>
9 <description>
10    <original_author id="name"></original_author>
11   <lifecycle_state>0</lifecycle_state>
12    <other_details id="MD5-CAM-1.0.1">FF0A2859</other_details>
13    </description>
14  <archetype_id>
15   <value>openEHR-EHR-ADMIN_ENTRY.example.v1</value>
16      <ontology>
17    <term_definitions language="pt">
18     <items code="at0000">
19       <items id="text">Example</items>
20      <items id="description">unknown</items>
21       <items id="comment"></items>
22    </items>
23     <items code="at0001">
24      <items id="text">Tree</items>
25       <items id="description">@ internal @</items>
26      <items id="comment" />
27     </items>
28     <items code="at0002">
29      <items id="text">Data</items>
30       <items id="description">*</items>
31       <items id="comment"></items>
32     </items>
33     <items code="at0003">
34       <items id="text">Hour</items>
35      <items id="description">*</items>
36       <items id="comment"></items>
37     </items>
38    <items code="at0004">
39       <items id="text">Source</items>
40       <items id="description">*</items>
41       <items id="comment"></items>
42    </items>
43   </term_definitions>
44 </ontology>
```

Figure 4. Example of an Archetype in XML

Fig. 5 illustrates the functionality of reuse of archetypes and shows the instance of the Admin_Entry constructor that was derived from importing the archetype written in XML and displayed in Fig. 4.

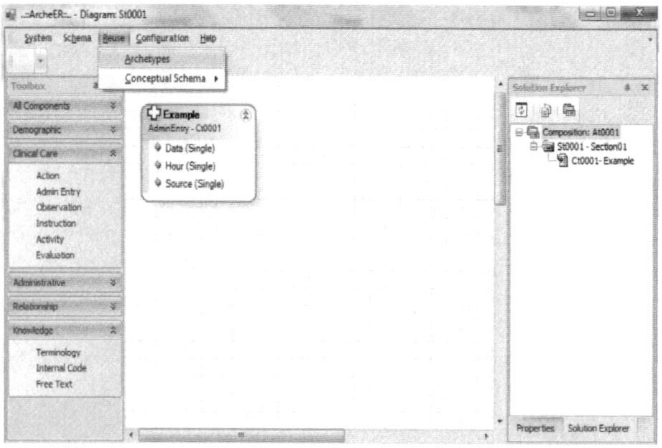

Figure 5. ArcheERCASE Functionality of Reuse of Archetypes

The reuse mechanism of ArcheER conceptual data schemas enables the reuse of one instance or all instances of ArcheERCASE modeling constructors that were used previously in the modeling of a given healthcare application. For example, in the modeling of an *emergency* outpatient care application, the DB designer can reuse a previously created ArcheER conceptual schema to model an ArcheER Section of *urgency*. For this, he must create a new ArcheER Section to represent the current context of *emergency*, and reuse all or some of the instances of the ArcheERCASE constructors previously chosen for the *urgency* section. It is relevant to note the DB designer can reuse the ArcheER conceptual schema entirely that was specified previously by another DB specialist, or create a new version of the previously designed schema, by extending the instances of the ArcheERCASE modeling constructors that are of interest to him.

IV. Results

In this section, we describe the main difficulties encountered in modeling HIS with the use of traditional approaches, and later, we comment on the advantages of modeling HIS using the ArcheER. In order to facilitate understanding, we show in Fig. 6 a data schema extracted from a HIS produced by manufacturers of a Health Software in Brazil. The HIS concerns an ambulatory emergency that is performed daily at an Hospital located in Northern Brazil.

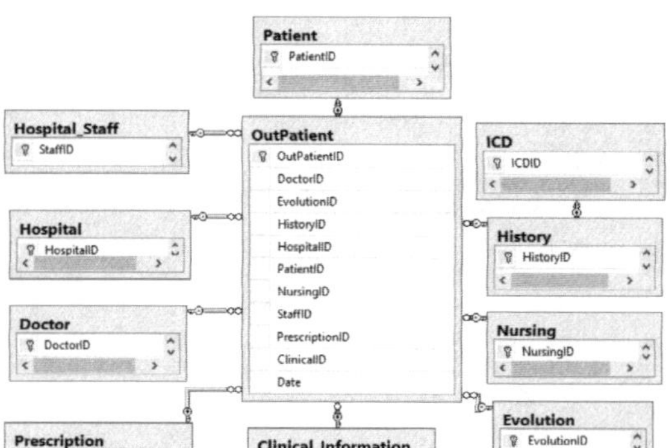

Figure 6. Legacy Data Schema

Observing the data schema, it is possible to see that the initial difficulty happens due to the variety of roles played by the actors in a health domain, such as, workers of a hospital, physicians responsible by patient care, nurses, and other health professionals, that sometimes act as health care providers, and at other times, may be seen as the patient who receives care itself. Besides, the current approaches of database modeling do not provide any constraints to limit this redundancy. Actually, in conventional modeling, for each role played by an actor in a health domain, new instances are created to represent it and, thus, data redundancy may be added to the Database Management System (DBMS). It is possible to see, in Fig. 6, that entities representing demographic information (i.e., Doctor, Hospital, Hospital_Staff, Patient and Nursing_Staff reflect this modeling practice, in other words, if an actor plays a role, new instances are created to each entity, making their information redundant in the EHR.

In the ArcheERCASE, actors are modeled in their more generic way, with new instances being created from the roles played, and therefore, an actor may play several roles in an organization and keeps its record unique. As shown in Fig. 7, the entity *Person_EHR* represents the most generic characteristics of the actor, while entities *Hospital_Staff, Patient, Nursing_Staff* and *Doctor* represent the roles played by this actor in EHR. To play some roles, the actor must have training that qualify it for the role, in this case the *Council* entity represents the professional record that the actor needs to have in order to play the role of a physician.

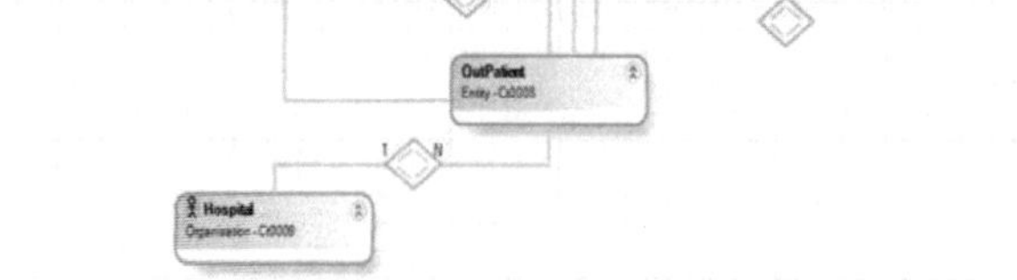

Figure 7. Demographic Conceptual Schema

Besides the roles played in a health domain, an actor can take the form of an organization that provides health services, or that is directly involved in the application context. In this sense, the entity *Hospital* represents the organization responsible by providing services to the patient. Besides the input of demographic information into the EHR modeling, another advantage of the ArcheER model is that, by means of the constraints specified, a demographic entity may only be related with other concepts of EHR (i.e., clinical care, administrative) by means of a role played. In this case, if necessary, only new instances of the roles played by an actor are created, keeping its most generic characteristics preserved, thus ensuring the uniqueness of EHR. As Fig. 8 shows, all relationship with the entity representing patient care (i.e., OutPatient) is being made by means of the roles identified in the described application.

Fig. 8 shows entities that model information of clinical care, administrative and knowledge. Entities *Snomed*, *List_Presc* and *ICD* show the knowledge modeled in the ArcheER conceptual schema. The first entity expresses the terminology and constraints of health care regarding the construction of laboratory examinations, while the entity *Item_Presc* models an internal coding that standardizes the prescription items of a hospital, and finally, the entity *ICD* represents the terminology used to define the patient diagnosis.

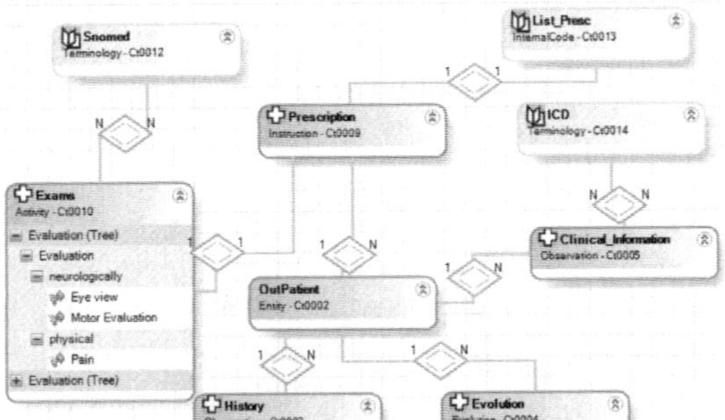

Figure 8. Clinical Conceptual Schema

For the modeling of clinical care information, ArcherER CASE provides the following entities types: *Admin_Entry, Observation, Evaluation, Instruction, Action and Evaluation*. All those types represent abstractions of clinical concepts found in a health domain. It is seen in Fig. 8 that the entities denoting the concepts of patient clinical care are: *Exams, Prescription, History, Evolution and Clinical_Information*. The importance of having modeling constructors that represent such concepts is justified by the following aspects. Firstly it helps in the understanding of how to identify and classify EHR clinical information, and secondly, each instance of a clinical care entity represents a potential archetype that may be reused.

V. Final Considerations

This article proposed a novel metamodel to help in the database modeling of HIS through a set of abstract classes whose instances are seen as a set of analysis patterns because they are useful to more than a single domain and help to build dual conceptual schemas based on reusable archetypes. This metamodel enables the generation of dual conceptual database schemas because the demographic characteristics of patients and information from the EHR are modeled separately from the constraints and standards associated with the clinical data of a specific domain.

Aiming at assessing the proposed metamodel, the ArcheERCASE modeling tool was presented, which has the following major contributions: (i) it is based on a reusable collection of analysis patterns denoted by conceptual data schemas generated according to the proposed metamodel; (ii) its data dictionary is stored in XML/ format to allows the schema exchange and interoperability; (iii) its documentation produced during the project (e.g., conceptual schema and data dictionary) permits further references and visualization, which makes future system maintenance easier; (iv) generates two-level conceptual schemas of data, allowing modifications and extensions to be conducted in the layer of archetypes, reducing dependencies on software developers and on development tools for computer systems. In fact, the impact of using a graphic drawing software in the dual modeling of HIS applications has so far not been studied; and (v) allows the reuse of archetypes specified in XML and stored in public domain repositories. The development of a query language based on the proposed metamodel and the specification of mapping rules to build ArcheER logical schemas object-relational are seen as suggestions of future work.

Acknowledgment

This work was partially supported by Fundação de Amparo à Ciência e Tecnologia do Estado de Pernambuco (FACEPE), under the grants APQ-0173-1.03/15 and IBPG-0809-1.03/13.

References

[1] C. C. Martínez, T. M. Menárguez, B. J. T. Fernández, and J. A. Maldonado, "A model-driven approach for representing clinical archetypes for Semantic Web environments," Journal of Biomedical Informatics, pp.150–164, 2009.

[2] V. Dinu and Nadkarni P, "Guidelines for the Effective Use of Entity-Attribute-Value Modeling for Biomedical Databases," International Journal of Medical Informatics, pp. 769-779, 2007.

[3] S. Garde, E. Hovenga, J. Buck, and P. Knaup, "Expressing clinical data sets with openEHR archetypes: A solid basis for ubiquitous computing," International Journal of Medical Informatics, pp. 334–341, 2007.

[4] B. Bernd, "Advances and Secure Architectural EHR Approaches," International Journal of Medical informatics, pp. 185-190, 2006.

[5] K. Bernstein , R. M. Bruun, S. Vingtoft, S. K. Andersen, and C. Nøhr, " Modelling and implementing electronic health records in Denmark," International Journal of Medical Informatic, pp. 213-220, 2005.

[6] J. Buck, S. Garde, C. D. Kohl, and G. P. Knaup, "Towards a comprehensive electronic patient record to support an innovative individual care concept for premature infants using the openEHR approach," International Journal of Medical Informatics, pp. 521-531, 2009.

[7] L. Lezcano, A. S. Miguel, and S. C. Rodríguez, " Integrating reasoning and clinical archetypes using OWL ontologies and SWRL rules," Journal of Biomedical Informatics, pp.1-11, 2010.

[8] M. Fowler, Analysis Patterns: Reusable Object Models, Addison-Wesley Professional, 1 ed., 1996.

[9] M. B. Späth and J. Grimson, "Applying the archetype approach to the database of a biobank information management system," International Journal of Medical Informatics, pp. 1-22, 2010.

[10] R. S. Pressman, Software Engineering: A Practitioner's Approach, McGraw-Hill Science/ Engineering/ Math, 7 ed., 2009.

[11] K. Hamilton and R. Miles, Learning UML 2.0, first ed., O'Reilly Media, 2006.

3D Human Heart Anatomy : Simulation and Visualization based on MR Images

Tawfik Chebbi[1], Rawia Frikha[2], Ridha Ejbali[2], Mourad Zaied[2]
[1]Higher Institute of Computer Science and Multimedia, University of Gabes, Tunisia
[2]REGIM-Lab: REsearch Groups in Intelligent Machines University of Sfax
e-mail: chebbit.tawfik@gmail.com, e-mail: frikha.rawia.tn@ieee.org
e-mail: ridha_ejbali@ieee.org, e-mail: mourad.zaied@ieee.org

Abstract— **Understanding the human heart anatomy is important in order to extract information and to understand how it works. Magnetic resonance imaging (MRI) can be a robust solution to extract some information about the heart anatomy. Data from multiple image planes can be combined to create a 3D model of the cardiac system. The shape of the human heart is an irregular shape that makes it difficult to model and it takes many hours to create a 3D shape of the human heart with a high details and precision. A new three-dimensional heart model has been developed including structural information from MRI. The method uses Marching Cubes (MC) Algorithm for the extraction of an equipotential surface (subsurface) of a 3D mesh structured and uniform model. In order to visualize the 3D virtual model created in a real environment, we use Augmented Reality techniques (AR).**

Keywords-3D heart; MRI; Marching Cubes; Segmentation; Augmented

I. INTRODUCTION

Cardiovascular diseases are the leading cause of death in many countries. Therefore, the study of the cardiac system has become a priority in computer science. Medical imaging technology gave the possibility to create a realistic 3D cardiac model from medical images.

The heart is the most vital organ in the human body that functions as the body's circulatory pump. Basically, the heart contains four chambers: two atria and two ventricles. The ventricles are responsible for pumping blood from the heart to the rest of the body, while the atria are the chambers that receive blood returned to the heart.

In this paper, we present a novel approach to create an anatomic model of the heart based on MRI.

The basic idea is to use medical imaging technology to create a virtual model of the heart. Our model can be used to get a 3D real time visualization of a specific patient heart and to help in diagnosis as a complement to medical imaging information. Our system allows users to create a 3D shape of the heart using MRI. In our study, we first use MRI to generate the virtual model. Then we use the AR to visualize it in the real world. The method uses the marching cubes algorithm to provide a 3D shape of the heart. The visualization of a 3D virtual heart in a real environment offer the possibility for the medical field students to better understand the anatomy of the cardiac system [1].

In Section 2 we describe the differences with existing works. In Section 3 we introduce the general architecture of our system and we prepare our data: MRI divided on multiple planes Sagittal, axial and coronal. In Section 4, to ensure a quality image of the model we apply a combined region growing and thresholding segmentation. In Section 5, we use the Marching cube algorithm to obtain the 3D model of the heart. Finally, we correct false faces in order to improve the model render quality.

II. RELATED WORK

In recent years, modeling of the human heart has been done successfully using medical imaging technology, as demonstrated by early works [2] and [3].

In this section, we provide a brief overview of some of the more distinctive work that has been done on cardiac 3D modeling. This will provide an overview of the main approaches for cardiac modeling.

Medical imaging provides the possibility to obtain important information, such as structural and functional. Using MRI or CT images we can create a 3D model of the heart. Neiderer et al. [4] created a specific-patient heart model. To create a specific-patient heart, it requires magnetic resonance images synchronized with ECG and breathing in order to reduce the noise and motion artefacts caused by to the cardiac cycle and breathing movements.

Heart tissue can also be personalized using MRI [5], such as the location and extension of the Myocardium. The CCS and the fiber orientation cannot be personized yet because of limited information. Also the mechanic behavior of the heart cannot be simulated with a high accuracy. With the exception of the work by Sermesant et al. [6], most models that have been built by the medical imaging/computer vision community incorporate only limited aspects of the physiology of the heart. Van assen et al. [6], made a significant amount of research on active shape based models for cardiac segmentation, they succeeded to create a 3D shape of the heart. In the other hand, Mitchell et al. [7], introduced a new model, it focus on modeling the entire cardiac volume, and not just the surface as surface models do. The main advantage of this method is: the shape deformations can be learned from a given training set. Sermesant created a model which simulates the electromechanical behavior of the heart in a numeric efficient way. By incorporating a priori knowledge about cardiac properties. Models based on tissue deformation [8], where the third dimension corresponds to time. This method estimate the cardiac wall motion with the help of a metric measuring the curvature properties of the surface. Matthews and baker [9] introduced a novel image alignment algorithm. This new algorithm can be used to align MRI slices in order to create 3D volume with it.

To obtain a high quality virtual model of the heart, one needs to prepare the data carefully because the final rendered model depends on it. A major factor that can affect the model quality is the technique used to extract 3D sub-surfaces.

In this paper we offer a new method to create a high quality virtual model of the human heart. The model we propose is meant to improve the segmentation stage. We use both thresholding and growing region segmentation and to improve the rendered quality of the model, we used the marching cube algorithm. For the visualization stage, we used the game engine unity 3D to create an augmented reality system.

.

III. DATA ACQUISITION

As described in Fig. 1, there are four primary steps in our approach to the 3D heart construction problem. Reconstructing a static heart model involves the following four successive steps:

a. Acquisition of MRI Data Sets.

b. Semi-automatic extraction of the structure information.

c. Interpolation and 3D reconstruction of the static heart model.

The overview of the system is shown in Fig. 1.

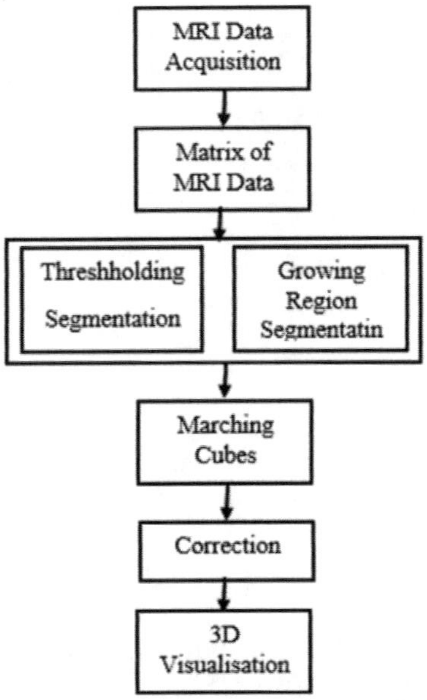

Figure 1. General Architechture of our system

We use MRI images for the construction of 3D heart proposed here. The images used for developing the 3D heart model are identical to the ones described in [11].

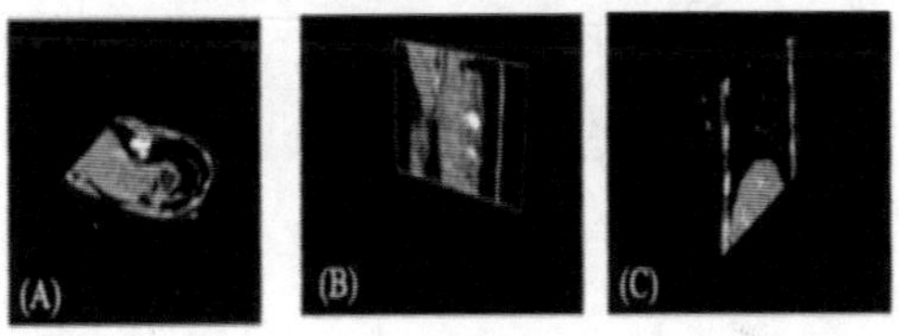

Figure 2. Different palnes, (A) Axial, (B) Sagittal and (C) Coronal

The shape of the 3D heart obtained using the MRI data was based on the axial, sagittal and coronal planes Fig. 2 of the human heart. We use 210 slices to cover the entire heart.

IV. SEGMENTATION

In this section, we describe the segmentation methods we used to correctly perform the segmentation of a 2D cardiac slices.

A. Thresholding

One of the most important tasks in 3D medical image reconstruction is segmentation because it affects directly the rendered quality and the results obtained. Each image slice is segmented individually to obtain the higher precision as we can get.

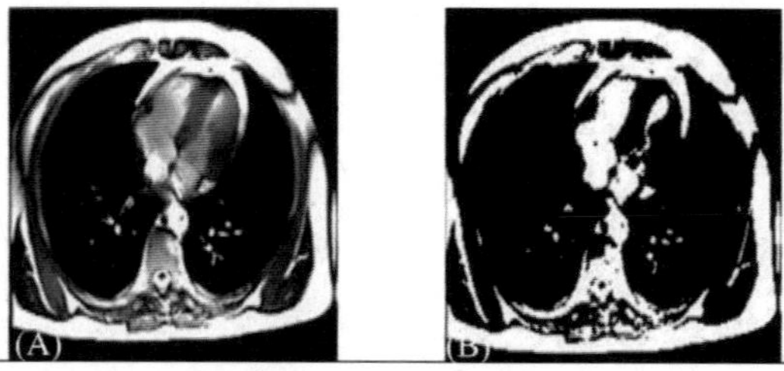

Figure 3. Result of segmentation using thresholing, (A) Original image, (B) Segmented image S=110

We start by fixing a constant S (a threshold [12]). If a pixel F (i, j) has a gray scale value higher than S, it will be assigned to category 1 (white color); otherwise, it will be assigned to category 2 (black color).

B. *Growing Region*

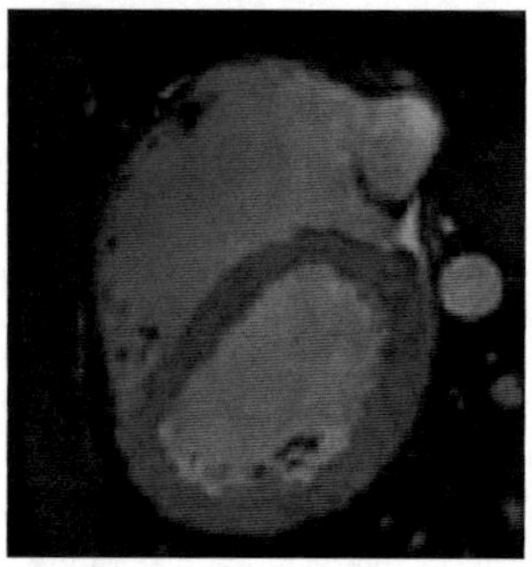

Figure 4. Growing region segmentation

The concept of "region" means an assembly of points with similar properties. Image segmentation based on region aims to partition an image into a set of regions with common characteristics. Region growing [13] is a method that is based on grouping pixels or sub regions into larger regions based on predefined properties (similar properties). The main idea is to start with a set of seed points and grow the regions by comparing each seed to its neighbor (4 or 8) pixels that have similar properties to the seed.

V. 3D Reconstruction of the Heart

The principle of the 3D reconstruction models from three dimensional stacks of 2D parallel images [14] of an atomic structure is done by rendering techniques, such as surface or volume that is based on an automatic or manual segmentation structures to reconstruct it using the 2D images. Marching cubes [15] algorithm is one of the most used algorithm in medical images reconstruction. So far, the marching cubes algorithm is used in lot of applications due to its relatively simple principle and strong quality of results.

The algorithm of Marching Cubes is based on surfaces to extract an equipotential surface (subsurface) of a 3D mesh structured and uniform model [16]. The marching cube algorithm is applied to a cube after the other. Marching cubes is based on a divide and conquer method to locate the surface in a logical cube created from eight pixels. The objective of the Marching Cubes algorithm is to create the 3D model of the anatomical structure interest.

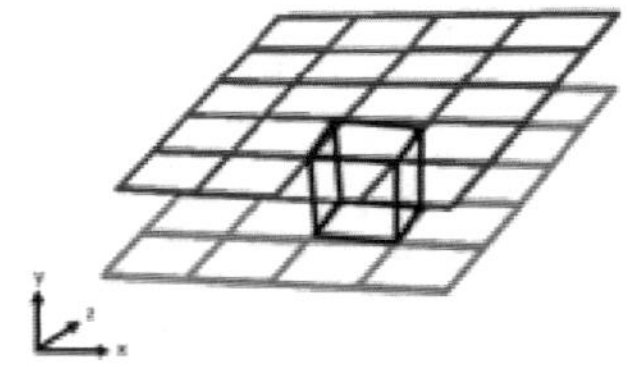

Figure 5. Marching Cubes

Principle:

- Create a cube Fig. 5
- Classification of the vertices on each cube
- Create an index for the cube
- Search Configuration corresponding for the 15 patterns
- Positioning the point of intersection of the surface with the cube using a Linear interpolation
- Calculate the normal for each vertex
- Interpolation normal for each vertex of the triangle
- Repeat steps for the other cubes

The grouping of surfaces obtained surfaces helps to obtain the approximation of the desired volume of the cardiac system. Paul Bourke invented a cube numbering system that allows to create an index for each case, based on the state of the vertex Fig. 6.

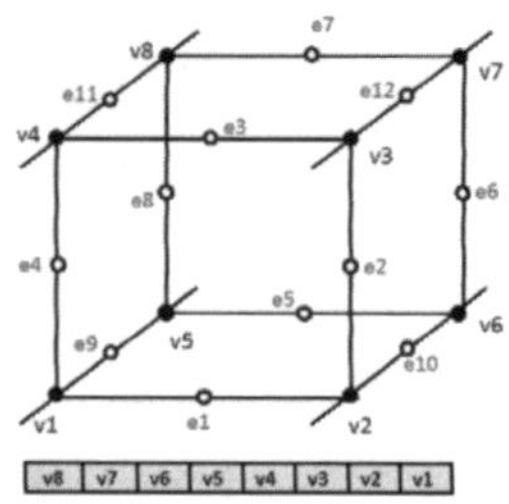

Figure 6. Cubes Numbering.

To create an index we must classify the vertices of cubes:

- 1 if it is inside the surface
- 0 if it is outside

Then, we need to create a surface topology in the cube, and since there are 8 vertices in the cube and each vertex is represented by two binary states inside and outside (0 and 1), then we have 256 case of surfaces which can intersect in a single cube or 256 possible configurations. By giving numbers to these 256 cases, we create a table to extract surface-edge intersections in each cube, given the labeling of a cubes vertices. The table contains the edges intersected for each case. But through rotational, symmetries and inversion internal / external points can be reduced to 15 only configurations that give 15 different triangles shown in Fig. 7

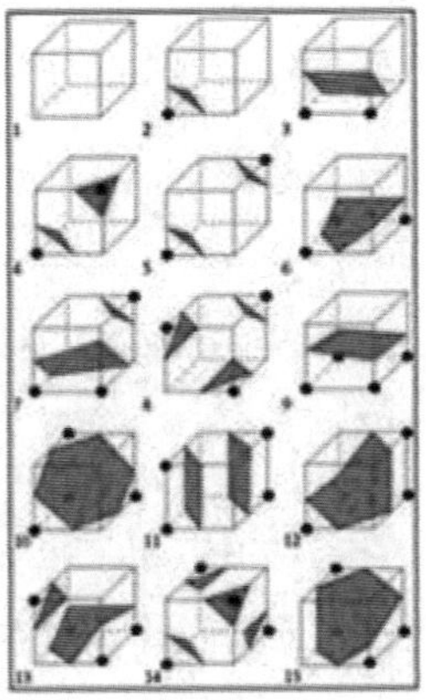

Figure 7. Trianguled Cubes.

Using the index to tell which edge the surface intersects, we can interpolate the surface intersection along the edge. We use linear interpolation, but have experimented with higher degree interpolations. Since the algorithm produces at least one and as many as four triangles per cube, the higher degree surfaces show little improvement over linear interpolation.

In summary, marching cubes creates a surface from a threedimensional set of data.

VI. RESULTS

We have applied MC to data obtained from MRI, as well as data generated from analytic functions. We present three case studies that illustrate the quality of the constructed surfaces and some modeling options. Each image was rendered at 512 by 512 resolution.

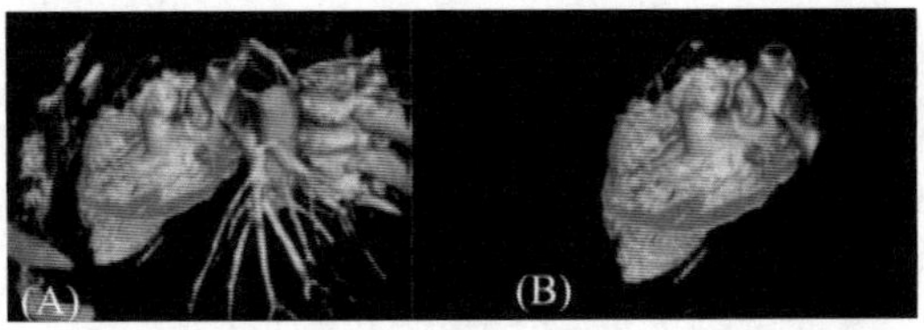

Figure 8. 3D Reconstruction using MRI, (A) without segmentation, (B) with segmentation

This 3D model is obtained after the elimination of the segmentation phase. We notice the existance of bones, veins and arteries. To isolate the 3D model of the human heart should always go through a segmentation phase. Sometimes this phase is made in a manual way. We found that the quality of rendered increases with increasing the number of pictures in the matrix that will interpolate. The heart appears as a single object whose geometry is complex. The appearance of false 3D geometric facets is due to the segmentation problem.

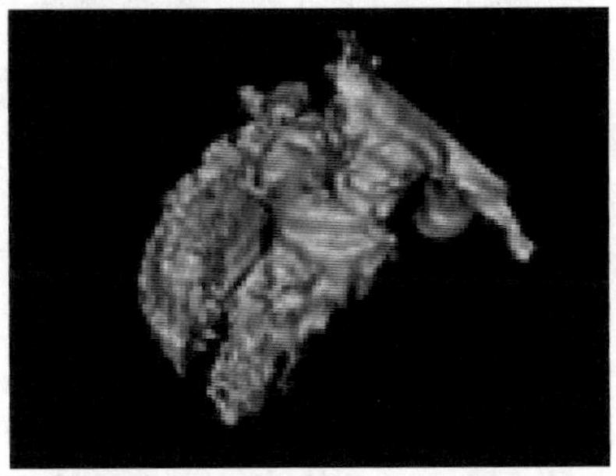

Figure 9. 3D construction using 24 slices

Linear interpolation between the different cuts is limited because of limitation of images. This affects the quality of 3D model of the cardiac system. One can notice the presence of the right and left ventricle, but the fabric is separated is not built.

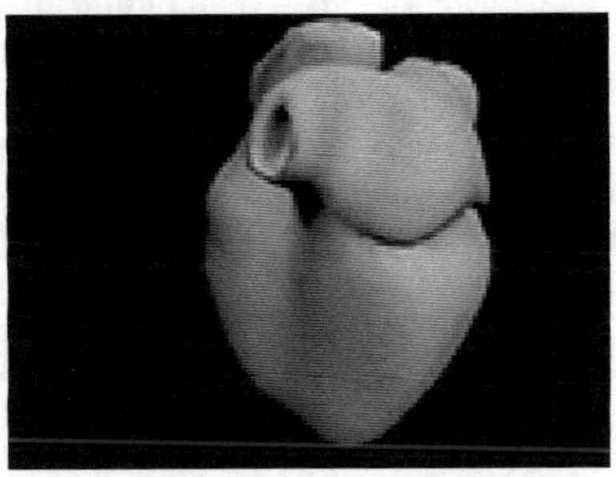

Figure 10. 3D construction using 210 slices with manual segmentation

This 3D model Fig. 10 is obtained after eliminating false faces. After using 210 images in the reconstruction phase, the model appears with a realistic effect. The phase of eliminating false faces remains manual for now . These false faces are generated in an automatic way to the noise of acquisition.

In this work, we have created a 3D Model of the human heart based on MRI, then we used the AR [17] to visualize the 3D model we have created in a real scene. The visualization system was developed using the Vuforia package in the game engine unity 3D, which provides efficient implementations and a high render quality of many advanced graphic techniques for the visualization of the heart geometry. This system is also based on high quality and real time rendering. To get the accurate position of data we use a 2D Marker Fig. 11, which we use to manipulate parameters of the visualization.

Figure 11. Marker used to track localization

Since we track the marker in each frame (100 times per second) we need to provide a way for users to easily initiate abort interaction with the simulation.

VII. CONCLUSION

We create a 3D human heart model based on MRI. We have applied MC algorithm to data obtained from MRI. Although the model was trained on a small sample of representative images (Fig.10), it shows excellent behavior for a wide range of images. 3D computational models of cardiac anatomy and function have benefited significantly from the revolution of medical imaging systems. Compared with previously published, the model proposed here is a human heart model with a high degree of realism and anatomical details developed to improve the understanding of the anatomy of the heart. Like most literary models this model is an approximation of heart. The level of realism and detail achieved is due in large part to the quality of images used in the construction of the model. Visual information about cardiac conduction system is still limited because of data transformation from 2D images to 3D information. As a future work, we are going to create a 3D moving heart based on TDM images.

ACKNOWLEDGMENT

The authors would like to acknowledge the financial support of this work by grants from General Direction of Scientific Research (DGRST), Tunisia, under the ARUB program.

REFERENCES

[1] B. Govind, S. Babyon, and G. Jankharia, Steadystate MRI imaging sequences: physics, classification and clinical applications, 2008.

[2] L. L. Creswell, J. S. Pirlo, W. H. Perman, M. V. Vannier and M. K. Pasque, Mathematical Modeling of the Heart Using Magnetic Resonance Imaging, 11.581-9, 1992.

[3] M. Lorgane and R. M. Gulrajani, A Computer Heart Model Incorporating Anisotropic Propagation: L. Model Construction and Simulation of Normal Activation 26.245-61, 1993.

[4] S. Neiderer, K. Rhode, R. Razavi and N. Smith, The Importance of Model Parameters and Boundary conditions in whole Organ Models of Cardiac Contraction. In : Imaging Model Heart, LNCS 5528. Berlin Heidelberg : Springe-Verlag, p. 348-56, 2009.

[5] M. Sermesant et al., Deformable biomedical models :application to 4D cardiac image analysis, 2003.

[6] V. Assen et al., SPASM : a 3D-ASM for segmentation of sparse and arbitrarily cardiac MRI data, 2006.

[7] S. Mitchell et al., 3D active apperance models : segmentation of cardiac MR and ultrasound images, 2002.

[8] G. hamarneh and T. Gustavsson, Deformable spatio-temporal shape models: extending ASM to 2D + time, 2004.

[9] I. Matthews and S. Baker, Equivalence and efficiency of image alignement algorithms.

[10] H.Ashikaga et al., Feasibility of image-based simulation to estimate ablation target in human Ventricular arrhythmia. Heart Rhythm, 2013.

[11] G. Evelin, Y. Lakshmi and G. Wiselin, MR brain Image Segmentation based on thresholding, 2013.

[12] L. Wang and M. Pei, Left Ventricle : Fully Automated Segmentation Based on Spatiotemporal Continuity and Myocardium Information in Cine Cardiac Magnetic Resonance Imaging (LV-FAST), 2015.

[13] D. Mendoza et al., Impact of Diastolic Dysfunction Siverity on Global Left Venticular Volumetric fillin gassessment by Automated Segmentation of routine cine Cardiovascular magnetic resonance, 2010.

[14] A. Dietrich and C. E. Scheidegger, Marching Cubes without Skinny Triangles, 2009.

[15] W. E. Lorensen and H. E. Cline, Marching Cubes: A High Resolution 3D Surface Construction Algorithm, 1987.

[16] Olov Engwall, A 3D Tongue Model Based on MRI Data, 2000.

[17] P.chinag , Augmented Reality Paper Clay Making Based on Hand Gesture Recognition , 2014.

Towards a Smart Car Seat Design for Drowsiness Detection Based on Pressure Distribution of the Driver's Body

Ines Teyeb, Olfa Jemai, Mourad Zaied and Chokri Ben Amar
REGIM-Lab: REsearch Groups in Intelligent Machines University of Sfax
Sfax, Tunisia
Email:ines.teyeb.tn@ieee.org, olfa.jemai@ieee.org, mourad.zaied@ieee.org, chokri.benamar@ieee.org

Abstract—**Driver fatigue is a serious problem causing thousands of road accidents each year. The major challenge in the field of accident avoidance systems is the development of technologies for detecting or preventing drowsiness at the wheel. In this paper, we present a novel approach for fatigue estimation based on the design of an intelligent seat able to anticipate driver fatigue through analysis of driver's body pressure distribution.**

Keywords–Fatigue; Vigilance; Body pressure; Drowsiness; Smart seat.

I. INTRODUCTION

Fatigue and sleepiness during driving are considered as a dangerous phase that threatens road safety. The decreased level of alertness, generated by involuntary transition from wakefulness to sleep is responsible for a high number of accidents.

Among the factors that promote accident risk, we mention drowsiness at the wheel due to the lack of sleep, driving for long journeys and night driving. Hence, the need of a reliable driver drowsiness detection system, which can alert drivers before a mishap happens.

In literature, diverse approches have been used to develop monitoring systems. The first category is based on physiological studies like eyelid closure, electrooculogram (EOG), cerebral, muscular and cardiovascular activity [1].

The second category is the vehicle oriented approach based on driver performance and unusual behavior of the vehicle. Its principle is to analyze variations in the steering wheel movements, in the lateral position of the vehicle and in the velocity [2]. The last category contains algorithms based on analysis of visual signs. Here, the symptoms of sleepiness are legible through the driver's face appearance and eyes/head activity. For this approach, many types of cameras have been cited in the litterature. As an example, we cite visible spectrum camera [3], IR camera [4] and stereo camera [5].

In this paper, we introduce a new drowsiness detection system based on one of the physical concepts related to the driver's body which is the distribution of the pressure on the seat and its variation in time. Our contribution is to invent a smart seat for vigilance monitoring in order to detect fatigue and biomechanical distraction via recognition of sitting position by analysis of the driver's body pressure distribution on the seat.

The plan of the paper is organized as follows: Section II presents some models of intelligent car seat for fatigue detection. Section III describes our proposed approach for intelligent seat design. Section IV ends with a conclusion and discussion of possible perspectives.

II. STATE OF THE ART

Among the examples of smart seat whose purpose is fatigue detection, we cite the Hearken project (Heart And Respiration In-Car Embedded Nonintrusive Sensor). It is developed by researchers from the Institute of Biomechanics of Valencia (IBV, Spain) [6]. The seat can calculate heart rate and breathing rate of the driver [7]. The solution proposed in this project to address the stated need is a nonintrusive sensing system of driver's heart and respiration embedded in the seat cover and the safety belt of a car. It will detect the mechanical effect of heart and respiration activity, filter and cancel the noise and artefacts expected in a moving vehicle(vibration and body movements), and calculate the relevant parameters [8]. To do this, the seat and the seat belt are equipped with invisible sensors . They are integrated in the seat cover. Besides, there is the Ford Biometric Seat which takes into account the vital functions of the driver and the ambient temperature of the vehicle. It is able to assess the driver's breathing rate. It include a seatbelt that integrates piezoelectric film for monitoring breathing patterns. There are also two conductive sensors located on both sides of the steering wheel that measures the heart rate and stress level of the driver. There are also two infrared sensors on the steering wheel's faade, likewise on the area where the conductive sensors are located. These infrared sensors measure the temperature of both sides of the face and as well as both hands [9]. In addition, there is the Nottingham Trent project(University's Advanced Textile Research Group at Plessey). This seat project attempts to wake the driver up if he starts to fall asleep at the wheel. It is based on an Electrocardiogram (ECG) sensor system stitched into a car seat that measures the driver's heartbeats. If this starts to slow down, signifying sleep, an alert will be sent to the driver in order to wake him up [10].

Companies such as Daimler or Volkswagen are working on similar ideas that use sensor within the steering wheel or cameras. We notice that the common point between these systems is that they are all based on the analysis of the vital aspects of the driver (heart rate and respiration rate). They are different from our approach which will be detailed in the next section.

As a first impression, we tried to invent an independent fatigue detection mechanism of the vital aspects of the driver already mentioned, such as body temperature, heart rate, etc) to avoid the risk of confusion with the vibration of the car despite the accuracy of the sensors because this project is still in the testing phase. We think that other than the vibration of the car, there are the environmental impacts such as climate change (rain, wind,etc.), that may influence the performance of sensors accuracy (in case of violent wind). The friction of the wind on the car can change the values given by the sensors.

III. PROPOSED APPROACH

Fatigue is a gradual decline in physical and mental alertness that may lead to drowsiness and sleep. Driver fatigue is characterized by various indices such as fixed eyes, heavy eyelids, back pain, leg numbness and incessant need to frequently change the position, etc. These indices are considered as relevant signs that highlight the state of fatigue by many organizations of driving and road safety associations such as ECF (French driving school) [11] which is a member of IFSEN (International Federation of Networks of Education for Security) [12].

In our project, we are interested in exploiting the growing need for position change caused by fatigue or drowsiness during driving as it is indicated in Fig. 1:

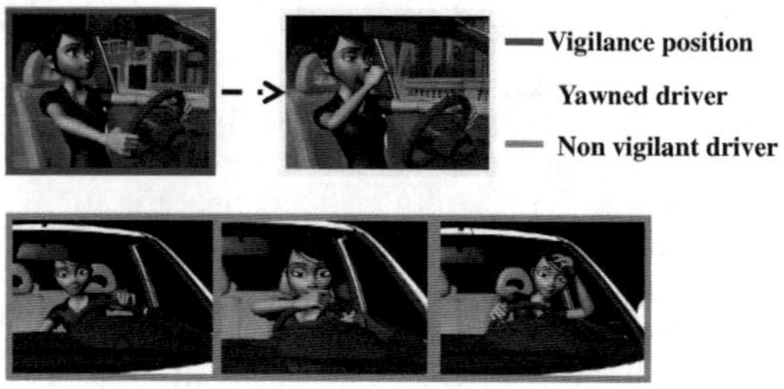

Figure 1. Examples of vigilant positions and fatigue ones

At the start of driving, the driver is usually vigilant. It adapts the good driving position (reference position). There should be no space between the seat and the driver's body. It must be "stuck" at the seat. However, he can't save this ideal driving position especially during long journeys and in special daytimes which promote fatigue and sleepiness [13].

The aim is to detect the fatigue and drowsiness state by analysis of pressure distribution change of the driver's body exerted on the seat. This change depends on the sitting position. It can be analyzed through a mesh of pressure sensors covering the seat surface. Fig. 2 mentions an illustration of this mesh of sensors.

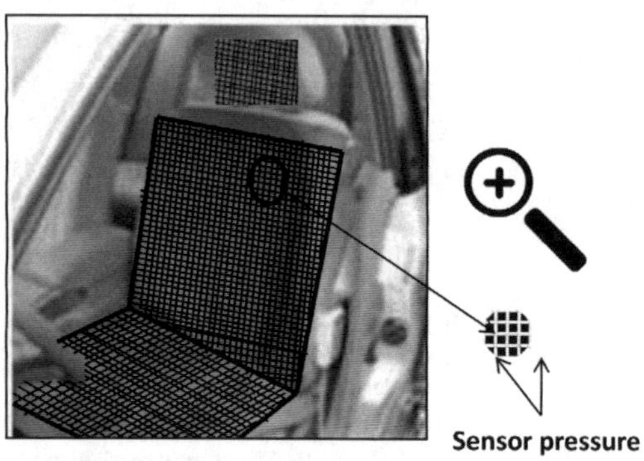

Figure 2. Mesh of pressure sensors

A. Interesting Seat Parts of Pressure Analysis

The most informative parts where the pressure change is more significant are the back cushion and the head support as indicated in Fig. 3. Indeed, our analysis is based on the 'all or nothing' rule (two states: zero pressure and high pressure) whose principle will be detailed in the next sections.

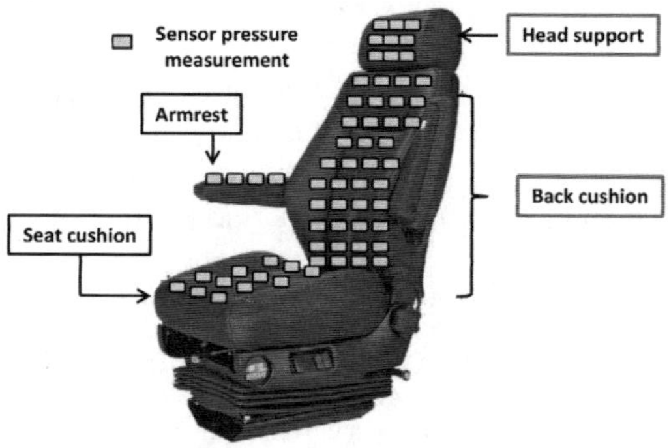

Figure 3. Different parts of the seat car

In the seat cushion, approximately there is only one state of pressure level (high value) because the weight of the driver's body is concentrated on this part whatever her position or her tilt's degree.

Regarding the efficiency of the pressure distribution on the armrest, it depends on the behavior of the driver(If he uses the armrest in case of right inclination or not).

By using specific embedded sensors, we can measure changes in driver's position during high activity and over long periods of time by analyzing the pressure changes over time.

B. Algorithm of Pressure Distribution Analysis

As we have already said, we will install a mesh of pressure sensors on the seat.

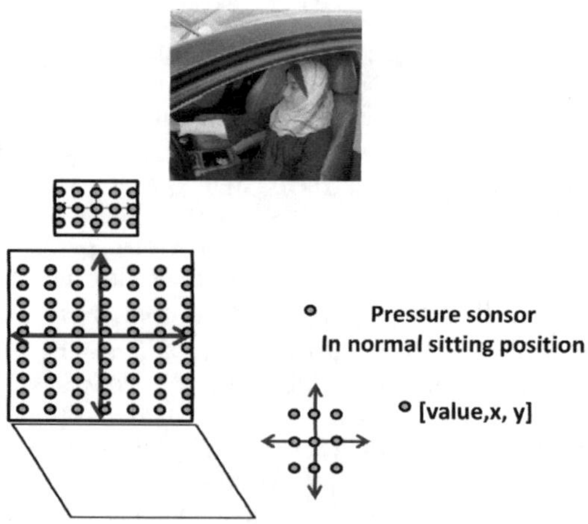

Figure 4. Reference sitting position

Each sensor is characterized by a specific address (x and y coordinates) and a value of force pressure as it is described in Fig. 4. The pressure is a fundamental physical concept. It can be seen as strength relative to the surface to which it applies. In mechanical field, pressure is defined locally from the component of the force normal to the surface on which it is exercised. If we consider an elementary surface dS with normal $\vec{n}$, undergoing a force $\vec{F}$, then the pressure p is defined by:

$$P = F/S \qquad (1)$$

with

- F: applied force in newtons
- S: application surface in cm^2

1) Body's pressure variation on different vigilance state

Fig. 5, mentions examples of the pressure distribution of driver's possible sitting position. Other than the change of

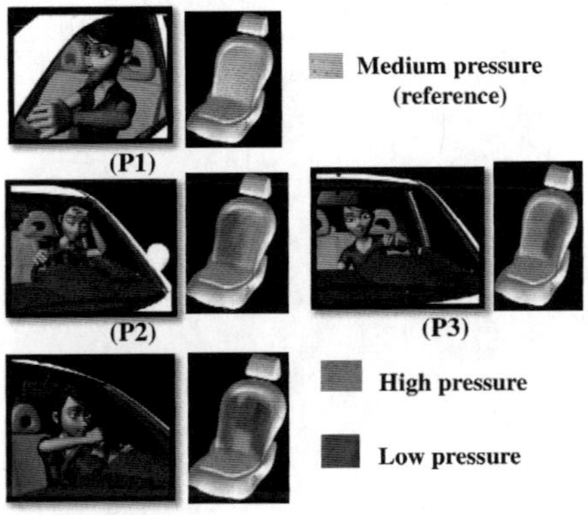

Figure 5. Examples of pressure distribution of some seating position

the seating position, this system allows us to recognize the driver's sitting position whether it is correct driving posture or not. For example, we notice for (P1) that the pressure distribution is approximately balanced on the seat's back cushion. For (P2), the left side is characterized by a high pressure value compared to that of the normal position, here the driver is moved more to the left side. The right part is characterized by a low pressure that may become null.

2) Right inclination

Fig. 6 indicates an example of pressure change in the case of right inclination.

After a tilt, there are areas in the seat where the value of the pressure becomes null because of the gap between some areas of the driver's body and the seat (there is no physical contact). We consider these notations as it is mentioned in the previous figure.

- black color: sensor with zero pressure
- yellow color: sensor with medium pressure (≤reference pressure)
- red color: sensor with high excess (>reference pressure)

As it is clear in the figure above, the pressure values vanish gradually from left to right by increasing the inclination degree. The black color dominates the left half of the sensor mesh but the right half is characterized by the dominance of red color

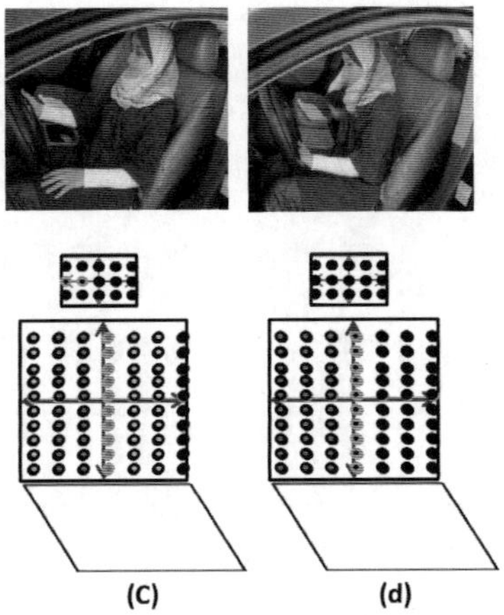

Figure 6. Cases of right inclination

(excessive pressure) because the body's weight is focused in this area. The recognition of inclination direction and degree may be known by analyzing the line sensor which represents the distance between the shoulders of the driver as it is explained in Fig. 7 : This figure shows the line of sensors

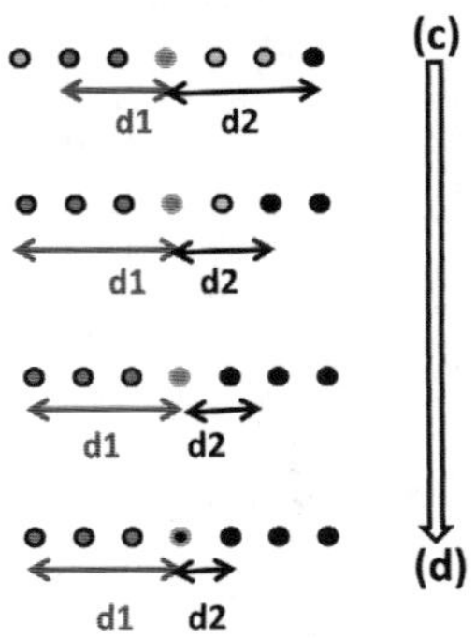

Figure 7. Characteristic distances of right inclination

at the shoulders of the cases (c)and (d) of the Fig. 6 and other intermediate states.

- d1: distance between the vertical central dorsal axis and the farthest pressure sensor with high pressure in the right part
- d2 = distance between the vertical central dorsal axis and the nearest sensor with zero pressure in the left part

When d1 is bigger and d2 is smaller, the inclination degree increases

3) Left inclination

Fig. 8 mentions an example of body pressure distribution on the case of left inclination

In this case, the pressure values vanish gradually from right to left by increasing the inclination degree. This idea is perceptible at the surface which is the shoulder area, as it is indicated in Fig. 9.

Here, the meaning of the distances d1 and d2 which is different from that in the case of right inclination

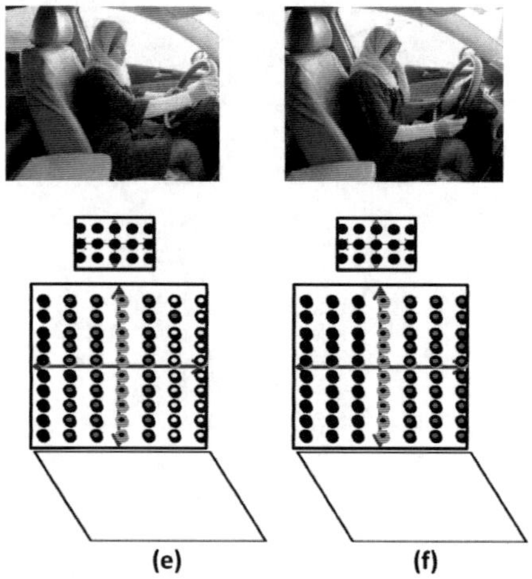

Figure 8. Cases of left inclination

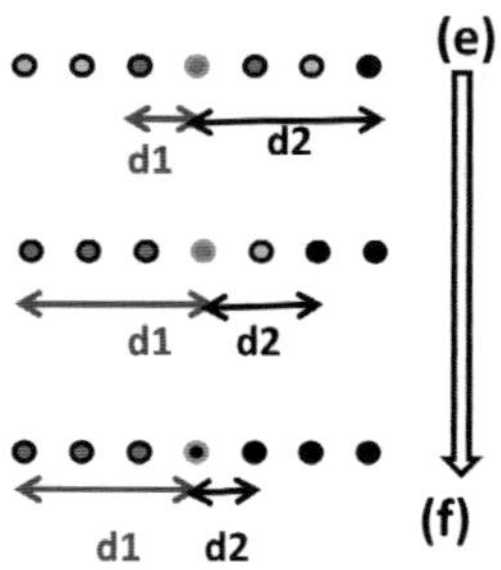

Figure 9. Characteristic distances of left inclination

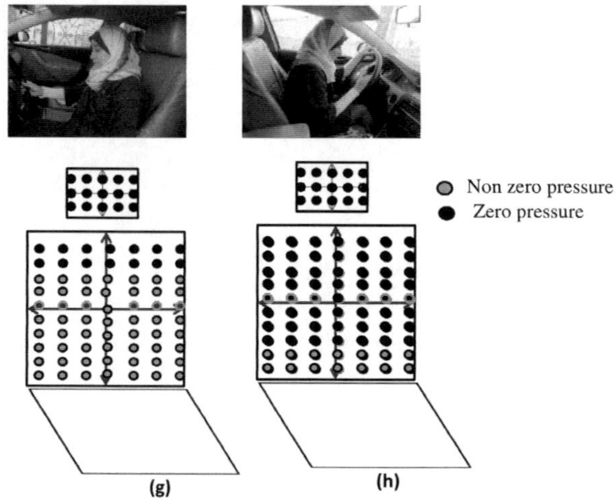

Figure 10. Cases of forward inclination

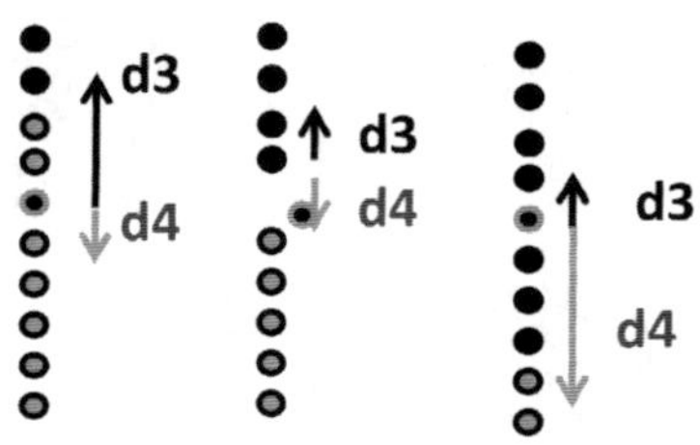

Figure 11. Characteristic distances of forward inclination

- d1 = distance between the vertical central dorsal axis and the nearest sensor with zero pressure in the right part
- d2 = distance between the vertical central dorsal axis and the farthest sensor with high pressure in the left part

4) Forward inclination

in Fig. 10, we cite an example for forward inclination

By increasing the inclination level (by moving from state g to h), the surface area with zero pressure becomes larger.

The following figure shows the distribution of pressure on the central column of the dorsal axis in various levels of inclination (cases (g) and (h) of figure 10 and another state). This idea is explained in Fig. 11.

- d3: distance between the center of the dorsal axis (horizontal axis) and the nearest zero pressure sensor (in the upper half of the back cushion)
- d4: distance between the center of the dorsal axis(horizontal axis) and the nearest non-zero pressure sensor(in the bottom half of the back cushion)

We note when d3 is smaller and d4 is bigger, the inclination degree increases.

Also, we note that in the head support there is no pressure (since no physical contact on this part in a forward inclination state). However, in a backward inclination case, it is possible that the pressure value at the head support increases compared to the normal state (reference position).

Fig. 12 shows different positions of the driver with or without contact with the head support.

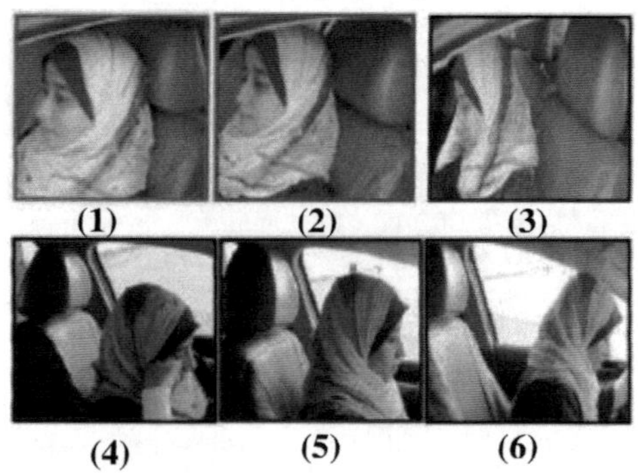

Figure 12. Head support in different driver positions

For example in image (1) which represents the reference position (vigilant state), the pressure distribution is balanced on the head support. However, in image(2), which shows a state of right inclination, there is a partial contact between the head and the head support. So approximately the left half of head support is characterized by zero pressure and the right half part is characterized by high pressure. For the rest of cases (4,5,6), we note that there is no contact at all with the head support.

The pressure distribution at this seat component differs according to the seat's dimensions and the driver's size.

C. Characteristics of the smart seat

1) Automatic activation

The system is activated automatically, as soon as the driver sits on the seat, the system loads to define the study area as it is indicated in Fig. 13.

2) Optimized system for pressure analysis

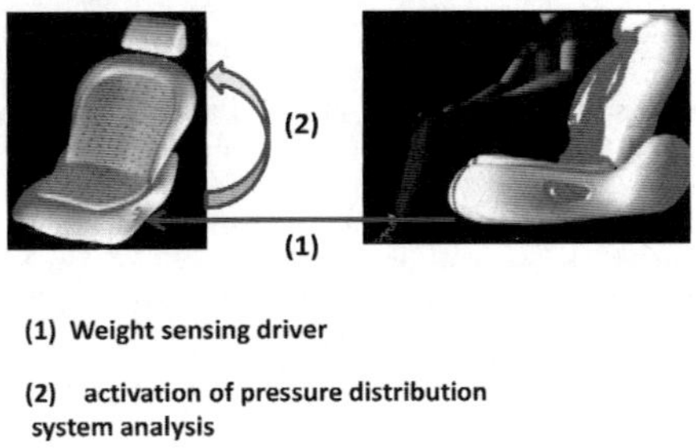

Figure 13. Automatic activation of the smart seat

We propose to add other algorithms that aim to optimize the data processing time (and thus the system response time) by the adaptation of analysis sensor surface which depends on the size of the driver. As soon as he sits on the seat, the system loads to define the study area according to the dorsal driver as it is mentioned in Fig. 14.

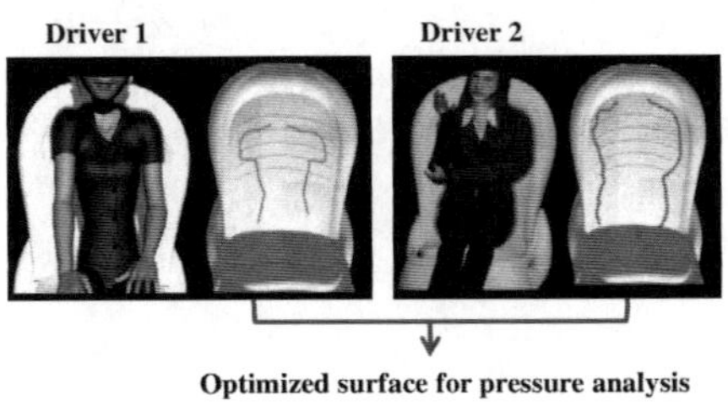

Figure 14. Illustration of the optimized system

D. Evaluation

A data collection is conducted in order to investigate whether different sitting position can be detected via analysis of body pressure distribution of the back of the driving seat. With a sheet sensors installed on the back of the driving simulator, pressure distribution is measured continuously in time, in which the pressure distribution can represent drivers posture. Four persons particpated in this study.

At this stage, three types of the actions were distinguished:

- Moving to the forward direction
- Moving to the left direction
- Moving to the right direction

The participant received five runs for data collection. The number of movements in a run differed from run to run depending on the sequence of the movements. The minimum was 8 and the maximum was 15 movements in each run.

The correct rate of movement detection was 100% for each driver (in general without specifying the movement direction).

This is done via a comparison between the pressure distribution of the reference position and other postions over time. If there is a change of the pressure's value of any other sitting position compared to the values of the reference position, we said that there is a driver movement.

In the following table (Table 1), we mean by RN the real number of a defined sitting position and GN mentions the generated number of recognized posture made by the smart seat in the test phase.

TABLE I. RESULT OF SITTING POSITION RECOGNITION FOR DIFFERENT MOVEMENT DIRECTION

		Driver 1	Driver 2	Driver 3	Driver 4
Right movement	RN	25	30	16	40
	RG	20	27	11	35
Left movement	RN	40	20	14	27
	RG	37	14	13	26
Forward movement	RN	19	36	15	20
	RG	17	34	14	19

The global recognition rate of different sitting position is mentioned in Fig. 15.

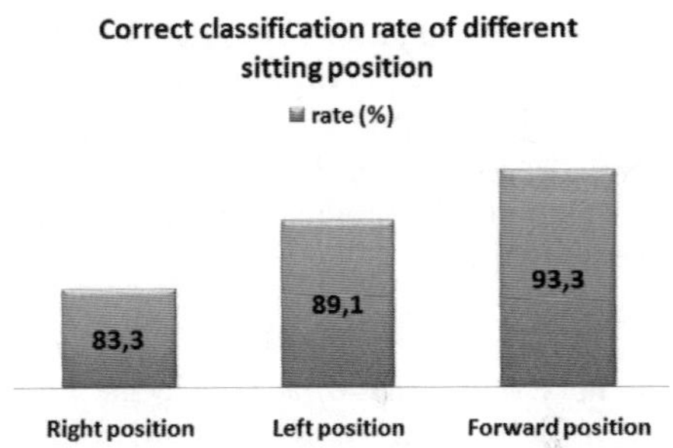

Figure 15. Global recognition rate of different sittig position

We aim to maximize the types of movements that can be recognized by the seat by adding other sitting positions to the three postures already mentioned.

E. Discussion

This approach allows us to detect the inclination's direction and degree of the driver in real time by comparing the distances d1 with d2 and d3 with d4. Thus comparison between the number of active sensors (non-zero pressure) with those at zero pressure).

Also, seeing that fatigue is characterized by incessant need of position change, we can calculate the frequency of position change which is equal to the number of inclinations times in a given time interval.

To differentiate the change in normal position (slight inclination) to those which denote fatigue or drowsiness, we must add the constraints of threshold and time which is the subject of our next work. If a specific threshold is reached (which is fixed experimentally and by medical experts), a timer will be triggered to calculate the inclination duration.

Added to that, in a previous work we have developed a drowsiness detection system based on a video approach by calculating eye closure duration using a classification system of eyes states based wavelets networks [14]-[18] and we have another system of vigilance measurement based on head posture estimation.

So it is possible to design a multi-parameter system based on pressure distribution,eyes blinking analysis and head position recognition [19].

The different sitting positions mentioned in the paper are just examples of the most common cases of drivers in general. Of course there are various other positions, but the principle is to follow the variation of the pressure distribution by analyzing the variation in the behavior of the sensors relative to the central axis of the seat. So, whatever the obtained position, its recognition takes place by applying the same principle. May be there are positions where there is a risk of recognition confusion, but we aim to generalize our approach on the maximum seating positions even with different degree of accuracy.

IV. CONCLUSION AND FUTURE WORKS

We propose a new method for fatigue estimation based on a design of a smart seat car using pressure sensors to analyse the pressure distribution of the driver's body in the time. Our method is different to those already cited in section II which exploit vital aspects of the driver, such as heart and breathing rate. Here, we exploit a physical concept which is the pressure force. The objective of this seat is to monitor driver's vigilance via sitting position recognition.

We aim to develop a multi-parameter vigilance monitoring system by combinig the previous systems already cited in the dicsussuion section.

ACKNOWLEDGMENT

The authors would like to acknowledge the financial support of this work by grants from General Direction of Scientific Research (DGRST), Tunisia, under the ARUB program.

REFERENCES

[1] T. Oron-Gilad, A. Ronen, and D. Shinar, cAlertness maintaining tasks (amts) while driving, Accident Analysis & Prevention, vol. 40, no. 3, 2008, pp. 851-860.

[2] J.H. Yang et al, Detection of driver fatigue caused by sleep deprivation, IEEE Transactions on Systems, Man and Cybernetics, vol. 39, pp. 694-705, 2009.

[3] T. D'Orazio, M. Leo, C. Guaragnella, and A. Distante, A visual approach for driver inattention detection, Pattern Recogn., vol. 40, no. 8, pp. 2341-2355, 2007.

[4] J. Heinzmann, D. Tate, and R. Scott, Using technology to eliminate drowsy driving, SPE International Conference on Health, Safety, and Environment in Oil and Gas Exploration and Production, pp. 15-17, 2008.

[5] Smart eye, http://www.smarteye.se [retrievd:05,2016]

[6] http://www.itemas.org/en/who-we-are/non-medical-centers/itcns/instituto-de-biomecanica-de-valencia-ibv/c/show/ [retrievd:07,2016]

[7] J. Solaza, H. de Rosarioa, P. Gameirob, and D. Bandec, Drowsiness and Fatigue Sensing System Based on Driver's Physiological Signals, Transport Research Arena, Paris, 2014.

[8] http://harken.ibv.org/index.php/about [retrievd:06,2016]

[9] http://www.biometricupdate.com/201208/ford-demonstrates-its-biometric-car-seat [retrievd:06,2016]

[10] Fabric based sensors to prevent drivers falling asleep at the wheel, July 2014, Nottingham.

[11] http://www.ecf.asso.fr/ [retrievd:05,2016]

[12] http://ifsen.org/ [retrievd:05,2016]

[13] Fatigue, Sleepiness, and Performance in Simulated Versus Real Driving Conditions SLEEP, Vol. 28, No. 12, 2005

[14] I. Teyeb, O.Jemai,T. Bouchrika, and C. Ben Amar, Detecting Driver Drowsiness Using Eyes Recognition System Based on Wavelet Network, 5th International Conference on Web and Information Technologies (ICWIT'13) proceedings, pp. 245-254,2013, may 09-12 Hammamet, Tunisia.

[15] I. Teyeb, O. Jemai, T. Bouchrika, and C. Ben Amar, A Novel Approach for Drowsy Driver Detection Using Eyes Recognition System Based on Wavelet Network. IJES: International Journal of Recent Contributions from Engineering, Science & IT, Vol. 1(1), pp. 46-52,2013.

[16] I. Teyeb, O. Jemai, M. Zaied and C. Ben Amar, A Novel Approach for Drowsy Driver Detection Using Head Posture Estimation and Eyes Recognition System Based on Wavelet Network, In The Fifth International Conference on Information, Intelligence, Systems and Applications (IISA 2014) proceedings, DOI: 10.1109/IISA.2014.6878809, pp. 379-384,2014, July 07-09, Chania, Greece.

[17] I. Teyeb, O. Jemai, M. Zaied, and C. Ben Amar, A multi level system design for vigilance measurement based on head posture estimation and eyes blinking, Proc. SPIE 9875, Eighth International Conference on Machine Vision (ICMV 2015), 98751P (December 8, 2015);doi:10.1117/12.2229616; http://dx.doi.org/10.1117/12.222966

[18] I. Teyeb, O. Jemai, M. Zaied, and C. Ben Amar, A Drowsy Driver Detection System Based on a New Method of Head Posture Estimation, The 15th International Conference on Intelligent Data Engineering and Automated Learning (IDEAL 2014) proceedings, Lecture Notes in Computer Science, Volume 8669, pp. 362369 ,2014, Salamanca, Espagne, Septembre 10-12.

[19] I. Teyeb, O. Jemai, M. Zaied and C. Ben Amar, "Vigilance Measurement System Through Analysis of Visual and Emotional Drivers Signs Using Wavelet Networks", Proc. of The 15th International Conference on Intelligent Systems Design and Applications (ISDA 2015), pp. 140-147,2015,Dcembre 14-16, Marrakech, Maroc.

Detection and Classification of Dental Caries in X-ray Images Using Deep Neural Networks

Ramzi Ben Ali, Ridha Ejbali and Mourad Zaied
REGIM-Lab.: REsearch Groups in Intelligent Machines, University of Sfax, ENIS,
Sfax, Tunisia
E-mail: {ramzi.benali.tn, ridha ejbali, mourad.zaied}@ieee.org

Abstract—**Dental caries, also known as dental cavities, is the most widespread pathology in the world. Up to a very recent period, almost all individuals had the experience of this pathology at least once in their life. Early detection of dental caries can help in a sharp decrease in the dental disease rate. Thanks to the growing accessibility to medical imaging, the clinical applications now have better impact on patient care. Recently, there has been interest in the application of machine learning strategies for classification and analysis of image data. In this paper, we propose a new method to detect and identify dental caries using X-ray images as dataset and deep neural network as technique. This technique is based on stacked sparse auto-encoder and a softmax classifier. Those techniques, sparse auto-encoder and softmax, are used to train a deep neural network. The novelty here is to apply deep neural network to diagnosis of dental caries. This approach was tested on a real dataset and has demonstrated a good performance of detection.**

Keywords-dental X-ray; classification; Deep Neural Networks; Stacked sparse auto-encoder; Softmax.

I. INTRODUCTION

The radiographs are essential to establish a good diagnosis and identify several problems that are impossible to visualize otherwise.

In orthodontics, dental radiography that is used frequently is the panoramic shot which offers a good "overview" of the teeth and jaws and provides the essential information for screening and diagnosis of several conditions and problems which can be detected at an early age.

Dental caries is an infectious disease. The enamel of the tooth is the first affected. A cavity forms in the tooth and then the decay spreads in depth. If the cavity is not treated, the hole expands and decay can affect the dentin (layer under the enamel) [1]. Pain is beginning to be felt, especially with the hot, cold or sweet things. Decay can affect the pulp of the tooth. We then speak about a toothache. Finally, a dental abscess may appear when the bacteria attack the periodontal ligament, the bone or the gum.

Cavities are very frequent. More than nine out of ten people would have had, at least one, tooth decay. In France, more than a third of 6 year-old children and more than half of 12 year-old children have been affected by this infection. In Canada, 57 percent of children aged between 6 and 12 years have had at least one tooth decay [2].

Dental radiography is an important element in the oral health follow up. It comes in addition to the visual examination done by the dentist. The x-ray allows dentist to "see" what is happening inside of the teeth and bones, thanks to x-rays of low intensity which can cross these structures. The types of radiography most common used by the dentist are: the retro-alveolar, the bite-wing, the panoramic radiograph [3].

The machine learning is defined as the ability to make an agent learn how to take a decision on the basis of observations [4]. In the biomedical context, the action of this agent is reflected by additional information to assist the dentists in making his decision. The patient management is found assigned to several steps, either at the level of diagnosis, of the treatment choice, or also in the surgical intervention. In the framework of this paper, the agent under focus has a role to classify biomedical images by machine learning with the intention of discovering clinically pertinent pathology patterns. These classification operations are based on decision-making tool. However, the inter patients variability poses many challenges for the traditional classification algorithms. These have for the most part been configured and parameterized on small data sets or on a very specific cohort.

During the last decade, the representations learning, a sub-domain of the machine learning, has experienced a huge comeback particularly in the computer vision domain. These representations algorithms have especially allowed crossing a significant step with regards to the objects recognition [7] and to speech recognition [8]. In machine learning, the model of Artificial Neural Networks (ANN) is a valuable tool. Although the ANN, was invented close to sixty years ago, it still remains an area of active research. Recently, with the deep learning, ANN has in fact allowed to dramatic improvements in many applications fields such as the computer vision. The increasing amount of available data and the computing power have made it easier to train high capacity models such as deep learning. However, the inherent difficulties involved in training such models, as an example the local minima, still have an important impact. The deep learning thus aims to find solutions through adding some regularization or improving the optimization. Unsupervised pre-training or dropout are examples of such solutions.

Our contribution is as follows: we propose a system of detection and classification of dental caries in X-ray images using deep neural network. This system can be very useful for dentists to classify dental X-ray images into tooth decay or normal tooth images. A stacked sparse auto-encoder and a softmax classifier [8] are used in our deep neural network.

This paper will be structured as follows: Section 2 presents the recent work. In Section 3, we will describe our methodology and demonstrate how to train and classify tooth images with deep neural networks with a stacked sparse auto-encoder and a softmax classifier. In Section 4, we will give some results of testing experiments. Finally, Section 5 concludes this paper.

II. Related work

Primarily, the detection of dental caries has been a visual process, principally based on visual-tactile examination and radiographic examination [1]. In the recent literature, several techniques have been developed for the detection of dental caries. Kositbowornchai et al. [9] developed a neural network to detect artificial dental caries using images from a charged coupled device (CCD) camera and intra-oral digital radiography. The main disadvantage of this method is that the evaluation of the system was done using teeth with artificial carries, which are completely different from naturally affected ones. Saravanan et al. [10] developed a new method to detect dental caries in its early stage using histogram and power spectral analysis. In this method, the detection of tooth cavities is done based on the region of concentration of pixels with regard to the histogram and based on the magnitude values with regard to the spectrum. The main drawback of this study is that this method depends only on the intensity of pixels. Berdouses et al. [11] developed a computer-aided automated methodology for the detection and classification of occlusal caries from photographic color images. This method is based on the segmentation of photographic color images.

Even though there are many methods for caries detection in early stage, it is still necessary to develop accurate carries detection method to help dentist.

The problem of the classical approach of forms recognition is that it is very difficult to build a good characteristics extractor and that it must be readjusted for each new application. The deep learning is a class of methods whose principles are known since the end of 1980s, but whose use was really generalized since approximately 2012.

One of the perspectives of the techniques of deep learning is the replacement of work which still is relatively laborious by algorithmic models of supervised learning, non-supervised (i.e., not requiring specific knowledge of the problem studied) or by techniques of extraction of hierarchical characteristics.

The idea is very simple: the training system consists of a series of modules, each one represent a processing step. Each module can be trained, with adjustable parameters similar to the weight of the linear classifiers. The system is trained end-to-end: to each example, all the parameters of all the modules are adjusted to approximate the output produced by the system of the desired output. The deep qualifying term comes from the arrangement of these modules in successive layers [12].

To be able to train the system in this way, it must be known in which direction and how much to adjust each parameter of each module. For this, it is necessary to calculate a gradient. The calculation of this gradient is done by the method of back-propagation, practised since mid-1980s. A deep architecture can be viewed as a multilayer network of simple elements, similar to the linear classifiers, inter-connected by training weight. This is what is called a neural network multi-layers.

The advantage of deep architectures stems from their capacity to learn to represent the world in a hierarchical manner. As all layers can be trained, no need to build a characteristics extractor by hand. The training will do it [13]. In addition, the first layers extract some simple characteristics and after that the following layers will combine to form more and more complex concepts.

III. Methodology

In this section, we will describe and motivate how to train and classify tooth images with deep neural networks with multiple hidden layers. Multiple hidden layers neural networks can be very useful in solving classification problems with complex data, such as images. Each layer can learn features at a different level of abstraction. We will use, in our deep neural, stacked sparse auto-encoders for features extraction and a softmax layer to classify the teeth images.

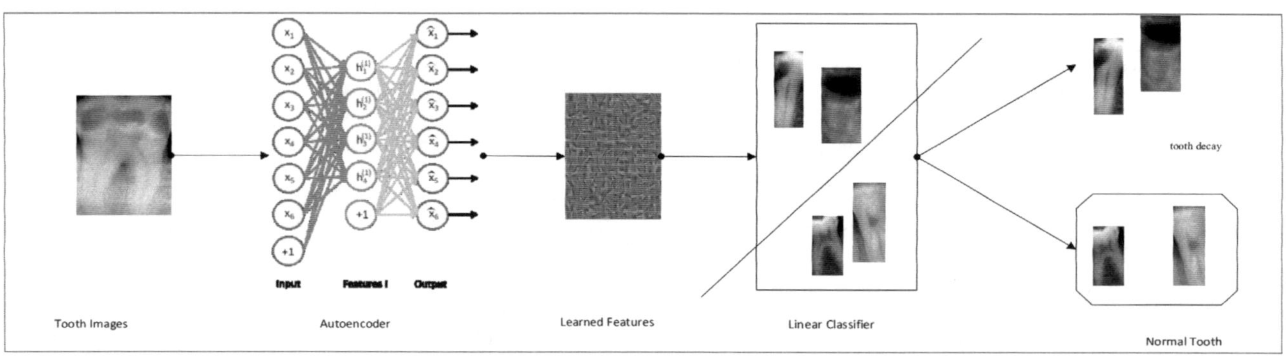

Figure 1. Shematization of our deep neural networks architecture

A. Stacked Sparse Auto-Encoder

A stacked auto-encoder is a neural network consisting of multiple layers of sparse auto-encoders in which the outputs of each layer is wired to the inputs of the successive layer [14].

In our work, we choose to use stacked sparse auto-encoder (SSAE) in our deep neural network. The size of tooth image is 64-by-64 pixels. The SSAE is trained, in an unsupervised fashion, in order to extract hidden features.

We begin by the training of the first auto-encoder without use of labels. The size of the input vector in the training data of the first auto-encoder is 4096 nodes. It will be minimized into 300 nodes in the first hidden layer. In the second step, we train another auto-encoder using data as the encoding of the inputs data provided by the previous auto-encoder. In this step, also, we decrease the size of the hidden representation to 150, so that the encoder in the second auto-encoder learns an even smaller representation of the input data. We repeat this step according to the number of the desired layers.

This method trains the parameters of each layer individually while freezing parameters for the remainder of the model. To produce better results, after this phase of training is complete, fine-tuning using back-propagation can be used to improve the results by tuning the parameters of all layers at the same time.

B. Softmax layer

The softmax classifier (SMC) is important in the field of machine learning because it can map a vector to a probability of a given output in binary classification. Softmax classifier is a supervised model which uses a logistic regression defined as:

$$h_\theta = \frac{1}{1+\exp(-\theta^T x)}$$

Where θ represents a vector of weight, and x is a vector of input values learned by the previous SSAE.

In the softmax function, we suppose that the labels were binary: $y(i) \in \{0,1\}$. We used this classifier to distinguish between decayed teeth and normal teeth. The SMC's parameter θ was trained to minimize the cost function. The output of this classifier, as we can see in Fig. 1, is two classes: decayed teeth or normal teeth.

As we can see in Fig. 3, our diagram of the stacked network is formed by the encoders from three auto-encoders and the softmax layer.

IV. EXPERIMENTAL RESULTS AND DISCUSSION

In this section we report the results of testing experiments we carried out to evaluate our deep neural network to classify dental X-ray images. The data set of images was collected from many dentists.

The aim of this work is to classify dental X-ray images into decayed or normal teeth images. So, we have used 1/3 of images for training each class and the rest of other images in the dataset were used for the classification test [14].

The size of input images is 64-by-64 pixels which is an entry vector having as dimension 4096. The images have been adjusted in such way that the value of the pixels is between 0 and 1. For each image, there are two possible labels, corresponding to decayed or normal teeth images.

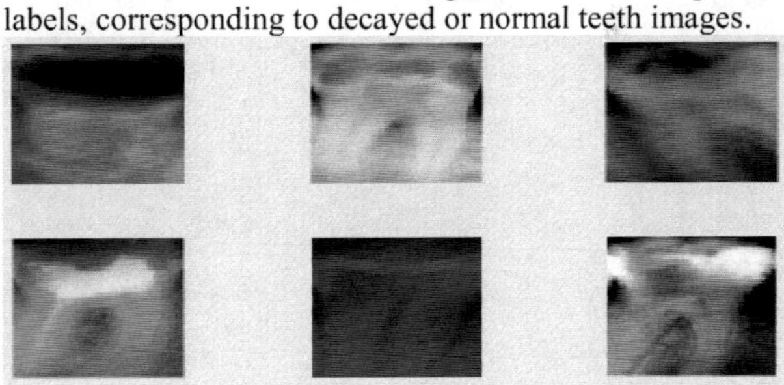

Figure 2. Some Dental X-ray images of our data set

As we can see in Fig. 2, we can view some of the images after loading the training data.

For this experience, all considered networks have a hidden layer containing 3 units and a layer of output. The structure of the different auto-encoders, as we can see in Fig. 3, is chosen in a consistent manner. Each experience has been repeated 20 times, with 500 iterations for the training and 400 iterations for the final learning.

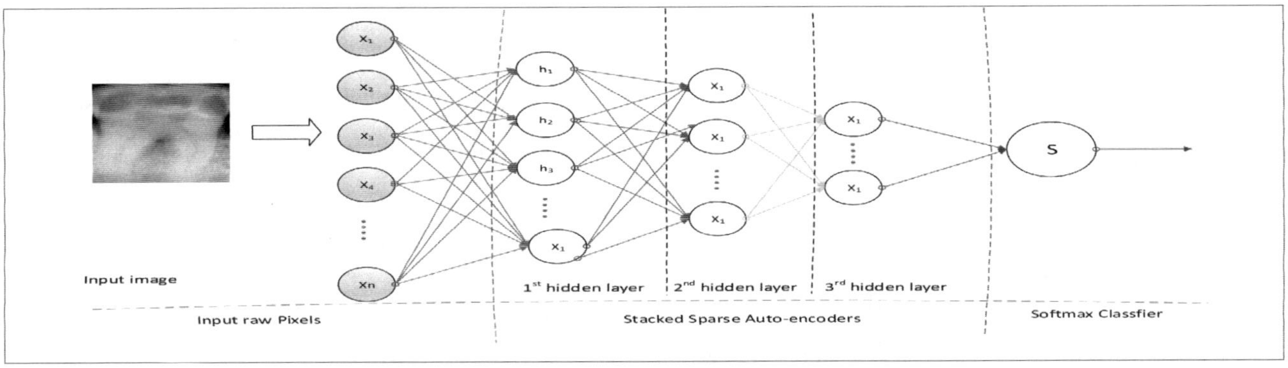

Figure 3. Shematization of stacked auto-encoder and a softmax classfier is to classify dental X-ray images into tooth decay or normal tooth images

To measure the quality of our classification system, we perform the result by the confusion matrix (Table 1). The classification test of our deep neural networks shows very good performance with a rate that reaches 97%.

TABLE I. QUALITATIVE RESULT OF OUR CLASSIFICATION APPROACH

Accuracy 97%		Target Class: Tooth Decay	Target Class: Normal Tooth	Class precision
Output class	Tooth Decay	48 %	1%	98%
	Normal Tooth	2%	49%	96.1%
	Class recall	96%	98%	

In this Table, 48% of all tooth images are correctly classified as decayed teeth. Similarly, 49% cases are correctly classified as normal teeth. 1% of all images are incorrectly classified as decayed teeth. Similarly, 2% of all data are incorrectly classified as normal teeth. Out of teeth decay predictions, 98% are correct, and for the normal teeth predictions, 96.1% are correct. For all teeth decay cases, 96% are correctly predicted as decayed teeth. For all normal teeth cases, 98% are correctly classified. Overall, 97% of the predictions are correct.

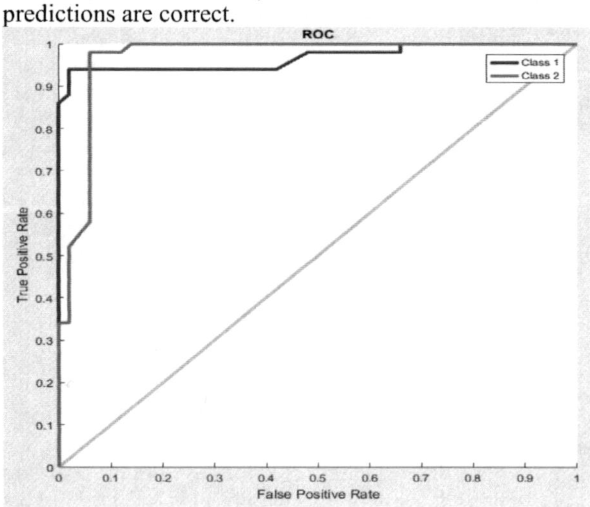

Figure 4. ROC Curve

Fig. 4 illustrates the performance of our classifier model by showing the TPR (True Positive Rate) against the FPR (False Positive Rate) for different threshold values.

V. CONCLUSION

In this paper, a deep neural network using Stacked Sparse Auto-encoder framework is presented for classification of dental X-ray images. The aim of this work is to classify dental X-ray images into decayed or normal teeth images.

In this work, we have used stacked sparse auto-encoder containing three hidden layers and a softmax classifier.

The conclusion we can draw from our experiments is: in comparison with the classic approach to random initialization of the network weight, this method promotes a convergence of the network to a better local minimum as well in classification with regression. This method gives a good result, as approved in Table 1. However, the accuracy and reliability of our results can be improved using a larger dental database.

The implementation of training strategies on really deep structures with several hidden layers is a future extension of this work.

ACKNOWLEDGMENT

The authors would like to acknowledge the financial support of this work by grants from General Direction of Scientific Research (DGRST), Tunisia, under the ARUB program.

REFERENCES

[1] M. B. Diniz1, J. Rodrigues, and A. Lussi, "Traditional and Novel Caries Detection Methods", Contemporary Approach to Dental Caries, Eds Ming-Yu Li, Chapter 6, 2012.

[2] C Badet and B Richard, " Dental caries", EMC-Dentisterie, 'pp. 40-48, 2004.

[3] R. Ben Ali, R. Ejbali, and M. Zaied, " GPU-based Segmentation of Dental X-ray Images using Active Contours Without Edges", 15th International Conference on Intelligent Systems Design and Applications, pp. 505 – 510, 2015.

[4] H. M.. El Damanhoury, K. S. Fakhruddin, and M. A. Awad, "Effectiveness of teaching International Caries Detection and Assessment System II and its e-learning program to freshman dental students on occlusal caries detection," European journal of dentistry , pp. 493–497, 2014.

[5] A. Vashishth, B. Kaushal, and A. Srivastava, " Caries Detection Technique for Radiographic and Intra Oral Camera Images," International Journal of Soft Computing and Engineering (IJSCE), pp. 2231-2307, Volume-4, Issue-2, 2014.

[6] Y. Bengio, A. Courville, and P. Vincent, "Representation learning : A review and new perspectives.", IEEE transactions on pattern analysis and machine intelligence, pp. 580-587, 2013

[7] A. Krizhevsky, I. Sutskever, and G. E. Hinton, "Imagenet classification with deep convolutional neural networks", In NIPS, pp. 1097–1105, 2012.

[8] J. Xu, L. Xiang, Q. Liu, H. Gilmore, J. Wu, J. Tang, and A. Madabhushi," Stacked Sparse Autoencoder (SSAE) for Nuclei Detection on Breast Cancer Histopathology Images," *IEEE Trans Med* ol. 35, issue 1, pp. 119-130, 2016

[9] S. Kositbowornchai,S. Siriteptawee,S. Plermkamon,S. Bureerat, D. Chetchotsak, "Anartificial neural network for detection of simulated dental caries, Int.J.Comput.Assist.Radiol.Surg., pp. 91–96, 2006.

[10] T Saravanan, MS Raj, K Gopalakrishnan, "Identification of Early Caries in Human Tooth Using Histogram and Power Spectral Analysis", Middle-East Journal of Scientific Research, pp. 871-875, 2014.

[11] E. D. Berdouses, G. D. Koutsouri, E.F. Tripoliti, G. K. Matsopoulos, C. J. Oulis, and D. I. Fotiadis. A computer-aided automated methodology for the detection and classification of occlusal caries from photographic color images. Comput Biol Med., pp.119–135, 2015

[12] N. Srivastava, G. Hinton, A. Krizhevsky, I. Sutskever, and R. Salakhutdinov, "Dropout : A simple way to prevent neural networks from overfitting", The Journal of Machine Learning Research, vol. 15, no. 1, pp. 1929–1958, 2014.

[13] D. Kumar, A. Wong, and D. A. Clausi, "Lung nodule classification using deep features in ct images," Computer and Robot Vision (CRV), 2015 12th Conference on, pp. 133–138, 2015..

[14] X. Zhang, H. Dou, T. Ju, Jun Xu, and S. Zhang, "Fusing Heterogeneous Features from Stacked Sparse Autoencoder for Histopathological Image Analysis", IEEE Journal of Biomedical and Health Informatics, 2015.

[15] A. E. Rad, I. B. M. Amin, M. S. M. Rahim, and H. Kolivand. "Computer-Aided Dental Caries Detection System from X-Ray Images", In Computational Intelligence in Information Systems Springer. International Publishing, pp.233-243, 2015.

Towards Agile Enterprise Data Warehousing

Mikko Puonti
and Timo Lehtonen

Solita, Tampere, Finland
Email: puonti@iki.fi
timo.lehtonen@solita.fi

Antti Luoto
and Timo Aaltonen

Department of Pervasive Computing,
Tampere University of Technology,
Tampere, Finland
Email: antti.l.luoto@tut.fi
timo.aaltonen@tut.fi

Timo Aho

Yle, The Finnish Broadcasting Company,
Helsinki, Finland
Email: timo.aho@iki.fi

Abstract—**Traditional business intelligence and data warehouse projects are very much sequential in nature. The process starts with data preparation and continues with the reporting needed by business measurements. This is somewhat similar to the waterfall model of software development and also shares some of its problems: the work is done in serial manner and the reaction time for possible design changes is often long. Agile principles are not well supported by the traditional serial workflow. By making the data preparation and reporting tasks parallel, it is possible to gain several advantages, such as shorter lead time and shorter feedback cycle. The solution proposed in this paper is based on enriched conceptual model that enables the business intelligence implementation process of different teams to change from serial to parallel workflow.**

Keywords–data warehouses; business intelligence; agile software development; scrum.

I. Introduction

Business Intelligence (BI) projects are traditionally following a pattern, where the work is actually done in serial tasks, which are strongly dependent on each other. This leads to long development cycles where some tasks need to be done before the next tasks can be even started. The problems of this approach include long feedback times and inefficient working process. The working method does not support the agile process models, such as scrum [1].

Scrum is an iterative project management approach to deliver software in incremental development cycles called *Sprints* that usually last from two to four weeks. Its benefits come from the ability to respond to the unpredictable environment changes as every sprint is planned separately.

In this article, we propose a process improvement to avoid the dependency of serial BI development tasks. The core of the idea is to rearrange serial development sprints to parallel ones by using a conceptual data model as a basis for a dimensional data warehouse (DW) model. The dimensional model is, on the other hand, an agreement between different development teams with different skills and, thus, a basis for communication between them. Research literature about combining BI with agile mindset exists but to the best of our knowledge none of them concentrate on how to organize work of teams in parallel way in agile BI project.

The expected benefits of our approach include shorter sprint cycle lengths, which leads to shorter customer feedback time. Also, it helps the DW modelers and BI reporters to concentrate on their work by reducing the fragmentation of development sprints, because of easier allocation of work. As a result, more development iterations can be done in the same time frame as with a serial workflow.

The proposed process improvement can be seen as a first step towards agile practices in BI projects and it can be later on combined with other agile practices.

The rest of this paper is structured as follows. In Section II, we introduce the necessary background for the paper by addressing the related work in agile BI processes. Section III presents the current and target states of the data warehousing and reporting process while Section IV introduces the approach from the viewpoint of data modeling. Finally, we draw some concluding remarks in Section V and outline our strategy for validating the expected benefits of the proposed approach in Section VI.

II. Related Work

The chosen related work concentrates on bringing miscellaneous agile practices to DW and BI processes. In general, incremental and iterative approaches are seen as beneficial in them but to the best of our knowledge, other authors have not discussed about organizing different teams' work in parallel so that traditionally done serial work could be done simultaneously. This is a gap we are trying to fill by improving the DW modeling process.

In [2], the authors categorize different agile BI actions in their literature review. Their categorization is based on previous work presented in [3] and identifies four agile BI action categories which are *Principles* (rules and assumptions derived from extensive observation and evolved through years of experience [4]), *Process models* (guidance to coordinate and control different tasks systematically which must be performed in order to achieve a specific goal [4]), *Techniques* (a way or style of carrying out a particular task) and *Technologies* (tools). The ideas presented in this paper fit to category *Process models* as the idea is to parallelize DW design tasks. The work in [2], also noted that agile principles are often discussed in a relation to agile process models, and in *Process models* category, Scrum can be seen as the most popular research topic between the years 2007 and 2013. We go through some of this previous work in the following paragraphs.

A process model called Four-Wheel-Drive (4WD) introduced in [5] utilizes six agile DW design practices (incremental process, iteration, user involvement, continuous and automated testing, lean documentation) that are based on software engineering methods. According to them, the impacts of an iterative and incremental process are better and faster feedback, improved change and resource management, clearer requirements and early detection of errors. They discuss incremental techniques in the light of risk analysis that balances between the value to users and the risk of releasing early. Similarly, our approach aims to enable ways of working more iteratively and incrementally while also making customer feedback easier but they don't have the viewpoint of parallelization which would also shorten the required time for DW projects.

In addition to direct process improvement, the work in [6] presents an optimization model for sprint planning in agile DW design, which is based on the team's ability to estimate a set of development constraints. In contrast to our work, we do not concentrate on the planning phases of sprints even tough the planning should be also easier in our parallel workflow where teams are working more in close collaboration. They aim to optimize the sprints by planning whereas we optimize time usage with work parallelization.

The work in [7] gives a description of a DW project that was executed in an agile manner. The lessons learned include successful usage of agile Enterprise Data Models, tools integrated to version control and continuous integration of the database. Even though their usage of Enterprise Data Model improved communication and collaboration by shortening feedback loops between different teams, they don't explicitly mention about making the workflow parallel, which is our goal. Our approach similarly improves the communication and collaboration between teams.

III. Data Warehousing and Reporting Process

According to [8], BI is a process that consists of two main activities: getting data in and getting data out. The first activity, i.e., (DW), is about collecting data from source systems to a single DW that combines the data. The data is then extracted to a useful form for decision support. Getting that data out is the part that receives the most attention as it eventually brings out the value even though the DW part is considered to be more laborious.

The skills and the tools needed for the two activities are different. Thus, the competence is diversed in DW and reporting teams. DW implementation work consists of modeling in addition to Extract, Transform, Load (ETL) loads and data integration with an ETL tool. An ETL developer needs technical knowledge of databases and data transformations while a report specialist makes visualizations and needs understanding of the data. The naming of the data items in report meta model utilized for analysis is done using business terms. Hence, a reporting specialist needs understanding of the customer's business process.

The data is the driver for the whole implementation of the reports. For analytical purposes, data is stored in a dimensional schema of a data mart [9, Chapter 1] by the DW team. Report implementation consists of two steps. In the first step, a meta model of data entities and the structure of the data is created, while in the second step, the actual report is created with a reporting tool. Testing of the reporting functionalities is commonly done by an end-user with the actual customer data. Thus, a prerequisite for the report development is an existing DW utilizing dimensional schema which is populated with the customer's data.

The diverse expertise of the different teams and the need of an existing DW before starting the report development results in lengthy workflow in current BI processes.

A. Current State

Currently, the way of working divides the design and implementation process of BI report into two teams, in which one team finishes the DW design work and another team continues by producing the specified report. Only after both the teams have finished their serial sprints, it is possible to gain feedback from the customer and start fixing the problems, starting again from DW work and continuing to reporting. This is presented in the Fig. 1.

Fig. 2 presents the current state of the workflow in a timeline. In the figure, *DW Sprint* includes actions, such as data integration, ETL and DW modeling (dimensional model) while *Reporting Sprint* consists of actions, such as creating a meta model for the report and creation of the actual report. The specification describes the business requirements and the visual guidelines for the report.

The result of the work in *DW Sprint* is a data mart that utilizes dimensional schema. The data mart and data loads in the data mart are done by an ETL developer. In the scrum process model, the DW implementation is done first in a *DW sprint* as can be seen in the Fig. 2. After the *DW sprint* deliverable (the data mart with customer's data) is available, the report implementation will be able to start. This dependency leads to a situation where there is first a *DW sprint* after which a *Reporting sprint* will follow. Implementation of a report requires at least two sprints, since in the first sprint the data comes available to the DW (DW sprint) and the actual report for the end user is implemented in the next sprint.

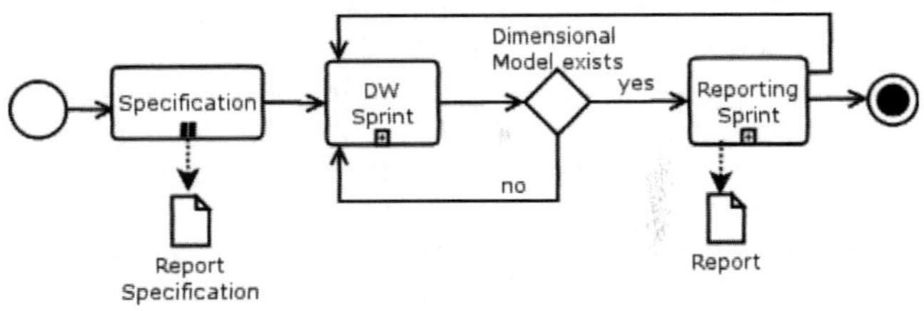

Figure 1. The current state of the process.

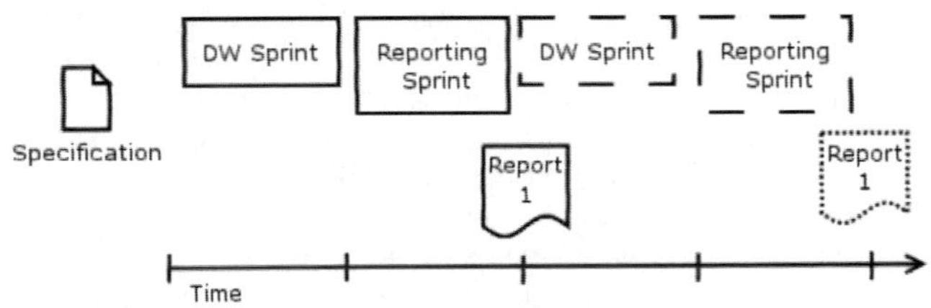

Figure 2. Workflow presented in a timeline.

B. Problem: Sequential Working

As a result of the diverse expertise in the teams and the need of an existing DW before reporting work, the full report development in *Reporting sprint* will not start before the first *DW Sprint* is finished, as it is presented in Fig. 1. The situation leads to a dependency between the DW implementation and report implementation.

The main problem of the current state is that getting feedback from the customer, which is based on the report, requires finishing both the sprints before it is possible to get feedback. After the feedback is received, the teams can start fixing the problems with new iterations of *DW sprint* and *Reporting sprint*. This also leads to fragmentation of work and excess waiting time between the sprints. Moreover, even though the workload is not as big as in the first iteration, it is still serial work and takes two sprints. If each sprint lasts for two weeks then completing both the sprints takes four weeks which multiplies to eight weeks after the feedback has been received and the corrections have been made. This is also illustrated in Fig. 2.

C. Solution: Parallel Working Enabled

As a solution to shorten the customer feedback cycle length and to defragment the DW and reporting work, we are targeting to parallelization of the serial sprints. The parallel team working is presented in Fig. 4. The parallelization is enabled by dimensional model based on conceptual model that contains information of the source systems. Based on the source system information in conceptual model, the dimensional model can designed at an attribute level with the support of interface specifications. A conceptual model presents associations between the modeled entities while the interface specification presents the attributes related to that association. The target state of the DW development process is presented in Fig. 3. The following aspects rise when comparing the current state to the target state.

1) Dimensional Model Based on Conceptual Model: Dimensional model represents *facts* which are business measures of the *dimensions*. The *dimensions* are grouping the business. Conceptual model consists of business entities and relationships between those entities. By adding information about a source system for an entity in a conceptual model, it is possible to get enough information of that entity without doing an exact logical data model. For creating the dimensional model, it is vital to know all the attributes of the *fact* and *dimension* tables. The attributes of each entity in a conceptual model can be solved out by looking at the interface of that entity. Each entity needs an interface from the source system to the DW and it the interface has to exist before the *DW Sprint* can start. The interface has the attribute information of the conceptual model entity, which makes it possible to create a dimensional model based on a combination of a conceptual model and an interface documentation.

2) Parallel Work of Different Teams: In the current state, the way of working was divided to serial sprints of different teams. The result of the completed DW sprint was a dimensional model which was utilized by reporting team. Thus, it would be beneficial, if the team could receive the dimensional model earlier to utilize it as a specification between them and the DW team. With the help of a dimensional model that is based on a conceptual model, it is possible to arrange the work so that the reporting team can to start developing the meta model for the reporting at the same time as the DW team starts the ETL work. In addition, the parallel way of working makes it easier for the teams to communicate with each other since they are concentrating on the same main goal, and further, the report can be produced in the end of the parallel sprints enabling customer feedback.

3) Shorter Feedback Cycle and Shorter Delay of Modifications: Since end-user is using the reports, getting useful feedback based on the report requires the report to include actual business data. Parallel working in *DW sprint* and *Reporting sprint* enables finishing the report in one sprint of calendar time. End-user can give feedback based on the report to both teams directly after the sprint. This is a huge difference to the DW team, which will get the feedback immediately after the sprint when compared to serial work in current state when the feedback was available only after the *Reporting sprint* was finished. This is beneficial because receiving feedback is more relevant when it is received directly and without delay. Faster feedback will also shorten the delay of starting the modification work. Therefore, making the modifications is easier since it requires less fragmented work and context switching.

Furthermore, parallel working shortens implementation time which also shortens the time that the end-user waits from giving the business needs to getting a report. In addition, the end-user is likely to be more participating in the process since the implementation time is shorter. According to [10], the end-user participation is such customer collaboration, which makes the product better. As an example of the effects in time, if a sprint lasts for two weeks, the parallel work ensures that delivering a new version of the report takes only two weeks. This is a notable improvement when compared to current state when delivering a report needed four weeks.

Data modeling is the key for communication between the teams and therefore it enables the parallelization of the work.

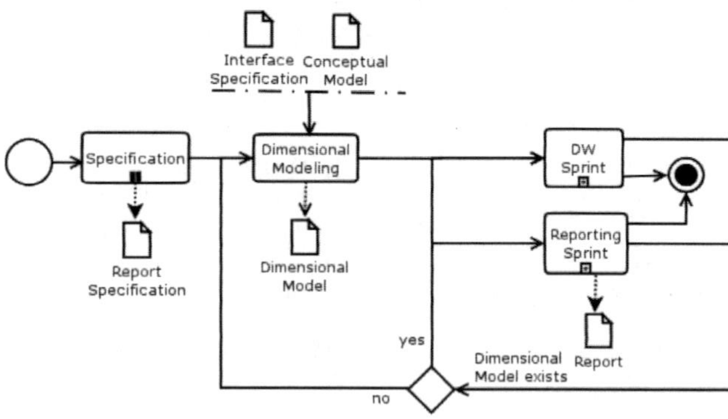

Figure 3. The target state of the process.

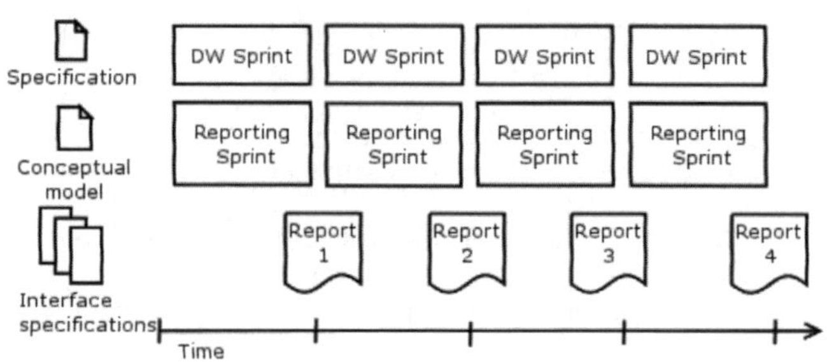

Figure 4. Sprints are parallel and feedback is faster.

IV. Data Modeling

Well managed data modeling is a crucial task for a DW project. Data modeling is about gathering the customers' data requirements and satisfying them with a DW solution.

According to [11], data modeling work is done on three design layers: logical, conceptual and contextual (by bottom-up order). Out of those layers, in this article, we are mostly interested in the conceptual and logical data modeling.

A. Conceptual Data Modeling

Conceptual data modeling is about modeling the user's data requirements in a conceptual manner using common concepts, such as entities and relationships. It describes the data and relationships between different data entities. Conceptual data modeling is a quick way to create a model of the problem domain with business representatives in a workshop, because the main entities come from the business domain and thus they have a business meaning. The collaboration between business stakeholders and data modelers is very important in order to tie the data intensive solution to the business processes.

Conceptual model can be utilized to ensure that all the participants share the same conceptual understanding of the modeled area [11]. In addition, it is a base that evolves to logical data model.

B. Logical Data Modeling

Logical data model presents all entities and their attributes. Each entity which has a primary key is marked in the model. Many-to-many relationships between entities are specified by creating an association entity between the entities. Creating a logical data model requires the following steps [12]:

- Specifying primary keys for all the entities.
- Finding the relationships between different entities.
- Finding all the attributes for each entity.
- Resolving many-to-many relationships.
- Normalisation.

The purpose of the logical data model is to provide a detailed specification for the physical relational database design [11]. In our context a logical data model is a tool for DW designers to produce a DW.

C. Dimensional Modeling

A dimensional model consist of fact and dimension tables in which the main items generally are *facts* and *dimensions* [9]. A *fact* represents a business measurement and is linked to several *dimensions*. A *dimension* groups and labels the measurements while it is also used to restrict the data set of measurements. Dimensional modeling is widely used modeling technique to offer data from DW to reporting tools.

D. Granularity of Data Modeling

The conceptual data model is important for communication between each participant in the project, especially for the business stakeholders, but it does not cover the detailed information needed in the implementation. The logical model, on the other hand, is more detailed but requires more work as it is relatively slow to model all the attributes and relationships of each entity.

The kind of data modeling described so far, is missing one critical piece of information as it does not tell where the data actually exists. The source system information is the most vital information in the reporting project. The needed granularity of data modeling is a mix of conceptual and logical data modeling enriched with information about the location of different entities. The combination of conceptual entities marked with the primary key attributes and information of source systems is the minimum required granularity of needed data model. A model should be enriched with the vital attributes, but the amount of attributes depend on how well the modelers know the domain. When the available information is well known and the business entity is clear, it is possible for everyone to understand the information even if it is not modeled in detail.

V. Conclusions

In this paper, we presented an idea to shorten the feedback cycle of BI projects. The proposed method consists of parallelizing DW and reporting team sprints by using a dimensional model as an agreement between the teams. Since modeling plays a crucial part in BI process, it is important to provide the dimensional model as early as possible. In this paper we claim this to be possible by developing dimensional model based on a combination of a conceptual model and the interface documentation of a source system.

Traditionally, reporting team starts working after DW team has offered a dimensional model with actual data. In our approach, reporting team can start working in parallel with DW team but initially without any actual data. The DW team implements ETL processes with small increments which gives then increasing amount of actual data to reporting team. It is worth noting that making the specifications in the new approach does not increase the overall process time. This is because interface specification is created implicitly anyway and conceptual model is very light weight to create.

As a result of the approach, the customer feedback cycle shortens which moreover makes the feedback more direct. Furthermore, because of parallel working, the communication between teams is more efficient and reaction time to feedback between teams is shorter. This is a step towards agile enterprise data warehousing where a bigger team consists of two separate teams with diverse competence.

VI. Future Work

As a future work, we are planning to conduct a case study in which we will utilize our ideas in an industrial BI project in a mid-sized Finnish software company. Moreover, we are eventually aiming at integrating the different teams (DW team and reporting team) so that the expertise of a person working in a BI project would cover both the required perspectives. That way, it is possible to reduce the amount of persons needed in a project.

The proposed idea is our first step towards agile BI projects, since it can be adopted with other agile principles, as well. To make the BI process even more agile and faster, we are studying how to shorten implementation time by generating ETL processes automatically based on modeling principles [13]. To get full advantage of these improvements, we also aim at creating release management practices to get our BI project closer to the continuous delivery.

Acknowledgment

The work was financially supported by TEKES (Finnish Funding Agency for Innovation) DIGILE Need for Speed program. We would also like to thank Solita and Yle for the possibility of doing this research.

References

[1] K. Schwaber, "Scrum development process," in the Proceedings of the Workshop on Object-Oriented Programming Systems, Languages and Applications Workshop on Business Object Design and Implementation, OOPSLA '95, Austin, Texas, pp. 117–134, October 1995.

[2] R. Krawatzeck, B. Dinter, and T. Duc Ang Pham, "How to make business intelligence agile: The agile bi actions catalog," in System Sciences (HICSS), 2015 48th Hawaii International Conference on, pp. 4762–4771, January 2015.

[3] R. Krawatzeck, M. Zimmer, and S. Trahasch, "Agile business intelligence - definition, maßnahmen und herausforderungen," HMD Praxis der Wirtschaftsinformatik, vol. 50, no. 2, pp. 56–63, January 2014.

[4] F. Tsui, O. Karam, and B. Bernal, Essentials of software engineering. Jones & Bartlett Publishers, 2013.

[5] M. Golfarelli, S. Rizzi, and E. Turrichia, "Modern software engineering methodologies meet data warehouse design: 4wd," in 13th International Conference, DaWaK 2011, Toulouse, France. Proceedings, pp. 66–79, August 2011.

[6] M. Golfarelli, S. Rizzi, and E. Turricchia, "Sprint planning optimization in agile data warehouse design," in Proceeding DaWaK'12 Proceedings of the 14th international conference on Data Warehousing and Knowledge Discovery, pp. 30–41, 2012.

[7] T. Bunio, "Agile data warehouse – the final frontier: How a data warehouse redevelopment is being done in an agile and pragmatic way," in Proceeding AGILE '12 Proceedings of the 2012 Agile Conference, pp. 156–164, August 2012.

[8] H. Watson and B. Wixom, "The current state of business intelligence," Computer, vol. 40, no. 9, pp. 96–99, September 2007.

[9] R. Kimball and M. Ross, The data warehouse toolkit: the complete guide to dimensional modeling. John Wiley & Sons, 2011.

[10] M. Fowler and J. Highsmith, "The agile manifesto," Software Development, vol. 9, no. 8, pp. 28–35, 2001.

[11] A. Sharp and P. McDermott, Workflow modeling: tools for process improvement and applications development. 685 Canton Street Norwood, MA 02062: Artech House, 2001.

[12] 1keydata, "Logical data model," http://www.1keydata.com/datawarehousing/logical-data-model.html, accessed: 2016-01-18.

[13] M. Puonti, T. Raitalaakso, T. Aho, and T. Mikkonen, "Automating transformations in data vault data warehouse loads," in Proceedings of the 26th International Conference on Information Modelling and Knowledge Bases, EJC 2016, pp. 219–235, June 2016.

Toward the Design and Implementation of the Hosted Private Cloud

Chia Hung Kao
Department of Applied Mathematics
National Taitung University
Taitung, Taiwan
Email: chkao@nttu.edu.tw

Hsin Tse Lu
Data Analytics Technology and Applications Research Institute
Institute for Information Industry
Taipei, Taiwan
Email: oliu@iii.org.tw

***Abstract*—In recent years, cloud computing products and services are widely used by enterprises, companies and individuals in their daily tasks. Among different cloud computing models, private cloud is more appropriate for small and medium business (SMB) from the perspectives of security, control and reliability. However, the complexity of deployment, configuration and management of cloud computing infrastructure causes additional efforts and costs, especially because SMBs usually do not have enough IT resources. Therefore, the hosted private cloud model is developed to achieve higher usability by masking the complexities from users, and keep the advantages of private cloud at the same time. In this paper, based on previous virtualization solution, the design and the implementation of hosted private cloud are introduced.**

***Keywords*–Cloud Computing; Private Cloud; Hosted Private Cloud.**

I. INTRODUCTION

Cloud computing has attracted considerable attention in recent years. As the related technologies grow and mature, cloud computing products and services are widely used by enterprises, companies and individuals in their daily tasks [1]. Public cloud services, such as Amazon AWS [2], Microsoft Azure [3], Google Cloud Platform [4] and so on, provide comprehensive computing, storage and network resources through Internet. On the other hand, hybrid cloud is the composition of multiple clouds, that achieves heterogeneous resource consolidation and keeps the benefits brought by individual clouds [5]. Finally, companies or organizations can build and manage their own private cloud to deliver necessary infrastructure, platform and application services internally. For SMBs, private cloud model is more appropriate from the perspectives of security, control and reliability [6]. However, the complexity of deployment, configuration and management of cloud computing infrastructure causes additional efforts and costs, especially because SMBs usually do not have enough IT resources (e.g., hardware, software and engineers). Therefore, the model of hosted private cloud is developed to achieve higher usability by masking the construction and management complexities from users and keep the advantages of private cloud at the same time.

Fig. 1 depicts the context diagram of the hosted private cloud. There are several actors, including Cloud Infrastructure Administrator, Hosted Private Cloud Administrator, Private Cloud Owner/User and Service Consumer, which are stated as the following.

- **Cloud Infrastructure Administrator**: Cloud Infrastructure Administrator is responsible for the construction, configuration, management and maintenance of physical hardware and environment. Computation resources, storage resources, networking, energy, security and so on are included. Different scale of cloud infrastructure is constructed and configured for further usage. Based on particular requirements and conditions, the administrator helps to add, configure, remove, monitor and maintain the components inside cloud infrastructure.
- **Hosted Private Cloud Administrator**: Hosted Private Cloud Administrator is responsible for the management of hosted private cloud built by underlying cloud infrastructure. Through the functionalities provided by hosted private cloud, the administrator can manage, monitor and allocate corresponding resources for multiple private cloud environments. Based on the monitoring information and the requirements from Private Cloud Owner/User, resources for private cloud environment can be managed and adjusted by Hosted Private Cloud Administrator. In addition, the administrator might configure security policies (e.g., network connectivity and isolation), backup and restore mechanism, failover plan and so on for better service quality of the hosted private cloud.
- **Private Cloud Owner/User**: When the hosted private cloud is built, Private Cloud Owner/User can register and request private cloud environment. Hosted Private Cloud Administrator evaluates the request from Private Cloud Owner/User and constructs corresponding

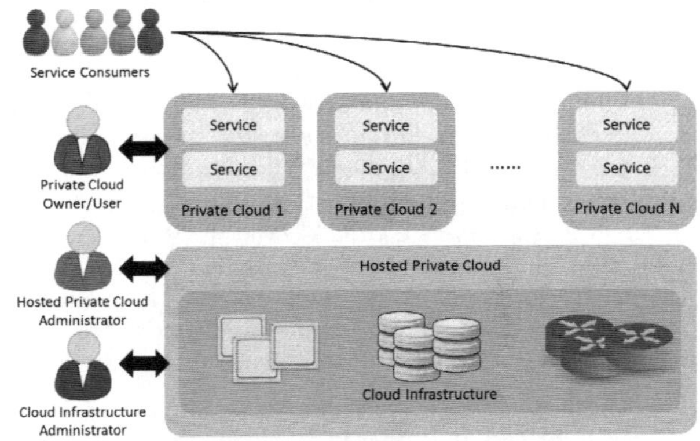

Figure 1. Context diagram of the hosted private cloud.

private cloud environment if the underlying resources are sufficient. Once the environment is built, Private Cloud Owner/User can manage and monitor the private cloud environment, and create corresponding environment (e.g., virtual machines, storage and networking) for services and applications. Another usage scenario for Private Cloud Owner/User is to provide service and application (e.g., disk images) directly for Hosted Private Cloud Administrator without creating private cloud environment from scratch. This facilitates the service and application deployment and eases the burden of construction of private cloud environment from Private Cloud Owner/User.

- **Service Consumers**: Service consumers are the end users who use the services built on private cloud environment.

In this paper, the design and the implementation of hosted private cloud are introduced. The hosted private cloud is modified and extended from previous virtualization solution, Cloud Appliance Kernel Environment (CAKE) [7][8]. It provides different tenants (Private Cloud Owner/User) with isolated resources to support their tasks and efficient management mechanisms for Hosted Private Cloud Administrator and Private Cloud Owner/User. Current deployment of the hosted private cloud is also described in this paper for further functional and performance evaluation [9].

The remainder of this paper is organized as follows. Section II reviews related studies. Section III introduces the virtualization solution, CAKE. Section IV describes the architecture of the hosted private cloud and Section V presents the deployment for functional and quality evaluation. Finally, Section VI presents conclusion and future works.

II. RELATED WORK

Moghaddam et al. [10] surveyed different architecture, models, deployment types, key technologies and characteristics of cloud computing. According to their survey, the "virtual private cloud" offered by public cloud service providers achieved both flexibility of public clouds and reliability of private clouds. Resources can be shared by different subscribers and the private cloud can be accessed through secure communication channel. Cardellini and Iannucci [11] presented an architecture for a reliable, scalable, flexible and modular private cloud. Authors also implemented a case study to evaluate the proposed private cloud architecture by Linux Terminal Server Project (LTSP). Mangal et al. [12] integrated private cloud and public cloud for more efficient resource utilization. Based on specific load conditions, the virtualization instances will be migrated to public cloud or back to the private cloud accordingly. Shtern et al. [13] designed a reference architecture (AERIE), which can create virtual private cloud on top of public clouds. The issues of security and data protection were considered and mitigated through the proposed design. In addition to academic studies, several commercial products or services of "managed private cloud" and "virtual private cloud" are available [14][15][16].

To sum up, the model of hosted private cloud achieves both flexibility and reliability and has attracted attentions of software companies, service providers and consumers. Unlike the consideration of complex or hybrid architecture and the provision of large scale cloud environment, the design of the hosted private cloud in this paper tries to build private environments for consumers like SMBs efficiently. Furthermore, the simplicity and manageability are also considered in the design for cloud infrastructure providers and hosted private cloud providers.

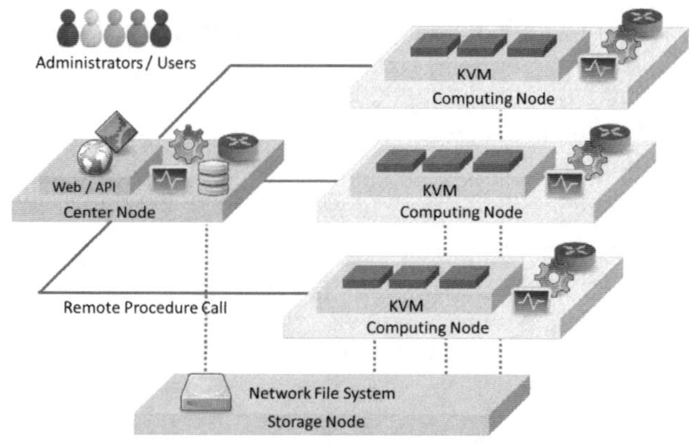

Figure 2. Overview of the CAKE architecture.

III. CLOUD APPLIANCE KERNEL ENVIRONMENT

CAKE, developed by Institute for Information Industry, is a server virtualization management solution based on Kernel-based Virtual Machine (KVM) [17]. It supports lifecycle management of virtual machines, and provides user friendly management console for administrators and users. CAKE is designed as an appliance based on commodity hardware. Thus, users can purchase or use existing hardware without any modification and install CAKE to build and manage private cloud efficiently. Based on different usage requirements, CAKE can be deployed as a single node service or multi-node cluster for virtualization capacity or high availability. As shown in Fig. 2, there are three major components in CAKE, including Center Node, Computing Node and Storage Node.

- **Center Node**: The major functionality of Center Node is to manage the virtualization environment built by all the Computing Nodes in the CAKE cluster. In addition, Center Node provides user management, network configuration, storage management, API service, backup and restore, and monitoring mechanisms. Users and administrators can login to Center Node to use and manage the virtualization environment through web interface.
- **Computing Node**: The Computing Node is the physical environment for virtual machines. It receives requests (as the form of remote procedure call) from Center Node and performs corresponding management tasks on virtual machines based on KVM through libvirt [18], including creation, deletion, boot, shutdown, configuration, migration and so on. Computing Nodes can be added to or removed from CAKE cluster dynamically based on resource requirements.
- **Storage Node**: The Storage Node is responsible for the preservation of images, templates, snapshots, and virtual disks of virtual machines. Currently, Network

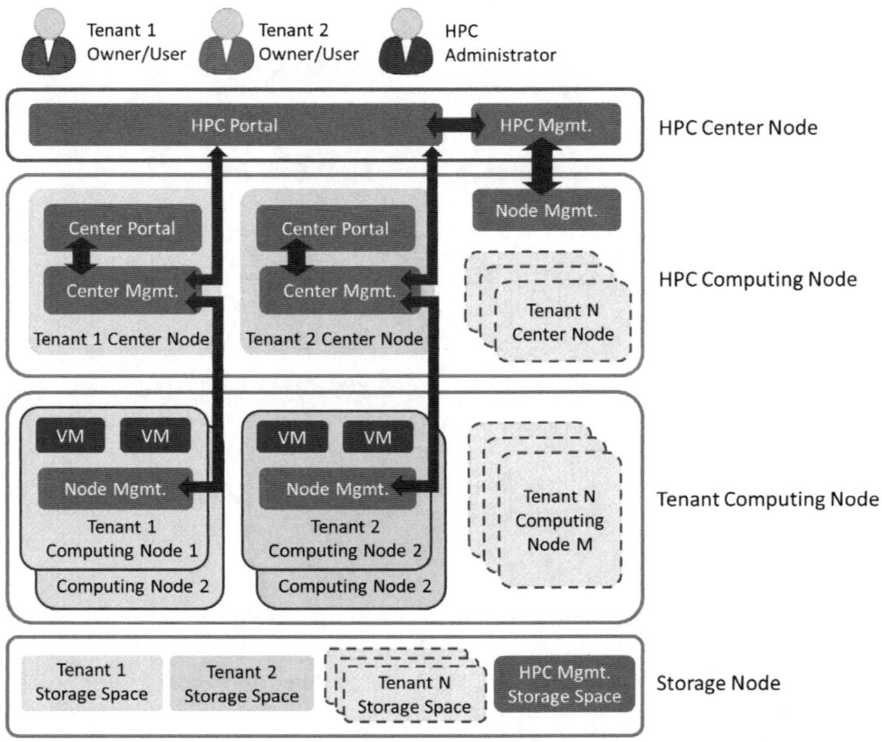

Figure 3. Architecture of the hosted private cloud.

File System (NFS) [19] is used in CAKE for simplicity and reliability. Center node and the computing nodes in CAKE cluster mount the NFS for all the operations in the virtualization environment.

IV. Architecture of Hosted Private Cloud

The operation model of CAKE is suitable for one specific organization, company or SMB. In other words, the multi-tenancy is not taken into consideration in the original design. Therefore, the design and implementation should be extended and modified to fulfill the requirements of hosted private cloud. Meanwhile, the original design and the operation model of CAKE can be leveraged to simplify the architecture design of hosted private cloud, and decrease the implementation effort. Fig. 3 shows the architecture of the hosted private cloud based on CAKE. The major modification is to add a higher layer for the management and monitoring of the overall hosted private cloud, which is achieved by one specific set of CAKE cluster. The specific CAKE cluster manages multiple virtualized CAKE centers, which are connected by particular CAKE clusters to construct multiple private cloud environments. Components of the hosted private cloud include Hosted Private Cloud (HPC) Center Node, Hosted Private Cloud (HPC) Computing Node, Tenant Center Node, Tenant Computing Node and Storage Node.

- **HPC Center Node**: The major functionality of HPC Center Node is to manage the overall hosted private cloud environment. As shown in Fig. 3, through HPC management module, HPC Center Node requests HPC Computing Node to perform the construction, configuration and management tasks on Tenant Center Nodes. It also provides web interface (HPC Portal) for HPC administrator to manage HPC cluster and tenants in the hosted private cloud environment. HPC administrators can add, delete, configure and monitor tenants and underlying resources accordingly. In addition, tenant owners and users can login with corresponding tenant identification to manage their private cloud environments. Monitoring data gathered by Tenant Center Nodes will be sent back to HPC Center Node for summarized information of the whole hosted private cloud environment. Finally, multiple HPC Center Nodes can be built and federated for the concern of high availability [20].
- **HPC Computing Node**: HPC Computing Node is the physical environment only for Tenant Center Node (virtualized CAKE Center). One HPC Computing Node can support the running of several Tenant Center Nodes. Based on the amount of managed tenants, HPC Computing Node can be added or removed by HPC administrator accordingly. In order to achieve high availability, HPC Center Node will detect the status of HPC Computing Node periodically. If HPC Computing Node is down for unknown reasons, HPC Center Node will trigger the migration task to move Tenant Center Node from failure HPC Computing Node to another. On the other hand, HPC administrator can perform migration manually due to maintenance requirements.
- **Tenant Center Node**: Tenant Center Node is virtualized CAKE Center and deployed on HPC Computing

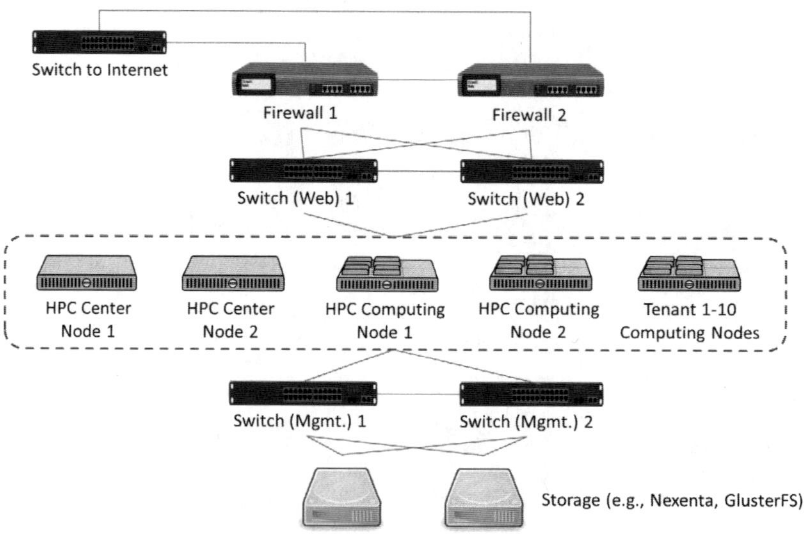

Figure 4. Deployment of the hosted private cloud.

Node. Similar to the operation model of CAKE, it helps to manage dedicated private cloud environment built by Tenant Computing Nodes. If new tenant should be built, HPC administrator can create Tenant Center Node from image template efficiently and associate allocated Tenant Computing Nodes.

- **Tenant Computing Node**: Tenant Computing Node is the physical environment for virtual machines operated by specific tenants. Similarly, it receives requests from particular Tenant Center Node and performs corresponding control and management tasks on virtual machines. Tenant Computing Node can be added to or removed from specific tenant based on requirements. If multiple Tenant Computing Nodes are deployed, the availability of virtual machines can be improved through the periodical check and migration request from Tenant Center Node.
- **Storage Node**: Multi-tenancy (e.g., access management and data isolation) should be taken into consideration in the hosted private cloud. Corresponding storage spaces should be configured and managed for different tenants. In addition, performance, scalability and availability are also important issues due to large amounts of usages simultaneously and continuously. Software-defined storage (e.g., Nexenta [21] and GlusterFS [22]) can be appropriate solutions for hosted private cloud.

V. Deployment

Currently, the deployment of the hosted private cloud is performed in one cabinet for functional and performance evaluation. Fig. 4 depicts the organization of hardware, networking and HPC nodes. The physical server used in the deployment is 2U 4-Node server. Two HPC Center Nodes and two HPC Computing Nodes are used in current deployment, which can be allocated in one physical 2U 4-Node server. With the above configuration, availability can be achieved to tackle possible failure situations. On the other hand, five 2U 4-Node servers are allocated for tenants. Each tenant uses two nodes in one physical server for fundamental virtualization capacity and availability. The hosted private cloud is anticipated to support ten tenants. Therefore, it is expected to provide 16 virtual machines for each tenant, and totally 160 virtual machines for the current setting of hosted private cloud in one cabinet. Based on further resource or operation requirements, physical servers can be added and configured to Tenant Computing Nodes for tenants. Nexenta and GlusterFS are deployed and evaluated in the hosted private cloud individually. Both storage systems can be configured to support the data access and space management of multiple tenants. In addition, Nexenta and GlusterFS provide failover mechanism for high availability requirement. Finally, virtual LAN (VLAN) and secure sockets layer virtual private network (SSL-VPN) can be created and configured through firewall and switch to enhance security and isolation of tenants in hosted private cloud. On the other hand, in order to achieve high availability of the whole environment, firewall and switch are federated and deployed with failover capability.

VI. Conclusion

In this paper, the design and the implementation of hosted private cloud are introduced. Based on previous virtualization solution (CAKE), the hosted private cloud is extended and modified to provide different tenants with isolated resources to support their tasks, and efficient management mechanism for administrators. Besides, it leverages the original design and operation model of CAKE that simplifies the architecture design of hosted private cloud and decreases the implementation effort. For future works, test cases based on real world usage scenarios will be designed and deployed for functional evaluation. In addition, different deployment scale of the hosted private cloud (e.g., from one cabinet to multiple cabinets) should be examined. Finally, the performance, reliability and availability will be evaluated for actual service delivery in future works.

REFERENCES

[1] W. Y. Chang, H. Abu-Amara, and J. F. Sanford, Transforming Enterprise Cloud Services. Springer, 2010.

[2] Amazon Web Services, URL: https://aws.amazon.com [accessed: 2016-06-24].

[3] Microsoft Azure, URL: https://azure.microsoft.com/en-us [accessed: 2016-06-24].

[4] Google Cloud Platform, URL: https://cloud.google.com [accessed: 2016-06-24].

[5] N. Leavitt, "Hybrid Clouds Move to the Forefront," Computer, vol. 46, no. 5, May 2013, pp. 15–18.

[6] R. L. Grossman, "The Case for Cloud Computing," IT Professional, vol. 11, no. 2, Mar.-Apr. 2009, pp. 23–27.

[7] G. Wang and J. Unger, "A Strategy to Move Taiwan's IT Industry From Commodity Hardware Manufacturing to Competitive Cloud Solutions," IEEE Access, vol. 1, May 2013, pp. 159–166.

[8] W. C.-C. Chu, C.-T. Yang, C.-W. Lu, C.-H. Chang, J.-N. Chen, P.-A. Hsiung, and H.-M. Lee, "Cloud Computing in Taiwan," Computer, vol. 45, no. 6, June 2012, pp. 48–56.

[9] K. Ye, Z. Wu, B. B. Zhou, X. Jiang, C. Wang, and A. Y. Zomaya, "Virt-B: Toward Performance Benchmarking of Virtual Machine Systems," IEEE Internet Computing, vol. 18, no. 3, May-June 2014, pp. 64–72.

[10] F. F. Moghaddam, M. B. Rohani, M. Ahmadi, T. Khodadadi, and K. Madadipouya, "Cloud Computing: Vision, Architecture and Characteristics," Proceedings of the 2015 IEEE 6th Control and System Graduate Research Colloquium, Aug. 2015, pp. 1–6.

[11] V. Cardellini and S. Iannucci, "Designing a Flexible and Modular Architecture for a Private Cloud: a Case Study," Proceedings of the 6th International Workshop on Virtualization Technologies in Distributed Computing Date, June 2012, pp. 37–44.

[12] G. Mangal, P. Kasliwal, U. Deshpande, M. Kurhekar, and G. Chafle, "Flexible Cloud Computing by Integrating Public-Private Clouds using OpenStack," Proceedings of the 2015 IEEE International Conference on Cloud Computing in Emerging Markets, Nov. 2015, pp. 146–152.

[13] M. Shtern, B. Simmons, M. Smit, and M. Litoiu, "An Architecture for Overlaying Private Clouds on Public Providers," Proceedings of the 2012 8th International Conference on Network and Service Management, Oct. 2012, pp. 371–377.

[14] IBM Cloud OpenStack Services, URL: http://open.ibmcloud.com/ [accessed: 2016-06-24].

[15] HPE Helion Managed Private Cloud, URL: https://www.hpe.com/us/en/solutions/cloud.html [accessed: 2016-06-24].

[16] Amazon Virtual Private Cloud, URL: https://aws.amazon.com/vpc/ [accessed: 2016-06-24].

[17] Kernel Virtual Machine, URL: http://www.linux-kvm.org [accessed: 2016-06-24].

[18] libvirt: The virtualization API, URL: https://libvirt.org [accessed: 2016-06-24].

[19] B. Pawlowski, C. Juszczak, P. Staubach, C. Smith, D. Lebel, and D. Hitz, "NFS Version 3: Design and Implementation," Proceedings of the Summer 1994 USENIX Technical Conference, June 1994, pp. 137–151.

[20] Pacemaker, URL: http://clusterlabs.org [accessed: 2016-06-24].

[21] Nexenta, URL: https://nexenta.com [accessed: 2016-06-24].

[22] GlusterFS, URL: https://www.gluster.org [accessed: 2016-06-24].

A General Solution for Business Process Model Extension with Cost Perspective based on Process Mining

Dhafer Thabet, Sonia Ayachi Ghannouchi, Henda Hajjami Ben Ghezala
RIADI Laboratory
National School for Computer Sciences
Mannouba, Tunisia
e-mail: dhafer.thabet@isetso.rnu.tn, sonia.ayachi@isgs.rnu.tn, henda.benghezala@ensi.rnu.tn

***Abstract*—Several organizations look for improving their business processes in order to enhance their efficiency and competitiveness. Business process management approach includes techniques allowing continuous business process improvement. Process mining is a business process management technique allowing to extract knowledge from event logs commonly available in today's information systems. Business process model extension is a process mining technique enriching a business process model with different perspectives useful for decision making support. Furthermore, financial costs incurred during business process execution is prominent information needed for business process improvement decision making in terms of cost reduction. We propose a solution for business process model extension with cost perspective based on process mining. The solution is based on cost extension of the high-level process structure, which is a meta-model enabling the integration of different perspectives into one model independently of its notation. However, the cost extension is designed only at the activity level and the general approach needs to be validated. In this paper, on one hand, we propose an improved version of the proposed approach providing cost extension including cost data description and analysis at both activity and business process levels, and on the other hand, we present implementation and tests of the improved solution on three simplified business process model notations: Petri Net, Event-driven Process Chain and Business Process Model and Notation.**

Keywords-Business Process Management; Business Process Improvement; Process Mining; Business Process Model Cost Extension; Cost Extended High Level Process Structure.

I. INTRODUCTION

The main concern of several organizations is to enhance their efficiency and competitiveness [3]. The Business Process Management (BPM) approach aims at, continuously, improving organizations' business processes [1][22]. The Process Mining (PMining) technique is used to analyze business processes based on event logs commonly available in today's information systems [1][22]. Event logs can be used to conduct three types of PMining [13][23][28]: (1) discovery: produces a BP model using event logs; (2) conformance: an existing process model is compared with the corresponding event logs to identify the eventual deviations; (3) enhancement: includes two sub-types: repair (improving the model to better reflect reality) and extension. The latter type allows to enrich the BP model with additional perspectives useful for BP improvement decision making support (examples: organizational, case and time perspectives).

Furthermore, organizations look to reduce the financial costs incurred during the execution of their business processes using different techniques. Management Accounting (MA) is the field defining how cost (and other information) should be used for planning, controlling, continuous improvement and decision making [10][30]. It includes several techniques such as: Activity-Based Costing/Management (ABC/M) [10][30]; Time-Driven ABC (TDABC) [14]; and Resource Consumption Accounting (RCA) [7][21]. The goal of these techniques is to measure costs incurred during process execution and to allocate them to the BP operations.

In order to facilitate access and interpretation of cost information for decision makers, it would be interesting to have these information associated to the corresponding BP model. Indeed, this enables decision makers to easily obtain accurate cost information about their business processes. Thus, we considered the issue of BP model extension with cost information based on PMining extension technique. In [24][25], we started by studying this issue for business processes modeled with Petri Nets. Thus, we proposed an approach and its implementation for Petri Net cost extension based on PMining extension technique. Furthermore, in [27], the proposed solution was improved according to recommendations we drew from interviews we conducted with experts in MA. Moreover, in [28], we proposed a generalized version of the proposed approach in order to make it independent of the BP modeling notation (not only Petri Nets).

The main research goal is BP model extension with cost perspective using PMining extension technique in order to support decision makers in their improvement decisions for cost reduction. The solution we proposed in [24][25] ensures a Petri Net model cost extension based on PMining extension technique. In [26], we improved the proposed solution with respect to recommendations drew from interviews with experts in terms of MA. The considered improvements concern three main levels: cost data structure, cost data description and cost data analysis. Besides, in [27], we generalized the proposed approach in order to support different BP modeling notations.

However, the generalized approach provides cost extension, cost data description and analysis, only at the activity level. Thus, it would be useful for decision makers to also get insight on cost information and knowledge at the BP level. For instance, this would provide information about the activities which incurred the highest cost value among the considered BP activities. Therefore, in this paper, the considered main research question is about the way to improve the proposed approach so that it provides cost extension, cost data description and analysis at both activity and BP levels. Moreover, this paper presents an overview about the implementation as well as the tests of the improved approach on three simplified BP modeling notations: PN, EPC and BPMN.

In the remainder of this paper, we give an overview about the related works, in Section II. Section III presents the proposed solution design, implementation and tests. Finally, a summary of the contribution, its limits and the future works are presented in Section IV.

II. Related Work

The work of Nauta in [18] is a proposal of an architecture to support cost-awareness in PMining. Nauta's solution, mainly, consists in annotating the initial event log -in eXtensible Event Stream (XES) format [12] - with cost information using a cost model. The cost annotation is performed, per cost type, in the final event of each task instance. Then, the obtained cost annotated event log -in XES format- is used to create cost reports [18].

The work of Wynn et al. [32][33] was motivated by the work of Nauta. Wynn et al. proposed a cost mining framework allowing cost reports generation and cost prediction. The cost report can be customized in different ways. The cost prediction looks for cost patterns so that it would be possible to predict cost consumption of an ongoing BP case [33]. The cost prediction is performed by proposing a cost extension of the transition system approach [29] to produce a cost-annotated transition system.

The technique proposed by Conforti et al. in [5] aims at predicting faults related to three dimensions of a BP, which are time, cost and reputation. It allows process participants to make risk-informed decisions when taking part in a BP. The technique relies on risk estimator trained using data extracted from event logs. For each state of a process execution where input is required from a participant, the estimator determines the severity and likelihood that a fault will occur if that input is going to be used to carry on the process execution. The technique offers the considered participant risk-based recommendations for reducing the number of faults and their severities [5].

Although cost reports, which are produced by the solution of Nauta, are used by management accountants to have details about the costs incurred by BP execution, they are not sufficient for better decision making support. Moreover, the generation of only tabular cost reports does not facilitate decision making. In the work of Wynn et al., cost reports are generated separately from the BP model, which may not facilitate support for decision makers with no MA background. Furthermore, the proposed cost prediction is mainly based on activities and resources of the considered BP while different other attributes could influence cost values. In addition, cost prediction aims at cost reduction for the current BP case but does not support improvement decisions for the whole BP. Similarly, in the work of Conforti et al., cost-related risk prediction is used to provide recommendations supporting reduction of cost-related faults for the current BP case but not for the whole BP improvement. Besides, all of the mentioned works do not provide BP model cost extension at different levels (particularly activity and BP levels) while it is important to present BP-related cost information from different points of view. Moreover, each of these works focus on a particular type of BP models, although the diversity of BP modeling notations.

Therefore, in this paper, we propose a solution using the cost annotated event logs, produced by the solution of Nauta, in order to extend BP models with cost perspective at BP and activity levels. Besides, the proposed solution takes into account the diversity of BP modeling notations.

III. Proposed Solution

In [27], we introduced the first version of the generalized approach for BP model cost extension based on PMining. In order to provide better support for decision makers in their improvement decisions, we considered to further improve the previous version of the proposed approach so that cost extension covers the activity level as well as the BP level. Moreover, the improved solution should be implemented and tested in order to be validated. In the following, we present the improved solution design, implementation and tests.

A. Proposed Solution Design

In the following, we present an overview about the proposed approach and the adopted general meta-model allowing cost extension at activity and BP levels.

1) Proposed Approach Overview: Fig. 1 shows an overview about the proposed approach. The BP model and the corresponding cost annotated event log are the inputs of the generalized approach. The BP model is extended with cost data extracted from the cost annotated event log. Thus, the obtained output of this step is a cost extended BP model. Then, the output is graphically displayed with respect to the corresponding notation. The following step is to handle the cost extended BP model in such a way to further support decision makers in BP cost reduction. Cost data can be handled at two different levels: the activity level and the BP level.

Firstly, activity level cost data is handled whether by description or analysis for each user-selected activity. On one hand, cost data description allows decision makers to get insight about each activity of the BP model from a cost point of view. Cost description is performed using user-customizable tables and graphics. Tables are used to present cost values with respect to the user-specified options. Graphics are used to represent views of average cost values based on different factors (resource, cost types, instances) and to visualize a comparison between recorded cost values and the user-expected ones. The user-defined cost values could be provided whether by a single cost expected value or a cost expected interval representing a cost value range between expected minimum and maximum cost values. On the other hand, cost data analysis supports decision makers to find out factors influencing on incurred cost values. Two cost analysis methods are considered. The first method consists in classifying resources into two groups by comparing resource-based average cost corresponding to the selected activity with a user-defined cost value or interval. This method supports decision makers to determine resources involved in incurring higher/lower cost values than the user-expected one for the selected activity. The second cost data analysis method deals with how to support decision makers to know which activity-related attributes (resource, time and other data attributes) influence activity cost values, and how. The method is based on using Machine Learning (ML) classification algorithms [9][23][31], which allow to extract knowledge about the influence of selected attributes on activity cost values. The inputs of a ML classification algorithm are: training examples, attributes and classes. In our case, for each selected activity of the BP model, training examples are the activity instances contained in the cost annotated event log. The attributes are the activity-related ones including resource, time and data attributes. If the user provides a single expected cost value, two classes are defined: C1 (respectively C2) represents activity instances having an average cost value (cost type is selected by the user) higher (respectively lower) than a user-estimated cost value. If an expected cost interval is provided (expected maximum and minimum cost values), in addition to C1 and C2 classes, a third class C3 is added to represent activity instances having an average cost value (cost type is selected by the user) between the user-expected cost interval bounds. The outputs are the inferred structural patterns represented, for instance, in the form of a list of classification rules, which represent a simple and expressive way to understand which attributes influence cost values, and how [27].

Secondly, BP cost data can be handled with two main ways. On one hand, the first way provides BP cost data description using tables or graphics. Tables represent numeric cost data values calculated according to user-customized options (computation modes and cost types). Graphics provide cost-related views based on different factors (BP instances, activities and cost types) and are also used to represent comparisons between recorded cost values and user-defined cost value or interval. On the other hand, the second way consists in analyzing BP cost data in order to support decision makers determining factors influencing cost values at the BP level. Cost data analysis includes two methods. The first method provides statistics about BP instances that incurred costs more/less than a user-defined cost value or interval. If the user chooses to provide a single cost value, the cost data analysis consists in calculating the percentages of BP instances that incurred costs more and less than the user-defined one. If the user provides an interval (expected maximum and minimum cost values), the cost data analysis consists in computing percentages of BP instances that incurred costs higher, in and lower than the user-defined cost interval. Then, the obtained percentages are displayed textually and/or graphically. The second BP cost analysis method aims at extracting knowledge about BP-related attributes (time and other data attributes) that influence BP cost values using ML classification algorithms. The input data include training examples, which are the BP instances (traces) contained in the cost annotated event log; attributes which are BP instances-related attributes including time and (if any) other data attributes; and classes which depend on the cost expected value(s) provided by the user. If a single value is provided, two classes are generated: C1 (respectively C2) represents BP instances with average costs higher (respectively lower) than the user-expected one. If an interval is provided, a third class C3 is generated representing BP instances with average costs within the provided interval. The outputs of this method are structural patterns representing knowledge about factors that influence BP-related cost values.

2) Cost-extended High-Level Process Structure: The high-level process structure is a general meta-model designed to embed information from different perspectives into the control flow and to make them as generic and reusable as possible [23]. As our goal is to incorporate cost information into the BP model, we considered to extend the high-level process structure with the data structure representing the cost perspective. The cost extended high-level process core data structure is shown in Fig. 2 as a UML class diagram. The yellow-colored classes together with their relationships represent the high-level process structure. The HLProcess is the central class and holds the high-level information independently of the BP model type. It holds a list of process elements (HLProcessElement) such as activities (HLActivity) for the process. Besides, each high-level process element is identified using the HLID class. The HLGlobal class holds information that is globally relevant for the BP. The HLModel class enables to match the nodes of an actual BP model to their corresponding elements in the HLProcess structure. The ModelGraph class represents the actual BP model. These classes represent the common elements that will be shared by all high-level processes, regardless of whether they refer to some Petri net model, or YAWL model, etc. [23][27].

As shown in Fig. 2, the cost data structure is represented by the grey-colored classes together with their relationships. The HLProcessCost class and the corresponding relationships represent cost information at BP level. It consists of a list of process instances costs each of which is represented by the ProcessInstanceCost class. Moreover, as HLProcessCost class represents cost information at BP level, it is associated to the HLProcess class. Each process instance cost consists of a list of activity instances costs (ActivityInstanceCost class).

Each activity instance cost consists in turn of elementary costs (ElementaryCost class). Each elementary cost has a value, a currency and a cost type (CostType class). Furthermore, each process instance cost is related to a process instance (ProcessInstance class) and each activity instance cost is related to an activity instance (ActivityInstance class). The ProcessInstance and ActivityInstance classes are generalized using the abstract Instance class so that for each process instance and activity instance, we retain the resources involved in its execution (Resource class), the corresponding time information (Time class) and, if any, other related data attributes (DataAttribute class). This way, HLProcessCost class holds cost information related to the whole BP and to each one of its activities independently of the BP model notation. Thus, the cost-extended HLPS shown in Fig. 2 allows to get cost information at both BP and activity levels.

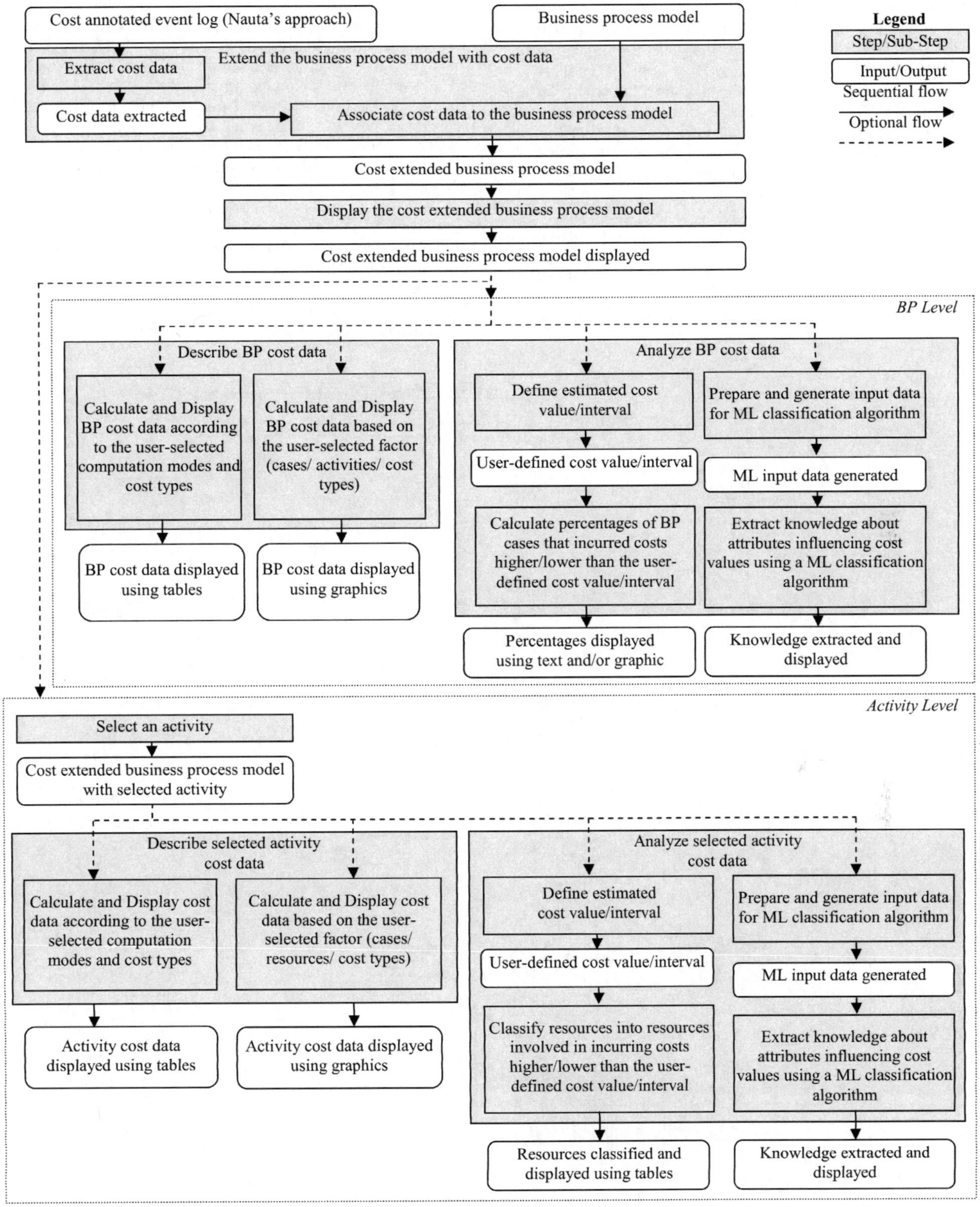

Figure 1. Improved approach overview.

B. Proposed Solution Implementation

The proposed approach is implemented as a tool for BP model cost extension. Table 1 shows the general architecture of the implemented tool. The left side column of Table 1 represents the required inputs for the implemented tool. The first input is the BP model file (PN or EPC or BPMN, etc.), which meets the corresponding meta-model (format). For this moment, the PNML [15], the EPML [17] and simplified BPMN [19] meta-models are implemented. Thus, the implemented tool supports PN, EPC and BPMN models corresponding, respectively, to the above mentioned meta-models. The second input is the corresponding cost annotated event log file, which meets XES format - the standard event log meta-model for PMining [12]. The central column of Table 1 shows the internal tool structure, which is represented by a UML component diagram. It is composed of three packages: CostExtendedHLPS, GUI and Main.

The CostExtendedHLPS package contains three sub-packages: HLProcess, HLModel and ModelGraph. The HLProcess sub-package consists of the high level process information classes and their relationships (HLProcess and related classes in Fig. 2) including cost data structure. The HLProcess sub-package uses the OpenXES plugin to import cost data from cost extended event log files. The HLModel sub-package contains the HLModel class and its sub-classes as shown in Fig. 2. The ModelGraph sub-package consists of the ModelGraph class and its sub-classes, which represent the different BP meta-models. For this moment, we implemented PN, EPC and BPMN meta-models using (respectively) the PNML framework [15], EPCTools [6] and BPMN Camunda [4] plugins. The GUI package contains all graphical user interfaces and their related classes whose role is to import input files and display processed results. Orchestration of the different packages is ensured by the Main package.

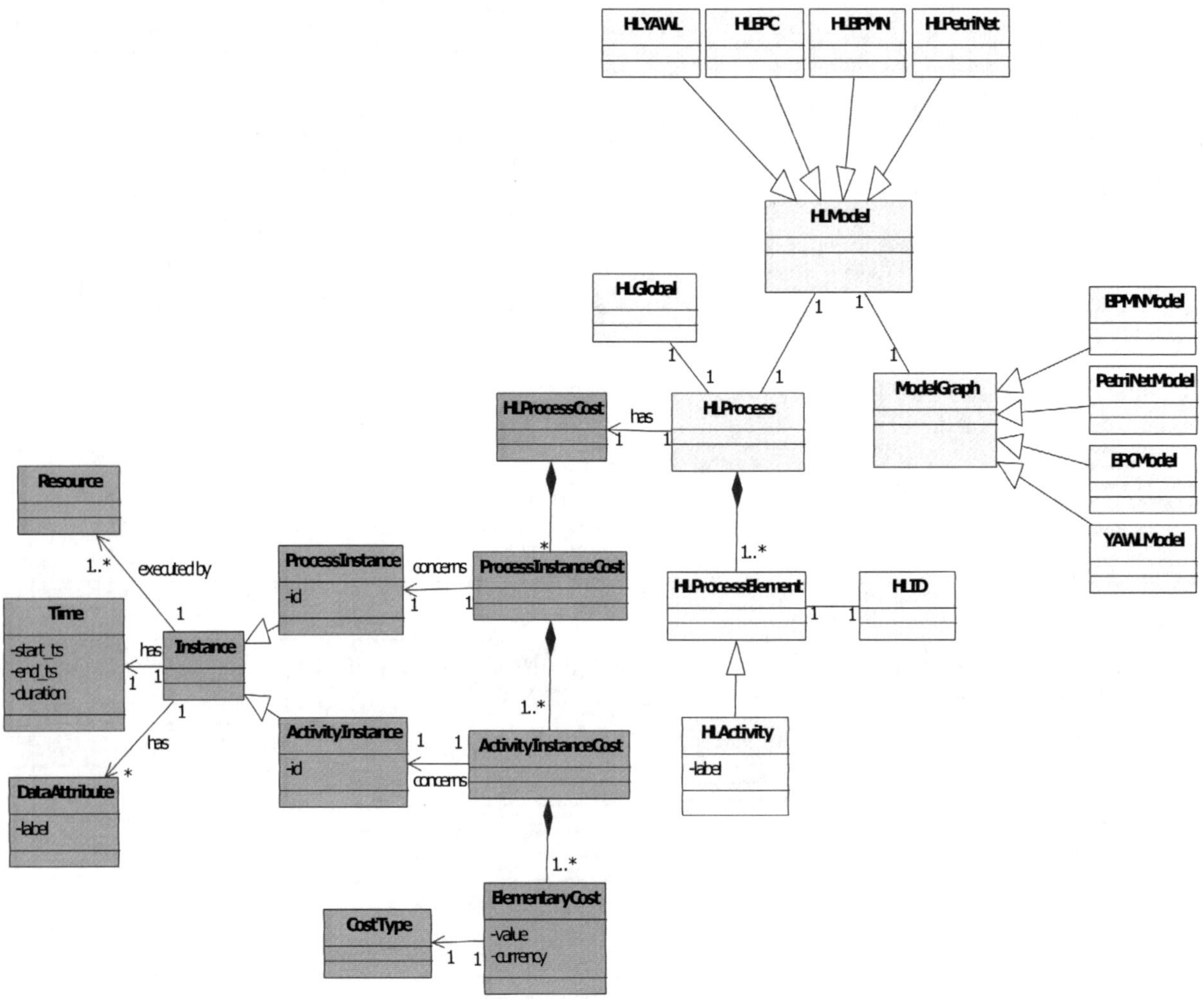

Figure 2. Improved cost-extended HLPS.

TABLE I. GENERAL ARCHITECTURE OF THE BP MODEL COST EXTENSION TOOL.

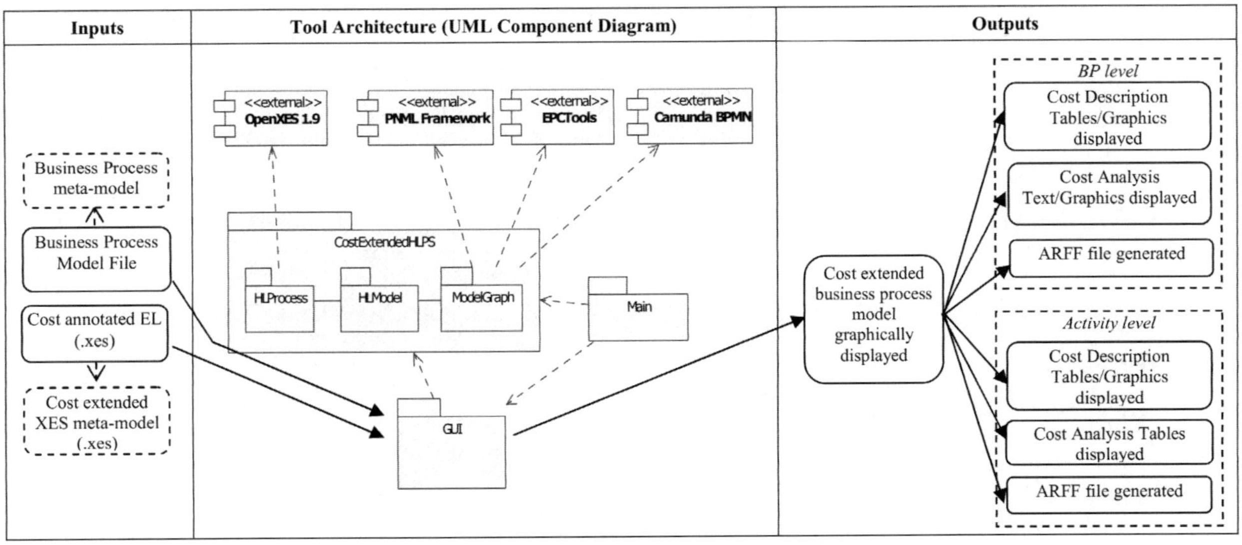

Depending on the user-selected option, the produced output concerns whether the BP level or the activity level. On one hand, the BP level outputs are computed for the whole BP and may be: (1) cost description results displayed whether with tables or graphics, or (2) cost analysis results displayed using text and/or graphics for BP instances costs statistics method and are generated as Attribute-Relation File Format (ARFF) file [31] for the ML classification-based method at BP level. Each generated ARFF file consists of attributes values and classes as presented in section III.A.1. Thus, the generated ARFF file can be easily imported into the Waikato Environment for Knowledge Analysis (Weka) system [31], which allows to pre-process the input data and provides several algorithms to apply for extracting knowledge about factors influencing cost values of the whole BP in different forms such as classification rules or decision trees. On the other hand, activity level outputs are calculated for each selected activity and may be: (1) cost description results displayed using tables or graphics, or (2) cost analysis results, which are displayed using tables for the cost-based resource classification method and are generated as ARFF files for the ML classification-based method at activity level. The generated ARFF file can be imported in Weka and classification algorithms can be applied to extract knowledge about factors influencing cost values of the selected activity.

C. *Proposed Solution Tests*

In order to validate the improved solution, we carried out tests using the same BP example with three different modeling notations: PN, EPC and BPMN. The test example is a simple phone repair process. The considered BP modeled with Petri Net notation is presented in [18][24]. The BP begins by the registration of the broken phone and then it is analyzed to determine the defect type. Depending on the severity of the defect, a simple repair or a complex repair is carried out. Then, the phone is tested to check whether it is fixed. If so, the repair details are archived and it is returned to the customer. If it is not fixed, the repair and then the test are restarted again. If the phone is still broken after the fifth repair test, the repair details are archived and the phone is returned to the customer. Otherwise, the customer is informed about the defect type after the defect analysis and before archiving the repair details [18][23].

This process example was already used as a test case example in Nauta's solution. We used the produced cost annotated event log (1000 cases obtained by simulation) together with its corresponding BP model (in PN, EPC and BPMN notations) as inputs for our tool test phase. In the following two sub-sections, the obtained results of the carried out tests are presented for each of the BP and the activity levels cost extensions with different BP modeling notations.

1) Tests Results of the Business Process Level Cost Extension: Fig. 3 (respectively Fig. 4) shows the obtained results after importing the BP example Petri Net (respectively BPMN) model file and the corresponding cost annotated event log file. The background frame of Fig. 3 (respectively Fig. 4) represents the main tool frame, which displays the corresponding Petri Net (respectively BPMN) model. The foreground frames of Fig. 3 illustrate cost data description at the BP level. The top left frame represents the BP level related cost description table with different computation modes (average, maximum and minimum) for all cost types (total, fixed, labour, variable overhead and material costs). The top right frame shows average total cost incurred by each activity of the BP using a pie chart indicating the activity that incurred the highest cost among them ("Repair (Complex)" activity in Fig. 3). The bottom right frame shows BP level related average cost per cost type: total cost is yellow-colored and other cost types are green-colored. The bottom left frame illustrates BP level related average cost based on BP cases together with two horizontal lines representing minimum (blue line) and maximum (green line) cost values provided by the user as the expected cost interval boundaries.

The foreground frames of Fig. 4 provide cost statistics about BP instances. As shown in the foreground left frame of Fig. 4, the selected cost type to be analyzed is "Total Cost" and the user chooses to enter an expected cost interval (500..800 AUD) instead of an expected cost value. Moreover, both textual and graphical display modes are selected. Then, when validating, BP cost statistics results are displayed. Textual results are displayed in the bottom of the foreground left frame of Fig. 4. The red (respectively blue, green)-colored text represents number and percentage of BP instances that incurred higher (respectively in interval, lower) average total costs than the user-provided cost interval. The foreground right frame of Fig. 4 represents graphically the obtained results using a pie chart. As shown in both foreground frames, 7.7% of BP instances incurred total costs more than 800 AUD, 7.2% of them incurred total costs less than 500 AUD and 85.1% of them incurred total costs between 500 and 800 AUD. Tests of ML-based cost analysis for the BP level is left for other BP examples as for the considered test example, there is no data attributes related to the BP instances (traces). The tests results of the BP level cost extension, presented in Fig. 3 and Fig. 4, remain valid for the three considered BP notations (PN, EPC and BPMN).

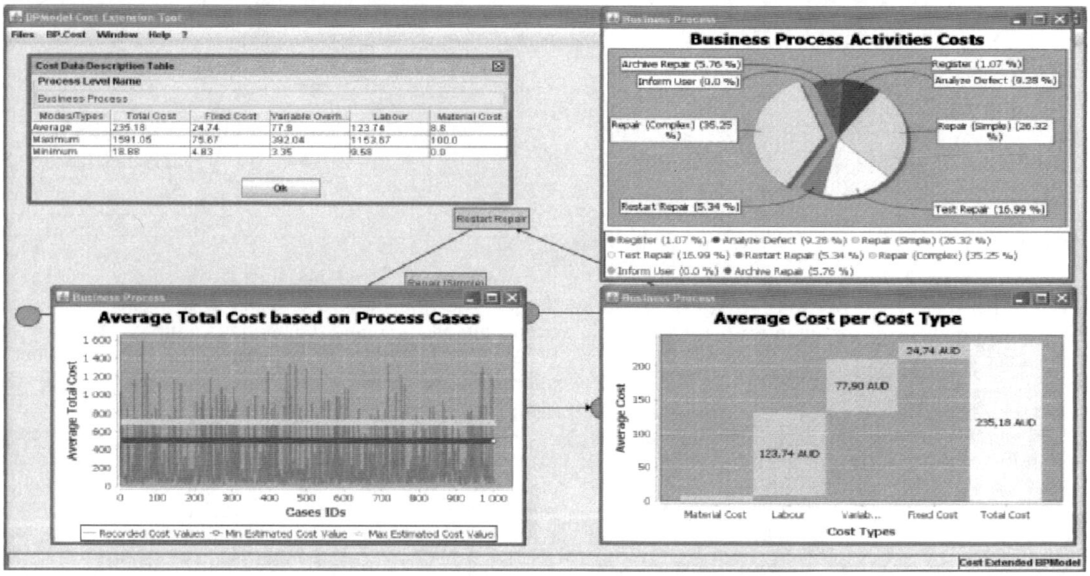

Figure 3. Cost data description (BP level) with PN notation.

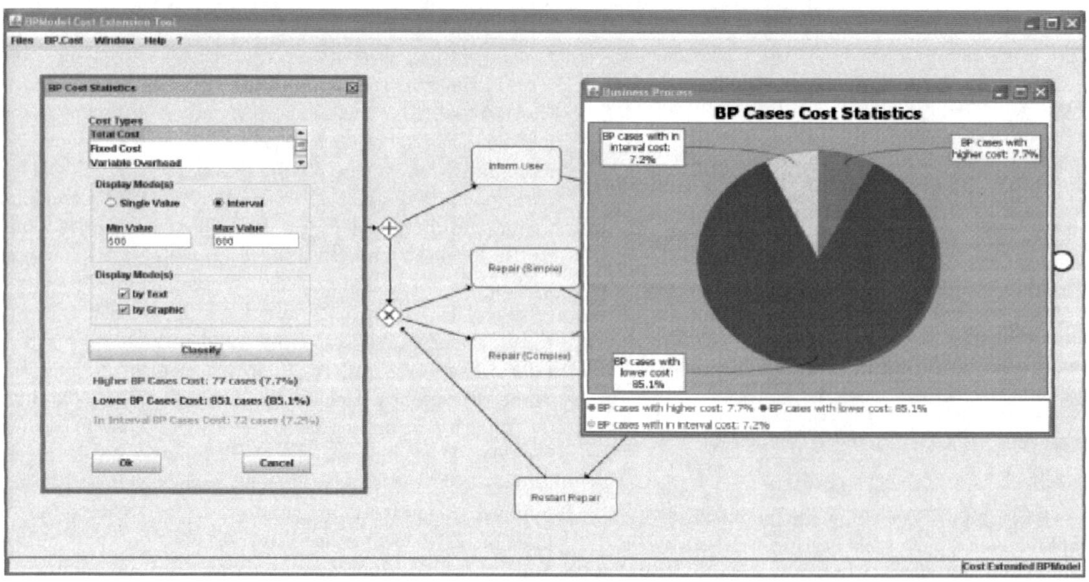

Figure 4. BP cases cost statistics (BP level) with BPMN notation.

2) Tests Results of the Activity Level Cost Extension: As shown in Fig. 5 (respectively Fig. 6), the background frame displays the obtained EPC (respectively BPMN) model after importing the corresponding BP model and cost extended event log files. The foreground frames of Fig. 5 show cost data description corresponding to the "Analyze Defect" function. The top left frame illustrates cost data description table corresponding to the "Analyze Defect" function with average, maximum and minimum computation modes and total, variable overhead, fixed and labour cost types. The top right frame shows blue bars each of which representing the average of total costs related to "Analyze Defect" function instances executed by a resource. The bottom right frame illustrates a curve representing the average total costs of the "Analyze Defect" function based on its instances and two lines representing the user-expected cost interval boundaries: minimum (blue line) and maximum (green line) cost values. The bottom left frame shows average cost per cost type for the "Analyze Defect" function: yellow-colored bar represents total cost and green-colored bars represent others cost types.

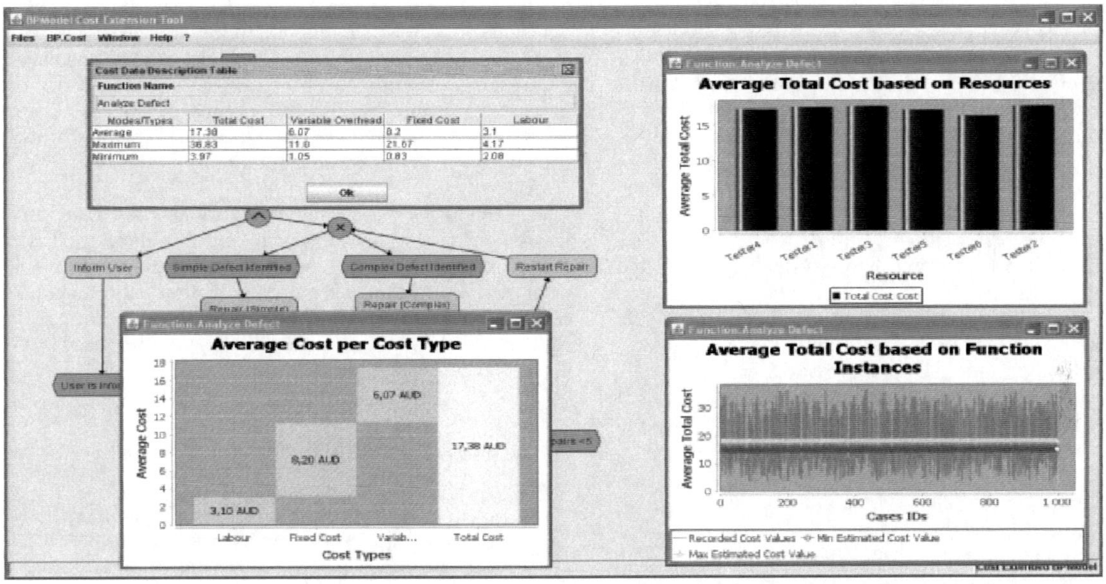

Figure 5. Cost data description for "Analyze Defect" function (activity level) with EPC notation.

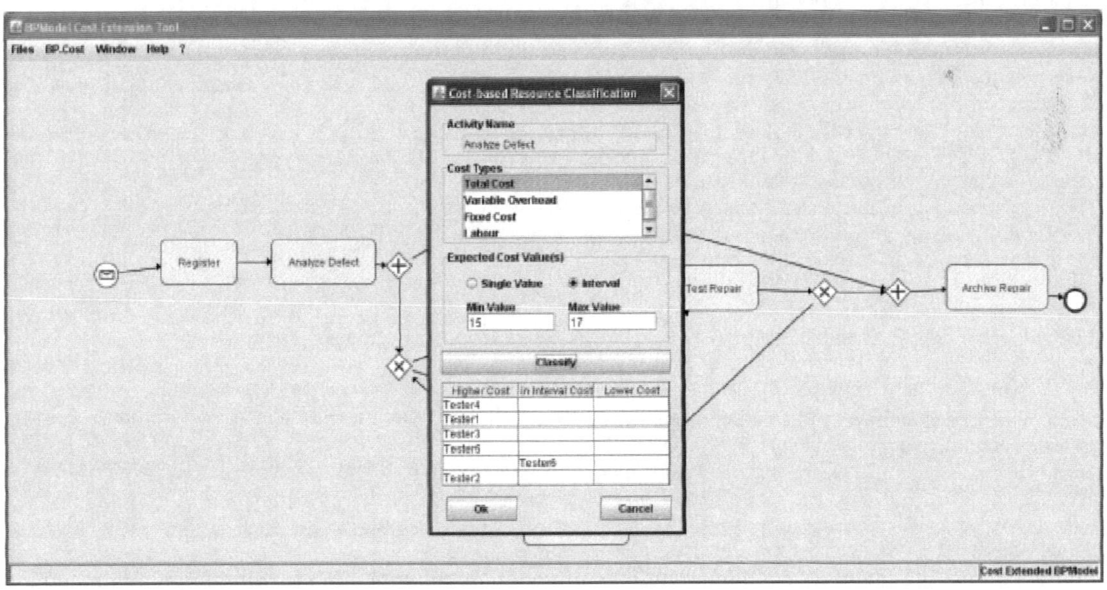

Figure 6. Resource classification based on total cost of "Analyze Defect" activity (activity level) with BPMN notation.

The foreground right frame of Fig. 6 shows test results of the first activity level cost analysis method, which is a cost-based resource classification for the "Analyze Defect" activity. As it is illustrated in Fig. 6, the user selected the "Total Cost" as the cost type to be analyzed. The provided expected cost interval for the considered activity ranges from 15 AUD to 17 AUD. Then, the provided result is displayed using a table showing three columns. The first column (respectively second, third) lists resources, which executed "Analyze Defect" activity instances with average total cost higher (respectively in interval, lower) than the user-expected cost interval. As shown in Fig. 6, the average total cost of "Analyze Defect" activity instances executed by "Tester6" is within the user-expected cost interval. However, the other resources are involved in incurring higher total costs than 17 AUD and no resources incurred lower total costs than 15 AUD. Furthermore, the second activity-level cost analysis (ML-based) method is tested on the "Analyze Defect" activity by selecting the total cost as a cost type and 17 AUD as the expected cost value. An ARFF file is automatically generated according to details presented in section III.A.1. Afterwards, the ARFF file is imported using Weka system. The selected attributes are: "resource", "duration", "phone type" and "defect type" attributes for the activity in hand. Then, we applied different classification algorithms among which we retained the J48 algorithm [31] as it provided the highest rate of correctly classified instances (100%). The obtained result is presented by the following classification rules:

```
If (phoneType = T1) Then
    Cost is lower
If (phoneType = T2) Then
    Cost is lower
If (phoneType = T3) Then
    Cost is higher
```

The obtained classification rules show that if the phone type is T1 or T2, the incurred total cost of the "Analyze Defect" activity is lower than the expected cost value (17 AUD). However, if the phone type is T3, the total cost exceeds the expected cost value. Then, it can be concluded that the total cost incurred during the execution of this activity depends on the "phone type" attribute and the influence of the other attributes on the corresponding total cost is not prominent. This indicates to decision makers that reviewing the repair of T3 phones is likely to lead to a solution to reduce costs incurred by the execution of "Analyze Defect" activity. The tests results, presented in Fig. 5 and Fig. 6 about the activity level cost extension, remain valid for the three implemented BP notations (PN, EPC and BPMN).

IV. Conclusion and Future Works

In this paper, we proposed an improved solution providing BP model cost extension at the activity level as well as the BP level based on Process Mining. In fact, we extended the proposed approach so that it offers cost description and analysis at both activity and BP levels. Besides, we improved the proposed meta-model (HLPS) in order to represent cost data at activity and BP levels. Moreover, we presented the implementation of the improved approach. Additionally, we described the obtained results of tests that we carried out on the implemented tool using a simple phone repair process as test example with three simplified modeling notations: PN, EPC and BPMN. Furthermore, the tests results show that the solution is extensible to cover different other business modeling notations. Therefore, the obtained proposal is a general BP model cost extension solution providing cost extension, description and analysis at activity and BP levels, which further improve decision making support for BP cost reduction.

However, the proposed solution has some limits especially for the ML-based cost data analysis. First, the provided BP level cost analysis does not include the influence of resources on BP costs while it may be important in cost reduction decision making. Second, selection of the classification algorithm is left for the user, which may be enhanced by guiding the selection in order to improve the quality of the generated results. Third, the proposed solution does not include means to simulate the impacts, of changes brought to the BP, on its incurred costs before applying real actions on the BP.

Currently, we are studying further cost data analysis improvements in such a way to provide more guidance for better decision making support. These improvements will be proposed and validated by coordination with data mining experts. In future works, we consider to carry out real world case studies in order to evaluate the proposed solution performances.

References

[1] M. Adams, N. Russell, A. H. M. ter Hofstede, and W. M. P. van der Aalst, Modern business process automation, Springer, Heidelberg, 2010.

[2] J. Billington et al., "The Petri Net Markup Language: Concepts, Technology, and Tools," In ICATPN'03, 24th International Conference on Applications and Theory of Petri Nets, Springer, pp. 483-505, 2003.

[3] P. Briol, Business process engineering: from elaboration to exploitation, Briol Patrice, 2008.

[4] Camunda Services, 2014. BPMN Workflow Engine. [online] Available at: <http://camunda.org/> [retreived: August, 2015].

[5] R. Conforti, M. de Leoni, M. La Rosa1, and W. M. P. van der Aalst, "Supporting Risk-Informed Decisions during, Business Process Execution," International Conference on Advanced Information Systems Engineering, 2013.

[6] N. Cuntz and E. Kindler, 2006. EPC Tools. [online] Available at: <http://www2.cs.uni-paderborn.de/cs/kindler/Forschung/EPCTools/> [retreived: August, 2015].

[7] D. Clinton and S. A. Webber, "RCA at clopay: here's innovation in management accounting with resource consumption accounting," In Strategic Finance, 2004.

[8] D. Gilbert, "The JFreeChart class library," 2014 (version 1.0.19) Installation Guide. [pdf] Available at: <http://garr.dl.sourceforge.net/project/jfreechart/1.%20JFreeChart/1.0.19/jfreechart-1.0.19.zip> [retreived: August, 2014].

[9] J. Han, M. Kamber, and J. Pei, Data mining: concepts and techniques, 3rd ed., Elsevier, United States of America, 2012.

[10] D. R. Hansen and M. M. Mowen, "Cost management: accounting and control," 2006, Thomson South-Western. United States of America.

[11] L. M. Hillah, E. Kindler, F. Kordon, and L. Petrucci, "A Primer on the Petri Net Markup Language and ISO/IEC 15909-2*," In CPN'09, 10th International workshop on Practical Use of Colored Petri Nets and the CPN Tools. Denmark, 2009.

[12] Hverbeek, "eXtensible Event Stream," [online] Available: <http://www.xes-standard.org> [retreived: June, 2013].

[13] IEEE Task Force on Process Mining, 2012. "Process Mining Manifesto," In BPM 2011 Workshops. Springer.

[14] R. S. Kaplan and S. R. Anderson, "Time-driven Activity-Based Costing". In HBS Working Paper, 2003.

[15] LIP6 (Laboratoire d'Informatique de Paris 6), 2012. PNML Framework download site. [online] Available at: <http://pnml.lip6.fr> [retreived: July, 2013].

[16] LIP6 (Laboratoire d'Informatique de Paris 6), 2013. PNML reference site. [online] Available: <http://www.pnml.org> [retreived: July, 2013].

[17] J. Mendling, 2005. EPC Markup Language (EPML). [online] Available at: <http://www.mendling.com/EPML/> [retreived: June, 2015].

[18] W. E. Nauta, "Towards cost-awareness in process mining," Master's thesis Eindhoven, 2011. [pdf] Available: <http://alexandria.tue.nl/extra1/afstversl/wsk-i/nauta2011.pdf> [retreived: April 2012].

[19] OMG (Object Management Group), 2015. BPMN 2.0. [online] Available at: <http://www.omg.org/spec/BPMN/2.0/> [retreived: August 2015].

[20] Process Mining Group, 2013. Process Mining: Research, Tools and Application. [pdf] Available: <http://www.processmining.org> [retreived: June, 2013].

[21] RCA Institute, 2008. Resource Consumption Accounting Institute. [online] Available: <http://www.rcainstitute.org> [retreived: April, 2012].

[22] M. Rosemann and J. vom Brocke, Handbook on business process management 1, Springer. Heidelberg, 2010.

[23] A. Rozinat, "Process mining: conformance and extension," PhD Thesis, University Press Facilities. Eindhoven, 2010.

[24] D. Thabet, S. A. Ghannouchi, and H. H. Ben Ghezala, "Towards business process model extension with cost perspective based on process mining - Petri Net model case," In ICEIS'14, 16th International Conference on Enterprise Information Systems, SciTePress, Portugal, pp. 335-342, 2014.

[25] D. Thabet, S. A. Ghannouchi, and H. H. Ben Ghezala, "Petri net model extension with cost perspective based on process mining," In ICMHIS'14, 9th International Colloquium of MHIS (Management High Institute of Sousse), Tunisia, 2014.

[26] D. Thabet, S. A. Ghannouchi, S. and H. H. Ben Ghezala, "Petri Net Model Cost Extension based on Process Mining - Cost Data Description and Analysis," In ICEIS'15, 17th International Conference on Enterprise Information Systems, SciTePress, Spain, pp. 268-275, 2015.

[27] D. Thabet, S. A. Ghannouchi, and H. H. Ben Ghezala, "Business Process Model Extension with Cost Perspective based on Process Mining - Cost Data Description and Analysis." In IBIMA'15, 26th International Business Information Management Association Conference, Spain, 2015.

[28] W. M. P. van der Aalst, Process Mining: Discovery, Conformance and Enhancement of Business Processes, Springer-Verlag. Berlin, 2011.

[29] W. M. P. van der Aalst, M. Schonenberg, and M. Song, "Time prediction based on process mining," Information Systems, vol. 36, no. 2, pp. 450-475, 2011.

[30] J. J. Weygandt, P. D. Kimmel, and D. E. Kieso, Managerial accounting tools for business decision making, John Wiley & Sons Inc. United States of America, 2010.

[31] I. H. Witten, F. Eibe, and M. A. Hall, Data mining: practical machine learning tools and techniques, Elsevier. Burlington, 2011.

[32] M. T. Wynn, W. Z. Low, and W. Nauta, "A framework for cost-aware process management: generation of accurate and timely management accounting cost reports," Conferences in Research and Practice in Information Technology, pp. 79-88, 2013.

[33] M. T. Wynn, W. Z. Low, A. H. M. ter Hofstede, and W. Nauta, "A framework for cost-aware process management: cost reporting and cost prediction," Journal of Universal Computer Science, vol. 20, no. 3, pp. 406-430, 2014.

Understandability Metric for Web Services

Usama Maabed, Ahmed El-Fatatry, Adel El-Zoghabi
Institute of Graduate Studies and Research, Alexandria University
Alexandria, Egypt.
e-mail: umaabed@alexu.edu.eg, e-mail: elfatatry@alexu.edu.eg, e-mail: zoghabi@alexu.edu.eg

Abstract-- This work is concerned with developing a quality index for Web service understandability. A major reason for poor search results in Web service repositories is the lack of proper descriptions for existing services and as a result such services are not counted in search results. We present a mechanism to specify and measure Web service interface quality. The mechanism includes metrics for both the registration and operation phases. The evaluation results show significant enhancement in the discovery process as a result of using the proposed mechanism.

Keywords—SOA; Web services; Usability; Discovery; Web service interface quality.

I. INTRODUCTION

Web service discovery is a major challenge for automatic Web service selection and integration. Discovery depends not only on Web service availability but also on the ability to understand the objective and the function of the available Web services, using the descriptive details. Web service description is often overlooked when working with a Web service to increase its quality. Even if a Web service follows all recommendations it will still be inaccessible if its description is difficult to comprehend. Several approaches and techniques have been proposed to address this challenge, including syntactic-based and semantic-based approaches [1][2]. Such approaches assume that correct and valid service descriptions already exist. In practice, the reality is different.

We analyzed more than 35,000 Web services from eight well-known datasets [3]-[7]. In these datasets, we found that only 49% of registered services are active. Further analysis of Web Services Description Language (WSDL) based Web services shows that only 19 % have a Web service description. Therefore, 81 % of Web services are not being considered in the syntactic discovery phase. Our findings are also supported by previous studies [8][9].

On other hand, the semantic approach suffers from "a cold-start problem" because it assumes that a corpus of previously annotated services is available [1] [2] [10].

Recently, Quality of Service (QoS) in Web service discovery has gained considerable attention as a vital research topic [8][11][12]. In this context, it is important to distinguish between two research domains within Web service discovery. The first approach focuses largely on Web service functionality and performance, such as response time, latency, availability, accessibility, and security. The second approach focuses on the quality of a Web service interface, largely assessing the Web service interface in terms of complexity. The importance of the second approach lies in the fact that without easily understandable Web service interface functionality, it is not reasonable to expect successful discovery or usability [11]. In general, the more details we can obtain about a Web service function and its domain, the more it becomes reachable and usable.

Analyzing a text or web site for its readability has a long tradition in literature. Different approaches and metrics have been employed to assess the readability of web sites, or to filter documents that match a user's reading ability [13]. However, there are some differences between a web site and Web service description. On the one hand, text in the web is presented is usually long and presented differently than a Web service description, which expected to be short and straightforward. On the other hand, Web service description needs to be comprehended not only by humans but also by agents in case of auto-discovery.

Given the differences in the presentation and nature of Web service, having an index that gives an indicator on the readability or clarity of Web service interface, becomes more essential. In this regard, we have also to consider the majority of currently deployed Web services that have no description or that have a poorly written description. For such cases, focusing only on the readability of the Web service description might not help in identifying the Web service domain or its functionality.

Our research aims at introducing a new approach for fixing the current problem of poorly written Web service descriptions and providing practical control over Web service interface quality to minimize and avoid such bad practices.

In this paper, we address this topic under several aspects. First, we consider the problem of text noise in Web service description and the attribute names used in the Web service interface. This noise represents additional text that are typically not part of the main context and might not help in classifying or understanding the Web service function. Obviously, this noise should not be considered when determining the readability or clarity of a Web service interface. One way to eliminate the noise is to provide hand designed filters for cleaning the interface contents of a particular Web service. The second step is to have a mathematic approach to measure the understandability of the Web service interface. In this regard, we considered the number of the extracted meaningful words from the filtered Web service interface. We used the well-known WordNet [14], which is an electronic lexical database that is available to researchers in computational linguistics, text analysis, and many related areas. We analyzed the web-service operations and input/output message parameter meaningful naming as part of the Web service usability and understandability characteristics. In addition, we considered sharing the clarity and understandability indexes to be available during the discovery phase as part of QoS improvement.

This approach will help service providers in improving their service quality by satisfying discovery needs and measures. Service registry moderators and brokers will gain the advantage of providing valid and well-defined Web services with better quality, based on better classification and clustering that supports service discovery and composition. Consumers will effectively use the shared interface quality metrics during registry queries to select services that match their quality needs and development constraints with minimal effort.

Thus, the main contribution of this work is to develop a novel approach that addresses currently poorly written Web service descriptions with a focus on developing the required control that can help in addressing such malpractice.

The rest of this paper is structured as follows: the related work and previous developed metrics are discussed in Section 2, followed by the research problem in Section 3. The solution requirements are defined in Section 4. In Section 5, we introduce the proposed framework. The experimental Evaluation and the research findings are discussed in Section 6. Finally, the conclusion and recommendations for future research are presented in Section 7.

II. Related Work

In software quality research, metrics for service interface quality have only recently gained attention [15]-[18]. In this Section, we summarize efforts in the area of measuring the quality and complexity of a Web service interface.

The first work on Extensible Markup Language (XML) metrics was presented in [19]; the work presents a set of five metrics based on Document Type Definition (DTD) specifications and the schema graph representation, adopting common metrics used for software to determine the characteristics of DTDs. The authors use product metrics in terms of size, structure complexity, structure depth, Fan-In, and Fan-Out.

McDowell et al. [15] focus on XML schema types and introduce two indices for measuring quality and complexity based on eleven metrics. The proposed metrics are Number of Complex Type Declarations, Number of Simple Type Declarations, Number of Annotations, Number of Derived Complex Types, Average number of Attributes per Complex Type Declaration, Number of Global Type Declarations, Number of Global Type References, Number of Unbounded Elements, Average Bounded Element Multiplicity Size, Average Number of Restrictions per Simple Type Declaration, and Element Fanning.

Lammel et al. [20] proposed a suite of metrics for XML Schema that primarily focused on schema size and complexity. The suite ranges from simple counters of various types of schema nodes, such as Number of global element declarations, Number of global complex-type definitions, Number of global simple-type definitions, and Number of global attribute declarations, to more involved metrics such as McCabe, depth, and breadth. Their work helped to introduce the fundamental metrics for the XSD language and identified the basic feature model of the XSD language at a basic level [21].

Qureshi et al. [16] focused on measuring the complexity of XML documents based on different structural characteristics. Their work aims to lower the complexity of XML documents and improve their reusability and maintainability. They used the Weight Allocation Algorithm (WA) and the Document Object Model (DOM) for tree representation. Weights are assigned to each element of XML trees, according to their distance from the root node. The algorithm provides a mechanism to gauge the quality and comprehensibility of XML documents.

Visser [22] presents a more advanced metric that considers the structure of a schema by adopting well-known measurement methods from graphs. The metrics are adaptations of existing metrics for other software artifacts, such as programs and grammars. As a prerequisite, a graph representation must be computed from a given XML Schema to measure, for example, how closely the graph structure is related to a tree structure in which the measures of reclusiveness are identified.

Basci and Misra [18] developed a structure-based metric that measures the complexity related to the internal architecture and recursion of XSD components. The metric has been empirically and theoretically validated using 65 public Web services.

H. Sneed [23] proposed a suite of metrics that contains various metrics to assess the complexity of service interfaces and to determine their size for estimating testing effort. The proposed metrics range from common size measurements such as lines of code and number of statements to metrics for measuring the complexity and quality of Web Services. The relevant metrics are Interface Data Complexity, Interface Relation Complexity, Interface Format Complexity, Interface Structure Complexity, and quality-related metrics covering Modularity, Adaptability, Reusability, Testability, Portability, and Conformity. Sneed defines the complexity of a service interface as the median value of its lingual complexity and its structural complexity. The lingual complexity of a service interface has been defined in terms of type and number of occurrences, and the structural complexity defined in terms of entities and relationships, in which entities are the instances of the data-types, messages, operations, parameters, bindings and ports defined in the schema. A relationship refers to compositions and cross-references.

Kumari and Upadhyaya [24] proposed an interaction complexity metric for black-box components based on measuring the complexity of their interfaces. The parameters they considered are the size of each component and the interaction with the component in terms of input/output interactions. Graph theoretical notions have been used to illustrate the interaction among software components and to compute complexity. The proposed measure has been applied to five cases chosen for their study and yielded encouraging results, which may further help in controlling the complexity of component-based systems to minimize both integration and maintenance efforts.

The review of the literature reveals that few studies focus on developing metrics that measure the quality of Web service interfaces. Existing metrics partially address this subject by focusing on the WS interface structure; these depend on counting a schema's components, or measuring the schema's complexity by considering different weights for each schema component. Although these metrics are important, they do not yield sufficient information about the clarity of a given interface and the understandability of each independent component. For instance, the count of service elements and types is more relevant to the service context and its functionality, which might vary from one domain to another. In addition, measuring the complexity of a schema's complex types or elements recursively by assuming that each of its sub-components has its own weight requires extra effort with no justified effect on the overall complexity measurement. To conclude, the metrics that measure schema complexity by counting components do not yield sufficient information about the complexity value of a given schema [18].

III. Problem Definition

Research into Web services has traditionally concentrated on issues such as service semantics, discovery, and composition. However, there has been little focus on currently deployed Web services. Investment in such services is far from efficient.

Although many efforts have been invested in finding new approaches to improve the semantic description of WS, most service descriptions that exist to date are syntactic in nature [25].

In an SOA context, Web service interface-related quality problems include poorly written Web service descriptions and a shortage of quality metrics for Web service interfaces. These two major issues also directly affect usability and the discovery process. This has been supported by different research findings. Zheng et al. [26] concluded that the WSDL files on the Internet are fragile. WSDL files may contain empty content, invalid formats, invalid syntax, and other types of errors.

In this Section, we summarize the defined issues with current Web services implementations, which is supported by previous researches.

A. *Web Service Description Poor Quality*

A major limitation of the Web services technology is that finding and composing services still requires manual effort. Although semantic web technology appears to be a promising approach for automated service discovery, it has several limitations [25] that can be summarized as:

- Most existing service descriptions are syntactic in nature.
- The vast majority of already existing Web services are specified using WSDL and do not have associated semantics.
- It is impractical to expect all new services to have semantic descriptions.
- From a service requester's perspective, the requester may not be aware of all terms related to the service request or domain knowledge.
- Introducing semantics into Web services has not yet moved to the industrial implementation phase.

Conversely, a search for semantic service descriptions conducted by Klusch and Xing [27] with a specialized metasearch engine, Sousuo, found no more than approximately 100 semantic service descriptions in prominent formats such as OWL-S, WSML, WSDL-S, and SAWSDL on the web. This number is very small compared with more than half a million sources indexed by the semantic web search engine Swoogle, and several hundreds of validated Web service descriptions in WSDL found by Sousuo on the web [25].

Having a quality model with suitable metrics has become crucial for assessing the Web service interface quality and its readiness for public use.

IV. Solution Requirements

In our research, it was necessary to measure a number of issues that have not been addressed or fulfilled, or have not been identified in Web services discovery. The main issues are currently registered but invalid Web services, poorly written WS descriptions, low usability, and the issue of sharing WS interface quality metrics. Controlling WS interface clarity and understandability is an important objective because it affects all other quality attributes such as usability, reliability, and maintainability. The following points represent our proposed approach to achieve better usability with a focus on WSs with poorly written descriptions.

A Web service interface specifies all of the information needed to access and use a service. The description should be rich, containing sufficient details and aspects of the service. Efficient and successful implementation of WSDL requires quality control with relevant metrics to ensure the required quality. The implementation details of a Web service are hidden behind their interfaces, which are published on the Internet and can be accessed through WSDL. WSDL consists of a set of operations, which are the access points for interacting with the outside computing environment. Such interfaces require metrics that are more relevant to its nature as a black box, with no access to its implementation source code.

To achieve a Web service with a high level of usability, we must consider the following.

- Describe the Web service functionality properly.
- Define Types and elements globally, facilitating reuse in other XML schemas and in the same XML schema documents.
- Design the Web service interface structure in terms of traceability and understandability.
- Use proper naming for attributes and elements within the schema documents and annotations.

V. Proposed Approach

Our approach to enhance Web service discovery and usability has two facets. One empowers the current WS descriptions using the extracted words from the types and element names. The second is the use of ISO/IEC 25010 standard [28] to develop a consistent model to evaluate Web service interface quality. We extend recent research efforts that focus on developing WS interface complexity metrics, and introduce clarity and understandability metrics. This approach addresses a Web service interface with a poor description by validating its clarity and quality, extracting distinct tokens from the used attributes and element names, and sharing this information through WSDL schema extension. The information is then utilized by service providers to improve their service quality and by consumers during discovery and selection.

A. *Dataset used in this research*

Throughout this research, we conducted several large-scale evaluations using popular WSDL datasets, which were obtained from well-known Web services providers. Because the main objective here is to improve the WS usability by consider its reachability through different discovery approaches, we consider some non-WSDL-based approaches during our analysis with initial focus on the syntactic part.

The QWS dataset [3] represents 2507 real WSDL files obtained from public sources on the Web. OPOSSum [6] is a database of service descriptions that has 1263 WSDL files. WS-DREAM [7] is a dataset that is composed of 3738 WSDL files that aim to reflect real-world data for Web Service researchers. Service-repository [4] is a directory of SOAP Web services. Servicefinder, Biocatalogue, Seekda, and Xmethods [29] are Web services catalogues.

We analyzed these datasets not only to support our research but also to provide a reusable dataset and practical feedback for promoting research on Web services interface quality. We applied the following procedure during our research:

- First, we tested the Web services availability and isolated the non-active Web services. The aim was to identify the bad files that had no active services, files referencing unavailable schema, files with local file references to schema files, or incomplete files.
- Second, we analyzed the active Web services to determine the problem size of Web services with no description. In this phase, we checked whether the published Web services had a description part. We also assessed the number of the meaningful words it contained. Meaningful words refers to words that cannot be considered part of stop-words, or terms which commonly appear across many service descriptions and can be found in a lexical database. The meaningful number of words is used to identify the Web service domain or classification or for clustering analysis. During this process, we addressed the duplication of Web service definitions that exist in some datasets. Primarily, we utilized the service name, host, and the Web service structure in identifying the duplications.

B. *Web Services availability and descriptions*

In this Section, we focus on two criteria: WS availability and WS description. We analyzed these parameters using previously defined datasets to identify active Web services that are valid for our research. Our analysis results are depicted in Fig. 1, which shows that the average percentage of active WSs is approximately 49%.

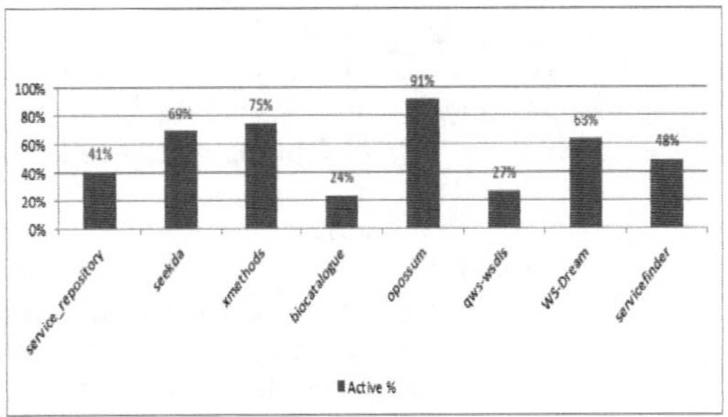

Figure 1. Active WS Percentage per Dataset

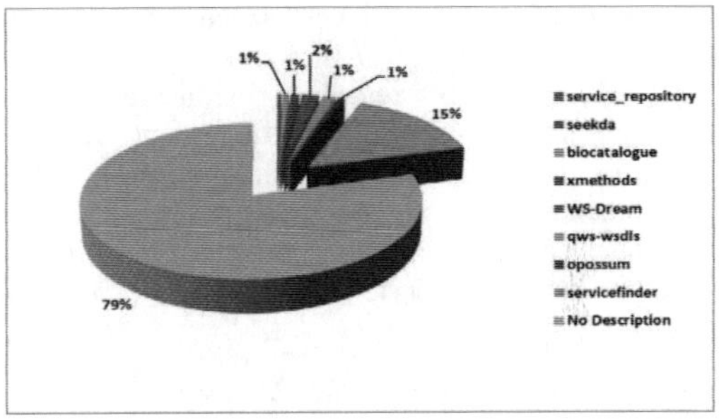

Figure 2. WSs with Description vs. WSs without Description

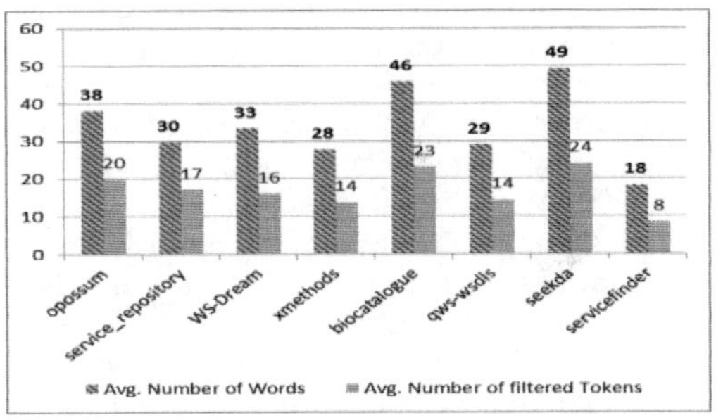

Figure 3. WS description - Avg. words vs. Avg. Token

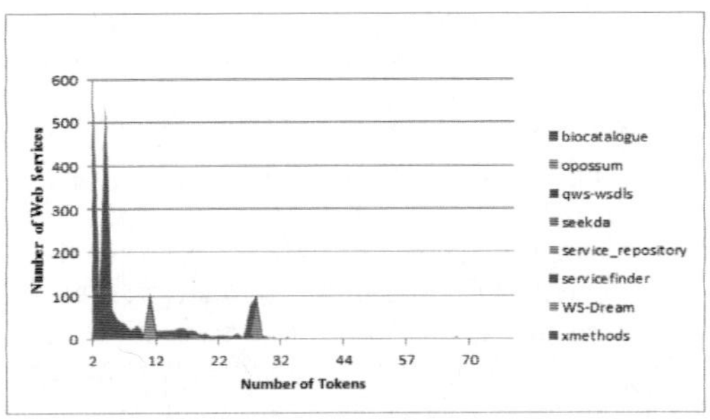

Figure 4. Number of Tokens Distribution

To understand the missing description problem of Web services, we considered in our analysis the complete collected active Web services after removing the Web services duplications. Fig. 2 shows that the total number of Web services that have descriptions is only 21% of the overall collected Web services.

Having collected the number of WSDL files with descriptions, the second step was to inspect the content of each file to evaluate the description part. To inspect the description, we applied the Information retrieval technique for removing the 'stopwords'. We used the stopwords to eliminate the terms that commonly appear across many service descriptions. For Web services with descriptions, Fig. 3 shows a comparison between the number of words found in the description part and the number of the extracted meaningful tokens.

As shown in Fig. 4, we found that the number of tokens in the Web service description ranges from 2 to 33 tokens. This shows that having a Web service description as a single criterion is insufficient to meet the quality requirement; there is also a need for a control on the size and meaning of the parts to ensure clarity and understandability requirements are met. This control must maintain both the minimum number of meaningful words contained in the Web service description and the operation names.

C. Web Service Interface Quality Metrics

Web service interface quality refers to the effort required to understand its functionality, structures, and the messages that are responsible for exchanges and for conveying Web service data between the service requestor and the service provider. Web service interface complexity can be measured by analyzing the XML Schema structure embedded in the WS interface. The focus of this Section is to propose a set of WSDL schema metrics to fill the gap caused by the missing clarity and understandability part of the WS interface quality control.

1) WS Interface Clarity and Understandability

In the previous sections, statistics show that only 21% of Web services have descriptions. In other words, approximately 80% of Web services are not considered during the normal syntactic search and discovery process. In this Section, we explain a new approach that depends on the parameter names of Web services: Web service name, endpoint, messages, and schema types. Throughout this research, we use the term "Clarity" to refer to the extent to which a Web service and its operations' naming are developed employing an appropriate and clear standard that is easily comprehended during the discovery process. This influences the understandability of the WS interface.

The Clarity Index measures the degree of syntactic understandability by parsing the Web service interface and extracting the meaningful parts (tokens) from the names of services, operations, and schema types. To calculate the Clarity Index, we compare the number of the extracted meaningful tokens to the overall number of terms used in these names for the overall elements used in the Web service interface. The same is applied on the service description part, which is measured by the following formula.

$$\text{Clarity}_{\text{Index}} = \left(\frac{\sum_{i=0}^{n} t_s}{\mathbf{n_s}} + \frac{t_{sd}}{\mathbf{n_{sd}}}\right) / \ 2 \qquad (1)$$

where t_s and n_s are the number of the extracted tokens and the total number of terms extracted from the WS interface, respectively. t_{sd} is the number of extracted tokens of the description part, and n_{sd} is the total number of the extracted terms from the description part.

Similarly, we consider Web service annotations to extend the clarity index to provide a more specific metric to measure the understandability sub-characteristic. We measure it with the following formula:

$$\text{Understandability}_{\text{Index}} = \left(\frac{\sum_{i=0}^{n} t_s}{n_s} + \frac{N_{An}}{N_E + N_{At}} + \frac{t_{sd}}{n_{sd}}\right) / \ 3 \qquad (2)$$

N_{An} is the number of annotations, N_E is the number of items, and N_{At} is the number of attributes.

As the main focus of this part of work is the Web services with no description, we focus primarily on the Clarity Index because the annotation part will also be missing, also we did not consider the readability index for Web service description, which will be consider on further work.

2) WSDL Quality Index

Although our main research focus is finding a solution to address current poorly written WS descriptions or WSs with no description, we found that it is important to address the overall quality of the WS interface.

As explained in the related work Section, most previous studies focused on the WS interface structure without considering the understandability of the provided information inside. The quality of the WS interface is influenced by how much effort is required to understand its element types during either manual discovery or auto-discovery.

It is important to distinguish between two different aspects of interface quality. First, the complexity of the WS interfaces largely focuses on the interface structure. Second, the clarity and understandability largely focuses on understanding the Web service interface in terms of ease of reading and understanding the WS functionality. The combination of both can provide the required WS interface Quality control. To illustrate our idea, we propose a WSDLQuality Index that extends the current efforts in this area by including the defined Understandability metric. The same approach is valid for any other developed WSDL quality metrics.

$$WSDLQuality\ Index = \text{Complexity}_{\ Index} + \text{Understandabity}_{Index} \qquad (3)$$

In the evaluation Section, we explain the importance of the Clarity Index in more detail.

D. Sharing WSDL Quality Metrics

A WS interface document initially defines the methods of the service and how they are invoked, but it lacks support for nonfunctional properties such as QoS. The WSDL standard allows several powerful techniques for extending its schema to include or redefine elements and attributes [30]. The standard also allows organizing and structuring its schemas by breaking them into multiple files. These child schemas can then be included into a parent schema. Breaking schemas into multiple files has several advantages. First, it creates reusable definitions that can be used across several Web services. Second, it makes the definitions easier to read because it breaks down the schema into smaller units that are simpler to manage.

In this context, two main proposals have been introduced. First, a registry-based extension is proposed that focuses largely on the UDDI and use its tModels to express the extra required fields, which is a straightforward means of defining quality attributes in this type of Web service registry [31]-[33]. Second, a WSDL-based extension is proposed that uses a simple WSDL schema to provide required QoS information such as using annotations, model-driven techniques, or semantic concepts [34]-[36].

In this study, we considered a WSDL schema extension for Web service clarity and quality metrics sharing without addressing the transformation or mapping to a web registry structure because this is already covered by many approaches, as explained in the previous Section.

Fig. 5 and Fig. 6 depict the WS quality schema (WSQ) used to share the WS interface quality. It is worth noting that the main goal is not to provide a comprehensive catalog for the description of the WSDL quality attribute but to show how we can share such characteristics and metrics.

```
<WSQ>
    <ClarityIndex>0.25</ClarityIndex>
    <ComplexityIndex>0.39</ComplexityIndex>
    <TokensList> PAY Transaction MAC Transaction Transaction MAC MAC
Transaction Transaction Transaction MAC MAC MAC MAC</TokensList>
    <DistinctTokens> mac, pay, transaction</DistinctTokens>
    <DistinctTokensTF> 7,1,6 </DistinctTokensTF>
    <ArrayOfTokenTF>
        <Token>mac</Token>
        <Token>pay</Token>
        <Token>transaction</Token>
        <TokenTF>7</TokenTF>
        <TokenTF>1</TokenTF>
        <TokenTF>6</TokenTF>
    </ArrayOfTokenTF>
    <AvailabilityIndex>0.95</AvailabilityIndex>
</WSQ>
```

Figure 5. Example of a schema extension

Sharing the WSDL quality metrics has a number of advantages. First, the characteristic of the proposed WSDL follows the current approaches for WS QoS sharing, which can effectively be used to specify and share not only Web service interface quality control-related measures but also the SLA and service-provider trustworthiness metrics. Second, it improves the Web service reachability, composition, and usability by providing detailed information about the WS interface such as the distinct tokens and its term frequency (TF).

These tokens support both automatic syntactic discovery of the Web service and the Semantic discovery approach by providing a means that can help in identifying the Web service domain and classification. Third, it removes the burden of repeating the same processing every time during the automatic discovery phase by the service requestor. In general, it helps in resolving the missing WS description problem by providing an alternative means for extracting meaningful tokens to empower the missing description part. In addition, it provides the required control to measure the clarity and quality of the Web service interface to filter out any improper services.

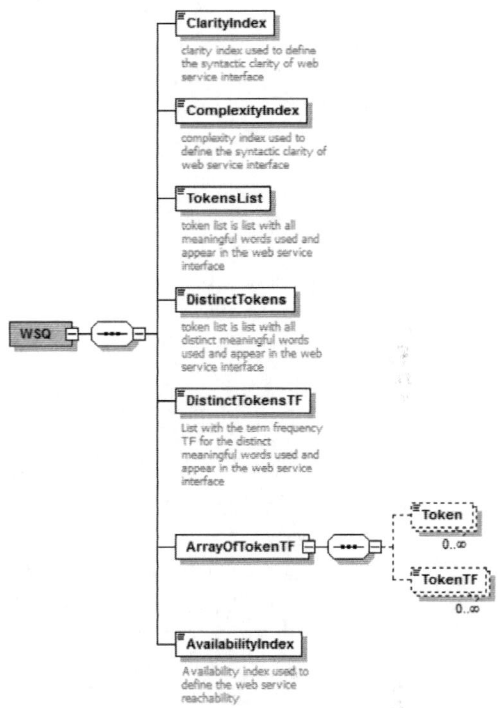

Figure 6. WSQ Schema Structure

VI. EXPERIMENTAL EVALUATION AND DISCUSSION

In this Section, we experimentally measure and compare the results of applying the Clarity Index to a list of Web services. In addition, we discuss the benefits of combining the complexity and clarity metrics to create a better WS interface Quality index.

The aim of this experiment is to show the capability of our approach to narrow the gap between Web services with and without a service description in terms of syntactic-based discoverability and usability. The results are summarized in Fig. 7, which shows the analysis of 10,000 active Web services, 52% of which have a Clarity Index greater than 40% and 79% of which have a Clarity Index greater than 30%. This shows that our approach can address and provide good support even for those Web services that have no description because it does not depend only on the description part but instead also relies on the attribute and element names used in the WS interface that we used to empower the description part.

Fig. 8 illustrates the Clarity Index similarity pattern of a Web service that has a description, and of the Web services

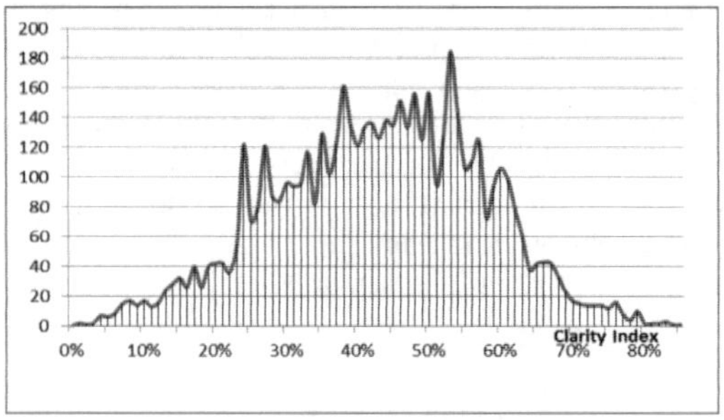

Figure 7. Clarity Index Distribution

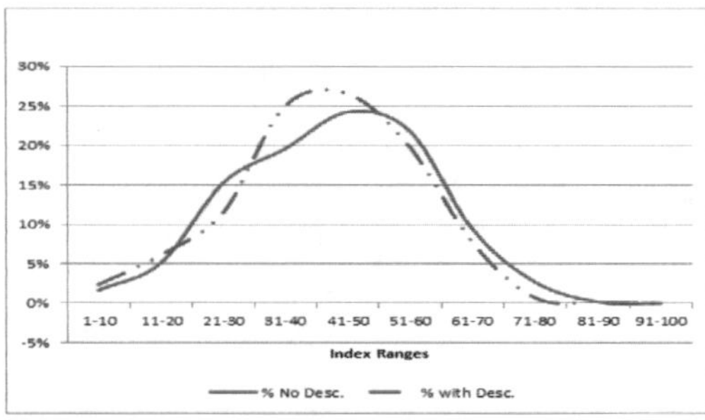

Figure 8. Clarity Index Pattern Comparisons

that do not have a description. The pattern matching reflects the understandability level of Web services, which allows the use of Web services with no description similarly to Web services with a description during the discovery process.

Note that in our previous analysis, 80% of the published Web services had no description. In other words, this number of Web services is out of the search and discovery scope. Our approach provides a means to recover this large number back into the search and the discovery process, which will be reflected also as better usability.

Fig. 9 shows the positive effect of considering all elements of the Web service interface against considering the description part only.

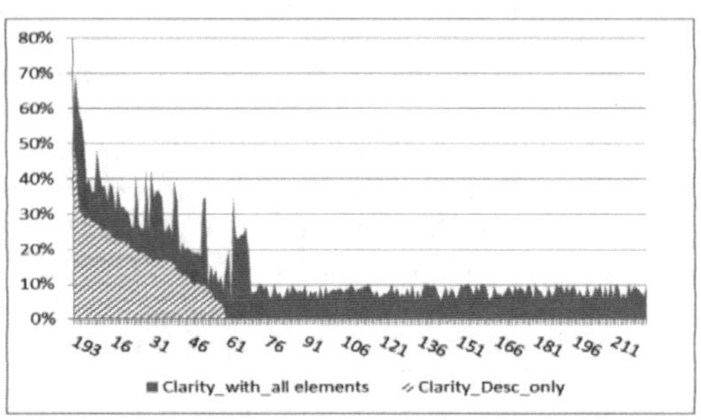

Figure 9. WS description Vs all elements Clarity Index

VII. CONCLUSION AND FUTURE WORK

In this study, our focus has been a practical problem of Web service discovery and usability, primarily WSDL-based Web services with poorly written descriptions. We developed a new approach to enhance the current Web service architecture capability that addresses the defined problem. Our approach is important for many reasons: first, it suggests an appropriate indicator of how Web service interface functionality is clearly described. This helps improve the automatic discovery and usability of Web services. Second, it helps in addressing the missing WS description problem by providing a technique for extracting meaningful tokens to empower the description missing part. Third, it provides a measure of interface clarity, which can be used during WS registration to filter out any unclear WS. Fourth, this approach is not limited to WSDL-based Web services but any other technologies as long a proper interface parser is available. In addition, we consider an approach to share the enhancement we introduce.

Our approach to share the WS interface quality metrics has a number of advantages. First, the proposed WSDL extension's characteristic follows the current approaches for WS QoS sharing. The proposed measure helps not only in WS interface quality control but also in the SLA and for service provider trustworthiness metrics. Second, it improves Web service reachability, composition, and usability by providing detailed information about the WS interface such as distinct tokens and term frequency (TF). These tokens support both the syntactic discovery of Web services and the semantic discovery approach by providing a mechanism that can help in identifying Web service classification. Third, the proposed approach helps in removing the burden of repeating the same processing every time during the discovery phase by the service requestor.

In this work, we focused mainly on Web service that has no description or a poor written description. For Web service with comprehended description, we are planning to consider the readability as a proxy for understandability and to extend the developed clarity and understandability indexes to include previously developed measurements as those used to study the readability of information including that returned by search engines. In addition, we are planning to study the advantage of having a common approach that consider different modern WS approaches such as JSON schema Apache Avro schemas, and other automated documentation generators.

REFERENCES

[1] S. Batra and S. Bawa, "Review of Machine Learning Approaches to Semantic Web Service Discovery," Journal of Advances in Information Technology, vol. 1, no. 3, pp. 146-151, 2010.

[2] M. Klusch and F. Kaufer, "WSMO-MX: A Logic Programming Based Hybrid Service Matchmaker," in European Conference on Web Services (ECOWS'06) , Zurich, 2006.

[3] E. Al-Masri and Q. H. and Mahmoud. [Online]. Available: http://www.uoguelph.ca/~qmahmoud/qws/. [Accessed March 2016].

[4] "Service-Repository," [Online]. Available: http://www.service-repository.com/. [Accessed Jan. 2016].

[5] J. Spillner. [Online]. Available: http://data.serviceplatform.org/. [Accessed Nov. 2015].

[6] U. Küster, "OPOSSum," [Online]. Available: http://fusion.cs.uni-jena.de/opossum/. [Accessed Jan. 2016].

[7] Z. Zheng and M. R. Lyu, "WS-Dream," [Online]. Available: http://www.wsdream.net. [Accessed Feb. 2016].

[8] M. Sabou, C. Wroe, C. Goble and G. Mishne, "Learning Domain Ontologies for Web Service Descriptions: An Experiment in Bioinformatics," in The 14th international conference on World Wide Web (WWW'05), Chiba, Japan, 2005.

[9] J. Fan and S. Kambhampati, "A snapshot of public Web Services," ACM SIGMOD Record, vol. 34, no. 1, pp. 24-32, 2005.

[10] C. Kiefer, A. Bernstein, H. J. Lee, M. Klein and M. Stocker, "Semantic Process Retrieval with iSPARQL," in The Semantic Web: Research and Applications, Innsbruck, Austria, Springer Berlin Heidelberg, 2007, pp. 609-623.

[11] J. Garofalakis, Y. Panagis and E. Sakkopoulos, "Web Service Discovery Mechanisms: Looking for a Needle in a Haystack?," in International Workshop on Web Engineering, Santa Cruz, 2004.

[12] E. Al-Masri and Q. H. Mahmoud, "Crawling Multiple UDDI Business Registries," in WWW '07 Proceedings of the 16th International Conference on World Wide Web, Banff, Alberta, Canada, 2007.

[13] L. Martin and T. Gottron, "Readability and the Web," Future Internet, vol. 4, no. 1, pp. 238-252, 2012.

[14] C. Fellbaum, WordNet An Electronic Lexical Database, Cambridge, MA ; London.: The MIT Press, 1998.

[15] A. McDowell, C. Schmidt and K.-b. Yue, "Analysis and Metrics of XML Schema," in Proceedings of the International Conference on Software Engineering Research and Practice, SERP '04, Las Vegas, Nevada, USA, 2004.

[16] M. H. Qureshi and M. H. Samadzadeh, "Determining the Complexity of XML Documents," in International Conference on Information Technology: Coding and Computing, ITCC 2005., Washington, DC, USA, 2005.

[17] Q. P. Thi, D. T. Quang and T. H. Quyet, "A Complexity Measure for Web Service," in KSE '09 Proceedings of the 2009 International Conference on Knowledge and Systems Engineering, Hanoi, Vietnam, 2009.

[18] D. Basci and S. Misra, "Measuring and Evaluating a Design Complexity Metric for XML Schema Documents," Journal of Information Science and Engineering, vol. 25, no. 5, pp. 1405-1425, 2009.

[19] M. Klettke, L. Schneider and A. Heuer, "Metrics for XML Document Collections," in Worshops XMLDM, MDDE, and YRWS on XML-Based Data Management and Multimedia Engineering — EDBT 2002, Berlin, 2002.

[20] R. Lammel, S. Kitsis and D. Remy, "Analysis of XML schema usage," in XML 2005 Conference, Atlanta, Georgia, USA, 2005.

[21] Y. Zhang, "Literature Review and Survey - XML Schema Metrics," University of Windsor, Ontario, Canada, 2008.

[22] J. Visser, "Structure Metrics for XML Schema," in XATA 2006, Portalegre, Portugal, 2006.

[23] H. M. Sneed, "Measuring Web Service interfaces," in 12th IEEE International Symposium on Web Systems,WSE 2010, Timisoara, Romania, 2010.

[24] U. Kumari and S. Upadhyaya, "An Interface Complexity Measure for Component-based Software Systems," International Journal of Computer Applications, vol. 36, no. 1, pp. 46-52, 2011.

[25] A. V. Paliwal, B. Shafiq, J. Vaidya, H. Xiong and N. Adam, "Semantics Based Automated Service Discovery," IEEE Transactions on Services Computing, vol. 5, no. 2, pp. 260-275, 2012.

[26] Z. Zheng, Y. Zhang and M. R. Lyu, "Distributed QoS Evaluation for Real-World Web Services," in IEEE International Conference on Web Services (ICWS 2010), Miami, FL, USA, 2010.

[27] M. Klusch and Z. Xing, "Deployed Semantic Services for the Common User of the Web: A Reality Check," in ICSC 2008, Santa Clara, CA, 2008.

[28] ISO/IEC, "ISO/IEC 25010:2011," [Online]. Available: http://www.iso.org/iso/home/store/catalogue_tc/catalogue_detail.htm?csnumber=35733. [Accessed Dec. 2015].

[29] J. Spillner. [Online]. Available: http://data.serviceplatform.org/. [Accessed Nov. 2015].

[30] D. Waldt, "Six strategies for extending XML schemas in a single namespace," [Online]. Available: http://www.ibm.com/developerworks/library/x-xtendschema/. [Accessed Jan. 2016].

[31] A. Blum and F. Carter, "Representing Web Services Management Information in UDDI," 2004.

[32] Z. Xu, P. Martin, W. Powley and F. Zulkernine, "Reputation-Enhanced QoS-based Web Services Discovery," in IEEE International Conference on Web Services. ICWS 2007, Salt Lake City, UT, 2007.

[33] C.-C. Lo, D.-Y. Cheng, P.-C. Lin and K.-M. Chao, "A Study on Representation of QoS in UDDI for Web Services Composition," in Complex, Intelligent and Software Intensive Systems, CISIS 2008, Barcelona, 2008.

[34] A. D'Ambrogio, "A model-driven wsdl extension for describing the qos of Web services," in The IEEE International Conference on Web Servicess (ICWS'06), Chicago, USA, 2006.

[35] Y. Kang, "Extended Model Design for Quality Factor Based Web Service Management," in Future Generation Communication and Networking (Fgcn 2007), Jeju , 2007.

[36] K. Zhu, Z. Duan and J. Wang, "Quality of Service in Web Services Discovery," in Advanced Management of Information for Globalized Enterprises (AMIGE 2008), Tianjin, 2008.

[37] G. Zuccon, "Understandability Biased Evaluation for Information Retrieval," in Advances in Information Retrieval, Springer International Publishing, 2016, pp. 280-292.

Towards an Open Smart City Notification Service

Luiz Cajueiro, Silvino Neto, Felipe Ferraz, Ana Cavalvanti
Recife Center for Advanced Studies and Systems (CESAR)
Recife – PE, Brazil
e-mail: {luiz.cajueiro, silvino.neto}@gmail.com, fsf@cesar.org.br, anapaula.cavalvanti@gmail.com

***Abstract*— Heterogeneity is a critical barrier to event processing in Smart Cities. Over the past few years many techniques have been proposed for message exchange between specific domains systems. However, identifying the context for all kinds of events is hampered due to the large number of protocols and formats that exist. Under these circumstances, this paper proposes a middleware for analyzing multiple events and to infer their respective contexts, thereby providing a flexible way of communication between distributed systems in different domains of a Smart City. Our studies have lead us to believe in the feasibility of the proposed approach, for it is an approach which reduces the burden of implementing/mapping all of the existing formats which can be activated in a given situation.**

Keywords:Middleware; CEP; Pub/Sub; Heterogeneous Systems; Smart City; Events; Google Cloud Platform.

I. INTRODUCTION

In one of our previous works [1] we presented the Platform for Real-Time Verification of Epidemic Notification (PREVENT), a cloud-based message-oriented middleware platform for real-time disease surveillance which uses the HL7-FHIR specification. FHIR is HL7's new specification that comprises of a set of international standards to exchange applications. This work originated in the need to allow PREVENT to receive messages which were structured in any given non-FHIR healthcare protocol. Through this experiment we observed that the heterogeneity problem faced by PREVENT is common to other systems in different domains. This fact has motivated our research to seek a common solution or framework to address this problem.

Cities are the main centers of human and economic activities. They have the potential to create and maintain means which generate development opportunities for their inhabitants. However, as cities grow they lead themselves into a wide range of complex problems [2][3]. Through technological innovation, the smart city concept emerges as an approach which promises to work in favor of more efficient and sustainable cities. Since its inception, the concept designed to enhance the potential for smart cities evolved from the specific projects implementation level to global strategies aimed at addressing the broader challenges of cities [2].

Each city is a complex *ecosystem* which consists of several subsystems working together to ensure the different services being provided (e.g., energy and water supply). Due to the growth of each of these ecosystems, the amount of information for decisions to be made becomes overwhelming. As a consequence, there are neither standard courses of action nor well-established ways to handle such a massive amount of data.

The intelligence used for this control is, in general, digital or analog - and almost inevitably human - pointing towards the utility of an automated process. In the context of smart cities, automation is a vital component for the connections between systems [4].

Most solutions applied in cities behave monolithically and are not interoperable [5]. Through communication between different systems, it is possible to achieve drastic changes in applications and services offered to citizens, thus enabling the concept of smart cities to become a reality [6]. Each one of these heterogeneous systems works and deals with specific functions which operate in each context. However, such an individualized approach is usually part of a bigger and more complex scenario, with many other applications involved. Thus, contextualized event sharing can provide the necessary triggers to generate a standalone flow in the treatment of occurrences arising in cities [5][7].

Different specific domain entities usually adopt a common domain communication protocol; but such a consensus can remain unknown to other areas or system domains. In a smart city there are various standards for communication as well as an extremely high and continuous flow of generated events. Protocols such as HL7-FHIR [1] bring standards to a specific domain where applications can be adapted to embrace solutions. On the other hand, trying to adapt legacy systems to communicate with these protocols can be too expensive in terms of cost and effort in a way that could lead the project to impracticability.

This paper proposes a cloud middleware for analyzing the different events arising in heterogeneous systems. It also provides a mechanism for events to be notified to the interested parties, considering topics of interest previously informed through the Publish/Subscribe (Pub / Sub) design pattern. A middleware with notification-based services (ASN), which applies discrimination filters based on context, may provide the required tools in order to enable Smart City mechanisms to ensure automation and efficiency in the treatment of events which may arise [8].

The proposed middleware adopts complex event processing (CEP) techniques, and a set of adaptive rules is used in order to establish the correlation between the information content of incoming events [9].

The remainder of this paper is organized as follows: Section 2 presents background concepts. Then, Section 3 describes adopted platform flows, processes and other architectural aspects of the middleware. Finally, Section 4 presents conclusions and discusses possible future works.

II. BACKGROUND

This section presents the concepts required for a better understanding of this paper.

A. Smart Cities

Smart cities have their origin in two main factors: (i) the increase in world population, which has caused a rural exodus and (ii) ecological awareness related to scarce natural resources [10].

This concept represents an innovation in the management of cities, as well as their services and infrastructure. It is based on the use of information technology to support the management of problems which occur in modern cities, making them more efficient and sustainable [2].

The smart city concept aims to provide an integrated system in which it is possible to achieve specific goals related to the improvement of cities management and in bettering inhabitants' lives, maximizing efficiency in the implementation of these activities.

1) Features of a Smart City

Implementations for smart cities may differ significantly depending on their focus. The Regional Science Center at Vienna's University of Technology [11] enumerates six aspects that define a smart city. These aspects represent the main challenges related to core areas:

a) SmartEconomy (Competitiveness): Based on the economic structure of cities, it focuses on promoting multiple sectors of the economy in order to maintain the stability of the whole economy if any of its sectors crashes.

b) SmartGovernance (Citizen Participation): Focuses on promoting the current governance model of co-existence (top-down) with informal initiatives, incorporating the format (bottom-up) for its functioning.

c) SmartEnviroment (Healthcare): Applied by reducing land consumption in the city's expanse and aiming for a more efficient use of the environment already used. It highlights the concern with natural conditions, pollution, environmental protection and resources for sustainable management.

d) Smart People (Social and Human Capital): Promotes initiatives in order to solve high unemployment levels, taking into account all citizens, regardless of age, gender, culture or social status.

e) SmartMobility (Transport and ICT): Aims at reducing pollution and congestion through alternative transport for cars and the provision of sustainable public transport, available to all citizens.

f) Smart Living (Quality of life): Promotes social cohesion, better health and a decrease in crime rates [10][12][13].

2) Projects:

Over recent years, many initiatives (public and private) have been proposed around the world in order to adapt urban areas to smart city issues. New initiatives propose the creation of new cities, projecting their smart infrastructure from the beginning of their construction. Some initiatives to achieve smart cities include:

- **Amsterdam**, Europe: Created by the merging of many organizations and companies. Named Amsterdam Smart City (ASC), it focuses on the application of smart city concepts for achieving three objectives: economic growth, a change in inhabitants' perception and a focus on improving quality of life [10].
- **Shanghai**, China: It is one of the first pilot cities in China to apply smart cities concepts. It aims to achieve gains in areas such as security and the development of information technology in city systems [12].
- **Rio de Janeiro**, Brazil [13]: A partnership with IBM has resulted in the construction of the Rio De Janeiro city center of operations. It aims to improve the monitoring and control of events in the city through cameras and a better integration between the city's service providers [10][11].

B. Publish/Subscribe

Publish/subscribe design pattern - or pub/sub - is widely used by services which work with interest-based notification. Due to its asynchronous decoupling property, it provides an elegant technique for the implementation of an infrastructure capable of providing a significant level of many-to-many communication. Such a feature enables independence between the entities involved. The pattern is widely used as a main component in projects from various fields, e.g., medical applications [14], air traffic management and industrial production [15].

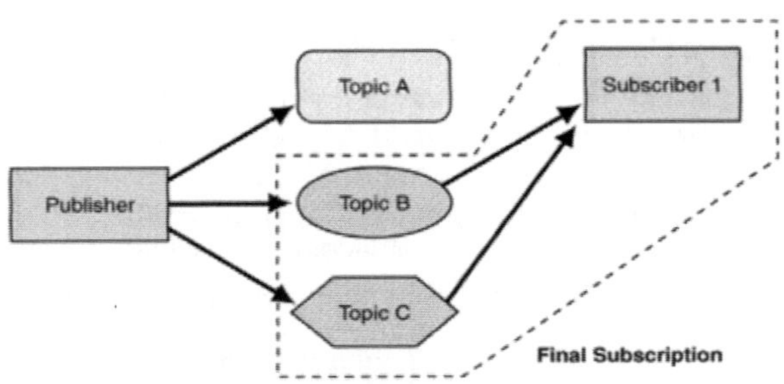

Figure 1. Publish/Subscribe Diagram

1) Pub/Sub Based Services

Pub/sub services are composed of three main components: (i) the publisher, (ii) the subscriber and (iii) a notification service (named broker) which will make the interconnection between subscribers and publishers. This architecture is based on the object-oriented design pattern Subject-Observer.

A pub/sub service starts when the publisher sends a message to the notification service, containing specific information, called an event. This event is evaluated using some fixed condition as a basis within the service and it is extracted as information and/or topic of interest. The service maintains a list of subscribers, which may be linked to one or more points of interest. Thus, the service retrieves subscribers that are interested in the event content and sends a notification to each one through the endpoint informed during the subscription process. Fig. 1 presents the topic-based subscription flow. A system may perform both publisher and subscriber roles, and the distinction between these roles is determined by whether or not it has sent an event, or just subscribed to a topic of interest [15][16].

Notification Services can define different behaviors depending on subscription models. They are:

- Channels-based: The notification service has a number of communication channels. Events are sent and received only by its subscribers, regardless of the content.
- Topics-based: Publishers assign to the sent event an identification tag with some default information. Also, subscribers report which tags of interest should generate notification for them, e.g., accidents, muggings, etc. [14].
- Type-based: Subscribers report interest in events belonging to any area of particular interest, such as public safety or health.
- Content-based: Some rules are defined, rules which the event content must satisfy. Events only generate notification if the defined rules are positively validated [17][18][19].

Such model efficiency is already well established and proven. Its use can be noted in many frameworks, as well as through the OMG Data Distribution Service (DDS) and Java Messaging Service (JMS) [15]. It is also available as a service on cloud platforms like Google Cloud Platform (Cloud Pub / Sub) [20] and Amazon Simple Notification Service (SNS) [21].

C. *CEP (Complex Event Processing)*

Complex event processing (CEP) has become important technology for big data processing because it enables the consumption of a lot of events in a relatively low period of time. CEP is part of an architecture that relies on the detection, use, analysis and generation of events. It is an efficient way to use rules to detect correlations between events within a certain scope of processing [9]. It has been used by many applications ranging from medical systems to real-time financial analysis, fault detection, and so on.

A CEP system consists of relationships between event generators, processing server and other systems called event consumers. Event generators can be sensors which monitor environments or other systems which notify when a specific scenario occurs (e.g., security vulnerabilities or price changes in stocks). Event consumers are typically decision-making systems that perform some action based on notification received by the CEP server. The existence of a server intermediating such communication is one major advantage of using a CEP server, since it eliminates the need for decentralized treatment in end systems for processing events generated by different channels. Fig. 2 shows the structure of a CEP system, as well as its relationship with its components [22].

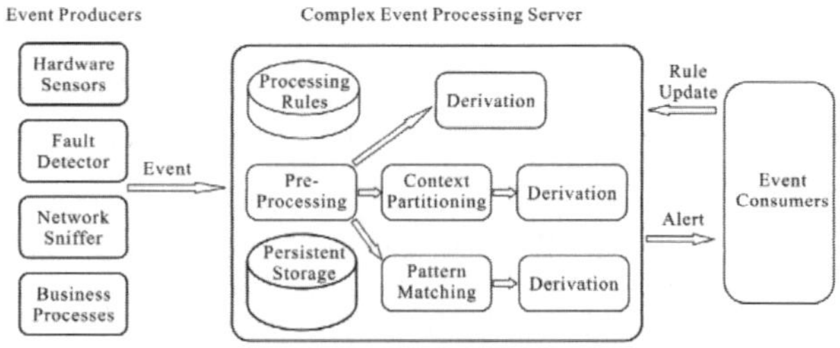

Figure 2. CEP System Structure

Two categories stand out among the existing processing models: Detection-oriented monitoring and aggregation-oriented monitoring [23].

- Detection-oriented model: The data are analyzed from a base, which consists of past events information. In this model, the goal is to find patterns from the processed content.
- Aggregation-oriented model: The data are analyzed in real time and each event received is processed individually [24].

Events are analyzed using a specific set of criteria. Among the most common are:

- Time: The event timestamp is used. Events are linked when they are in a specific range of creation.
- Location: The correlation is performed through the place where the events occurred.
- ID: Events can embed some default identifier for its context.

The unified analysis of temporal and geospatial data allow the identification of heterogeneous events in a Smart City, enabling information sharing between domain-specific systems for processing events.

After the analysis step, a further evaluation is performed in order to determine whether any action will be taken. This kind of trigger is widely used in applications that require to run a procedure in response to external events.

Unlike other client/server approaches (in which the client typically sends a request to the server and expects its completion before sending a new one), in CEP systems communication is made in a single direction. The event generator sends requests continuously and does not wait for an answer. When a consumer system wants to change or create specific criteria, it must send a message to the server, and then it will be notified whenever that new rule is identified [20]. This flow can be seen in Fig. 2 [22].

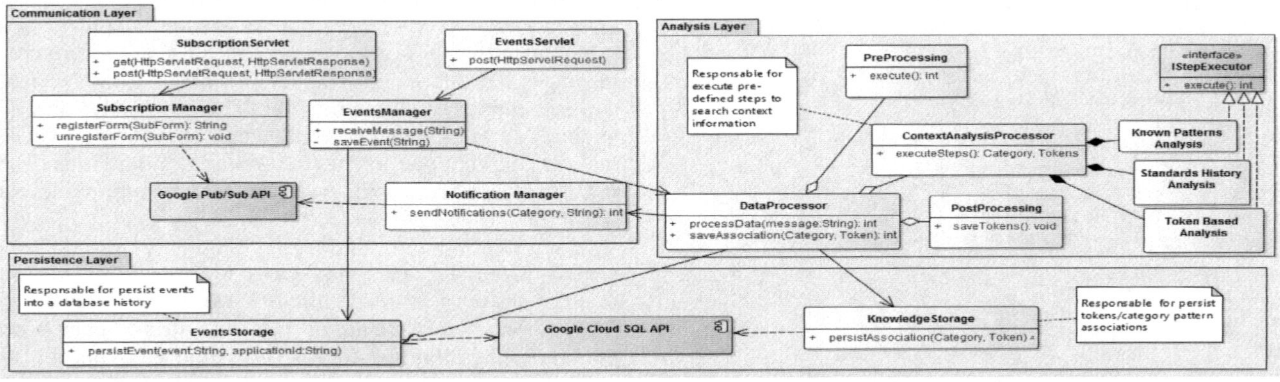

Figure 3. Interaction Class Diagram of the Layers

III. MIDDLEWARE

Heterogeneity is a major barrier for processing events generated in smart cities. There are several standards on the market, such as FHIR [1] (specified for medical use), FIX [25] and ISO 8583 [26] (specified for the financial industry). However, due to the amount of existing protocols and formats, the ability to recognize, in a simple way, the context for all kinds of events generated in a smart city is compromised [13].

Aiming to mitigate the impact of mapping and implementing all the possibilities of existing formats, this middleware is designed for analyzing and inferring in which category a received event will be categorized.

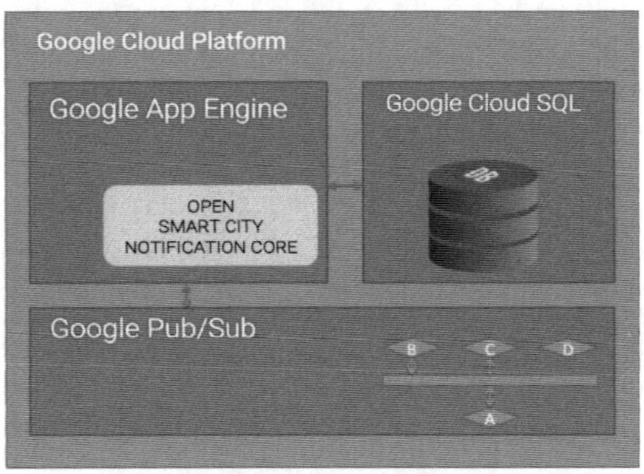

Figure 4 - Middleware Deployment Architecture

This section discusses the flows, processes and other architectural aspects of the middleware. The middleware is designed with a division into three layers. The communication layer is responsible for managing information exchanged with stakeholders. The processing layer performs context analysis and, finally, a layer for persistent data control (Fig. 3). The middleware composition is conducted by independent modules, which can be replicated on multiple servers, thus promoting scalability to meet a lot of requests. The proposed structure is based on events, and, in this model, other systems and entities will provide inputs for the middleware.

A. Composition

This work adopts the Google Cloud Platform (GCP), a set of cloud-based scalable services. This platform does not directly address the heterogeneity problem, but it provides the necessary infrastructure and, in addition, facilitates the creation of similar instances. Among the services provided by the platform, Google App Engine (GAP) has been chosen to deploy the application, since it provides automatic resizing as the number of requests increases. GAP also provides automatic resources management if the number of requests increases. Moreover, the application is held in a container which can be replicated and run on multiple servers, providing high scalability for the middleware.

For data storage, the proposed middleware adopts Google Cloud SQL for events information maintenance and other system persistence requirements. Message-oriented modeling has been adopted in order to promote communication with subscribers, through the use of the Google Pub/Sub platform, which provides mechanisms for sending and receiving messages asynchronously. Fig. 4 illustrates the middleware structure in the cloud platform.

System processing flow consists of three general steps, which are: (i) subscription step, in which systems of interest subscribe to the topics of interest. Next, there is (ii), the analysis and processing step, in which the events are caught and handled, and, finally, (iii) sending notification to subscribers. These steps are further detailed as follows:

B. Subscription Step

The proposed middleware implements the design pattern publish/subscribe, adapting underwriting issues by topic, type and content-based analysis (Section 2). In order to perform the signature process, the system provides a REST service and a GET method called "subscribe", through which the subscribers must specify a list of topics (or areas) of interest, as well as an endpoint to be triggered as to when a notification should be sent, due to its processing result (Fig. 5 - A).

```
subscribe
{
    "topic":[integer],                    (A)
    "name":"string-value",
    "endpoint":"string-value"
}
subscriptionForm{
    "topic":[integer],
    "subscriptions":[                      (B)
        "subscription"":{
            "name":"string-value",
            "endpoint":"string-value"
        }
    ]
}
```

Figure 5 - Subscriptions JSON Format

Furthermore, the application also provides a protocol for batch registration. Thus, governance agencies can manage entity groups to be notified whenever a given event type occurs. Therefore, the application provides a method called "subscribeForm", which should contain a list of endpoints return as well as information for filtering interests (Fig. 5 - B). The system returns an ID to subscribers in application methods, and such an ID can be used by authorities updating or canceling its subscription. Such an identifier can also be used if the source system wants to inform any event to the system.

Figure 6. FHIR-Based Message

C. Event Arrival and Analysis

Whenever a new event arrives it is saved in the database and attached to the source system ID. Also, the event content is forwarded to the analysis module.

The review process attempts to discover in the event message one or more key tokens which are content and syntax identifiers. Therefore, all the received and interpreted messages are stored in database records. This database contains references to the messages source systems, as well as finding tokens which made the interpretation possible, so that data can be used for future message interpretation. The middleware performs a three-step process in order to make a structural analysis of the received text message.

Each step performs a different type of search, and if any step is successful, no other needs to be performed. The middleware must be trained before it can run the analysis. The precondition of training reflects the need to enter a set of rules and known message formats into the database, as well as a token list attached to specific contexts. Such information is taken in the following steps:

1) Known Patterns Analysis: The system searches for a known format identifier in the message. In Fig. 6, for example, search terms are "ICD10", "ResourceType" and "Diagnostics Report". Identifiers recognition is achieved by comparing message structure with the patterns previously registered in the middleware training phase. Whenever the number of combinations meets a specific threshold, the system sets the message topics of interest.

2) History Recovery: Whenever a message does not contain a known pattern identifier the system verifies if it fulfills a set of tokens for historically interpreted messages. Thus, it is possible to assess whether a pattern has already been used and accepted previously, thereby ensuring greater reliability in the results. In the example of Fig. 7 the terms "occurrences", "casualites" and "periodoInDays" have been classified as tokens for the context of a previous analysis.

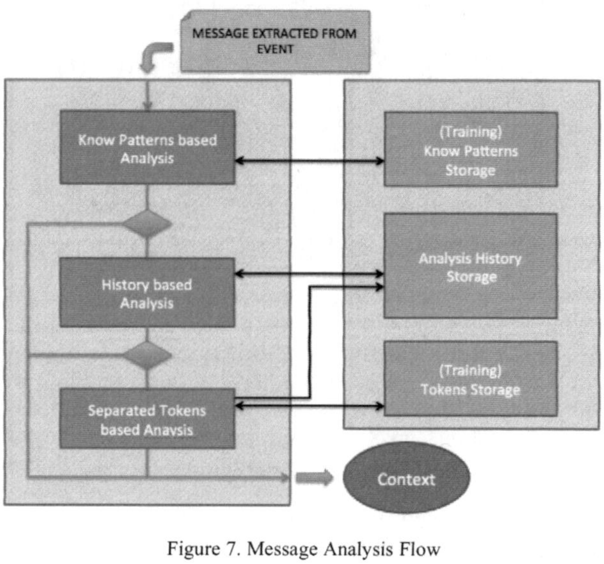

Figure 7. Message Analysis Flow

3) Sundry tokens-based analysis: In the case that no pattern has been identified in a message, the system uses a set of predefined tokens which are already linked to some context and which have been stored in the training process. Whenever the amount of combinations meets a defined threshold, the system will consider the message and token group as a new pattern, storing them in the database. In Fig. 6, the terms: "Diagnostic" and "Hospital" have been added to the training stage and linked to the health context. All data saved at that step is used for future history recovery. Fig. 7 illustrates the flow described in the preceding steps.

D. Notification dispatch to subscribers

Through topics of interest information derived in the previous step, the system searches for signatures callback information in the database. Such information is submitted to the pub/sub communication module. Due to the pub/sub adopted engine, all notifications are sent through multiple asynchronous threads. Notification messages are targeted to endpoints reported in the registration step, either for individual subscribers or forms submitted by third parties, to receive a notification message. The sent message's body incorporates in textual representation the original received message in the processed event.

IV. CONCLUSION AND FUTURE WORK

This paper has presented and discussed aspects related to the requirements for information sharing over multiple domains. The information is derived from events of heterogeneous systems that are spread across different systems which comprise a Smart City.

Besides these aspects, many obstacles and difficulties have been raised, resulting from the existence of the numerous communication protocols and formats which are used by each one of these systems. It is believed that the development of the proposed middleware can lead to a complete solution in order to perform the identification and dissemination of events/occurrences in smart city environments.

It is important to mention that this work is currently in progress. In order to clarify the next objectives, a list of targeted milestones has been introduced, as follows:

1) Implementation: Developing the proposed architecture, promoting the adoption of the chosen Cloud Platform framework.

2) Case Study: The simulation of a heterogeneous environment uses the PREVENT framework as a subscriber to receive reports through our middleware. To validate the capacity of analysis and conversion, messages in a non-FHIR format will be delivered to our middleware. As the main expected output our middleware should be able to convert, process and send the messages received(using the knowledge it has been trained for) as events which are understood by the PREVENT plataform.

3) Training Data: As discussed in Section 3, the proposed middleware requires an initial loading of data in order to identify the default messages in the event. This step consists of collecting required data for training the pattern recognition engine adopted by the middleware.

As the output for the listed items, in addition to the success rate obtained for context inference this technique also aims to extract metrics related to middleware performance; for example, the response time for processing and delivering notifications for processed events.

REFERENCES

[1] S. Neto, M. Valéria, P. Manoel, and F. Ferraz, "Publish/subscribe cloud middleware for real-time disease surveillance," *ICSEA 2015 Tenth Int. Conf. Softw. Eng. Adv.*, no. c, pp. 150–157, 2015.

[2] M. Andres, "Smart Cities Concept and Challenges: Bases for the Assessment of Smart City Projects," *Transp. Res. Centre, Univ. Politécnica Madrid, Prof. Aranguren s/n, Madrid, Spain*, pp. 11–21.

[3] S. P. Pawar, "Smart City with Internet of Things (Sensor networks) and Big Data," *Academia.edu*, no. 9860027825, p. 10.

[4] M. Jung, J. Weidinger, W. Kastner, and A. Olivieri, "Building Automation and Smart Cities: An Integration Approach Based on a Service-Oriented Architecture," *Adv. Inf. Netw. Appl. Work.*, pp. 1361–1367, 2013.

[5] S. Wahle, T. Magedanz, and F. Schulze, "The OpenMTC framework - M2M solutions for smart cities and the internet of things," *2012 IEEE Int. Symp. a World Wireless, Mob. Multimed. Networks, WoWMoM 2012 - Digit. Proc.*, pp. 2–4, 2012.

[6] J. Wan, D. Li, C. Zou, and K. Zhou, "M2M communications for smart city: An event-based architecture," *Proc. - 2012 IEEE 12th Int. Conf. Comput. Inf. Technol. CIT 2012*, pp. 895–900, 2012.

[7] A. Elmangoush, H. Coskun, S. Wahle, and T. Magedanz, "Design aspects for a reference M2M communication platform for Smart Cities," *2013 9th Int. Conf. Innov. Inf. Technol. IIT 2013*, no. MARCH 2013, pp. 204–209, 2013.

[8] A. Chanda, K. Elmeleegy, A. L. Cox, and W. Zwaenepoel, "Composite Subscriptions in Content-Based Publish/Subscribe Systems," vol. 3790, no. December, pp. 42–59, 2005.

[9] B. Schilling, B. Koldehofe, and K. Rothermel, "Efficient and distributed rule placement in heavy constraint-driven event systems," *Proc.- 2011 IEEE Int. Conf. HPCC 2011 - 2011 IEEE Int. Work. FTDCS 2011 -Workshops 2011 Int. Conf. UIC 2011- Work. 2011 Int. Conf. ATC 2011*, pp. 355–364, 2011.

[10] S. Pellicer, G. Santa, A. L. Bleda, R. Maestre, A. J. Jara, and A. G. Skarmeta, "A global perspective of smart cities: A survey," *Proc. - 7th Int. Conf. Innov. Mob. Internet Serv. Ubiquitous Comput. IMIS 2013*, pp. 439–444, 2013.

[11] R. Giffinger, "Smart cities Ranking of European medium-sized cities," *October*, 2007. [Online]. Available from: http://linkinghub.elsevier.com/retrieve/pii/S026427519800050X 2016.07.11

[12] X. Lin, H. Quan, H. Zhang, and Y. Huang, "The 5I Model of Smart City: A Case of Shanghai, china," *2015 IEEE First Int. Conf. Big Data Comput. Serv. Appl.*, pp. 329–332, 2015.

[13] Y. Fujiwara, K. Yamada, K. Tabata, M. Oda, K. Hashimoto, T. Suganuma, A. Rahim, P. Vlacheas, V. Stavroulaki, D. Kelaidonis, and A. Georgakopoulos, "Context Aware Services: A Novel Trend in IoT Based Research in Smart City Project," *Comput. Softw. Appl. Conf. (COMPSAC), 2015 IEEE 39th Annu.*, vol. 3, pp. 479–480, 2015.

[14] J. Singh, D. M. Eyers, and J. Bacon, "Disclosure Control in Multi-Domain Publish / Subscribe Systems," *ACM Int. Conf.*

Distrib. event-based Syst., no. Ic, pp. 159–170, 2011.

[15] C. Esposito and M. Ciampi, "On security in publish/subscribe services: A survey," *IEEE Commun. Surv. Tutorials*, vol. 17, no. 2, pp. 966–997, 2015.

[16] M. Corporation, "Publish/Subscribe," 2004. [Online]. Available from: https://msdn.microsoft.com/en-us/library/ff649664.aspx 2016.07.11

[17] A. Carzaniga, M. Papalini, and A. L. Wolf, "Content-based publish/subscribe networking and information-centric networking," *Proc. ACM SIGCOMM Work. Information-centric Netw. - ICN '11*, no. 1, p. 56, 2011.

[18] R. Baldoni, L. Querzoni, and A. Virgillito, "Distributed Event Routing in Publish / Subscribe Communication Systems : a Survey," *Tech. Rep.*, pp. 1–27, 2005.

[19] J. L. Martins and S. Member, "Routing Algorithms for Content-Based Publish / Subscribe Systems," *Communications*, vol. 12, no. 1, pp. 39–58, 2010.

[20] Google, "Google Cloud Platform," 2015. [Online]. Available from: https://cloud.google.com/appengine/docs/whatisgoogleappengine 2016.07.11

[21] Amazon, "Amazon Simple Notification Service (SNS)," 2016. [Online]. Available from: https://aws.amazon.com/sns/ 2016.07.11

[22] H. Chai and W. Zhao, "Towards Trustworthy Complex Event Processing," pp. 1–4.

[23] D. B. Robins, "Complex Event Processing," *2010 Second Int. Work. Educ. Technol. Comput. Sci.*, p. 10, 2010.

[24] M. Antunes, D. Gomes, and R. Aguiar, "Semantic-Based Publish/Subscribe for M2M," *2014 Int. Conf. Cyber-Enabled Distrib. Comput. Knowl. Discov.*, pp. 256–263, 2014.

[25] P. B. P. Tongkamonwat, "IFIX: A new information exchange framework for financial organizations," *Adv. Informatics Concepts, Theory Appl. (ICAICTA), 2015 2nd Int. Conf.*, vol. 16, pp. 1 – 5, 2015.

[26] ISO, "ISO 8583-1:2003," 2003. [Online]. Available from: https://www.iso.org/obp/ui/#iso:std:iso:8583:-1:ed-1:v1:en 2016.07.11

A Set of Support Tools to Software Process Appraisal and Improvement in Adherence to CMMI-DEV

Leonardo Possamai Mezzomo, Sandro Ronaldo Bezerra Oliveira
Graduate Program in Computer Science
Federal University of Pará
Belém, Pará, Brazil
e-mail: leopossamai@gmail.com, srbo@ufpa.br

Alexandre Marcos Lins de Vasconcelos
Informatics Center
Federal University of Pernambuco
Recife, Pernambuco, Brazil
e-mail: amlv@cin.ufpe.br

***Abstract*—Adopting standards and reference models for quality software processes is essential to ensure a competitive software industry. However, despite the increasing number of standards and models, only a small proportion of software organizations adopt them. This paper presents a set of support tools for software process appraisal and improvement through their adherence to the CMMI-DEV (Capability Maturity Model Integration for Development) model. The purpose of this set of support tools is to assist software organizations in the implementation of the CMMI-DEV model. It is expected that these tools will be readily adopted by software organizations because they are based on models and standards that are generally accepted. Furthermore, this set of support tools employs free (non-proprietary) technologies to reduce costs.**

Keywords-software engineering; software quality; process appraisal; process improvement; software tool.

I. INTRODUCTION

Currently, there is a much greater need to develop software than design or create a tool or use a particular programming language. There have also been collective, complex and creative endeavors in this area since the quality of a software product relies heavily on the people, organizations and procedures needed to create it and make it available [1].

Quality is not only a question of market differentiation that can enable an organization to sell more and increase its profits, but also a prerequisite that the organization must meet to be able to put its product on the global market. In the domain of software development, quality can be defined as a set of characteristics that must be satisfied to ensure the software product caters for the needs of its users [2]. Thus, before the quality of the product can be achieved, a software development team must find a solution to guide them about what, how and when to do something. It is believed that the key to software quality lies in the quality-based process that is used to achieve it [3].

According to Humphrey [4], a software process consists of a set of software engineering tasks required to transform a user's requirements into software. In defining this process, some information is necessary about areas such as: activities, resources, consumed and generated work-products, procedures, paradigms and technology, and a software life cycle model [5]. Thus, a software process can be regarded as a set of tasks or activities that must be performed by a team to ensure a good product or service.

While the organizations have been implementing their processes, they have also carried out an appraisal as a means of improving them [6]. A software process cannot stay immutable in time, and as a result, reflects the "critical points" that lead to unwanted problems in product development. The processes must constantly undergo refinements and modifications so that they can increase their ability and flexibility during the projects. This means that they need to be continuously improved [1].

The aim of the Organizational Process Appraisal and Improvement process is to determine how the organization's processes help it to achieve its business goals and to support, implement and deploy measures that will lead to continuous improvement [6]. Although it is an independent process, it is essential that the process definition stage is deployed.

As there has been a good deal of discussion about the appraisals and continuous improvements of the processes, software engineers and organizations still have difficulties in defining their processes, because there is no software process that can be generically used by different organizations [7]. However, the process must be improved and continuously refined with each new project to enable it to deal with the requirements and expectations of the market and the organization. In this way, the process can increase the efficiency and productivity of the organization as a whole. These observations have driven a large number of studies on the creation of quality models and methods for improving processes [1] [8].

To make improvements in these processes, it is important to appraise them. The appraisal process addresses many factors, such as their assets (tasks, activities, procedures, tools, etc) and the products that are the outcome of the projects. Thus, providing support for the adoption of continuous improvement strategies is essential [1].

At present, Organizational Process Appraisal and Improvement process are employed in the quality models. The purpose of these models, guidelines and standards is to guide organizations about the use of good practices and the implementation of these processes. The main guidelines include the following: the Capability Maturity Model Integration (CMMI) [6], the Brazilian Software Process Improvement program (MPS.BR) [9] and the International

Organization for Standardization / International Electrotechnical Commission (ISO / IEC) 12207 [10].

The purpose of this paper is to define an approach about the Organizational Process Appraisal and Improvement process that is aligned with the Capability Maturity Model Integration for the Development (CMMI-DEV) quality model. This approach consists of: a) process mapping between the assets included in the quality models, b) a process framework for mapping and c) free tools of systemic support for the activities defined in the framework. Thus, it is expected to simplify the implementation of the appraisal process and assist organizations that are seeking to improve, standardize and institutionalize their software development processes, through the application of organizational assets for their software projects. These tools are based on free standards and technologies and are the outcome of the Software Process Improvement: Development and Research (SPIDER) project [11], carried out at the Federal University of Pará (UFPA).

As well as this introductory part, Section II discusses the software process appraisal and improvement stages, and it also examines related works. Section III sets out the appraisal and improvement tools. Section IV discusses the analysis of the tools and their application in industry and their adherence to the CMMI-DEV model. Section V analyzes the results obtained from this. Finally, Section VI summarizes the conclusions and makes recommendations for future work.

II. Background and Related Works

This section provides an overview of the CMMI-DEV model, the fundamental concepts of the software process with regard to improvement and appraisal, and some related works.

A. *The CMMI-DEV Model*

The CMMI is a maturity model for process improvement, created by the Software Engineering Institute (SEI) to integrate areas of knowledge in a single model, such as Systems Engineering (SE), Software Engineering (SW), Integrated Products and Process Development (IPPD) and Supplier Sourcing (SS) [6].

Currently, the CMMI is in version 1.3 and is composed of three models, which are as follows: CMMI-DEV, which is concerned with development processes, CMMI for Acquisition (CMMI-ACQ), which deals with acquisition processes, as well as product and / or sourcing services, and CMMI for Services (CMMI-SVC), which focuses on service processes such as maintenance and evolution.

The CMMI structure consists of many elements that are grouped into three categories, which are: a) required components (Specific and Generic Goals), b) expected components (Specific and Generic Practices) and c) informative components (Subpractices, Examples of Work Products, and others). These components assist in the interpretation of the model requirements. Thus, the CMMI-DEV comprises twenty-two process areas, each of which has its own purpose and specific goals supplemented by generic goals, since they are related to all the process areas. The specific goal is to define the characteristics, which are unique for each process area, while the generic goals define the characteristics that are common to all the process areas. Each specific goal has a set of specific practices, which are activities that must be carried out to accomplish the goal. The generic goals have generic practices as well.

B. *Software Process Appraisal and Improvement*

To determine how the standard processes can assist the organization, the disciplined process appraisals must be performed by means of a process appraisal model, which is employed for assessing the process capability based on a reference model [12]. It is possible to determine the way that the processes can be assessed for a specific project in the organizational unit by analyzing the results obtained of the strengths and weaknesses of these appraisals and the risks involved. As a result, improvements can be made on the basis of information obtained in the standard processes of the organization and this can be applied to the standard processes by making changes in their existing capabilities or by replacing them with subprocesses that are more efficient or effective [13].

According to CMMI [6], the purpose of the Organizational Appraisal and Improvement process, called the Organizational Process Focus (OPF) process area, is to determine how the standard processes of the organization can a) assist an organization in achieving its business goals and b) support the organization by helping it to plan, implement and deploy continuous improvement in processes based on an awareness of its strengths and weaknesses. The main objective of the OPF process area is to conduct systematic appraisals, plan and implement the improvements that are found necessary by these appraisals and provide experience in the use of the standard processes of the organization.

The main goals of business process improvement are: (i) to understand the characteristics and factors that affect process capability, (ii) to plan and implement the activities that modify the process in response to business needs, and (iii) to assess the effects and benefits obtained and compare them with the cost of making changes in the processes [13].

Once the potential improvements in the standard processes of the organization have been identified, they are analyzed and transformed into action items that must be realistic and aligned to the roles and responsibilities defined in the organization. These action items should be planned and implemented, and not only take account of the resources available, but also the risks inherent in the changes that have to be implemented in the organization's standard processes [14].

An efficient way to identify possible areas of improvement in future projects would be to conduct "post-mortem appraisals", which entail making an appraisal after the execution of all aspects of a project, including its products, processes and resources [15]. Collier *et al.* [16] propose an appraisal process that follows 5 stages: (i) establishing a mechanism for collecting information for the project (usually by a survey), (ii) collecting objective information about the project (usually by measures related to the execution of the project), (iii) conducting an in-depth meeting (a structured meeting involving members of the project with the aim of collecting information that was not obtained in the first attempt to do this), (iv) leading the project that traces the activities of a single day (a meeting, where key players come together to evaluate the main events that have taken place during the project and the information obtained and thus assess the main problems and their possible associated causes), and (v) publishing the results.

After the improvements in the standard processes have been implemented, it is important to support the appropriate use of processes and other organizational process assets in the organization's projects and monitor their use to ensure that the implemented improvements have the desired effect and avoid having asny adverse effects on the projects [14].

C. *Related Works*

In [17], WebAPAEE was proposed for a process management environment based on free software. It was designed between 2004 and 2005 as a cooperative venture between academic and scientific institutions, in particular the Software Engineering Laboratory (LabES) at UFPA.

With regard to the process appraisal, the scope of the project is still limited. Currently, the environment is suitable for the definition of metrics and the collection of estimates and measurements, but there is no mechanism in the environment to enable an appraisal of the task of collecting that has been carried out. Furthermore, currently there is an ongoing project in the software environment to provide a more complete and integrated support for the measurement and analytical procedures. It is clear that there is not yet an integration of this kind. Although the process improvement, is discussed in [18] in an implementation strategy based on the Initiating, Diagnosing, Establishing, Acting and Learning (IDEAL) model [19], the project is only able to support the improvement, but lacks a tool that is integrated in the environment.

In [3], there is a software process implementation for the environment, called ImPProS, which is involved with Process Definition, Simulation, Implementation, Evaluation and Improvement through the use of tools that support the software process and software development. Among the approaches that form the environment, it is worth highlighting the ProEvaluator and ProImprove, which carry out the process evaluation and improvement activities respectively. However, this environment has some drawbacks: with regard to evaluation, the ProEvaluator supports the automation of only a few activities included in the MPS.BR Assessment Method [20], and on the question of improvement, the support tool only implements the activities of the IDEAL model, but does not integrate these activities with the results of the evaluation, and thus does not provide a cycle for process improvement.

Finally, Montoni *et al.* [21] present a Software Development Environment (SDE), called TABA Station that supports project management activities, improvements in software product quality and increased productivity. The TABA Station [22], which has been operating since 1990, is a meta-environment that seeks to generate a software development environment that is suited to organizational features, software processes and specific projects. The main dsriving-force behind this is the fact that the application domains and specific projects have their own characteristics, and it is essential that these features are present in a customized way in the environments used by software engineers for the application development.

In this environment, there are tools intended for process evaluation and improvement, called AvalPro and Pilot. The former supports the Processes and Product Quality Assurance team [23], while the latter is designed to carry out an evaluation of the improvement proposals of a process in a systematic, planned and controlled way by carrying out pilot schemes [24]. It was not found that the tools are based on quality models and unclear what their relationship is with other tools embedded in the environmental domain.

Finally, in [33] Portela *et al.* present a tool focused on software process enactment, which has been previously appraised and improved, called Spider-PE. It should be pointed out that this work differs from the paper on the Spider-PE tool in some respects. For example, the tools discussed in this work are concerned with generating and implementing the results of the software process appraisal and improvement, while Spider-PE receives as input the process has already been appraised and improved, i.e. these tools are dependent and are used in sequence during the implementation of process lifecycle.

The selection criteria of the tools described in this section are that they should be available for download and further analysis. Also, it must be possible to use them in the development scenario of Brazilian software organizations that adopt a software process improvement program using CMMI-DEV or another model.

The weaknesses of these tools are as follows: they do not provide different ways of conducting software process appraisals (objective criteria or metrics), they do not record the results of appraisals carried out over a period of time, they do not keep a historical record of improvement items generated from the results of the appraisal, they do not make full use of all the activities, principles and techniques suggested by the IDEAL model, and they do not evaluate the results of the improvements implemented in the software processes. All these features are suggested in the adherence of the OPF process area included in the CMMI-DEV.

Unlike these other environments, the proposal, set out in detail in this paper, is an appraisal tool integrated into the process for the modeling and definition tool, called Spider-PM, and a tool for process improvement, called Spider-PI, defined by the mapping of the appraisal and improvement process found in the Brazilian Reference Model of SPI for Software (MR-MPS-SW) and CMMI-DEV models and ISO/IEC 12207 standard.

III. A SET OF SUPPORT TOOLS FOR PROCESS APPRAISAL AND IMPROVEMENT

The set of supporting concepts adopted in this paper defines a set of technologies that can be integrated and thus assist in the software process appraisal and improvement. In this domain, there are tools, techniques, procedures, processes, roles, methodologies, frameworks, languages, standards, patterns, and so on.

A. A Framework for Software Process Appraisal and Improvement

A process framework was designed to make the organization concerned about the quality of its appraisal and improvement processes, not only adherent to the MR-MPS-SW model but also the other model and standard. All the activities in the framework originate from the assets (activities, practices, expected results) included in CMMI-DEV, MR-MPS-SW and ISO / IEC 12207.

Three flows were used to prepare the framework. One of them is called a macro-flow and contains macro-activities and two of them are formed of specific activities. The macro-activities are called Process Appraisal and Process Improvement; each of them consists of a set of other activities that structure the specific flows. The framework was modeled by means of the Business Process Modeling Notation (BPMN).

Fig. 1 shows a general flow between the macro-activities. In this flow, there is a need to appraise and improve a process. The exclusive gateways help to clarify the possible steps that can be followed. The first exclusive gateway determines the existence of a process, and allows it to be further assessed or improved by specific activities. Thus, it is important that there is already a process (as defined above), and that there is input to the macro-activity "Appraising Process". There is also another exclusive gateway that allows a process to be improved, if it can find opportunities for improvement at the end of the appraisal.

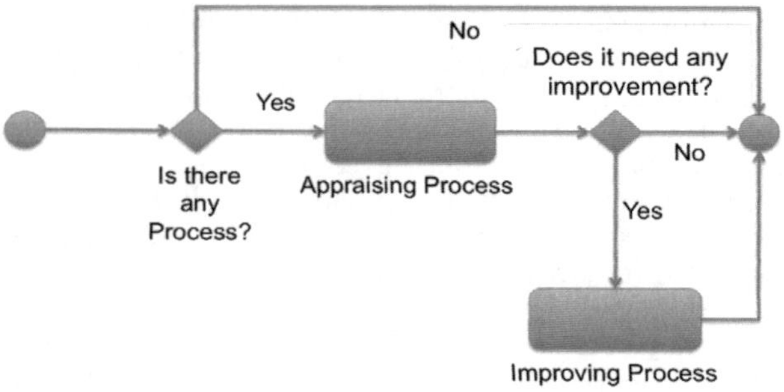

Figure 1. FlowChart showing the Macro-Activities of the Framework

The activities that form the flows that are directed at the process appraisal and improvement goals are included in the macro-activities. These activities are as follows: the Appraising Process, activities related to appraisal based on objective criteria or metrics, and the Improving Process, activities related to the implementation of improvements from the IDEAL model.

The appraisal framework, in which the activities are described as features in Section B, begins with an activity that provides information about the use of the process and can be checked before the process is used. After this, the appraisal needs and goals are defined and the type of appraisal is chosen from the metrics (metrically – using the Spider-MSControl tool [31]) or objective criteria (objectively - using the Spider-CL tool [32]). The activities, included in the appraisals that are based on metrics, follow a simple flow from the definition of goals and measurements, and then the collection and analysis of the measurements. The other type of appraisal includes a set of activities that involve the definition of questions and the application of surveys, which are later drawn on to conduct the data collection and analysis. However, the two types of appraisal generate a report, which serves as input for process improvement.

The report on the generated improvements at the end of the appraisal is considered to be critical for the improvement activities. In this domain, the framework is formed of seventeen activities, which are described in Section C as features that are based on an improvement model called IDEAL. The IDEAL model is an organizational improvement pattern that serves as a guide for initiates. It plans and implements the improvement actions and provides a usable and easy approach to understand the stages that are needed to establish a successful process improvement program [19].

The evaluation of the prepared framework was submited to the judgment of experts in software process appraisal and improvement (included in the MR-MPS-SW, CMMI-DEV and ISO / IEC 12207) through the completion of a questionnaire. These experts were contacted by email, and were sent the framework documents and survey with objective questions about the work proposed. The purpose of the survey was primarily to evaluate the correctness and suitability of the framework to support people and organizations when they use the solution that supports the quality models and standards.

The survey had sixteen objective questions, divided into two parts:

- (i) Expert Profile - this was designed to characterize the expert's level of knowledge, regarding the process models and appraisal methods, time of experience, and the role/function of the software process appraisal, and
- (ii) Approach Evaluation - this concerns the correctness and completeness of the mapping and the framework, and determines whether the process framework can serve as a reference-point for software process appraisals and improvements in an organization or if it adheres to the designed mapping.

In addition to objective questions, the survey also had a space for comments so the expert could provide any additional information that needed to be reviewed.

The expert had considerable knowledge of quality models and software process appraisal and improvement, as well as five years' practical experience of making appraisals and improvements in the processes included in MPS.BR, CMMI-DEV and ISO / IEC 12207 models. Thus, the need for the expert to have sufficient knowledge and experience in both quality models and standards was an ideal condition that had been achieved.

With regard to the results of the evaluation, the framework was considered to be suitable, and was able to address a few of the suggestions made for corrections.

B. The Software Process Appraisal Tool

The Spider-PM tool is a General Public License (GPL) tool that supports the process modeling and definition, by means of the Software & Systems Process Engineering Metamodel Specification (SPEM) standard. The Spider-PM tool also supports the software process appraisal.

Since the software process appraisal is a crucial skill, it should be noted that the use of tools to support the appraisal process is of great importance, as confirmed by Hunter, Robinson and Woodman [25] "Tools to visualise software assessment data are therefore of value both to software producers who wish to improve their processes compared with their competitors, and for software procurers who wish the assess the processes of potential contractors against those used in the industrial sector involved.".

Currently, most process appraisals only involve recording the information in documents and spreadsheets. This means it takes more time to write the work manual, since it is more difficult to handle the appraisal information [26].

The appraisal tool integrated to Spider-PM is designed to systematize the activities of the appraisal process by complying with quality models and standards. This tool was developed from preliminary studies, which included a preparation of process mapping based on quality models and standards and the design of a process framework. Hence, the input for this tool is the software process defined in the Spider-PM, which consists of activities, tasks, resources, work products, roles, and others assets that will be appraised in an automated way. This tool has the following features:

- Appraisal Creation: this enables a new appraisal to be recorded. In this feature, the user can create an appraisal, by filling some of the spaces,
- Appraisal of Reading: this shows the users all the process appraisals that have been created. It makes possible to list all the appraisals created or else it can deal with queries that are included in three filters,
- Appraisal Setup: this enables the appraisal to be initialized. The graphical interface of this feature has a component that lists all the appraisals with the "Created" status, so that they can be automatically initiated,
- Appraisal Storage: this enables the reports produced by the appraisal to be stored in the tool,
- Appraisal Diagnosis: this allows the appraisal to be diagnosed after the reports have been loaded in the repository (see Fig. 2). This means that the user can select the process and the appraisal is carried out in the dialogue box. Then the tool generates a diagnosis chart, which shows the number of strengths, weaknesses, opportunities and threats achieved as the result of an appraisal. The graphical interface of this feature has a component that lists all the appraisals with the "Finished" status,
- Diagnosis of Reading: this shows the users all the diagnosis items of the appraised processes that have been created,
- Appraisal Consolidation: this gathers together and disseminates the information generated by the appraisals.

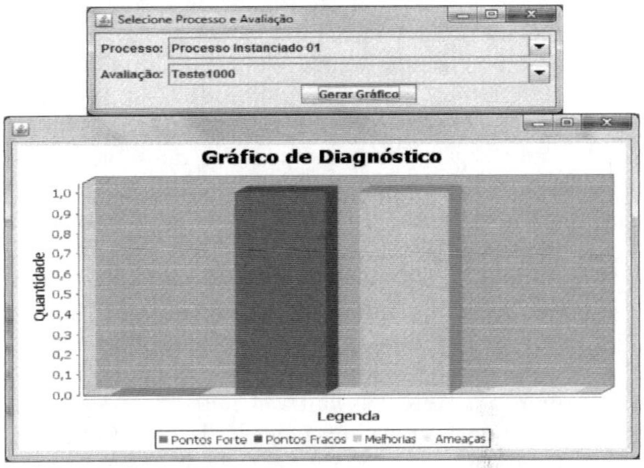

Figure 2. Screen for the Generation of the Diagnosis Chart

The following section describes the support tool that is employed to improve the software process on the basis of the appraisal results obtained.

C. Spider-PI: The Software Process Improvement Tool

Spider-PI also has a General Public License (GPL) and is designed to systematize the business process improvement activities in compliance with quality models and standards. It was developed from preliminary studies, which included the preparation of process mapping based on quality models and standards, and the design of the process framework. The input for this tool comprises the results of the appraisal generated by the Software Process Appraisal Tool. This is formed of the strengths, weaknesses, opportunities and threats that will be addressed in an automated way. This tool has the following features:

- New Improvement Creation: this enables new improvements to be recorded. In this feature, the user can "create an improvement", by filling some fields of the feature,
- Improvement Setup: this enables the improvement to be initialized. The graphical interface of this feature has a component that lists all the improvements with the "Created" status, which can be automatically initiated,
- Improvement Display: this shows users all the process improvements that have been created,
- Defining the Reason for Improvement: this enables the users to create the reason / goal of the improvement,
- Defining Improvement Practices: this allows the users to define the necessary practices required to make the improvement,
- Defining the Improvement Domain: this allows the

users to create the goals, existing works and benefits, which can be achieved / obtained by the improvement,

- Defining the Improvement Sponsorship: this enables the sponsor to give his / her approval of the improvement implementation and to give continuous support,
- Defining the Improvement Infrastructure: this provides the information about the infrastructure designed for the improvement, such as the human effort that must be expended to make the improvement,
- Characterizing Improvement Practices: this makes it possible to characterize the current practices and set out the goals for achieving the improvement implementation,
- Defining the Improvement Procedures: this enables the users to define the procedures that must be followed for the completion of the improvement,
- Defining the Priorities for the Implementation of Practices: this sets out the range of priorities for implementing the improvement in the practices,
- Defining the Improvement Plan: this allows the improvement implementation plan to be defined,
- Creating the "Improvement Solution": this prepares the improvement solution,
- Testing the "Improvement Solution": this tests the improvement solution that has been formulated,
- Deploying the "Improvement Solution": this enables the "improvement solution" to be deployed,
- Analysis and Validation of the Improvement: this validates the improvement, as shown in Fig. 3. The user selects the improvement practice that has been implemented in the process. After this, the system displays the planned state (both before and after the improvement has been made). Then, the user performs the validation of the practice implementation in the process on the basis of a set of criteria and metrics that have been previously defined. As a result, this user can report the experiences obtained from the improvement implementation. At the end of this feature, a status is defined to show the "improvement practice" that has been implemented by the user,

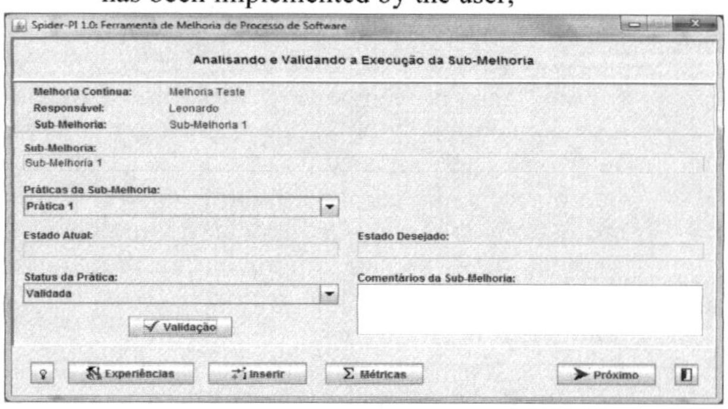

Figure 3. Screen showing the Analysis and Validation of the Improvement Implementation

- Proposing Future Activities: this allows future activities to be carried out so that they can be performed with a view to bringing about an improvement.

These tools are designed as desktop environments, using Java programming language and other free technologies, such as Eclipse 3.7 Integrated Development Environment (IDE), MySQL 5.5 Database Management System (DBMS), Hibernate 4.0 for object-relational mapping, XStream a simple library for serializing objects into eXtensible Markup Language (XML), and iText as the library for creating and manipulating the Protable Document Format (PDF). For a full description of the tools and each feature, see the work of Mezzomo [27].

It should be emphasized that these tools are used in sequence, and follow the management lifecycle of the software process: definition, execution, evaluation and improvement. These tools interoperate with each other as follows: (i) the definition tool generates a software process with the assets (Spider-PM), (ii) this process should be planned, executed and managed by the allocated staff (Spider-PE [33]). Then (iii) the process can be appraised by objective criteria and / or metrics to identify the strengths, weaknesses, opportunities and threats (Appraisal Tool), and (iv) the appraisal results are implemented by means of the improvement practices in the software process (Spider-PI).

IV. TOOLS EVALUATION

This section describes the evaluation of tools in the software industry and their adherence to CMMI-DEV.

A. Application in the Software Industry

The tools were used during the implementation of CMMI-DEV Maturity Level 3 in a Brazilian software development organization called Emprel, and gave support to the practices included in the Organizational Process Definition (OPD) and OPF process areas. The organization was assessed at this level and obtained a certificate issued by the CMMI Institute.

The users of the tools stated that their use facilitated the generation of historical data. As a result of the continuous appraisal process, there was a greater improvement in traceability made by the appraisals, together with the process versions that were established. This led to a more efficient and effective means of managing the implementation of the OPD and OPF process areas. It can be stated that the tool helped the organization in the following areas:

- Establishing organizational process needs,
- Appraising the business processes of the organization,
- Identifying the process improvements of the organization,
- Establishing process action plans,
- Implementing process action plans,
- Deploying organizational process assets,
- Adopting standard processes,
- Monitoring the implementation,

- Incorporating experiences into the assets of the organizational process.

B. Adherence to CMMI-DEV

The analysis of the adherence of the tools was conducted through the mapping of the features outlined in Section III with the specific practices included in the OPF process area that can be found in CMMI-DEV. A specific practice can be defined as "the description of an activity that is considered important in achieving the associated specific goal, i.e. it describes the activities that are expected to result in the achievement of the specific goals of a CMMI process area" [6]. In the OPF process area of CMMI-DEV, there are nine specific practices. The details of each of the recommendations for the specific practices listed in the first column of Table I, can be obtained by consulting the official guide of the CMMI-DEV model [6].

TABLE I. ADHERENCE BETWEEN THE APPRAISAL AND IMPROVEMENT TOOL TO CMMI-DEV

OPF Specific Practices	Process Tool Functionalities	Degree of Adherence
SP1.1 Establish Organizational Process Needs	Appraisal Creation	Fully Implemented
SP 1.2 Appraise the Organization's Processes	Appraisal Setrup	Fully Implemented
SP 1.3 Identify the Organization's Process Improvements	Appraisal Diagnosis, Appraisal Consolidation	Fully Implemented
SP 2.1 Establish Process Action Plans	Defining the Improvement Practices, Defining the Improvement Domain, Defining the Improvement Plan	Fully Implemented
SP 2.2 Implement Process Action Plans	Creating the Improvement Solution, Testing the Improvement Solution	Fully Implemented
SP 3.1 Deploy Organizational Process Assets	Deploying the Improvement Solution	Fully Implemented
SP 3.2 Deploy Standard Processes	Deploying the Improvement Solution	Fully Implemented
SP 3.3 Monitor the Implementation	Analysing and Validating the Improvement	Fully Implemented
SP 3.4 Incorporate Experiences into Organizational Process Assets	Proposing Future Actions	Fully Implemented

It can be seen that the features of the tools implement all the CMMI-DEV specific practices of the OPF process area, and hence it can be assumed that the tools are adherent to CMMI-DEV and support the process appraisal and improvement.

V. OBTAINED RESULTS

This section describes the obtained results of this work in both the academic world and industry.

A. In the Academic World

An initial version of this thesis proposal has been published and presented at a conference called Workshop of Theses and Dissertations in Software Quality (WTDQS) [28]. This research can be characterized as a subproject of the SPIDER Project, and was accepted in the 2011/2012 cycles of the Brazilian Program of Software Quality and Productivity. In 2011, the framework employed in the implementation of the tools was published in the Symposium of Computer Technology at Santarém (SIGES) [29] and Conference of the Peruvian Society of Computing (CSPC) [30] conferences. The framework and tools were the subject of a dissertation that was defended at the Federal University of Pará (Graduate Program in Computer Science) [27].

The main academic results were as follows: the training of one post-graduate student in Computer Science, the training of two students from a scientific background, and the dissemination of knowledge about process appraisal and improvement in subjects involving experimental software engineering applied to practical projects. Thus, the knowledge used for the development of software tools served to improve the practical understanding of the concepts defined by the quality models.

B. In Industry

The authors took part in consultation projects related to process improvement and made use of the technologies examined in this paper. First, the tools were used by organizations, which are partners of the SPIDER project, such as Jambu Tecnologia and GOL Software, both located in Belém city, and SWQuality and Emprel, located in Recife city. Basically, the tools assisted in the appraisal and improvement stages by defining and monitoring the projects. On the other hand, the activities carried out by the Framework are widely adopted in the implementation of the CMMI-DEV Maturity Level 3 in organizations in which the authors act as consultants; these are, located at Porto Digital (Recife city) and Farol Digital (João Pessoa city).

The main results for industry were as follows: the support given for the implementation of practices on software process appraisal and improvement that are included in the quality models, the systematic implementation of the appraisal and improvement process, and the training of business teams in software process appraisal and improvement. Thus, the tool can be seen as providing support for the implementation of quality models as well as for the education of personnel in the area of software process appraisal and improvement.

VI. CONCLUSION

The development of organizational process appraisal and improvement tools is intended to support the process appraisal and improvement activities that involve the good practices defined by the quality models and standards. However, our goal is to facilitate the adoption of these models and standards for software development organizations by means of these tools. A striking feature of this proposal is the fact that the tools are open source, and can thus enable the academic community and / or industry to assist in their development and evolution. The use of tools can also help the software organizations to achieve more satisfactory levels of discipline through the combination of techniques and methods that assist in the appraisal and improvement of its processes.

The main contribution to science made by this work concerns the automated application of practices in CMMI-DEV on organizational process appraisal and improvement, which involve tools and their integration with other management support tools. As well as this, the software process improvement programs continually benefit from the results that generate value to the organization.

In a future work, which is already in development, the integration of these tools with other tools will be made available in a SPIDER project. This entails a joint implementation of the other process areas included in CMMI-DEV, such as configuration management, measurement and analysis.

It should be stressed that this work has provided a set of basic support tools for the implementation of an organizational process improvement program. These tools are integrated with other tools that support different process areas included in the CMMI-DEV. Moreover, this work forms a part of a master's thesis for the Graduate Program in Computer Science and also a scientific research project at the Faculty of Computing, Federal University of Pará.

ACKNOWLEDGMENTS

The authors would like to thank the Dean of Research and Postgraduate Studies at the Federal University of Pará (PROPESP/UFPA) by the Qualified Publication Support Program (PAPQ), for the financial support.

REFERENCES

[1] A. Fuggetta, "Software Process: A Roadmap", In: Proceedings of The Future of Software Engineering, (ICSE'2000), Ireland, pp. 25-34, 2000.

[2] L. Morais, "Software Quality - Unraveling an essential requirement in the development process", Revista de Engenharia de Software, ed. 29, ano 3, pp. 34-38, 2010

[3] S. R. B. Oliveira, "ProDefiner: A Progressive Approach to Software Process Definition in a Process Centered Environment Domain", Tese de Doutorado, CIN/UFPE, Brazil, 2007.

[4] W. S. Humphrey, Managing the Software Process, The SEI Series in Software Engineering, Addison-Wesley, 1989.

[5] R. A. Falbo, "Knowledge Integration in a Software Development Environment", Tese de Doutorado, COPPE/UFRJ, Brazil, 1998.

[6] SEI – Software Engineering Institute, "CMMI for Development – V 1.3", 2010, Available: http://www.sei.cmu.edu/reports/10tr033.pdf, [retrieved: July, 2016].

[7] A. Koscianski and M. S. Soares, Software Quality - Learn the More Modern Methodologies and Techniques to Software Development, 2ed, São Paulo: Novatec, 2007.

[8] P. Kruchten, Introduction to RUP – Rational Unified Process, Rio de Janeiro: Ciência Moderna, 2003.

[9] SOFTEX – Associação para Promoção do Software Brasileiro, "MPS Software General Guide 2012", 2013, Avaiable: http://www.softex.br/wp-content/uploads/2016/04/MPS.BR_Guia_Geral_Software_2016-com-ISBN.pdf, [retrieved: July, 2016].

[10] ISO/IEC, "ISO/IEC 12207: Systems and software engineering – Software life cycle processes", Geneve, 2008.

[11] S. Oliveira, M. Souza, W. Lira, E. Yoshidome, and J. Furtado, "A System Solution Proposal of a Free Software Tools SUITE to Support the Implementation of MPS.BR Model", Revista do Programa Brasileiro de Qualidade e Produtividade em Software, pp. 103-107, 2011.

[12] ISO/IEC, "ISO/IEC 15504-1: Information Technology - Process Assessment - Part 1: Concepts and Vocabulary", Geneve, 2004.

[13] W. A. Florac and A. D. Carleton, Measuring the Software Process – Statistical Process Control for Software Process Improvement, Addison-Wesley, 1999.

[14] S. Zaharan, S. Software Process Improvement – Practical Guidelines for Business Success, Addison-Wesley, 1998.

[15] S. L. Pfleeger, Software Engineering: theory and practice, 2nd edition, Prentice-Hall, Inc., ISBN 0-13-029049-1, 2001.

[16] B. Collier, T. DeMarco, and P. Fearey, "A defined process for project post mortem reviews", IEEE Software, pp. 65-72, 1996.

[17] E. Sales, M. Sales, A. Costa, C. Reis, and R. Reis, "WebAPSEE Pro: An Environment to Support hte Software Process Management", In: VI WAMPS, Brazil, pp. 228-237, 2010.

[18] B. França, E. Sales, C. Reis, and R. Reis, "Using the WebAPSEE Environment in the Implementation of the MPS.BR level G at CTIC-UFPA", In: VIII SBQS, Brazil, pp. 310-317, 2009.

[19] B. Mcfeeley, "IDEALSM: A User's Guide for Software Process Improvement", Software Engineering Institute Handbook, Carnegie Mellon University, CMU/SEI-96-HB-001, 1996.

[20] J. M. C. Xavier, "ProEvaluator: A Tool for Software Process Assessment", Dissertação de Mestrado, UFPE, Brazil, 2007.

[21] M. Montoni, G. Santos, S. Figueiredo, R. Silva, R. Barcelos, A. Barreto, A. Barreto, C. Cerdeiral, P. Lupo, and A. Rocha, "A Software Process and Product Quality Assurance Approach to Support Knowledge Management in TABA Station", In: V SBQS, Brazil, pp. 87-99, 2006.

[22] G. H. Travassos, "The Tools Integration Model of TABA Station", Tese de Doutorado, COPPE/UFRJ, Brazil, 1994.

[23] J. Andrade, "Software Process Assessment in TABA Environment", Dissertação de Mestrado, COPPE-UFRJ, Brazil, 2005.

[24] R. C. Silva Filho, A. R. C. Rocha, and G. H. Travassos, "An Approach for Improvement Proposal Evaluation in Software Processes", In: VI SBQS, Brazil, pp. 485-499, 2007.

[25] R. Hunter, G. Robinson, and I. Woodman, "Tool Support for Software Process Assessment and Improvement", University if Strathclyde, Department of Computer Science, 1997.

[26] J. Neiva, "The Proposal for a Framework and Systemic Support for Process Assessment Based on MA-MPS, SCAMPI and ISO/IEC 15504", PBQP Software, SEPIN/MCTI, pp. 121-127, 2010.

[27] L. P. Mezzomo, "A Framework for Software Process Assessment and Improvement Adhering CMMI, MR-MPS-SW and ISO/IEC 12207", Dissertação de Mestrado, UFPA, Brazil, 2015.

[28] L. P. Mezzomo and S. R. B. Oliveira, "A Proposal of Tools to Support the Organizational Process Evaluation and Improvement Process in Software Quality Models and Standards Domain", WTDQS - SBQS, Brazil, pp. 35-42, 2012.

[29] L. P. Mezzomo and S. R. B. Oliveira, "Framework for Organizational Process Definition, Evaluation and Based on Quality Models", I SIGES, Brazil, pp. 56-66, 2011.

[30] L. P. Mezzomo and S R. B. Oliveira, "An Approach to Software Process Definition, Evaluation and Improvement in the Software Quality Models and Standards Domain", X CSPC, Peru, pp. 97-106, 2011.

[31] T. S. A. Costa, B. W. F. V. Silva, D. J. S. Teixeira, G. P. Silva, P. J. S. Souza, A. I. X. M. Batista, S. R. B. Oliveira, and A. M. L. Vasconcelos, "Spider-MSControl: A Tool for Support to the Measurement Process using GQIM Approach", In: Software

Engineering and Applications, USA, pp. 55-62, 2015, Avaiable: http://www.spider.ufpa.br, [retrieved: July, 2016].

[32] R. S. Barros and S. R. B. Oliveira, "Spider-CL: A Tool for Support to use Objective Criteria in the Software Quality Domain", In: ERIN, Brazil, pp. 112-120, 2010, Avaiable: http://www.spider.ufpa.br, [retrieved: July, 2016].

[33] C. Portela, A. Vasconcelos, S. Oliveira, A. Silva, and E. Silva, "Spider-PE: A Set of Support Tools to Sotware Process Enactement", In: The Ninth International Conference on Software Engineering Advances, France, pp. 539-544, 2014.

A New Algorithm to Parse a Mathematical Expression and its Application to Create a Customizable Programming Language

Vassili Kaplan
Zurich, Switzerland
e-mail: vassilik@gmail.com

Abstract—**This paper presents an algorithm to parse a string containing a mathematical expression. This algorithm represents an alternative to other parsing algorithms, e.g., the Dijkstra "shunting-yard" algorithm. The algorithm presented here, has the same time complexity, but in our point of view it is easier to implement and to extend. As an example of extending this algorithm, we also present how it can be used to implement a fully customizable scripting programming language. The reference implementation language will be C++.**

Keywords: software development; software engineering; algorithm; parsing; scripting language; programming language.

I. Introduction

There are already a few parsing algorithms. E. Dijkstra invented his "shunting-yard" algorithm to parse a mathematical expression in 1961 [1]. The Look-Ahead Left-to-Right (LALR) parser was invented by F. DeRemer in 1969 [2]. It is based on the so called "bottom-up" parsing. The LALR parser can be even automatically generated by YACC [3]. There are also a few algorithms for the "top-down" parsers, e.g., a Recursive Descent Parser [4], which is based on the LL(k) grammar (Left-to-right, Leftmost derivation) [5]. The ANTLR [6] is a widely used tool to automatically generate parsers based on the LL(*) grammar. In particular, the ANTLR can even generate the Recursive Descent Parser.

Why would we want to develop yet another parsing algorithm if there are so many around, including even the parser generating tools? Aside from its own interest, we believe that it is much easier to implement in an object-oriented language. It is also much easier to extend, i.e., to add your own functionality. As an example of extending the language, we will show how one can implement a scripting language from scratch, without using any external libraries. One can add new functions to the language on the fly. One can also add programming language keywords in any human language with just a few configuration changes, which we will also illustrate in this article.

We have presented an alternative to this algorithm in [7][8][9]. We call this alternative algorithm the "split-and-merge" algorithm, because, analogous to other parsing algorithms, it consists of two steps. In the first step, we split the whole expression into the list of so called "cells". Each cell consists of a number and an "action" to be applied to that cell. In the second step, we merge all the cells together according to the priorities of the "actions". In this article, we extend this work and show a more generalized parsing algorithm.

There is already a reference implementation of a scripting language using the split-and-merge algorithm in C# [10]. But the language described there was not very mature. In particular, there is a section towards the end of the article that mentions some of the missing features. Here, we are going to show how to implement those features, and a few more.

For simplicity, we will continue calling the parsing algorithm as the "split-and-merge" algorithm and the scripting language created by using that algorithm as **C**ustomized **S**cripting in **C**++ using the **S**plit-and-merge algorithm ("CSCS").

The rest of this paper is organized as follows. Section II presents the split-and-merge algorithm. Section III shows how to register variables and functions with the parser. Section IV addresses writing of custom functions in CSCS. Section V describes the try, throw and catch control flow statements. Section VI shows how to provide CSCS keywords in any human language. Summary and conclusions appear in Section VII.

II. The Split-and-Merge Algorithm

Here, we are going to generalize the split-and-merge algorithm described in [7][8][9]. The algorithm can parse not only a mathematical expression but any language statement. A separation character must separate all the statements. We define this separation character as a semicolon, ";".

The algorithm consists of two steps.

In the first step, we split the given string into the list of objects, called "Variables". Each "Variable" consists of an intermediate result (a number, a string, or an array of other Variables) and an "action" that must be applied to this Variable. In in [1][2][3], we called this "Variable" a "Cell" and it could have only a numerical result.

The last element of the created list of Variables has a so called "null action", which, for convenience, we denote by the character ")". It has the lowest priority of 0.

For numbers, an action can be any of "+", "-", "*", "/", "%", "&&", "||", and some others. For strings, only "+" (concatenation) and logical operators "<", "<=", ">", ">=", "==", "!=" are defined.

Listing 1 contains a part of the Variable definition:

```
struct Variable {
  string toString() const;

  bool canMergeWith(const Variable& right);
  void merge(const Variable& right);

  void mergeNumbers(const Variable& right);
  void mergeStrings(const Variable& right);

  static int getPriority(const string& action);
  // ------------------
```

```
    double numValue;
    string strValue;
    vector<Variable> tuple;
    string action;
    string varname;
    Constants::Type type;
};
```

Listing 1: Variable data structure

The separation criteria for splitting the string into Variables are: an action, an expression in parentheses, or a function, previously registered with the parser. We are going to describe how to register a function with the parser in the next section. In case of an expression in parentheses or a function, we apply recursively the whole split-and-merge algorithm to that expression in parentheses or the function argument in order to get a Variable object as a result. So, at the end of the first step, we are going to have a list of Variables, each one having an action to be applied to the next Variable in the list. See the main parsing cycle of the first part of the algorithm in Listing 2.

```
do { // Main processing cycle of the first part.
  char ch = data[from++];
  string action = Constants::EMPTY;
  bool keepCollecting =  stillCollecting(data, from,
                         parsingItem, to, action);
  if (keepCollecting) {
    // The char still belongs to the previous operand
    parsingItem += ch;

    if (contains(to, data[from])) {
            continue;
    }
  }
  ParserFunction func(data, from, parsingItem,
                      ch, action);
  Variable current = func.getValue(data, from);

  char  next  =  from  <  data.size()  ?  data[from]  :
        NULL_CHAR;

  bool done = listToMerge.empty() &&
    (action == NULL_ACTION || next == END_STATEMENT);
  if (done) { // Not a math expression.
    listToMerge.push_back(current);
    return listToMerge;
  }
  current.action = action;
  listToMerge.push_back(current);
  parsingItem.clear();
} while (from < data.size() &&
        !contains(to, data[from]));
```

Listing 2: The split part of the split-and-merge algorithm

The second step consists in merging the list of Variables created in the first step, according to the priorities of their actions. The priorities of the actions are defined in Listing 3.

```
unordered_map<string, int> prio;
    prio["++"] = 10;
    prio["--"] = 10;
    prio["^"]  = 9;
    prio["%"]  = 8;
    prio["*"]  = 8;
    prio["/"]  = 8;
    prio["+"]  = 7;
    prio["-"]  = 7;
    prio["<"]  = 6;
    prio[">"]  = 6;
    prio["<="] = 6;
    prio[">="] = 6;
    prio["=="] = 5;
    prio["!="] = 5;
    prio["&&"] = 4;
    prio["||"] = 3;
    prio["+="] = 2;
    prio["-="] = 2;
    prio["*="] = 2;
    prio["/="] = 2;
    prio["%="] = 2;
    prio["="]  = 2;
```

Listing 3: Priorities of the actions

Two Variable objects can only be merged together if the priority of the action of the Variable on the left is greater or equal than the priority of the action of the Variable on the right. Otherwise, we merge the Variable on the right with the Variable on its right first, and so on, recursively. As soon as the right Variable has been merged with the Variable next to it, we return back to the original, left Variable, and try to re-merge it with the newly created right Variable. Note that eventually we will be able to merge the entire list since the last variable in this list has a null action with the priority zero.

The implementation of the second step is shown in Listing 4. The function merge() is called from outside with the mergeOneOnly parameter set to false.

```
Variable Parser::merge(Variable& current, size_t&
 index, vector<Variable>& listToMerge, bool mergeOne) {
  while (index < listToMerge.size()) {
    Variable& next = listToMerge[index++];

    while (!current.canMergeWith(next)) {
      merge(next, index, listToMerge,
            true/*mergeOne*/);
    }
    current.merge(next);
    if (mergeOne) {
      break;
    }
  }
  return current;
}
```

Listing 4: The merge part of the split-and-merge algorithm

*A. Example of parsing 1 – 2*sin(0)*

Let us see the algorithm in action, applying it to the "1 – 2*sin(0)" string. "1-" and "2*" tokens are parsed and converted into Variables directly, without any problem:

Split(1 – 2*sin(0)) →
  Variable(numValue = 1, action = "-"),
  Varaible(numValue = 2, action = "*"),
  Split-And-Merge(sin(0)).

To proceed, we need to process the "sin(0)" string first, applying the whole spilt-and-merge algorithm to it.

When the parser gets the "sin" token, it maps it to the sine function registered earlier (we will discuss registering functions in the next section). Then the parser evaluates the sin(0) and returns 0 as a result.

Therefore, the result of splitting the original string "1 – 2*sin(0)" will be a list consisting of three Variables:

1. Variable(numValue = 1, action = "-")
2. Varaible(numValue = 2, action = "*")
3. Varaible(numValue = 0, action = ")")

In the second step of the algorithm, we merge the resulting list of variables one by one.

Note that we cannot merge directly the first Variable with the second one since the priority of the action of the first Variable "-", is less than the priority of the action of the second variable, "*", according to the Listing 3. Therefore, we need to merge first Variables 2 and 3. The priority of the "*" action is greater than the priority of the null action ")" (the last Variable in the list has always a "null" action). So we can merge 2 and 0: applying the action "*", the result will be 2 * 0 = 0. The resulting variable will inherit the action from the right Variable, i.e., the "null" action ")".

Now we return back to the first Variable and merge it with the newly created Variable(numValue = 0, ")"). Applying action "-" to the both variables we get the final result: 1 – 0 = 0. Therefore, the split-and-merge("1 – 2*sin(0)") = 0.

Using the algorithm above with the recursion, it is possible to parse any compound CSCS expression. The architectural diagram of the split-and-merge algorithm and its usage to parse a string appears in Figure 1. Here is an example of the CSCS code:

```
x = sin(pi^2);
cache["if"] = -10 * x;
cache["else"] = 10 * x;
if (x < 0 && log(x + 3*10^2) < 6*exp(x) ||
              x < 1 - pi) {
  print("in if, cache=", cache["if"]);
} else {
  print("in else, cache=", cache["else"]);
}
```

The code above has a few functions (sin(), exp(), log(), print()) and a few control flow statements (if, else). How does the parser know what to do with them?

III. Registering Variables and Functions with the Parser

All the functions that can be added to the parser must derive from the ParserFunction class. Listing 5 contains an excerpt from the ParserFunction class definition.

```
class ParserFunction {
public:
  ParserFunction(const string& data, size_t& from,
       const string& item, char ch, string& action);

  Variable getValue(const string& data, size_t& from){
    return m_impl->evaluate(data, from);
  }
protected:
  virtual Variable evaluate(const string& data,
                            size_t& from) = 0;
  Variable::emptyInstance;
  static StringOrNumberFunction* s_strOrNumFunction;
  static IdentityFunction*       s_idFunction;
}
```

Listing 5: The ParserFunction class definition

The Identity is a special function, which is called when we have an argument in parentheses. It just calls the main entry method of the split-and-merge algorithm to load the whole expression in parentheses:

```
class IdentityFunction : public ParserFunction {
public:
  virtual Variable evaluate(const string& data,
                            size_t& from) {
    return Parser::loadAndCalculate(data, from);
  }
};
```

The parser will call the evaluate() method on any class deriving from the ParserFunction class as soon as the parser gets a token corresponding to the function registered with the parser. There are three basic steps to register a function with the parser:

- Define the function keyword token, i.e., the name of the function in the scripting language, CSCS, e.g.:

```
static const string SIN; // in Constants.h
const string Constants::SIN = "sin"; // in .cpp
```

- Implement the class to be mapped to the keyword from the previous step. Basically, the evaluate() method must be overridden. E.g., for the sin() function:

```
class SinFunction : public ParserFunction {
public:
  virtual Variable evaluate(const string& data,
                            size_t& from) {
     Variable arg = Parser::loadAndCalculate(
                            data, from);
     return ::sin(arg.numValue);
  }
};
```

loadAndCalculate() is the main parser entry point, which calculates the value of the passed expression.

- Map the object of the class, implemented in the previous step, with the previously defined keyword as follows:

```
ParserFunction::addGlobalFunction(Constants::SIN,
                              new SinFunction());
```

The addGlobalFunction() method just adds a new entry to the global dictionary used by the parser to map the keywords to functions:

```
void ParserFunction::addGlobalFunction(const string&
                name, ParserFunction* function) {
  auto it = s_functions.find(name);
  if (it != s_functions.end()) {
    delete it->second;
  }
  s_functions[name] = function;
}
```

Similarly, we can register any function with the parser, e.g., if(), while(), try(), throw(), etc.

We can also define local or global variables in the same way. In the next section, we are going to see how to define functions in CSCS and add passed arguments as local variables to CSCS.

IV. Writing Functions in CSCS

To write a custom function in the scripting language, two functions had to be introduced in C++, FunctionCreator and CustomFunction, both deriving from the ParserFunction base class. As soon as the Parser gets a token with the "function" keyword, it will call the evaluate() method on the FunctionCreator object, see Listing 6.

```
Variable FunctionCreator::evaluate(const string& data,
                                   size_t& from) {
  string funcName = Utils::getToken(data,
```

```
                                  from, TOKEN_SEPARATION);
  vector<string> args =
         Utils::getFunctionSignature(data, from);
  string body = Utils::getBody (data, from, '{', '}');
  CustomFunction* custFunc = new CustomFunction(
                               funcName, body, args);
  ParserFunction::addGlobalFunction(
                          funcName, custFunc);
  return Variable(funcName);
}
```

Listing 6: The function creator class

Basically, it just creates a new object, CustomFunction, and initializes it with the extracted function body and the list of parameters. It also registers the name of the custom function with the parser, so the parser maps that name with the new CustomFunction object, which will be called as soon as the parser encounters the function name keyword.

So all of the functions that we implement in the CSCS code correspond to different instances of the CustomFunction class. The custom function does primarily two things, see Listing 7. First, it extracts the function arguments and adds them as local variables to the Parser (they will be removed from the Parser as soon as the function execution is finished or an exception is thrown). It also checks that the number of actual parameters is equal to the number of the registered ones (this part is skipped for brevity).

```
Variable CustomFunction::evaluate(const string& data,
                                   size_t& from) {
  vector<Variable> args = Utils::getArgs(data, from,
                                   START_ARG, END_ARG);
  // 1. Add passed arguments as locals to the Parser.
  StackLevel stackLevel(m_name);

  for (size_t i = 0; i < m_args.size(); i++) {
    stackLevel.variables[m_args[i]] = args[i];
  }
  ParserFunction::addLocalVariables(stackLevel);

  // 2. Execute the body of the function.
  size_t funcPtr = 0;
  Variable result;

  while (funcPtr < m_body.size() - 1) {
    result = Parser::loadAndCalculate(m_body, funcPtr);
    Utils::goToNextStatement(m_body, funcPtr);
  }
  // 3. Return the last result of the execution.
  ParserFunction::popLocalVariables();
  return result;
}
```

Listing 7: The custom function class

Secondly, the body of the function is evaluated, using the main parser entry point, the loadAndCalculate() method.

If the body contains calls to other functions, or to itself, the calls to the CustomFunction can be recursive.

Let us see this with an example of a function implemented in CSCS. It calculates the so called Catalan numbers (named after a Belgian mathematician Eugène Catalan), see Listing 8.

```
// Catalan numbers function implemented in CSCS.
// C(0) = 1, C(n+1) = Sum(C(i) * C(n - i)), i: 0-> n
// for n >= 0. Equivalent to:
// C(n) = 2 * (2*n - 1) / (n + 1) * C(n-1), n > 0
function catalan(n) {
  if (!isInteger(n)) {
    exc = "Catalan is for integers only (n="+ n +")";
    throw (exc);
  }
  if (n < 0) {
    exc = "Negative number (n="+ n +") supplied";
    throw (exc);
  }
  if (n <= 1) {
    return 1;
  }
  return 2 * (2*n - 1) / (n + 1) * catalan(n - 1);
}
```

Listing 8: Recursive calculation of Catalan numbers implemented in CSCS

The Catalan function above uses an auxiliary isInteger() function:

```
function isInteger(candidate) {
  return candidate == round(candidate);
}
```

isInteger() function calls yet another, round() function. The implementation of the round() function is already in the C++ code and is analogous to the implementation of the sine function that we saw in the previous section.

To execute the Catalan function with different arguments, we can use the following CSCS code:

```
try {
  c = catalan(n);
  print("catalan(", n, ")=", c);
} catch(exc) {
  print("Caught: " + exc);
}
```

It gets the following output for different values of n:

```
Caught: Catalan is for integers only (n=1.500000) at
  catalan()
Caught: Negative number (n=-10) supplied at
  catalan()
catalan(10)=16796
```

Since the exception happened at the global level, the exception stack printed consisted only of the catalan() function itself.

The CSCS code above contains try(), throw(), and catch() control flow statements. How are they implemented in C++?

V. Throw, Try, and Catch Control Flow Statements

The throw() and try() control flow statements can be implemented as functions in the same way you saw the implementation of the sine function above. The catch() is not implemented as a separate function but is processed right after the try() block.

Both implementations derive from the ParserFunction class as well. First we show the more straightforward one, the throw() function:

```
Variable ThrowFunction::evaluate(const string& data,
                                  size_t& from) {
    // 1. Extract what to throw.
    Variable arg = Utils::getItem(data, from);

    // 2. Convert it to string.
    string result = arg.toString();

    // 3. Throw it!
    throw ParsingException(result);
}
```

The try() function requires a bit more work. Here is an excerpt:

```
Variable TryStatement::evaluate(
      const string& data, size_t& from) {
  size_t startTryCondition = from - 1;
  size_t stackLevel =
         ParserFunction::currStackLevel();
  ParsingException exception;
  Variable result;
  try {
    result = processBlock(data, from);
  }
  catch(ParsingException& exc) {
    exception = exc;
  }
```

First, we note where we started the processing (so later on we can return back to skip the whole try-catch block). Then, we simply process the try block, and if the exception is thrown, we catch it. In the parser code, we throw only exceptions of type ParsingException, which is a wrapper over the C++ std::exception.

If there is an exception, then we need to skip the whole catch block. For that, we go back to the beginning of the try block and then skip it.

```
if (!exception.msg().empty()) {
  from = startTryCondition;
  skipBlock(data, from);
}
```

After the try block, we expect a catch token and the name of the exception to be caught, regardless if the exception was thrown or not:

```
string catch = Utils::getNextToken(data, from);
if (CATCH_LIST.find(catch) == CATCH_LIST.end()) {
  throw ParsingException("Expected a catch but got ["+
                         catch +"]");
}
string excName = Utils::getNextToken(data, from);
```

The reader may have noticed that when checking if the "catch" keyword was following the try-block or not, we didn't compare the extracted token with the "catch" string, but with a CATCH_LIST. The reason is that the CATCH_LIST contains all possible translations of the "catch" keyword to any of the languages that the user may supply in the configuration file. How is a keyword translation added to the parser?

VI. PROVIDING KEYWORDS IN DIFFERENT LANGUAGES

One of the main advantages of writing a custom programming language is the possibility to have the keywords in any language (besides the "base" language, understandably chosen to be English).

Here is how we can add the custom keyword translations to the CSCS language.

First, we define them in a configuration file. Here is an incomplete example of a configuration file with Russian translations:

```
function     = функция
include      = включить
if           = если
else         = иначе
elif         = иначе_если
return       = вернуться
print        = печать
size         = размер
while        = пока
```

The same configuration file may contain an arbitrary number of languages. After reading the keyword translations, we add them to the parser one by one:

```
void addTranslation(const string& originalName,
                    const string& translation) {
  ParserFunction* originalFunction =
  ParserFunction::getFunction(originalName);
  if (originalFunction != 0) {
    ParserFunction::addGlobalFunction(
         translation, originalFunction);
  }

  tryAddToSet(originalName, translation, CATCH,
           CATCH_LIST);
  tryAddToSet(originalName, translation, ELSE,
           ELSE_LIST);
  // other sets
}
```

First, we try to add a translation to one of the registered functions (like sin(), cos(), round(), try(), throw(), etc.). Then, we try to add them to the sets of additional keywords, that are not functions (e.g., the "catch" is processed only together with the try-block, the "else" and "else if" are processed only within the if-block, etc.

The tryAddToSet() is an auxiliary template function that adds a translation to a set in case the original keyword name belongs to that set (e.g., CATCH = "catch" belongs to the CATCH_LIST).

Here is the implementation of some CSCS code using Russian keywords. The code below just goes over the defined array of strings in the while loop and prints every other element of that list:

```
слова = {"Это", "написано", "по-русски"};
разм = размер(слова);
и = 0;
пока(и < разм) {
  если (и % 2 == 0) {
    печать(слова[и]);
  }
  и++;
}
```

VII. CONCLUSIONS AND FUTURE WORK

In this paper, we presented an algorithm to parse a string containing an expression and then we saw how we can apply this algorithm to parse a customized scripting programming language, that we called CSCS.

The implementation of the sin() function and throw() and try() control flow statements was shown. We saw that implementing a math function and a control flow statement is basically the same: one needs to write a new class, deriving from the ParserFunction class, and override its evaluate() method. Then one needs to register that function with the parser, mapping it to a keyword. The evaluate() method will be called by the parser as soon as the parser extracts a keyword corresponding to this function. For the lack of space, we didn't show how to implement if(), while(), break, continue, and return control flow statements but they are all implemented analogously. The same applies to the prefix and postfix ++ and -- operators, that we did not have space to show.

Using the above approach of adding a new function to the parser, anything can be added to the CSCS language as long as it is possible to implement it in C++.

Even though the time complexity of the split-and-merge algorithm is the same as of the Dijkstra's algorithm (and the split-and-merge might be a bit slower since it uses a lot of recursions), we believe that the main advantage of the split-and-merge algorithm is in that it is easier to extend and add user specific code. It can be extended in two ways: one is to add new functions or control flow statements, and the second is to add keyword translations in any human language.

For the future, we plan to focus on extending the CSCS language: adding more features and more functions. CSCS already supports if-else, try-catch, throw, while, function, return, break, continue, and include file control flow statements; arrays with an unlimited number of dimensions (implemented as vectors) and dictionaries (also with an unlimited number of dimensions, implemented as unordered maps). We plan to add a few other data structures to CSCS as well.

We also plan to add more common operating system functions, for example a task manager, listing processes with a possibility to kill a process and a process scheduler system. The challenge there is that these functions are operating system dependent and require multiple implementations for each operating system. One could also add some external libraries, which hide the implementations for different operating systems, but our goal is not to have any external libraries at all.

Another idea is to extend CSCS towards a functional programming language, something like F# - where a few very short language constructs implement quite a few language statements behind the scenes. We believe that this is easy to implement using the split-and-merge function implementation approach.

References

[1] E. Dijkstra, "Shunting-yard algorithm", https://en.wikipedia.org/wiki/Shunting-yard_algorithm Retrieved: June 2016.

[2] F. DeRemer, T. Pennello, "Efficient Computation of LALR(1) Look-Ahead Sets". Transactions on Programming Languages and Systems (ACM) **4** (4): 615–649.

[3] Yet Another Compiler Compiler, YACC, https://en.wikipedia.org/wiki/Yacc. Retrieved: June 2016

[4] Recursive Descent Parser, https://en.wikipedia.org/wiki/Recursive_descent_parser Retrieved: June 2016.

[5] LL parser, https://en.wikipedia.org/wiki/LL_parser Retrieved: June 2016.

[6] ANTNLR, https://en.wikipedia.org/wiki/ANTLR Retrieved: June 2016.

[7] V. Kaplan, "Split and Merge Algorithm for Parsing Mathematical Expressions", ACCU CVu, 27-2, May 2015, http://accu.org/var/uploads/journals/CVu272.pdf Retrieved: June 2016.

[8] V. Kaplan, "Split and Merge Revisited", ACCU CVu, 27-3, July 2015, http://accu.org/var/uploads/journals/CVu273.pdf Retrieved: June 2016.

[9] V. Kaplan, "A Split-and-Merge Expression Parser in C#", MSDN Magazine, October 2015, https://msdn.microsoft.com/en-us/magazine/mt573716.aspx Retrieved: June 2016.

[10] V. Kaplan, "Customizable Scripting in C#", MSDN Magazine, February 2016, https://msdn.microsoft.com/en-us/magazine/mt632273.aspx Retrieved: June 2016.

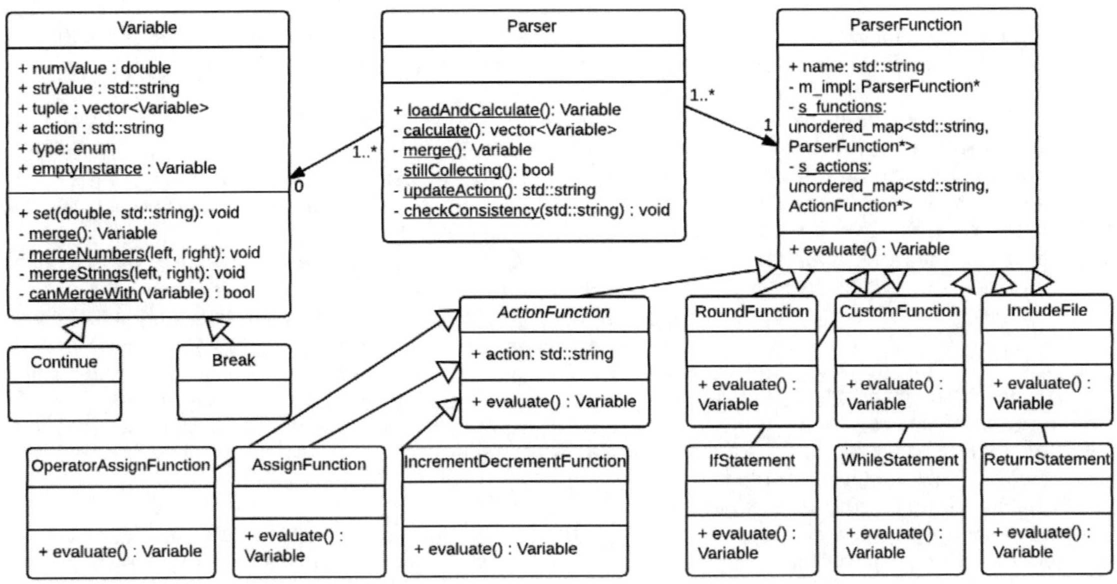

Figure 1. The Parser Framework UML Class Diagram

Proposed Data Model for a Historical Base Tool

Karine Santos Valença, Edna Dias Canedo, Ricardo Ajax D. Kosloski, and Sérgio A. A de Freitas
Faculdade UnB Gama - FGA
University of Brasília (UnB)
Caixa Postal 8114 – 72405-610
Brasília, DF, Brazil
E-mail: valenca.karine@gmail.com, ednacanedo@unb.br, ricardoajax@unb.br, sergiofreitas@unb.br

Abstract - Measurement processes, specifically in Software Engineering, are of great relevance to the success of an organization, though relevant data can only be obtained from systematic measurements. In this case, it is important to note that to attain proper results, the necessary inputs for collecting measures must be collected by the organisation itself. Therefore, organisations should have a measurement historical database that should be kept updated. In this paper we present a proposal where the users can define their metric using a historical database system built on the basis of metamodelling, so that they can create their metric, registering this metric in the system and, if necessary, modifying the definition of the metric without making changes to the application's source code. Furthermore, based on this metamodel, a data model was developed to support the application's software development. So, the use of our metamodel to build an organisational historical database software system means to boost the creation of new metrics, or to update the definitions of the metric already in existence and, in this way, improve the users' agility and flexibility to maintain the organisation's metric. The improvement in this aspect will reflect on the capability of the organisation to take advantage of the results from its measurements processes.

Keywords - Measurement; Systematic Mapping; Metamodelling; Goal Question Metric; Database.

I. INTRODUCTION

Measurement processes are fundamental for many types of organisations as regards their knowing, controlling, and streamlining their productive processes [6]. The Software Engineering domain is no different, as measurement processes allow the teams to understand its capabilities and thus allowing the planning and execution of solid software projects with respect to its costs, scopes, quality, risk and other variables [7]. Measurement processes cover a wide range of elements, amongst which the sub processes that define, collect, analyse, and report the results to the whole organisation and that are very important to support many different kinds of actions [6], [22].

In order to improve the organisation's agility and efficiency in the use of their measurement data, it is important that the majority of these sub processes is done in the most automated possible way. Moreover, the speed of their acquisition and precision of the measurement records will be vital to allow the continuous and critical analysis of comparative studies (benchmarking), as they are fundamental to support decisions about corrective and preventive actions, as well as for improvement opportunities in the organisation itself [14]. Beyond this, the actions and the measurable results of the organisation should be continuously evaluated to show that such actions and measurable results are always aligned with the improvement goals of the organisation [2], [22].

Based on corrective and preventive actions, the organisations should adjust their metric, which can be a big problem for their historical database systems if the organisation were to do huge maintenance work in the code of already-implemented applications.

A possible solution to boost the speed and efficiency in the updating of the organisation's historical database would be to deal with metamodelling resources.

In this kind of solution, the users could define the features of the metric adopted by the organisation without necessarily proceeding with code maintenance to run the organisation's historical database.

In this paper, the solution proposed has as one advantage the possibility to generate several measurements that comply with a given standard assumed by the organisation, by just defining or updating the definition of its metric.

This work aims at, as a general goal, using the concepts of metamodelling as a practical application to improve the maintainability of the software development organisation's historical database systems.

This paper is structured as follows: Section II presents the method for research used in this study, as well as the research questions that were defined. Section III presents a view of the results found until now, and Section IV provides the conclusions and our expectations for future work.

II. RESEARCH METHOD

Research was done as a systematic mapping literature review theory, to define research questions, find relevant publications, select the publications, and extract the data related to the research questions [17].

Questions related to the subject were proposed and a search strategy was created to answer them. The search strategy was the one defined by the Experimental Software Engineering area, to build a reliable knowledge base from the use of query strings applied to academic publications databases such as the ACM, IEEE, amongst others [20]. The publications that met the search criteria were selected to be part of the study.

A. Research Questions

Research questions were raised that were aligned with the goal of this work, to build a solid knowledge base that would lead to a metamodelling proposal for a measurement system. The measurement is the cornerstone of an experimental study, being defined as the mapping of the experimental world towards the formal or relational domain. The main goal of the mapping is to characterise and manipulate the attributes of empirical entities in a formal way. Instead of directly judging, based on real entities, the numbers or symbols are assigned to such entities, and the appraisal is done based on such numbers and symbols. The number or symbol attributed to the entity via the mapping is named measurement. The attribute of the entity under measurement is named metric [20].

The questions prepared were:

(QP1) What does the literature characterise as metamodelling?

(QP2) What is a measurement and what is its relevance in Software Engineering?

(QP3) Which metamodelling resources can be used to build a flexible measurement historical base?

(QP4) What data model can be used to create a flexible historical base tool?

B. Search Strategy

The search strategy included a manual search of publications found in the Computer Science and Software Engineering areas. For each item, and using related key-words, the research sources were the ACM Digital Library, IEEE Xplore, SpringerLink, and Science Direct.

The key words were picked according to the survey questions. At first, key words with a wider coverage were defined, to find the largest number possible of related publications. More precise, key words were defined during the execution of the survey, to answer some specific questions. Table 1 shows the key words used in the search and the number of papers found in each academic database.

Along with the publications found, we also discovered new research sources, using the snowball technique, to find research objects. This works as a chain where a research object provides other research sources which, in turn, spawn other sources, and so on [21]. As an example, paper [13] holds a simplistic definition of what the Goal Question Metric (GQM) method is and the reasons to use it. A reference to that section leads to publication [2], a paper with over 400 mentions, according to Google Scholar.

TABLE I. NUMBER OF PAPERS FOUND FOR EACH KEY WORD

Key word	ACM	IEEE Xplore	Springer Link	Science Direct
Metamodelling	697	539	2,088	1,189
Metamodelling software	466	275	1,722	802
GQM Method	11	41	936	519
Measurement metamodel	38	63	1,436	1,676
Goal Question Metric Metamodel	0	1	614	557

C. Criteria for Inclusion and Exclusion

After implementing and executing the search strategy, publications were included that had a title or abstract that referred to the theme of our research and published between 1989 and 2016. Year 1989 was chosen as a starting point since the oldest information of relevance to the theme occurred that year.

The exclusion criterion filtered out the papers with fewer than 10 mentions according to Google Scholar. As it is expected, the papers that were not widely referenced might not have the expected quality, or have a superficial approach of the subject.

With the goal of screening the publications, we read the abstract of the publications finally listed and verified whether they addressed some of the points raised earlier. From then on, 28 publications had been listed which, after a more detailed reading and analysis were cut down to 19 publications.

III. RESULTS

This section describes the results obtained after the systematic mapping of the selected papers.

A. Analysis of the First Research Question

(QP1) What does the literature characterise as metamodelling?

To answer this, a characterisation of metamodelling was done to then answer what metamodelling is. The following results were obtained.

Mellor, Clark, and Futagami define model as a grouping of components that describe physical and abstract things, or a hypothetical reality [16]. Rothenberg [18] characterises models as an abstraction from reality as models cannot represent all of its aspects. Thus, we can characterise models as a group of elements aimed at expressing/simplifying a given reality.

Models cannot represent reality with all of its particularities and, moreover, one could say that models do not need to represent all the aspects of reality. In creating a model, one can consider only the points that are relevant for the proposal and, as a result, using models allows dealing with reality in a more simplistic way, reducing its complexity and irreversibility [18].

Another important point of this simplicity relates to the visual representation of the model. In [15] it is said that 'each model will be expressed using a combination of text and multiple complementary and interrelated diagrams'. As a result, with the reduction of the aspects that would be represented, the model is visually cleaner and more organised.

To begin understanding what metamodelling is, it is interesting to look at the origin of the word. The word 'metamodel' is a variant of 'model' and thus it is understood that metamodelling is a specific kind of modelling [9]. Metamodelling is the act of producing metamodels. The word meta, according to the Oxford Dictionary, is of Greek origin and means 'behind' or 'after'. In the meaning that we seek, a metamodel means that which is behind a model.

In [14] a metamodel is defined as a model for a modelling language. For example, a model for the Unified Modelling Language (UML) is described by an UML metamodel which defines how models can be structured, as well as the elements they may contain [15]. The work presented by Clark [3] also states that a metamodel describes a modelling language with a higher level of abstraction than that of the modelling language [3]. To simplify these definitions we may conclude that a metamodel defines how a model should be constructed.

A metamodel is also considered as a model, although the metamodel captures the main features and properties of the language that will be modelled and, apart from that, a metamodel has its own architecture, named meta-metamodel which defines how metamodels should be described [3]. Thus, it is understood that the difference between a common model and a metamodel is that the information represented by a metamodel is actually a model [9].

The use of metamodelling has its benefits. It allows the definition of languages without the need for implementing technologies, focusing on the domain of the problem and promoting an increase of productivity throughout the development process [3].

B. Analysis of the Second Research Question

(QP2) What is a measurement and what is its relevance in Software Engineering?

As presented in [6] a measurement is 'the process through which numbers or symbols are assigned to attributes of entities in the real world in such a way as to describe them according to clearly defined rules'. This means that, through measurement, it is possible to describe something, through observation and recording, assigning numerical values to its characteristics.

The work presented Kan [11] states that a 'measurement is crucial to the progress of all sciences. Scientific progress is made through observations and generalizations based on data and measurements…' It is no different in Software Engineering, and measurements have a very important role to play in the success of organisations, as such measurement processes allow the software teams come to grips with their capacities. As a result, with measurements it is possible to carry out solid project planning that will not overshoot the planning done as regards the scope, quality, risk, and project length, as the measurement allows one to gain knowledge on the processes [7]. Apart from that, there are many characteristics in software projects that can be measured [12], strengthening the importance of measurement in this area.

Measurement in the domain of Software Engineering corresponds to the successive process of defining, collecting, and analysing data in the software development process, to understand and control the processes [19]. That is, through measurement, several useful items of information are studied and analysed and, through them, one can discover how the process is executed, what results are being generated in it, and also learn about managing the process, making the process better.

In the domain of measurement, and within Software Engineering, an approach is used, named Goal Question Metric (GQM) to define the measurements. GQM is an approach based on the premise that the measurements should be defined based on the measurement goals of the organisation, which in their turn generate questions which, again in their turn, can be answered via metric. Apart from that, the structure of the GQM provides a framework to interpret the measured data, using the established metric, and their associations with the questions put forward and the results measured, which serve as inputs to meet the measurement goals. [2].

The GQM method consists of defining goals and then refining them into questions aimed at characterising the object of the measurement, and supporting the interpretation of the data on the goals [2], [19]. It should be pointed that, for the questions to support interpretation in a satisfactory manner, the research points should be set on an intermediary level of abstraction [19], that is, neither being so specific, as regards the metric, nor abstract as regards the goals.

For each question, it is suggested that the measurement team creates hypotheses for them, and such hypotheses will be compared with the results obtained during the interpretation stage [19]. Defining the hypotheses is important as it serves to gauge the level of knowledge of the team on the processes executed.

The hypotheses are then refined into metric which is data aimed at answering the questions in a quantitative manner. The metric can either be objective or subjective [2].

The definition of the metric in the GQM is done on a top-down direction, meaning that at first a general perspective of the measurement is defined (the goal of the measurement) and after that it is processed into finer detail until the entire specification is reduced to base elements (metric) [5]. The method has 4 stages [19]:

Planning stage: Selection of the project to apply the measurement to; project definition, characterisation, and planning.

Definition stage: Definition and documenting of the goals, questions, metric, and hypotheses.

Data collection stage: Collection of the present data for the measurement project.

Interpretation stage: Analysis of the data as related to the set metric, answering to the questions raised; after that the evaluation takes place - whether the goal been reached.

An important activity takes place during the data collection stage. In it, a definition is made as to how the data will be collected, and how they will be filled in/entered, and how the data will be stored in a database [19]. It is important to store this data as, with the analysis of such historical data one will be able to identify patterns and also plan more adequately, as well as improve the processes in the organisation [7].

C. Analysis of the Third Research Question

(QP3) Which metamodelling resources can be used to build a flexible measurement historical base?

The metamodelling language requires a specific metamodelling architecture. The traditional metamodelling architecture has 04 meta-levels [3]:

M3: holds the meta-model that describes the properties all metamodels can display.

M2: holds the metamodel that captures the language.

M1: hold the application, and can contain the classes of an object-oriented system or the table for a relational database.

M0: holds the data of the application developed.

In using this architecture, the authors of work [8] propose a conceptual framework for measurement. Level M3 holds an abstract language for metamodel definition. Level M2 holds generic metamodels that will serve to create specific models. This level consists of the measurement metamodel and the domain metamodels that work to represent the types of entities eligible for measurement. Level M1 is that where the specific models are and it consists of the measurement and domain models. And Level M0 holds the data the users record in the applications [8].

Apart from the use of the architecture for the construction of a metamodel, one should define the abstract syntax, after defining the syntactic rules and the meta-operations, and define the concrete syntax, and define the semantics and, lastly, establish the relation with other modelling languages [3].

A metamodel should describe the concrete and abstract syntax, as well as the semantics of the model. The concrete syntax relates to the notation that facilitates the presentation and construction of the models, and may be text-based or visual-based. The abstract syntax describes the definition of concepts, the relationships that exist between them, and how they blend to create models [18]. Semantics gives meaning to each concept, in a well-defined and well-set manner [10]. The merger of these three factors allows the construction of a coherent and well-structured metamodel.

After the study on how to build a metamodel, a study was done of metamodels that had already been put forward by other authors on measurement. Figure 1 shows the measurement metamodel, using the GQM method, developed based on [4], [8], [19].

According to the GQM method, it is expected that a measurement project should have several goals, if it intends to measure in an intentional manner [2].

A measurement goal has a standard structure, a template, as proposed by Basili [2]; this proposal states that a goal has the object to be measured, the characteristic of the object, the standpoint, and the proposal for measurement. For example, the goal of 'Maximising client satisfaction with the software product', has the 'software product' as an object, 'satisfaction' as a characteristic, the 'client' as a standpoint, and 'maximising' as the proposal.

This template was finely tuned in the work of [19] that proposes the following structure: analysing (the object of measurement), for a proposal of (the goal of the measurement), as regards the (focus on object quality), from the standpoint of (those that measure the object), and in the domain of (the realm where the measurement will be made).

Using this template allows greater compliance with the GQM method as it is more aligned with its proposals and definitions. Based on these templates, Table 2 was built with the structure of the goal, with the GQM method [2], [19].

Following the definition of the goal, it will be refined into several questions, aimed at characterising the object that will be measured. The questions, on their turn, are answered by a metric that aims at answering with quantitative information [2].

A metric can consist of several measures and the latter defines the structure for the measurement values [4]. To define this structure it is necessary to choose the measurement unit (table, column, percentage, hours, etc.), the scale to be used (integers, real, etc.), and the type of scale (Scale types are nominal, ordinal, interval, ratio, and absolute).

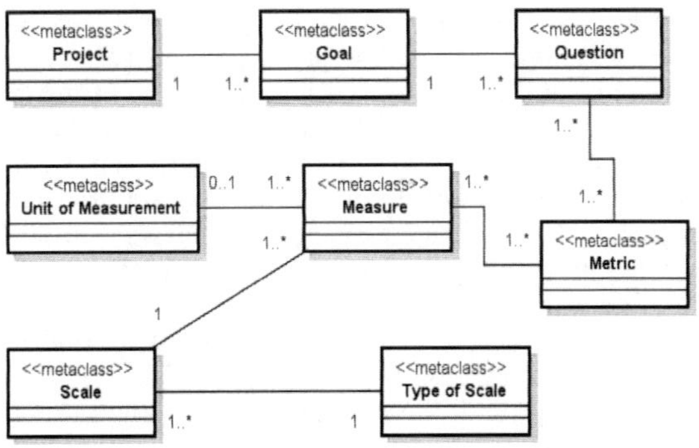

Figure 1. Metamodel proposed for measurement, using the Goal Question Metric method

TABLE II. GOAL STRUCTURE AS PROPOSED BY THE GQM METHOD

Analyse	Goal of measurement
For the proposal of	The goal of the measurement (understanding, improving, or controlling)
As regards	The focus on the quality of the object to be measured
From the standpoint of	The people that measure the object
In the domain of	The environment where the measurement takes place

Scale types are nominal, ordinal, interval, ratio, and absolute. In the nominal scale the categories for attributes should be jointly exhaustive (all categories as a whole should cover the possibilities of the category of an attribute) and mutually excluding (the attributes may be classified in only one category). In an ordinal scale the attributes may be compared amongst them in an ordinal manner, but this scale does not provide information on the magnitude of the difference that exists between points of the scale. The interval scale allows knowing the difference between two points of the scale. This type of scale requires a well-defined measurement unit that can be considered a standard and that is repeatable. The ratio scale is similar to the interval one, as in the proportional scale it is possible to find the difference between two points of the scale. However, in the proportion scale it is possible to find an absolute zero and non-arbitrary [11]. The absolute scale is merely a count of some element in the entity and it allows any arithmetical analysis [6]. Most of the measurements are done in the interval scale and that of the arbitrary proportion [11].

Having created the measurements, one should define how the measurements relate to each other to create a metric. This means defining the function of measurement for that metric. This is an important stage as it is from this function that the result of the metric is obtained.

To better explain metamodelling, the following example was created: The project of a given software company has, as one of its measurement goal, to 'Analyse the software product to improve its quality from the standpoint of the clients'. Faced with this, the clients were asked a set of questions. One of these questions was: 'What is the quality of the software product developed by the company?' To answer it, a metric was raised, namely 'average errors per class'. This metric has two dimensions: the numbers of errors found and the number of classes in the project. The unit for measurement 'number of errors found' is the quantity of Errors and, for measurement 'number of classes' it is the quantity of Classes. The scale for both measurements is of integers from 0 to infinite and the type of scale is the absolute scale.

Figure 2 was created to better illustrate what information the user should provide to define a metric in the proposed measurement system. In this figure the example is about one measurement called Average error per class.

One metric holds many measures. The measures blend through mathematical operators or functions to define a metric, that is, a metric can be obtained through a mathematical combination of its dimensions. It should be pointed that the metric 'Average errors per class' is obtained with the combination of two independent variables, 'Number of Errors' and 'Number of Classes'. This combination is done with the use of the 'average' function, which is a resultant from a mathematical formula that blends the independent variables to calculate the dependent variable, i.e., 'average errors per class' would be the 'number of errors' <divided by> 'number of classes'. What the users need to do to define the 'average errors per class' metric is to blend the two measures, using this operator. Each measure will have a measurement unit and also a scale. In the example given above, both measures have the same scale, although they can be different, even when belonging to the same metric. Having defined the metric, it is necessary to choose the type of scale.

Another example, if the metric Productivity = Size/Effort, then size and effort are the basic measurements (independent variables) used to calculate productivity. Thus, the productivity metric is obtained with the blending of these measurements and the <divided by> operator. They have a scale, a measurement unit, and a type of scale.

In order for a user to define one's metric one should first record the measurements (independent variables), use the mathematical operators or functions that were previously defined in the application and blend them as the 'calculation formula' for the metric (dependent variable).

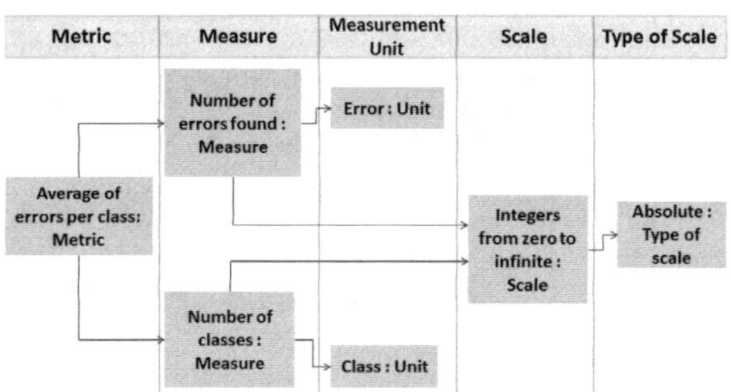

Figure 2. Definition of metric using the proposed metamodel

D. Analysis of the Fourth Research Question

(QP4) What data model can be used to create a flexible historical base tool?

To answer this, we thought about what data would be required for a user to enter in order to carry out measurements with the use of the GQM method. And as a result the data form below was created:

Project – defined by:
- Project name; Project description;
- Company name
- And Start date:

Measurement Goal (as described by GQM Method):
- Analyze:
- For a proposal to:
- As regards:
- From the standpoint of:
- In the domain of:

Questions – defined by:
- Question; Description of question:

Metric – defined by:
- Name of metric;
- Description of metric;
- Date of calculation.

Measurement function:
- Measurement 1:
- Measurement 2;
- Measurement no.:
- Another value:
- Function:

Measurement:
- Name of measurement:
- Description of measurement:
- Date of collection:
- Value:

Measurement Unit:
- Name of measurement unit:
- Description of measurement unit:

Scale:
- Name of scale:
- Number set:
- Minimum number:
- Maximum number:

Type of scale:
- Name of type of scale:
- Description of type of scale:

Based on this data form it was possible to create a data model. The data model created went through a verification procedure and a validation walk-through, the latter being an informal technique to ascertain software product quality [1]. As a result, after the creation of the model, those who took part in the walk-through did an analysis of the model to try and find inconsistencies in it. Those who took part in the verification and validation procedure are students of the Software Engineering School at the Gama UnB School, enrolled in and attending the Software Verification and Validation classes. This discipline has the following pre-requisites for students to attend: Metric and Estimates for

Software, Software Quality, and Advanced Software Development. Apart from that the lecturer of this course followed the process, to give his feedback regarding the model proposed.

Following the analysis work the model was explained to the participants, to solve eventual queries. After that the items the participants considered wrong were discussed and a consensus was reached on the model. The model was re-structured based on these discussions and a check list was produced to verify whether the model had been corrected in its entirety.

The data model derived from the metamodel proposed as it has all the metaclasses of the metamodel, apart from including the attributes of such classes and other tables for standardisation the model.

IV. CONCLUSION

Based on the study presented, it is possible to see the contribution of measurements to software development companies, allowing people to learn about the performance and quality of their processes and products developed. Thus, when using metamodelling in a measurement system, it is expected that an increase in productivity and in measurement activities will take place. Apart from that, metamodelling also grants additional flexibility in the definition of metric as it allows users to create their own metric, no longer being dependent of existing ones.

With the proposal made in this work it will also be possible to create an application that allows users, apart from creating their own metric, to store such measurement data in a historical data base and, due to the flexibility metamodelling allows, it will be possible to make several changes to those metric without the need to do maintenance on the source code.

As a result, in the continuation of this work, the data model proposed in this paper will be used to create an application that will allow users to define their own metric and record them in a historical data base. The development process in its initial stage and we expect that several organisations might benefit from it, cutting their costs with system maintenance, especially in legacy systems.

REFERENCES

[1] O. Balci, Validation, verification, and testing techniques throughout the life cycle of a simulation study. Proceedings of Operations Research, pp. 121-173, 1994.

[2] V. R. Basili, Software Modelling and Measurement: The Goal Question Metric Paradigm. Computer Science Technical Report Series, CS-TR-2956 (UMIACS-TR-92-96), University of Maryland, College Park, MD.1992.

[3] T. Clark, P. Sammut, J. Willans, Applied metamodelling: A foundation for language driven development, 2nd Ed. Ceteva, 2008.

[4] E. Damiani, A. Colombo, F. Frati, and C. Bellettini, A Metamodel for Modelling and Measuring Scrum Development Processes. LNCS, pp. 74-83, 2007.

[5] B. El-Haik, and A. Shaout, Software design for six sigma. Wiley. 2010.

[6] N. Fenton, and S. Pfleeger, Software Metric. Boston: PWS Pub., 1997.

[7] W. A. Florac, R. E. Park, and A. D. Carleton, Practical Software Measurement: Measuring for Process Management and Improvement Pittsburgh, PA, 1997.

[8] F. García, M. Serrano, J. Cruz-Lemus, F. Ruiz, and M. Piattini, Managing software process measurement: A metamodel-based approach. Information Sciences, pp. 177-182, 2007.

[9] P. C. González, and B. Henderson-Sellers, Metamodelling for software engineering. John Wiley. 2008.

[10] D. Harel, and B. Rumpe, Meaningful modelling: what's the semantics of "semantics"? Computer. 37, 10, pp. 64-72, 2004.

[11] S. Kan, Metric and models in software quality engineering. Addison-Wesley. 1995.

[12] L. Laird, and M. Brennan, Software measurement and estimation. Wiley-Interscience. 2006.

[13] L. Lavazza, Providing automated support for the GQM measurement process. IEEE Softw. 17, 3, pp. 56-62, 2000.

[14] C. Lokan, T. Wright, P. Hill, and M. Stringer, Organisational benchmarking using the ISBSG Data Repository. IEEE Softw. 18, 5, pp. 26-32, 2001.

[15] S. Mellor, MDA distilled. Addison-Wesley. 2004.

[16] S. Mellor, A. Clark, and T. Futagami, Model-driven development - Guest editor's introduction. IEEE Software, pp. 14-18, 2003.

[17] K. Petersen, R. Feldt, S. Mujtaba, and M. Mattsson, Systematic mapping studies in software engineering, Proceedings of the 12th International Conference on Evaluation and Assessment in Software Engineering (EASE), British Computer Society, Swinton, UK, pp. 68-77, 2008.

[18] J. Rothenberg, Artificial intelligence, simulation & modelling. Chapter: The Nature of Modelling, John Wiley &Sons, Inc., New York, NY, USA, pp. 75-92, 1989.

[19] R. Solingen, and E. Berghout, The goal/question/metric method. The McGraw-Hill Companies. 1999.

[20] E. A. G Amaral, G. H. Travassos, "Em Busca de uma Abordagem para Empacotamento de Experimentos em Engenharia de Software". In. Proceedings of the 2nd JIISIS - Jornada Ibero-Americana de Engenharia de Software e Engenharia de Conhecimento. Salvador, Brazil. 2002.

[21] W. Vogt, Dictionary of statistics and methodology. Sage Publications. 1993.

[22] ISO/IEC 15939:2007 - Systems and software engineering — Measurement process, International Organisation for Standardization, Geneva, Switzerland, 2007.

Analysis of Expectations of Students and Their Initial Concepts on Software Quality

Luis Fernández-Sanz, José Amelio Medina, Josefa Gómez-Pérez
Dept. of Computer Sciences, Universidad de Alcalá
Alcalá de Henares, Spain
Email:{luis.fernandezs, josea.medina, josefa.gomezp}@uah.es

Sanjay Misra
Covenant University
Ota State, Nigeria
Email: ssoapm@gmail.com

Abstract— **Quality is everywhere in every discipline. Software quality has been included in all regular education programs both at undergraduate level and in postgraduate programs with more or less intensity and wideness. However, several authors have questioned the real effectiveness of software quality education related to the real understanding of the concept. This paper analyses the expectations of students with and without working experience in software development regarding software quality education and the preferences and the ideas expressed before the training courses.**

Keywords-software quality; education; curriculum; quality culture.

I. INTRODUCTION

Quality is one of the three typical dimensions for managing every project in the well-known iron triangle first presented in [1] no matter if it is an industrial or a software one. Although later than other engineering sectors, software development also embraced the challenge of quality as part of its regular responsibilities, facing the challenge of adapting methods to the peculiar nature of software [2]. Independently from its value as a market trend or real management goal, software quality management is one of the topics included in educational programs at undergraduate level and in postgraduate programs. However, some contributions (e.g. [3]) have identified intrinsic problems in understanding the concepts related to software quality, then looking for new perspectives for a correct understanding of software quality. This conflict was also described in [4] when they wrote "If you are a software developer, manager, or maintainer, quality is often on your mind. But what do you really mean by software quality? Is your definition adequate? Is the software you produce better or worse than you would like it to be?" Even the authors conducted a small survey to 27 readers to know more on several aspects of this conflict. This is consistent with some results already presented many years ago [5] related to perception of students (postgraduate with some experience) regarding software quality and some of its associated concepts, observing some improvement in the perception of software quality as well as some changes in preferred topics after completing the specific course in the area.

Obviously, when dealing with software quality in software engineering education there are several references which doubt of the capability of regular programs to embed the idea of quality in students' mind. For example, [6] think that quality is central and critical in software development but that it is usual computer science faculty do not devote enough attention to teaching their students how to develop high-quality software (at least looking at the curriculum design and implementation). Of course, the recommendations for really effective curricula in software engineering are also frequent and are always including the topic of software quality and associated methods and techniques (see e.g. [7]). Of course, the most general models for software engineering education are always considering software quality has a pillar of the curricula in software engineering: e.g., the well-known Software Engineering Body of Knowledge (SWEBOK) [8] devotes one of its 10 Knowledge Areas to Software Quality Analysis.

As a summary, we can say that software quality is always clearly present in practically 100% of educational programs in software engineering but it seems to be a topic which frequently raises questions on the real impact on students. However, the consequences of the unsatisfactory results of the education on software quality go beyond the limits of possible deficiencies in the qualification of (future) software professionals. As software engineering is mainly a human activity, not just a technical matter of technology, perceptions of software engineers deeply impact the results in term of productivity and quality. The work with Human and Organizational Factors (HOF) and nontechnical issues highlight that the people involved in the software development process are as important as the processes and the project.

Different studies have shown how these factors lead to improvements in products, increases in productivity, or decreases in production costs. As an example, [9] provides the outcomes of a study carried out in a professional environment. It shows that certain organizational factors, that might not affect project success, negatively affect software quality: among the factor of influence there is a wrong quality culture or a lack of sense of quality achievement. Additional discussion and information could be found in [10]. Although there are different aspects which confirm the practical impact of misconceptions on software productivity and quality, poor understandings of quality principles has been identified as relevant in effectiveness of software projects. Moreover, these barriers may hinder the achievement of good results in educational programs. The main goal of this study is the analysis of the expectations of students to know how working experience and learned concepts may influence their attitude towards software quality.

The paper is organized as follows. Section II describes the educational experience where the data on students' opinions and expectations were collected. The analysis of results is provided in Section III, while Section IV outlines some conclusions and suggests some future lines of action.

II. EDUCATIONAL EXPERIENCE ON SOFTWARE QUALITY

Authors frequently teach courses on quality managements systems and software quality in different undergraduate and postgraduate computing programs. Our experience tend to show that theoretical or rather abstract or high level concepts imply a more difficult understanding than those more connected to low level practical work. Given that software quality management works at a higher corporate/organizational level, especially those students without working experience tend to be less connected to the corresponding ideas.

Together with our concerns on the real effects of courses, we wanted to check several aspects on the expectations of students when they are exposed to software quality education. Thanks to the collaboration of students, we collected information from several courses where we got a reasonable variety of profiles and education levels which provides some representativeness to results. The selected courses and groups of students were the following ones:

G1: Undergraduate in 2nd and 3rd year of Informatics Engineering program at University of Alcalá with two different courses "Software Engineering" and "Advanced Software Engineering" where there are 20 hours devoted to software quality: 39 respondents (Madrid).

G2: Undergraduate in 2nd and 3rd year of Information Systems program at University of Alcalá with two different courses "Software Engineering" and "Advanced Software Engineering" where there are 20 hours devoted to software quality: 14 respondents.

G3: Undergraduate in 4th year of Information Systems and Informatics Engineering programs at University of Alcalá with a specialized course on "Software quality, testing and maintenance" with 60 hours: 11 respondents (Madrid).

M1: Students enrolled in the Master program on IT Project Management at University of Alcalá with specific courses on "quality management and software quality" with a total of 100 hours: 9 respondents.

Although the topics in all courses are very similar, the approach in each of them is obviously different depending on the specific educational goals, previous courses, students' background and profile as well as duration. In fact, biggest differences are evident when comparing teaching to undergraduate and to postgraduate students. It is important to remark that all the students have attended previous courses on other aspects connected to software quality such as software testing and configuration management. However, there was a general scheme of points taught in each course:

- Concept of quality and differences between software and other products. Other concepts related to quality and management by processes.
- Corporate perspective: quality management systems and continuous improvement. Standards and frameworks for software process improvement (ISO, CMMi, etc.)
- Project quality management: software quality assurance, activities and techniques
- Software quality evaluation: models and metrics

INITIAL QUESTIONNAIRE

1. Write a definition of quality: ____________________

2. So, which of the following phrases is most adjusted to your idea of quality?

□ Highest possible level, no matter who is the customer
□ Something associated to expensive and luxurious products
□ Product has some guarantee in case of problems
□ Balance between price and value
□ Concept to be customized to specific needs of the customer

3. Have you ever heard about software quality?

□ Informal chat with colleagues
□ Commercial presentations
□ Articles or conference papers
□ Books (whole or chapters) related to this topic
□ You know quality standards and have worked with them
□ You do not have any references about this but you guess its importance

4. So, your idea about software quality is:

(1) Unfavourable impression: it is useless or impractical
(2) Rather unfavourable impression: it represents a great effort to get poor results
(3) Neutral impression: we need to improve and we can do it but it is essential to know how to do it
(4) Favourable impression: we are able to achieve good results by applying certain techniques
(5) Very favourable impression: it is incredible that we are not still applying these techniques.

5. In your opinion, who or what should encourage the adoption of quality techniques in the practice? (you can mark several options)

□ Quality department
□ Management
□ Software professionals and technicians
□ The need of satisfying legal dispositions or standards
□ Customers, contracts or market pressure
□ Others (please indicate) ____________________

6. Which of the following topics do you consider as the most important for this course? Put them in order of preference from 1 to 5 (have you ever heard about them?)

□ ISO 9001 (ISO 9000-3)	*Heard □*
□ Quality management systems	*Heard □*
□ Testing, reviews, audits	*Heard □*
□ Software process improvement	*Heard □*
□ Quality control and evaluation (metrics)	*Heard □*

Have you ever worked in professional software development (<u>undergraduate students</u>)? □ Yes □ No

Figure 1. Initial questionnaire

Questionnaire in Fig. 1 was used for information collection from students, the same for all the groups. This form is replicating the one already used in a previous study [5] where it is described the design considerations as well as the methodological considerations. The idea was being able to compare some results in the future. Each form had 4 closed multiple choice questions as well as to open questions apart from a question on real working experience in software projects. Only undergraduate students were asked about their working experience since all master students were experienced. It was clearly commented to students that there were not correct answers to the questionnaires, that it was aimed at capturing their ideas freely expressed. Only graduate students and experienced undergraduate students were asked about which techniques they would intend to use in their job after the course. Of course, questionnaires were anonymous.

Only after collecting all the information, the teacher was allowed to exploit the activity to organize a free debate on their perceptions and the reflections associated to them.

III. ANALYSIS OF RESULTS

Given the small samples, the main goal of the analysis is getting descriptive information of the ideas expressed through the questions. Specific goals are the following:

G1. Which is the initial concept of quality for those attending the course? (question 1)

G2. Is the concept of quality different between experienced and unexperienced? (questions 1 and 6)

G3. Which is the opinion on quality of those attending the course? (question 2).

G4. Is the opinion on quality different between between experienced and unexperienced ? (questions 3 and 4)

G5. Knowing if opinion on quality is the same between students with working experience and those without it? (question 4)

G6. Which is the opinion on who should be the promoter/sponsor of quality? (question 5).

G7. Knowing if the idea that people tend to make responsible only to the quality department of the whole results of the organization? (question 5)

G8. Which is the opinion on orientation to customer? (question 6)

We present the results extracted from questionnaires in Table 1, separating results for unexperienced and experienced students to enable an easier analysis of data.

1) As seen on the Table 1, most part of respondents knew or has heard about software quality (only 3% remain ignorant before the course). This is not exclusive of those inexperienced students (2.2%) although one experienced did not have previous references. It is remarkable that 28.4% of experienced and 16.4% of inexperienced have worked with standard or have been working in practical application to projects.
2) Many respondents have acquired knowledge through theoretical or practical courses (approx. 40% of experienced and 53 % of inexperienced. Although there is a slight difference (13.8% of experienced vs 12.3% of inexperienced), there is not much impact of commercial information (while teachers thought before this experience it was the opposite).

TABLE I. RESULTS FOR WITH AND WITHOUT EXPERIENCE

	Experience (31,81%)	No experience (68.18%)
# students	35	75
Concept of quality		
Requirements and need	37.1 %	34.66 %
Customer satisfaction	14.3 %	12 %
Guarantee	0	24 %
Tools and maintenance	2.86 %	2.66 %
Correct function	20 %	10.66 %
No losing time	2.86 %	1.33 %
Product value	14.3 %	5.33 %
Process	8.57 %	4 %
Void answer	0 %	5.33 %
Ideas on quality		
Highest possible level	25.71 %	13.33 %
Luxury/expensive	0 %	1.33 %
Guarantee	5.71 %	8 %
Value-price balance	22.85 %	28 %
Customization	45.71 %	49.33 %
Previous references		
Speech/debates	7.32 %	8.64 %
Commercial presentations	6.5 %	3.64 %
Theory in courses	23.6 %	30.5 %
Practical work in course	16.3 %	23.2 %
Articles and conferences	9.75 %	10 %
Books	7.32 %	8.64 %
Working with standards	13.8 %	7.73 %
Practice in projects	14.6 %	5.45 %
No references	0.81 %	2.22 %
Quality idea	4.08	3.85
Motivator/sponsor		
Quality department	28.8 %	20.2 %
Top management	5.08 %	5.64 %
Professionals/technicians	20.3 %	24.02 %
Every employee	39 %	33.9 %
Customers/market	6.78 %	15.3 %
Other	0	0.81 %
Customer orientation:		
Information for use	2.86 %	25.33 %
Satisfy customer specification	0	2.66 %
Satisfy customer needs	51.4 %	37.33 %
Features and requisites	8.57 %	2.66 %
Post-sales service	0 %	0 %
Developing services and systems oriented to customers	2.86 %	0 %
Product reliability and maintainability	0 %	0 %
Information for choosing product	14.3 %	16 %
Do not know	2.86 %	0 %

Void	8.57 %	9.33 %

3) Initial idea on software quality is rather high as our informal observation was suggesting: average for experienced is 4.08 while unexperienced scored 3.85, both numbers really high. When we compare undergraduate (4.02) and graduate students (4.22) differences are also small. Only 4 people (0.02%) started with level 2 (Rather unfavourable).
4) Frequent misconception in old fashion quality organizational cultures detected by Crossby [11] where majority of people believes that quality is a only responsibility of the quality department seem s to be still alive in a good number of undergraduate students (25.1 %) while is really reduced in master students (7.14%). It is worth to remark the high proportion of undergraduate and postgraduate who think that the main responsibility for quality is on the shoulders of the own software professionals. It is important to note that the largest percentage of people is correctly thinking that quality is a responsibility of all workers in the organization, more clearly for experienced students (57.14%) than for unexperienced (34.2%). Finally, market/customers is the main driver and motivator for quality for 15.2 of postgraduate students versus 7.14% of the undergraduate ones. In general there is a good consistency with the current philosophy of quality in the organizations.
5) From the definitions of quality written by students we can see that the most mentioned concept is the one referred to requirements and needs, similar for experienced (37.1%) and unexperienced students (34.6%). The second most mentioned option is customer satisfaction with 14.3% and 12% respectively. The most relevant difference between both groups of students appear in the option of focusing quality as a guarantee procedure (maybe allowing refund if customer is unsatisfied): 24% of undergraduate mentioned that while none of postgraduate did.
6) When expressing their idea of product/service quality the idea that quality concept has to be adapted to the needs of each customer is accepted by the majority (45.71% experienced and 49.33% unexperienced). Both groups reject the idea of associating quality with expensive/luxurious products while both groups consider relevant the existence of a proper balance between price and value.
7) When dealing with the concept of customer orientation, we want to highlight that information for using the product is the main aspect for 25.33% of unexperienced students while satisfying customers' needs was chosen by 37.33% while 51.4% of experienced students chose customer satisfaction letting the information for using the product as the last option.
8) There is a wide variety in the initiatives which inspire more interest in students for putting them into practice. It is interesting to note that there were no other options apart from the ones shown in the questionnaire. Adoption of techniques, tools and quality standards keep a good medium level (between 30% and 50%) while certification activities score low, maybe because they are considered as options out of the decision power of the respondents.

We decided not to analyze differences among the different courses as the sample numbers were small and the goal was focused on general expectations of students only distinguishing the impact or working experience. Analyzing the effects of the different courses was not meaningful since they are a non-representative subset of the official syllabus available for software quality education: i.e., results could not be applicable to other designs of software quality courses. Regarding the analysis of post-course results, we collected data confirming that our courses finally helped fix the misconceptions on software quality work (e.g., thinking that not everybody has a direct responsibility in quality), but we are not discussing here in order to avoid mixing the analysis of expectations with the analysis of educational effectiveness of our courses.

IV. CONCLUSIONS

First valuable result for us has been a better knowledge on the expectations and the initial idea that our students have in mind before starting the courses. This has already served us to adjust the pedagogical methods and the details of topics to better fit our teaching activity to the students profile and background. It has also enabled a more solid discussion of stereotypes on quality, creating new materials and activities to better debate on the implications of the different views of software quality (see e.g., [3]). It was really useful to find out that still a relevant number of students think that the main responsibility of quality relies on the quality department instead of accepting that every worker is essential to assure quality results, thus trying to convince them with the basic ideas from [11]. Also knowing the main interests in the field of software quality has helped us in reconsidering the way of explaining and teaching each topic in the course.

The contribution of our work is clearly focused on knowing which are the attitudes and the conceptions regarding software quality of students and professionals. It is well-known that an effective quality management strategy has to rely on the contribution of everybody to achieve the quality goals. As an example, discovering that a relevant percentage of professionals are still thinking that the quality department is the main responsible of quality is very important to the practical implementation of software quality management: organizations simply cannot assume that professionals are coming with clear ideas so teams can directly start to work with processes and method for software quality. This is also an important lesson for other educators in software quality: techniques and methods are essential but they are useless if the attitudinal and conceptual part is not worked.

We expect to cumulate more data during the present academic year to enlarge samples so more sophisticated analysis using multivariate analysis. We are also already using an after-course questionnaire to evaluate the evolution of the quality concepts from the initial idea brought by students to the outgoing one which will guide their professional activity. We expect that students (as happened in [5]) will raise the value given to quality while they also tend to improve the perception and correct understanding of the concept of quality.

ACKNOWLEDGMENT

This work has been partially funded by European Commission for project ICEBERG no. 324356 (7h Framework Programme IAPP Marie Curie program).

REFERENCES

[1] APM. A History of the Association for Project Management 1972-2010. Buckinghamshire: Association for Project Management, 2010.

[2] R.S. Pressman, Software engineering. A practitioner's approach, McGrwa-Hill, 2015.

[3] I. Tervonen and P. Kerola, "Towards deeper co-understanding of software quality", Information and Software Technology, vol. 39, Issues 14–15, pp. 995-1003, 1998.

[4] B. Kitchenham and S.L. Pfleeger. "Software quality: The elusive target". IEEE software, 13(1), 12, 1996.

[5] L. Fernández, J.J. Dolado. "Students expectations in Sofwtare Quality Education", Inspire'96. International Conference On Software Process Improvement - Research Into Education & Training, , C. Hawkins, M. Ross, G. Staples, H. Wickberg (eds.), Londres: SGES Publications, 1996.

[6] T.B. Hilburn and M. Townhidnejad. "Software quality: a curriculum postscript?". ACM SIGCSE Bulletin, 32(1), 167-171, 2000.

[7] M. Jazayeri. "The education of a software engineer". In Proceedings of the 19th IEEE international conference on Automated software engineering (pp. 18-xxvii). IEEE Computer Society, 2004.

[8] A. Abran, P. Bourque, R. Dupuis, and J.W. Moore. "Guide to the software engineering body of knowledge-SWEBOK". IEEE Press, 2001.

[9] M. Lavallée, P.N. Robillard."Why Good Developers Write Bad Code: An Observational Case Study of the Impacts of Organizational Factors on Software Quality". International Conference on software Engineering (ICSE2015), pp. 16-24.

[10] L. Fernández-Sanz,, and S. Misra. "Influence of human factors in software quality and productivity". In Computational Science and Its Applications-ICCSA 2011, pp. 257-269. Springer Berlin Heidelberg.

[11] P.B. Crossby, Quality is free. The art of making quality certain, McGraw-Hill, 1979.

iGuard: A Personalized Privacy Guard System for Cloud Service Usage on Mobile Devices

Chien-Wei Hu
Institute of Computer and Communication Engineering,
National Cheng Kung University,
Tainan, Taiwan
chienwei@nature.ee.ncku.edu.tw

Hewijin Christine Jiau
Department of Electrical Engineering,
National Cheng Kung University,
Tainan, Taiwan
jiauhjc@mail.ncku.edu.tw

Kuo-Feng Ssu
Department of Electrical Engineering,
National Cheng Kung University,
Tainan, Taiwan
ssu@ee.ncku.edu.tw

***Abstract*—Users encounter privacy threats when they use cloud services through mobile devices. A user leaves a large amount of usage data on the server sides. Leaving a single piece of usage data on the server side may seem harmless to user's privacy, but if usage data is all taken together, the sensitive information can be leaked. To detect privacy leakages, various privacy measurements have been proposed. However, it's not easy for the user to find suitable privacy measurements because he does not have the background knowledge. Moreover, the user also does not know what is available to be used for protecting his privacy when he finds privacy leakages. In this work, iGuard, a personalized guard system for cloud service usage on mobile devices, is provided. iGuard provides a customized privacy measurement plan which fits in the user's personal situation. The plan is executed to detect possible privacy leakages when the user is using cloud services. To resolve the leakages, iGuard also provides workable privacy protection strategies. The user can apply one of the strategies and see its effect on the privacy measurement results. According to the results, the user can tune his strategy continuously until he is satisfied with the results. By continuously tuning, the user can manage the privacy-utility trade-offs of using cloud services.**

Keywords–privacy measurement; privacy protection.

I. Introduction

Users enjoy all kinds of conveniences provided by cloud services through mobile devices anytime and anywhere. Cloud services enable users to access all kinds of data and use various software on the Internet. In 2014, twelve percent of the EU population used cloud services for document editing. The proportion was even higher (23%) among the population aged 16-24 [1]. But the truth is that cloud service providers are also interested in tracking user information, e.g., user preferences, personality traits, and relationship statuses. Privacy threats increase when users access cloud services through mobile devices. Mobile devices are equipped with various sensors to collect users' contextual information, such as geolocation information. When a user performs an operation on a cloud service, not only data that the user enters into the cloud service but also contextual information is sent to the cloud service. The cloud service gets more data than the user inputted manually, but the user does not know what the cloud service gets additionally. Besides, leaking a single piece of usage data to the cloud service may be harmless to user's privacy. But a user's profile, such as his routines and preferences, will be revealed if all the usage data on the server side is aggregated and further analyzed.

The revealed user information is collected further and reused without the user's awareness and permission [2]. The management of user data on cloud services might not be trustworthy [3]. Cloud service providers might use user data for various purposes, or sell the data to others who need to perform data aggregation. More user information might eventually be mined for all kinds of purposes, and the user will not have any control over those purposes. In fact, the user has the right to know what can be revealed from his usage data, but cloud service providers do not respect this right, still collecting user information without notifying the user. If the user wants to be aware of data leakages from his usage data, he must apply appropriate privacy measurements on the usage data by himself. A privacy measurement focuses on a kind of usage data and detects a specific user privacy leakage from the data. There are various privacy measurements available currently. For example, the privacy measurement proposed by Liao et. al [4] can be used to detect leakages of the user's transportation routines from Global Positioning System (GPS) data. Even though the user does not expose any GPS data to the cloud service, another privacy measurement proposed by Valkanas and Gunopulos [5] can be used to detect user's location information leakages from general textual information on social network services. A user has his own combination of cloud services in use and personal privacy preferences. Among all these different privacy measurements, the user has to select privacy measurements that fit in his situation and performs the privacy measurements on suitable timing. However, the user may not have the background knowledge to select and perform the privacy measurements. A general user knows how to operate a cloud service, but he may not know the usage data that will be sent to the cloud service, let alone the privacy measurements that are available for detecting privacy leakages. Even though the user discovers a privacy leakage, he may not have the knowledge to avoid the privacy leakage while keeping using the cloud service.

In this work, iGuard, a personalized guard system for cloud service usage on mobile devices, is proposed. According to the user's personal situation, his combination of cloud services in use and privacy preferences, iGuard selects appropriate privacy measurements for the user. iGuard collects usage data sent to the cloud services and triggers corresponding privacy measurements on suitable timing for detecting possible privacy leakages. If privacy leakage is detected, the user will receive a warning from iGuard. iGuard provides privacy protection strategies for the user. The effect of the applied protection strategies is reflected in the results of the privacy measurements so that the user can improve his strategies continuously based on the results. Contributions of this work are outlined as follows.

1) In this work, user-centric privacy protection is provided. The user-centric privacy protection focuses on personal privacy measurements and customized privacy protection strategies. The personal privacy measurements detect critical privacy threats, and the customized privacy protection strategies help mitigate the threats.
2) iGuard, a system that implements the user-centric privacy protection, is provided. As types and amount of user data collected by cloud services increase, demands of new privacy measurements also increase to provide comprehensive user privacy protection. iGuard takes the extension of privacy measurements into consideration, and is flexible for adding new privacy measurements.

The remainder of this work is organized as follows. In Section II, an overview of related work is provided. The user-centric privacy protection is illustrated in Section III. Details of the iGuard system is described in Section IV. In Section V, two case studies of using iGuard are provided. Finally, this work is concluded in Section VI.

II. RELATED WORK

Privacy leakages caused by using cloud services have been identified in previous work. Chairunnanda et. al [6] indicated that users' identities were constructed from their typing patterns. Liao et. al [7] showed that users' daily activities and movements were identified from raw GPS data collected by mobile devices. Ferrari et. al [8] observed that users' mobility patterns in an urban environment were extracted from their participation in social networks. Valkanas and Gunopulos [5] demonstrated that user's location information was exposed from general textual information about their surroundings in social networks without using a GPS-enabled device. Murukannaiah and Singh [9] indicated that users social circles could be identified by bringing together contextual information and users' online social interactions. These work provides various privacy measurements on different privacy leakages. iGuard utilizes suitable privacy measurements and makes privacy measurement plans for users according to their personal settings.

Protection strategies that alleviate the identified privacy leakages are also proposed. Stenneth and Yu [10] used a trusted thirdparty server as the mediator between user devices and cloud services, and applied the k-anonymity technique to hide identifications of the user devices. Zhang et. al [11] used noise data to obfuscate cloud services. The authors generated noise service requests and injected these requests into real customer service requests. The noise service requests' occurrence probabilities were identical to customer service requests so that cloud service providers could not distinguish them from customer service requests. Customers' privacy was consequently protected. Ren et. al [12] partitioned data into data fragments and stored them to different cloud services. Beresford et. al [13] created a modified version of the Android operating system that allowed users to 'mock' access to the resources of user devices for cloud services. Guha et. al [14] proposed the Koi platform which avoided leaking privacy-sensitive information by masking low-level lat-long information from applications. Kasai et. al [15] proposed a service provision system that selected the best-working services for users according to the minimal personal information provided by the users. Among all these privacy protection strategies, iGuard provides users the ones that solve their identified privacy leakages. Users can select the preferred one and apply it for protecting their privacy.

III. USER-CENTRIC PRIVACY PROTECTION

A user uses cloud services through the mobile device to solve daily problems, and the combination of cloud services in use varies from person to person. Furthermore, information exposure that causes "privacy leakage" to a user also varies from person to person, since the definition of "sensitive information" is different for every user. Some users take their political views as sensitive information but others do not. Some users mind revealing their home addresses, but others do not. Every user has his own sensitive information list describing personal information that should not be exposed to others. As a result, iGuard applies user-centric privacy protection to take the user's personal situation into consideration. The process of the user-centric privacy protection is shown in Figure 1. Details of each step of the process are described as follows.

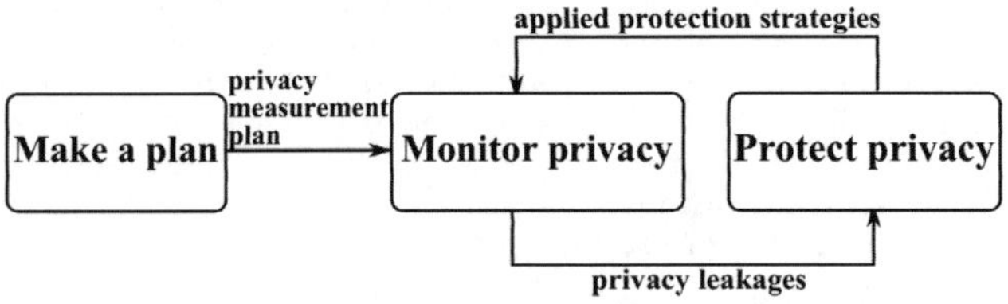

Figure 1. The user-centric privacy protection process.

- **Step 1. Make a plan.** Privacy monitoring is performed according to a customized privacy measurement plan, which is made based on the user's personal situation. The privacy measurement plan is the base to ensure the user's privacy when he is using cloud services. The privacy measurement plan defines the privacy measurements which should be applied and the timing of triggering these privacy measurements. Selection of the privacy measurements is based on
  1) the type of cloud services in use,
  2) the type of usage data that is sent to the cloud services, and
  3) the user's sensitive information list.

  A privacy measurement does not need to be triggered in real time when the user is using a cloud service. It can be a summary of user operations in a period of time, e.g., a day or several hours. The frequency of applying a privacy measurement is decided according to the user's preference and characteristics of the privacy measurement.

- **Step 2. Monitor privacy.** When the user is using a cloud service through the mobile device, usage data sent to the cloud service should be evaluated for privacy concern. In this step, corresponding privacy measurements are triggered. The privacy measurements take the usage data as input and indicate potential privacy disclosure threats. The user will receive warnings if privacy leakage is detected. He reviews details of the warning and takes further actions for protecting his privacy (step 3).
- **Step 3. Protect privacy.** The user can apply privacy protection strategies to alleviate the privacy leakages. Privacy protection strategies are divided into two categories.
  1) Changing user behavior. Changing the way that a user uses the cloud service will also change the usage data received by the cloud service. The user can thus hide his sensitive information by changing his behavior. For example, a user checks his e-mails most frequently when he is at work. If the user's working hours are detected from his usage frequency, he can confuse the cloud service by using the cloud service as evenly as possible in different time periods of a day.
  2) Applying third-party privacy protection services. There are a variety of privacy protection services available to protect the user's privacy. These services can insert noises to normal usage data [11], use fake data to replace real data [13], or suggest the best-working cloud services that fit the user's privacy requirements to replace the cloud service in use [15]. By applying these privacy protection services, the user can keep his privacy safe while using the cloud service as normally as possible.

  The user can apply more than one privacy protection strategies, and observe their effects on the results of the privacy measurements (step 2). The user can change or adjust the strategies to find one that best fits his personal situation, and balances the trade-offs between cloud service utilities and privacy protection.

IV. IGUARD SYSTEM

The system overview of iGuard is depicted in Figure 2. Components of iGuard are divided into three parts.

1) **Packet collector**. To detect possible privacy leakages, iGuard has to collect usage data which is sent to cloud services. Packet collector is responsible for collecting mobile device packets to further extract usage data from them.
2) **iGuard client**. iGuard client is the interface between the user and iGuard server. It is implemented as an application installed on the mobile device to interact with the user. iGuard client allows the user to review results of the privacy measurements, and send his personal preferences to iGuard server. Once privacy leakage is detected, iGuard client generates instant notification to the user.
3) **iGuard server**. iGuard server consists of four components: plan maker, privacy measurement coordinator, service agent, and strategy suggester. The four components collaborate to complete the whole process of user-centric privacy protection.

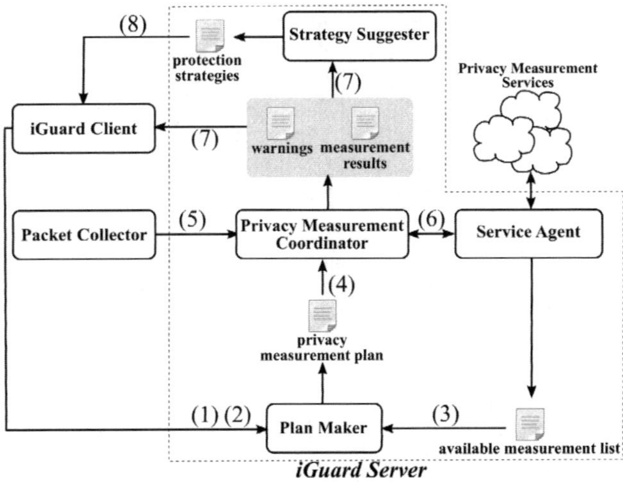

Figure 2. iGuard system overview.

In the following, the ways that the components of iGuard server achieve user-centric privacy protection are illustrated.

A. *Make a Plan*

Making a personalized privacy measurement plan includes the following three steps.

1) **Acquire types of usage data that will be sent to cloud services**. Applications are client-side interfaces for cloud services. Permissions of an application reveal the types of data that will be acquired by its corresponding cloud service. At the beginning, iGuard client collects all the applications installed on the mobile device and their permissions. iGuard client sends the information to plan maker (1). Plan maker analyzes permissions of the applications and gets the types of usage data collected by the cloud services behind the applications. If a new application is installed on the mobile device, plan maker will be notified about the new-installed application and update the privacy measurement plan.
2) **Confirm the user's sensitive information list**. In this step, plan maker checks the user's sensitive information list. A sensitive information list describes a user's personal information that should not be exposed to others. Initially, iGuard client provides a generalized sensitive information list to the user. Once the user tunes the list to get a personalized sensitive information list, plan maker will receive the updated list from iGuard client (2).
3) **Check available privacy measurements**. Plan maker gets the list of available privacy measurements from service agent (3), which is responsible for communicating with third-party privacy measurement services. In the available measurement list, privacy measurements provided by the third-party privacy measurement services are described. For each of the privacy measurements in the list, its type of input

data, focused privacy leakage, and suggested detection frequency are provided. Plan maker selects the privacy measurements, which not only fit in the types of usage data but also can detect leakages of sensitive information. Plan maker then creates a privacy measurement plan, which defines the corresponding privacy measurements and their triggering frequency when the cloud services are used.

After a privacy measurement plan is created or updated, plan maker sends it to privacy measurement coordinator for performing privacy monitoring (4).

B. Monitor Privacy

When the user is using the cloud service, mobile phone packets sent to the cloud service are acquired by packet collector. Packet collector can be a component which embeds either in a modified version of the Andriod operating system or in software-defined networking [16]. Packet collector then copies the packets to privacy measurement coordinator (5). Privacy measurement coordinator identifies the cloud service in use and extracts the usage data sent to the cloud service. Privacy measurement coordinator accumulates the usage data until the triggering time of the corresponding privacy measurements specified in the privacy measurement plan comes. To trigger a privacy measurement, privacy measurement coordinator activates the corresponding privacy measurement service through service agent (6). Service agent is responsible for communicating with privacy measurement services. Once it receives measurement results from the privacy measurement service, service agent passes the measurement results back to privacy measurement coordinator. Privacy measurement coordinator keeps the measurement results for user review in the future. If privacy leakages are identified in the measurement results, privacy measurement coordinator will generate warnings to iGuard client and activate strategy suggester (7).

As all sorts of portable devices are invented and widely used, new types of usage data are exposed to cloud services, such as the user's daily amount of exercise and heart rate. Demands for new privacy measurements increase to detect new privacy risks caused by the usage data. To flexibly add new privacy measurements, service agent applies the service-oriented architecture (SOA). Third-party privacy measurement services are assumed trustworthy. They are self-contained units which provide privacy measurement functionality. The mechanism for communication between service agent and privacy measurement services is described in authors' another work [17]. A privacy measurement service can join iGuard by registering to service agent. If a new privacy measurement service successfully registers to service agent, service agent will update the available measurement list. Service agent also updates the available measurement list when a privacy measurement service becomes unavailable. Once the available measurement list is updated, service agent will notify plan maker to update the privacy measurement plan.

C. Protect Privacy

The goal of privacy protection strategies is to confuse cloud services so that sensitive user information will not be inferred from the usage data. Strategy suggester collects privacy protection strategies that can work on a specific type of usage data. Taking GPS data as an example, the user can turn off the GPS sensor, change his route, or use a privacy protection service to insert fake GPS data into his usage data. Strategy suggester provides possible protection strategies (8) according to the type of usage data that causes the privacy leakage. Regarding more than one privacy leakages, the user can apply several protection strategies at the same time. The effect of the applied strategies will be reflected in the results of future privacy measurements. The user can tune and change the privacy protection strategies until he is satisfied with the results.

V. Case Studies

GPS data is common in the usage data exposed to cloud services. The case studies demonstrate not only that extra user sensitive information will be leaked from the GPS data, but also the ways that iGuard assists user in detecting the leakages and fixing them. To make the case studies as real as possible, real telecommunications service usage data with user's GPS locations is used to simulate the user's usage data exposed to a location-based cloud service. The telecommunications service usage data is provided by Mr. Malte Spitz, a German Green Party politician and Executive Committee member. He acquired the usage data from his telecommunications service provider. The usage data can be downloaded on ZEIT Online [18]. This data set was collected from August 2009 to February 2010, and contained 30,374 location-based usage data. It is assumed that the location-based service collects the user's GPS locations to provides contextual information for him, such as the weather, traffic conditions, nearby restaurants which are open, etc. It is assumed that this location-based service always runs in the background and collects the user's locations regularly to update the contextual information. The user can also actively query the location-based service for further information. When the user is actively using the location-based service, his locations will be collected more frequently than normal. So, the behavior of the location-based service in collecting the user's GPS locations is close to the telecommunications service. The location-based usage data of the telecommunications service is used to simulate the usage data collected by the location-based service. In the case studies, iGuard is applied to eliminate the privacy issues which result from exposing the user's personal schedules and home address to the location-based service.

At the beginning, iGuard makes the privacy measurement plan, as shown in Figure 3. In Figure 3, two privacy measurements which aim at GPS data are selected. One is for detecting personal schedule leakage, and the other is for detecting user's home address leakage from the exposed GPS data. For each privacy measurement, the type of the target usage data, the cloud service which the usage data is exposed to, the frequency to perform the privacy measurement, and the privacy measurement service which is in charge to perform the privacy measurement are displayed. Currently, those two privacy measurement services are implemented by authors as third-party privacy measurement services. If the user unchecks the box before a privacy measurement, the privacy measurement will not be performed. Results of these two privacy measurements are shown in the following.

A. Case 1: Personal Schedule Leakages

Since the location-based service is frequently used in the user's daily life, user's usage frequency reflects his personal

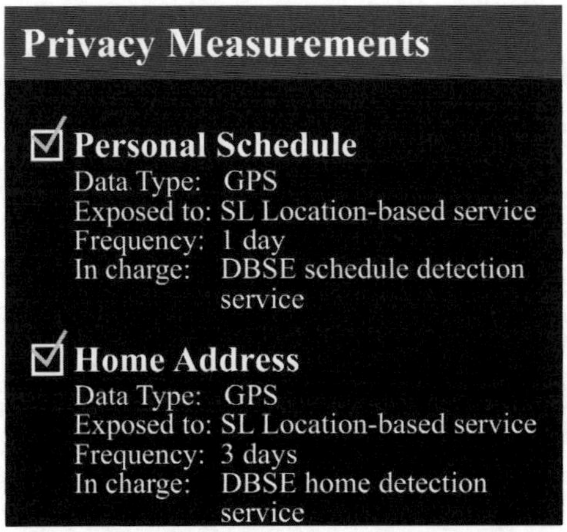

Figure 3. The privacy measurement plan.

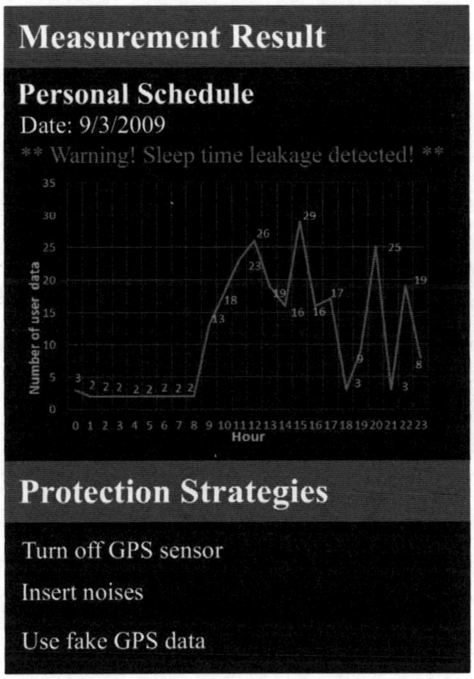

Figure 4. The privacy leakage for personal schedule.

schedule, especially the sleep time. The user will not use the location-based service when he is sleeping. A time duration that the usage frequency is steady but relatively low can be the user's sleep time. This privacy measurement checks the number of usage data transmissions to the location-based service in each hour of a day to find possible sleep time leakages. The privacy measurement is performed once a day and takes usage data of the whole day as the input. In fact, the measurement results of the usage data for each day from August 2009 to February 2010 are similar. The sleep time is leaked almost every day from the usage frequency of the service. In this case study, the usage data on 09-03-2009 is selected as the example to demonstrate the privacy leakage, as shown in Figure 4. In the measurement results, there is a relatively low and steady curve in the time duration 1:00-8:59, which is a hint for the sleep time leakage. Below the measurement results, privacy protection strategies for GPS data are suggested. If the user selects to insert noises to his future usage data to change his service usage frequency, iGuard will suggest corresponding privacy protection services that are available to assist the user in completing the work. In this work, a noise inserting service is implemented to assist user in inserting noises to his usage data. The service inserts noises that are similar to the normal usage data [11]. The new measurement results are show in Figure 5. The measurement results show that the privacy leakage is eliminated by the strategy.

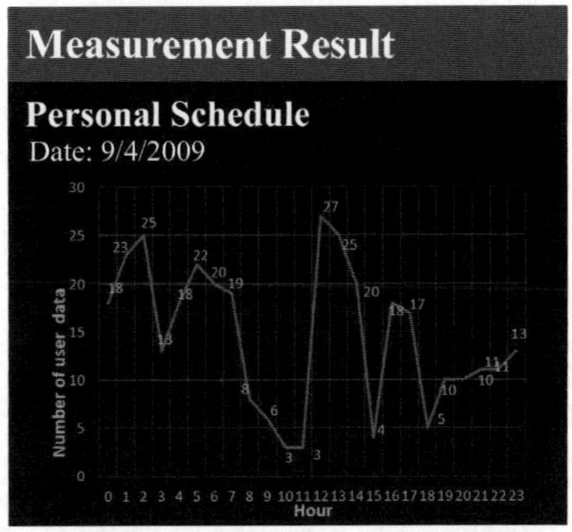

Figure 5. The measurement results after a privacy protection strategy is applied.

B. Case 2: Home Address Leakages

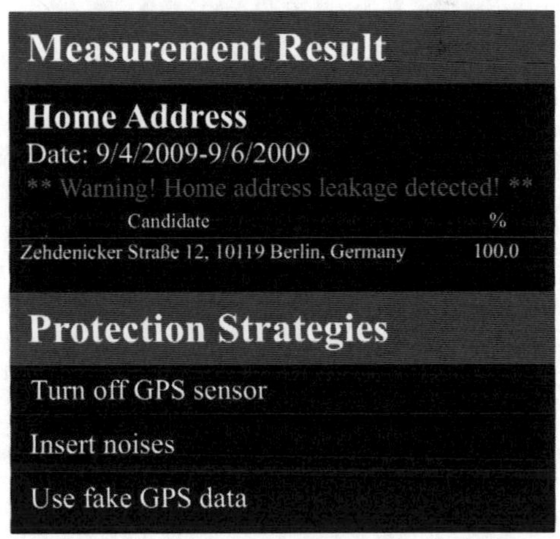

Figure 6. The privacy leakage for home address.

Most people stay at home to sleep at night. If the user's locations in sleep time are exposed to cloud services, his home address is likely to be exposed, too. This privacy measurement checks the user's locations exposed to the cloud service in sleep time for possible home address leakages. The privacy measurement is performed every three days according to the privacy measurement plan. The user is assumed to be sleeping during 1:00 AM to 4:00 AM. The privacy measurement calculates the percentage which the user stays at a location in the period of time. In this case study, the usage data from 09-10-2009 to 09-12-2009 is used as an example to demonstrate the home address leakage, as shown in Figure 6. The measurement results show that the user only stays at one location during the sleep time of these three days. The location can indicate the user's home address. The user can select to insert noises with fake GPS data when he is at home. The fake GPS data is mixed with real ones and the percentage of fake data can even be higher than real data. As a result, the user can mislead the location-based service to wrong home address information so that the home address leakage can be prevented.

VI. Conclusion and Future Work

iGuard plays the role of a mediator, which links available privacy measurements and privacy protection strategies to the user. According to the user's personal situation, iGuard performs customized privacy measurements for the user and suggests workable strategies to protect his privacy. In the user's view, the user will enjoy comprehensive privacy detection and protection as available privacy measurements and protection strategies linked to iGuard extend. In the view of providers for services of privacy measurement and privacy protection, they benefit from increasing users of their services. iGuard creates a win-win situation for both of users and service providers handling privacy issues.

In the future, iGuard will be extended for various user devices, such as smart home systems in Internet of Things (IoT), and assist users in managing their privacy for all devices in use. iGuard will provide users a comprehensive protection strategy that considers users' personal preferences and handles all privacy issues caused by using the devices. Thus users can enjoy simple and effective way to keep their privacy while utilizing all services through various devices.

Acknowledgment

The authors would like to thank the anonymous reviewers for their valuable suggestions that improved this paper. This research was supported in part by the Ministry of Science and Technology of Taiwan under Contracts MOST 104-2221-E-006-158 and MOST 104-2221-E-006-040.

References

[1] H. Seybert and P. Reinecke, "Internet and Cloud Services - Statistics On The Use by Individuals." http://ec.europa.eu/eurostat/statistics-explained/index.php/Internet_and_cloud_services_-_statistics_on_the_use_by_individuals, Dec. 2014. [Online; retrieved: Jun. 15, 2016].

[2] K. Shilton, "Four Billion Little Brothers?: Privacy, Mobile Phones, and Ubiquitous Data Collection," *Communications of the ACM*, vol. 52, no. 11, pp. 48–53, Nov. 2009.

[3] S. Subashini and V. Kavitha, "A Survey on Security Issues in Service Delivery Models of Cloud Computing ," *Journal of Network and Computer Applications*, vol. 34, no. 1, pp. 1 – 11, Jan. 2011.

[4] L. Liao, D. J. Patterson, D. Fox, and H. Kautz, "Learning and Inferring Transportation Routines," *Artificial Intelligence*, vol. 171, no. 5-6, pp. 311–331, Apr. 2007.

[5] G. Valkanas and D. Gunopulos, "Location Extraction from Social Networks with Commodity Software and Online Data," *2012 IEEE 12th International Conference on Data Mining Workshops (ICDMW)*, pp. 827–834, 2012.

[6] P. Chairunnanda, N. Pham, and U. Hengartner, "Privacy: Gone With the Typing! Identifying Web Users by Their Typing Patterns," *2011 IEEE Third International Conference on Privacy, Security, Risk and Trust (PASSAT) and 2011 IEEE Third Inernational Conference on Social Computing (SocialCom)*, pp. 974–980, Oct. 2011.

[7] L. Liao, D. J. Patterson, D. Fox, and H. Kautz, "Building Personal Maps from GPS Data," *Annals of the New York Academy of Sciences*, vol. 1093, no. 1, pp. 249–265, 2006.

[8] L. Ferrari, A. Rosi, M. Mamei, and F. Zambonelli, "Extracting Urban Patterns From Location-Based Social Networks," *Proceedings of the 3rd ACM SIGSPATIAL International Workshop on Location-Based Social Networks*, pp. 9–16, 2011.

[9] P. Murukannaiah and M. Singh, "Platys Social: Relating Shared Places and Private Social Circles," *IEEE Internet Computing*, vol. 16, no. 3, pp. 53 –59, May-Jun. 2012.

[10] L. O. Stenneth and P. S. Yu, "Privacy-Aware Mobile Location-Based Systems," *Proceedings of the 1st International Workshop on Mobile Location-Based Service*, pp. 79–88, 2011.

[11] G. Zhang, X. Liu, and Y. Yang, "Time-Series Pattern Based Effective Noise Generation for Privacy Protection on Cloud," *IEEE Transactions on Computers*, vol. 64, no. 5, pp. 1456–1469, May 2015.

[12] P. Ren, W. Liu, and D. Sun, "Partition-Based Data Cube Storage and Parallel Queries for Cloud Computing," *2013 Ninth International Conference on Natural Computation (ICNC)*, pp. 1183–1187, Jul. 2013.

[13] A. R. Beresford, A. Rice, N. Skehin, and R. Sohan, "MockDroid: Trading Privacy for Application Functionality on Smartphones," *Proceedings of the 12th Workshop on Mobile Computing Systems and Applications*, pp. 49–54, 2011.

[14] S. Guha, M. Jain, and V. N. Padmanabhan, "Koi: A Location-Privacy Platform for Smartphone Apps," *Proceedings of the 9th USENIX Conference on Networked Systems Design and Implementation*, 2012.

[15] H. Kasai, W. Uchida, and S. Kurakake, "A Service Provisioning System for Distributed Personalization With Private Data Protection," *Journal of Systems and Software*, vol. 80, no. 12, pp. 2025 – 2038, 2007.

[16] R. Jin and B. Wang, "Malware Detection for Mobile Devices Using Software-Defined Networking," *Proceedings of the 2013 Second GENI Research and Educational Experiment Workshop*, pp. 81–88, 2013.

[17] C.-W. Hu and H. C. Jiau, "Trust Circle: Promoting Collaboration and Data Sharing Between Data Providers and Data Consumers in IoT," submitted for publication.

[18] K. Biermann, "Betrayed by Our Own Data." http://www.zeit.de/digital/datenschutz/2011-03/data-protection-malte-spitz, Mar. 2011. [Online; retrieved: Jun. 15, 2016].

Trust-Oriented Protocol for Continuous Monitoring of Stored Files in Cloud

Alexandre Pinheiro[1], Edna Dias Canedo[2], Rafael Timóteo de Sousa Júnior[1] and Robson de Oliveira Albuquerque
[1]Electrical Engineering Department
[2]Faculdade UnB Gama
University of Brasília, UnB
Brasília - DF, Brazil
E-mail: tenpinheiro@dct.eb.mil.br, ednacanedo@unb.br, desousa@unb.br, robson@redes.unb.br

Abstract — **The speed, availability, scalability and low cost are main attractive of cloud services. However, building safe storage services from a customer point of view, mainly when this service is being hosted on public cloud infrastructure, whose service providers are not fully trustworthy, it is an obstacle to be overcame. There are common situations, where owners of large data amount need to store them for a long time, but they will not necessarily need to access them. This time can vary from few years to decades, in accordance with applicable laws of each country. In these cases, important aspects as integrity, availability and privacy must be considered when making decision on adoption of cloud services. Considering the damage whose information loss or its leakage may cause, this paper presents a protocol, which through an independent checker, allows a periodic monitoring on stored files in cloud using trust and cryptography concepts to ensure data integrity. Moreover, this paper also presents a protocol reference implementation and the performed tests results.**

Keywords-protocol; trust; cloud data storage; integrity; data monitoring.

I. INTRODUCTION

Companies, institutions and government agencies generate large amounts of information in digital format, such as documents, projects, transactions records etc., every day. For legal or business reasons, this information needs to remain stored for a long period of time and this has become an issue for IT managers.

The use of cloud services for storing sensitive information started to gain relevance, along with its popularization, cost reductions and an ever-growing supply of Cloud Storage Services (CSS). However, ensuring integrity and confidentiality still has to be evaluated in such services in order to protect information.

CSS for data storage are fast, cheap, and almost infinitely scalable. However, reliability can be an issue, as even the best services sometimes fail [1].

A considerable number of organizations consider security and privacy as obstacles to the acceptance of public cloud services [2].

Data integrity is defined as the accuracy and consistency of stored data. This condition indicates that the data has not changed and has not been broken [2]. CSS should provide mechanisms to confirm data integrity, while still ensuring user privacy.

Considering these perspectives, this paper proposes a protocol based in outsourced service which provides the CSS customers the constant assurance of the existence and integrity of their files without the need to keep copies of the original files or expose its contents.

This paper is structured as follows: Section II reviews works related to data integrity in the cloud. Then, Section III proposes a new protocol named Trust-Oriented Protocol for Continuous Monitoring of Stored Files in Cloud (TOPMCloud). A detailed analysis of the TOPMCloud is shown in Section IV. The Section V shows a TOPMCloud implementation. A resume of obtained results are presented in Section VI. Section VII ends this paper with some conclusions and outlines future works.

II. RELATED WORK

In order to try to guarantee the integrity of data stored in CSS, many research works suggested solutions with both advantages and disadvantages regarding the domain analysed in this paper.

The protocol proposed by Juels and Kaliski [3] enables the CSS to prove a file subjected to verification was not corrupted. To that end a formal and secure definition of proof of retrievability was presented and introduced the use of sentinels. Sentinels are special blocks, hidden in the original file prior being encrypted and then used to challenge the CSS. In the work of Kumar and Saxena [4], a scheme was presented, based on [3] where one does not need to encrypt all the data, but only a few bits per data block.

George and Sabitha [5] proposed a solution to improve privacy and integrity. The solution was designed to be used in tables and it was divided in two parts. The first, called 'anonymisation' is used to identify fields in records that could identify their owners. Anonymisation uses techniques such as generalisation, suppression, obfuscation, and addition of anonymous records to enhance data privacy.

The second, called 'integrity checking', uses public and private key encryption techniques to generate a tag for each record on a table. Both parts are executed helped by trusted third party called 'enclave' that saves all the data generated that will be used for deanonymisation and integrity verification.

A new encrypted integrity verification method is proposed by Kavuri et al. [6]. The proposed method uses a new hash algorithm, the Dynamic User Policy Based Hash Algorithm. Hashes on data are calculated for each authorised cloud user. For data encryption, an Improved Attribute-Based Encryption algorithm is used. Encrypted data and its hash value are saved separately in CSS. Data integrity can be verified only by an authorized user and it is necessary to retrieve all the encrypted data and its hash.

Another proposal to simultaneously achieve data integrity verification and privacy preserving is found in the work of Al-Jaberi and Zainal [7]. Their work proposed the use of two encryption algorithms for every data upload or download transaction.

The Advanced Encryption Standard (AES) algorithm is used to encrypt client's' data which will be saved in a CSS, and a RSA-based partial homomorphic encryption technique is used to encrypt AES encryption keys that will be saved in a third party together with a hash of the file. Data integrity is verified only when a client downloads one's file.

In the work of Kay et al. [8], a data integrity auditing protocol that allows the fast identification of corrupted data using of homomorphic cipher-text verification and recoverable coding methodology was proposed. Due the methodology adopted, both the total auditing time and the communication cost could be reduced. Checking the integrity of outsourced data is done periodically by a trusted or untrusted entity.

In the work of Wang et al. [9], it is presented a security model for public verification for storage correctness assurance that supports dynamic data operation. The model guarantees that no challenged file blocks should be retrieved by the verifier during the verification process and no state information should be stored at the verifier side between audits. A Merkle Hash Tree (MHT) is used to save the hashes of authentic data values and both the values and positions of data blocks are authenticated by the verifier.

In the work of Jordão et al. [10], an approach was presented that allows inserting large volumes of encrypted data in non-relational databases hosted in the cloud and after that performs queries on inserted data without the use of a decryption key. Although not the main focus of the work, this approach could be used to verify the integrity of stored content in the cloud through the evaluation of responses to queries with previously calculated results.

The proposed solutions in [5][7][8][9] are using asymmetric cryptographic algorithms which are admittedly slow compared to symmetric algorithms. The solution proposed by Kavuri et al. [6] needs to retrieve whole file to check it. In the work of Juels and Kaliski [3], and in the work of Kumar and Saxena [4], small changes in the file can remain unnoticed until the whole file to be recovered.

Thus, unlike the works cited above, this paper presents a protocol that only uses symmetric encryption to check file integrity. Furthermore, it uses a challenge/response-based technique for checking the integrity without download the file. Finally, our solution checks all file bytes so that any change, no matter how small, will be identified quickly.

III. PROTOCOL OBJECTIVES

The main objective of protocol is to make possible utilization of an outsourced service allowing client to constantly monitor the integrity of their stored files in CSS, without having to keep copies from original files or reveal its contents.

A. *Protocol requirements*

One of the main requirements of this protocol is to prevent the CSS provider from offering and charging a client for a storage service that in practice is not being provided. Other premises are low bandwidth consumption, quick identification of a misbehaving service, providing strong defenses against fraud, avoiding the overloading of CSS, ensuring data confidentiality and also giving utmost predictability to the Integrity Check Service (ICS).

B. *Protocol operating principle*

The basic operating principle of the protocol begins with the encryption of the original file, followed by its division into 4096 small chunks, which in turn are grouped randomly to form each data block with distinct 16-chunks. Hashes will be generated from these data blocks and together with the addresses of the chunks which formed the data block are sent to the ICS.

The selection and distribution of chunks used to assemble the data blocks is done in cycles. The number of cycles will vary according to the file storage period. Each cycle generates 256 data blocks without repeating chunks.

The data blocks generated in each cycle contains all of the chunks of the encrypted file ($256 * 16 = 4096$).

Each hash and its chunk addresses will be used only once by the ICS to send an integrity verification challenge to the CSS provider. On receiving a challenge with the chunk addresses, the CSS reads the chunks from stored file, assembles the data block, generates a hash from data block and sends the hash as answer to the ICS.

Chunks number per file as well as chunks number to compose each data block was chosen through mathematical simulations. These simulations seek to find small numbers that minimize the required time to fully check a file, but large enough to make it impossible to save hashes from all possible data blocks without taking up more disk space than the original file.

To finalize, the answer hash and the origin hash are compared by ICS. If the hashes are equal, it means the content of evaluated chunks in the stored file is intact.

C. *Protocol architecture*

The protocol architecture is based in three components: i) customers; ii) storage services in the cloud; and iii) an integrity check service. The interaction between the architectural members is carried out through an exchange of asynchronous messages.

The protocol consists of two distinct processes. The first, called "File Storage Process", which is run on demand and has the client as its starting point. The second called 'Verification Process' is instantiated by an ICS and executed continuously to verify one CSS.

An ICS can simultaneously verify more than one CSS through parallel instances of the Verification Process. An overview of the TOPMCloud protocol architecture is shown in Figure 1.

1) *File Storage Process*

File Storage Process is responsible for preparing the file to be sent to the CSS and for generating the information needed for its verification by ICS.

In Figure 1, each stage from 'File Storage Process' are named with the prefix 'Stage FS-' followed by the number of the stage and, if necessary, by its stage sub-process number.

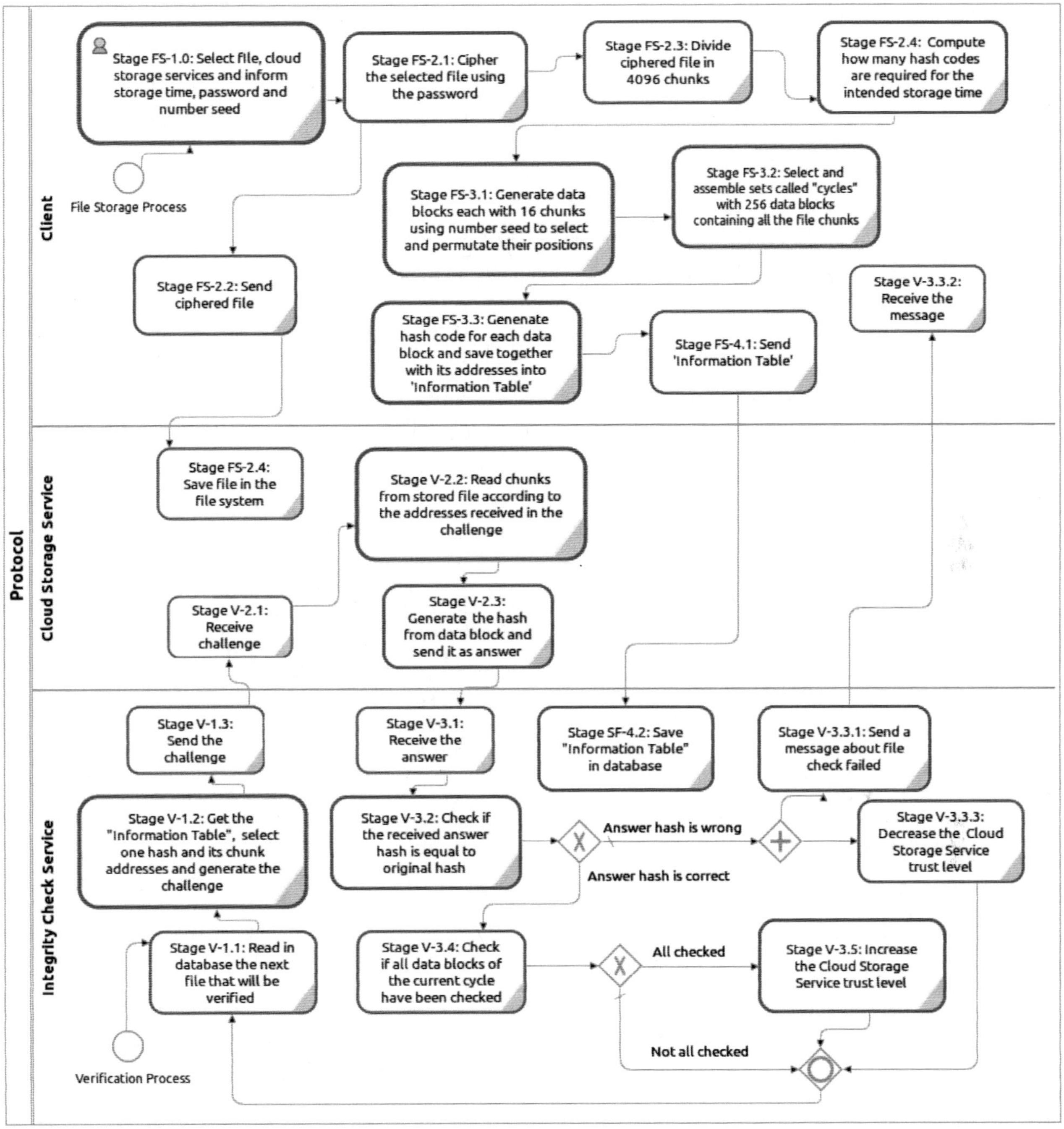

Fig. 1. TOPMCloud Protocol.

The process goes as follows. First, the user should select a file, a password, a number seed, and the time in years for which it intends to maintain the monitoring of file integrity. The password will be used to generate the secret key used to encrypt chosen file.

The number seed will add extra entropy to the process that creates a random seed used to warrant an unpredictable selection and distribution of the data that forms the source of the hash codes to be used to check file integrity.

One or more CSS should also be selected. Considering the need to ensure the recoverability of files, selecting more than one provider is important to provide redundancy, given that customers will not keep a copy of the original files.

In the next stage, data blocks are generated from random union of 16 chunks of the original file. For this, after the split, each file chunk receives an address code between 0 and 4095, represented in hexadecimal format (000 - FFF).

An algorithm developed for this purpose will make the selection of chunks and permutation of their positions for each data block.

The algorithm uses the number seed provided by user to creates the random seed which will be used to add an extra layer of the entropy to the pseudo-random sequence generator that chooses the sequences of address codes.

The algorithm is also responsible for grouping data blocks in sets called 'cycles'. Each cycle consists of 256 data blocks that have all the 4096 chunks of the original file. This stage is shown in Figure 1 as sub-processes 'FS-3.1', 'FS-3.2', and 'FS-3.3'.

Finally, in the last stage is built a data structure named 'information table'. It contains record header made up by a file identifier, the chunk size in bytes, the body records amount, the total number of cycles, and a checksum. Each record on the table represents a data block and contains fields with the address codes of the 16 file chunks, their cycle number and hash code. The 'information table' is sent to ICS and the file sent to CSS is deleted from the customer.

2) Verification Process

This process is designed to periodically check the integrity of files saved in CSS. Furthermore, it assigns a trust level for each CSS according to the check results.

Trust is recognized as an important aspect for decision-making in distributed and auto-organized applications [11][12]. Marsh [11] provided a clarification of trust concepts, presented an implementable formalism for trust, and applied a trust model to a distributed artificial intelligence (DAI) system in order to enable agents to make trust-based decisions.

Trust and security have become crucial to guarantee the healthy development of cloud platforms, providing solutions for concerns such as the lack of integrity and privacy, the guarantee of security and author rights.

The verification process consists of the following stages: In ICS, selecting the next file to be checked, generating the challenge and delivering it to CSS; In CSS, receiving the challenge, reading the chunks from saved file according to the challenge, assembling the data block, generating the data block hash, rendering and sending the answer to ICS; and in ICS again, receiving and checking the answer. The sub-process from "Verification Process" shown in Figure 1 follows the same previously used rules, but are prefixed with 'Stage V-'.

In the first stage, the ICS verifies what next file should have its integrity checked in a given CSS, performing the same procedure in parallel with each other registered CSS.

After selecting the file, its information table is read and the number of the last checked cycle is retrieved. When the file is new or when the last checked cycle has already been completed, a new and not yet checked cycle is randomly chosen.

After that, the next not-verified record that belongs to the selected cycle is selected from information table. The challenge is assembled using the address codes obtained from selected record, the file chunk length, the file identifier and a challenge identifier. When ready, the challenge is sent to CSS and the pool of challenges that are waiting for an answer is updated.

In the second stage, the CSS receives the challenge and concurrently retrieves all chunks from saved file. Chunks are retrieved according to address codes and length received in the challenge. All chunks retrieved are concatenated forming a data block, and from it, a hash is generated. This hash is packaged together with the challenge identifier and sent as response to the ICS.

In the third stage, the ICS receives the answer, finds the challenge in the pool, reads the original record from the information table and compares the received hash with the hash that gave rise to the challenge. If they do not match, a message is sent to client reporting the error. Whenever a file verification process fails, the CSS trust level is immediately downgraded. The sub-processes from 'V-3.1' to 'V-3.6' show this stage in Figure 1.

When the ICS does not receive an answer from the CSS on a challenge, after the wait time has expired, the original challenge is re-sent and the wait time is squared. After the 10th unsuccessful attempt, the challenge is considered failed and the same procedures described in the third stage are adopted.

If the response hash and the original hash are equal, then a flag will be saved in the information table record, indicating that the data block represented by its hash was successfully verified. After that, case there is no other record in the current cycle to be checked, this means that all of data blocks of the file saved in CSS have already been successfully verified and the CSS trust level must be raised.

To end the stage, the trust level classification process will be done. Upon completion of this stage, the process is re-executed from the first stage.

3) Trust Level Classification Process

Whenever a verification process fails, the trust level of the CSS verified will be downgraded. When the current trust level value is greater than zero, it is set to zero, when the trust value is in the range between 0 and -0.5, it is reduced by 15%. Otherwise, it is calculated the value of 2.5% from the difference between the current trust level value and -1, and the result is subtracted from trust level value. These calculations are shown in the source code below.

```
IF (TrustLevel > 0) THEN
    TrustLevel = 0
ELSE IF (TrustLevel >= -0.5) THEN
    TrustLevel = TrustLevel - (TrustLevel * -0.15)
ELSE
    TrustLevel = TrustLevel - {[(-1) - TrustLevel] * -0.025}
```

However, whenever a checking cycle is completed without failures (all the data blocks of a file have been checked without errors), the CSS trust level is raised. If the current trust level value is less than 0.5, then the trust level value is raised by 2.5%. Otherwise, it is calculated the value of 0.5% from the difference between 1 and the current trust level value, and the result is added to trust level value. These calculations are shown in the source code below.

```
IF (TrustLevel < 0.5) THEN
    TrustLevel = TrustLevel + (TrustLevel * 0.025)
ELSE
    TrustLevel = TrustLevel + {[1 - TrustLevel] * 0.005}
```

The trust level in a CSS will affect the verification periodicity of its files and the time needed to get a complete file cycle. When the verification of all the data blocks in a cycle has been successfully concluded, this means that all the chunks of the original file were tested.

The minimum percentages of stored files on each service that will be verified per day, as well as the minimum percentage of data blocks that will be checked by file and per day, according to trust level, are shown in Table I. The values 1 and -1 that respectively represent blind trust and complete distrust are incompatible with the object of classification and will not be considered.

TABLE I. CLASSIFICATION OF THE TRUST LEVELS

Trust Level	Value Range	Files verified by day	% from file verified by day	Data Blocks verified by day
Very high trust	]0.9, 1[	15%	~ 0.4%	1
High trust	]0.75, 0.9]	16%	~ 0.8%	2
High medium trust	]0.5, 0.75]	17%	~ 1.2%	3
Low medium trust	]0.25, 0.5]	18%	~ 1.6%	4
Low trust	]0, 0.25]	19%	~ 2.0%	5
Low distrust	]-0.25, 0]	20%	~2.4%	6
Low medium distrust	]−0.5, −0.25]	25%	~ 3.2%	8
High medium distrust	]−0.75, −0.5]	30%	~ 4.0%	10
High distrust	]−0.9, −0.75]	35%	~ 4.8%	12
Very high distrust	]-1, -0.9]	50%	~5.6%	14

Whenever the value of the trust is zero, a fixed value is assigned to determine the initial trust. Thus, if the last check resulted in a 'positive assessment', a value of +0.1 is assigned for trust; otherwise, if a fault has been identified, the assigned value is -0.1.

IV. PROTOCOL ANALYSIS

As a prerequisite to define the characteristics of the proposed protocol we took into consideration the following assumptions: low consumption of network bandwidth; predictability and economy in consumption of ICS resources; fast identification of misbehaving services; privacy; resistance against fraud, and no overloading of the CSS.

Thus, the proposed logical division of the file into 4096 chunks, grouped into blocks of 16 chunks each, aims at minimizing the storage service overhead by reducing the amount of data to be read for each verification, and enabling the parallel execution of searching and recovering each data chunk.

Fast identification of badly behaved services also helped to determine the proposed values. The protocol uses a random selection of 16 file chunks in the data block, to allow checking the integrity of various parts of the file in a single verification step.

Privacy is attained with the use of 256-bit hash codes to represent each data block, regardless of their original size. The hash codes allow the ICS to perform the validation of files hosted in storage services, without necessarily knowing their contents.

Furthermore, the use of hash codes in combination with a fixed amount of data blocks, providing predictability and low usage of the network bandwidth. It is possible to pre-determine the computational cost required to verify the integrity of a file, the whole time foreseen for its storage, regardless of its size.

There is also the possibility to predict the total number of data blocks, as it varies according to the time predicted for the file storage, so that each hash code and the chunk addresses that formed the data are used only once, uniquely and exclusively as a challenge to the CSS. Calculations were made based on a worst-case scenario, i.e., the hypothetical situation where the CSS remains throughout the file storage period rated as 'Very High Distrust'.

According to Table 1, in a CSS rated as 'Very High Distrust', it is necessary to check at least 14 data blocks of each file a day. As the data blocks generation is performed in cycles with 256 blocks each, to determine the total number of data blocks to be generated (2), it is necessary to first calculate the total number of cycles (1).

$$Cycles = ROUND\left(\frac{(14*366)*Years}{256},\ 0\right) \quad (1)$$

$$Data\ Blocks = Cycles * 256 \quad (2)$$

From the definition of the number of blocks, it is possible to determine the size of the 'information table' and, therefore, the computing cost to transfer and store it in an ICS.

Finally, fraud resistance is obtained by means of a selection and swapping algorithm that assigns the entropy needed to render as impracticable any attempt to predict which chunks are in each data block, as well as the order in which these chunks were joined. A brute force attack, generating hash codes for all possible combinations of data blocks, is not feasible as the number of possible combinations for the arrangement of 4096 file chunks in blocks with 16 chunks each is of about 6.09×10^{57} blocks (3). Consequently, to generate and store 256-bit hash codes for all possible combinations of data blocks would need about 1.77×10^{47} TB in disk space (4).

$$A_{n,p} = \frac{n!}{(n-p)!} \rightarrow A_{4096,16} = \frac{4096!}{(4096-16)!} \cong 6.09 \times 10^{57} \quad (3)$$

$$Disk\ Space\ (TB) = \frac{(6.09 \times 10^{57}) * 256}{8 * 1024^4} \cong 1.77 \times 10^{47} \quad (4)$$

V. IMPLEMENTATION

The implementation of TOPMCloud protocol was divided in three stages. At first stage, all processes of customer responsibility were implemented. At second stage, all processes of ICS responsibility were implemented, and finally, at third stage, all processes of CSS responsibility were implemented.

For each stage, we developed an application, all of them using components of Java EE technology as JPA, EJB and CDI. For the client, we developed a desktop application, whereas for ICS and CSS, we developed Web Service (WS) applications. The utilized application server was Glassfish and, as Database Management System (DBMS), we chose PostgreSQL.

The main customer application tasks are: encrypting the file; dividing it into equal chunks; assembling data blocks; generating their hashes and joining them in cycles; generating the information table and sending it to the ICS; and, finally, sending the encrypted file to CSS. For task of encrypting file, we chose the AES-256 algorithm using Cipher-Block Chaining (CBC) operation mode.

Raffle process of file chunks to compose each data block was implemented using the SHA1PRNG algorithm, a pseudo-random number generator. Due to its high speed, security, and simplicity, we adopted the algorithm Blake2 [13] as cryptographic hash function for this work.

At second stage, we implemented all necessary routines for ICS provider executing the file monitoring using WSs. The main tasks implemented by ICS application are: receiving information tables and saving them in your database; generating challenges and sending them to CSSs; monitoring and receiving answers about challenges; and ranking trust level from monitored CSSs.

At third and last stage, as well as in previous stage, we implemented all necessary routines to the CSS answering the challenges to ICS using WSs. The main tasks in CSS application are: receiving and saving challenges in your database; processing challenges; and sending response to ICS. Challenges reception, their processing and responses delivery are carried out in parallel and asynchronously.

VI. RESULTS

The scenario used to test the application and to verify TOPMCloud efficiency was composed of three Virtual Machines (VM) (a customer, a ICS and a CSS). These VMs shared resources from a computer equipped with an Intel core i7 2.4 GHz, 12GB of RAM memory, and a 1TB SATA Hard Disk 5400 RPM.

Five tests were performed with three different large file sizes. The average results are presented in Table II.

TABLE II. TEST RESULTS

File size	Times spent to:			
	encrypt file	**compute file hash**	**compute data block hashes (for 1 year)**	**check one data block**
5 GB	4.0 min	23.4 s	32.0 min	0.11 s
9 GB	7.1 min	91.1 s	71.8 min	0.88 s
14 GB	10.6 min	137.0 s	108.6 min	1.20 s

In order to simulate a file integrity breakdown and determine the number of days required to identify the fault, tests were performed on a CSS classified as 'low trust'. The same three previously tested files were monitored, however only the 5 GB file had changed its contents. The characteristics and results of each test are presented in Table III.

TABLE III. FAULT SIMULATION TESTS

Bytes changed	File percentage	Location	Affected chunks	Days required to find fault					
				T1	**T2**	**T3**	**T4**	**T5**	**Average**
4688	0.000085%	random choice	1 or 2	10	9	22	12	15	~14
55006658	1.0%	end of file	41	3	7	6	6	3	5

With the aim to determine the maximum number of days required to complete a file check cycle (all its data blocks being checked at least once) on each trust level, we did simulations using the percentages defined for each trust level in Table I. The results are presented in Figure 2.

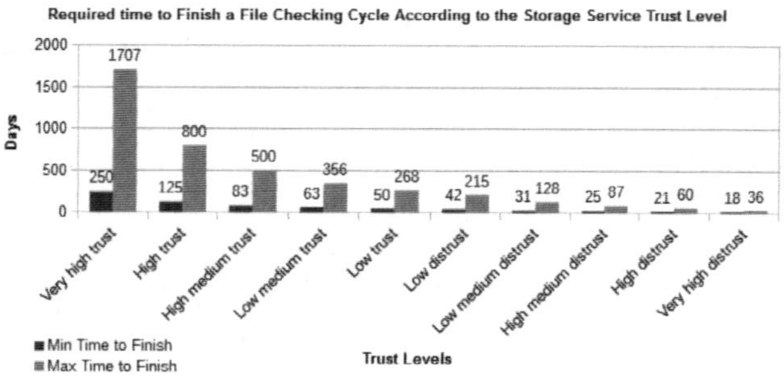

Fig. 2. Number of days required to complete a file check cycle.

This time variation is intended to reward services with fewer failures, minimizing consumption of resources such as processing and bandwidth. Moreover, it allows prioritizing the protocol for checking files that are stored in services that have already failed, reducing the time required to determine if there are any corrupted or lost files.

VII. CONCLUSION AND FUTURE WORK

In this paper, we proposed a protocol to ensure the integrity of stored files in CSS through an ICS hosted by a third party. The protocol named TOPMCloud allows periodic and qualified monitoring of file integrity using trust concepts without confidentiality compromising.

Based on CSS behaviour, the checking frequency can increase or decrease, reducing overload on services that never fail or checking more quickly all stored files in CSSs that have already failed.

As it can be seen in Section VI, TOPMCloud provides a efficient control over file integrity. Even on very large files, time spent checking each data block does not overload the CSS. Variation in number of days required to identify the same fault, which was purposely inserted in the file, obtained in subsequent tests, confirms the randomness of the selection process of each data block sent as a challenge to CSS.

Another important result obtained was the speed to identify a fault, even interfering in only 2 from 4096 file chunks, the average period for its identification was only two weeks.

As part of future works, we intend to formalize and validate the protocol using Petri nets. We will conduct tests simulating the protocol behaviour with CSSs classified in all trust levels. Furthermore, we want to add a mechanism to ensure that, only when authorized by a customer, a ICS could send challenges to CSS.

REFERENCES

[1] S. T. Tandel, V. K. Shah, and S. Hiranwal, "An implementation of effective XML based dynamic data integrity audit service in cloud," in International Journal of Societal Applications of Computer Science, vol. 2, issue 8, pp. 449-553, 2014.

[2] P. Dabas and D. Wadhwa, "A recapitulation of data auditing approaches for cloud data," in International Journal of Computer Applications Technology and Research (IJCATR), vol. 3, issue 6, pp. 329-332, 2014.

[3] A. Juels and B. S. Kaliski, "Pors: proofs of retrievability for large files" in 14th ACM Conference on Computer and Comunication Security (CCS), Alexandria, VA, pp.584-59, 2007.

[4] R. S. Kumar and A. Saxena, "Data integrity proofs in cloud storage," in Third International Conference on Communication Systems and Networks (COMSNETS), Bangalore, pp. 138-146, 2011.

[5] R. S. George and S. Sabitha, "Data anonymization and integrity checking in cloud computing," in Fourth International Conference on Computing (ICCCNT), Communications and Networking Technologies, Tiruchengode, pp. 758-769, 2013.

[6] S. K. S. V. A. Kavuri, G. R. Kancherla, and B. R. Bobba, "Data authentication and integrity verification techniques for trusted/untrusted cloud servers," in International Conference on Advances in Computing, Communications and Informatics (ICACCI), New Delhi, pp. 2590-2596, 2014.

[7] M. F. Al-Jaberi and A. Zainal, "Data integrity and privacy model in cloud computing," in International Symposium on Biometrics and Security Technologies (ISBAST), Kuala Lumpur, pp. 280-284, 2014.

[8] H. Kay, H. Chuanhe, W. Jinhai, Z. Hao, W. Xi, L. Yilong, Z. Lianzhen, and W. Bin, "An efficient public batch auditing protocol for data security in multi-cloud storage," in 8th ChinaGrid Annual Conference (ChinaGrid), Changchun, pp. 51-56, 2013.

[9] Q. Wang, C. Wang, J. Li, K. Ren, and W. Lou, "An enabling public verifiability and data dynamics for storage security in cloud computing," in 14th European Symposium on Research in Computer Security (ESORICS), Saint-Malo, pp. 355-370, 2009.

[10] R. Jordão, V. A. Martins, F. Buiati, R. T. Sousa Jr, and F. E. Deus, "Secure Data Storage in Distributed Cloud Environments," in IEEE International Conference on Big Data (IEEE BigData), Washington DC, pp. 6-12, 2014.

[11] S. P. Marsh, "Formalising Trust as a Computational Concept", Ph.D. Thesis, University of Stirling, 1994.

[12] T. Beth, M. Borcherding, and B. Klein, "Valuation of trust in open networks," in 3Th European Symposium on Research in Computer Security (ESORICS), Brighton, pp. 1-18, 1994.

[13] J. Aumasson, S. Neves, W. O'Hearn, and Z. Winnerlein, "BLAKE2: Simpler, Smaller, Fast as MD5," in Applied Cryptography and Network Security, Springer Berlin Heidelberg, pp. 119-135, 2013.

Smart Cities Security Issues: An Impeding Identity Crisis

Felipe Silva Ferraz, Carlos André Guimarães Ferraz, Ademir Gomes

CESAR-Centro de Estudos e Sistemas Avançados do Recife
Recife, Brazil
Email: fsf@cesar.org.br

Informatics Center
Federal University of Pernambuco
Recife, Brazil
Email:{fsf3, cagf}@cin.ufpe.br

Engineering department
Federal Rural University of PE
Recife, Brazil
Email: ademir.ferraz@gmail.com

Abstract — **Cities have changed the manner in which population is distributed around the globe. Beginning in the 70s, a large number of people began to migrate from the countryside to a metropolis. In such a scenario, it is necessary to build city systems and provide citizens with different methods to interact with these systems. Further, citizens play an important role in building this interoperable environment, and they are required to provide data and information about themselves in order to improve the functioning of the systems. However, citizens do not want their personal and private data to be disseminated in the city. This study explores problems in information security, and, more specifically, those related to identifier and identity management in the context of a smart city environment. This study proposes to address such problems by using an architecture that separates identifiers from data, thus creating a multiple identity infrastructure.**

Keywords- Identity; Security; Smart Cities;

I. INTRODUCTION

The first decade of the 21st century has seen a major change in population distribution in the world. Owing to revolutions in industry and changes in commerce, many people began to migrate from the countryside to big cities [1] [2].

In order to deal with this new scenario in which a majority of the population lives in metropolises, cities are imposing an additional load on their core systems such as the Education, Public Safety, Transportation, Energy and Water, Healthcare, and Government systems [3]. Thus, cities have been created and developed, and citizens have been empowered technologically owing to the increasing number of instrumented and interconnected urban solutions and systems.

To develop this ubiquitous and intelligent ecosystem, several studies are focusing on the concept of a smart city. This concept involves better management of the infrastructure and data of a city [3]. In a smart city, better urban performance must not depend solely on its hardware infrastructure or the physical concepts of infrastructure, but must start taking into account the social interactions, the large amount of generated data, and a faster deployment of information and services to every citizen. The adoption of a smart city solution is becoming increasingly inevitable in order to present entities with an interoperable environment, which is capable of influencing web-based systems in data storage and sharing, and inter-communication among systems and other entities. Henceforth, entities will serve as a reference for various aspects of a smart city system such as citizens, sensors, and services.

Issues related to the development of smart cities into interoperable urban environments pose a fundamental hurdle in solving complex problems of core systems in cities [3]. Further, one of the most critical barriers that prevent mainstream users (or citizens) from adopting the smart cities solution is the uncertainty concerning the safety of their data in the various collaborative systems, which form part of a unified set of systems that address the problems of urban environments.

It is important to provide citizens with the means to manage their own identity across ubiquitous and interoperable systems [4]–[6]. This solution must not compromise the environment solution in any manner and must increase the privacy and anonymity of the citizen. Hence, for citizens, identity management is a key enabler for the evolution and maintenance of smart cities [7][8].

This study enumerates a set of security issues, identity issues in particular, that remain to be addressed from the perspective of a smart city. It also presents a reference architecture based on the management of identifiers. This architecture aims to increase security in the environment of smart cities, and provides entities (citizens, services, and sensors) with a method to interact with systems by using unique IDs for each system. Finally, an analysis of these issues is performed for the proposed architecture.

This manuscript is organized as follows: After a brief introduction, the concepts of smart cities are introduced in Section II. In Section III, security analysis of smart cities is presented. The proposed architecture is described in Section IV. Section V consists of the evaluation of the proposed architecture. In Section VI, the conclusion is presented and future work is discussed.

II. SMART CITIES: AN IDENTITY CRISIS

The current level of urbanization in smart cities has attained an unprecedented economic and social growth; large cities now accommodate a majority of the world population and an increasing percentage of the most skilled, educated, creative, and entrepreneurial men and women in the world [1]. Today, more than 50% of the people on the planet live in large cities. According to the United Nations, this number will increase to 70% in less than 50 years [1]. This city growth or emergence of urban life is leading to unprecedented pressure on the infrastructure of the city owing to an increasing demand for basic services that result in exponential overloading [3].

The smart city concept is based on intelligence, connection, and instrumentation. Another perspective, represented in Fig. 1, demonstrates three main characteristics in a smart city definition; it is an environment that is instrumented, interconnected, and intelligent [7]. A system that has only one or two of the above mentioned three characteristics results in a scenario in which a vital part will be missing.

In spite of various studies and protocols related to information security, the number of vulnerabilities in connected applications has increased during the past few years [9]. Therefore, smart city systems require a distinct approach to address specific information security challenges [10][11].

According to [3][6][12][13], Smart city solutions depend on a high degree of connectivity in order to enable their systems (such as Education, Government, Traffic, Security, Resources, and Health) to create an interoperable network, thus offering citizens more powerful, accurate, and innovative [14] services. Thus, one of the major challenges in smart-city development is related to information security in the scope of interoperable systems [1]. Information security is a critical issue owing to the increasing potential of cyber-attacks and incidents in critical sectors of a smart city.

In addition to deliberate attacks, such as those from disgruntled employees, industrial espionage and terrorists, information security must also address accidental compromises of the information infrastructure owing to user errors, equipment failures, and natural disasters. Vulnerabilities may allow an attacker to penetrate a network, gain access to control software [11][15], and modify load conditions to destabilize the system in an unpredictable manner. In order to protect a smart city effectively, various security problems must be addressed according to a specific design or plan.

The belief that a traditional security approach based on privacy maintenance, authorization, and authentication can simply be added to the critical infrastructure of a city to make it safer as the city becomes smarter does not correspond to the actual scenario [4].

A. *Distinct concepts: Identity versus identifier*

Identity is not absolute. An identity describes an entity within a specific scope. In our context, an entity could be a citizen, computer, service, sensor, organization, or one of many other actors of a smart city environment.

In formal terms, the identity of an entity, within a scope, is the set of all characteristics attributed to this entity within that scope. For example, one could have an identity related to an educational system that contains information about the educational record, courses taken, and/or grades received; another possible identity could be related to the resource systems of a citizen, and the data stored may include the amount of energy or water consumed in the home of a citizen. Therefore, identities are only valid within a specific field and represent more than simply information that distinguishes one entity from another; they also represent who the entity is, along with its characteristics.

In order to uniquely identify an entity, it is necessary to rely on identifiers and not only on identities. This distinction between identity and identifier is essential, and is not always correctly understood. The confusion is understandable because, in common phrasing, identity is almost synonymous with personal data or information used to identify an entity, which, in turn, is understood to be a unique identifier. Identifiers (such as a user name, sensor identifiers, social number, passport number, serial number, or serial ID) are also valid and guaranteed to be unique only within a scope.

Thus, instead of considering an entity with a single identifier to represent a single identity across different systems, it is more natural to view an entity as a collection of multiple identifiers (a set of sets), each with its own scope, that can represent different identities of the same entity because the entity is identified differently within different possibilities. Note that this concept is aligned with the idea that privacy ensures that information about a person does not leak from one scope to another.

The goal of permitting citizens to manage their own identities encompasses the integration of the identity of a citizen across multiple systems and services and the ability to provide a joint response to the needs arising from daily events. This goal also includes the ability to control the type of information about the citizen that is released to a particular system or at a particular time; however, anonymously aggregated data are made more widely available [6].

Thus, identity management is a key enabler for future cities. A unified identity system, which may be able to integrate itself with multiple identity providers, and different methods of authentication and identification are necessary to manage the extensively "wired" nature of the city and the density of data transactions, systems, and solution diversity [6].

Citizens or entities can use their identities to gain access to services and systems and utilize through the benefits that they have to offer. This is a method to integrate several solutions (systems and services); eventually, entities and services repeat their identification artifact at various instances of time and in various situations.

Ideally, every citizen and/or entity should have various identifiers corresponding to various identities, each of which is composed of the scope combined with several attributes that are either exposed or used to validate a claim without revealing information. The use of multiple identifiers and identities limits the exposure of truly important credentials, thus minimizing the risk of abuse and identity theft, while allowing the exposure of less critical information that is helpful to participants in the ecosystem of the city such as retailers, building operators, service providers, and governments [6].

Citizens are responsible for their identities, for the information that constitutes such identities, and the condition under which this information can be exposed.

Smart cities will pass through information security problems. This paper alerts to security problems, more specifically, the problems generated by the relation of identity and identifiers. The following sections will depict some of this eminent identity threats in the scope of a smart city.

B. Identity management is not a primary objective

For users and administrators, Identity Management and Information Security are not primary concerns. Sometimes, issues with privacy are also ignored depending on the purpose of an interaction. Citizens, entities, and users, in general, are more focused on the task that must be executed rather than on the manner in which that task will identify the responsible entities.

An identity management system should focus on methods to simplify daily tasks while offering the security, transparency, and privacy that a user needs. Citizens expect an Identity Management system to be secure and transparent, and privacy to be enforced in such a manner that daily tasks become easier and not more complex. Although these are latent concerns for many users and citizens, it has been demonstrated that they are unwilling to invest money and/or time to increase security measures in any aspect of the interaction with a system or set of systems in spite of the hidden problems that such investments could avoid [8].

C. Sensing that I have been followed

Owing to the nature of a smart city, which must be an interoperable and interconnected environment and utilize various sensors (physical or social), the sensors are used to collect data from several city scenarios. This data enables urban systems to implement better city management.

Based on this assumption, it is extremely important that the information used by System B and that is originally from System A cannot be traced back to its source. Further, information provided by a citizen to improve System C must not be used to determine where that citizen is or what the citizen does [11].

Therefore, it is important to ensure that the described interchange of data has resources that prevent tracking of an entity identity.

D. Identity trust is a sensitive matter and must be earned

In recent times, account managers have been accused of fraud related to identity theft. If the person responsible for identity management is a suspect, the question of whom a citizen can entrust with identity data arises. The answer for this question must be deeply analyzed, taking some risk assessment into account. Each unique authentication and/or authorization service is susceptible to failures or attacks. Services are also vulnerable to theft because mistakes could occur. These mistakes, in addition, could create a data disclosure related to ID.

Various privacy policies are presented by approximately 20 Identity Providers (IdPs)—some focus on preserving the privacy of user transactions, some focus on enabling a single sign on environment, and others focus only on identity privacy [8][15].

E. Various types of system and services access

Identity management systems, or just IdM, have been used to create different sets of access rights. These rights offer different risk profile, thus it assumes different relations between users, identity provides, and relying parties. Unfortunately, users and system designers are not aware of this discrepancy in access rights. This may promote a set of unacceptable risks; the distinction between membership and ownership of a specific resource is fundamental.

In the context of cities, IdM were first used to centralize access rights managements to business systems and in educational environment to grant students access to wireless areas, digital libraries, laboratories and/or grade systems. In either case, identity management was used to verify whether a certain citizen is a member of a group, and not the owner of a right. Even more, IdM systems are used to enforce ownership of a resource.

Illegal accesses to different types of account could impact finances and the correct use of a system. In this context, the danger involved in using IdM systems will mainly affect a user, in a Smart City context; it may impact citizens and sensors. This affects an identity management system by enforcing membership, through the creation of different trust relations, rather than enforcing data ownership. Both cases, an identity management scheme that enforces membership is conceptually different from an IdM system that promotes ownership [16].

F. The paradigm of a single access point

Identity management systems require the user and the accessed system or service to place a large amount of trust in the identity provider. A significant part of identity and identifier information is stored with the provider; in this scenario, entities can take no action other than simply trusting the identity server and service to preserve their privacy, identifiers, and security, and to properly secure their information. However, mistakes can occur and privacy-sensitive information can become public, a group of attackers can focus their effort on invalidating the server, or a bottleneck from entities to service could be created, thus making the service unavailable [8][17].

Thus, the identity provider becomes the single point of failure. In different providers, the IdP is a critical and unique point of access, and hence, it creates a threat that allows security measures and definitions to be converged at a single point. However, this point can also become the focus of intense attacks.

G. An easy "phish" to catch even in the ocean

Today, identity management solutions provide the user with a single authentication mechanism, and the user is unable to authenticate a new IdP and Relying Party (RP). This feature is necessary in order to avoid phishing attacks in which the attacker makes users believe that their identity data and credentials must be revealed. With the extent of identity management increasing, phishing attacks based on obtaining IdP and login credentials will most likely increase [8][18].

Hence, it is necessary to create and define a centralized solution in which it is feasible to moderate the number of points in the transactions performed in order to reduce the possible locations where a phish could occur. This feature would also allow data to be updated when a system flaw or compromise occurs.

H. *To be or not to be, an identity crisis*

One of the many advantages of identity management for citizens is that the entities do not need to remember every single identifier that may be used in order to access various solutions. In some scenarios, an entity requires only one identifier, e.g., a user name and password, in order to log in and receive a multisite token.

Based on this perspective, it would be suitable to have a single identity provider that uses a single user name/password or another authentication token to guarantee and apply a broad identification feature across different systems.

Based on a less optimistic view, this much-needed feature may not be feasible owing to the fact that users may not trust a single identity provider having access to all their services, tokens, and systems [8].

I. *What you are looking at and should not: Privacy issues*

Every day, solutions responsible for identifier management are requested to intervene in numerous transactions from different users on the Internet. Based on the approach, these solutions mediate transactions from entity to entity, RP, devices, systems, services, and components involving personal data information, thus registering data related to who connects with whom.

This property raises obvious privacy concerns owing to the fact that a user is prompted to provide identity (and/or identifiers) information in order to connect with different services using a unique identifier. This information is sent to an environment that audits those transactions [5][19][20].

J. *Linkability across domains*

A smart city uses an interconnected and interoperable environment to provide applications and solutions that have the opportunity to interact with each other, thus exchanging data. In this context, a broad linkability across all the systems involved in a smart city is potentially harmful and can result in the risk of a viral effect being created [20].

If the boundaries that delimit the connections between systems are not well protected, a system may encounter a scenario in which a value is changed in System A, and the use of this changed value by System B may corrupt the information created or stored in System B. The consequence of this behavior is known as viral effect because a system will affect another system, thus propagating a situation throughout the environment, which, in this case, is a city.

Identity Management plays an important role by providing a user the capability to track an entity across all the systems using that entity. To maintain privacy, it should be possible for users to keep their information and data private, or to create a scenario in which it is not possible for a domain to resolve "who" an identifier is in another domain, thus preventing the domain from maintaining records of who an entity is and what the entity has been doing [8].

K. *Where has my data gone?*

Smart systems, within the context of urban environment or smart cities, may utilize devices such as smartphones, tablets, and other gadgets. These devices provide smart systems with a wide range of data and information. Depending on the data type handled by these devices, it is possible to store personal data such as messages, pictures, appointments, bank account, and contacts.

In addition to being responsible for enabling communication with everyone, mobile devices have changed the way common citizens handle their daily tasks. A smart device has become a vault for storing and saving valuable and sensitive data that is accessible instantly. This model could create a sensitive scenario in which valuable information could be lost if the applications and solutions responsible for storing, saving, and accessing data are not well implemented and lack security measures [11][15][20].

L. *Crossed access to information in data centers*

In this scenario, we address situations related to undesired access to information resulting from exploitation of breaches on the server side.

This issue deals with a situation that is beyond the authentication and authorization of a particular entity. The focus must be on correct restrictions and definition of boundaries in an interoperable environment.

For example, while accessing information related to the education of a student, a given entity (application) can recover criminal records related to this citizen although the solution should use only information related to Educational Services. This situation may occur if both the systems share a common space or permissions that must be respected in order to avoid this kind of behavior are not implemented [11][15][20].

III. SMART CITY SECURITY ARCHITECTURE

OAuth, Security Assertion and Markup Language (SAML), and OpenID are solutions for authentication and authorization of assets. They are based on the assumption that each ID will be created as a unique identifier for a set of systems.

The assets could be any type of information or entities such as documents, data, and photos. Through the mentioned technologies adoption, it is feasible to create mechanisms that make it possible to transfer the responsibility of ensuring security to a third party, which could be a known server (Facebook, Google, etc.), or to implement the same approach in an in-house solution. However, the demands of a smart city are considerably different from the ones addressed by these solutions. It is important to define demand-specific solutions in order to solve specific problems.

As previously mentioned this paper intends to present identity security issues under the scope of s smart city, nonetheless it also slightly presents an architecture proposal that detaches identity, identifier and data, thus mitigating the identity security issues [21].

A. *Objective*

The main objective of the proposed architecture is to be a layer in which an identifier is transformed into another one. The new identifier will be generated from a combination of an entity ID and the accessed service.

This mechanism will enable an entity to maintain the secrecy of its identity from a unique service and within an environment composed of several systems and services.

This approach will be valid even when the same entity accesses different sets of services. The new ID is created from a combination of two other identifiers, and hence, the resultant ID will be unique for each service accessed by the same entity.

B. *General view*

This sub-section describes the general components of the proposed architecture. Fig. 1 shows three layers with several components.

Each component represents a framework or technology that is well-known and adopted to guarantee information security in applications and solutions in a smart city context.

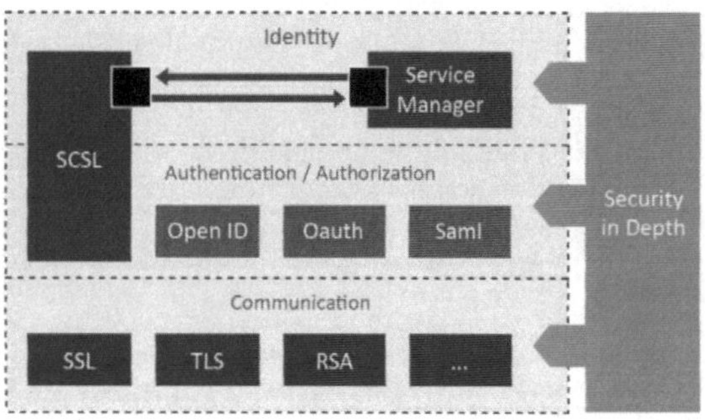

Figure.1 Architecture General view.

Each layer in Fig. 1 is described below:

Identity: It represents the portion of the reference architecture responsible for managing identifiers. It is composed of two core components: a Smart City Security Layer (SCSL) and Service Manager.

SCSL: It is an architectural module responsible for receiving a set of information and combining this information to create a new identifier for an entity.

Service manager: It is a module responsible for managing services that are used by SCSL and, indirectly, by the entities. In a following subsection more details about the Service Manager and SCSL will be explained.

Authentication/Authorization: It represents the part of the proposed architecture responsible for authentication and authorization. In this layer, various technologies such as OAuth, OpenID, and SAML are available and should be combined with the remainder of the solution.

Security in Depth: According to Schumacher et al. [17], it refers to the adoption of several security measures in various parts of a system, or solution, in order to increase overall security. This transversal module represents the need for security measures in different sections of the code responsible for service and identifier management, i.e., the implementation must take into account good practices related to security such as avoiding security risks indicated by the Open Web Application Security Project (OWASP) [22].

Communication: The proposed architecture explores the manner in which identifier management can increase security. The communication from an entity to SCSL and from SCSL to a service uses security communication protocols such as Security Sockets Layer (SSL) and Transport Layer Security (TLS).

C. *A unique identity provider*

The proposed architecture is a mechanism based on the concept of change identifiers involved in a system relation. A system relation is related to an entity sending and receiving values from a different set of services.

In Section IV(B), the general view, with the basic components to be adopted, was explored. In the proposed architecture, the adoption of SAML, OpenID, or OAuth is recommended for the authorization and authentication process. Further, two integrated components must be developed. These two components, SCSL and Service Manager, are responsible for providing the basic infrastructure for an entity to communicate with a service through the Internet by managing different identifiers for different identities of the same entity.

The Service Manager functions as a name register service that is responsible for receiving an address from a service. This address represents a system that will handle requests from entities. The address is made secure and is stored, and an identifier for that address is created and sent back to the requester.

This service identifier must be used by any entity that wishes to communicate with the service through SCSL.

Fig. 2 represents the basic flow associated with the architecture mechanism that is responsible for changing the ID.

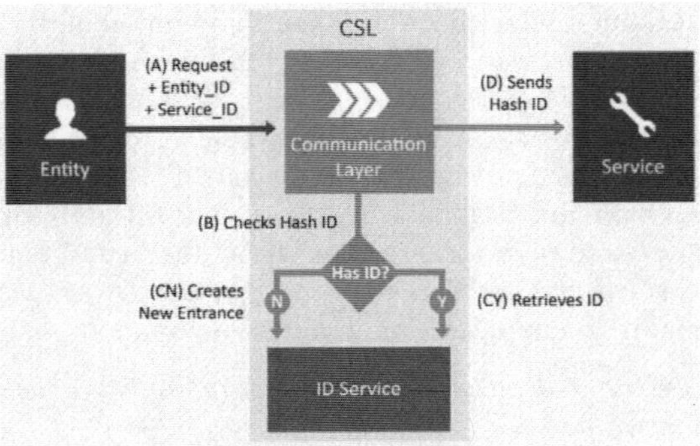

Figure 2. SCSL basic flow.

Fig. 2 is composed of:

Entity: A component that requests information from a service. A citizen, a sensor, or a service that is interoperating with another service can be an Entity. Thus, any actor of a city can be an Entity.

Service: It represents any service contacted by an entity. The Service is composed of systems of an urban environment.

Communication Layer: It represents a contact point between an Entity and a Service, and is responsible for transforming the identifier sent by the entity to the correct ID that must be used within the service.

ID Service: It is a component responsible for storing and managing information that is used to generate the correct ID.

The basic flow in Fig. 2 shows an Entity sending a message composed of an Entity_ID, Service_ID, and a packet.

This message is processed in SCSL, where Entity_ID is combined with Service_ID. In our case study, we combined these values to generate a 256-bit hash value.

This hash value is verified with an internal database. If the hash value does not already exist, a new register will be created with the service ID, the entity ID, and the hash value. If it already exists, it is passed to the service or used to retrieve the original ID of the Entity. This hash value is used as the Entity ID, and then, the packet is sent to the service that is retrieved from the Service Manager using the transmitted Service_ID.

D. Sequence Diagram

The sequence diagram in Fig. 3 depicts the flow implementation for registering a service and sending a message using the proposed architecture.

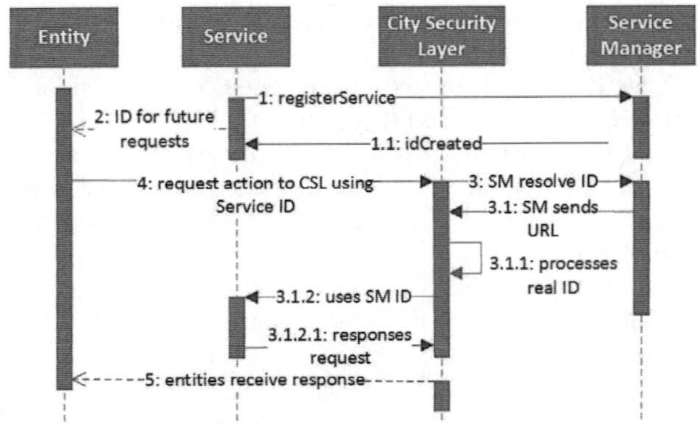

Figure 3. Platform sequence diagram.

In this scenario, a Service must initially register itself by sending a message to the Service Manager.

This action will provide the Service with an ID that is used in future requests by devices, sensors, citizens, etc.

An Entity sends a message to SCSL using this ID. The message contains the Service ID, the Entity ID, and the packet containing the data to be transmitted. The data packet format could be JSON, XML, or Plain Text.

The city security layer will execute the process described in Section IV(C), and the entity ID will be modified to the ID that must be used in the service context.

Finally, after the change in identifier, the data packet contained in the original message will be forwarded to the service.

IV. VALIDATION

In order to conduct the case study, an infrastructure was created using AWS.

This structure is composed of four sets of virtual machines. The first has the instances responsible for data generation; the second group presents the scenarios; the third group is the SCSL implementation, and the last group represents city systems.

The instance type used in this process is t2.medium, which has two vCPUs (equivalent to a 1,25GHz) and 4 GB of memory RAM.

The Relational Database Service chosen for SCSL is db.t2.medium with two vCPUs and 4 GB of memory RAM. For the set of machines responsible for the systems, we selected a db.t2.small with one vCPU and 2 GB of RAM.

With regard to the responsibilities of each set of machines, please note the following:

City systems: responsible for simulating urban services. This is composed of three systems: Natural Resources, Educational, and Government. Each system is composed of a set of web services, which in turn are built using Representational State Transfer Application Program Interface (REST API) implemented using JAVA APIs [29].

Each system uses one EC2 instance (t2.medium) and one RDS instance (db.t2.small).

SCSL: represents the implementation responsible for service management and ID changes.

The service manager is deployed in one EC2 (t2.medium) and one RDS (db.t2.small). The ID manager is deployed in one EC2 (t2.medium) and in one RDS (db.t2.medium).

Note that the RDS instance used for SCSL has more resources because every request passes through SCSL for ID changing.

Data generator: Responsible for generating random data used by the systems. This uses three Virtual Machine (VM) instances, where each instance generates random data for one system exclusively.

The generated data is sent in the form of a JSON request composed of an entity ID that represents the ID to be changed in SCSL, a service ID that represents the service to be requested, and nested JSON packet that contains data related to the service to be requested. In addition, the generator is responsible for creating a different and random amount of data for each system used by the applications. This means that, for example, the educational system can have a random number of Schools, each School can have a random number of Courses, and each Course can have a random number of Students. [29].

Scenarios: Scenarios 1, 2, and 3 represent a client application that consumes data from the system in the form of JSONs. Each scenario is deployed in a separate instance.

A. *ID changed and functionalities preserved.*

The first test used the proposed systems, and built applications to create and consume the information. Afterward, SCSL was included as a step after the applications and before the system to verify whether the applications continued to work as designed.

The changes needed to implement SCSL required each application to adopt the consumed/requested services by changing them to call the SCSL service using the Service_ID instead of directly calling a desired service.

In addition to these changes, no more updates were required, and the applications worked without modifications.

B. *Different and unique ID created. Separting data from IDs..*

Systems may be composed of different services in order to create a unique solution. For example, the education system uses services related to Grades, Schools, and Classes. Thus, a system can opt to use a unique ID for every service (e.g., the same Student_Number to identify student grades and classes), or it could use different IDs for each service (e.g., Student_Number for grades and Student_Number_Year for the classes taken by a particular student in a given year).

The option selected for TbE was to use different IDs per service. In this case, the result is that several IDs were created for different scopes of the same system. To validate the strengths of the proposal, IDs were revealed through applications; and in the services, an attempt was made to recover more information using the breached IDs. It was not possible to recover information from that entity in the services and system. This indicates that the IDs are indeed different from one service to another.

C. *ID captured in an application did not compromise the system*

This topic discusses how solutions that use different systems behave if the IDs from one system are revealed. Nevertheless, even if all IDs are breached from all services, no corruption or recovery could be found within a different scope (in this case, systems in different scenarios).

D. *Entities separated from their data*

The architecture core proposes the creation of a unique and different ID for each relationship between an Entity and a Service. By doing this, the architecture achieves a separation from an Entity to its Identity. Assuming that each Identity is composed of an Identifier and its contextual Data, the architecture achieves a separation of an Entity from its Data.

E. *Compartmentalization and security in depth*

Compartmentalization is a concept explored by Schumacher et al. in [17]. For this concept, the authors explored the gains related to defining separate compartments per functionality.

The first topic, ID changed and functionalities preserved, explored data corruption with a unique system by exposing the ID of a service that is part of an environment with a set of services. In this case, because of the basic capability of changing IDs, the services and system in their entirety were unharmed.

The second topic, IDs within systems were independently maintained, explored the ID of a system that has been breached without compromising a second system that has a relation to the first. In the third topic, ID captured in an application did not compromise the system, when corruption began in an application (or on the client side), the systems using those IDs are still safe.

These three behaviors (service-to-service, system-to-system, and application-to-system/service) indicated that, although we are considering a unique application that consumes services, the three main components (applications, SCSL, and services) were isolated from ID discovery. Finally, the last topic, Entities separated from their data, explored the… result of SCSL appliance, in which a entity is separated from its identity, and therefore, separated from its data.

Through the mentioned characteristics and gains it can be proved that the identity is safer into an interoperable environment; moreover, entity privacy is demonstrated to have increased.

V. EVALUATION

The main strength of SCSL is its ability to provide a citizen with a ubiquitous mechanism in which the entity is required to provide the environment with only one identifier, allowing the ID service to retrieve and build different identifiers, thus different identities, for each requested system.

The adoption of this approach enables identity management to be handled differently because the actual identification of a citizen or sensor will be hidden from the system responsible for the data, and, therefore, from eventual breaches in such systems.

The following subsection depicts the impact of the proposed architecture in order to validate how the introduced issues are addressed by this approach.

A. *Identity management is not a primary objective*

Identity management will still remain a secondary objective; however, the use of the SCSL approach permits this concern to be less important.

The proposed approach will ensure that an Identity System is responsible for dealing with identities and identifiers, thus diminishing the need for citizens to be concerned about this particular aspect.

B. *Sensing that I have been followed*

The main strength of the proposed architecture is in being a solution that separates real IDs from operational IDs used by city systems. Thus, only the central ID manager will have the ability to retrieve the ID of a citizen; however, the information related to each ID will not be available to the central ID manager. This information will be maintained in the city system.

The city system has only partial information; the actual ID is not available to this system. Thus, each component of the environment will have certain part of the entire data, and therefore, linking information to an ID, and an ID to a citizen will not be possible.

C. *Identity trust is a sensitive matter and must be earned*

Let us consider a scenario in which citizens would not need to be worried about identity issues by allowing a single third party to be responsible for managing their identifiers. This situation would probably increase their trust because the third party will have access to identifiers and not identities, and therefore, the data of citizens will be safe in the system.

The notion that, even if the data system is breached, the identity will remain in safety, is a powerful motivation for trusting SCSL.

D. *Various types of system and services access*

This issue deals with problems related to identity management systems that are responsible for applying various types of access rights and permissions. Although OAuth and other frameworks have been specified as authorization and authentication frameworks that could be used with the remainder of the solution, we do not believe that identifier management addresses this issue.

E. *The paradigm of a single access point*

The adoption of a single system responsible for identity and identifier management will enable the strength to be focused at a single point, thus increasing the overall security. The system responsible for the identifiers is the one that must be secure; this situation is equivalent to protecting the keys in a key-locker system. One does not need to protect the entire environment but only the portion that is capable of identifying the rest of the environment.

However, significant attention must be given to this characteristic owing to the fact that if the solution fails, the entire city will be unable to function because it will not be possible to resolve an entity ID.

F. *An easy "phish" to catch even in the ocean*

This issue is not addressed by the proposed approach because authentication and authorization concerns are beyond the scope of this proposal. Although we have suggested the adoption of OAuth, SAML, or OpenID as authentication and authorization handlers, our focus is on identity management.

G. *To be or not to be, an identity crisis*

The existence of a single identity manager enables the citizen and other city entities to refer to a unique point using a single identifier to access all other identities that the entity may have within the entire environment. This notion permits one identifier to be multiplexed by N other identifiers by a third party, thus avoiding problems related to managing a group of IDs.

H. *What you are looking at and should not: Privacy issues*

Privacy issues are partially solved by identity and identifiers management. As mentioned earlier, the primary consequence of the adoption of the proposed architecture is a separation of data and citizen identifiers, and, thus a separation of identity and identifiers.

Thus, even if certain data is revealed, it will not be possible to determine the entity that the data belongs to or the data of a specific entity. Therefore, the information of a citizen will remain private.

I. *Linkability across domains*

This issue is addressed by SCSL owing to the capability already mentioned earlier. The same entity account will be identified differently in each system and/or service of a city; thus, the maintenance of linkability across domains will be difficult for an attacker. In order to validate an ID recovered from a system, an attacker must initially pass through the identification service, and then, discover the equivalent identity in a secondary system.

J. Where has my data gone?

As mentioned in section IV, the primary strength of the three (OAuth, SAML and OpenID) standards lies in interoperability and authentication, and therefore, they do not impact the issue discussed in Section III. A similar reasoning applies to SCSL; it proposes to change the manner in which identifiers are sent and used by systems, and therefore, it does not impact this issue.

K. Crossed access to information in data centers

This issue is addressed by SCSL. Although an attacker can compromise a system, gather information about a citizen, and access other systems through the compromised system, the attacker will have the perception that the system databases are composed of different entities. An entity will be presented differently for each system or service.

VI. CONCLUSION

The development of new collaborating systems based on the current systems that support a city is an urgent need in order to enable urban environments to deliver better service to citizens and improve the current infrastructure. Further, this development plays a crucial role in the creation of new methods to sustain the changes in the composition of cities.

The new proposed paradigm, related to an interoperable environment of city systems, poses various challenges such as performance, usability, availability, privacy, and information security. Security concerns are a challenge that must be addressed. The absence of a solution to this problem will result in citizens avoiding the use of the offered solutions, and therefore, the development of smart cities will be affected.

This study explored a set of identification and privacy problems that continue to pose challenges and addressed questions that must be answered in order to offer a more secure environment to citizens. An approach based on identifiers and identity separation architecture was presented and analyzed. It has been demonstrated that the proposed architecture improves the privacy and anonymity of citizens.

In future work, we intend to conclude an ongoing study related to validating performance issues related with the adoption of the proposed architecture. Further, we will evaluate various new security issues in smart cities and deploy a cloud-based system for the identity service.

REFERENCES

[1] S. Dirks and M. Keeling, "A vision of smarter cities: How cities can lead the way into a prosperous and sustainable future," IBM Inst. Bus. Value. June, 2009.

[2] IBM. Ibm smarter healthcare. http://ibm.co/bCJpHX, 2012. " [Online] Available: 20 – July -2016 ".

[3] F. Ferraz, C. Sampaio, and C. Ferraz, "Towards a Smart City Security Model Exploring Smart Cities Elements Based on Nowadays Solutions," ICSEA 2013, no. c, pp. 546–550, 2013.

[4] Y. Wang and Y. Zhou, "Cloud architecture based on Near Field Communication in the smart city," in 2012 7th International Conference on Computer Science & Education (ICCSE), 2012, no. Iccse, pp. 231–234.

[5] A. Martinez-Balleste, P. Perez-martinez, and A. Solanas, "The pursuit of citizens' privacy: a privacy-aware smart city is possible," IEEE Commun. Mag., vol. 51, no. 6, pp. 136–141, Jun. 2013.

[6] C. Harrison, B. Eckman, R. Hamilton, P. Hartswick, J. Kalagnanam, J. Paraszczak, and P. Williams, "Foundations for Smarter Cities," IBM J. Res. Dev., vol. 54, no. 4, pp. 1–16, Jul. 2010.

[7] P. (2010). Harrison, C., Eckman, B., Hamilton, R., Hartswick, P., Kalagnanam, J., Paraszczak, J., & Williams, "Foundations for Smarter Cities," IBM J. Res. Dev.

[8] R. Dhamija and L. Dusseault, "The Seven Flaws of Identity Management: Usability and Security Challenges," IEEE Secur. Priv. Mag., vol. 6, no. 2, pp. 24–29, Mar. 2008.

[9] J. M. Gonçalves, "Privacy and Information Security in Brazil? Yes, We Have It and We Do It!," 2010 Seventh Int. Conf. Inf. Technol. New Gener., pp. 702–707, 2010.

[10] A. Bartoli, J. Hernández-Serrano, and M. Soriano, "Security and Privacy in your Smart City,"cttc.cat, pp. 1–6.

[11] F. S. Ferraz and C. A. G. Ferraz, "Smart City Security Issues: Depicting Information Security Issues in the Role of an Urban Environment," in 2014 IEEE/ACM 7th International Conference on Utility and Cloud Computing, 2014, pp. 842–847.

[12] C. Balakrishna, "Enabling Technologies for Smart City Services and Applications," 2012 Sixth Int. Conf. Next Gener. Mob. Appl. Serv. Technol., pp. 223–227, Sep. 2012.

[13] W. M. da Silva, A. Alvaro, G. H. R. P. Tomas, R. a. Afonso, K. L. Dias, and V. C. Garcia, "Smart cities software architectures," in Proceedings of the 28th Annual ACM Symposium on Applied Computing - SAC '13, 2013, p. 1722.

[14] M. Batty, K. W. Axhausen, F. Giannotti, a. Pozdnoukhov, a. Bazzani, M. Wachowicz, G. Ouzounis, and Y. Portugali, "Smart cities of the future," Eur. Phys. J. Spec. Top., vol. 214, no. 1, pp. 481–518, Dec. 2012.

[15] M. Sen, A. Dutt, S. Agarwal, and A. Nath, "Issues of Privacy and Security in the Role of Software in Smart Cities," in 2013 International Conference on Communication Systems and Network Technologies, 2013, pp. 518–523.

[16] G. Alpár, J. Hoepman, and J. Siljee, "The identity crisis. security, privacy and usability issues in identity management," arXiv Prepr. arXiv1101.0427, pp. 1–15, 2011.

[17] M. Schumacher, E. Fernandez-Buglioni, D. Hybertson, F. Buschmann, and P. Sommerlad, Security Patterns: Integrating Security and Systems Engineering (Wiley Software Patterns Series). John Wiley & Sons, 2006.

[18] I. D. Addo, S. I. Ahamed, S. S. Yau, and A. Buduru, "A Reference Architecture for Improving Security and Privacy in Internet of Things Applications," 2014 IEEE Int. Conf. Mob. Serv., pp. 108–115, Jun. 2014.

[19] A. Ukil, "Connect with Your Friends and Share Private Information Safely," 2012 Ninth Int. Conf. Inf. Technol. - New Gener., pp. 367–372, Apr. 2012.

[20] F. S. Ferraz and C. A. G. Ferraz, "More Than Meets the Eye In Smart City Information Security: Exploring security issues far beyond privacy concerns," in 2014 IEEE International Conference on Ubiquitous Intelligence and Computing/International Conference on Autonomic and Trusted 2014 IEEE 11th Intl Conf on Ubiquitous Intelligence & Computing and 2014 IEEE 11th Intl Conf on Autonomic & Trusted Computing and, 2014, vol. 677–686, p. 9.

[21] F. S. Ferraz, C. Candido, B. Sampaio, C. André, and G. Ferraz, "Towards A Smart-City Security Architecture Proposal and Analysis of Impact of Major Smart-City Security Issues," in SOFTENG 2015: The First International Conference on Advances and Trends in Software Engineering Information, 2015, no. c, pp. 108–114.

[22] OWASP, "OWASP Top 10 - 2013: The ten most critical web application security risks," 2013.

Predicting Unknown Vulnerabilities using Software Metrics and Maturity Models

Patrick Kamongi, Krishna Kavi, Mahadevan Gomathisankaran

Department of Computer Science and Engineering
University of North Texas
Denton, TX 76203, USA
Emails: patrickkamongi@my.unt.edu, kavi@cse.unt.edu, mgomathi@unt.edu

***Abstract*—We face an increasing reliance on software-based services, applications, platforms, and infrastructures to accomplish daily activities. It is possible to introduce vulnerabilities during any software life cycle and these vulnerabilities could lead to security attacks. It is known that as the software complexity increases, discovering a new security vulnerability introduced by subsequent updates and code changes becomes difficult. This can be seen from the rate of new vulnerabilities discovered after a software release. IT Products' vulnerabilities sometimes remain undiscovered for many years. In this paper, we report our study of IT products' source codes using software maturity models and the history of vulnerabilities discovered. We use this data to develop a model to predict the number of security vulnerabilities contained in a product, including undiscovered vulnerabilities. Our proposed approach can be used to explore proactive strategies for mitigating the risks due to zero-day vulnerabilities.**

Keywords–Vulnerabilities; Metrics; Models.

I. Introduction

Any software product that is in production goes through a series of changes throughout its lifecycle as a result of feature changes or bug fixes among other factors. As any given software product matures, it has been shown that it is vulnerability-prone and that its security vulnerabilities do get discovered throughout its maturity. For the last decade or so, we have seen a rising trend of security vulnerabilities in software products being disclosed on a regular basis [1]. This observed trend calls for an increased security awareness and demands new approaches to stay ahead of this alarming fact.

The type of security vulnerabilities that are discovered and leveraged by malicious actors before the relevant software provider becomes aware of and fixes them, are known as zero-day (0day) vulnerabilities. The worrisome nature of 0day vulnerabilities is due to the endless number of approaches that a malicious actor might employ to abuse a given software product. The security community and software product vendors sponsor bug bounty initiatives in an attempt to stay ahead of the large number of vulnerabilities hidden in software products currently in use. A portion of these hidden vulnerabilities in software products are being discovered using assessment techniques targeting some aspects of the software's design, implementation and use; such as static code analysis and dynamic binary analysis but still undisclosed vulnerabilities remain, and this serves as the motivation for our research.

An estimation of the potential number of undetected or unreported security vulnerabilities is useful because it may lead to proactive strategies for protecting IT assets. In this work, we want to address the following types of questions:

- To what extent do software complexity metrics correlate with the number of vulnerabilities disclosed for any given software product instance?
- Can we extrapolate a list of specific software metrics that shows a high correlation with regard to the above question?
- Can we predict the number of undisclosed vulnerabilities for any given software product?

Previous research has attempted to predict software error (or bug) incidences using software change history [2]. Software metrics have also been used to predict vulnerability prone codes in any given software [3]. Various techniques have been used to study the trend of vulnerabilities in software products [4] [5]. In this study, we explore the correlation between software change history and maturity with the number of vulnerabilities each software release may contain and subsequently exposed.

The main contributions of our work are:

- Sweep: a toolkit that automates software complexity metrics generation and analysis.
- A methodology for using the Sweep toolkit to automatically generate a dataset for any given software product. The produced dataset contains information on all software releases for the given software product along with the relevant software metrics and number of reported vulnerabilities for each release in a timeline fashion.
- A proof of concept predictive web service endpoint, based on a machine learning regression classifier trained on the dataset produced by the Sweep toolkit. This endpoint is leveraged in an automated fashion to predict the number of unknown vulnerabilities for any given software product instance.

The rest of this paper is organized as follows. In Section II, we present our proposed methodology towards building a predictive model for estimating the number of unknown vulnerabilities. In Section III, we present our experimental study and its evaluation. Section IV contains related works pertinent to this study. Finally, Section V contains conclusions of our work thus far, along with possible extensions and future direction of our research.

II. Our Predictive Methodology

In this section, we present our novel model for predicting the number of unknown vulnerabilities for any given IT Product. We start by presenting our data collection approach in Section II-A, then the details of how we designed and validated our prediction model in Section II-B.

A. Data collections

For this study, we have devised a generic and automated data collection approach for any software product that has its various release source codes available and written in known programming languages. The data of our interest is based on each studied software product's release complexity metrics, and a timeline trend of the number of disclosed vulnerabilities.

For each IT Product (software product), we start by collecting details about the product's releases (with an identifying name), the number of releases and the number of vulnerabilities already reported. We also analyze the source code of each released version of the IT Product and then compute various software metrics for the given source codes. The collected data is stored in a dataset file as comma-separated values (CSV). The following describes the process for collecting data for any IT product.

1) Select the IT Product to analyze.
2) Download all of this IT Product's released versions and source code for these versions.
3) For each release, represent it using a Common Platform Enumeration (CPE) [6] format as its unique identifier for cataloging the product version and its data into our datasets.
4) For each of the above releases, use our lookup index to match and find all reported or known vulnerabilities and store this information using a timeline trend.
5) Perform software source code analysis for each released version, and store all computed software metrics data [7].

Since in most cases the size of the source code for each release is very large, we leverage the capabilities of the *Understand 4.0* [8] tool for static code analysis and software metrics generation. To alleviate the complexity involved in collecting the data of our interest for any given software product manually, we designed and implemented the Sweep-toolkit to automate data collection and avoid any human error during this process.

Sweep-toolkit is designed as a lightweight framework that implements various plugins to orchestrate the data collection for this study. The currently implemented plugins offer these functionalities:

- Use of the *Understand* [8] command line tool (*und*) to automate the metrics generation for each IT Product's release source codes by automatically generating and executing relevant batch files.
- An automated approach to analyze and summarize the generated metrics for each IT Product release.
- A workflow engine to build and ensure that each IT Product release is represented in a CPE format.
- A Lookup index of the known vulnerabilities [1] and affected IT Products in CPE format.
- An orchestration application to automate and march in all these above functionalities towards data collection for any given IT Product and returns a dataset file which is set to be used in the predictive model experiment (Section II-B).

As described above, by passing relevant details of any given IT Product to the Sweep-toolkit, a dataset is generated as a result of the toolkit execution. The generated dataset is made of a set of 124 features that would represent collected data on each of the analyzed IT Product instances. In Section III, we illustrate a case scenario used for this study as a proof of concept of our proposed predictive model.

Sweep-toolkit [9] is developed for a Linux environment, with its plugins implemented in Python 3.x, Java and Bash scripts (approximately 2K lines of code).

B. Predictive model

In this section, we introduce our model for predicting vulnerabilities and show how we validated our model.

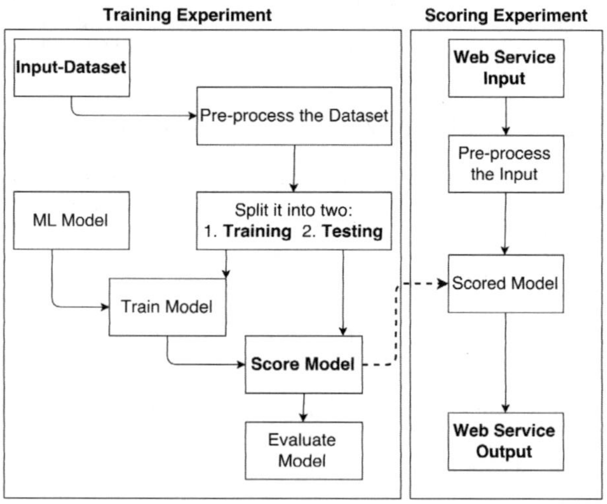

Figure 1. Predictive Model - Framework

In an attempt to address our posed research question of whether we can predict the number of undisclosed vulnerabilities for any given software product, we base our solution on the data that can be collected for this software product using our Sweep-toolkit as discussed in the previous Section II-A. Once a dataset is generated for the software product of interest, we proposed to design and train a machine learning regression classifier to build a model that should be able to predict the number of vulnerabilities for any other release of this software product.

For any predictive experiment, the more data you have the more accurate the trained model becomes. With this in mind, among all of the data collected around the 124 features found in any given dataset, we leverage a feature scoring method to identify which set of features correlate well with the number of disclosed vulnerabilities for each of the studied software product releases. Then, we start by exploring different machine learning regression techniques to find one that best fits our collected data. For this study, we leverage Microsoft Azure – Machine Learning Studio [10] to design our predictive model.

Azure Machine Learning Studio provides many easy to use building blocks for designing a predictive solution.

We build our predictive model along these easy to follow steps, which are also illustrated in Fig. 1:

- Create a machine learning workspace within Azure ML Studio for each relevant IT Product's dataset.
- Upload the data generated by Sweep-toolkit for the IT product into Azure Datasets, and design predictive models within Azure ML Studio.
- Train and Evaluate the models and identify the best model.
- Score and publish the best model as a web service.

Some specific aspects that drive our predictive model are our choices for the regression classifier module and feature scoring method. In Section III, we provide details on these choices and how they strengthen the prediction experiment for any given IT Product.

C. Prediction workflow

Our approach to predict the number of unknown vulnerabilities for any given software product follow this workflow:

- Start by generating a dataset for the given IT Product as illustrated in Section II-A.
- Using the above dataset, build and test a predictive experiment within Azure ML Studio as illustrated in Section II-B. Once the above predictive experiment has completed successfully, a trained model and web service will be produced as a result.
- Using a subset of the dataset that was reserved for validation, ensure that the trained model is scoring well against this validation data.
- Then, we expose a middleware application which leverages the above predictive web service endpoint to receive input data as illustrated in Fig. 1 and to return the predicted total number of vulnerabilities along with other associated metadata (such as the prediction accuracy and error rates).
- We can now perform dynamic prediction for any of this IT Product's releases, by first passing the release version source code details for data collection. Then using the generated data as input to the above middleware application, we get the predicted number of vulnerabilities for the assessed software product release.
- The predicted number can then be interpreted with two views, one for the overall accumulated number of vulnerabilities and the other view for the unknown numbers of vulnerabilities (this can be easily computed by subtracting the known vulnerabilities from the predicted ones by taking into consideration the prediction error rate). Since predicted vulnerabilities cannot be classified based on the potential threats that can result from their exposure, we separate them from known vulnerabilities such that users can be aware of the potential risk to their software.

This proposed prediction workflow can be repeated as needed to update the dataset and trained model, as the assessed IT Product's code base changes and new vulnerabilities are getting disclosed.

III. Experimental Study and Evaluation

In this section, we take an in-depth look at a case study of an IT Product that serves as a proof of concept for this work.

A. Use case: OpenSSL – software product

The discovery of the *OpenSSL's* Heartbleed bug [11] in 2014 revealed that this vulnerability remained unknown for two years before it was discovered. Heartbleed and other similar types of vulnerabilities serve as the motivation for our research among other facts that are presented in Section I.

For a proof of concept, we looked at different open-source IT Products and selected the *OpenSSL* [12] software product as our first pick for this study. We selected OpenSSL due to its critical role that it plays in Transport Layer Security (TLS) and Secure Sockets Layer (SSL) protocols. In addition, many other software products rely on it (since it is commercial grade and open source) to build complex softwares and services (this has a wider reach, since any new discovered software vulnerability within OpenSSL package impacts other critical software products that rely on it). Then, we selected OpenSSL due to its maturity (which enable us to collect enough data needed for our study and predictive models). Our selection parameters here, should be applicable in selecting any other software product to study and validate our proposed prediction models.

Using our prediction workflow presented in Section II-C, we apply it to the *OpenSSL* software product.

1) OpenSSL – dataset generation: We downloaded and analyzed 154 OpenSSL versions which are released in these categories: 0.9.x, 1.0.0, 1.0.1, 1.0.2, 1.1.0, and fips [12]. Using our Sweep-toolkit, we pass as input the directory path to all of the OpenSSL versions' uncompressed directories of source codes. Once Sweep-toolkit completes its execution, it returns a dataset for OpenSSL.

This OpenSSL dataset has 154 entries (one per each OpenSSL version), where each entry contains collected data for all specified 124 features (CPE-Name, Year-1999, ..., Year-X, ,..., Year-Current, #CVEIDs, Understand-Metric-1, .., Understand-Metric-n). With:

- *CPE-Name* representing each analyzed OpenSSL release (i.e., *cpe:/a:openssl:openssl:1.0.0f*).
- *Year-1999* representing the number of disclosed vulnerabilities in the year 1999 (which is the first year recorded in NVD data feeds [1]). The other data for the following years are included as well, up to the current year (i.e., for the above CPE instance, in the Year-2014, Sweep-toolkit found 22 disclosed vulnerabilities).
- *#CVEIDs* representing the accumulated number of known vulnerabilities (i.e., 50 is the total number of disclosed vulnerabilities for the above CPE instance example).
- *Understand-Metric-1, ..., Understand-Metric-n* representing all computed software metrics supported by the Understand tool [7] (e.g., the above CPE instance has a *SumCyclomatic* value of 43479, and the other metrics data are provided accordingly).

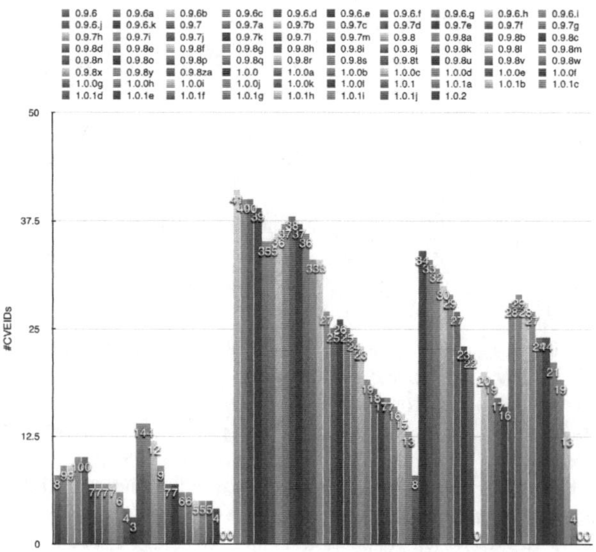

Figure 2. OpenSSL Releases vs. Disclosed Number of Vulnerabilities

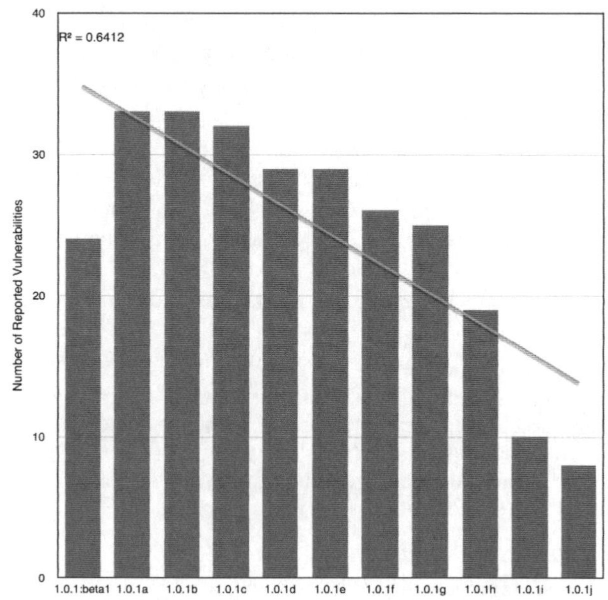

Figure 3. OpenSSL:1.0.1 – Minor Releases Linear Trend

2) OpenSSL – Predictive experiment: Consider tracking product releases (minor and major) and vulnerabilities detected for the OpenSSL product as shown in Fig. 2. By slicing one of the observed trends in Fig. 2, Fig. 3 shows that there is a decreasing trend in terms of vulnerabilities between major releases of the OpenSSL product.

We predict a similar behavior with other IT products since this trend reflects a behavior similar to software maturity or improved quality over time. Here we see the maturity of OpenSSL in terms of the number of reported vulnerabilities over time. We also make the following preliminary observations from the data collected so far, along with this small sample illustrated in Fig. 2 and 3.

- The history of reported vulnerabilities have shown a decreasing trend throughout each IT Product's minor releases (i.e., OpenSSL:1.0.1.:a, b, c, ..., j) in terms of the number of vulnerabilities, with exceptions for some limited distribution versions (see Fig. 3).
- The average number of reported vulnerabilities spiked whenever the rate of minor releases was high after a major release of an IT Product (i.e., for OpenSSL, this is clearly observed by grouping each of the trends (release families) shown in Fig. 2).
- The newly discovered vulnerability in a current IT Product release affects some of the previous releases due to the fact that the versions share a technology (with unknown vulnerabilities), such as common library, framework, design pattern, and so on.
- The straight line in Fig. 3 reflects the evaluated R^2 value (coefficient of determination) which appears to be above 0.5 when using Linear, Polynomial and Exponential trend estimations. However, while using logarithmic and power trends, the R^2 value was less than 0.5. This hints that there is value in knowing how these data can be used to predict the number of vulnerabilities, although we need a more carefully designed approach to correlate the data with vulnerabilities.

To improve our model and produce a high coefficient of determination with the prediction of the number of vulnerabilities, we considered all the features of the vulnerability details and generated source code metrics to build a predictive model as presented in previous Sections. Using Azure ML Studio [10], we built our predictive experiment as illustrated in Fig. 1.

Typically, the first step is to understand the nature of the training dataset which requires preprocessing to remove noisy data and selecting the most significant features that lead to highly confident predictions. Azure ML Studio offers necessary tools to facilitate this pre-processing task such as: *Project Columns, Filter Based Feature Selection.* For the *Filter Based Feature Selection* module, we used the *pearson correlation* feature scoring method selected for identifying the best contributing features (about 25). Another important aspect to decide was on the amount of training data needed for each machine learning technique and this is defined by the *Split* module (using a 50% split to avoid any bias) of Azure ML Studio.

The goal of our research is to predict the number of vulnerabilities for any given IT Product version based on the data we collected. We needed to identify a machine learning algorithm to train and predict using the generated OpenSSL dataset. We found that regression based models are well suited for our purpose. We explored all available Azure ML Studio's [10] machine learning regression models, and determined that a *Boosted Decision Tree Regression* [13] is the best for our predictions. Then, by following the easy to use predictive framework illustrated in Fig. 1, we trained and scored our chosen model using the generated OpenSSL dataset (from the previous section) targeting the #CVEIDs feature name (as presented in Section III-A1) and included its evaluation results in Table I. We present a detailed discussion of our results in Section III-B.

Note that the number of OpenSSL releases used to train

TABLE I. USING OUR LABELED OPENSSL DATASET TO EVALUATE ITS BOOSTED DECISION TREE REGRESSION MODEL

Number of Desired Features	Mean Absolute Error	Relative Absolute Error	Coefficient of Determination
5	7.995	0.618	0.597
10	3.341	0.258	0.927
15	3.347	0.258	0.926
25	3.780	0.292	0.917
40	3.985	0.308	0.912
65	3.851	0.297	0.916
80	3.597	0.278	0.918
95	3.597	0.278	0.918

our model is less than the total number available because the originally produced dataset was divided into sub-datasets for training, testing and validation.

Table II shows a comparison of the number of reported vulnerabilities and the number of predicted vulnerabilities for some OpenSSL releases used for the training experiment (with the selection of 25 desired features selected by the Filter based feature selection as described previously). To use any of the predicted number of vulnerabilities, one has to account for the estimated Mean Absolute Error. The slight differences in the known vulnerabilities and the scored number is a result of the chosen training dataset, and automatically selected number of features. Since, our interest is to predict the number of unknown vulnerabilities for any subsequent prediction, we consider the upper bound predicted value including the error rate.

TABLE II. SAMPLE OF SCORED OPENSSL INSTANCES

OpenSSL Releases	Known #Vulnerabilities	Predicted #Vulnerabilities
cpe:/a:openssl:openssl:0.9.8s	22	17.139
cpe:/a:openssl:openssl:1.0.1f	53	41.747
cpe:/a:openssl:openssl:0.9.7g	35	30.823
cpe:/a:openssl:openssl:1.0.1g	52	43.777
cpe:/a:openssl:openssl:0.9.6m	30	37.448

3) OpenSSL – Predictive Model Validation: In Table III, we present a comparison of the OpenSSL releases sample used to evaluate and validate the scored predictive model. These results tell us how well our model was able to score against our validation dataset.

- Mean Absolute Error : 2.927
- Root Mean Squared Error : 4.068
- Relative Absolute Error : 0.203
- Relative Squared Error :0.059
- Coefficient of Determination :0.940

TABLE III. SAMPLE OF OPENSSL INSTANCES FOR VALIDATION

OpenSSL Releases	Known #Vulnerabilities	Predicted #Vulnerabilities
cpe:/a:openssl:openssl:1.0.1a	60	52.498
cpe:/a:openssl:openssl:1.0.0h	46	46.815
cpe:/a:openssl:openssl:0.9.8m	34	33.867
cpe:/a:openssl:openssl:1.0.2c	15	15.729
cpe:/a:openssl:openssl:1.0.2d	14	11.526

TABLE IV. OPENSSL'S VERSIONS – PREDICTED NUMBER OF VULNERABILITIES

OpenSSL Instances	Known #Vulnerabilities	Predicted #Vulnerabilities
openssl-1.0.0:beta1	0	11.054
openssl-1.0.0:beta2	0	11.054
openssl-1.0.2:beta1	0	11.667
openssl-1.0.2:beta2	0	11.667
openssl-1.1.0:pre2	0	8.641
openssl-engine:0.9.6m	0	11.148
openssl-fips:2.0.9	0	11.148
openssl:0.9.8zd	0	5.489
openssl:1.0.0t	0	8.843

4) OpenSSL – Prediction of Unknown Vulnerabilities: Transforming the previously built predictive model for OpenSSL into a web service endpoint is straightforward. In Table IV, we show some examples of the predicted number of vulnerabilities for some versions of OpenSSL releases using our published web service. These OpenSSL instances have no currently known vulnerabilities, therefore the predicted number reflects the unknown vulnerabilities that may be discovered using different assessment techniques (to be explored in our future work).

B. Discussions

In Table I, we presented our model evaluation results using the "Boosted Decision Tree Regression" technique for predicting vulnerabilities for the OpenSSL software product. The following preliminary observations can be made from these results and our overall study experience.

- The studied *OpenSSL* dataset fit well with the selected machine learning technique, yielding a high coefficient of determination above 0.5 (which is better than a random guess prediction).
- The scored *OpenSSL* predictive model shows a positive correlation between the known vulnerabilities (#CVEIDs) and predicted ones (Scored Labels), which can be viewed via the scatter plot generated within the Azure ML Studio workspace. This reaffirms one of our hypotheses that we can predict the number of vulnerabilities contained in an IT Product using software metrics and vulnerability disclosure history.
- The coefficient of determination of the scored model is at the lowest, when the desired number of features is set to 5. By taking a close look at the automatically selected 5 features (Year-2010 to Year-2014), it reveals that they are all about the vulnerability disclose history timeline per *Year-X* (this is due to the fact that the trained model targets the accumulated total number of vulnerabilities (*#CVEIDs*) and this targeted feature is a result of these found vulnerabilities timeline).
- The coefficient of determination is improved and reaches its highest, when the desired number of features is increased from 5 to 10 or a higher value. This improvement in the prediction accuracy is a result of our feature selector capabilities used to identify additional and unique features that are part of the computed software metrics (to name a few: *CountLineCodeExe, Knots, CountPath, SumEssential, Cyclomatic*, etc.). Depending on the desired prediction

accuracy, a matching model is scored to build a predictive web service.

Table IV contains results of our evaluation of the *OpenSSL* dataset for new or beta instances (or releases) of the product with no reported vulnerabilities thus far. It should be noted that these two OpenSSL instances (*openssl-1.0.2:beta1* and *openssl-1.0.2:beta2*) have very similar source code bases, therefore we predict that both versions will likely contain the same number of vulnerabilities. These vulnerabilities should be viewed as the potential number of vulnerabilities that will likely be discovered in these products. This information can be used to plan for defensive mechanisms to mitigate security risks due to the unknown vulnerabilities.

C. Recommended Proactive Strategies

Ideally one should be able to implement countermeasures to patch or mitigate risks due to known vulnerabilities. Some organizations provide defensive mechanisms for some known vulnerabilities of popular IT products [14] [15]. However, the rate at which new vulnerabilities are being detected and reported is making it difficult to maintain up-to-date lists of patches. Moreover, as we have shown in this work, IT products very likely contain unknown or yet to be discovered vulnerabilities. Thus it is necessary to explore additional (beyond patching) defensive measures to increase our confidence in IT products. We include some recommendations in this regard.

- Any unknown pattern or behavior observed for an IT Product being assessed via security penetration testing approaches or monitored via deployed security infrastructures can serve as an indicator that zero day (or undiscovered) vulnerabilities are present or being exploited in the IT Product of interest. Therefore, these unknown behaviors can be categorized in our predicted number of unknown vulnerabilities which in turn should raise an awareness to stress test the IT Product to find them.
- We recommend exploring various software rejuvenation techniques in an attempt to mitigate some malware that may be exploiting hidden or unknown vulnerabilities before taking a foothold in the product. It has been shown that software rejuvenation [16] can minimize security risks due to malware. It has also been shown how the cost of rejuvenation can be used to plan the frequency of rejuvenation schedules.

IV. Related Work

Yonghee et al. [17] attempted to understand whether there is a correlation between software complexity measure and security, primarily focusing on the JavaScript Engine in the Mozilla application framework. They show a weak correlation, primarily because of the small number of features used. In our study, we expanded on the number of software metrics and used product releases to obtain higher correlations to reported vulnerabilities. Our predictive model works well when there is a large number of product releases and the product has a mature user base.

Other prior works have explored various software properties to serve as indicators of vulnerabilities where they used techniques such as software complexity and developer activity metrics [18] [19] [3]. Then using these software metrics coupled with some empirical models, there are works [20] [21] [22] [23] that have proposed solutions towards representing and predicting trends in software vulnerabilities. Our research has some key concepts similar to these works, but we extend the scope in terms of automatic data analysis and vulnerability prediction.

V. Conclusion and Future Work

In this paper, we presented our novel approach for predicting the number of unknown vulnerabilities in a given IT Product. We have shown how to generate a dataset that represents product maturity in terms of source-code base growth and vulnerability disclosure history. We have shown how to use such a dataset and develop a model that results in accurate predictions. We used the Azure cloud based machine learning framework for this purpose. We validated our approach for the *OpenSSL* IT product. We plan to broaden our experimentation to support any open-source software product and extend the number of features to include in the relevant dataset.

Our proposed approach for analyzing the source code of a given IT Product and leveraging its vulnerability disclosure history toward building a predictive model serves as a basis for building other solutions. A planned solution that can leverage our model is to categorize the predicted number of vulnerabilities into threat types (i.e., STRIDE [24]) using some inherent IT Product properties along with some actionable threat intelligences and, in turn, propose relevant mitigation techniques to counter these vulnerabilities and threats.

The other aspect of our work that we plan to extend is the ability to design and train our predictive model in a generic way that would allow IT Products that may need a different machine learning and training approach. We plan to group IT products into different categories, identify representative features of products that belong to a group and provide suggested approaches that result in highly accurate prediction of security vulnerabilities. We plan to expand on the IT product features to enhance our prediction accuracies using security threat intelligence reports, inherent vulnerabilities associated with different programming languages and development platforms.

Acknowledgment

The authors would like to acknowledge Mr. David Struble, former Senior Software Technologist in Raytheon Company's Net-Centric Systems group, for his editorial contributions to this paper. Our research is supported in part by the NSF Net-centric and Cloud Software and Systems Industry/University Cooperative Research Center and its member organizations.

References

[1] "National Vulnerability Database," 2016, URL: https://nvd.nist.gov/ [accessed: 2016-07-12].

[2] T. L. Graves, A. F. Karr, J. S. Marron, and H. Siy, "Predicting fault incidence using software change history," in IEEE Transactions on Software Engineering," IEEE, vol. 26, no. 7, pp. 653–661, 2000.

[3] I. Chowdhury and M. Zulkernine, "Using complexity, coupling, and cohesion metrics as early indicators of vulnerabilities," in Journal of Systems Architecture," Elsevier, vol. 57, no. 3, pp. 294–313, 2011.

[4] M. Bozorgi, L. K. Saul, S. Savage, and G. M. Voelker, "Beyond heuristics: learning to classify vulnerabilities and predict exploits," in Proceedings of the 16th ACM SIGKDD international conference on Knowledge discovery and data mining," ACM, pp. 105–114, 2010.

[5] S. Zhang, D. Caragea, and X. Ou, "An empirical study on using the national vulnerability database to predict software vulnerabilities," in Database and Expert Systems Applications," Springer, pp. 217–231, 2011.

[6] "Common Platform Enumeration (CPE)," 2016, URL: http://scap.nist.gov/specifications/cpe/ [accessed: 2016-07-12].

[7] "What Metrics does Understand have?" 2016, URL: https://scitools.com/support/metrics_list/ [accessed: 2016-07-12].

[8] "Understand Scitools," 2016, URL: https://scitools.com/ [accessed: 2016-07-12].

[9] "Sweep-Toolkit," 2016, URL: https://github.com/kamongi/sweep-toolkit [accessed: 2016-07-12].

[10] "Microsoft Azure Machine Learning," 2016, URL: https://studio.azureml.net/ [accessed: 2016-07-12].

[11] "Heartbleed Bug," 2016, URL: https://web.nvd.nist.gov/view/vuln/detail?vulnId=CVE-2014-0160 [accessed: 2016-07-12].

[12] "OpenSSL," 2016, URL: https://www.openssl.org/ [accessed: 2016-07-12].

[13] "Boosted Decision Tree Regression," 2016, URL: https://msdn.microsoft.com/en-us/library/azure/dn905801.aspx [accessed: 2016-07-12].

[14] "Apple security updates," 2016, URL: https://support.apple.com/en-us/HT201222 [accessed: 2016-07-12].

[15] "Adobe – Security Bulletins and Advisories," 2016, URL: https://helpx.adobe.com/security.html [accessed: 2016-07-12].

[16] C.-Y. Lee, K. M. Kavi, M. Gomathisankaran, and P. Kamongi, "Security Through Software Rejuvenation," in The Ninth International Conference on Software Engineering Advances (ICSEA)," IARIA, pp. 347–353, 2014.

[17] Y. Shin and L. Williams, "Is complexity really the enemy of software security?" in Proceedings of the 4th ACM workshop on Quality of protection" ACM, pp. 47–50, 2008.

[18] Y. Shin, A. Meneely, L. Williams, and J. A. Osborne, "Evaluating complexity, code churn, and developer activity metrics as indicators of software vulnerabilities," in IEEE Transactions on Software Engineering," IEEE, vol. 37, no. 6, pp. 772–787, 2011.

[19] Y. Shin, "Exploring complexity metrics as indicators of software vulnerability," in Proceedings of the 3rd International Doctoral Symposium on Empirical Software Engineering, Kaiserslautem, Germany, 2008, URL: http://www4.ncsu.edu/~yshin2/papers/esem2008ds_shin.pdf [accessed: 2016-07-12].

[20] Y. Shin and L. Williams, "An empirical model to predict security vulnerabilities using code complexity metrics," in Proceedings of the Second ACM-IEEE international symposium on Empirical software engineering and measurement," ACM, pp. 315–317, 2008.

[21] O. H. Alhazmi, Y. K. Malaiya, and I. Ray, "Measuring, analyzing and predicting security vulnerabilities in software systems," in Computers & Security," Elsevier, vol. 26, no. 3, pp. 219–228, 2007.

[22] O. H. Alhazmi and Y. K. Malaiya, "Modeling the vulnerability discovery process," in 16th IEEE International Symposium on Software Reliability Engineering, 2005. ISSRE 2005.," IEEE, pp. 10–pp, 2005.

[23] ——, "Prediction capabilities of vulnerability discovery models," in Reliability and Maintainability Symposium, 2006. RAMS'06. Annual," IEEE, pp. 86–91, 2006.

[24] "The STRIDE Threat Model," 2016, URL: http://msdn.microsoft.com/en-US/library/ee823878(v=cs.20).aspx [accessed: 2016-07-12].

A Catalog of Best Practices about Supplier Agreement Management and Agile Practices

Elisiane Monteiro Soares, Sandro Ronaldo Bezerra Oliveira
Graduate Program in Computer Science
Federal University of Pará
Belém, Pará, Brazil
e-mail: elismclean@gmail.com, srbo@ufpa.br

Melquizedequi Cabral dos Santos, Alexandre Marcos Lins de Vasconcelos
Informatic Center
Federal University of Pernambuco
Recife, Pernambuco, Brazil
e-mail: {mcs6, amlv}@cin.ufpe.br

***Abstract*—With the growth of the market related to the software development industry, it is necessary to adopt practices that can assist this area in an agile way. This can enable the management of activities related to software acquisition to be defined more effectively, both for those who provide the system, and for those who acquire it. This paper proposes a catalog of best practices using the agile principles that are included in some methodologies. These are designed to manage the software acquisition process in the organizational context of software development, based on the SAM (Supplier Agreement Management) process area of the CMMI-DEV (Capability Maturity Model Integration for Development). The purpose of this catalog is to support the software organizations in the definition and implementation of their processes that are based on quality improvement programs.**

Keywords-software engineering; software quality; process improvement; acquisition; supplier agreement management; agile practices.

I. INTRODUCTION

The software is of an abstract and intangible nature, which means that quality software development is a complex and challenging task for software organizations [1].

Some software development organizations are looking for new strategies to address these challenges, such as the acquisition of parts of the products or services offered to customers. This can improve the quality of the process and the end product that will be delivered to them. Another strategy involves the use of Software Process Improvement programs such as the CMMI-DEV model. This provides guidance for the application of best practices of CMMI in a development organization, to help organizations improve their skills in a systematic way and thus meet their deadlines and develop software [2].

Another approach adopted by organizations is the Agile Methodology, which aims to help teams work rapidly and efficiently through short and time-boxed iterations for planning product increments, and speed up the development procedure. This task may be essential for an organization that wishes to stay in the competitive market, when there is a need for continuous improvement in software products so that they can meet the increasing needs of their customers [3]. The adoption of agile practices in software development has occurred in response to the need to produce software of quality, at great speed that satisfies the user's needs. The software projects often require this speed and productivity to meet the demands and challenges of the market. As a result, the Information Technology (IT) areas have had to invest in quality, monitoring and governance capacity. This task is a real problem in the context of software development and it is essential for companies to achieve quality and agility in their development to meet their deadlines and ensure cost / risk control effectiveness [1]. Other problems may be related to the following: difficulties with the planning team, difficulties in reviewing the product requirements based on traditional models, dissatisfaction of the business area with software development projects, and a low response rate with regards to the development process carried out to meet market demands.

Some experiences with software development might be successful in delivery of the product, owing to the use of an outsourcing strategy. However, organizations are still having problems with the planning, implementation and management of the acquisition process of goods or services from suppliers. This is due to the fact that it is difficult to maintain control of the development process of these suppliers. There are also problems in managing the quality of the goods and services acquired, which may be caused by poor planning, and thus lead to a delay in delivery and unplanned costs [4].

In another study [11] we performed a Systematic Literature Mapping (SLM) [5]; this was a 'secondary' study based on a review of the evidence contained in primary studies and its purpose was to identify, analyze, interpret and report all the key primary research findings in the study area.

The justification of this study lies in the fact that the management of the Acquisition Process is of great importance to software development organizations and its management, as well as to software maturity models [6]. However, these models specify processes that require more time for implementation, when what is needed to meet the market demands is an acquisition process that is not carried out in a bureaucratic and systematic way, but is flexible, agile and with quality.

The main goal of this work is to develop and evaluate a Catalog of Best Practices based on the concepts of an agile methodology for managing the software acquisition process in the context of software development organizations. This catalog must comply with the guidelines set out by the SAM process area of CMMI-DEV, and are concerned with agile methodologies. It aims to provide a solution to support organizations that can contribute to agility, make cost reductions and control the time needed to implement the acquisition process.

In addition to this introductory section, this paper is structured in the following way: in Section 2 there will be a review of related works and this will outline the background of this work, Section 3 will describe the catalog of best practices produced by SAM and the agile practices, Section 4 shows the expected results, and Section 5 concludes the work with some final considerations.

II. RELATED WORKS AND BACKGROUND

This section provides an overview of the concepts of the SAM process area in CMMI-DEV and an overview of systematic literature mapping performed in another work, and examines some related works.

A. *Supplier Agreement Management Process Area in CMMI-DEV*

In this work, the CMMI-DEV is the focal point of the study, since it has a process area that can support the SAM in the acquisition of goods and services in development projects. The CMMI for Development has 22 process areas that have a set of best practices and these address the question of carrying out activities for goods and services development, using practices that cover the lifecycle of the products from their conception to their delivery and maintenance [2], (as shown in Table I). It also a) helps to integrate organizational functions that have traditionally been separated, b) sets out process improvement goals, c) establishes a set of priorities to provide guidance for processes quality, and d) provides a benchmark for the evaluation of current processes [2].

TABLE I. CMMI PROCESS MATURITY LEVELS.

Level	Categories			
	Project Management	**Process Management**	**Engineering**	**Support**
5		Organizational Performance Management		Casual Analysis and Resolution.
4	Quantitative Project Management.	Organizational Process Performance		
3	Integrated Project Management, Risks Management.	Organizational Process Definition, Organizational Process Focus, Organizational Training	Requirements Development, Technical Solution, Product Integration, Verification, Validation.	Decision Analysis and Resolution.
2	Requirements Management, Project Planning, Project Monitoring and Control, **Supplier Agreement Management.**			Configuration Management, Process and Product Quality Assurance, Measurements and Analysis.
1	Process ad hoc.			

The purpose of the SAM process area is to manage the acquisition of goods and services from suppliers [2]. The scope of the SAM process area covers the acquisition of products, services and goods and services components that can be delivered to the customer or included in a product or service system [2]. This area involves the following specific practices: determining the type of acquisition, selecting suppliers, drafting supplier agreements, fulfilling the supplier agreement, accepting the acquired products, and ensuring the delivery of the goods.

B. *An Overview of a Systematic Literature Mapping*

In another study [11], a SLM was performed through a research partnership between students and lecturers at the Federal University of Pará and University of Pernambuco The aim of this was to identify key data on how the software acquisition process could be combined with agile methodologies. This stage showed that there are gaps in this area since the SAM process area was carried out by means of agile practices in the software development environment, and also showed the significance of the study undertaken in this paper.

The selection of the studies followed several phases and the work was carried out by two or more researchers to reduce the risk of bias in the selection [5]. The complete research protocol is available in [11]. This research was performed in four phases; it was conducted by two researchers and three reviewers.

Phase 1 consisted of a) an automatic search to access the sources and execute a string to locate the relevant studies in accordance with the criteria defined in the protocol, and b) a manual search to access the conference and download all the studies related to the research topic.

In Phase 2, each study selected in the previous phase was analyzed by two researchers, based on the analysis of the title and abstract. Any duplicate studies were discarded together with those that were clearly irrelevant to the search according to the inclusion and exclusion criteria.

In Phase 3, list of Phase 2 was consolidated and all these studies were evaluated by two researchers who applied the inclusion and exclusion criteria, through a complete reading. If there were conflicts of opinion between the researchers, a meeting was held to reach a consensus, and if the disagreement persisted, the matter was solved by the reviewer.

On the basis of the consolidated list of Phase 3, a quality assessment was conducted in Phase 4 together with a data extraction of all the studies from a complete reading of the studies. The studies were analyzed by two researchers to evaluate the quality, through the application of quality criteria. The data extraction was performed by two researchers and the results were documented in a form, and the extraction review was conducted by the reviewers.

Fig. 1 summarizes the phases and the number of identified studies from each SLM phase. Before the selection, a meeting was held to clarify the concepts and discussions about the inclusion and exclusion criteria, so that the concepts were understood by all the participants.

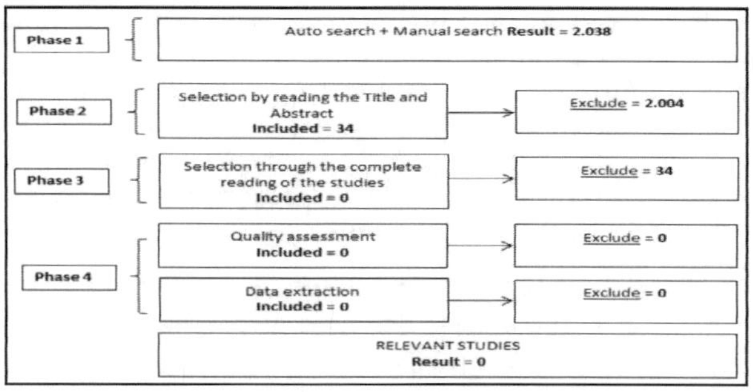

Figure 1. The study selection process

The findings suggest that there is a lack of research on the subject, due to the fact that no relevant data have been disclosed about how the SAM process area of CMMI-DEV can be combined with agile methodologies. In view of this, this result confirms that there is a gap in knowledge about the investigated area, which confirms the relevance, feasibility and innovativeness of this research study.

C. Related Works

The related works to this research were considered to be relevant if they addressed the following issues: (1) the need to support the systematic implementation of maturity models, (2) the study of software acquisition, (3) the use of agile methodologies in the context of software development, (4) the use of agile methodologies in the context of software process improvement. Some studies relating to the topics mentioned are described below.

Furtado's research study [7] supports the systematic implementation of maturity models, and carried out a task based on process improvement models and standards. This work defined a proposal for the acquisition process by means of a process framework and a tool to support the implementation and execution of the process for acquiring software and related services. On the basis of this framework, this paper confirmed the compatibility of the activities that compose it, with regard to the SAM process area of CMMI-DEV. Thus, it was able to determine which of its activities can be mapped to the agile practices, so as to define the catalog of best practices proposed in this paper.

With regards to the research studies on software acquisition, an approach was adopted to define the processes required for the acquisition. These included different contexts, and defined a software acquisition process to enable the reuse of process components in the definition and implementation of acquisition processes, and support the organizations that implement the software acquisition more efficiently. However, this work did not include the agile concepts in its approach [8].

A related work about the use of agile methodologies in software development, showed some of the advantages of agile methodologies of software compared with traditional methods. This study discussed the main features and practices of agile methodologies, and made comparisons with traditional methodologies, by emphasizing that agile methodologies are based on people rather than processes and planning [9]. However, it was restricted to show the advantages and disadvantages of eXtreme Programming (XP) and Scrum, without focusing on the acquisition procedure.

Another study [10] analyzed quantitative and qualitative data collected from the literature and two Brazilian organizations that employed the XP agile methodology. The main contribution of this work is that it identified features from the Agile and CMMI association and the implications of this application.

As a result, this methodology gave an account of fusion that was incomplete, since it was found that there are only a few quantitative reports. These were insufficient either to provide a definitive opinion about this "incomplete" fusion or to define in which cases the fusion would generate better results. It should be noted that the research was confined to dealing with an agile methodology - XP.

From the analysis of the works above, it is clear that the acquisiton process implemented in an agile way was not within the scope of these projects. As a differential, this study will provide an implementation of the main agile approaches with regard to the framework [7] that are compatible with the SAM process area of CMMI-DEV, and provide the necessary basis for setting up the Catalog of Best Practices by employing agile methodologies to support the acquisition process in the context of software development organizations.

III. The Catalog of Best Practices for SAM and Agile Practices

The first mapping was carried out within the framework presented in [7], which included the SAM practices, and the second mapping of activities resulted from the first one that had agile methodologies (XP, Scrum and Feature Driven Development (FDD)). This provided evidence that the application of agile practices can be used in the context of a software acquistion procedure. This document was prepared as follows: all the activities, which are in the framework phases, were related to the SAM practices that resulted from each activity and confirmed the level of agile practice that was needed to assist in the implementation of the procedure.

On the basis of the obtained results from the previous mapping, a catalog of practices was recommended, which included the suggestions for agile practices that can be implemented in activities performed in a traditional software development organization. When evaluating the catalog, the experts in the area of Software Quality used a peer review technique to determine the effectiveness of the agile practices with regards to the proposed acquisition procedure.

A. The Agile SAM Workflow

The activities included in the catalog were identified by aligning the framework activies of the software and related service acquisition processes [7] with the SAM process area of CMMI-DEV [2]. In this way the research was able to identify the best practices defined for the software acquisition process that can support organizations to form acquisition agreements based on agile practices.

The catalog comprises of 4 activities: (1) Preparing the

Acquisition, (2) Selecting the Supplier, (3) Monitoring Acquisition, and (4) Accepting the Acquired Product. The macro workflow can be seen in Fig. 2.

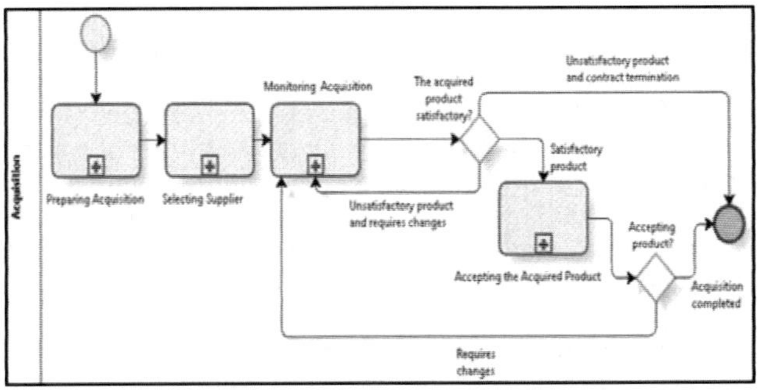

Figure 2. The Agile SAM Macro Workflow

In the first activity, Preparing the Acquisition, the activities about acquisition planning are carried out and include the following: establishing the needs and desired outcomes, setting out the project stakeholders, defining and prioritizing the stakeholders' requirements, reviewing the requirements, conducting a technical feasibility analysis, developing an acquisition strategy, defining and agreeing on the acquisition schedule, defining the criteria for the product acceptance, setting out the criteria for supplier selection, preparing and approving the acquistion plan, and identifing the potential suppliers.

The aim of the second activity, Selecting the Supplier, is to identify and select the supplier that meets the expectations of the acquisition. This consists of the following 7 activities: receiving the proposals, giving an operational opinion, providing a technical opinion, selecting the supplier, preparing and negotiating an agreement, ensuring the agreement terms are fully understood, and drawing up the agreement.

During the third activity, Monitoring Acquisition, the control and monitoring of the acquisition are performed. This includes the following activities: reviewing the agreement terms, agreeing to the changes, tracking issues, and monitoring the supplier processes. In this activity the question of whether the product being developed is satisfactory or not is determined. If it is unsatisfactory, there are two alternatives for the customer that have to be evaluated: implementing the necessary changes or terminating the agreement; this finalizes the acquisition process. But if the product is satisfactory the activity is carried out.

In the fourth activity, Accepting the Acquired Product, it is determined if the product can be accepted by the customer. The following activies are carried out: evaluating the product delivered by the acquisition, complying with the agreement, and accepting the product. During this activity, it is still necessary to confirm if the product will be accepted, because when necessary, it is susceptible to change. However, if no inconsistencies are found, the acquisition is completed together with the acceptance of the product.

B. The Catalog of Agile Best Practices

The catalog of agile best practices was developed on the basis of the results obtained by mapping the 4 activities identified and the agile practices that can be used in these activities. This was achieved by determining if the use of the agile practices was compatible with all the activities present in the macro workflow, and a total of 25 activities were required for the acquisition procedures. Some of the agile practices that may be used in each activity of the catalog are outlined in the subsection below.

1) Activity 1: Preparing the Acquisition

In this activity eleven tasks have been described for the implementation of the guidelines for the agile practices.

Before the 'Establishment of the Needs and Intended Results' task can be carried out, a meeting must be held to discuss the needs and desired outcomes from the acquisition, and to compile a Product Backlog with the list of required features. At this meeting, questions will be raised about the reasons for the acquisition and what requirements and restrictions there are of the product that will be purchased. By employing the Scrum agile methodology, the Product Backlog will be prepared and this contains the specifications of the items needed for the product, as well as a description of them. This backlog will be displayed in CANVAS for the benefit of the team involved.

In 'Setting out the Project for the Stakeholders', a meeting will be to define the Project to the stakeholders. The following items will be determined to identify the stakeholder, during the meeting: Who are the people that can affect the project? What is the responsibility of the project? How can each stakeholder help (positive factor) and adversely affect (negative factor) the acquisition? What are the degrees of influence of each stakeholder? This information is required to fill the Stakeholders Definition CANVAS.

In the 'Defining and Prioritizing the Stakeholder Requirements' task, a meeting should be held to define the order of priority of the items that form the Product Backlog, which is compiled during the 'Establishment of the Needs and Intended Results' task. In this case, the following information will be added to the Backlog: a column called "Priority Value", the aim of which aims is identify the priority according to the degree of its importance to the project in the range of 1 to 10. These values can be classified as follows, 1-3 Low Priority, 4-6 Average Priority and 7-10 High Priority. There is another column called "Priority Level" that shows the degree of priority of each item. This forms the backlog that can be defined, since it is represented in an incremental way, "1" being the most representative item (High Priority) within a project. In this way, it is possible to identify the features that require most attention.

In 'Revising the Requirements', after the requirements for the acquisition have been defined, an attempt should be made to check if all the items listed in the Backlog are in accordance with the stakeholders needs and establish if there are any inconsistencies and conflicts that affect the cost-effectiveness of each item. This activity is based on the Scrum agile practice called Sprint Review, which should be carried out in each cycle by the supplier. It is a means of determining if the purchaser's needs are actually being met and what changes may be required when necessary. The information will be displayed in CANVAS by Checklist. The details of each Backlog item must be put on a card, which will consist of a single identification (ID), item name and its description. The ID is important because it is used during the review of each item, since if any inconsistency is found, this identification will be used in an "inconsistency" card representing the revised item, the description of the problem identified and the change required to correct the problem. If no problem is identified in the Backlog item, it will be marked as Checked (√).

In 'Performing the Technical Feasibility Analysis', a meeting should be held to check the technical feasibility and preparation of CANVAS. Thus, the following questions must be checked:

- Is the solution or the proposed technology practical?
- Does it already have the necessary technology?
- Does it already have the necessary technical knowledge?
- Is the schedule reasonable?

These questions will be analyzed in the light of the available resources, existing restrictions for the project and the quality and the time required for the Project. Feedback must be given for each question.

In the 'Developing a Procurement Strategy' task, a meeting will be held to develop an acquisition strategy based on the results obtained in 'Performing the Technical Feasibility Analysis' task. This is because these results provide the necessary support for planning a consistent strategy with the acquisition needs, that takes account of the viable alternatives, risk analysis, costs and benefits of each option. The results of this task will be displayed in CANVAS, which specifies the acquisition strategy that will be adopted.

In the 'Defining the Acquisition Schedule' task, the reviewed points of the acquisition will be defined and monitored. This meeting should define the day of the month in which these revisions will be made. The times of the daily and / or weekly meetings will also be set, since they are important for checking the activities and the progress made in the proposed acquisition, in all its phases. These dates should be defined and agreed among the stakeholders. Thus, a schedule with the acquisition activities should be generated, which will be displayed together with the specifications for the activities in Kanban (Work CANVAS), which is responsible for implementing the scheme and setting dates for its achievement. Each completed activity is given a Checked (√) to show that it has been its implemented.

In 'Defining the Accepted Criteria for the Purchased Product', a meeting will be held to examine these criteria. This involves drawing up a list of project tasks and work products that must be delivered at the end of this project. These should include a 'Checklist for Product Acceptance' with the specifications required for the product that need to be met.

In 'Defining the Supplier Selection Criteria', a planned meeting should be held to choose the criteria that will be used for the supplier selection process. This meeting will comprise those responsible for acquisition management, and will discuss the relevant criteria to be considered when choosing a supplier, such as budgeting, preparing a schedule for product development, the necessary knowledge for carrying out the project and experience in previous projects. A Supplier Selection Checklist should be generated.

The 'Preparation and Approval of the Acquisition Plan' task, should make use of some of the work products generated in other tasks, such as the schedule, the Supplier Selection Checklist, and the Product Acceptance Checklist. A list of the products that need to be supplied should also be prepared, as well as a definition of the stakeholders' responsibilities for the acquisition procedure. On the basis of this information, the plan will be prepared that specifies the best way to proceed with the acquisition. This plan will be sent to the Work CANVAS so that the stakeholders are informed.

In the 'Identifying the Potential Suppliers' task, a survey will be initially made conducted of the information about the suppliers, such as the criteria listed in the Work CANVAS, which makes it easy for stakeholders to view the list of suppliers that have been analyzed in this activity. Thus, the most suitable suppliers for the project will be identified. Each feature will have an identification, and this ID will be used as a reference-point to show which suppliers that meet each of these requirements. In the last column the suppliers that come closest to meeting the required criteria will be defined, and thus become the potential suppliers.

2) Activity 2: Selecting the Supplier

In this activity, seven tasks have been described below, together with the implementation guidelines based on agile principles and practices.

In 'Receiving Proposals', the suppliers proposals will be forwarded to the person responsible for the acquisition project, who will evaluate its contents, on the basis of the criteria for the potential suppliers. These include the specifications of the "unserved criteria", providing the suppliers with better proposals and displaying them in the Work CANVAS the Suppliers Proposals List.

In the 'Issuing the Operational Opinion' task, a meeting will be held that includes the acquisition management team. The purpose of this is to conduct an analysis of the proposal by comparing the different features of the suppliers and to establish if its proposed solution will actually work. The feedback will be provided by the PIECES Operational Assessment Framework, i.e. it will take account of Performance, Information, Economy, Control, Efficiency and Services. These are checked as follows:

- Performance: Does the current operation mode provide suitable throughput and response time?

- Information: Does the current operation mode provide the end user and managers with accurate, useful, relevant and timely information?
- Economy: Does the current operation mode offer information services that are cost effective for the organization?
- Control: Does the current operation mode provide efficient control services to prevent fraud and to ensure the accuracy and security of the data and information?
- Efficiency: Does the current operation mode make maximum use of available resources? and
- Services: Does the current operation mode provide a reliable service? Is it flexible and extensible?

The 'Issuing Technical Feedback' task will take place after the previous task and will involve an analysis of questions related to supplier features with regard to the availability of technical resources and the necessary professionals to implement the proposal.

The 'Selecting Supplier' task will be carried out by the team responsible for the product acquisition and is concerned with discussing the features of the suppliers that have already been identified and revealed in the operational and technical feedback. On the basis of this information, the team selects the most advantageous proposal that meets the specifications of the required product. A Supplier Analysis and Selection CANVAS will evaluate proposals, together with the specification of the selected supplier and the rationale for selecting or not selecting each supplier. After this, a notification about the acceptance of the selected proposal will be made.

In 'Preparing and Negotiating a Agreement', a meeting will be be arranged for those responsible for the acquisition management and the supplier. This task involves holding a discussion about the agreement terms, expectations and obligations of those involved (the purchaser and supplier), and addressing questions about: costs, the schedule, items to be reviewed and the monitoring to be performed, etc. A list should be drawn up of the main terms to be agreed among those involved .

In the 'Ensuring the Agreement Terms are Fully Understood' task, all the agreement terms will be checked. This is to ensure, that they are understood by all those involved in the acquisition. If there is any question or suggestion about the agreement items, these will be discussed and analyzed, and any necessary measures taken for entry, modification or deletion of the term. At the end of the meeting everyone should be aware of what is expected to be agreed. A checklist of items that will be carried out should be prepared, as well as the agreement and the justification for the inclusion or not of the agreement items.

In the 'Issuing the Agreement' task, which is undertaken on the completion of the previous task, the provisions that will form the agreement will have been defined and agreed. Thus, the agreement will be issued at a meeting that will be attended by the acquirer and the supplier who are selected as the people responsible for issuing and signing the agreement.

3) Activity 3: Monitoring Acquisition

In this activity four tasks have been described below, together with the implementation guidelines based on the agile principles and practices.

The 'Reviewing the Agreement Terms' task will be carried out by those responsible for acquisition management and the suppliers and involves checking all the items contained in the Agreement. An analysis will be conducted to determine which are relevant and if there any inconsistencies, and decisions will be made about the necessary changes. Thus, a CANVAS should include the list of agreement terms with a checklist of possible changes, the proper justification for the amendment of items and / or the inclusion of agreement terms.

The 'Agreeing the Changes' task requires a meeting that will be attended by the acquisition management team and the supplier for analysis of the changes identified in the previous task. Thus, a changed card is required and the inclusion of the change information in the agreement must duly agree among those involved.

The 'Tracking the Problems', will be attended by the acquisition management team and involves discussing the problems found and the proposed solutions for each situation. Thus, a problem tracking CANVAS should be generated, which will have TO DO, DOING and DONE status. This CANVAS consists of the following: the project activities and the identification of problems found in each of these activities, a proposed solution, the names of those responsible for each solution, and the starting date and completion date of the corrections made.

In the 'Monitoring the Supplier Process' task, a meeting will be held that will be attended by the acquisition management team and the supplier. The aim of this is to determine what processes are used by the supplier, to check whether the supplier is able to meet expectations of the acquirer or if it is carrying out its activities in accordance with the agreement. Thus, a Checklist about the analysis of processes performed by the supplier should be generated, based on criteria for monitoring the execution of processes.

4) Activity 4:Accepting the Acquired Product

In this activity three tasks are described below, together with the implementation guidelines using the agile principles and practices.

The 'Evaluating the Product Delivered' task involves evaluating the product by taking account of the product acceptance criteria. This will be carried out by the acquisition team and the supplier, so that the supplier is provided with knowledge of any inconsistencies or problems found in the product. Thus, a CANVAS with a checklist of acceptance criteria for a product (that includes functional and non-functional requirements), is given the status of "Attended" or "Not Attended", together with a) the justification for this status, b) recommendations for the correction of the problems found, and c) a desription of the situation of each checked item.

The 'Maintaining the Agreement Compliance' task involves holding a meeting with the acquisition management team and the supplier who conduct a detailed analysis of attendance of each item included in the agreement. Thus, a CANVAS with the checklist of attendance with the agreement items should be generated.

In 'Accepting the Product Delivered', which takes place after the product evaluation and the verification of the attendance with the agreement, a meeting is held to formalize the product acceptance and the signing of the Acceptance Agreement by the stakeholders takes place. This agreement must include at least the following information: Name of the Project, Goals of the Acceptance Agreement, Description of the items being delivered, Identification of the stakeholdersthat sign the agreement (acquirer and supplier), and Signature Date.

C. The Evaluation of Catalog

The evaluation of this work was initially made to check if the compatibility of the activities that form the acquisition process framework of software and related services [7] with regard to the practices included in the SAM process area of CMMI-DEV [2]. For this reason, for an expert in Software Quality and Process Improvement areas was sent a questionare to obtain feedback about its evaluation and obtain opinions and suggestions for its improvement.

After this, the evaluation was conducted of the mapping of agile practices that are compatible with the framework activities included in theSAM process area of CMMI-DEV. This was sent to an expert to give feedback about its validity and obtain some opinions about it.

Finally, the Catalog of Best Practices also had its validity confirmed through a peer review carried out by an expert. An attempt will also be made to validate its application in the definition of a process for a software organization, which will involve an evaluation of the efficiency and effectiveness of this catalog to support this activity and bring about an improvement in the organizational process.

IV. Expected Results

The research product is a catalog of best practices about SAM with agile activities that can be used to implement each activity present in the macro workflow. This catalog was examined by an expert in the area of software quality, and will then be submitted to a critical analysis of its validity, usability, compatibility with models and standards, and feasibility for use in an organizational environment.

In this way the validity of its agile activities can be confirmed and with the aid of the catalog, its evaluation will enable improvements to be made to any failings detected by the peer review of an expert.

V. Conclusion

This work has shown the importance of using processes for improvement in an organizational environment, especially with regard to the software acquisition process. Its objective is to know and apply the findings of the literature in the area of software development.

To achieve this goal, we conducted in another work [11] a SLM in the preliminary studies of the research area of this paper, to determine what gaps there are and their degree of importance. After this phase the mapping of an acquisition process framework with agile practices was performed, to provide the necessary basis for preparing the catalog of best practices using agile methodologies for the management of the software acquisition process.

In future work in this research area an experiment should be carried out where the catalog can be used in a study case. This should be conducted in a software development organization so that comparisons can be made with regard to the situation of an organization before and after the implementation of the practices included in the catalog. Thus, we intend to evaluate this together with the members of the organization to ensure that the necessary improvements in the catalog are made to allow it to be adaptated to real situations faced by the organization.

Acknowledgment

The authors would like to thank the Dean of Research and Postgraduate Studies at the Federal University of Pará (PROPESP/UFPA) by the Qualified Publication Support Program (PAPQ) for the financial support.

References

[1] I. Sommerville, "Software Engineering", 9. ed. São Paulo: Pearson Prentice Hall, 2011.

[2] SEI – Software Engineering Institute, "CMMI for Development – V 1.3", 2010, Available: http://www.sei.cmu.edu/reports/10tr033.pdf, retrieved: July, 2016.

[3] J. F. Abrantes, "Experimental studies on mobility in the Software Development and its Use in Testing Process", Tese de D.Sc., COPPE/UFRJ, Brazil, 2012.

[4] J. A. Calvo-Manzano, T. San Feliu, and A. Pursche, "The forgotten practices of subcontracting", In Information Systems and Technologies (CISTI), Brazil, pp. 1-4, 2010.

[5] B. Kitchenham and S. Charters, "Guidelines for performing Systematic Literature Reviews in Software Engineering", Keele University and Durham University Joint Report, EBSE 2007-001, 2007.

[6] SOFTEX – Associação para Promoção da Excelência do Software Brasileiro, "MPS.BR - Acquisition Guide", 2013, Available: http://www.softex.br/wp-content/uploads/2013/07/MPS.BR_Guia_de_Aquisicao_2013.pdf, retrieved: July, 2016.

[7] J. C. C. Furtado, "Spider-ACQ: An Approach to the systematization of Products and Services Acquisition Process Based Quality Multi-models", Masters Dissertation, PPGCC/UFPA, 2011.

[8] E. D. Nunes, "Definition of Software Acquisition Processes for Reuse", Masters Dissertation, COPPE/UFRJ, Brazil, 2011.

[9] M. S. Soares, "Agile Methodologies Extreme Programming and Scrum for Software Development", Revista Eletrônica de Sistemas de Informação. vol. 3, p. 8-13, 2004.

[10] C. Santana, C. Gusmão, L.Soares, C. Pinheiro, T. Maciel, A. Vasconcelos, and A. Rouiller, "Agile Software Development and CMMI: What We Do Not Know about Dancing with Elephants", Conference: Agile Processes in Software Engineering and Extreme Programming, 10th International Conference, XP 2009, Pula, Sardinia, Italy, pp. 124-129,2009.

[11] M. C. Santos, E. M. Soares, S. R. B. Oliveira, and A. M. L Vasconcelos, "A Systematic Mapping about SAM and Agile Practices", Available: https://www.dropbox.com/s/x0xh8i1653nnqkp/protocolo1.docx?dl=0, retrieved: July, 2016.

Integrating Service Design Prototyping into Software Development

Tanja Sauvola[1], Simo Rontti[2], Laura Laivamaa[3], Markku Oivo[1], Pasi Kuvaja[1]

[1]M3S research unit, University of Oulu
e-mail: firstname.lastname@oulu.fi
[2] University of Lapland
e-mail: firstname.lastname@ulapland.fi
[3]e-mail: lsmeds@ulapland.fi

***Abstract*—Customer-driven service design is becoming an integral part of continuous software development. The fulfilment of needs is manifested through customer behaviour patterns that are often difficult to identify and validate for R&D. This paper investigates how customer involvement in software development can be achieved through experience prototyping. First, participatory action research with four cases is presented. As a result, the benefits, challenges and critical factors for successful service prototyping are identified. Second, a practical model is proposed for integrating service design as sprints within the software development process. Based on the study, the deployment of these methods can be adopted through an organisational culture that invests in the needed mindset, expertise, timing and placement. Contextual and motivating user involvement is important throughout the software development process. A number of important subjects that need further studies, such as service design performance measurement and customer data management, were also identified.**

Keywords*—*customer involvement; service design; software development; experience prototyping

I. INTRODUCTION

Today, software is transforming almost all industries and is the main driver for innovation [1]. Elbert stated that all companies are in the software business either directly with IT solutions or indirectly with products in which software is critical for value creation, such as embedded systems, or value delivery, such as services. In today's highly competitive and fast-changing markets, software intensive industry is evolving towards a value driven and adaptive real-time business paradigm [2]. Hence, we live in a world of data overload, where any argument in product development can find supporting data. It is easy to find information to support our assumptions, but testing them with customers and then taking corrective actions is still hard [3]. Customer involvement and understanding customer needs are essential in software development in order to build successful products and services. According to Humble, after failing to deliver value for customers, the second largest risk in product development is building the wrong thing the right way and overinvesting in unproven opportunities. For this reason software companies need to continuously collect customer feedback and validate assumptions during the development process in order to build a product that is the best fit for customer needs [3][4][5]. However, customer needs are often difficult to identify and they can change rapidly. Obtaining tacit and complex knowledge from customers is hard, as interacting and talking to customers may often be misleading, e.g., asking customers for information that they are not able to provide, such as what product to develop or technologies it should contain [6]. Agile methods [7][8] and Lean Startup [9] philosophy are addressing these issues by offering a range of techniques for more flexible ways of working. The aim is to produce a definition of a new service concept or the 'minimum viable product', which is to be implemented in markets as fast as possible with minimum effort, allowing us to measure how customers react and then validate findings.

Service design (SD) is an ascendant field of research where cultural, social and human interaction are connected [10]. The customer-driven SD approach aims at products and services that are useful, usable and desirable from the user's point of view and efficient from the service or product producer's point of view [11]. Service design has already taken place in the business-to-consumer (B2C) context, but it is also recognised as a useful approach in the business-to-business (B2B) context as well as in the internal development of organisations' processes [12]. More recently, a few process models and working practices, such as Lean UX [13], user story mapping [14] and design sprint models [15][16], have been introduced under both service design and user experience (UX) design titles and attempt to synthesise service design thinking, agile software development and lean start-up philosophies.

In this study, using four case projects from Finnish companies, we examine the role and impact of the experience prototyping methods of service design in software development contexts. Therefore, the main research question is:

RQ: How can service design be integrated into software development through a collaborative experience prototyping approach?

In exploring this we also ask:

- What are the benefits, challenges and critical factors of collaborative experience prototyping in software development?
- What is the position and role of service design in software development?

The contribution of the paper is twofold. First, we present a participatory action research study with four cases, where we identify the role of SD and benefits, challenges and critical factors of experience prototyping in the software development context. Second, we outline a practical model for integrating SD in the software development process in order to increase customer insights and solve problems that are relevant for customers and thereby deliver value.

The rest of the paper is structured as follows. Section II presents the background and related work for this study. Section III presents study design and research method. In Section IV, we present and discuss our results from the empirical study and outline the findings in a practical model for integrating service design in software development projects. Finally, Section V concludes this paper and suggests topics for future research.

II. Background and Related Work

A. *Customer involvement in software development*

Today, software is developed in rapidly changing and unpredictable markets, with complex and constantly changing customer requirements and the added pressure to shorten time-to-market [17]. Agile methods, which are widely adopted in the software industry [18], facilitate more flexible ways of organising software development activities in order to better meet the dynamic and unpredictable conditions in the business environment. Many different agile methodologies have been devised, such as Extreme Programming, Scrum, Kanban and Lean software development, which to some extent share the underlying mindset but use different implementations [2]. As stated by Nerur et al., agile methods are people-centric, recognising the value that competent people and their relationships bring to software development. In addition, agile methods focus on improving customer satisfaction through collaboration, active participation of relevant stakeholders and embracing change. The value of agile methods depends largely on an organisation's ability to learn. [19]

In the Agile software engineering literature [8][19], customer involvement is seen as the direction software companies should take to transform their practices throughout the development process. Typically, this is addressed by having a product owner represent the customer point of view [4]. However, recent studies show that even though ways of learning about customers are increasing, software companies often find it challenging to obtain timely and accurate feedback from customers to support research and development (R&D) decision-making processes continuously [4][5]. Customer involvement is studied widely in areas such as participatory design, user-centric design, usability engineering, human aspects of software engineering and requirements engineering [20].

Customer involvement is an abstract concept that refers to ways in which customers play roles in the software development process and the extent of their participation. Customer involvement is referred to as direct interaction using techniques based on active customer participation [21]. Through the years, a long list of practices and methods has been introduced to enable user participation and involvement. Although user participation seems to be a beneficial and well-understood approach in product development, direct user involvement may not always be feasible. The situation is especially difficult in business markets when a wide physical or cultural gap exists between suppliers and customers and there can be multiple organisations and management layers between developers and users. The SD approach introduced in the next section offers a method to bridge this gap.

B. *Service design approach*

SD is a methodological approach, which can be used for customer involvement during the software development process. It is a holistic, multidisciplinary field that helps to innovate and improve existing products and services as well as make them more useful and desirable for customers [22]. Service design provides methods and tools for concretising and understanding user motivations and emotions during the development process for all the stakeholders involved. In B2B markets in particular, a large number of internal and external stakeholders must be considered, such as users, decision makers, developers, etc. The SD approach integrates the themes of a customer's emotions and experiences in the innovation process and concretises them for the benefit of value co-creation efforts [23].

Service design offers an outside-in-development approach, where products and services are developed holistically from customers' and end-users' point of view. In the B2B context, it means studying both the client business' and the end-users' processes, needs and wants. SD views the entire customer journey before, during and after the actual service in order to design the process fluently and support customers' goals [19]. Another key concept is the touchpoint through which the product or service is experienced; touchpoints are anything that can be designed in order to direct user experience in the desired direction [24]. This includes not only software user interfaces but also phone service, face-to-face communication, social media, signs, service premises, prints, physical tokens and their interconnection from the customer point of view. The touchpoint concept can also be looked at from the software development point of view (inside-out), as a link to customers through traditional product development phases: requirements, development, verification and validation and post-deployment where qualitative and quantitative data is collected [5].

The concept of co-creating value is defined by Srivastava and Verma as systematic and structured process based on collaboration with external stakeholders to generate value for the company as well as for the customers [25]. In the SD process, customers are not considered merely as feedback informants but as active participants from the beginning to the end of the process. In the process, customers may be targets of study via qualitative methods, such as interviews and observation, or customers can be asked to produce the customer data themselves using self-documentation methods, such as design probes [26]. Co-design is emphasised in SD, which refers to the process in which stakeholders are involved in concrete productive design tasks. These workshop sessions typically include collaborative prototyping and other means of expressing the information needed in the design process facilitated by design professionals [27]. Recently, the workshop-based SD process has led to the compression of service design into a short but efficient design sprint as the pre-development phase in a lean and agile software development process [15][16].

According to Buchenau and Fulton Suri, experience prototyping is a key method in co-design sessions, serving as an efficient medium for concretising and empathising with customer insight. The aim of experience prototyping is to represent and prototype different design concepts and ideas. Prototypes are defined as 'representations of a design made before final artefacts exist'. To them the term 'experience design' consists of methods that make it possible for designers, customers and users to reach a common understanding of the forthcoming results (products or services) of the ongoing project. Experience prototypes may include suggestive staging; 'quick and dirty' card mockups, taking the roles of both customer and service provider and enacting service situations. Experience prototyping has three roles in the design process: understanding customer insight findings, exploring new ideas and communicating concepts to others. [28]

Pinheiro lists three main goals for how early experience prototypes can be used in a project: '(1) set the context for users to participate in idea generation and co-design, (2) service enactment, or role-play, to explain or lean from a complex concept and (3) test to validate specific service interactions or the entire service journey'. The experience prototype can serve as an earlier, more inexpensive and efficient version of the minimum viable product (MVP) emphasised in Lean Startup philosophy. [15]

Several methods and facilities have been developed in order to enhance the facilitation of co-design and holistic experience prototyping. The Service Innovation Corner (SINCO) is a service prototyping environment concept developed at the University of Lapland [29]. SINCO consists of the environment and a set of tools for co-design and experience prototyping. In SINCO, technological equipment and digital material, such as photos, videos, and sounds, are used to create the atmosphere of actual service moments for prototyping and re-enactment. The SINCO set-up has two 117' background projection screens perpendicular to each other to provide the background scenery and enable partial yet immersive spatiality [30]. SINCO methods and tools were applied in this research when conducting co-creation workshops with the case companies. Fig. 1 summarises the research setting and the interrelations of the key concepts of this paper.

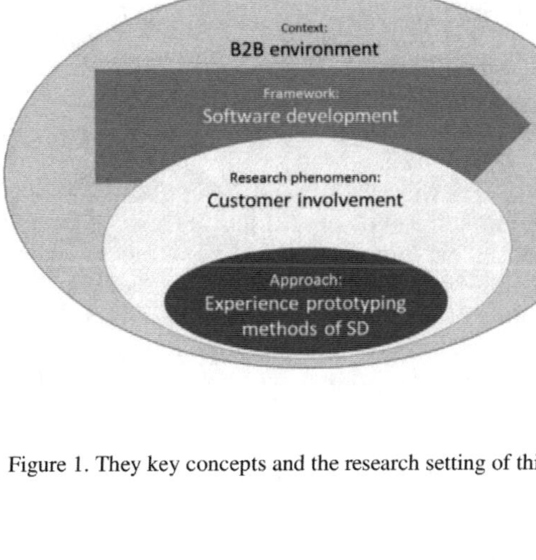

Figure 1. They key concepts and the research setting of this paper.

III. Research Design

In this section, research methods and settings, data collection activities and analysis are presented.

A. *Research method*

The aim of this paper is to study the role and impacts of experience prototyping methods of service design in the software development context. We apply the multiple case study approach, which adopts an interpretive approach [31]. The multiple-case study is suitable for this study because it allows the researchers to study the phenomenon in a real life setting as well as a cross-case analysis of the data. The general research framework for this study can be characterised as participatory action research (PAR), as described by Whyte, with the research activities taking place in empirical context advancing both science and practice [32]. PAR is a social process involving practitioners in the research from the initial design of the project through data gathering and analysis to final conclusions and actions arising out of the research. Methods to achieve the research goal include end-user interviews, role plays and data and information visualisations. They also include experience prototyping in the SINCO environment where both customers' and end-users' tangible and intangible needs and wants were examined with scenarios including images, video and audio material. The approach to these methods is also PAR, in that it studies a situation and a set of problems to determine what the facts through self-reflective iterative cycles. This can also be described as a co-learning process between researchers and workshop participants resulting to organisational learning and change [32][33].

B. *Case companies*

The study uses empirical data from four case companies in Finland. We refer to the companies as Company A, B, C and D. The four companies were selected using convenience sampling from a group of Finnish leading-edge companies participating in two large national research programmes. Company A is developing embedded software solutions for specialised markets in the wireless and automotive industry. It also provides B2B product development services and customised solutions for wireless communications. The focus of the case was to increase user insights of special devices used in specialised market segments, such as public safety. Company B is an SME operating in metal industry, manufacturing hydraulic cylinders and offering cylinder maintenance services for big industry clients. The focus of the project in the company was to develop a digital maintenance service. Company C operates in the software industry, offering a variety of IT solutions focusing on data security operations, mainly in B2B and B2C markets.

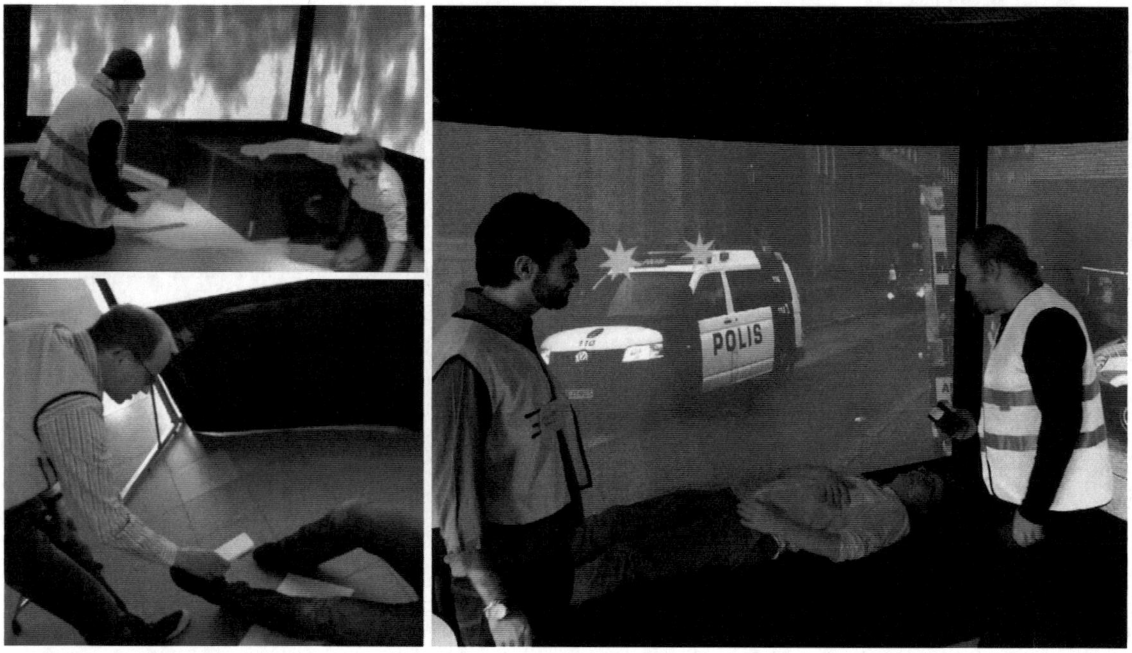

Figure 2. Example of the SD workshops: Experience prototyping public safety communication use cases in the SINCO.

Company D is a multinational bank operating on both B2B and B2C markets. The focus of the case project was to analyse and improve online banking services.

C. *Data collection and analysis*

Empirical data was collected from December 2013 to March 2014 (Companies B and D) and from November 2014 to September 2015 (Companies A and C), using semi-structured interviews with open ended questions [n=11], workshops [n=12], group discussions [n=10], field diaries by the service design team during workshops [n=13] and secondary data [n=29]. The interviewees and workshop attendees were selected by a key contact person from each company who was asked to nominate experts from various departments, such as product management, R&D, validation and verification, sales and marketing and, in some cases, contact centre and customer counter functions. The interview guide allowed us to conduct the interviews in the form of a discussion with each interviewee that lasted approximately 1–2 hours.

The workshops (Fig. 2), besides being an integral part of the service design sprints, can be considered as participative action research cycles, producing data about the research phenomenon [31]. In the workshops, SD was turned into action through service design sprints affiliated to the company's existing R&D, business development or marketing processes. All workshop participants had a lot of experience of working in the company on multiple projects. Workshops lasted approximately between 3–5 hours and were facilitated by 1–3 service designers. Workshops and interviews were video and audio recorded and transcribed for analysis. In addition, participatory observation was used as a research method in this study. These field diary notes were important, as the emerged emotions during the workshops, such as frustration, anger or laughter, were observed and documented carefully. In addition, secondary data was collected from the case companies: (1) process models and other documents, (2) both individual and group interviews of the potential end-users and (3) material from workshops and presentations.

In our study, we assess three aspects of validity, i.e. construct validity, external validity and reliability, as identified by Runeson et al. [30]. Prior to data collection, the research design that also included the data collection process was carefully considered. The activity involved selecting appropriate companies and roles for the interviews and providing all interviewees with introductory materials (e.g., study objectives, the structure of the workshops and interviews, etc.). Threats to the reliability of the study findings were mitigated by three researchers involved in all the phases of the research process. In particular, data collection and analysis was performed in continuous collaboration following the general techniques for case study analysis and used the QSR NVivo tool [1]. During the analysis, all materials, including transcripts, field notes, audio and video files and other related material, were stored in NVivo. All transcribed interviews were carefully read and coded by themes. The results were produced by looking for themes related to the research question.

[1] www.qsrinternational.com

IV. Result Analysis and Discussion

Based on the empirical findings, this section presents and discuss the identified benefits, challenges and critical factors of service prototyping in a software development context (Tables I, II and III). Additionally, a practical model for integrating service design sprints into the software development process is outlined and discussed (Fig. 3).

A. *Experience prototyping in software development*

The use of SD experience prototyping methods has benefits and challenges. The findings from each case study company show, that at their best, these methods can nourish and support innovation and development culture. The most important offering of the workshops, according to many of the participants, was the liberalisation of mindsets. Experience prototyping methods also allow for the efficient constitution of a complete understanding of all stakeholders' viewpoints. These methods were seen as pleasant and motivating but also challenging because participants had to step out of their comfort zone. According to workshop participants, they were able to develop significant knowledge, skills, and emotions by experience prototyping in an emergent process that empowered people to engage in discovery, reflection and even action (Fig. 2). Testing of business hypotheses and assumptions in product development could be then turned into faster and more accurate decision-making and value creation. Table I categorises and describes the identified benefits and Table II categorises and describes the identified challenges of experience prototyping based on the research data. In Table III, we also identified critical factors that need to be considered in order to successfully implement experience prototyping within company processes.

TABLE I. Identified Benefits of Experience Prototyping

Benefit	Description
Improved Communication	SD methods help to improve communication between all the stakeholders (e.g., management, sales, development team, customer and end-users). Collaborative prototyping sessions also increase transparency in the organisation by uncovering grassroots knowledge to be exploited in development even on strategic and business level.
Instant feedback	Presents an opportunity to get instant and direct feedback from the end-users.
Increased motivation and innovation	SD methods motivate development teams, customers and end-users to innovate, co-develop and more actively participate in the development process. SD methods also support and sustain innovation process.
Mindset change	It brings out the user oriented mindset and changes the viewpoint from insight-out to outside-in. Customer journey walkthrough and empathising the customer role inherently leads to customer-centric development approach (outside-in) instead of just pushing new technology based features (inside-out).
Learning and decision making	This accelerates the decision-making, e.g., via more efficient distribution and understanding of the information. In the process, tacit knowledge is converted to tangible knowledge. This is an opportunity to find behaviours and patterns about which users are not aware. Learning process with different levels: individual, team and organisational.
Identification and prioritisation of features or potential market segments	SD methods help stakeholders to identify and prioritise features as well as avoid building unnecessary functions based on deeper understanding of end-user needs. It may also help to identify new potential products/services or market segments and even reduce time to market.
Value creation	Value can be created from intangible end-user experiences and emotions. Quick and cost effective way to test new ideas before any development work is done.

TABLE II. Identified Challenges of Experience Prototyping

Challenge	Description
Facilitation	Special skills and environment are needed to facilitate SINCO workshops. Companies do not have the premises nor facilitation capabilities.
Stakeholder availability	Due to increasing demands and hectic business schedules, it may be challenging to find suitable time for all stakeholders to participate in a workshop at the same time. In the B2B context, involving end-users may be challenging.
Measurement and data management	Lack of systematic ways to collect customer data and identify metrics for how to measure customer value and no practices for documenting and integrating workshop results back to the existing processes. Video was identified as an effective medium to document and communicate experience prototypes but companies' IT systems don't necessarily offer suitable ways to store and tag videos.
Timing and placement of the workshop	Proper timing and placement of the workshop with the company's process. In two of the cases, the involvement of end users and the whole SD sprint took place too late in the development process.

TABLE III. Identified Critical Factors of Experience Prototyping.

Critical factor	Description
Service design expertise	In-house and outsourced service design expertise is utilised. In-house service design expertise is needed to pursue the co-creation model forward and to be able to facilitate and/or purchase facilitation on demand. The outsider view was needed to help companies apply an outside-in customer-centric development approach.
Preparation	Understanding the business challenge and the context is critical. Preparations phase consists of brief from the case company, collecting information (benchmarking, observations, mystery shopping etc.) and information analysis for scenarios formation. Defining which information will be collected as the result of the workshop session, and how.

Critical factor	Description
Facilitation	The facilitator must be able to direct the participants and experience prototyping session as well as rapidly build mock-ups during the session. Facilitator defines the point of view through which matters are analysed. Also, proper rhythm of different collaboration modes: presenting background information, enacting and gathering and analysing insights unveiled in the drama (role play) are important.
Involvement of real customers and end users	Involving real users to both the customer insight phase (in workshop and during the preceding field study) and concept testing is critical in order to validate the findings.

Our results indicate that, typically in the B2B context, there is no direct interface between the development team and users. Often this is due to the intermediaries in the supply chain. We also noticed that even if the link between the development team and the users does exist, this opportunity is rarely fully utilised, and typically users are involved too late in the process. For development teams, this may lead to a situation where it is difficult to understand the reasons behind the requirements and validate which features bring real value. Experience prototyping workshops acted as a tool for innovation, communication and interpreter emphasising stakeholder experiences, thus allowing different points of views to be discussed. It provided instant and detailed insight about end-user motivations in different situations and the possibility to test various different service or development options. In experience prototyping workshops, involving real users is necessary in order to enable deep customer insight efficiently as well as test and validate the findings. By observing the workshop sessions, we noticed that sessions that were too long are challenging and may become a tiresome activity, especially when the methods used were unfamiliar to most of the participants. Therefore, it is important to balance the time between the workshops and discussion activities and provide clear instructions to the attendees.

Essentially, the challenge for companies today is no longer how to solve technical issues but rather how to solve problems that are relevant for customers and end users. This requires changing the company culture and mind-set from 'insight-out' technology and features first thinking towards more customer-centric 'outside-in' approach.

B. Integrating service design sprint into software development processes

The role of SD varied with to R&D phase and the lifecycle point of the software being developed. The roles and the positioning of the service design sprints against software development process in the case companies is presented in Table IV.

Through the findings from the company cases, we identified that SD experience prototyping could to be considered as a new development strategy. In all cases, the companies' company culture was identified as a key factor to support change and encourage constant learning. SD methods provide one set of tools for gaining this lacking user knowledge. As a result of our study, we present a practical model of how to introduce SD experience prototyping into Agile Scrum process as sprints (Fig. 3.). In the model, user knowledge is used for continuous learning during the Scrum process, which can be used to test, validate and prioritise features, update the product roadmap, improve the product or service and ultimately result in better customer satisfaction. The model builds on the possibility of learning and executing small tasks that are delivered as an MVP to customers.

In the proposed model, the SD experience prototyping sprints take place in three phases of the agile software development process. The first SD sprint focuses on customer insight and analysing the customer journey through the holistic service experience in which the software product is part. The involvement of real customers and end-users is crucial during this first SD sprint. The first SD sprint results in the product backlog of the MVP or script for the minimum

TABLE IV. THE ROLES AND THE POSITIONING OF THE SERVICE DESIGN SPRINTS AGAINST THE SOFTWARE DEVELOPMENT PROCESS

Company	Role of SD sprint	Positioning of SD sprint
A	Novelty customer involvement platform to validate the holistic user experience of a communication device and its ecosystem	Indirect link to ongoing software development, complementing product backlog, validating overall product/service quality (software development being one sub problem of the design, manufacturing and delivery of the electronic device/platform under development)
B	Pre-development tool for a new maintenance service concept. Providing a service vision and come up with a roadmap for IT service development.	SD sprint as a pre-development phase of software development, online-software concept/backlog as a core deliverable of the SD sprint
C	Make corporate internal operations and knowledge visible through gamification and prototyping.	Pre-development phase, online service portal concept/mockup being a central deliverable of SD sprint.
D	Validate and finish the user experience of new service concept consisting of new online channels already being in implementation phase.	Indirect link to already ongoing software development, complementing product backlog, validating overall product/service quality

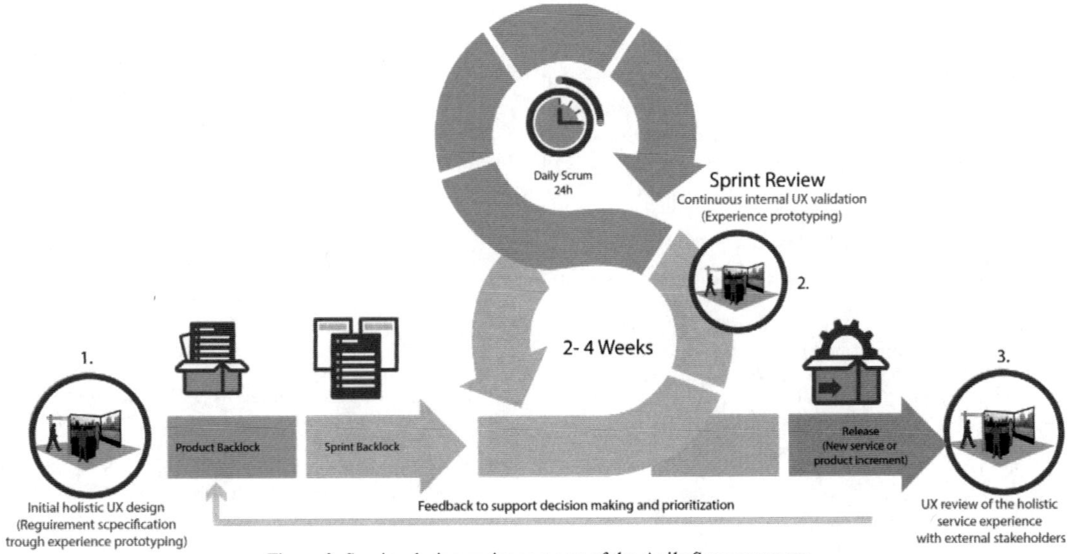

Figure 3. Service design sprint as a part of the Agile Scrum process

valuable service. The second position, where holistic user experience prototyping takes place, happens during the software development sprint as company's internal holistic user experience (UX) check point tool. The aim is to validate and integrate the developed individual software features into a common vision of the holistic outside-in service experience at regular intervals. The third experience prototyping sprint takes place before actual commercial launch of a service. Depending on the case, this sprint may have different foci. The first is evaluating the product or service concept with customers and other external stakeholders in order to accept and refine the critical points of the customer journey before deployment. The second purpose is to educate relevant stakeholders (e.g., sales, marketing and support) of the software use cases and customer experience related sales arguments. The responsibility of coordinating the SD sprints falls naturally to the product owner. The actual facilitation of the experience prototyping sessions requires hiring or purchasing special service design expertise, or it may fall under UX designers' responsibility as new expertise with the need for education and training.

V. CONCLUSION

Users expect nothing less than great products that are easy to use and bring value regardless of technology, platform or context. Delivering value in constantly changing markets and meeting customer needs are key success factors for any business. The objective of this paper was to study the role and impact of experience prototyping in software development projects, including its benefits, challenges and critical factors.

Our study shows that during the case projects, the role of SD was to concretise customers' and end-users' needs to internal stakeholders and to innovate, validate and create new product or service concepts holistically. The methods to achieve the aim included end-user interviews, followed by workshops and role plays, data and information visualisations as well as experience prototyping during the workshops in the SINCO environment. In general, SD methods enhance the software development process and benefit both the developers and users by enabling companies to develop customer-centric products and services that are useful, desirable and competitive in the market. We identified a number of benefits of experience prototyping in the software development context, such as instant feedback, faster and more accurate decision-making, continuous learning as well as focusing the development effort on things that bring value to users are some of the perceived benefits. Furthermore, we identified challenges and critical factors that could block the use of SD methods during development activities, such as stakeholder availability, special skills and the environment needed for workshop facilitation, etc. Based on the results, we present a practical model of how to integrate SD prototyping sprints in software development processes. The model builds on existing software development practices with short learning and iteration cycles, where customer experience can be improved by arcing out the situation, making quick improvements and prototyping the experience again. In the proposed model, the SD experience prototyping sprints take place in three phases (before, during and after) of the agile software development process.

It is important to note that due to the methodological nature of our research, generalisation based on the results is inherently limited. However, our research results offer a fruitful ground for future studies on using experience prototyping or other SD methods in software development practices. Our future research will aim to validate the proposed model in an empirical context. For future research, it could be important to identify mechanisms that can be used to analyse and incorporate workshop results into software development processes and identify metrics for analysing customer value.

ACKNOWLEDGMENT

This work was supported by TEKES (Finnish Fund for Technology and Innovation) as part of the 'Need for Speed' project (http://www.n4s.fi/) and 'Value through Emotion' project. This work has been done in co-operation with research group (M3S) from the University of Oulu and University of Lapland.

REFERENCES

[1] C. Elbert, 'Looking into the future'. *IEEE Software*, vol. 32, no. 6, pp. 92–97, 2015.

[2] J. Järvinen, T. Huomo, T. Mikkonen and P. Tyrväinen, 'From Agile software development to Mercury business' In *Software Business. Towards Continuous Value Delivery*, Cyprus: Springer, vol. 182, pp. 58–71, 2014,

[3] J. Humble and J. Molesky, *Lean Enterprise: How High Performance Organizations Innovate at Scale*, CA, USA: O'Reilly, 2015.

[4] H. H. Olsson and J. Bosch, 'Towards continuous customer validation: A conceptual model for combining qualitative customer feedback with quantitative customer observation', in *Software Business: 6th International Conference, ICSOB*, Portugal, pp 154-166, 2015.

[5] T. Sauvola, L. E. Lwakatare, T. Karvonen, P. Kuvaja, H. H. Olsson and J. Bosch. 'Towards customer-centric software development, a multiple-case study', in *41st Euromicro Conference on Software Engineering and Advanced Applications (SEAA)*, Portugal, pp 9-17, 2015.

[6] A. Griffin, 'Obtaining customers' needs for product development', in K.B. Kahn, *The PDMA Handbook of New Product Development*, 3rd Ed., Hoboken, NJ: Wiley, pp. 213–230, 2013.

[7] J. Highsmith, *Agile Project Management: Creating Innovative Products*. New York, NY: Addison-Wesley, 2009.

[8] T. Dybå and T. Dingsøyr, 'Empirical studies of agile software development: A systematic review', *Information and Software Technology*. vol. 50, pp. 833–859, 2008.

[9] E. Ries, *The Lean Startup. How Constant innovation Creates Radically Successful Businesses*. UK: Penguin, 2011.

[10] S. Miettinen and A. Valtonen, (Eds), *Service Design with Theory. Discussions on Change, Value and Methods.* Rovaniemi, Finland: Lapland University Press, 2012.

[11] E. Kuure and S. Miettinen, 'Learning through action: Introducing the innovative simulation and learning environment Service Innovation Corner (SINCO)', presented at World Conference on E-Learning, 21-24 October, Las Vegas, NV, USA, pp. 1536-1545, 2013.

[12] B. Reason, 'Mind your own business. Service Design in a B2B'. *Touchpoint Journal, Service Design Network*, vol. 1, no. 3, January 2010.

[13] J. Gothelf and J. Seiden, *Lean UX. Applying Lean Principles to Improve User Experience,* USA: O'Reilly, 2013.

[14] J. Patton, *User story mapping. Discover the whole story, build the right product.* Sebastopol, CA, USA: O'Reilly, 2014.

[15] T. Pinheiro, *The Service Startup. Design Gets Lean.* USA: Hayakawa, Altabooks and Createspace, 2014.

[16] J. Knapp, J. Zeratsky and B. Kowitz, *Sprint. How to solve big problems and test new ideas in just five days.* New York, NY, USA: Simon & Schuster, 2016.

[17] G. G. Claps, R. B. Svensson and A. Aurum, 'On the journey to continuous deployment: Technical and social challenges along the way,' *Information and Software Technology*, vol. 57, pp. 21–31, 2015.

[18] P. Rodríguez, J. Partanen, P. Kuvaja and M. Oivo, 'Combining lean thinking and agile methods for software development: a case study of a Finnish provider of wireless embedded systems detailed', in *47th Hawaii International Conference on System Sciences, IEEE,* pp 4770 – 4779, 2014.

[19] S. Nerur and V. Balijepally, 'Theoretical reflections on agile development methodologies'. *Communications of the ACM—Emergency Response Information Systems: Emerging Trends and Technologies,* vol. 50, no. 3,pp 79-83, 2007.

[20] U. Abelein and B. Peach, 'Understanding the influence of user participation and involvement on system success—A systematic mapping study,' *J. Empirical Software Engineering,* vol. 20, pp. 28–81, 2013.

[21] S. G. Yaman, T. Sauvola, L. Riungu-Kalliosaari, L.Hokkanen, P. Kuvaja, M. Oivo and T. Männistö, 'Customer involvement in continuous deployment: a systematic literature review', in *Requirements Engineering: Foundation for Software Quality, 22nd International Working Conference, REFSQ,* Sweden, pp 249–265, 2016.

[22] M. Stickdorn and J. Schneider, *This Is Service Design Thinking: Basics, Tools, Cases.* New York, NY, USA: Wiley, 2012.

[23] S. Miettinen, S. Rontti and J. Jeminen, 'Co-prototyping emotional value', in *19th DMI: Academic Design Management Conference. Design Management in an Era of Disruption*, London, UK, pp. 2-4, 2014.

[24] J. Howard, 'On the origin of touchpoints. design for service research, patterns and observation'. [Online]. Available: https://designforservice.wordpress.com/2007/11/07/on-the-origin-of-touchpoints/

[25] R. M. Srivastava and S. Verma, *Strategic Management. Concepts, Skills and Practices,* New Delhi: PHI Learning, 2012.

[26] T. Mattelmäki, *Design Probes.* Finland: University of Art and Design Helsinki, 2006.

[27] Y. Lee, 'Design participation tactics: The challenges and new roles for designers in the co-design process'. *CoDesign—Internal Journal of CoCreation in Design and the Arts,* vol. 4, no. 1, pp. 31–50, March 2008.

[28] M. Buchenau and J. Fulton Suri, 'Experience prototyping', in *Proc. 3rd Conference on Designing Interactive Systems: Processes, Practices, Methods, and Techniques* (DIS '00), ACM, USA, pp. 424-433, 2000.

[29] S. Rontti, S. Miettinen, E. Kuure and A. Lindström, 'A Laboratory Concept for Service Prototyping—Service Innovation Corner (SINCO)', in *Service Design and Innovation Conference (ServDes 2012),* Helsinki, Finland, pp. 229-241, 2012.

[30] S. Rontti, S. Miettinen, E. Kuure and A. Lindström, 'Agile techniques in service prototyping', in *Service Design with Theory. Discussions on Change, Value and Methods*, S. Miettinen and A. Valtonen, Eds. Rovaniemi, Finland: Lapland University Press, pp. 189–196, 2012.

[31] P. Runeson, M. Höst, A. Rainer and B. Regnell, *Case Study Research in Software Engineering: Guidelines and Examples.* NJ: Wiley, 2012.

[32] W. F Whyte, *Participatory Action Research,* USA: Sage, 1991.

[33] J. M. Chevalier and D. J. Buckles, *Handbook for Participatory Action Research, Planning and Evaluation.* Ottawa: SAS2 Dialogue. [Online]. Available: http://www.participatoryactionresearch.net/sites/default/files/sites/all/files/manager/Toolkit_En_March7_2013-S.pdf, 2013

Business Model Canvas as an Option for Co-Creation of Strategic Themes of SAFe Portfolio

Eriko Brito
Recife Center for Advanced Studies and Systems (CESAR)
Recife – PE, Brazil
e-mail: eriko.brito@outlook.com

Felipe Furtado
Recife Center for Advanced Studies and Systems (CESAR)
Recife – PE, Brazil
The Open University
Walton Hall, Milton Keynes, MK7 6AA , United Kingdon
e-mail: furtado.fs@gmail.com

Abstract—**This article discusses the use of the Business Model Canvas (BMC) technique as a co-creative option for the elaboration of strategic themes of the Scaled Agile Framework (SAFe). The proposed model is different from SAFe, although it quotes the technique as an alternative, and establishes a process for using BMC in conjunction with formulating strategic themes. It is work-in-progress which exploits a visual way of thinking about strategy and the SAFe approach to corporate management. Evaluation of the proposal will use focus group techniques and the opinions of specialists will be surveyed.**

Keywords—Business Model Generation; SAFe; Agile Methods; Strategic Planning.

I. INTRODUCTION

In the mid-60s, strategic planning established itself as "the best way" to design and implement strategies. Early strategic systems are currently viewed as instruments that guarantee that strategic decisions will be developed without errors at tactical and operational levels. However, planning does not exactly occur in this way [1].

Mintzberg [1] dedicates four chapters to analyzing typically related problems and defines the fallacies of strategic planning as follows: **a)** The fallacy of prediction - attempting to design the future based on predetermined steps, **b)** The fallacy of detachment, - an erroneous understanding that functional units of a company have the autonomy to define and implement strategies, **c)** The fallacy of formalization which sees to it that strategic planning is "written in stone," rigid, inflexible, and follows a fixed pattern.

Parallel to the context presented so far in this paper, software engineering gained experience of agile management models. Melo [2] in his study which had 466 participants, presented a series of benefits when agile practices were adapted. VersionOne reported in its ninth and tenth annual report on agility status, [3][4], that interest had grown in frameworks such as Large-Scale-Scrum (LeSS), Disciplined Agile Delivery (DAD), Scrum of Scrums and Agile Portfolio Management (APM), and set out to scale best practices of agile management, especially the SAFe model.

Of these models, SAFe is the only one to present, within its structure, an explicit openness to strategic management and does so by defining strategic themes and the project portfolio backlog, these being options which, respectively, are analogous to objective strategy concepts [5], and portfolio projects [6].

Having historically dealt with similar complexities while at a tactical level, the management area/project planning has sought to simplify its processes as a result of the emergence of agile models based on design thinking and co-creation [7]. The role that the BMC plays in this is to be regarded as a collaborative technique for innovation in business models and strategic planning.

Given these correlations, this paper presents a process option for using the BMC technique, suggested but not sketched out by Leffingwell [8], to co-create SAFe strategic themes, thereby introducing agile practices of software engineering into corporate strategic management.

The structure of this paper is as follows. Section II presents the research method and Section III presents the theoretical basis of research on strategic planning, SAFe, BMC, and Blue Ocean Strategy. Section IV discusses the proposal, and puts forward a roadmap for using BMC with SAFe. Lastly in Section V, some conclusions are drawn and suggestions for future studies are made.

II. RESEARCH METHOD

Initially, a theoretical study was conducted on the SAFe model and a detailed understanding was formed on how the process of setting strategic themes at the portfolio level occurs. This concept was the starting point for introducing the BMC technique which had already been suggested by Leffingwell [8] as an option for formulating strategic themes. Next, a Table of equivalence between processes for formulating strategic themes and good strategic planning practices was compiled in order to determine analogies. Fig. 1 illustrates this process as a whole.

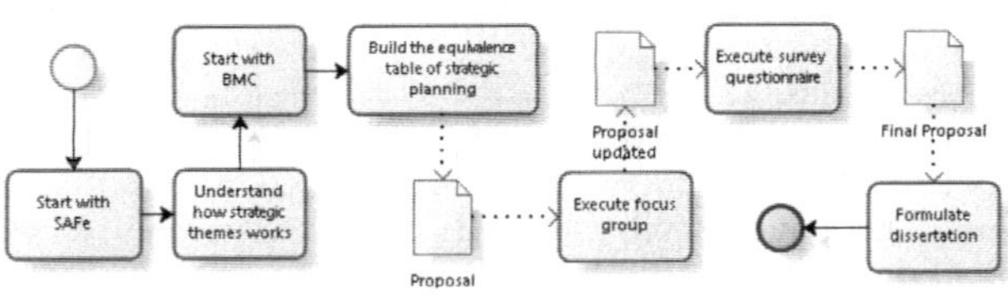

Figure 1. Research method.

For conceptual support of the equivalence between the methods when the research was being undertaken, the literature was reviewed with a view to seeking references in the fields of project management, portfolio management, strategic planning, and agile operations.

The proposal will be evaluated by applying two techniques: **a)** Focus groups [9], as this is a research method which has to be well-planned and structured in which, arising from group discussion. insights about diverse contexts are obtained, and **b)** a Survey of the opinions of specialists [10], which is a broad tool for gathering information from which comparisons, adjustments and explanations can be made.

III. Background Review

The background review presents the main concepts used in this work as follows.

A. *Strategic Planning*

For Drucker [11], strategic planning is a systematic continuous process of decision-making that involves controlled risks to achieve the strategic objectives.

In terms of processes for formulating a competitive strategy in one plan, Porter [12] has three main steps: **a)** What is the business currently achieving. This addresses the implicit and explicit identification of current strategies, **b)** What is happening in the environment? This aims to identify the capacity of competitors, industry, society and their strengths and weaknesses and, **c)** What should the business do? This relates to support for testing the strategic assumptions, making a survey of alternative strategies, and choosing the strategies for business that will add the greatest value to it.

One option for addressing the steps/questions a, b and c proposed by Porter [12] is to use SWOT analysis, an acronym for Strengths, Weaknesses, Opportunities, Threats. The technique is presented by Kotler and Keller [13] as a corporate overview, as an instrument to monitor the dimensions of the company internally consisting of its strengths and weaknesses, and externally, of mapping the opportunities and threats.

B. *Scaled Agile Framework (SAFe)*

Stettina and Hörz [14] introduce an alternative to the challenges placed in management with agile processes which they call the Scaled Agile Framework (SAFe). This adds an agile philosophy to managing the software of project portfolios and also, among other techniques, recursion processes and activities. The model is divided into four major thematic groups, namely, portfolio, value chain, programs, and staff. The model presents how to scale the agility of software engineering as an option that corporate management ought to consider.

The level of a Portfolio, Fig. 2, should be designed and monitored to ensure that the strategic view is maintained and that key resources are allocated to the value chain of the business. This is supported by strategic themes which act as connectors between the business strategy and the vision of the portfolio [8].

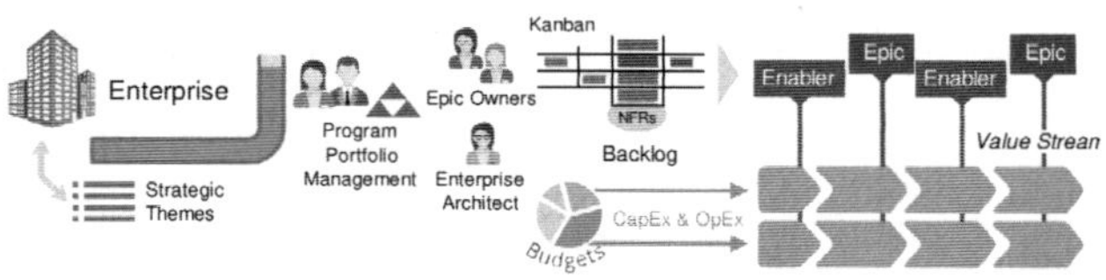

Figure 2. Portfolio level. Adapted from [8].

C. *Business Model Canvas (BMC)*

In general, the starting point of any discussion of a particular model of business should be that the business itself is thoroughly understood [15]. The BMC is a tool that provides a unified reading of business models which addresses four key areas: clients, supply, infrastructure and financial viability structured into nine thematic blocks as see in Fig 3.

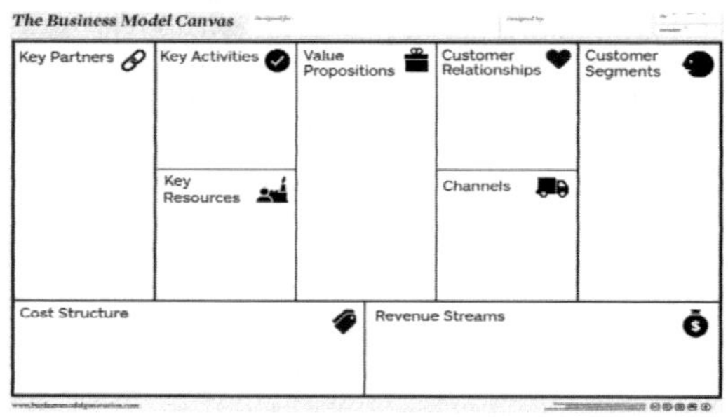

Figure 3. BMC. Adapted from [15].

The process of modeling business or a strategy which uses BMC is conducted in a single frame, preferably printed on an A1 sheet of paper using blocks of adhesive notes (post-its), during stakeholders' meetings. These post-its are used to fill the BMC until a thorough understanding of the process has been formed or the strategy reviewed.

D. *Blue Ocean Strategy (BOS)*

Designed for the purpose of formulating market differentiation strategies, BOS is presented by Kim and Mauborgne [16] as a technique for use by a company in a red ocean, where the business effort and formulation strategies are focused on competition, for a context where concurrence is irrelevant because the market is vast and has not yet been explored.

As an option to create business strategies to gain access to this unexplored and vast market, Kim and Mauborgne [16] present a framework with four actions to create value which minimizes the impact on costs, namely, a) Which of the factors that the industry takes for granted should be eliminated? b) Which factors should be reduced well below the industry's standard? c) Which factors should be raised well above the industry's standard? and d) Which factors should be created that the industry has never offered?

The first question causes a company to reflect on the possibility of eliminating the points over which it has been competing in its segment for a long time but which offer no noticeable differences. The second leads the company to think about the products and services that have been oversized in their cost structure, thus adversely affecting its competitive position in the market. The third reflects on the relationship with the client, the need for rediscovery, and to improve the services and products the company offers and provides. And finally, the fourth question prompts a company to discover new sources of value for customers, thereby generating new market demands.

IV. PROPOSAL: BMC AS AN OPTION FOR SAFE

Leffingwell [8] considers that strategic themes may represent points of connection, see Table 1, between the corporate strategic objectives presented by Olsen [5] and the backlog portfolio of projects, and that formulating both of them requires a large collaborative effort and many hours of teamwork.

TABLE I. STRATEGIC PLANNING AND STRATEGIC THEMES

Strategic Planning	***Strategic Themes***
Where are we now?	Mission, Principles, Skills and Environment
How do we get there?	Financial Goals and Budget
Where are we going?	Vision and Business Direction

Fig. 4 is adapted from [8] to represent the BMC entry point in the flow of SAFe and this is used to formulate the strategic themes by mapping how they are supported.

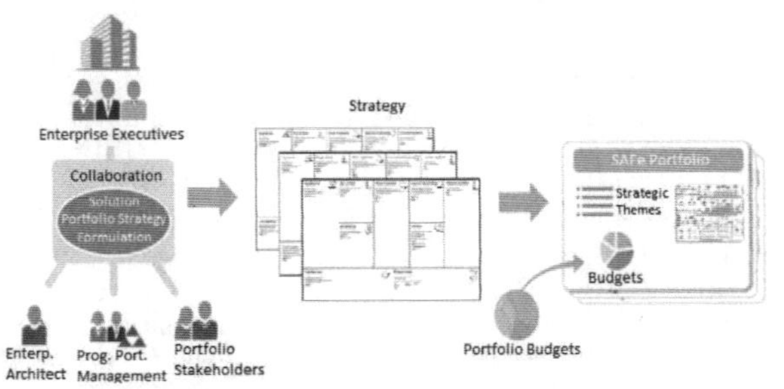

Figure 4. BMC in strategic themes flow. Adapted from [8].

Steps for deriving strategies with the BMC were organized into four groups of processes, see Fig. 5: a) Identify the current model, b) Analyze the internal scenario, c) Analyze the external environment and, d) Formulate the strategic themes.

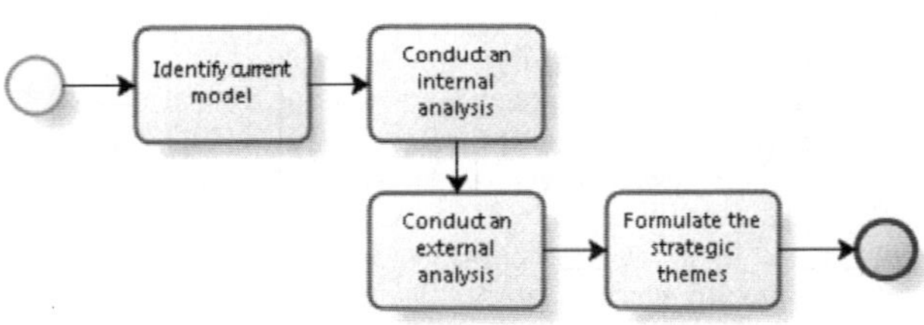

Figure 5. Derivation of strategies using the BMC.

The following paragraphs discuss how to deploy the four groups of processes to fill the BMC and formulate strategic themes.

A. *Identify current model*

With the help of a moderator, stakeholders must record the actual situation of the company on the BMC, current strategies or their proposals for current values. Each thematic group should reflect its context.

Finally, the BMC must be 100% completed which will result in the model giving a picture of the company´s current business model or its strategies. There are no restrictions on using more than one BMC framework to reflect all the company's value propositions.

B. *Conduct an internal analysis*

After the current scenario has been mapped, the next step is to analyze the internal environment. The assessments suggested by Osterwalder and Pigneur [15] can be used to map the strengths and weaknesses. New post-its can be used to record findings on the canvas and marked (S) for the strengths and (W) for the weak points, as illustrated in the example in Fig. 6.

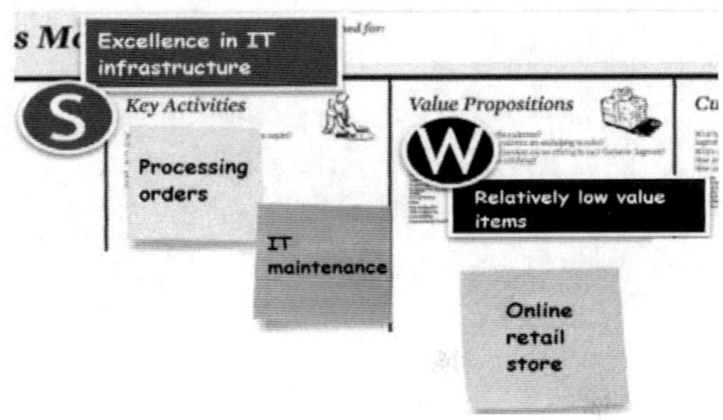

Figure 6. Strengths and weaknesses.

C. *Conduct an external analysis*

After having identified the strengths and weaknesses of the current model, the next step is to look at the opportunities and resident threats of the external scenario. The assessment of opportunities and threats may occur according to Kotler and Keller [13]. The record of these points requires the inclusion of new post-its with descriptions which should be marked with (T) for threats and (O) for opportunities. Fig. 7 illustrates an example.

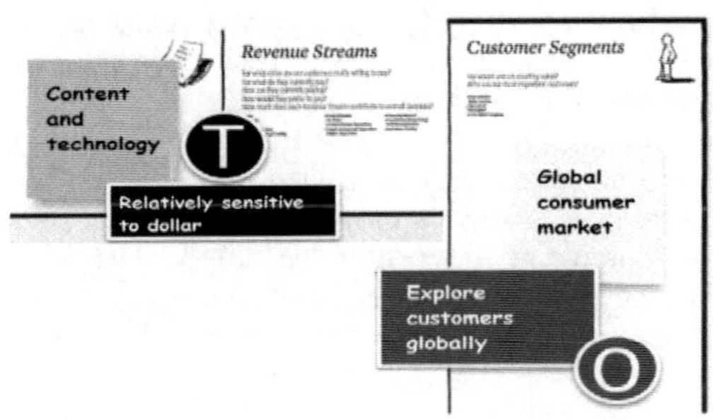

Figure 7. Opportunities and threats.

At the end of this phase, it is expected that the BMC will show the current model and highlight the strengths, weaknesses, opportunities and threats. This will reflect two situations discussed by Osterwalder and Pigneur [15], namely: a) A picture of where the company is and, b) Suggestions for future actions.

D. Formulate the strategic themes

The strategic themes can now be formulated, bearing in mind that, as they are strategic objectives as defined by Kotler and Keller [13], they should be specific and limited in time. To establish these correlations, Osterwalder and Pigneur [15] make use of BOS [16] so as to demonstrate that the BMC is a natural extension of BOS and that together they help in understanding the cause and effect relationship between these two techniques.

The BMC can then be factored into regions as shown in Fig. 8 and be used to tap into the strategic themes as follows: a) Can costs be reduced by eliminating or reducing canvas components? b) What new values can be created or improved for clients without significantly impacting costs?

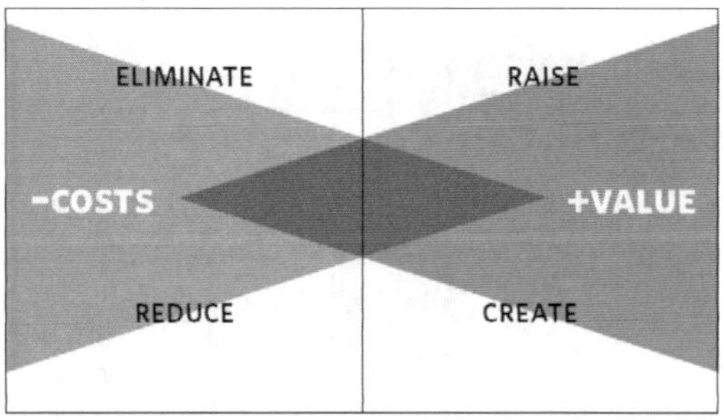

Figure 8. BOS and BMC. Adapted from [15].

Since the corporate strategic themes were derived, they can follow the SAFe flow to the phase of mapping its influence.

V. FINAL COMMENTS AND NEXT STEPS

This work in progress discussed a proposal for how to use the BMC, as a visual co-creative option, to create the strategic themes on SAFe portfolio level.

In terms of future actions, the strategy presented will be evaluated in a focus group and survey with experts. Evaluations need to be made of other models and techniques such as Lean Canvas [17], Strategy Model Canvas [18], and Lean Startup [19], so as to ensure that they have the same capability as BMC in formulating strategies.

As a continuation of the research, the following matters will be investigated: a) The influence of corporate strategic themes on results, b) The Project Model Canvas [20], as an option for preparing the portfolio backlog, c) The evolution of the research by identifying details of equivalence between the models and, d) Evaluating the final proposal by using focus group techniques and conducting a survey on the views of specialists.

REFERENCES

[1] H. Mintzberg, “Rethinking strategic planning part I: Pitfalls and fallacies,” Long Range Planning, vol. 27, no. 3, pp. 12–21, 1994.

[2] C. De Melo, V. et al, “Agile methods in Brazil: the state of practice in teams and organizations” Relatório Técnico RT-\-MAC-2012-\-03. Dep. Ciência da Comput. IME-USP., no. 2010, p. 9, 2012.

[3] VersionOne, “9th Annual State of Agile Survey,” pp. 1–17, 2015.

[4] VersionOne, “10th Annual State of Agile Survey,” pp. 1–16, 2016.

[5] E. Olsen, Strategic Planning For Dummies. Indianapolis, Indiana: Wiley Publishing, Inc., 2011.

[6] A Guide to the Project Management Body of Knowledge, Fifth Edition. Newtown Square, Pennsylvania 19073-3299 USA: Project Management Institute, Inc, 2013.

[7] E. Brito, R. Costa, A. Duarte, P. De Pós-graduação, and I. Ppgi, “About the Use of Model Canvas in Data Management Plans for Digital Curation Research Projects.” VIII Brazilian e-Science Workshop, Brasília, 2014.

[8] D. Leffingwell, “Scaled agile framework,” 2016. [Online]. Available: http://scaledagileframework.com. [Accessed: 02-Feb-2016].

[9] J. Kontio, J. Lehtola, L. Bragge, “Using the focus group method in software engineering: obtaining practitioner and user experiences”. Redondo Beach, CA: International Symposium on Empirical Software Engineering (ISESE), 2004.

[10] S. L. Pfleeger and B. A. Kitchenham, “Principles of Survey Research Part 1 " Turning Lemons into Lemonade Systems / Software , I n c . What our series will discuss Description of the Lethbridge survey,” vol. 26, no. 6, pp. 16–18, 2001.

[11] P. F. Drucker, Introduction to Adminsitration, São Paulo: Pioneira Thompson Learning, 2002. ISBN 8522101305.

[12] M. E. Porter, Competitive strategy: Techniques for analyzing industries and companies. Simon and Schuster, 2008.

[13] P. Kotler and K. L. Keller, Marketing Management. Pearson, 2011. ISBN 0132102927.

[14] C. J. Stettina and J. Hörz, “Agile portfolio management: An empirical perspective on the practice in use,” *Int. J. Proj. Manag.*, vol. 33, no. 1, pp. 140–152, 2015.

[15] A. Osterwalder, Y. Pigneur, A. Smith, and T. Movement, *Business Model Generation*. Hoboken, New Jersey: John Wiley & Sons Inc, 2010.

[16] W. C. Kim and R. Mauborgne, *Blue Ocean Strategy: How to Create Uncontested Market Space and Make the Competition Irrelevant*. Boston, Massachusetts: Harvard Business School Publishing Corporation, 2005.

[17] A. Maurya, *Running Lean*, Second. O'Reilly Media, Inc., 2012.

[18] L. C. Passos, “Strategy Model Canvas.” Sergipe, AL, 2015. [Online].Available: http://www.strategymodelcanvas.com.br/. [Accessed: 02-Feb-2016].

[19] E. Ries, *The Lean Startup: How Today's Entrepreneurs Use Continuous Innovation to Create Radically Successful Businesses*. 2011.

[20] J. F. Júnior, *Project Model Canvas: project management without bureaucracy*. Brasil, Elsevier, 2014.

A Synchronous Agile Framework Proposal Combining Scrum and TDD

Marcia Maria Savoine [1], Vanessa França Rocha [1], Carlos Andrew Costa Bezerra [1], André Magno Costa de Araújo [2], Joyce Karoline Maciel Matias [1]

ITPAC – President Antonio Carlos Tocantinense Institute Araguaina, Brazil [1], Federal University of Pernambuco Recife, Brazil [2]

e-mail: savoine@gmail.com, vanfranrocha@gmail.com, andrew@r2asistemas.com.br, amcaraujo@gmail.com, joycekarolpaz@gmail.com

Abstract — **Optimizing processes in software development are becoming increasingly more popular. For that reason, the consuming market demands more efficiency and quality. To achieve that, some methodologies are adopted in order to ensure that real value will be delivered to the customer. This paper relates a series of good practices based on team management features described in Scrum, and the development and source code testing covered in the TDD methodology. By specifying a framework structure with such features, this work allows software factories use a lean model, facing the reality of their projects in several aspects (e.g., team management, code development and testing).**

Keywords- Software Development; Methodologies; Scrum; TDD.

I. INTRODUCTION

The continuous improvement in productivity and organizational processes depend on the use of software as a competitive advantage [1].

Therefore, new methodologies and techniques are adopted to handle processes in software production quality as well as providing training to professionals, aiming to manage and develop products efficiently and in short time.

In harmony with such fast-paced world, Agile methodologies propose structured practices and organized steps throughout the software development cycle. More specifically, Scrum aims to manage all the processes that take place within each project event to obtain a detailed and complete overview of the features developed and their deadlines.

On the other hand, in Test-Driven Development (TDD), the process is apparently simple - tests are written before writing the code itself, not only in order to address shortcomings, but to meet the features in a reliable and predictable manner [2].

Considering the Agile methodologies, it is noticed that small and medium-sized software factories usually find it substantially difficult to fully employ Agile practices, as the size and complexity of the project, possible lack of control, poor staff training and difficult conciliation with existing processes are some of the points that hinder the adoption of these methodologies [3].

This work aims to determine the features offered by both agile methodologies (Scrum and TDD) and asserts when software factories should use each one as a model according to the reality of each project.

This paper presents a theoretical and practical framework for systematic association of Scrum and TDD combining the strengths of both (i.e., responsive management and agile development, respectively) through an exploratory research carried out in the documentation and guidelines of the investigated methodology. It is also dedicated to compare both methodologies to raise similarities and differences towards proposing a method using an association of both to a conceptual framework throughout the software development cycle.

This paper is structured as follows: Section 2 presents the related work; Section 3 presents Agile methodologies concepts, for Scrum and TDD respectively. Section 4 presents a comparative analysis of the studied methodologies. Section 5 shows a framework with the proposed combination and use of both methodologies. Last but not least, Section 6 presents conclusions and future work.

II. RELATED WORK

This research focused mainly on finding works in which the main concern was assessing the use of the Scrum framework to manage activities and the team, and the use of code management in TDD. The main point those works had in common was indicating that the use of TDD with Scrum provided benefits to the software development and design. Sinialto and Abramhamsson [4] show that there is an improvement in the code and application test coverage. However, Janzen and Saiedian [5] show that TDD makes developers more confident during code maintenance, hence leading to higher productivity and possibility of delivery on time.

Puleio [6] points out that for a new project that was meant to replace an existing legacy service with a new one after long meetings, the team opted to use Scrum for project management, TDD and pair programming. Soon after, they decided to fully embrace XP (Extreme Programming) practices. After several difficulties encountered and solved, the project was successful, leading the team to conclude that the code tests could be done following agile methods.

Despite the growing popularity of Agile methodologies, there is a limited amount of literature that combines Agile methodologies and software testing, especially concerning how to perform the tests and integrate with Scrum. For this reason, Van den Broek et al. [7] performed an analysis based on a case study on the use of tests in a Scrum team. Afterwards, the authors proposed a visual model that integrates testing and some Scrum activities.

Our research relates to the work in Van den Broek et al. [7] since they propose a visual model that integrates testing activities and Scrum. However, we noticed that there are factors affecting the adoption of Scrum and TDD, as the latter is only used to test the practices in Scrum. Our work used practices, characteristics, Scrum roles and artifacts from both Scrum and TDD equally, in order to improve processes where one fails and another completes.

III. AGILE METHODOLOGIES

Agile methodologies aim to accelerate software development and delivery, as a means to make pieces of new software more frequently available to clients and improving the participation of all stakeholders. Therefore, Agile methodologies have specific characteristics, but maintain the same core principles throughout the life cycle of software development [8]. These principles are customer engagement, incremental delivery, people over process, accepting changes, and keeping it simple.

Having the core principles in mind, in subsections A and B the specificities of the Scrum framework and TDD methodology addressed in this work are described in detail.

A. *Scrum*

Scrum is used for managing Agile software projects iteratively and incrementally. In this sense, Sutherland [9], states that the Scrum framework aims to capture the way the teams really work, giving them the tools to organize themselves and, most importantly, quickly improve the speed and quality of their work.

In Fig.1, one may notice that, initially the Product Owner and Stakeholders set the Product Backlog, which is followed by prioritization of the sprints (Sprint Backlog). At the end of the Sprint a product increment is delivered to the customer.

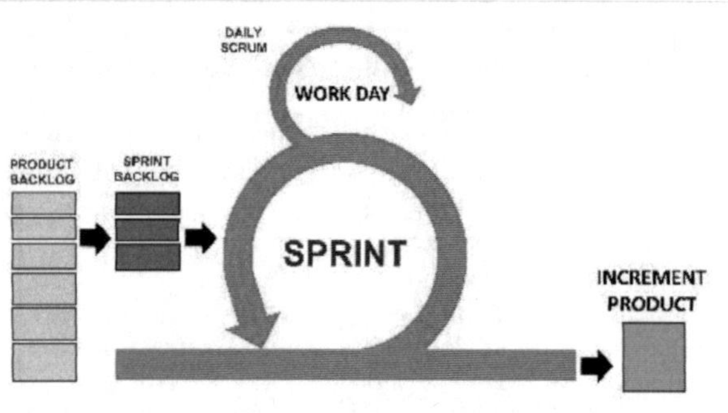

Figure 1. Scrum Cycle. [10]

Scrum consists of three roles that are responsible for executing events and building artifacts. They are:

- Product Owner: responsible for prioritizing the Product Backlog (list of requirements) and getting important information from the stakeholders.
- Scrum Master: ensures that all the work occurs smoothly and in an organized fashion without interruptions, acts as a facilitator or conductor in Scrum meetings and assists the interaction between the Product Owner and the development team.
- Team Members: people who carry out development and testing. The team must be organized and have deep product knowledge.

Scrum implements an iterative and incremental skeleton through fully decentralized roles and responsibilities [11]. In Scrum, Events and Artifacts are:

- Product Backlog: List of requirements, design features, extracted from user history.
- Release Backlog: The product is set to be developed in parts (Sprints). In the end of each Sprint, the delivery of completed increments is called Release Backlog.
- Sprint Backlog: each Sprint aims to add an important part of the Release Backlog.
- Daily Scrum: At the end of each day of development all members in the team come together for the Daily Scrum, a short meeting lasting around 15 minutes.

Despite Scrum's goal being to deliver value to the customer in the form of relevant features in the final product, members of a Scrum project team should use some artifacts to support the decentralized and simple management [12].

The great advantage of Scrum is achieving the delivery of a functional product with higher quality and lower cost, with a team that works in less time. Unlike other methods, it consists in a pre-determined time-box to verify and validate whether what is being done is what was actually established and whether it is adaptable to the format and type of project.

Scrum proposes a new software management framework, which is based on self-organization, motivation, ownership and pride of a team in carrying out their acquisitions. As it is adaptable, Scrum provides the right support for the team, and accommodates phases that are important to the quality of the software production, such as testing activities that are a trend among renowned software factories [13].

B. *TDD*

TDD is a methodology focused on software quality, in particular the quality of implementation and testing. TDD increases the reliability of the system and raises the assurance that what was executed is in accord with the proposed requirements [14].

According to Aniche [15], TDD is a software development methodology that is based on the repetition of a small cycle of activities. First, the developer writes a test that fails. Then, the developer fixes what is missing and makes the test passes, implementing the desired functionality. Finally, they perform the refactoring of the code to remove any duplication of data or code generated in the process, as shown in Fig. 2.

These three rules of TDD bring immediate benefits when applied: class design with very low linkage; software documentation on tests; flexibility; and debugging time reduction.

Conditions that should be tested are loops, operations and polymorphisms; however, tests should be applied only to those conditions written by the developer himself. This allows the testing to be compatible with the logic used in the development, covering all the code characteristics [16].

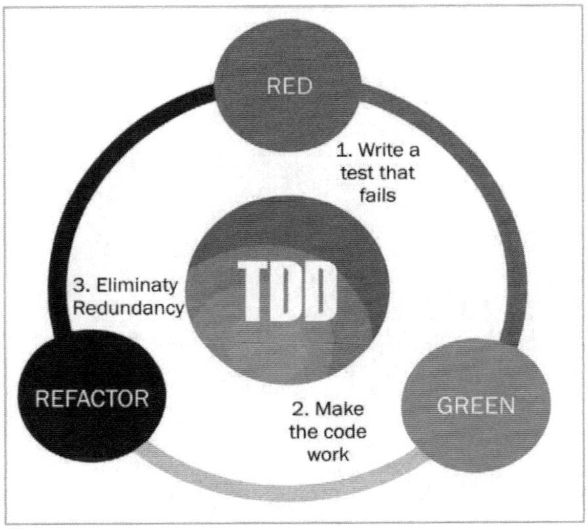

Figure 2. TDD Cycle. [16]

The main reasons for the adoption of TDD according to Kaufmann and Janzen [17] are presented below: the development is set by first considering the objectives, then thinking about the possible solutions; the understanding of the system can be achieved by reading the tests; unnecessary code is not developed; there is no piece of code without test; once a test is working, it is known that it will always work and it also serves as a regression test; tests allow progress to be made in the software, because they ensure that the changes do not alter the operation of the system.

The feedback provided by TDD promotes significant improvement in the design of classes, helping the programmer to encode more cohesive and less coupled classes, reducing the occurrence of errors and software maintenance costs.

IV. COMPARATIVE ANALYSIS BETWEEN THE AGILE METHODOLOGIES SCRUM AND TDD

We held a comparative analysis described aiming to highlight the similarities and weaknesses in both methodologies, and trying to identify where the inconsistencies of a method could be complemented by practices of the other. This was done after realizing that the use of Scrum focuses on management of software projects which had great feedback from self-manageable and self-organized teams, with a strong contribution from the Scrum Master. In this way, Scrum and TDD have different applications, as the latter focuses on software quality by building code based on programming and testing standards.

A. *Specific Features*

The presented features were selected based on the theoretical framework of Section II, paying attention to their relevance and degree of understanding, and also considered specificities to indicate essential activities found in software projects and executed by a software factory. These characteristics must objectively state individual and similar points of methodologies that make direct reference to the core Agile principles and the structure of the methodologies in the study. Thus, we selected the following:

- Self-organizing team: team organization and work among members who can, for the most part, find the best solution to manage and carry out their work.
- Project supervisor: responsible for monitoring the team giving the necessary support, supervising the work done and what remains to be done;
- Results of the development report: measures the evolution of product development and is presented periodically;
- Setting steps: Breaking the project into phases or stages;
- Quality code: code analysis based on the architecture and coding standards;
- Small steps: Process in which the project has its phases broken into smaller parts;
- Time reduction: Gain of time based on an architecture without design;
- Cost reduction: Savings generated by the use of the methodology;
- Simplicity: Doing only what is necessary;
- Feedback: Returning information to the team and customer;
- Project delivery: All increments are fully tested, guaranteeing they work together and providing a quality delivery.
- Adaptable to change: Product is flexible for adjustments and redesigns;
- Testing responsible: Team person who assumes the function of tester;
- Format test: How the tests are applied to software.

By observing the behavior of each methodology in each pinpointed feature, we analyzed the individual weaknesses and characteristics that are complementary or overlapping, as well specific practices, roles and artifacts (Table 1), which are indicators that help and guide teams through the development process. For example, practices 6 and 7 are complete when executed together; on the other hand, item 8 in "Roles" highlights that such a feature does not exist in the TDD methodology; however, it exists in Scrum, and the Scrum Master benefits if he decides to adopt both methodologies. Likewise, the item 10 in "Artifacts" shows there are no structures in TDD to address progress besides tests, and Scrum complements it.

The final analysis highlights the strongest features, structure and procedures of each method. Thus, although those are meant for different segments – in the software development context where there is a close attention scenario for good practice that values quality, scalability and effective results - the application of both methodologies in a synchronized and adjusted fashion, maintaining their individual characteristics, may contribute for better results.

TABLE I. ESSENTIAL CHARACTERISTICS OF THE AGILE METHODOLOGIES OF SCRUM AND TDD

			AGILE METHODOLOGY	
N°	**INDICATORS**		**SCRUM**	**TDD**
1	**Practices**	Self-Organizing Teams	The team self-organizes activities	Not specified
2		Setting Steps	*Sprints*	Test Cycle
3		Small Steps	Division in sprints for development of releases	Baby Steps guarantee features are broken in as many parts as needed
4		Simplicity	Produce only the necessary	Simplification of procedures and code
5		Feedback	The staff and customer	Continuous feedback to the team
6		Adaptable to Change	Changes in the project and its project type	Test suite ensuring changes without loss of performance and functionality
7		Format test	Parallel-running implementation	Written test before implementing functionality
8	**Roles**	Project Supervisor	Scrum Master	Not specified
9		Testing responsible	Developer	Developer
10	**Artifacts**	Evolution report on the results	Daily Scrum and Burn Down	Automatized tests
11		Project Delivery	Whenever it is all done	Not specified
12		Code Quality	Not specified	Compliance with Object Oriented Programming
13		Time Reduction	Deliver something functional for the customer in a short time	Development and maintenance since it optimizes the process and reduces errors
14		Cost Reduction	The less time, less charges will be applied	Software maintenance error correction or projection errors

V. PROPOSED SYNCHRONOUS USE OF SCRUM AND TDD

We developed a proposal based on the analysis performed with the purpose of exploring characteristics and attaining better comprehension of possible coexisting use of both methods in the form of a synchronous framework that exemplifies the interaction of Scrum and TDD as Agile methodologies and how their integration can be made so they may coexistence in harmony.

According to the framework structure shown in Fig. 3, the integration of Scrum and TDD is applicable to a self-organizing team (item 1) which values the simplicity in the processes and also in the code (item 2) and follows the lead of a Scrum Master. Setting out small steps for each *Sprint* (item 3), the organization achieves in reductions in time and cost (items 4 and 5), as the team produces only the necessary and minimizes errors and do-overs. The developer (item 9) is responsible for coding and testing following the standards established by TDD (items 7 and 8), and presents its findings to the Scrum Master and the team at every Daily Scrum. The code documentation that comes down to testing as set out in TDD is available to be evaluated and improved by the team, therefore enabling the Scrum Master to measure (item 10), not only what is being done, but how it is being done, ensuring quality to the team and to the end customer. At this point of the framework, we stress the ability to adapt to change (item 11), with documented and tested code and a self-organizing team ending the cycle with continuous feedback with the customer and the team (items 12 and 13); this guarantees that, when the software is considered ready (item 14), it will have high quality levels, ensuring the adaptation and survival of the project even when facing changes to the original delivery.

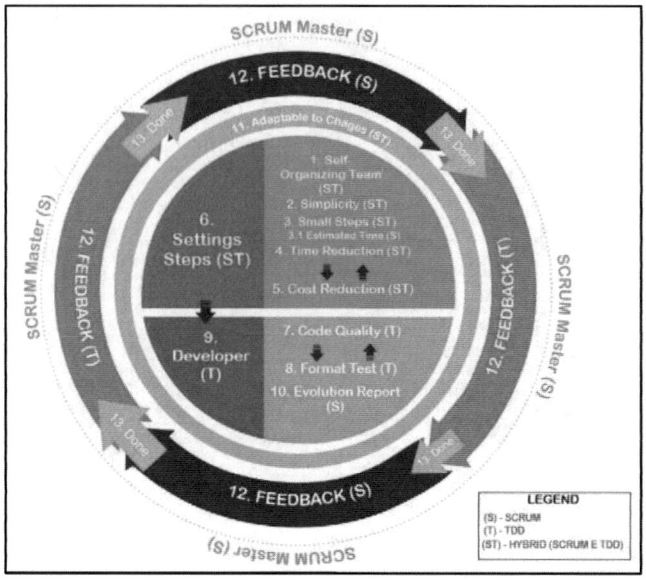

Figure 3. Proposed Framework for combineduse of Scrum and TDD

The presence of the Scrum Master (Scrum methodology) is in evidence because they are present throughout the framework cycle, facilitating and enhancing the work of the entire team, ensuring that the framework is followed, and seeking for continuous improvement.

As stated by Silva and Lemos [18], the role of the Scrum Master is analogous to that of an orchestra conductor. Both should provide guidance and steady leadership to a team of talented professionals who work together to create something that no one can do alone.

Thus, through the proposed framework, we sought to address characteristics of the two methodologies which, by coexisting, may further contribute to the success of the project and the quality of software.

VI. CONCLUSION

This paper presents two aspects within the agile context: the management team which is involved throughout the software process with Scrum and the team that actually develops the lines of code and performs tests using TDD. No methodology by itself includes both strands effectively; therefore, to address this situation we studied both methodologies and proposed a framework which can be used in software factories.

Based on the analysis and the framework presented, it is clear that the differences and similarities found in both methodologies make them more useful when used in tandem, as they guarantee software is produced avoiding problems in the code due to continuous testing, which prevents new errors and corrections during future implementations, eventually reducing time and cost. Thus, the combined use of Scrum and TDD is strongly recommended, as it will bring clear gains to the project by indicating the increase in staff quality, product and codes, and then covering the whole process of development, evolution and maintenance of software grounded on best practices and ensuring full feedback on all processes and practices.

In the future, we intend to develop a tool to assist in software development by proposing a set of coexisting Scrum and TDD methodologies, confirming the efficacy of the proposed framework and performing its validation in a real scenario of a software project.

REFERENCES

[1] J. Herbsleb and D. Moitra, “Global Software Development”, EUA: IEEE Software. 2011.

[2] S. Freeman and N. Pryce, “Growing Object-Oriented Software, Guided by Tests”.Addison-Wesley Signature Series, 2010.

[3] C. Andrade, J. Lopes, W. Barbosa and M. Costa, “Identifying difficulties in the implementation and contract management in agile projects in Belo Horizonte”. DOI - 10.5752/P.2316-9451.2014v3n1p18. Abakós , v. 3, 2014, p. 18-37.

[4] M. Siniaalto, P. Abramhamsson, "A Comparative Case Study on the Impact of Test-Driven Development on Program Design and Test Coverage". Finland: First International Symposium on Empirical Software Engineering and Measurement (ESEM 2007), 2010.

[5] D. Janzen, H. Saiedian, "On the Influence of Test-Driven Development on Software Design". USA: 19th Conference on Software Engineering Education & Training (CSEET'06), 2011.

[6] M. Puleio, "How not to do Agile Testing". USA: AGILE 2006 (AGILE'06), 2006.

[7] R. van den Broek, M. M. Bonsangue, M. Chaudron and H. van Merode. "Integrating testing into Agile software development processes". Lisboa: Model-Driven Engineering and Software Development (MODELSWARD) 2nd International Conference on, 2014.

[8] I. Sommerville, “Software Engineering”, Boston: Pearson. 2007.

[9] J. Sutherland, “Scrum: The Art of Doing Twice the Work in Half the Time”, New York: Crown Business. 2014.

[10] K. Schwaber, “Agile Project Management witch Scrum”, Reedmond: Microsoft Press. 2013.

[11] K. Schwaber, “Scrum Guide”, Harvard Businner Review, Boston, IV, p. 163-179., 2013.

[12] Z. Požgaj, N. Vlahović, V. Bosilj-Vukšić, "Agile Management: A Teaching Model Based on SCRUM". MIPRO-IEEE, 26-30 May, Opatija, Croatia. 2014.

[13] A. Pham and P. Pham, “Scrum in Action: Agile Software Project Management and Development”, Course Technology, 2011.

[14] K. Beck, “Test-Driven Development By Example”. Estados Unidos: Addison Wesley, 2002.

[15] M. Aniche “Real World Test-Driven Development”, São Paulo: Code Crushing, 2013.

[16] K. Beck, “Test-Driven Development”, 1 st. ed. Addison-Wesley Professional, 2002.

[17] R. Kaufmann, D. Janzen., “Implications of Test-Driven Development A Pilot Study”. In: 18th Annual ACM Conference on Object-Oriented Programming System, Languages and Application (OOPSLA 2003). New York: ACM, 2003.

[18] W. Silva and L. Lemos “SCRUM: A New Approach to Software Development Front of Current Competitive Scenario Demand”, Rio de Janeiro: Fluminense Federal University. 2008.

AUTHOR INDEX

AUTHOR INDEX